Teaching Elementary Science

SIXTH EDITION

Teaching Elementary Science

William K. Esler

University of Central Florida,
Orlando

Mary K. Esler

Orange County Public Schools,
Orlando

Wadsworth Publishing Company
Belmont, California
A Division of Wadsworth, Inc.

Education Editor: Suzanna Brabrant
Editorial Assistant: Dana Lipsky
Production Editor: Karen Garrison
Managing Designers: Kaelin Chappell and
 Cloyce Wall
Print Buyer: Randy Hurst
Art Editor: Nancy Spellman
Text and Cover Designer: Kaelin Chappell
Cover Image: The Photo Source/Superstock
Compositor: Thompson Type
Printer: R. R. Donnelly and Sons

*This book is printed on
acid-free recycled paper.*

Photographs on pages 2, 7, 19, 30, 52, 59, 79, 118, 123, 124, 127, 153, 157, 160, 161, 176, 179, 186, 198 left, and 201 by Mary Esler.

Photographs on pages 12, 13, 15, 44, 180, 182, 198 right, and 483 by William Esler.

1 2 3 4 5 6 7 8 9 10 — 97 96 95 94 93

Library of Congress Cataloging-in-Publication Data
Esler, William K.
 Teaching elementary science / William K. Esler, Mary K. Esler. — 6th ed.
  p. cm.
 Includes bibliographical references and index.
 ISBN 0-534-17700-X
 1. Science — Study and teaching
(Elementary) I. Esler, Mary K. II. Title.
LB1585.E84 1993   92-4815

P R E F A C E

To the Reader

This sixth edition of *Teaching Elementary Science* is dedicated to the same purpose as the original text. That purpose is helping pre-service and in-service elementary school teachers acquire the skill, knowledge, and attitudes that will enable them to teach "good" science in their classrooms. As science educators, we are fully aware of the conditions existing in many of our elementary schools that work against the implementation of quality science instruction. We are confident, however, that many of these problems disappear when confronted by a determined and properly prepared teacher.

Since a great variety of science programs and materials exists in elementary classrooms today, this book does not emphasize one curriculum. A program that prepares a teacher to teach one or two curricula is of no use to the teacher who is not fortunate enough to be in a school that has the appropriate materials. The alternative to this approach is to identify the skills, knowledge, and attitudes that enable a teacher to operate in many situations. Good science teachers, in whatever type of program, have certain common characteristics:

1. *The ability to relate science instruction to the cognitive and affective development of children*. When students are continuously assigned tasks that are inappropriate, too easy, or too hard, the result is boredom and frustration for both teachers and students. Understanding your students' intellectual structure and development can help you to formulate learning tasks that match their abilities. Understanding the wide range of your students' cognitive skills and being aware of those tasks that can strengthen each skill can also help you formulate procedures that will keep children challenged. The nature of the learner is introduced in Chapters 1 and 2, and the reader is reminded throughout Section One of the relationships of that nature to the learning process.

   The child's attitudes toward the teacher and the subject matter are closely related to the nature of the learning activities. Thus, you should understand the nature of the child's involvement as he or she is engaged in learning tasks. This will help you to structure classroom activities to provide maximum attitudinal changes. Present research indicates that children of diverse cultural backgrounds develop intellectually in much the same way. Therefore, the teaching techniques demonstrated in this book should serve you well, whatever your students' socioeconomic and cultural differences.

2. *The ability to understand and implement inquiry techniques*. To operate well with the inquiry mode of teaching, you should clearly understand the procedures and possible outcomes of each inquiry technique. Chapter 3 summarizes and describes three basic inquiry techniques and procedures for teaching an inquiry lesson. Examples of teaching episodes are presented in dialogue form in this chapter and elsewhere. This method of presenting inquiry lessons is intended to help you understand the nature of inquiry as well as to apply inquiry techniques in your classroom.

   Learning centers and other types of individualizing instruction are commonplace in today's elementary schools. In Chapter 8, you will find an extensive treatment of techniques for adapting individualizing procedures to teach science in the elementary school classroom.

3. *The ability to implement didactic teaching techniques in your teaching*. Didactic or direct teaching procedures are used by most teachers to teach science content. Chapter 4 contains a detailed discussion of didactic teaching procedures that due to familiarity are often neglected. Skills for didactic teaching, just as those of inquiry, must be developed with study and practice to achieve optimum results.

4. *The ability to plan instruction to include both the process and the content of science*. Herein lies the greatest challenge and perhaps the greatest contribution this book has to offer — the presentation of the Inquiry-Concept-Information (I-C-I) sequence for planning and carrying out science instruction. This sixth edition of *Teaching Elementary Science* attempts to provide considerable information and rationale for the use of the recommended implementation sequence of *inquiry teaching* to develop *scientific concepts* followed by *information-gathering* learning activities. By involving children with inquiry activities, you can help them develop both a conceptual framework and the skills necessary for doing science; this is true regardless of the nature of their curriculum materials. After studying the information presented in this textbook, you should also be able to reorganize noninquiry programs to include sizable elements of inquiry learning.

Procedures for helping you implement one or more of the inquiry techniques in a content-oriented textbook program are presented in Chapters 4 and 5. In these chapters you will find a description of the sequence of *inquiry, concepts,* and *information* that will ensure that children understand the science processes even as they experience science lessons based on a textbook.

5. *The ability to adapt your science program to individualize instruction for both normal and exceptional children in your classroom and to integrate science with reading, language arts, mathematics, and social studies.* Information contained in Chapters 7 and 8 will help you to develop the skills and insights necessary to do this.

6. *Know and understand some of the major concepts of science.* Many elementary school teachers lament that they do not know enough science to teach it. Indeed, some knowledge of the content of science is essential to good teaching. The ideal science teacher would probably be a person who combines a knowledge of the subject matter and skills of science with an understanding of the nature of children.

   Section Two of this book is designed to explain both the subject matter and how to present it in the classroom. Each broad topic — such as magnetism or electricity — is organized in terms of the big ideas, or their concepts and subconcepts. This conceptual organization simplifies the presentation of science content, and it provides ideas around which to organize your teaching. A brief overview of each concept and subconcept of science is accompanied by complete lesson plans that can guide you in introducing the concept to elementary school children. Section Two reviews seventeen broad topics of science and contains over two hundred lesson plans. Section Two may be regarded as a basic curriculum guide for teaching science in the elementary school.

7. *A knowledge of sources of elementary science programs, manipulatives, print, film, and graphic media, including computer applications for science education in the elementary school.* Chapter 6 provides a comprehensive overview of general equipment and materials. Chapters 6 and 8 describe procedures and suitable materials for computer use in the elementary school science classroom. Selected appendixes provide names and addresses of appropriate sources of materials for teaching science to children.

8. *Understand the problems confronting our society that result from applications of science to technology.* Chapter 9 discusses intervention and suggests ways to guide children as they consider problems of the environment, medicine, and more. The general problem-solving techniques presented in Chapter 9 are a natural extension of the science process skills discussed earlier in the text.

In summary, this book attempts to: (1) show why you should teach science in such a way as to challenge the child intellectually and to help the child maintain a high level of curiosity while enjoying what is taught; (2) provide models for inquiry and didactic teaching that you can use in the classroom; (3) present an overview of natural science organized into a conceptual framework; and (4) show you how to use inquiry and didactic techniques to reshape content-oriented programs so that you can develop your students' science skills. It is our hope that this book will help you operate a successful skill-oriented inquiry science program, regardless of the materials with which you must work.

Acknowledgments

We wish to express our appreciation to our friends and colleagues at the University of Central Florida who have offered support and criticism of the first five editions of the book: to Jack

Armstrong and Margaret While, who examined its methods and content in the crucible of the classroom.

A special thanks is owed to Suzanna Brabant, education editor, and Karen Garrison, production editor, who made it almost a pleasure to scrutinize what existed to make this edition better. Their openness and friendly persuasions were most helpful in spurring us on in our revision efforts. Several reviewers were of help in appraising the sixth edition; their thoroughness and honesty were appreciated. They are: Delmar Janke, Texas A & M; Esther Railton-Rice, CSU Hayward; Ellsworth Starring, Rhode Island College; Robert L. Stevenson, Western Kentucky University; Deborah J. Tippins, University of Georgia; Marvin Tolman, Brigham Young University; L. Kay Walker, Northern Arizona University.

And most of all, we express our appreciation to those for whom the book was written. Many students and college instructors have read and reacted to it, and their suggestions have been invaluable to us in maintaining the timeliness and clarity of its content.

CONTENTS

Section One
Organizing to Teach Children Science

Chapter 2
How Children Learn Science 26

Chapter 3
Teaching Science by Inquiry 50

Chapter 7
Integrating Science with Other Subjects 133

Chapter 8
Individualizing Science/Science for Exceptional Children 149

Chapter 9
Teaching Children to Solve Problems of Science, Technology, and Society 175

Section Two
Units of Study for Elementary School Science

PART ▪ A
Investigating Living Things

PART ▪ B
Understanding Physical Science

Teaching Elementary Science

"[She] that invents a machine augments the power of [humankind]."

—H. W. BEECHER

Organizing to Teach Children Science

How to Use Section One of This Book

This book has two parts. Section One is the "how to teach" part; Section Two is the "what to teach" part.

The nine chapters in Section One should be read sequentially. The presentation of ideas is accumulative—that is, to understand material in the later chapters, you must sometimes know terms and concepts that were presented in the early chapters.

At the end of each chapter of Section One, you will find a list of extending activities. These activities are meant to add depth and understanding to previously learned concepts. You can gain a minimal level of understanding without doing the extending activities. They are provided as enrichment exercises. Do them as time and energy permit.

Suggestions for using Section Two will be found in the introductory pages to that section.

We hope you find what follows to be a helpful preparation for teaching science. Good luck to you as you read the book and later, as you put your ideas into practice in the classroom.

CHAPTER 1

An Introduction to Elementary School Science

Look What's in This Chapter

In this chapter we want to share with you our sense of the interesting and exciting nature of science and scientific investigation. We'll discuss how science can be incorporated into the elementary school curriculum to enhance the curiosity, skills, and knowledge of children as they explore the world in which they live. You will learn about the history of teaching science by inquiry or problem-solving methods, and you'll become familiar with three elementary school curricula developed in the 1960s and 1970s, which provided much of the style, structure, and substance found in current elementary school science programs. Finally, you will gain a glimpse into the future of science teaching in the elementary school as we look at several curriculum projects now on the market or under development.

Figure 1–1 ■ Curiosity Is the Starting Point for Science

The beginning of science is wondering. A prehistoric man is startled by a shooting star streaking across the sky. An ancient Egyptian stares into a sunlit well. A boy on a beach watches the soaring, twisting flight of a bird. Each of these scenes contains a common element, curiosity. In each instance curiosity is a beginning, a force that may drive a person to seek an explanation of the phenomenon he or she has witnessed. Curiosity is the same across the barriers of time, race, and geography.

Scientific Inquiry Helps Children's Curiosity to Grow

Science begins with the child. Questions such as "What is a shooting star?" and "How can birds fly?" have been asked by thousands of children and have, throughout history, elicited a hundred different answers. Obviously some of these an-

swers were wrong. But the important point is that the children never stopped asking the questions. They saw and wondered and sought an answer (Figure 1–1).

Children are naturally curious about their environment. Young children observe and openly seek to understand what they see. Some teachers derive their greatest pleasure from helping young children to pursue their enthusiastic involvement with nature. In no other activity are children quite so open and questioning, quite so willing to express their feelings and their thoughts. Science, teachers find, is the near-perfect vehicle for helping children to develop their thinking skills. This, then, is the pleasant task of the modern elementary science teacher—helping children to investigate their world and to acquire the skills and knowledge necessary to *understand* the world around them.

Science—A Process for Answering Questions About Nature

The enterprise called science is the natural extension of human curiosity, of asking questions about the world around us and searching for the "best" answers. What science is *not* is a set of facts. Those who work with science know that what is fact today is questioned tomorrow, and often ridiculed as nonsense a year from now. As teachers we must help our students to think of science as a quest, not as an acquisition, as an ongoing enterprise, not as a finished task.

Effects upon Children of Learning Science Through an Inquiry Process

Later in this chapter you will become acquainted with elementary school science programs that all use procedures of questioning and investigation as methods for teaching science. These methods parallel the natural experiences of children with their environment—exhibiting

Children exploring their environment.

curiosity, asking questions, and attempting to find solutions.

Investigations of activity-oriented, inquiry-based elementary science programs developed in the 1960s and 1970s revealed some surprising and interesting things. While performing the activities of these science programs, children developed in areas other than those intended by the curriculum designers! Activity-oriented, inquiry-based elementary science:

1. Enhances the I.Q. scores of primary-grade children.
2. Increases student-initiated content-relevant speech among ghetto children.
3. Increases language and general knowledge.
4. Develops measuring skills.
5. Increases mathematics concepts.
6. Increases number skills.
7. Increases social studies skills.
8. Increases listening skills.
9. Improves visual perception skills.
10. Develops logical thinking.
11. Teaches science process.
12. Serves as a reading readiness program for early primary-grade children.
13. Enhances the curiosity of children.
14. Improves attitudes of children toward science and school.

The list of benefits derived from inquiry-based science is not yet complete; others continue to be added as researchers conduct their investigations of the science programs in a variety of settings. For example, manipulative science programs are proving to be easily adapted and especially effective with a wide variety of exceptional children, ranging from the mainstreamed educable mentally retarded and learning disabled to the physically handicapped and the sight and hearing impaired. (Science for exceptional children is considered in Chapter 8.)

How can all of these good things happen to children as the result of doing science? Does it sound too good to be true? The research findings are clear and conclusive. These benefits and more result when children pursue science, exercising their curiosities and their science skills.

The Nature of Science: Model Building

Because the activities employed in teaching science emulate the practices of scientists in investigating and discovering new answers to questions about our environment, it is important to understand the nature of science itself.

There is a fable wherein three blind men are asked to describe an elephant. The first blind man feels the animal's tail and says, "The elephant is like a rope." The second blind man feels its trunk and says, "The elephant is like a snake." The third blind man feels its leg and says, "The elephant is like a tree trunk." (See Figure 1–2.)

Obviously the conclusions of all three blind men were inadequate, but the procedure that they used is frequently employed in science. Each man gathered the evidence that was available to him and attempted to form a mental image of the nature of the unknown animal. That their images were inexact reflected the lim-

itations of the evidence with which each man had to work. How might the three blind men have contrived to describe the elephant more exactly? They might have pooled their information. They might also have made further observations, perhaps in some systematic way, with each man investigating some portion of the animal. At each step of their investigation, as they met to transmit and discuss their observations, a new, more exact image of the elephant would be formed. Eventually, after extensive observation and hypothesizing, they might have gained a good idea of what it looked like. The blind men would have formed a theory or model of the elephant's structure.

This is how science works. The process of building mental images that explain the nature of the unknown is called model building. A scientific model is a theory formulated to explain and integrate all of the information that is known to pertain to a particular natural phenomenon. As additional information is accumulated, it is tested against the accepted model. The model or theory may have to be altered to accommodate the new data. It may even have to be replaced with a new model.

Model building is sometimes a tortuous process. Consider how the model of the solar system was developed. Based on direct observation, the ancient Greeks and Arabs built a model of the universe that placed the earth in the center of a huge sphere. All other heavenly bodies were located on the sphere. This model corresponded to the known data. Later, more careful observations of the night skies revealed that certain stars seemed not to circle the earth in a perfect orbit but rather to wander back and forth among the other stars. The old model was amended to include the new observations. Two "stars"—Mercury and Venus—were then pictured as traveling in small, circular orbits of their own, while they circled the earth in a large orbit. (See Figure 1–3.) Subsequent observations revealed even more discrepancies that required further adjustments in the existing model.

Ptolemy's model became very complex—it was not until the sixteenth and seventeenth

Figure 1–2 ▪ "Scientists" at Work

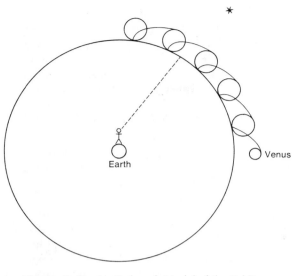

Figure 1–3 ■ Ptolemy's Model of the Orbit of Venus

centuries that astronomers like Copernicus and Galileo decided that too much of the data did not fit the earth-centered universe model. They discarded it for a brand new one that had the earth and the other planets moving about the sun.

The process of model building and refutation of the earth-centered universe took place over a span of two thousand years. Today, because scientists have accumulated knowledge and sophisticated instruments with which to work, model building generally progresses faster. But the process remains essentially the same—gathering data, formulating a model, modifying the model to accommodate new information, or throwing it out altogether in favor of a better one. The development of the atomic model, for example, is reviewed in Chapter 14.

Historical Development of Elementary Science Teaching

Science has long been studied in elementary schools in the United States. But the nature of its content and the methods of teaching it have changed over the last one hundred years. All school programs in nineteenth-century America were dominated by the influence of faculty psychology. Its basic tenet was that the child's mind could be trained by rigorous exercises; he was made to memorize information and to develop classic methods of thought. In the clapboard-sided elementary schools of the East and the log-cabin schoolrooms of rural America, the teacher was often a stern taskmaster, and motivation was drawn chiefly from the hickory switch. Into these strongly teacher-centered schools, a new approach to science was introduced in the 1850s. It was called object teaching.

Object teaching in this country is often traced directly to the Swiss educator Johann Heinrich Pestalozzi (1746–1827). In the European variety of object teaching, children were taught to observe and study natural phenomena. Object teaching was given a big push in this country when the National Education Association supported the Oswego Plan, developed in Oswego, New York.

Under the Oswego Plan, children were directed to describe in detail animate and inanimate objects. The purpose of the method is described by Hermann Krusi, a writer of that period, who stated that children would study objects "in which they are interested, and which tend to cultivate their perceptual faculties; and at the same time, lead them to name the object, to describe its parts, and to state the relation of these parts. Thus language is also cultivated; and from the observation of a single object, the pupil is led to compare it with others, and the first steps in classification are taken."[1] It would seem that the method of object teaching should help children learn to observe and communicate, two important first steps toward "doing" inquiry science. Unfortunately, in actual practice, object teaching exercises were often very highly structured. The trick for the student was to memorize an "approved" list of characteristics.

---

[1]Quoted by Herbert A. Smith, "Historical Background of Elementary Science," *Journal of Research in Science Teaching* 1, no. 3 (1963): 200–205, 223.

He did not learn to interpret and understand what he observed. In fact, it was assumed that children were incapable of interpreting phenomena. Their learning role was confined to description and memorization. The lack of a textbook for directing the lessons placed a heavy burden on the teachers, many of whom were untrained in science. Lessons were often confined to obvious descriptions of objects. The methodology of object teaching was ill suited to the demands of American society, and at the close of the nineteenth century this method of instruction began to lose its popular acceptance.

America was then in the throes of one of the greatest population migrations in the history of the world. Immigrants from Europe were pouring into the large eastern cities at the rate of a million a year. At the same time, an agricultural society was becoming industrialized. These factors produced a new trend in science teaching called nature study.

The avowed purpose of nature study was to acquaint or reacquaint big-city dwellers with nature and thereby influence them to leave the city for the farm. Unfortunately, faculty psychology still dominated the thinking of educators in the 1890s, and even nature study consisted of formalized memorization exercises. Nature study began to wane by the end of the first decade of the twentieth century.

To meet the needs of the people in the eastern cities, science in the 1920s was often taught as health and hygiene. The colleges lost some of their influence over the public school curriculum, and highly compartmentalized science courses such as zoology and physiology were combined into more general subjects such as biology. It was in the early 1920s that the present emphasis on science as inquiry first appeared.

John Dewey (1859–1952), a prominent educator often called the father of progressive education, contended that the methodology of science is at least equal in value to the actual knowledge accumulated. In the schools that practiced Dewey's philosophy, science was often used to solve practical problems of community health, water supply, and so forth. Problems were selected for study, and methods for finding solutions were given a pragmatic and utilitarian base. Dewey's methods of instruction are making a strong comeback with the current emphasis on problem solving in today's elementary school classrooms.

The 1927 doctoral dissertation of Gerald S. Craig, a graduate student at Columbia University, is considered a landmark work in the development of elementary school science teaching. Craig pointed out the utilitarian aspects of science in the areas of health and safety and expressed the belief that science was important to a citizen's general education. He observed that the laws and principles of science can be applied to solve everyday problems. Knowledge of natural law and scientific methods, Craig believed, would help citizens to cope with life in a changing society. Craig was among the first to emphasize the affective dimension of teaching science as an investigation, rather than as a rote exercise.

Since the 1920s, science as inquiry has slowly gained favor to become the strongest single influence upon science teaching to date. Three yearbooks of the National Society for the Study of Education (NSSE) were devoted to science; they, too, are thought to have had considerable influence in this area. The *Thirty-first Yearbook* (1932) stressed the need to:

1. Sequence and articulate science instruction.
2. Differentiate science programs for special groups of students.
3. Determine the ultimate purposes and goals of science instruction.
4. Stress the major generalizations as objectives for science teaching.

The *Thirty-first Yearbook* greatly influenced later research and study in the field of science education. The *Forty-sixth Yearbook* (1947) stressed the affective areas of science instruction, the development of methods for instruction, and procedures for evaluating instruction. The *Fifty-ninth Yearbook* (1960) sought to expand the use of inquiry and processes as the objectives and methods of science instruction.

The 1960s may some day be viewed as the most important decade in the development of science education. A spectacular era of curriculum development began in the late 1950s—one that may never again be matched. Dozens of experimental curriculum programs were spawned in an atmosphere of international competition aimed chiefly at the Soviet Union. Millions in federal funds were spent to help educators, psychologists, and scientists develop the programs best suited to attain two goals—scientific literacy for all citizens and greater competence for those who chose to specialize in science-related vocations. Today, to help realize these goals, the programs begun in the sixties are being refined, and their use in the public schools is being expanded.

Federally Funded Elementary School Science Programs of the Sixties and Seventies

During the late 1950s many working scientists felt that what was being taught as science did not reflect what science really was. Professional scientists working in curriculum projects therefore attempted to define contemporary science by restructuring established conceptual schemes. A conceptual scheme is a small group of concepts around which the child's day-to-day science experiences are built. Because the structures of the new elementary science curricula were formulated and edited by professional scientists, they reflect what these scientists believe to be real science.

The work of the psychologist was no less important than that of the scientist to the development of the new elementary science programs. The psychologist's role was to reconcile the child's cognitive development with the task requirements for pursuing specific learning activities. He attempted to determine whether the child was cognitively ready to pursue a particular concept.

Teachers participated in both the planning and development stages of the curriculum development process. The one characteristic that distinguished the new science programs from the old ones was their developmental nature. Massive federal support, along with considerable funding from private foundations, enabled the curriculum designers to test and revise their materials. The materials of all the major science curriculum programs were proven teachable in the classroom, often with thousands of children, before they were released for general use. Unlike some textbook material of the past, the suggested activities, if properly handled, are almost guaranteed to work with children.

The 1960s' science programs have other characteristics in common. In each program children become involved with materials. They become experimenters and discoverers. Essentially, then, the science classroom becomes a laboratory. A teacher in such a program drops the authoritarian role so familiarly associated with classroom instruction and becomes a guide and consultant. Her new role is one of making suggestions and asking questions as the children carry out the activities.

The programs of the sixties and seventies often required the teacher to pay more attention to classroom management. Children must be taught to distribute, return, and care for materials. Some exercises require the children to group and regroup, and most activities provide them with at least some freedom of movement. Most children require directions for operating and limits within which they may make individual choices. Maximum learning will take place when the children are free to interact with one another, but only in an atmosphere that is orderly and free from extensive irrelevant activity.

Three of these science programs are: the Science—A Process Approach (SAPA) program of the American Association for the Advancement of Science; the Science Curriculum

Improvement Study (SCIS); and the Elementary Science Study (ESS). These particular programs were chosen for study because the materials for each are widely available commercially and because they are perhaps the best known of the elementary science projects. Furthermore, they represent three different philosophies. Thus, they provide a cross section of the thinking of present-day science curriculum specialists.

Science—A Process Approach (SAPA)

The primary objective of the Science—A Process Approach program is to have children acquire the skills of doing science. (The particular skills are discussed in detail in Chapter 4.) The process skills were originally defined in the course of an attempt to analyze how research scientists operate. This procedure, called task analysis, yielded eight primary and five integrated process skills. (See Chart 1–1.) The long-range objective of the Science—A Process Approach program is to have the learner become proficient in as many of these skills as possible. Though the program deals with an appreciable amount of science content, this content is a by-product

rather than a primary goal. *All answers to questions concerning the structure and articulation of learning activities are formulated to promote the development of process skills.*

SAPA II is a revision of the original modularized program, providing flexibility. A year's work consists of fifteen modules each in a separate drawer. The modules are grouped into clusters according to similarities in process and content. Program designers state that certain "key clusters" of SAPA II contain materials for developing important process skills and should receive priority. Other clusters may be scheduled according to the desires of the classroom teacher. SAPA II also provides separate pack-

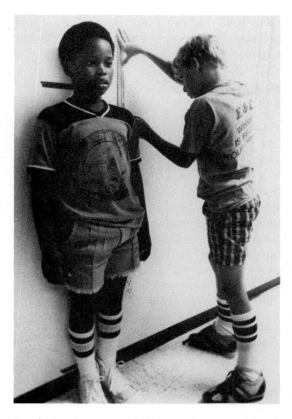

Developing the process skill, measuring, an activity of the SAPA program.

Chart 1–1 ▪ The Process Skills of the Program*

Primary Skills	Integrated Skills
Observing	Formulating Hypotheses
Classifying	Controlling Variables
Measuring	Interpreting Data
Communicating	Defining Operationally
Inferring	Experimenting
Predicting	
Using Time/Space Relationships	
Using Numbers	

*See Chapter 4 for a detailed description of the nature of the process skills.

"Stringing beads," an activity of the SCIS program.

ages for certain special topics called learning chains. Xerox literature reports the availability of learning chains in the areas of the metric system, special education, and reading readiness.

There is no textbook for the SAPA program. The children learn by participating in activities. The teacher is provided with a series of small booklets that serve as teachers' guides. These guides contain detailed descriptions of a few teaching activities designed to help the children to acquire a well-defined skill or skills. They also provide a set of behavioral objectives for the activities, a sequence chart showing how the skills being taught are related to other skills, a rationale for teaching the skill, a vocabulary list, a materials list, a generalizing experience, and individual and group evaluation procedures.

The Science Curriculum Improvement Study (SCIS)

The designers of the Science Curriculum Improvement Study project sought to develop an elementary school science program around the conceptual structure of science as it is viewed by contemporary scientists. A few basic concepts of science were chosen as being widely applicable and useful, and the subject matter was built around them. These concepts were chosen from both the physical and the life sciences. Chart 1–2 shows all six levels of the SCIS program in final edition and the concepts introduced in each unit. The kindergarten unit called "Beginnings" was added to the program to provide introductory readiness activities.

The SCIS program differs fundamentally from the SAPA program. Since the goal of the SCIS program is that the child obtain scientific literacy[2] the answers to most questions of program development were decided on the basis of concept development. The skills of doing science are taught throughout the SCIS program, but they are not the fiber from which the curriculum

---

[2]In their book, *A New Look at Elementary School Science* (Chicago: Rand McNally, 1967), Robert Karplus and Herbert D. Thier define scientific literacy: "The individual must have a conceptual structure and a means of communicating that enables him to interpret the information as though he had obtained it himself. We will call this functional understanding of scientific concepts 'scientific literacy.'"

Chart 1–2 ▪ The SCIS Final Edition Program

Beginnings (Kindergarten)

color	odor	quantity
shape	sound	position
texture	size	organisms

Life Sciences		**Physical Sciences**	
ORGANISMS:		MATERIAL OBJECTS:	
organism	habitat	object	serial ordering
birth	food web	property	change
death	detritus	material	evidence
LIFE CYCLES:		INTERACTION AND SYSTEMS:	
growth	biotic potential	interaction	system
development	generation	evidence of interaction	interaction-at-a-distance
life cycle	plant and animal metamorphosis	SUBSYSTEMS AND VARIABLES:	
genetic identity		subsystem	
POPULATIONS:		evaporation	solution
population	food web	histogram	variable
food chain	community	RELATIVE POSITION AND MOTION:	
ENVIRONMENTS:		reference object	polar coordinates
environment	range	relative position	rectangular coordinates
environmental factor	optimum range	relative motion	
COMMUNITIES:	producers	ENERGY SOURCES:	
photosynthesis	consumers	energy transfer	energy source
community	decomposers	energy chain	energy receiver
food transfer	raw materials	MODELS: ELECTRIC AND MAGNETIC INTERACTIONS:	
ECOSYSTEMS:		scientific model	electricity
ecosystem	oxygen–carbon dioxide cycle	magnetic field	
water cycle	pollutant		
food-mineral cycle			

---

is woven. Concept development is somewhat sequential, and so is the SCIS program.

Although SCIS is basically a laboratory program, the children are not expected to discover all concepts for themselves. The general scheme of instruction includes the sequence of exploration, invention, and discovery. The students observe and explore a phenomenon. The teacher "invents" an idea, such as magnetic fields or points of reference, to serve as an organizer. And then the students are guided to discover further relationships about the phenomenon.

The Elementary Science Study (ESS)

The Elementary Science Study is not a science program. Rather, it is an attempt to provide a great variety of materials from which an ele-

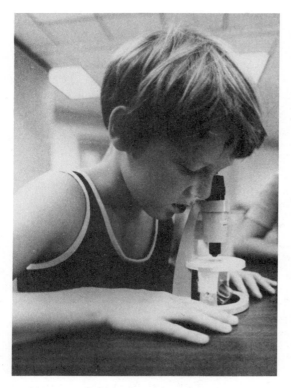

Looking at small things through a microscope, adapted from the ESS program.

All units of the ESS program provide for long periods of unstructured time that children use to follow their curiosity. Perhaps a statement from the *Introduction to the Elementary Science Study* best expresses the philosophy of the program developers:

The Elementary Science Study units differ widely, but they share a common approach to the teaching of science in elementary schools. Rather than beginning with a discussion of basic concepts of science, ESS puts physical materials into children's hands from the start and helps each child investigate through these materials the nature of the world around him. Children acquire a great deal of useful information, not by rote but through their own active participation. We feel that this process brings home even to the very young students the essence of science—open inquiry combined with experimentation.

It is apparent that children are scientists by disposition; they ask questions and use their senses as well as their reasoning powers to explore their physical environments; they derive great satisfaction from finding out what makes things tick; they like solving problems; they are challenged by new materials or by new ways of using familiar materials. It is this natural curiosity of children and their freedom from preconceptions to difficulty that ESS tries to cultivate and direct into deeper channels. It is our intention to enrich every child's understanding, rather than to create scientific prodigies or direct all children toward scientific careers.[4]

The developers of the ESS program feel that their materials and methods do teach children both science content and skills. Certain units are designed to develop such skills as weighing, graphing, and using instruments. Certainly throughout the program the learner is invited to become a good observer, to learn to manipulate materials, to develop strategies for dealing with problems, and to strengthen his or her ability to make intuitive responses.

The variety of topics covered by more than fifty units of ESS material is so great as to defy

mentary science program can be built. The developers of the ESS materials do not expect that any school would ever use all of the study's more than fifty units. Rather, they believe that science teachers and supervisors should have a plethora of topics and materials from which to choose. Then they can construct programs especially suited to local teachers, local children, and local communities.

The variety of ESS topics appears endless, but there is a unifying theme that ties them all together. This theme, one of investigation and discovery, grew out of the philosophy that holds that a large part of the child's time should be spent "messing about in science."[3]

---

[3]David Hawkins, "Messing About in Science," *Science and Children* 2 (February 1965): 5–9.

[4]Elementary Science Study, *Introduction to the Elementary Science Study* (New York: McGraw-Hill, 1966), 1. Reprinted by permission of the Elementary Science Study of Education Development Center, Inc.

any reasonable system of classification. The following are some of the units made and distributed by ESS:

Gases and "Airs"	"A" Blocks
Kitchen Physics	Primary Balancing
Small Things	Mobiles
Behavior of Mealworms	Pendulums
Growing Seeds	Mystery Powders
Microgardening	Light and Shadows
Bones	Peas and Particles
Batteries and Bulbs	Changes

The Effect of the Federally Funded Curricula on Elementary School Science in the Eighties and Nineties

These science curricula have had a definite impact on teaching. New textbook series are emphasizing child-centered activities and a laboratory approach to science teaching. Several commercial textbook companies are now providing programs that specify manipulative materials. This emphasis upon child-centered activity is almost certainly due to the success of the experimental curricula.

Through institutes and in-service programs, thousands of elementary school teachers have been trained in one or more of the new curricula. The training of elementary school science specialists has had an impact upon the general level of science instruction in the elementary schools of the nation.

The federally funded science programs have contributed greatly to the art of teaching by defining many of the cognitive, problem-solving skills. Their methodologies have been extensively published. Where these methodologies deal with questioning skills, indirect teaching techniques have benefited.

Finally, these science programs with their accompanying philosophies have affected teacher training. Graduates of many teacher-training institutions now understand the process skills and appreciate the need to develop children's problem-solving abilities.

In all these ways, the curricula of the 1960s and 1970s have affected the teaching of elementary science. The laboratory-based elementary school science programs have left their impact on the programs of the 1980s and 1990s.

Can You Teach One of These Curricula?

The developers of the SAPA and the SCIS programs preferred that the teachers who used them be specially prepared. They felt that if you were familiar with their materials, philosophy, and teaching techniques, you would do a better job of teaching their programs. They were probably right. However, this does not mean that you cannot use the programs without special training. Indeed, this book is based on the premise that if you develop the skills described herein, you can teach *any* curriculum effectively. The methodology of these programs is basically one of discovery, experimentation, and rational inquiry. If you have the necessary skills for teaching science by one of these inquiry methods, you need only familiarize yourself with the materials of any new program in order to use it. Good science teaching is good science teaching, regardless of the curriculum.

Science Education in the Twenty-first Century

As the last years of the twentieth century approach, our society finds itself awash in a giant wave of change. In the minds of many, our way of life on earth is being fundamentally altered, and the schools as social institutions reflect this social transition. Our society is moving from the product-based economy that has characterized the mature stages of the industrial revolution to an information- and service-based economy. We are moving from an era wherein 90 percent of the workforce was engaged in manufacturing products into one in which it is projected that fewer than 10 percent of American workers will be engaged in manufacturing, with about 90 percent in service occupations. Many of the service vocations will require technical knowledge to develop and operate highly automated, robotically operated plants and to repair and service complex, electronically operated equipment. In the schools there is a dramatic shift away from a primary concern for minimal competencies suitable for training a manufacturing workforce toward an emphasis on academic excellence. Many political and educational leaders see this as a dramatic and long-term process, and science is among the most important subject fields to be affected. In the closing years of this century (and well into the twenty-first century), literacy in science may well be among the most important goals of public education in the nation.

Science teaching in the near future may be equally important to our society both as a vehicle for teaching processes that allow us to deal with societal problems and as a body of knowledge. The values of science, such as the spirit of inquiry, objectivity, and devotion to rational problem solving, will be extremely important as we deal with such dilemmas as world hunger, dwindling energy supplies, and environmental pollution. Science teaching in the future will serve to teach both a body of information and the processes of rational thought.

Elementary Science Curricula for the Twenty-first Century

A number of new elementary science curricula and curriculum frameworks designed to meet the needs of children and society into the new millennium are appearing on the scene. We will take a brief look at three of them: Science and Technology for Children, of the Smithsonian Institution's National Science Resource Center;

Activities that Integrate Mathematics and Science (AIMS), of the AIMS Education Foundation; and Project 2061, of the American Association for the Advancement of Science.

Science and Technology for Children (STC)

Science and Technology for Children is a curriculum program of the National Science Resources Center, an affiliate of the Smithsonian Institution. This twenty-four-unit program, designed for grades 1 through 6, reflects an attempt by the NSRC to revolutionize science teaching in the elementary schools of this country. It is an activity-based curriculum wherein children learn science by doing science.

The Science and Technology for Children curriculum has four units for each grade level, 1 through 6; each unit is comprised of approximately sixteen lessons. A unit is designed to provide eight weeks of instruction. The units of study are developed around four central themes:

Theme One, Observing, Measuring and Identifying Properties, is applied to the units of all six grade levels.

Theme Two, Seeking Evidence/Recognizing Patterns and Cycles, is developed in the units of grades 2 through 6.

Theme Three, Identifying Cause and Effect/ Extending the Senses, is associated with the units of grades 4 through 6.

Theme Four, Designing and Conducting Experiments, is found primarily in the units of grade 6.

Prior to being introduced in the marketplace, each unit of study of the STC program is thoroughly field-tested and reviewed by prominent scientists and educators. The program also provides teachers with a variety of ways to assess student progress, including postunit assessments and student progress checklists. Many of the units provide for the introduction of computer-assisted instruction, trade books, and other media to enrich the learning process. Units also contain many activities where the science instruction is integrated with language arts, mathematics, and social studies instruction.

Following is a summary of the units by grade level:

Grade 1: Organisms; Weather; Measuring and Weighing; Properties of Objects.

Grade 2: The Life Cycle of Butterflies; Soils; Mirrors and Magnifiers; Changes.

Grade 3: Plant Growth and Development; Food Chains and Webs; Chemical Tests; Sounds and Signals.

Grade 4: Ourselves; Rocks; Floating and Sinking; Electric Circuits.

Grade 5: Microworlds; Bottle Biology; Food Chemistry; Structures, Machines and Inventions.

Grade 6: Experiments With Plants; Animal Behavior; It's About Time; Magnets and Motors.

The developers of the Science and Technology for Children program have attempted to provide an affordable science curriculum for elementary schools by restricting the use of expensive materials and equipment. Each unit contains a Teacher's Guide and a set of Student Activity Books, as well as the manipulative materials. The supplier for the Science and Technology for Children curriculum materials is:

The Carolina Biological Supply Company
2700 York Road
Burlington, NC 27215

Although at this writing all of the units of STC are not available for evaluation, many science educators agree that the program contains many positive elements, derived both from past experiences and from research of former curricula—namely, the hands-on approach to learning, the development of science skills and attitudes, and the use of the scientific process of experimentation. Other educators have expressed concerns that the tendency of new curricula, such as STC to introduce technology into the curriculum, and to deal with fewer topics of science may dilute the coverage of the broad scope of science. These concerns will likely be debated for many years to come.

Activities that Integrate Mathematics and Science (AIMS)

Many educators have advocated exploiting the natural relationship between mathematics and science by developing a curriculum that uses the naturally motivating activities of hands-on science to make the study of mathematics more interesting to elementary school children. Until now, no single curriculum development effort has succeeded in making inroads on a national scale. It now appears, however, that the AIMS materials created by the AIMS Educational Foundation of Fresno, California, are doing just that.

AIMS is dedicated to creating materials that integrate the study of elementary school science and mathematics in ways that are stimulating to both teachers and children. The developers of the AIMS materials offer a number of reasons that the study of math and science should be integrated to an appreciable degree in both elementary and middle schools. They maintain:

1. Math and science are integrated in nature and therefore should be integrated in the school classroom. Science educators who have advocated the integration of these subjects for several decades support this position. (Please see Chapter 7.)

2. In inquiry science as in real life, many math skills and science processes can be interwoven in a single investigative activity. This integration not only extends the amount of classroom time that science is studied, but also enriches the ways in which mathematics is studied.

3. The AIMS materials capitalize on the natural curiosity of children by presenting

Books and materials from AIMS Educational Foundation.

problem questions that are related to the students' real world; students become creative problem-solvers through investigating scientific phenomena and real-life problems.

4. Because of their participatory nature, the AIMS activities cause children to become active in the process of solving problems rather than remain merely observers in a directive teaching process.

5. The activities are enjoyable, and therefore children are more motivated to tackle intensive mathematics learning activities without the usual "math anxiety."

What Is Project AIMS?

Project AIMS developers describe their curriculum development project as a dynamic, expanding idea, not a finished product. They continue to add to their current array of short, paperback activity books that integrate the problem-solving processes of inquiry science with the study of mathematics. Great effort is made to select interesting and topical materials that are motivating to children and easy to incorporate into the elementary and middle school classrooms. The writing style and artwork are designed to be informal and to appeal to young readers, but the books present real problems for investigation, and the processes employed by students result in their acquisition of numerous math and science skills and attitudes.

Project AIMS also produces mathematic posters that have a problem-solving emphasis, laboratories that contain colorful and appropriate manipulative materials to be used with the AIMS activity books, and science posters that demonstrate investigative process. Project AIMS is also undertaking Project Setup, which produces printed materials designed to be utilized with selected interactive, problem-solving computer software.

Following is a brief summary of the Project AIMS activity books for integrating mathematics and science in the elementary and middle schools.

K–1 Series

Fall into Math and Science (Book 1)

Glide into Winter with Math and Science (Book 2)

Spring into Math and Science (Book 3)

The K–1 series is a collection of experiences related to the appropriate holidays and seasonal environments. Examples: collecting nuts and leaves, enjoying the Christmas season, growing crystal gardens, studying seeds, and exploring the "sounds of music."

Grade 2 Series

Seasoning Math and Science (Book A) Fall/Winter

Seasoning Math and Science (Book B) Spring/Summer

Examples: doing counting, graphing, and measuring activities using seeds, olives, bird nests, popcorn; building toothpick and gumdrop molecules; making balloon rockets, and so on.

Grades 3–4 Series

Jaw Breakers and Heart Thumpers (Book A)

Hardhatting in a Geo-World (Book B)

Popping with Power (Book C)

Overhead and Underfoot (Book D)

Examples: foods and body basics, including heart rate and exercise; structure and design, including soap bubbles and bridges; energy and conservation, including simple machines, melting ice cubes and others; weather and the natural environment, including cloud formations, building a hydrometer, barometer, and wind vane; soil composition; and insect travel. This series emphasizes the use of problem-solving investigations.

Grades 5–9 Series

Math + Science, A Solution (Book 1)

The Sky's the Limit (Book 2)

From Head to Toe (Book 3)

Fun with Foods (Book 4)

Floaters and Sinkers (Book 5)

Down to Earth (Book 6)

Our Wonderful World (Book 7)

Pieces and Patterns, A Patchwork in Math and Science (Book 8)

The titles of these middle-grade books are descriptive of their contents. Each book contains more than twenty investigations that involve students in the problem-solving process and require them to apply skills and knowledge related to both mathematics and science.

Other books published by AIMS are: *Primarily Bears* (K–6), *Water Precious Water* (2–6), *Critters* (K–6), *Out of This World* (5–9). Because Project AIMS continues to develop new materials all the time, others may be available at this reading. AIMS publishes many of its books in combined Spanish/English versions to facilitate their use with bilingual students. To secure sample lessons and a catalog of AIMS materials write to:

AIMS Education Foundation
P. O. Box 7766
Fresno, CA 93747

Project 2061

The American Association for the Advancement of Science has underway a curriculum reform effort for K–12 science that is known as Project 2061. This project, a long-term effort designed to be completed in three phases, was begun in the mid-1980s. Phase I was completed in 1989 with the publication of a report, *Science for All Americans*.

Phase I

The major goal of Phase I of Project 2061 was to define scientific literacy for students graduating from K–12 school programs in terms of the concepts, skills, and attitudes they acquire. Scientific literacy is broadly defined by this reform project through goal statements in science, including the social and behavioral sciences, and in mathematics and technology. The titles of the chapters in *Science for All Americans* that comprise the goal recommendations provide some insight into the breadth of scientific literacy as defined by the project:

1. The Nature of Science
2. The Nature of Mathematics
3. The Nature of Technology
4. The Physical Setting
5. The Living Environment
6. The Human Organism
7. Human Society
8. The Designed World (Technology)*
9. The Mathematical World
10. Historical Perspectives (of science)*
11. Common Themes (for example, Systems, Models, Constancy, and so on)*
12. Habits of Mind (Values, Attitudes, Skills)*

   *Indicates material added by author for purposes of clarity.

Goals listed and defined under each of these topics provide direction for curriculum designers who create programs of study. The development of such programs is the primary purpose of Phase II of the project.

Phase II

To attain their goal of reform in science education in the nation's schools, those involved in Project 2061 have undertaken to create five different curriculum models in five different school districts across the country. The teams that will develop these K–12 curricula for science, mathematics, and technology include teachers at all levels of instruction in fields that run the gamut from science and math to social studies and technology. Each curriculum model will be designed to achieve the recommendations of the Phase I report, but the curricula are expected to vary in emphasis, style, and the degree to which they diverge from current models. Having diversity in the curriculum models will provide choices for teachers, schools, and school districts that utilize the programs.

Some of the basic premises that will guide the curriculum designers of all five projects are:

1. Concepts, relationships, and thinking skills will be stressed, not the accumulation of facts.
2. The boundaries used in the traditional organization of science and mathematics will be "blurred" and new and creative organizational schemes will be tried.
3. The interrelationships of science, mathematics, and technology will be emphasized, and the final product will be an integration of these subjects.
4. Instruction in science in the K–12 school programs should resemble the nature of the scientific enterprise and feature questioning, inquiry, and the processing of data.
5. Themes that reappear again and again in the natural world, such as systems, change, and so on, may gain wider attention in the study of science and mathematics.

While the curriculum writing teams are creating the models of science, mathematics, and technology curricula, others involved with Project 2061 will be expending great effort to gain support from political leaders, educators at all levels, university personnel, business and industry, and the general public to enhance the success of their comprehensive reform project. These efforts will lay the groundwork for Phase III of the project.

Phase III

After the curriculum development teams have created the five instructional models (in about 1992), massive implementation efforts will begin in earnest. They will involve locating and training hundreds of curriculum change experts who will be agents to disseminate information to all levels and areas of community leadership across the country. It is probably safe to state that Project 2061 will have a major impact upon the nature of science, mathematics, and technology instruction at all levels in the nation's schools.

Thematic Patterns of Elementary School Science Instruction

Although we believe the three curriculum projects presented here serve as models of science instruction that will dominate elementary science teaching in the coming decades, it is true that many other forces will also come to bear, including the efforts made by those who publish science textbooks. However, overviews we've given of these three projects, Science and Technology for Children (STC), Activities that Integrate Math and Science (AIMS), and Project 2061 reveal some constants that may be the guiding principles for many other elementary school science curriculum models:

an emphasis on skill development

an emphasis on investigation and inquiry

the use of direct, hands-on learning activities

the integration of traditional subject matter, both within the study of science and across subject matters

the recognition of major, recurring themes as a framework for science curricula

an emphasis upon conceptual schemes and relationships and less attention to memorizing facts

a stronger relationship between science and technology instruction

It will be interesting in fifteen or twenty years to examine the nature of elementary school science teaching and assess the accuracy of our predictions.

Summary

Young children are curious. Given the chance to explore and communicate, the child is likely to remain curious all his or her life.

Science activities that are laboratory centered and employ techniques of inquiry help children to overcome many deficiencies. Such programs used with young children have been found to enhance growth in I.Q., oral communication skills, reading skills, mathematics skills, and social studies skills. In addition, they develop logical thinking, science processes, curiosity, and positive attitudes. The nature of laboratory-oriented, inquiry-based elementary science programs makes them particularly useful in the development of basic skills in many subject areas.

As a matter of convenience, complex conceptual patterns are often explained with scientific models. Models represent a workable relationship among observed phenomena. A scientific model takes all known observations into account. As new information is gained, the old model must be modified to accommodate it. Or the old model may be discarded altogether in favor of a new one. This is what happened when the Ptolemaic earth-centered theory of the universe was replaced by the sun-centered theory. Today both theories have been replaced with a theory that describes the sun as a single star in an island of millions of stars, with this island separated from other islands by vast distances.

The goals of modern elementary school science include the acquisition of knowledge, manipulative skills, intellectual skills, and investigative and objective attitudes. These ambitious goals may best be reached by programs based upon methods of problem solving and manipulative activities. All of the curricula developed in the 1960s reflect these methods of instruction.

Science teaching has undergone a number of transitions in this country. It began as a rote memory exercise with the hickory stick and the harsh discipline of the colonial schoolhouse and later evolved into object-teaching exercises attributed to the Swiss educator Pestalozzi and adopted in this country as the Oswego plan. Social purpose became paramount in the evolution of the science curriculum at the turn of the twentieth century. Nature study was instituted to attract the masses of immigrants from the swollen cities of the eastern seaboard to the farmlands of the Midwest, and public health problems led to the teaching of health, which was often incorporated into science lessons. The softening of university entrance requirements and the development of the comprehensive high school led to the study of general science and biology and away from the narrower science fields, such as zoology and physics. The Progressive Education movement founded by John Dewey led to the introduction of problem solving into the science curriculum in the 1930s.

Many new elementary science programs were initiated in two decades, 1960 to 1980. Most of the successful ones were developed by professional scientists, psychologists, and teachers. All of these science curricula had several characteristics in common. The learning activities were child centered and laboratory oriented. The learning activities were tried out on children and then reconstructed several times. Teachers were required to assume an indirect, supervisory role.

Science—A Process Approach is a highly structured science program that helps children to acquire the skills for doing science. Eight primary and five integrated process skills were identified. Activities were formulated to help children progress from the simplest of these skills to the most complex.

The primary goal of the Science Curriculum Improvement Study is to make children scientifically literate. Through exploration, invention, and discovery in their laboratory-oriented units, the children work toward this goal. The program includes two sequences of basic concepts, one in life science and one in physical science.

The most unstructured of these science curricula is the Elementary Science Study. It is comprised of units that can be taught in any order. There are no restrictions. The teacher is free to custom tailor a science program to suit his or her needs. The single unifying characteristic of all units of the ESS program is an unstructured, discovery approach to teaching.

The impact of the federally funded science programs on elementary education has been greater than their actual use in classrooms would imply. Their emphasis on pupil involvement and manipulation of materials has affected the nature of commercial programs throughout the 1980s and into the 1990s. The indirect approach to teaching, the development of questioning skills, and concern with the development of higher-level cognitive skills—all characteristics of these curricula—have significantly affected the nation's teacher-training programs.

Elementary school science curricula of the twenty-first century are exemplified by three programs: Science and Technology for Children (STC), of the Smithsonian Institution's National Science Resource Center; Activities that Integrate Mathematics and Science (AIMS), of the AIMS Education Foundation; and Project 2061, of the American Association for the Advancement of Science.

The STC program is comprised of four units for each of the grade levels, 1 through 6. The program was designed around four themes: 1. Observing, Measuring and Identifying Properties; 2. Seeking Evidence/Recognizing Patterns and Cycles; 3. Identifying Cause and Effect/Extending the Senses; 4. Designing and Conducting Experiments. The STC program uses hands-on activities to teach scientific skills and attitudes; attempts to integrate science with other subjects in the elementary curriculum; and utilizes computers, trade books, and other media in its instructional activities. All materials of STC are field-tested in school settings prior to their release for sale to educators.

The AIMS Foundation utilizes interesting, activity-based problem-solving activities of science as a basis for integrating mathematics and science in the elementary and middle grades. The curriculum materials of AIMS consist of paperback booklets, each of which contains twenty or more problem-solving activities that utilize the skills of both mathematics and science. AIMS materials are generally utilized to enrich and integrate ongoing school programs and do not possess the scope and sequence structures that are required of a stand-alone curriculum. The AIMS Foundation considers their curriculum to be dynamic in nature as new units are constantly under development.

Project 2061 is a comprehensive K–12 science curriculum effort of the American Association for the Advancement of Science. This comprehensive project began in the mid-1980s with Phase I, which was designed to identify scientific literacy for all students in American schools. This phase has been completed, and based on the scientific knowledge, skills, and attitudes identified by leading scientists and educators, Phase II was begun, the development of curriculum materials for the elementary grades. At five different school sites across the country, each of which possesses a unique set of cultural and socioeconomic attributes, a separate curriculum will be created. The goal has been to complete these curricula by 1992. During Phase III, thousands of experts will be identified across the country to act as change agents in assisting school districts to utilize materials from one or more of these curricula in their elementary schools. These premises on which Project 2061 is based are expected to guide the development and implementation of elementary science instruction well into the twenty-first century.

Extending Activities

1. Critique any one of the three science programs for the twenty-first century (STC, AIMS, or Project 2061). Discuss how well the program will serve our children, schools, and nation during the coming two decades.

2. Discuss with your peers how mathematics skills such as counting, measuring, and graphing may be developed using science activities.

3. From an elementary textbook choose a single scientific topic such as magnetism, electricity, or plant life. Try to write a small number of concepts that would provide a basis for understanding the topic.

4. A model of the solar system has all of the planets circling the sun in approximately the same plane. Suppose you are an astronomer and discover a dark outer planet that travels in a different plane and in a different direction. What options do you have in reconciling the old model and your new data?

Bibliography

Champagne, A., and L. Hornig. "Issues of Science Teacher Quality, Supply and Demand." *Science Education* 71, no. 1 (January 1987): 57–76.

Craig, G. S. "Certain Techniques Used in Developing a Course of Study in Science for the Horace Mann Elementary School." Ph.D. dissertation, Columbia University, 1927.

Dykstra, D. "Science Education in Elementary School: Some Observations." *Journal of Research in Science Teaching* 24, no. 2 (February 1987): 179–182.

Esler, W., and K. Merritt, Jr. "Teaching Reading Through Science Experience Stories." *School Science and Mathematics* 76, no. 3 (March 1976): 203–206.

Gagné, R. M. "The Learning Requirements for Inquiry." *Journal of Research in Science Teaching* 1 (1963): 144–153.

Gega, P. *Science in Elementary Education*, 5th Ed. New York: Macmillan, 1986.

Girard, G. T. "Impact of NSF Science Curriculum Projects." *School Science and Mathematics* 79, no. 1 (1979): 3–6.

Hawkins, D. "Messing About in Science." *Science and Children* 2 (February 1965): 5–9.

James, R., and S. Smith. "Alienation of Students from Science in Grades 4–12." *Science Education* 69, no. 1 (January 1985): 39–46.

Lawson, A., K. Costenson, and R. Cisneros. "A Summary of Research in Science Education—1984—Elementary School Science." *Science Education* 70, no. 3 (June 1986): 213–221.

Marcuccio, P. "Forty-Five Years of Elementary School Science! A Guided Tour." *Science and Children* 24, no. 4 (January 1987): 12–14.

Nager, R., and J. Penick. "Perceptions of Four Age Groups Toward Science Classes, Teachers, and the Value of Science." *Science Education* 70, no. 4 (July 1986): 355–364.

Rutherford, F. "The Character of Elementary School Science." *Science and Children* 24, no. 4 (January 1987): 8–11.

Schoenberger, M., and T. Russell. "Elementary Science as a Little Added Frill: A Report of Two Case Studies." *Science Education* 70 (1986): 519–538.

Wagner, A., and C. Lucas. "Philosophical Inquiry and Logic of Elementary School Science Education." *Science Education* 61, no. 4 (1977): 549–558.

Project AIMS, AIMS Education Foundation, P. O. Box 7766, Fresno CA 93747 (free catalog and sample activities).

American Association for the Advancement of Science, *Science For All Americans*; A Project 2061 Report on Literacy Goals in Science, Mathematics and Technology, 1333 H Street NW, Washington D.C. 20005 (AAAS Publication 89-01s, 218 pages, paperback).

Curriculum Projects

Science and Technology for Children, Carolina Biological Supply House, 2700 York Rd., Burlington NC 27215.

CHAPTER 2

How Children Learn Science

Look What's in This Chapter

The purpose of this chapter is to acquaint you with the development of children's minds—specifically, with those operations that affect their abilities to perform and learn science. You will examine the levels at which children process cognitive input, feelings, and motor activity, and you'll consider their implications for learning. Through the eyes of the world's foremost theorist, you will discover how children are thought to develop their abilities to acquire and process information and how to identify the stages that define this growth. You will also become acquainted with several of the most commonly employed patterns or models of teaching and learning as they apply to science teaching. You'll learn how scientific concepts may be arranged in terms of complexity and used to structure children's learning of science. Finally, you'll become aware of some of the common misconceptions children have regarding their world—and how this affects their understanding of science.

The skilled teacher blends a chosen teaching technique with an understanding of children and a thorough knowledge of the subject matter. Though interesting, bustling, well-ordered activities appear to unfold effortlessly under the direction of a skilled teacher, each act, and nearly every word, should result from a deep understanding of children and of their learning processes.

Types of Involvement

Picture two third-grade classes that meet in adjoining rooms. Peek through the window in the door of Mrs. Smith's room, and you will see thirty children leaning over their desks, writing. A closer look reveals that the children are looking up definitions of scientific terms and copying them into their notebooks. All of the children are quiet and are obviously working on their assignments. Now move next door to Mrs. Jones's room. Here we see several groups of children dropping various objects into pans of water. There is some noise, and we overhear the children talking: "But all of the wood pieces didn't float." "The boat made of aluminum foil floated. Not all metals sink." "How are the things alike that floated, or sank?"

Would you say that Mrs. Smith's or Mrs. Jones's class was most involved with what they were doing? If involvement means simply being occupied, then both classes would appear to be highly involved. But involvement no longer means merely being physically engaged in activity. It also refers to the mental operations taking place. Are the intellectual requirements for performing Mrs. Smith's vocabulary assignment different from those for Mrs. Jones's problem-solving activity? Obviously they are. The child's level of involvement with the learning activity is considered to be higher in problem solving than in memorizing situations. A higher noise level in the classroom does not necessarily mean a lower level of involvement. Within limits, the opposite may be true. Children who are highly involved

with a problem may be moving about the room, manipulating materials, and talking to each other.

Levels of Intellectual Activity

Intellectual activities may be classified in order of complexity. Obviously it is more complicated to solve an algebra problem than to name the capital of Ohio or to match an inventor with his or her inventions.

Knowledge

The lowest level of cognitive activity, according to one widely accepted classification system,[1] is the acquisition of knowledge by memorization. This includes memorization of knowledge at all levels—from simple terminology and facts to principles, generalizations, and theories. In short, this activity consists of acquiring any information through the exercise of memory.

Comprehension

Demonstrations of various levels of comprehension rank just above memorization. Comprehension is manifested in such acts as paraphrasing or translating information into the pupil's own language, explaining and summarizing communications, and determining the implications of given information.

Application

The application of information to problem situations ranks above comprehension in terms of complexity. Here the learner must select from a number of processes, skills, or theories those that will help him to solve his problem. He must

---

[1]Benjamin B. Bloom, ed., *Taxonomy of Educational Objectives, Handbook I; Cognitive Domain* (New York: David McKay Co., 1956).

then apply his selections in some orderly sequence to realize his goal.

Analysis

Analysis generally involves the detailed examination of a statement or process according to some preconceived logical system. The learner may examine the parts of the statement or process individually, reorder them, or substitute others to test the structure as a whole. A child would be operating at the analysis level, for instance, by examining a model of an atom to see if it conforms to all he knows about atoms.

Synthesis

This level is especially important for science, for synthesis means putting parts together to form a new and unique whole. Children who are doing individual discovery and experimental activities are thought to be operating mainly at the synthesis level, as they derive hypotheses and devise methods for testing them.

Evaluation

This is the highest level of cognitive activity. Now that humans have found ways to destroy ourselves and our environment, it has become increasingly urgent that scientists form a humanistic system of values. Now that science may even create life itself, the scientist is faced with awesome decisions. Many of these issues may be discussed even by elementary school children.

The categories of cognitive activity do not have clearly defined boundaries. Thus, a teacher may find it impossible to categorize with certainty any one particular intellectual act. Simply establishing its general place among the range of cognitive acts may have to do. A product that was unique to one pupil would be deemed synthesis; the same product, if it were previously learned information for a second pupil, would be classified as knowledge. A teacher can, however, structure science activities that will challenge the majority of the class at a particular cognitive level. To do so, he or she must understand the process by which the child's cognitive structure develops and know what prior experience in science the pupils have had. Armed with this information, the teacher can successfully predict where the pupils' behavior will fall on the continuum of cognitive activity. Let us examine a series of activities that might be performed by a first-grade class studying a unit on plants and animals. Try to determine the cognitive level required for each activity.

1. From memory, the children name three animals with feathers and three animals with fur.

2. The children indicate an understanding of bird structure by completing an unfinished drawing.

3. After a discussion of how birds' body parts are related to their eating habits, the children are shown a picture of several birds and are asked what each bird might eat.

4. The children are shown a picture of a hardwood forest habitat. They are asked such questions as: Why does the squirrel live here? and How can the fox live?

5. When asked how they think water gets from the ground to the tops of plants, the children say that the water must creep up the middle of the stem.

6. The children say that people should not throw trash on the park grounds because the park becomes dirty and other people want to use it.

Each of the learning activities listed above represents a major cognitive level of Benjamin Bloom's taxonomy. They are listed in order of increasing complexity. Did you recognize them all? As you reexamine the six learning activities, think about the intellectual requirements of each. Does not each activity call for a different kind of cognitive skill?

Chart 2–1 summarizes the levels of the cognitive domain and gives examples of student behavior on each level.

Chart 2–1 ▪ Levels of the Cognitive Domain and Examples of Identifying Student Behavior

Cognitive Domain	Examples of Student Behavior
Knowledge (Level 1)	The student will: recall memorized facts.
	recite memorized facts.
	list memorized facts.
	enumerate memorized facts.
	write memorized facts.
	Note: A fact may be as simple as a single word or as complex as a law, a principle, or a process.
Comprehension (Level 2)	The student will: translate information.
	interpret information in his or her own words.
	rewrite a statement in his or her own words.
	edit statements from other sources.
	extrapolate new meaning from information.
Application (Level 3)	The student will: use rules, laws, generalizations in a new problem situation.
	apply known solutions to new events.
	employ guides (road maps, charts, graphs) for solving everyday problems.
	apply new skills in effecting solutions to problems.
	construct models for solving problems.
Analysis (Level 4)	The student will: illustrate a relationship among parts of a whole.
	take apart the elements of an object or event.
	interchange equivalent parts.
	separate events for more careful study.
	reorder the parts for clearer conceptualizations.
Synthesis (Level 5)	The student will: derive a unique approach to a given situation.
	formulate a hypothesis.
	produce a new plan of operation.
	contribute unique ways of viewing well-worn solutions.
	develop research problems.
Evaluation (Level 6)	The student will: render an opinion based on relevant data.
	give a point of view supported by valid evidence.
	judge the worth of an object or event based on external criteria.
	judge the worth of an object or event based on internal criteria.
	support a position following careful analysis of a situation.

Attending to Attitudes

An elementary science class will often present to the astute observer a wide range of attitudes toward the learning activity it is engaged in. Some children may be *receiving* the instruction at a low level of awareness, or with controlled or selected attention. Most of them are probably *responding* to the instruction at levels of enthusiasm ranging from mere acquiescence to real enjoyment and satisfaction. The teacher must remember that if a point is to be internalized,

Are these children involved with the learning activity?

and if it is to have lasting meaning for the children, they must receive it with at least some *willingness to respond*. Ideally, they will receive it with a sense of satisfaction. Only then will the children *value* the experiences to the extent that they become a part of their own system for understanding similar experiences.

Structuring science experiences so as to provide the most positive response may have far-reaching effects. A child who has internalized a great many generalizations and skills may *organize the values* gained in the science classroom into a system that will serve in other areas. Desirable habits such as delaying decisions until all the evidence is in, considering all the possible results of an action, and keeping an open mind may best be cultivated with activities to which the child willingly responds and from which he or she gains some measure of satisfaction.

Chart 2–2 summarizes the levels of the affective domain and gives examples of student behavior on each level.

Psychomotor Activity

The psychomotor domain was the last of the three domains of learning to be named in Bloom's classification system. As developed by Anita J. Harrow (1972), this domain encompasses mind-body skill development from the reflexive actions of infants who grasp anything that is placed in their palms to the complex nondiscursive communication of pantomime. Chart 2–3 summarizes the levels of the psychomotor domain and provides examples of child behavior for the various levels.

Behaviors of Levels 1 and 2 of the psychomotor domain are not normally taught in the elementary school. However, some theorists believe that the lack of proper development of these two levels leads to problems at the higher levels. Some special programs exist wherein individuals who experience perceptual difficulties are put through a series of "patterning" activities to develop Level 2 basic fundamental movements.

Chart 2–2 ■ Levels of the Affective Domain and Examples of Identifying Student Behavior

Affective Domain	Examples of Student Behavior	
Receiving (Level 1)	The student will:	listen by turning to the correct page.
		observe by pointing to the event.
		give attention by sitting up straight.
		be aware of the assignment by doing it.
Responding (Level 2)	The student will:	answer a question.
		perform a task.
		turn in work.
		volunteer for a job.
Valuing (Level 3)	The student will:	follow the safety rules.
		exhibit acceptable behavior.
		initiate a task.
		complete a job on time.
Organization (Level 4)	The student will:	resolve conflicting values.
		change an opinion.
		alter a belief.
		adhere to a position.
		defer making a judgment.
Characterization by a Value or Value Complex (Level 5)	The student will:	behave in a predictable manner in a laboratory situation.
		voluntarily take a summer science course.
		have identifiable personality characteristics in harmony with the tenets of a scientific attitude.

Level 3 perceptual abilities are often associated with the "readiness" construct that is applied to children of primary-grade age levels. Manipulative activities of the kindergarten and first-grade levels of several laboratory science programs are commonly employed to develop the perceptual abilities of children and their readiness for reading instruction. While the development of physical abilities (Level 4 of the psychomotor domain) does not appear to be directly linked with classroom instruction, many educators believe that children must achieve Level 4 abilities prior to developing the skills associated with Level 5 (skilled movements). Laboratory science programs for the elementary school require that students perform many skilled

(Level 5) movements. In these programs children might: use a dropper to transfer a measured amount of liquid, use a graduated cylinder to measure liquid volume, use hand tools such as a screwdriver and pliers, measure objects with a meter stick, and many other acts. Nondiscursive communication (Level 6) is frequently employed in "self-concept" development programs where children are taught to explore human emotion through such activities as making happy faces, sad faces, angry faces, and so on.

It is theorized that psychomotor abilities are progressive, the more complex movements encompassing skills of the lower levels. Psychomotor skills may be developed only by the child being physically involved. Activity-oriented

Chart 2–3 ▪ Levels of the Psychomotor Domain and Examples of Identifying Child Behavior*

Psychomotor Domain	Examples of Child Behavior	
Reflexive Movement (Level 1)	The child will:	grasp an object placed in his palm.
		withdraw a hand from potential danger.
		jump at a sudden loud noise.
Basic Fundamental Movement (Level 2)	The child will:	raise arms on command.
		hop on one foot.
		crawl with proper movement.
Perceptual Abilities (Level 3)	The child will:	walk a balance beam.
		distinguish between two similar geometric shapes.
		describe the texture of objects.
		copy a line drawing.
Physical Abilities (Level 4)	The child will:	walk on all fours like a bear for thirty feet.
		lift a weight equal to one-half his body weight.
		jump over an obstacle one-half his body height.
Skilled Movements (Level 5)	The child will:	pour a liquid from one container to another.
		use a platform balance to accurately measure the weight of objects.
		draw a line freehand.
Nondiscursive Communication (Level 6)	The child will:	communicate an idea by pantomime.
		mimic an animal so that others may identify it.
		move rhythmically in conjunction to music.

*Information in this chart was derived chiefly from Anita J. Harrow, *A Taxonomy of the Psychomotor Domain* (New York: David McKay Co., 1972).

science programs can help a child to develop psychomotor skills. Conversely, certain psychomotor skills, especially at the perceptual abilities and skilled movement levels, are necessary for doing laboratory science activities.

Levels of Involvement with Science

Maximum cognitive involvement occurs when the child is engaged in finding the solution to a problem that has immediate meaning and importance to him. The higher cognitive levels that deal with decision making and analysis of data are best exercised when each child works individually on a solution. The best way to ensure that the child becomes involved is to let him operate as an independent investigator; in general, involvement decreases in proportion as the child is denied the chance to perform individually. The teacher who wants pupils to derive the maximum benefit from experiences in science provides opportunities for individual investigation.

For various reasons, not all elementary school science lessons may be done on an individual basis, with each child manipulating materials and making an investigation. There is often not enough equipment, or the teacher must personally provide the apparatus required for a lesson. Other factors that reduce the possibility of individual investigation are classroom safety, fear of disciplinary problems, and the nature of the science concept being taught. Most teachers find that it is much easier to supervise the activities of several groups of children than to control a classroom of individual operators. This, they feel, is particularly important when the activity might possibly be dangerous. Also, the teacher sometimes wishes to present a concept or skill that all the children need to possess in order to cope with succeeding lessons. Such a presentation might involve an experiment teaching them to account for variables or to construct graphs.

Realistically, the teacher must often work with pupils whose levels of involvement are reduced according to the nature of the concept being taught, their own characteristics, and the materials available. The various levels of involvement are:

1. Individual investigation.
2. Group investigation.
3. Pupil-teacher problem-solving discussion.
4. Pupil demonstration.
5. Teacher demonstration.
6. Teacher-centered activity.
7. Seatwork.

Depending on how the activities are structured, the levels of involvement may overlap and in some cases interchange with one another on the hierarchy. It should generally be the teacher's goal to begin planning on the level of individual investigation. Then descend as necessary. In this way the maximum involvement possible under the given conditions is provided.

The Development of the Child's Thinking Processes— Piaget's Theory

Teachers are often deceived by their own wishful thinking into overestimating the level of understanding of children. This occurs especially in the primary grades. This self-deception occurs because they assume that children perceive in the same way as adults. They do not. Many six-year-olds, for instance, have learned to count to a hundred but have no concept of "numberness" beyond, say, ten. Often they cannot even make a one-to-one correspondence. Children will learn the labels for numbers, properties of objects, and procedures in order to satisfy the demands of adults without always understanding meanings and relationships. One well-known comedian has a first-grade child saying, "Yeh man, two and two is four. What's a four?" It is verbal mimicry that often misleads well-meaning educators into believing that children really understand the related concepts.

Studies conducted by Jean Piaget (1896–1980) that have been widely substantiated indicate that the child's cognitive development takes place in four main, sequential stages: the sensory-motor stage, the preoperational stage, the concrete operations stage, and the stage of formal logic.

The Sensory-Motor Stage

In the period immediately following birth an infant has no sense of permanence. That which is not in the field of vision does not exist. During the period that is thought to last typically from birth to about eighteen months, the child develops this sense of permanence. That is, he or she comes to know that objects that are not in his field of view do not vanish, but still exist somewhere. The child begins to recognize shapes and sizes and to relate people and objects to physical needs: that is, some people and objects cause pleasant things to happen, and others cause unpleasant things to happen. The child also begins to gain a concept of self. Toward the end of the sensory-motor stage, the child can recognize himself in a family picture or in a mirror. Many authorities feel that a healthy and rich environment during the sensory-motor stage is very important to the child's subsequent intellectual development.

The Preoperational Stage

This stage lasts from eighteen months to about seven years of age. Early in this stage, the child begins to speak and to think. The thinking process, however, is restricted by perceptual limitations, for the child can focus upon only one dimension of an object at a time.

At this level of development, children are deceived by many of their observations. They are fooled by a bit of clay that is shaped first like a ball and then like a hot dog (conservation of substance). They cannot tell if a short, wide bottle contains more liquid than a tall, narrow bottle (conservation of liquid volume). They cannot understand that when objects are spread over a larger area, the number of objects does not increase (conservation of number). These and other conceptual limitations prevent the preoperational child from understanding transitions in shape, size, time, and number.

Later in the preoperational stage, children begin to acquire the ability to mentally reverse some operations. They can recognize, for instance, that a ball of clay that has been shaped into a hot dog can be reshaped back into a ball. The child is then said to be able to *conserve substance*.

A child's ability to conserve does not arrive in one great jump. There appears to be a *transitional stage*, during which the child may state that the ball and the rod have the "same amount of stuff," without being able to say why. His uncertainty may become very apparent when the examiner divides one of the clay balls into several parts. A real conserver would still maintain that the three small balls together have as much "stuff" as the whole ball. He would explain that nothing is changed except the shape; that nothing was added or taken away. The transitional conserver becomes confused and can provide no reasonable explanation.

The various conservation abilities do not develop simultaneously. A child may be able to conserve mass or weight, but not volume or density. Thus, the same child may be in several stages of development at once.

Piaget-like Child Study Exercises

Conservation of Substance

Show a child two balls of modeling clay of the same size. Ask: "Do the balls contain the same amount of clay? Do they have the same amount of stuff?" Then shape one ball into a hot dog or pancake (Figure 2–1). Now ask: "Now do the balls contain the same amount of clay? Do they still have the same amount of stuff?" Whatever the child answers, ask him: "Why is that?"

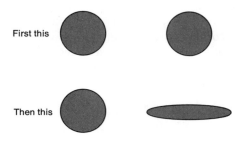

Figure 2–1 ■ Conservation of Substance

Conservation of Liquid Volume

Show a child two identical tumblers containing the same amount of water. Ask: "Do the tumblers contain the same amount of water?" Empty or fill the tumblers until the child agrees that they contain the same amount of water. Then pour the water from one tumbler into a third, tall, thin tumbler (Figure 2–2). Now ask: "Now do both tumblers contain the same amount of water?" Whatever the child answers, ask him: "Why is that?"

Conservation of Number

From a pile of beans remove one bean and have a five- or six-year-old child remove one, too. Let the child place his bean in a tall, thin jar while you place your bean in a short, wide jar (Figure 2–3). Repeat this operation until all the beans are gone from the pile, being careful to remove each of your beans as the child removes one of his. Ask the child: "Do both jars contain

Figure 2—2 ■ Conservation of Liquid Volume

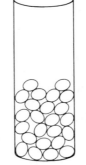

Figure 2—3 ■ Conservation of Number

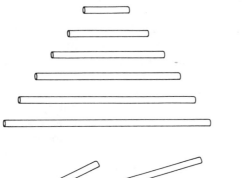

Figure 2—4 ■ Serial Ordering

the same number of beans?" Whatever the child answers, ask him: "Why is that?"

Serial Ordering

Give a child six sticks of different lengths. Tell him to put the sticks in order from shortest to longest. If the child completes this task, hand him three additional sticks that are different lengths than any of the original sticks. Tell the child to put the three sticks in their proper places in the ordered set. (See Figure 2—4.)

One-to-One Correspondence

From a pile of chips remove one chip at a time, placing them in a row. Each time you place a chip, ask the child to place a chip beside it. When both rows contain ten chips, ask the child: "Do both rows contain the same number of chips?" After the child agrees that both rows contain the same number of chips, spread apart the chips in one row so that the row becomes longer (Figure 2—5). Ask: "Do both rows still contain the same number of chips?" "Why is that?"

The Concrete Operations Stage

This stage lasts from about age seven to age eleven. A child in the concrete operations stage has the conservation abilities just described. The first conservations that appear are usually those associated with number. Then come those

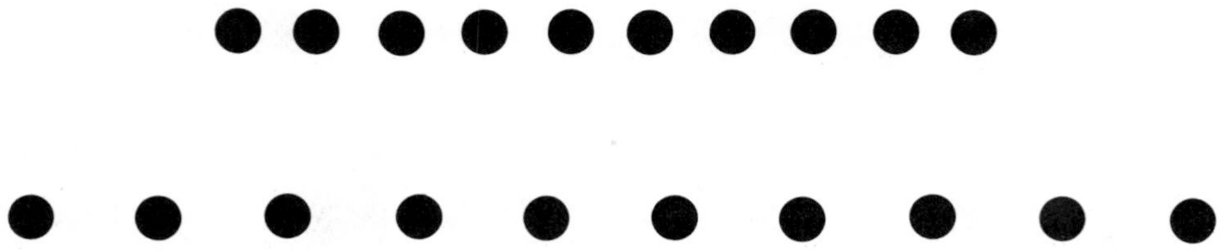

Figure 2–5 ■ One-to-One Correspondence

dealing with mass, weight, and length, and last of all, volume and density.

A child in the concrete operations stage can perform simple logical operations such as classifying objects by similarities and differences and ordering objects and ideas according to some property. He can, for instance, mentally manipulate concepts of girls, boys, and people. If you asked a child in the advanced concrete operations stage whether there were more boys or people in his class, he would probably say, "Boys are people and so are girls, so there are more people than boys." The same child might also be able to place sticks in order according to their length. He could place an additional stick of a different length between the proper two sticks in the ordered set. He sees the additional stick as being both shorter than something and longer than something else.

The child in the concrete operations stage experiments mostly by trial and error, and the trials are rarely related to one another. He cannot mentally consider multiple possibilities for seeking solutions to problems. He must physically manipulate, or see manipulated, concrete objects that represent the variables of the problem. This explains the present-day emphasis on involving children physically in science experiences. Many children are in the concrete operations stage in many of the conservations throughout much of their elementary school experience.

The Formal Operations Stage

At around eleven, the child enters the formal operations stage. He is now fully capable of performing logical operations, but has had only limited experience with them. He can mentally and systematically examine the consequences of combining various factors; he need no longer rely upon manipulating concrete objects. For example, a child in the formal operations stage is given three vials (Figure 2–6). Two contain a neutral liquid, while one contains a basic solution. He is asked to choose which vial contains the basic solution, using the fewest possible drops of indicator. He might think like this: "The indicator will turn a basic solution pink. I might pour some liquid from vials one and two together and test the combined solution. If the combined solution does not turn pink, I will know that vial three is the basic solution. If the solution does turn pink, I can put some indicator in vial one. If vial one does not turn pink, the basic solution is in vial two. If vial one does turn pink, the basic solution is in it. Thus, I can solve the problem using no more than two drops of indicator."

In this example the child is mentally manipulating all the possibilities that might lead to the solution. He can make the tests mentally and consider the implications of the results. He can experiment on a purely intellectual basis. Many educators forget this. They are caught up in the immediate success of primary-grade science programs based upon the manipulation of objects. But once the child has reached the formal operations stage, he no longer needs to manipulate objects. Now he can mentally test that which is not demonstrable. He can visualize the structure and appreciate the reasonableness of the scientific model.

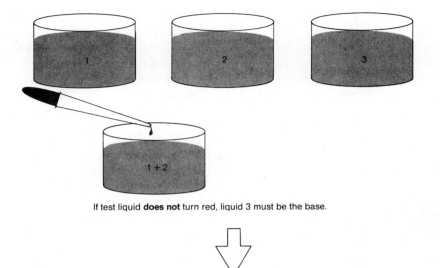

If test liquid **does not** turn red, liquid 3 must be the base.

or

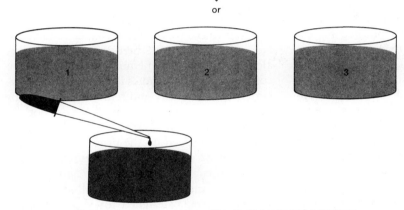

If test liquid **does** turn red, then either liquid 1 or liquid 2 is the base.

then

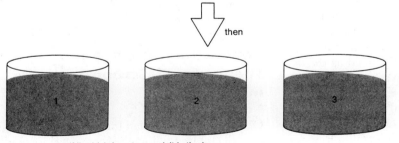

If liquid 1 **does** turn red, it is the base.
If liquid 1 **does not** turn red, then liquid 2 is the base.

Figure 2–6 ■ A Logical Operation

Fifth- and sixth-grade teachers must remember that in any one class there are usually pupils in both the concrete and formal operations stages. And even children who can handle abstractions may sometimes learn more easily when new ideas are introduced with some physical demonstration of the principle involved. The teacher must provide manipulative experiences for those requiring them and must challenge the abstract reasoning ability of the most advanced pupil. This is a big assignment.

Elementary Science and the Developmental Process

Piaget's theory that children move through a series of developmental stages on the way to intellectual maturity has received worldwide support. Psychologists have replicated his experiments with children of many nationalities and widely varying cultures. The results were startling. The children of Switzerland, Mozambique, and the African bush country all appeared to be going through the same sequence of developmental stages. The only differences in the intellectual development of the children of these widely diverse cultures was the age at which the child typically acquired the various conservations. Children all over the world appear to perceive given physical conditions and respond to standard questions in much the same way.

According to Piaget, the child's intellectual development is affected by four factors: *maturation, experience, social transmission*, and *equilibration*. Maturation is defined as the development of the child's nervous system. Experience is the child's direct association with objects in his or her physical environment. Social transmission is association with people and institutions. The fourth factor, equilibration (or self-regulation), is the key to the whole Piagetian theory.

Piaget believed that when a child encounters new facts or observations he tends to assimilate them if they fit easily into his existing knowledge structures. If the facts or observations are novel and cannot be assimilated, then intellectual dissonance is set up. To remove the dissonance, the existing knowledge structures must be modified. Equilibration is the act of restoring intellectual harmony and equilibrium. For example, the cognitive disturbance that results when a child sees clay balls remolded into hot dogs eventually results in the mental reversing of the act. The child remolds the hot dogs back into balls in his own mind. It is only by reversing the process that the mental dissonance is reduced. Equilibration, in this case, leads to the ability to reverse the process.

What can a science program do to enhance the young child's intellectual development? It can provide him with the chance to interact with physical objects. This is especially important to children who have had little chance to manipulate objects at home. Interaction with objects alone cannot result in equilibration or develop conservations, but studies indicate that such experiences help clarify and cement conservations still in the transitional stage. We do not yet know just how much experience with the environment can speed up the process of cognitive development, but most science educators consider that its advantages far outweigh any possible disadvantages. This is why all of the newer science curricula designed for young children rely heavily on manipulative experiences as a basic method of instruction.

Implications of Piagetian Theory for Classroom Instruction

One thing that Piagetian theory has taught us is that all children follow the same developmental pattern regardless of culture and general ability. Only the ages at which conservations typically appear are different. This important point explains why elementary science programs that employ many concrete experiences appear to work with slow children as well as with the culturally deprived. With proper attention to concrete experiences and ample time for the children to explore, special science programs for the many different kinds of children are not necessary.

A second implication is that classroom teachers must keep in mind that children perceive things differently. In most classrooms, teachers will find a range of developmental stages. Even in the middle school grades there are children who are preoperational in some conservation tasks, while others are in the stage of logical operations. If middle-grade teachers must choose between using manipulative materials or structuring more abstract lessons for those children able to perform abstract operations, they should choose the manipulative materials. For the nonconservers in their class, the concrete is *necessary*, for the logical thinkers it almost always is *helpful*.

A third implication for the classroom teacher is that mere physical activity is not enough to ensure the proper intellectual development of children. Ideas must also be manipulated. While Piaget advocated accepting all of a child's ideas, he also provided alternatives for the child to consider. If a child says that moisture on an aquarium came in the window, the teacher might say "Good," and after a pause say, "Could it possibly have already been in the room somewhere?" The teacher should always be indirect and never force the idea. In this way, children examine how they arrive at ideas, which leads to mentally testing the ideas' truths.

Allied to allowing a child to examine the sources of his or her own ideas is examining the processes involved in problem solving. After the class has solved a problem, the teacher may ask "How did we arrive at this answer?" and help the class retrace the steps taken in arriving at a solution. By adding the intellectual manipulation to concrete activities, the teacher is more likely to help children in their intellectual development.

Brain Research and Piaget[2]

The human brain is a wondrous organ so complex in its working that it defies comprehension. Three pounds of highly specialized cells enable humans to see, smell, feel, hear, and to remember, create, and solve complex problems. Although knowledge is far from complete, researchers are discovering more about the hundred billion nerve cells and the quadrillion intercellular connections that make up the adult brain.

Researchers have identified about twenty different nerve hormones that affect the transmission of signals among nerve cells of the brain. These complex proteins are synthesized within the brain tissue and operate in the synapses between neurons. Chemicals that stimulate or decrease the production of brain hormones can affect mental health, mood, and basic needs, such as hunger and the sex drive. Other research indicates that brain tissue is affected in its development and function by sustained activity. As more is learned about the physiology and chemistry of the brain, it may be useful to relate new understanding to theories derived from less empirical data, such as Piaget's theory of cognitive development.

As part of his theory of cognitive development, Piaget stressed the importance of high levels of interaction of children with their environment and other people to ensure optimum development of their cognitive structure. Researchers have discovered strong evidence of the importance of activity to neuronal development. They found that cats raised in an environment of only vertical lines later did not respond normally to horizontal lines. Apparently the brain structure that would enable the cats to see horizontal lines did not develop.

Other researchers found that animals raised under environmentally impoverished conditions

---

[2]Reprinted from W. K. Esler, "Brain Physiology: Research and Theory." *Science and Children* 20, no. 5 (March 1982): 44, 45.

had fewer synaptic connections among their brains' nerve cells. These scientists extrapolated that a human's intellectual potential was directly related to the richness and variety of personal experiences; that is, stimulation enriched the brain's capacity. Some observers theorize that the inability of the Japanese to pronounce the letter *L* is the result of a lack of early verbal experience since that sound is not present in their native language.

A system of brain cells that enables a person to demonstrate a skill is best developed before a child's brain reaches physical maturity, when opportunities lost may never be fully compensated. Attempts to develop skills that were neglected in a child's formative years have met with limited success. Many research physiologists support Piaget's conclusion that an array of childhood experiences is important to the development of the brain's neural structure.

Specific Skills

If the premise that early and frequent stimulation is necessary for proper development of brain cells and their electrical pathways is accepted, then it would be well to speculate concerning the development of specific mental skills. Brain-wave studies show that showers of electrical activity are scattered throughout the brain. Complex processes, such as creating an experiment or interpreting data, appear to require the correlated function of much of the cerebrum and midbrain. If optimal development of brain structure and function depend upon experience and activity, then Piaget's emphasis upon experience in the development of cognitive skills was significant. Also, the verbal interaction that is a vital social transmission as children discuss and probe their environment provides stimulation to many brain centers, building synaptic connections and helping to maintain high levels of hormone production.

Many of the followers of Piaget advocate that teachers follow classification and other problem-solving activities with a discussion of

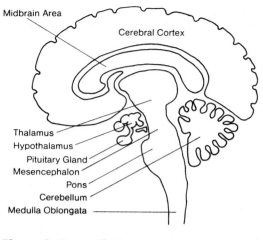

Figure 2–7 ■ The Brain

alternative methods and procedures that students might have used to achieve solutions. The complex brain activity required by such discussions may serve to create and strengthen neural pathways among many different areas of the brain.

The more researchers learn about the physiology and chemistry of the brain, the more they verify the educational applications of Piaget's theory. (See Figure 2–7.) Understanding the principles of maturation, experience, social transmission, and equilibration (self-regulation) has a base in the growing understanding of the intricate function of the brain.

Gagné's Behavioristic Learning Model

Another frequently applied theory of learning is that of Robert M. Gagné. Gagné's learning hierarchy is based upon the notion that all learning must proceed from the simple to the more complex in well-defined stages. Each step of the evolving content or skill is to be defined by careful examination of the entire learning sequence. In practice the curriculum designer starts by de-

Chart 2–4 ▪ A Sample Graphing Hierarchy Related to Gagné's Learning Levels

Gagné's Learning Levels*	Sample Prerequisite Skills
Level 1: Signal Learning (involuntary actions related to emotions, fright, joy, etc.)	These responses are too emotional and undefined to be related to a learning hierarchy.
Level 2: Stimulus-Response (voluntary motor learning)	Repeating words when spoken by the teacher. Repeating number words when spoken by the teacher.
Level 3: Chaining (joining together simple stimulus-response behaviors to form a self-acting sequence)	Using a pencil to copy words. Writing numbers in sequence.
Level 4: Verbal Chaining (naming objects, using descriptive adjectives to name objects)	Recognizing by name the variables to be considered. Writing numbers by 100s and 500s.
Level 5: Multiple Discrimination Learning (placing objects and events with one or more common properties in a set)	Distinguishing lines of a great slope from the lines of a lesser slope. Recognizing proper scales for axis. Interpreting and constructing simple graphs.
Level 6: Concept Learning (identifying sets of events that differ in outward appearance as a class)	Relating slope to a change in a variable. Knowing units of measure employed. Interpreting simple graphs.
Level 7: Principle Learning (combining acquired concepts)	Skills of interpolation and extrapolation of data. Skills of reading data from axis. Interpreting graphs.
Level 8: Problem Solving (the application of learned principles)	Interpreting a line graph of the world's population growth.

*For a complete treatment of Gagné's learning hierarchy, see Robert M. Gagné's *The Conditions of Learning* (New York: Holt, Rinehart & Winston, 1965), Chapter 7.

fining the final desired product—usually a complex, problem-solving skill. He then attempts to define the learning necessary to achieve this goal. The prerequisite skills are then defined in successive steps until the simplest possible contributing skills and knowledge are determined. After the skills knowledge hierarchy is constructed, the curriculum designer formulates a behavioral objective for each skill-knowledge cell. He then constructs a learning activity and evaluation procedure for each cell, establishing a hierarchical learning pattern. The learner begins with the simplest learning activities and progresses systematically toward the final complex, problem-solving skill.

Examine Gagné's eight learning levels in Chart 2–4. Do you see in principle how the learning hierarchy is employed in designing learning sequences for children? A brief consideration of the sample prerequisite skills reveals that the chart is greatly simplified. At the lower levels, a very large number of primitive learned responses are required to develop the higher skill level. In practice, learning hierarchies have become very complex with many prerequisite skills at each learning level. However, the theory demonstrates that learning must take place in well-defined steps with the learner moving from the simple tasks to the more complex concepts, principles, and skills.

Using the Behavioristic Model in the Classroom

The most commonly employed behavioristic curricula are the reading and math programs that utilize student performance checksheets, which cross grade levels and, even within a single grade, represent a carefully structured behavioral hierarchy. In these programs each student is expected to master the skills that are lower in the hierarchy before continuing on to the next level. In elementary school science, the Science—A Process Approach (SAPA) program utilizes this same type of organization. The student is required to master the subject matter by working through an array of tasks and objectives arranged in order from the simple to the more complex. Procedures of diagnosis and remediation are almost universally tied to this behavioristic model.

Bruner's Discovery Learning Model

Jerome Bruner more than any other person has successfully applied the principles of Piaget's child development theories to the education of children. The result is the mode of learning that is most often called discovery learning. The principal characteristics of Bruner's discovery are:

1. The child's involvement with the learning process.

2. The teacher's role as a guide and advisor in the child's search for information rather than as an expositor of information.

3. The common use of concrete materials as a beginning for the learning process.

The advantages of discovery learning according to Bruner are fourfold:

1. Discovery learning helps the child learn how to learn independently.

2. Discovery learning shifts the motivation of the learner from that of seeking external rewards (extrinsic motivation) to internal satisfaction (intrinsic motivation).

3. Discovery learning equips the learner with *practiced* procedures (heuristics) for solving problems.

4. Discovery learning helps the learner to retain more (he who does, understands and remembers) and to recall more useful information.

Bruner's presentation of the way a child absorbs and processes information closely parallels that of Piaget. A growing child passes through three distinct stages according to his mental representation of information: the enactive representation stage, the ikonic representation stage, and the symbolic representation stage. The enactive representation stage parallels Piaget's sensory-motor stage wherein the child is principally developing motor skills and an awareness of self and surroundings. In the ikonic stage the child's mental representations are greatly affected by his perceptions, and his perceptions are egocentric and unstable. He has yet to develop a control over his perceptions that permits him to view the world about him with a patterned consistency. When an internal control mechanism develops, the child moves into Bruner's stage of symbolic representation. At the heart of symbolic representation is the development of language and the ability to represent the outside world in terms of words and ideas. The child who begins to symbolically process information is moving into the logical operations stage as described by Piaget.

While Bruner provides many provocative ideas, he has not supplied an operational definition of discovery learning. He has not spelled out for the teacher those specific teaching acts that ensure that a discovery lesson is taking place. In the following chapters, inquiry teaching has been operationally defined in three different modes—rational, discovery, and experimentation—to provide specific procedures for each form of teaching by discovery.

Using the Discovery Model in the Classroom

In Chapter 3 you will find numerous examples of discovery learning. In its broadest definition, discovery occurs anytime the learner uses her higher cognitive skills to find new relationships or meanings in a given situation. Discovery takes place when a kindergarten teacher permits the children to place various objects in a pan of water and observe which ones sink and which ones float. It is also discovery when a fifth-grade teacher directs her students to construct a graph of the distance a metal object travels when sliding down an incline plane at various angles. The students, on their own, may discover the relationships between the angle of the incline and the distance the metal object slides across the table. There generally are no preliminary requirements for teaching a discovery lesson, other than to consider the general ability of the students to make the necessary associations.

Ausubel's Verbal Learning Model

Verbal learning taught by direct methods of instruction such as lecture and seatwork has maintained a strong following over the years. Recent research on effective teaching has indicated that when highly specific information that might be committed to memory is the desired learning objective, direct instruction is the most efficient mode. The current model of direct instruction includes the parameters of whole class instruction as compared to group or individual instruction, maximizing children's time engaged in tasks that represent easily attainable goals, and providing constant feedback to children on their completed tasks. The direct or verbal learning model is more effective with primary-grade children who are being taught the basic skills of reading and mathematics. The direct teaching techniques, according to research, appear to lose much of their effectiveness with upper elementary-grade children, and with children of high socioeconomic status and high I.Q.

David P. Ausubel, long-term advocate of verbal learning, has maintained that verbal learning technique, in which a body of information is highly organized and the learner is presented with an outline of the structure (advanced organizers), is much more efficient in terms of instructional time expended on learning and so permits the learner to experience a broader range of subject matter. Even Ausubel, however, conceded that discovery learning is necessary when children are in the concrete stage of cognitive development.

In this text we will emphasize the theories of Piaget and Bruner as starting points of the learning process. We will demonstrate procedures for introducing science to children through the use of manipulative materials and inquiry teaching methods. Gagné's hierarchical learning will be shown to be useful in information-gathering learning activities that follow the development of concepts and skills through the use of inquiry procedures.

Using the Verbal Learning Model in the Classroom

The verbal learning model is often thought of as one that encompasses traditional teaching methods. A second-grade teacher assigns children to complete a worksheet that contains new vocabulary words by first using a dictionary to locate definitions and then writing them on the worksheet. A sixth-grade teacher lectures her class on the culture of the Navajo Indians. A fourth-grade student copies his science words ten times to prepare for a test. And a third-grade teacher assigns her children to read a chapter in the science textbook and answer the questions that appear in the book. Each of these activities—especially if they are conducted after the students have been provided with an outline of the subject matter for the week (advanced organizers)—can be considered verbal learning.

Concept Learning

The general definition of the term *concept* is that it is a notion, a thought, or idea. The concepts of children cover many levels of thinking, ranging from unstructured intuitions to untested thought to well-developed and tested ideas. The nature of concept development in children is central to a teacher's understanding of the ways in which children process their sensory interactions with the world around them. Let's take a few minutes to consider the ways children develop concepts and conceptual frameworks.

A child's understanding of the world would appear to grow in three distinct stages. Initially, a child learns to recognize the properties of objects. A child learns that a kitten is soft and furry and has four legs and a tail. She has formed the concept of kitten. Then she may begin to group kittens together according to these and other attributes, excluding other animals that do not share them. Finally, she is able to predict the behaviors of the animals in the group—they will meow and not bark, they will sharpen their claws on the furniture, and so on. Thus, she has formed a concept of kitten, learned to classify kittens excluding other animals with dissimilar attributes, and can predict behaviors and possibly solve problems employing the concepts she has formed.

Let us examine how the growth of concepts is used to structure children's learning in science.

A third-grade teacher may provide students with experiences in observation that permit them to conclude that: (1) plants respond to water (roots of a geranium grew toward a wet area); (2) some plants respond to touch (a Venus'-flytrap closed when touched); and (3) plants respond to light (bean plants in a light-tight box grew toward an opening). The children conclude that plants are living things and are sensitive to the conditions of their environment. Several weeks later, as the class is studying simple animal life, they observe that mealworms respond to a light source. One child in the class

Children forming concepts about their world.

states, "That's not surprising. They are living things and all living things respond to their environment." Most of the other children agree. The concept that had been formed regarding plants has been expanded to include animals. The children have formed a scientific concept based on their observations and have used it as an organizing idea for handling new information on tropisms. Thus, dealing with the concepts of science serves two purposes: (1) isolated facts and observations are rendered understandable, and (2) conceived relationships provide a conceptual framework for organizing new information. Contrast this with the old style of science teaching, in which the students would have memorized the names of the tropisms of plants and the sensitivities of animals as separate, unrelated entities. The advantages of the new organization are apparent. The organization of the curriculum parallels the children's conceptual development, making what is learned more understandable and useful to the learner. The levels and placement of the concepts of science in the elementary school curriculum are discussed in Chapter 4. See especially Concept Mapping and the Organization of Science Concepts.

Understanding Children's Misconceptions

Children enter kindergarten having acquired many ideas about their natural world. They continue to acquire new information every day in their normal activities outside of school. This spontaneous knowledge is developed from children's contact with their environments and through social transmissions from parents, siblings, and others. Often these preconceptions are not congruent with the parallel concepts we attempt to teach in elementary school science programs; the discrepancies may confuse children and get in the way of their ability to learn the school material.

Misconceptions of children, sometimes called "alternative frameworks," can be described generally as being of two types, phenomenological and vocabulary-based. Phenomenological misconceptions are those associated with misinterpretations of natural phenomena, for example, heavy objects always sink in water and lightweight objects always float, or the earth is essentially a flat surface. These interpretations of their observations may have been acquired spontaneously by children as the result of their limited experiences, or they may have been passed on from some other person, often an authority figure in their lives. Vocabulary-based misconceptions are generally the result of the elementary school child's limited experiences. For instance, children consider the word *animal* to refer to dogs, cats, rabbits, and other familiar animals, although the formal concept of the word *animal* as taught in elementary school science programs encompasses all living things that are not plants. When teachers speak of insects or people as being animals, the young learner often is confused by the broader scientific definition. Similarly, the word *work* is sometimes a source of misconception problems for elementary school children. To a child, work occurs any time a person expends an effort, especially when that person gets tired and perspires. In science, work occurs only when an object is moved. When teachers present concepts that conflict with children's "alternative frameworks," children have difficulty assimilating the new information and often become confused. Sometimes children simply reject the formal, school-based concept in favor of the more familiar, informal one. Or they may build a dual, parallel system of concepts in order to remove the cognitive dissonance.

Dealing with Children's Misconceptions

The first step in dealing with the misconceptions/preconceptions/alternative frameworks of children is to recognize that they exist. Concepts grow normally and naturally in children's cognitive structure as they gain additional experience and information. Second, the teacher must try to spot the conflicts that arise between children's preconceptions and the more formal, scientific concepts presented to them.

The teacher can define students' preconceptions by using questions to arrive at a group definition or concept statement when possible. Third, the teacher should categorize the misconception as phenomenological or vocabulary-based. The goal is to correct the misconceptions that are based upon scientific phenomena and clarify the differences between the definitions of the informal use and formal scientific use of like words when the misconception is vocabulary-based. The fourth step involves structuring learning activities that will accomplish these goals and carrying them out.

Correcting Phenomenological Misconceptions

Once you have determined, through questioning, that a phenomenological misconception exists, the best way to correct it is to use hands-on experiences. This is especially true for those phenomena that may be closely examined in the classroom. For instance, the common notion among children that all metals sink in water may be examined by structuring "sink or float" exercises where children are permitted to place metal objects of all shapes and configurations in a pan of water and witness the results. Some dish- or boat-shaped metal objects will float. *Use these experiences to build upon the child's preconception, rather than try to destroy it.* For instance, after the children have stated on their own that some metal objects float, summarize their experience by saying, "We have seen that while it is true that many metal objects sink in water, other metal objects float. What do the metal objects that float have in common?" The misconception that the earth is flat can be attacked with models such as globes, or with a trip outside to the schoolyard to ask, "Looking across the schoolyard could we tell if the ground is flat or curved one centimeter upward or downward?" Conclude this activity back in the classroom by asking the children whether a man as small as an ant could see the curve in the globe, or would the surface of the globe look flat to him? As a teacher you may not always be successful in replacing children's conceptual structures regarding natural phenomena, but providing direct experience and, through the use of questions, opening the minds of the children to the alternative interpretation is an important first step in the process.

Correcting Vocabulary-based Misconceptions

Defining words in the *context* of their use is an accepted and desirable practice for correcting vocabulary-based misconceptions. Language arts teachers spend a great deal of effort helping children acquire this skill. We should do the same thing in science. To introduce the scientific concept that animals include all living things that are not plants, first have the students define the word *animal* in their own terms. (The characteristics of animals may be demonstrated later.) You may wish to write a statement of their definition (concept) on the chalkboard. Then have the children name all the living things they can think of that are not plants. (For purposes of this discussion it is assumed that the concept of living and nonliving things has been previously discussed.) You may want to ask such questions as "What about insects? Are they plants?" Do the same for frogs and snails and so on. When the children have listed a large number of creatures, including many that did not appear in their original definition, you might say to the class, "Your definition of animals included many of the animals you see around you in your homes and neighborhood. Scientists have a different definition for the word *animal*. All of these things you have listed are called animals by scientists. Can we write a sentence that defines animals as a scientist would?" Help the children to construct a statement conveying the idea that all living things that are not plants are called animals. Then, using this definition, provide a number of examples of animals and nonanimals. In this way—by clarifying the general use of a term as it is common to children and then formulating the science definition—you help children to accommodate the new information with their preconceptions of the word or concept. You preserve the value of their preconception while helping them to acquire an expanded structure for a concept.

The preconceptions or misconceptions of children in science can seriously affect their ability to assimilate new knowledge. But if the teacher will recognize the existence of children's misconceptions, define them in the children's own words, categorize them as they relate to natural phenomena or vocabulary, and take steps to help children accommodate the science concepts and their own alternative conceptual frameworks, many of the learning problems related to this concern will disappear.

Summary

The chief characteristic of today's elementary school science program is student involvement. All modern programs avoid using memory as the primary mode of learning. They seek to engage children in problem-solving activities that exercise higher-level cognitive operations. Cognitive activities are classified by Bloom's taxonomy as: knowledge, comprehension, application, analysis, synthesis, and evaluation.

The learner's attitudes, how he or she receives and values what takes place in the classroom, are defined by the affective domain of the taxonomy. The categories of the affective domain are: receiving, responding, valuing, organization, and characterization. Psychomotor skills are categorized as reflexive movement, basic fundamental movement, perceptual abilities, physical abilities, skilled movements, and nondiscursive communication.

Piaget's research offers fresh insight into the child's cognitive development. Children's perceptions of the physical world are affected by the limitations of their cognitive structure. Knowing this has helped science curriculum developers to shape experiences for children that are within their ability to perform. Exercises to further the development of the cognitive structure are included in many programs. Commonly in these programs the children manipulate concrete objects. Logical operations are reserved for the intermediate grades.

Gagné's theory of learning—based on eight levels of learning—provides a framework for curriculum developers to construct programs based upon a learning hierarchy. The levels of learning are: signal learning, stimulus-response learning, chaining, verbal chaining, multiple discrimination learning, concept learning, principle learning, and problem solving.

Bruner advocates discovery learning for its advantages in the areas of retention, learning how to solve problems, a shift to intrinsic motivation, and developing the tools for problem solving. Critics such as Ausubel state that discovery techniques are inefficient and offer no real advantages over lecture and demonstration.

Children learn concepts in stages of increasing sophistication, with the highest level enabling them to make predictions about similar or related phenomena and to generalize from a pool of data based upon a learned concept. Since children learn according to this pattern, it makes sense to teach them in a like manner, in a succession of evolving conceptualizations.

Elementary school children form many concepts informally outside the school setting. These preconceptions often are incomplete or conflict with the concepts formally presented in a science curriculum; this causes conflict for the learner and confuses the acquisition of the new concepts. These misconceptions are of two varieties, phenomenological (misconceptions about natural phenomena) and vocabulary-based (misconceptions about vocabulary).

In dealing with the misconceptions of children in science the teacher should (1) recognize the existence of the misconceptions, (2) define the misconceptions in the children's own words, (3) categorize the misconceptions as related to science phenomena or to vocabulary, and (4) take steps to help students to accommodate their own alternative conceptual framework and the formal concepts of the science curriculum. These accommodations are attained through using hands-on science activities for the phenomena-related misconceptions and through defining both the children's informal alternative frameworks and the formal frameworks of science for the vocabulary-based misconceptions, and then demonstrating the acceptability of each.

Extending Activities

1. Make a list of immediate and long-range affective child behaviors that might be associated with science teaching. Example: The child repeats classroom activities at home.

2. If possible, conduct the Piaget-like child study exercises with a number of children between the ages of four and nine. Make a record of the children's responses and compare the results of your interviews with those of your peers.

3. The following is a common elementary school science activity:

   Materials: food-warming candles, one large, burning candle used as a source of fire, three glass jars of different sizes, a flat metal pan. The concept to be taught is: A candle requires oxygen (air) to burn.
   a. Write a description of a discovery lesson that would teach the desired concept.
   b. Write a description of a verbal learning lesson that would teach the concept.

      Hint: When a jar is inverted over a burning candle, the fire will go out.

4. Describe an activity or lesson that would permit the students to broaden the concept learned in Activity 3 to be: All fire requires oxygen (air) to burn.

5. A child observes that the outside of a cold soda bottle is moist and concludes that the soda is "leaking" through the glass. What can you do to correct this misconception? Write a detailed description of your procedure.

Bibliography

Arzi, H., R. Ben-Zvi, and U. Daniel. "Forgetting versus Savings: The Many Faces of Long-Term Retention." *Science Education* 70, no. 2 (April 1986): 171–188.

Ausubel, D. P. "In Defense of Verbal Learning." *Educational Theory* 21 (1961): 23.

Baird, W., and C. Borich. "Validity Considerations for Research Ability on Integrated-Science Process Skills and Formal Reasoning Ability." *Science Education* 71, no. 2 (April 1987): 259–269.

Beck, D. H. "Functional Implications of Changes in the Senescent Brain: A Review." *Canadian Journal of Neurological Science* 4 (November 1978): 417–424.

Bruner, J. S. "The Act of Discovery." *Harvard Educational Review* 31 (1961): 21–32.

DeWied, D., and D. H. Versteeg. "Neurohypophyseal Principles and Memory." *Brain* 101, no. 3 (September 1978): 403–445.

Esler, W. K. "Brain Physiology: Research and Theory." *Science and Children* 20, no. 5 (March 1982): 44–45.

Gagné, R. M. *The Conditions of Learning.* New York: Holt, Rinehart & Winston, 1965, Chapter 7.

Greenough, W. T., R. W. West, and T. J. Voogd. "Synaptic Plate Perforations: Changes with Age and Experience in the Rat." *Science* 203 (December 1978): 1096–1098.

Hansl, N. R., and A. B. Hansl. "Learning and Memory Improvement Through Chemistry: Dream or Reality in the Offing?" *Phi Delta Kappan* 61, no. 4 (December 1979): 264–265.

Harrow, A. J. *A Taxonomy of the Psychomotor Domain.* New York: David McKay, 1972.

Hills, G. "Students' 'Untutored' Beliefs About Natural Phenomena: Primitive Science or Commonsense?" *Science Education* 73, no. 2 (1989): 155–158.

Humphrey, J. *Teaching Elementary School Science Through Motor Learning.* Springfield, Ill.: Charles C Thomas, 1975.

Inhelder, B., and J. Piaget. *The Growth of Thinking from Childhood to Adolescence.* New York: Basic Books, 1958.

Kovacs, G. L., B. Bohus, and D. H. Versteeg. "The Effects of Vasopression on Memory Processes: The Role of Noradrenergic Neurotransmission." *Neuroscience* 4, no. 11 (1979): 1529–1537.

Krathwohl, D. R., B. S. Bloom, and B. B. Masia. *Taxonomy of Educational Objectives. Handbook II: Affective Domain.* New York: David McKay, 1964.

Nabveh-Benjamin, et. al. "Use of the Ordered Tree Technique to Assess Students' Initial Knowledge and Conceptual Learning." *Teaching Psychology* 16 (December 1989): 182–187.

Pines, A., and L. West. "Conceptual Understanding and Science Learning: an Interpretation of Research Within a Sources-of-Knowledge Framework." *Science Education* 70, no. 5 (1986): 583–603.

Saunders, W., and D. Sheradson. "A Comparison of Concrete and Formal Science Instruction upon Science Achievement and Reasoning Ability of Sixth-Grade Students." *Journal of Research in Science Teaching* 24 (1986): 39–51.

Shuell, T. "Cognitive Psychology and Conceptual Change: Implications for Teaching Science." *Science Education* 7, no. 2 (April 1987): 239–250.

Stephens, J., T. Betswenger, and S. Dyche. "Misconceptions Die Hard." *The Science Teacher* 53, no. 6 (September 1986): 65–68.

Stryker, M. P., and H. Sherk. "Modification of Cortical Orientation Selectivity in the Cat by Restricted Visual Experience: A Re-examination." *Science* 190 (November 1975): 904–906.

Trowbridge, J., and J. Mintzes. "Students' Alternative Conceptions of Animals and Animal Classification." *School Science and Mathematics* 85, no. 4 (April 1985): 304–316.

Yore, D. "The Effects of Lesson Structure and Cognitive Style on the Science Achievement of Elementary School Children." *Science Education* 70, no. 4 (July 1986): 461–472.

CHAPTER 3

Teaching Science by Inquiry

Look What's in This Chapter

Now that you have an understanding of the nature of science and science teaching and of how children learn science, you are ready to acquire the information and skills necessary for teaching children science by the method of inquiry or problem solving. You will learn about four models for inquiry teaching—Rational (of which there are two types), Discovery, and Experimentation—and you'll begin to acquire the skills for using them. You will become acquainted with the important art of asking questions and dealing with student responses; you'll see how learning outcomes change as your questioning and your reactions to students' responses change. Finally, you'll learn about a variety of procedures for introducing inquiry science lessons to children.

Let us look in on four classrooms in an elementary school. Teacher A gives her pupils some seashells, with instructions to discover what they can from them. Teacher B has his students experimenting to test the hypothesis that warm air rises. Teacher C, using a demonstration, presents a problem to his class, and by asking questions leads the pupils to the answer. Teacher D requires her pupils to solve a problem by asking questions that can be answered yes or no. The activities in the four classrooms seem quite different. But each teacher is teaching by inquiry. Though each is employing a different technique, all four lessons have something in common. In each case, the pupils are involved in problem solving. And in each case they are developing manipulative and higher-level cognitive skills. To recognize teaching by inquiry, ask yourself two questions:

"Are the children required to go beyond the given information to gain new insights?" And: "Are the children problem solving—looking for answers or generalizations original to them?" If the answer to both questions is yes, then regardless of the nature of the activity, the class may be said to be involved in an inquiry lesson. Though the variations among lessons are numerous, inquiry learning activities may be classified into types. In this book they are placed in one of three categories: the rational approach, the discovery approach, and the experimental approach. Each of these methods is discussed in detail below.

Initiating Inquiry in the Classroom: Some Concerns

In spite of the emphasis given it in professional literature, science textbooks, and teacher-training programs, inquiry as a method for teaching science is still not accepted by some teachers. There are several reasons for this.

1. It is believed that teachers must understand the subject matter more thoroughly than with other methods.

2. Teachers must accept the often new and alien role of an indirect, facilitative leader.

3. Teachers must master new skills: they must learn to ask good questions and to properly handle student response.

4. Teachers sometimes fail in their early attempts to conduct inquiry lessons.

5. The students do not know how to react to the often new and strange atmosphere of inquiry.

In the following chapters we will deal with each of these concerns. Teachers who employ the inquiry model to teach science do not necessarily need to know more science content than traditional teachers, for in inquiry science the emphasis is on teaching some important concepts, not memorizing a lot of facts. Inquiry science teachers focus on the teaching and learning processes that help children to come to their own understanding of the world around them. Teachers should understand some major concepts of science, but they have less need to pose as an authority figure and "fountain of knowledge." The other skills necessary for being an effective inquiry science teacher are easily defined and acquired when approached with a positive attitude. Learning to ask questions, responding to student answers, and directing student-centered learning can provide you with some of the most satisfying experiences you'll encounter in teaching. Perhaps even more important, these interactions may provide many students with knowledge, skills, and pleasurable memories of your science classroom.

Why Teach by Inquiry?

Mentally review the contents of Chapters 1 and 2. Some desirable goals mentioned in those chapters were:

1. Maintaining children's curiosity.

2. Involving children in learning activities that require a high degree of cognitive skill.

Is this inquiry teaching?

3. Developing children's positive attitudes toward science.
4. Providing concrete experiences for children who have not reached Piaget's formal operations stage.

We also have read of the advantages of discovery learning as viewed by Bruner that have to do with increased self-direction, a shift to intrinsic motivation, learning how to solve problems, and increased memory. Will inquiry help us to achieve our goals? As you read this chapter and examine the nature of inquiry teaching, contrast the nature of inquiry procedures with that of more traditional methods—reading and memorizing—and decide for yourself.

Chapter 4 gives an additional reason for using inquiry techniques: they help children to develop process skills, the skills of doing science.

Teaching Children Problem Solving Using the Rational Inquiry Approach

The rational approach to teaching science to children in the elementary school is basically a method wherein the teacher uses manipulative materials to present a phenomenon to children either by demonstration or through a hands-on activity, and then guides them through questioning to arrive at a generalization of science. There are some variations in these techniques depending on which of two different groups of children they are used with. The first group includes primary-grade children, children from low socioeconomic backgrounds, low achievers, and some children with exceptionalities (dependent learners). The second group includes intermediate-grade and older children who do not fit into those categories listed for group one and who may be categorized as independent learners. We will call the teaching techniques for these two groups Type One and Type Two Rational Inquiry.

Type One Rational Inquiry: For Primary-Grade and Dependent Learners

To become acquainted with the Type One Rational Approach, let us sit in on Mrs. Wright's second-grade class as she takes them through a science lesson. The children have just observed Mrs. Wright rubbing two inflated balloons on a child's wool sweater. Then, suspending each balloon from a string, Mrs. Wright brings them close together. The two balloons repel one another vigorously (Figure 3–1). Mrs. Wright asks: "What happened? What did we see?" A number of children wave their arms in the air. Mrs. Wright looks at Susan. "They won't touch; the balloons moved away from one another." *Mrs. Wright*: "Yes, they did, didn't they. Would someone else like to tell me what they saw?" *Cedric*: "They fly apart like something is pushing them around." *Mrs. Wright*: "That's a good description, Cedric. Can anyone guess what is really pushing the balloons apart?" *Another student*: "Maybe the wind blew them." *Mrs. Wright*: "That is an idea. Are there others?" *A student*: "I think they got electricity on them from rubbing." *Mrs. Wright*: "Very good. What if I told you that they did get electricity on them when we rubbed them? What can we say about electricity on balloons?" *A student*: "Balloons

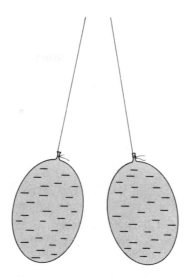

Figure 3–1 ■ Charged Balloons

with electricity on them push each other." *Mrs. Wright*: "Very good. Can anyone else tell me what we found out?" *Students*: "Balloons that are rubbed on sweaters will push on each other." *Mrs. Wright*: "That's fine. Can we write that on the board?"

Note Mrs. Wright's use of open-ended questions. Note that she makes supporting and encouraging responses to the children's answers and that she accepts and clarifies student responses and moves the discussion toward the desired goal. To perform well with the rational approach, the teacher must learn to ask the proper questions and to employ selected reinforcement.

Questioning in Rational Inquiry Lessons

Following are two groups of questions, A and B. What is the difference between the kind of response one might expect from a Group A question as compared to a Group B question?

Group A

"Which planet is closest to the sun?"

"What is the name of the movable part of an airplane wing?"

"How many legs does a grasshopper have?"

"What is Archimedes' principle?"

Group B

"What do you think?"

"What did you hear? See?"

"Why do birds fly south in the winter?"

"How can we move this large weight?"

Answers to Group A questions depend on the recall of prior knowledge. To answer Group B questions the learner must exercise his senses and higher-level cognitive skills. Group A questions tend to restrict mental activity to the recall of specifics. They invite responses only from those pupils who think they have the answers the teacher wants. Such questions might be termed closing questions, for they tend to close the classroom interaction to all other students. Group B questions might be termed opening questions, for they invite responses from all students and require a great range of cognitive skills. This does not imply that by simply asking opening questions, a teacher can trigger an outpouring of high-level cognitive activity on the students' part. It takes skill and patience to employ opening questions properly while directing the students to an acceptable generalization or conclusion.

Use of Selected Reinforcement

To teach by the rational inquiry method, one must have the students' cooperation. Some teachers attempt this technique only to find that the students do not respond. The teacher may discard the method and label the students lazy or dull when the problem was more related to her teaching technique. Do not expect too much too soon when employing the rational inquiry method with children who have had little or no experience with it. Children who have only been asked yes-or-no, know-it-or-don't-know-it questions may not be ready to offer opinions and best-solution answers the first time they are asked. They may not even believe the teacher really wants such answers. Many of them have been passive learners, unable to compete in a fact-oriented environment. Such children must be enticed to respond to open-ended questions.

An open classroom atmosphere where the children successfully solve problems is often achieved only after a period of training. One procedure for shaping student behavior during rational inquiry activities is selective reinforcement.

The basic premise of selective reinforcement is that all student responses are acceptable. The student is never told, "No, you are wrong." The strength of the reinforcement for each student response serves to guide and direct the flow of the verbal interaction toward the desired principle or generalization. Consider the effect on an elementary school class of each of the following teacher reactions to a student statement.

1. No, that's not right.

2. Uh, huh, that's one idea. Does anybody have another idea?

3. Very good, Jane. Can we expand upon Jane's idea? Can we add anything to that?

4. A good thought, but how can we explain . . . ?

5. Yes, Joe, the lack of oxygen might cause this. But have you considered . . . ?

Response number one is negative and rejecting. Such responses do not encourage other children to offer conjectures or opinions. Response number two is rather neutral. It directs the students away from the response toward other solutions to the problem. Response number three is strongly accepting. It directs the class to pursue Jane's thinking further. *Response three accepts a student idea and calls for further response.* Responses four and five accept the student response, but point out some incongruency. They provide direction for further thinking about the problem. Sometimes the teacher must offer guidance or supply additional information by saying: "What if I told you that . . . ?" or "Have you thought that . . . ?" or "What about this . . . ?" Using reinforcing responses such as two through five above, and furnishing additional guidance when required, a teacher may indirectly guide a class from the presentation of a problem to a successful conclusion that takes the form of a scientific concept. The ultimate test of the teacher employing the rational inquiry technique is whether she permits the students to formulate the solution to the problem. *For any rational inquiry lesson to be considered a success, the final response or generalization must come from the students, never from the teacher.* The teacher then asks several children to state the desired scientific principle in their own words. This serves to reinforce the concept.

Type Two Rational Inquiry: For Intermediate-Grade and Independent Learners

The primary differences in teaching Type One and Type Two Rational Inquiry are in the pace of the questioning and responses and the way the teacher reacts to student responses. Let's take a look at Mr. Wood's fifth-grade science class. Prior to the lesson Mr. Wood made a title card for the activity by writing the words "The Food Chain for a Woods and Pasture Habitat" on a long, narrow strip of posterboard. Using small magnets taped to the back of the title card, he affixed it to the metal chalkboard. Mr. Wood then randomly placed smaller cards on the chalkboard in the same way. These cards contain the words *grass, woody weeds, pine trees, hickory trees, mice, rabbits, foxes, cougars, hawks, buzzards, quail,* and *squirrels.* For ten minutes, the students take turns going to the chalkboard and drawing arrows with white chalk between those things that were eaten and those that did the eating. Each student also circles the thing that was eaten, the food source, with red chalk and the thing that did the eating with yellow chalk. When the students have completed drawing all the possible lines and circles, Mr. Wood asks: "What do we have here?" and leans back on his desk. After about ten seconds of silence, student A says: "It's a kind of diagram of what animals who live in a woods or pasture eat." Mr. Wood makes no response, and his expression remains passive and unchanged. Stu-

dent B then offers: "It shows that some things are eaters and also a food source. Mice and squirrels, for instance." Mr. Wood remains silent for five or six more seconds, then asks: "What would happen if one year all the hickory trees died?" *Student C:* "I guess that would be tough on the squirrels. They might die off." Student B: "And that could affect the hawks. They eat squirrels." "And the foxes, too" (Student E). As the student responses slow and then stop, Mr. Wood asks, "What if the grasses were affected by a fungus or other disease. What would happen?" The students continued to offer responses to Mr. Wood's questions and in reaction to the answers of other students. Finally Mr. Wood says, "We call this diagram on the chalkboard a food web. What does this food web show?" "That all the life in the web is interdependent." "That what happens to one plant or animal affects all the others." "If one plant or animal dies it is important to everyone." The student responses come one after the other without any reaction from Mr. Wood.

Do you see the important differences between how Mr. Wood handled the questioning for his fifth-grade class and the techniques of Mrs. Wright with her second-grade class? Of course it is obvious that Mr. Wood used almost no positive reinforcement. His reaction to student responses was generally neutral And he waited for long periods, sometimes ten seconds or more, for students to respond to his questions. He also refrained from reinforcing student responses, waiting in silence until other students spoke. Student talk was built on student talk. The secret of obtaining maximum student input into problem-solving situations is to refrain from reinforcing student responses and use "wait-time" after both the teacher's questions and the student responses.

As you can see, the use of selective reinforcement of Type One Rational Inquiry makes it best fitted for primary-grade students and other students who are for one reason or another dependent upon the teacher for motivation and direction. The constant reinforcement fulfills the students' needs, but at the same time also motivates the students to continue. As students mature and become more self-directed, it is a good idea to begin to reduce the amount of reinforcement they receive and gradually work toward the Type Two Rational Inquiry mode. Of course, some students with special needs will require reinforcement for a much longer time than others.

Questioning Effectively: Allowing Sufficient Wait Time

Especially in Type Two Rational Inquiry, knowing how to question effectively is important. By reviewing tapes of classroom episodes, a researcher discovered that teachers ask questions at the rate of two or three per minute on the average, and they permit only one second for a student to begin to reply before restating the question or directing it elsewhere. After receiving an answer to a question, the teacher will ask another question or comment upon the answer before a second passes. The nature of the questions and the rapid-fire questioning had a detrimental effect upon the quality of the teaching-learning interaction. It was also discovered that teachers spend about 20 percent of their time passing out positive and negative rewards to student answers. "Good, that's right" and "No, I don't think so" are typical teacher reactions to student answers. Constant right-wrong reinforcement of student responses tends to cut short student responses and focus their attention upon what they think the teacher wants.

When teachers attempt to increase their average wait time following both their own questions and student responses to five seconds or longer and reduce the frequency of right-wrong reactions to student responses, some interesting things happen. These are:

1. The length of student responses increases.
2. The number of student-initiated responses increases.
3. Failure to respond decreases.
4. Teacher-centered talk decreases and child-to-child talk increases.
5. The amount of inferential and speculative thinking increases.
6. The number of questions asked by the students increases.
7. Contributions of "slow" students increase.
8. Discipline problems decrease.

The Discovery Approach

All science teachers should try to involve their students at least sometimes in the individual discovery of relationships among observed phenomena. According to Piaget's theory, the chance that discoveries will be made is maximized when each student is personally manipulating material and data.

Pure Discovery

A teacher might provide each child with some wires, lamps, and dry cells and give him time to manipulate these materials. He would offer no guidelines for using the materials except those pertaining to the children's safety and the care of the equipment. Some children might discover how to make the lamp light up. Others might discover series and parallel circuits (Figure 3–2). Each child would manipulate and learn at his own rate. The approach is called pure discovery when no guidance is provided.

During pure discovery lessons, different groups in the class may investigate different problems. The teacher becomes an advisor and guide, moving from group to group. He may help one group to clarify a problem by suggesting that they list all known information. To a group that poses a hypothesis, the teacher may say: "How can we test this? How can we find out?" Each investigating group discovers what it can about its own problem, and in its own way. At the end of the lesson each group may report its findings to the rest of the class.

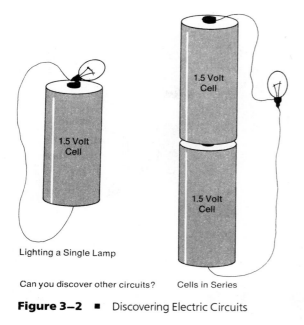

Lighting a Single Lamp

Can you discover other circuits?   Cells in Series

Figure 3–2 ■ Discovering Electric Circuits

more than one lamp burn?" or "Can you keep one lamp burning when the second lamp is unscrewed from its receptacle?" Such organizing questions make the lesson one of "guided" discovery. The amount of guidance the teacher provides during a discovery lesson is usually dictated by such factors as his teaching objectives and the amount of time available. Many teachers must continually remind themselves during a discovery lesson not to interject questions and comments that would reduce the freedom of the discovery process below the level originally planned.

At the conclusion of a guided discovery lesson, class members might list the things they have discovered on the chalkboard and perhaps draw diagrams of the electric circuits they have made. Then, using the questioning techniques of rational inquiry, the teacher may help the students form a generalization from their data.

Discovery with Very Young Children

Five-, six-, and seven-year-old children can discover many things about their environment. The objectives for a discovery lesson for a kindergarten class often do not encompass scientific generalizations as such. Rather, they serve to develop manipulative and observational skills. For example, children in a kindergarten class are given a packet of paper shapes—triangles, squares, rectangles, and circles (Figure 3–3). There are three of each shape, each one a different size and color. The teacher tells the children: "Put the pieces that look the same in the same pile." Some children may put all of the circles together in spite of the different sizes and colors. They have focused on the shape of the figures. Other children may classify the objects according to color, others according to size. They are discovering that the objects have more than one property and may be grouped in several ways. The children are learning to classify. Developing such skills is certainly a worthy objective for discovery lessons involving young children.

The teacher who operates a pure discovery classroom must be tolerant of noise, movement, and uncomfortable questions—all of which he is sure to get. A rule of thumb for the discovery teacher is to refrain from answering questions directly. Rather, he should help students to organize their thoughts and investigations so as to answer their own questions as often as possible. If the child asks: "What is inside a light bulb that makes it light?" the teacher may answer: "How might you find out?" If the child asks, "Why do all bulbs go out when one bulb in a series circuit is removed?" he might say: "Trace the current through the circuit. See where it goes."

Guided Discovery

Some teachers may want all their students to make a few similar discoveries, to have some experiences in common. If a teacher conducting a "batteries and bulbs" exercise wants the students to discover series and parallel circuits, he might ask such questions as: "Can we make

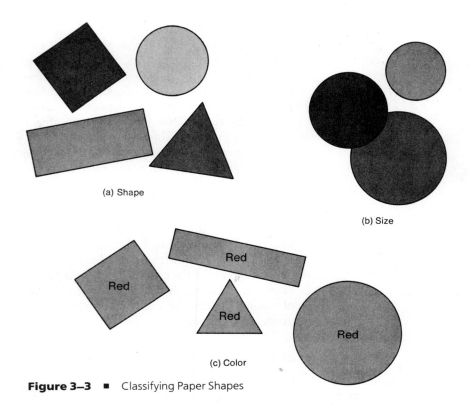

(a) Shape

(b) Size

(c) Color

Figure 3–3 ■ Classifying Paper Shapes

Discipline and Discovery

Some teachers with years of classroom experience are afraid to put manipulative materials into children's hands. They are afraid to let children investigate freely. Such teachers conjure up visions of utter chaos and open wounds. In short, they fear they will lose control of the class, particularly of those students who are difficult to handle. If the classroom is not managed properly, these fears may quickly come true. However, with proper management procedures, nearly any group of youngsters may safely be introduced to discovery activities. Experienced teachers have found the following guidelines helpful in *initiating* discovery lessons.

1. Divide the children into groups of four to six students each.

2. Give each child in the group a job; appoint a leader (responsible for directing the group participation of members, following group rules, and so on), recorder (responsible for recording group procedures and findings), materials handler (obtains, returns, and is responsible for manipulatives), manipulators (performs manipulation of material agreed upon by the group), and perhaps a safety director and a quality control officer (monitors all proceedings for proper procedures and care).

3. Carefully review with the class the responsibilities of all the role assignments.

4. Have students develop a set of rules or guidelines for the class or group.

5. Give directions for the activity prior to passing out materials. Collect materials prior to the discussion following the activity. (Do it this way until you judge the children can handle it otherwise.)

Is this better than reading about electricity? How?

6. Permit only the materials handler from each group to leave the group area.

7. Move among the groups as they work, assisting when needed.

8. Try to maintain discipline through the group leader.

9. When transferring students into and out of groups, move a few at a time in order to prevent noise and commotion.

Note: Issues related to safety in handling materials in the science program will be dealt with in detail in Chapter 5.

As a class gains experience in group work and develops a measure of self-control, some of these restrictions may be modified or removed. One pleasant surprise outcome of the group discovery lesson is its effect upon those students, especially boys, who are ordinarily considered behavior problems. Quite often such boys do well with the manipulative and problem-solving aspects of discovery learning. The positive effect of this success often carries over into other subjects. Probably more behavior problems are solved by the proper use of group discovery than are created or expanded by the technique.

Forming Permanent Working Groups

If you are planning to organize your science class so that group work is done frequently, it may be well to organize permanent working groups. Creating healthy working groups in which children work industriously and in harmony may take some time and effort. Some teachers prefer to assign each member of the group a task. One child may be the leader, one the recorder, two may be the experimenters who do most of the manipulating of materials, and another child may be the process controller who monitors the work of the group and suggests ways to improve measurements and procedures. The assigned tasks of the group members may be rotated periodically so that the children experience a variety of roles. When initially forming working groups, teachers should take time to define the various roles of the group members, stressing the importance of each job and the need for cooperation. Groups that are not working well together may require further counseling or a shifting of jobs among group members. It may also be necessary to sometimes move children from one group to another. The achievement of healthy working groups is a goal worth investing some time and energy in. No teaching situation is more pleasant than a classroom of five or six healthy working groups working independently on problems of interest.

Cooperative Learning in the Elementary Science Classroom

A number of schemes designed to promote cooperative learning among students has been introduced into the elementary schools in recent years. The group science model just presented possesses most of the characteristics typical of these cooperative learning schemes. One difference between our group science model and some other plans is the recommended size of the groups. We suggest four to six students to a group; cooperative learning designers suggest only two or three. Because many of the learning activities in these programs do not involve manipulative materials and are not necessarily of a problem-solving nature, the difference in recommended group size is understandable. Having fewer children in a group would double or triple the amount of manipulative materials necessary for an entire class. Groupings of four to six students should present few additional problems for teachers who wish to incorporate features of cooperative learning into their science classrooms, provided the procedures and guidelines presented in the preceding section are followed.

Evaluating student progress is another important consideration for those interested in cooperative learning. Cooperative learning programs stress the interdependence of students in performing learning activities. For example, students are assigned group grades for projects and assignments. To evaluate individual student progress, a teacher may question just one student from a group or collect only one paper from a group. If any individual testing occurs, all members of the group are responsible for seeing that each student achieves an acceptable score. In the science class this approach might mean that students would submit only one group report after completing a laboratory lesson. All of the members of the group would share in the teacher's evaluation of their work. Teachers who adopt the cooperative learning model for their science classrooms should construct an evaluation plan for the class and make sure all students and parents understand it. Teachers can also help students and parents to understand the cooperative learning philosophy by emphasizing that the positive outcomes of the process are worth the break from traditional grading practices.

There is some evidence that cooperative learning, when used in elementary school classrooms, improves student performance. However, most of this research has been conducted in situations other than grouped elementary science laboratory activities. For further information see D. Johnson, et al., in the chapter bibliography.

The Experimental Approach

We have seen two forms of inquiry teaching to this point. With the rational approach the teacher employs questioning and reinforcing techniques to direct children toward the solution to a problem. Discovery has the teacher giving materials to the children and guiding them in their observations and reasoning processes. The experimental approach is the third mode of inquiry teaching. Experimental inquiry most simply described is a procedure of making a statement that you think is true and finding a way to test the statement. A child may say, "I think heavy balls fall faster than lighter balls." How can you test this? Or a child may question, "Which absorbs more water, cloth or paper?" How can you find the answer? In the experimental approach the plan for testing the truth of a statement or for answering a question is discussed and decided prior to using the materials. This is the essential difference between discovery and experimentation. In discovery the materials are manipulated first without a formal plan of action. In experimentation the manipulation of materials follows the development of a plan of action.

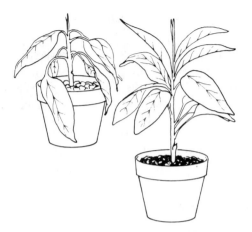

Figure 3–4 ■ What Could Have Caused This?

Selecting a Problem

The first time she does a science lesson involving experimentation, a teacher should choose a topic with which she is familiar, shaping it to her purpose. The topic may be one that she has taught before to another class or even to her present one. Since most children are familiar with growing things, the teacher might choose to investigate the question: What factors affect the growth of plants?

Establishing the Problem

To be worthy of investigation, a problem must be a problem to the children. A teacher may establish the children's interest in a variety of ways. She might show the class a sickly plant and ask why they think it is dying. A more direct way to introduce the problem would be simply to ask: "What things (variables) affect the growth of plants?" (See Figure 3–4.) While primary-grade children may name a number of variables that affect the growth of plants, they should be expected to consider only one variable

at a time in their experiment unless they have a great deal of guidance. To deal with multiple variables the children must be in the formal operations stage—this generally means the upper two grades of elementary school.

Formulating Hypotheses

The children might suggest such variables as water, temperature, sunlight, and fertilizer. The teacher may accept all these suggestions and may add any others she wants the children to consider. All student ideas may not be dealt with in the experiment that follows—only those readily tested with the time and materials available.

Next the teacher asks the children to say how they think the suggested variables will affect the growth of plants. Some typical hypotheses might be:

1. Plants require sunlight to grow.
2. Plants require water to grow.
3. Plants grow better in warm places.
4. Plants grow better when fertilizer is added.

If the children make an erroneous hypothesis, include it in the list as stated. Let the test of the hypothesis correct the misconception.

Structuring Tests for Hypotheses

The teacher then asks the class: "How might we test hypothesis 1?" The children might suggest placing some plants in sunlight and others in the dark. For hypothesis 2, the children might suggest watering some plants and not watering others; for hypothesis 3, placing some plants in a refrigerator and others in the room; and for hypothesis 4, adding fertilizer to some plants but not to others.

Controlling Variables

The teacher may ask the class: "How can we be sure when testing hypothesis 1 that it is the sunlight and not something else that is causing a difference in our plants?" He wants the children to say that everything about the plants will be the same, except that the experimental plants will be placed in the dark, while control plants are placed in the sunlight. The test for each hypothesis should involve experimental and control plants, the only difference between them being the single variable being tested. The teacher may also want to have the children suggest using more than one plant in each experiment. And of course, the class may choose to test only one or two of the hypotheses.

Making Operational Definitions

The teacher may ask the class: "How will we know that the variables we are testing affect the growth of plants?" The children may respond by suggesting that the plants be measured periodically. The class has operationally defined growth in their experiment in terms of the height of the plants. Their definition applies only to the immediate problem. Operational definitions serve to define variables in the context of the materials and the conditions of the immediate experiment. Growth might also be defined in terms of the thickness of the plants' stems, the number of leaves, or other factors. Other terms that might require operational def-

initions are warm and cold, water (how much), sunlight (how much or where), and fertilizer (what kind, how much).

Operational definitions need to be made for three different types of variables:

1. the manipulated variable—that variable that will be changed or adjusted during the experiment, for instance, the amount of water given to the plants

2. the responding variable—that variable that is to be observed and/or measured, for instance, the height of the plants in centimeters

3. constant variables, those that remain the same for both the experimental plants and the control plants, for instance, the sunlight, temperature, and fertilizer

In every experiment there will be one variable that is manipulated, a second that is to be observed and/or measured as it responds to the effects of the manipulated variable, and all other variables that are to remain the same for all the plants.

Experimenting

The teacher must decide how the actual experiment will be conducted. All the tests of the hypotheses could be done as teacher demonstrations. Or each hypothesis could be tested by a different group, and each group could then share its results with the others. A third choice would be to have each group or individual test each hypothesis. The choice depends largely on the amount of time and equipment available.

Recording and Interpreting Data

The students may need to be reminded that scientists make observations first. Then they interpret them. The children are simply to record what they observe concerning the growth of plants. After they have completed all their observations, they may interpret them to accept

Chart 3–1 ▪ Characteristics of Three Inquiry Techniques

Technique	Emphasizes Verbal Interaction with Peers	Emphasizes Children's Manipulation of Materials	Utilizes Problem-Solving Skills	Emphasizes Verbal Interaction with Teacher	Emphasizes Step-by-Step Laboratory Procedures
Rational Approach	Type One Moderate Type Two Strong	Weak Weak	Moderate Strong	Strong Strong	Weak Weak
Discovery Approach	Strong	Strong	Strong	Weak	Moderate
Experimental Approach	Strong	Strong	Strong	Moderate	Strong

or reject the hypothesis in question. Perhaps as each group reports its findings, the class as a whole may make the interpretations.

To summarize the experimental technique for doing inquiry:

1. Select and establish the problem.
2. Formulate hypotheses or problem questions.
3. Structure tests for the inferences.
   a. Make operational definitions.
   b. Decide how to control variables.
   c. Conduct the experiment.
   d. Record and interpret data.

Obviously the children in the preceding sample lesson received a great deal of direction from the teacher. As the pupils gain more experience with the experimentation process, they should receive less and less direction. The eventual goal is to have them define and investigate a problem independently with only minimal help from the teacher.

Experimenting with Very Young Children

Teachers and students tend to consider the experimental approach suitable only for the intermediate grades. They are wrong. Why not investigate the effect of a single variable such as water on the growth of plants with six- or seven-year-old children? The essence of experimenta-

tion is the kindergarten teacher asking her class: "How can we find out if our plants need water to live?"—and after having worked out the plan with the children, have them water one plant and not the other. Is there not a manipulated variable (the water) in this exercise? A control (the watered plant)? Are not the children required to make observations?—To form a conclusion based upon their observations? This is experimentation. To help very young children experiment, one must keep the exercise simple, usually investigating a single variable. Controls, formulation of hypotheses, use of operational definitions, and the interpretation of data are part of the exercise, but these terms themselves are not used, and the formality of the experimental procedure is not stressed. Experimenting is introduced to young children simply as a common-sense way to approach a problem or question.

Contrasting the Inquiry Techniques

You have just been introduced to three models of inquiry teaching: the rational approach, the discovery approach, and the experimental approach. These are the tools that enable the teacher to conduct an inquiry science program. Chart 3–1 will help you to compare the three inquiry techniques. Can you think of other characteristics to add to the chart?

Many science curricula prescribe inquiry techniques as basic teaching procedures. Teachers who can use one or more of these techniques will have an advantage when confronted with one of these programs. Chapter 4 will demonstrate that inquiry procedures help children to develop the skills of doing science. The reader will find that any science program, even one that is textbook-oriented, may be reorganized to emphasize inquiry procedures. *Teachers who have acquired the skills of inquiry teaching can generally operate effectively with any science program. This gives them a great deal of independence. They are freed from the need to use any one science curriculum.*

Some Formats for Introducing Inquiry Lessons

Several formats can be used to introduce inquiry lessons to young children. Four of the easiest are described below.

Demonstration with a Problem

Mr. Simpson showed his class a flask containing about five centimeters of water. The flask was closed with a stopper that had two glass tubes projecting from it. (See Figure 3–5.) When he inverted the flask, water began spraying from one tube into the flask. Water ran from a second tube to a container underneath the flask. "O.K.," he said, "explain why this is happening." Mr. Simpson then used the Type Two Rational Inquiry technique to help the students to construct an explanation for the "magic fountain": When the flask is inverted, water drains from the flask into tumbler B, producing a low pressure in the flask. The pressure of the atmosphere pushing down on the surface of the water in tumbler A forces water up the tube and into the low pressure region that has formed in the flask. The fountain will operate as long as the water supply in tumbler A lasts. (Notice also in

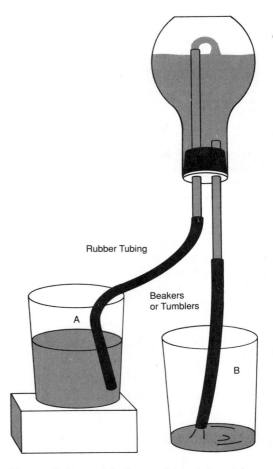

Figure 3–5 ■ Mr. Simpson's Magic Fountain

Figure 3–5 that tumbler A is positioned slightly higher than tumbler B.)

Discrepant Event

Mr. Simpson called the biggest girl in the class to the front of the room. He handed her a funnel that had a Ping-Pong ball inside and asked her to blow the ball as high as possible out of the funnel. (See Figure 3–6.) To everyone's surprise, neither this girl nor any other boy or girl in the class could blow the ball out of the funnel at all. This result is a discrepant event—one that causes a dissonance in the mind of the observer. It represents an unexpected outcome.

Figure 3–6 ■ Mr. Simpson's Discrepant Event

Figure 3–7 ■ Why Won't the Soda Come Up the Straw?

For children many demonstrations may be discrepant events. A balloon rubbed on a sweater "sticks" to the wall of the classroom. A paper napkin is crumpled and placed in the bottom of a tumbler; when the tumbler is inverted and forced under water in a sink or aquarium and then removed, the napkin is still dry. A nail can be suspended from a horseshoe magnet even if a piece of cardboard is placed between the magnet and the nail. As you examine many of the activities in this textbook, consider how children would react to them. To the children they are discrepant events.

Anecdote (with Demonstration)

Mr. Simpson told his class about a girl who, while drinking Coke, filled the opening around the straw with bubble gum and soon found it was no longer possible to draw the Coke up the straw. While he talked, he performed the acts described. (See Figure 3–7.)

Invitation to Inquiry

At times it is not possible to provide manipulative materials to introduce inquiry activities. However, it is still possible, even in the absence of direct observational and manipulative experiences, to provide children with learning activities that help develop problem-solving and critical thinking skills. In the place of direct experiences, the teacher may pose problems verbally or pictorially or provide data for analysis. This procedure is called invitation to inquiry.

Examples of invitation to inquiry lessons are:

1. An anecdote: The teacher tells a personal anecdote that presents a problem, and the children attempt to solve the problem. For example, the teacher may tell a story of camping in the mountains, boiling a three-minute egg and finding it was not well cooked. She may ask, "Why do you think this happened?" "Can you help me solve my problem?" (At higher altitudes water boils at a lower temperature.)

2. Interpretation of data: The teacher writes data such as the following on the board.

   World Population in Various Years
1850	1,200 million persons
1900	1,500 million persons
1950	2,300 million persons

Figure 3–8 ■ What Is Wrong with the Picture? How Can We Fix It?

The teacher might ask, "What do these numbers tell us about the world's population?" or "Can you predict the world's population in the year 2000?" "What do you think the population was in 1800?"

3. Pictorial stimulator: the teacher presents a problem situation through visual stimulation—a board drawing, pictures from magazines, filmstrips (with words blocked out), movies (with the sound turned off), or other visual media. Inquiry techniques are employed to solve problems that grow out of these stimulations. For one example of a pictorial stimulator see Figure 3–8.

Developing Oral Questioning Skills

You have just learned some special ways to use oral questioning techniques in the classroom. Now let us consider the skills required to direct verbal interaction outside the context of a formal inquiry session. With proper use of questions, almost any lesson can take on some of the characteristics of inquiry. Once acquired, the general skills of questioning may be used

to teach any subject in the elementary school curriculum.

To direct classroom discussion, the teacher must be able to elicit responses from the students, probe for ideas among the students, and help the students to close the discussion. Questions used by the teacher during open discussion may be classified, then, as eliciting, probing, and closure seeking.

Eliciting Questions

Eliciting questions are those questions employed to: (1) encourage an initial response, (2) encourage more students to participate in the discussion, and (3) rekindle a discussion that is lagging or dying out. (See Chart 3–2.)

Initial Responses

Eliciting questions designed to encourage an initial response are usually opening questions such as: "What did you see?" or "What do you think caused that?" Fact-oriented or closing questions may be used to elicit an initial response from a class if the information solicited is common to the backgrounds of most of the children. Such background-oriented questions, though requiring specific answers, still encourage most of the children to respond. Examples of such questions are: "How is ocean water different from lake water?" "What happens to tree leaves in the fall?"

Expanding Participation

Either opening or closing questions may be used to expand participation in a discussion. The teacher must decide whether to address the question to the whole class or to an individual student. A question addressed to the whole class and that tends to bring additional students into the discussion might be: "Can *anyone else* think of another reason?" To encourage a particular student to participate, the teacher might say: "John, you have had some good ideas in the past; what do you think should be done to protect our rivers?" Closing questions may also be used to expand participation. An inventive

Chart 3–2 ■ Purposes and Examples of Eliciting Questions

Purpose	Examples
1. To encourage initial responses	*Open-Ended* What did you see? What do you think? Can you guess why? *Background-Oriented* Who can describe a frog? What are the colors in a rainbow?
2. To expand participation	Can anyone else . . . ? Sue, you have good ideas; what do you think about . . . ? Carol, in your opinion, what is the best car sold today?
3. To rekindle a dying discussion	Can we summarize the data we have mentioned so far? If I told you . . . , what would you say?

teacher may "trap" a reluctant student into responding by asking him to answer a background-oriented question and expanding upon his answer:

"John, you like dogs. Can you give the names of several kinds of dogs?"

"What are the differences in their appearance?"

"How does this make them better able to do different things like hunt and run?"

"Does the size or strength of wild animals affect the way they live?"

With this series of questions the teacher helped a reluctant student to relate the familiar to the unknown.

Rekindling a Dying Discussion

Classroom discussions of science-related topics sometimes degenerate and lose direction as students aimlessly restate ideas. When this happens, the teacher can rekindle the discussion with the spark of organization. He may help the students to classify their ideas, and to see new relationships among them, by asking: "Can we list on the chalkboard what we know about river pollution so far?" Or the teacher may ask the students to consider the issue from a different point of view. She might ask: "What if you owned a factory that would have to close down if the waste products could not be put in the river?" Sometimes the teacher must supply information that seems necessary if the lesson is to progress. In discussing air pollution, the children have centered their remarks upon the effects of the automobile. When their statements become repetitious and lack new insight, the teacher says: "What if I told you that factories contribute more to air pollution than cars do. Should we shut down all factories?" The discussion should take on new direction and vigor.

Probing Questions

Probing questions seek to expand or extend *ideas.* While eliciting questions are concerned with inviting responses, probing questions are concerned with the quality of the responses.

Chart 3–3 ▪ Purposes and Examples of Probing Questions

Purpose	Examples
1. To extend ideas	Are there any other ideas?
	What else might we say about this?
	Noncommittal teacher responses.
2. To redirect ideas	Does anyone have another idea?
	Is there a better way?
	Do you recall what Susan said a while ago?
3. To justify ideas	How did you arrive at that, Joe?
	Where did you get your information, Joe?
4. To clarify ideas	Can you say that in other words?
	Debbie, can you explain what Ronnie just said?
	What did you mean by the term *responding variable,* Jack?

Probing questions tend to (1) extend ideas, (2) redirect ideas, (3) justify ideas, or (4) clarify ideas. (See Chart 3–3.)

Extending Ideas

To obtain as many ideas as possible about a given topic, a teacher may simply ask: "Does anyone have any other ideas?" or "What else might we say about this?" Sometimes the teacher will get more ideas if he remains completely noncommittal in response to student comments. As students offer ideas, he may say absently, "Uh huh," or "I see."

Redirecting Ideas

When a discussion is headed the wrong way, the teacher may say: "That is interesting, but what was it that Susan said just now?" or "That is one way to set up the experiment, but might there be an easier way?" All such questions will tend to redirect the discussion and help it to move where the teacher wants it to go.

Justifying Ideas

Sometimes a teacher may want a student to explain his reasons for saying something, or to describe his reasoning process. She may ask: "Why did you say that?" or "How did you arrive at that?" In asking a student to justify a response, the teacher is putting him on the spot. She must be careful not to let the process become threatening. By continuously requiring students to justify their responses, the teacher may frighten the more timid ones away from the discussion.

Clarifying Ideas

When a student's response is not clear, the teacher may ask him to state his idea in different words. Or he may ask some other student to explain what was said. The teacher may ask: "Can you say that in other words, Sam?" or "Sally, can you tell us what Jim said?" or "What did you mean by the word *mammals,* Sam?" Ideas expressed by the students should always be understood by the majority of the class.

Closure-Seeking Questions

Closure-seeking questions are used to help students form conclusions, solutions, or plans for

Chart 3–4 ▪ Purposes and Examples of Closure-Seeking Questions

Purpose	Examples
1. To classify ideas	What are the most important ideas we have expressed here?
	Which facts favor continued use of the rivers for dumping wastes?
2. To suggest investigation procedures	Where can we find out about water pollution? (Library research)
	What is our hypothesis?
	What variables affect the fish that live in polluted streams?
	How can we test our hypothesis?
3. To interpret data (Library research)	Can we draw any conclusions from our reports?
	Does industry have any right to use rivers to dump wastes?
(Experimentation)	Can we make a chart or graph of our data?
	Shall we accept our hypothesis?
	How could we have improved our experiment?

investigating problems. Closure-seeking questions are often used to: (1) help students to classify ideas, (2) invite students to suggest procedures for investigating a problem, and (3) help students to form conclusions by interpreting data. (See Chart 3–4.)

Classifying Ideas

While probing for ideas during a discussion, the teacher may not find it convenient to have the students evaluate what they are saying. Obviously not all ideas are equally valuable. When enough ideas have been obtained from the class, the teacher may ask: "What are the important things we have said today about water pollution?" or "What facts support industries in their use of rivers for dumping wastes?"

Suggesting Investigation Procedures

After a problem has been clarified, the teacher may ask the class how it could be investigated. If the problem does not lend itself to laboratory investigation, but is better solved by library research, the teacher may ask: "What do we need to know?" or "Where can we find this information?" To establish procedures for in-

vestigating empirical problems, the teacher may ask: "What is our hypothesis?" "What are the variables we must consider?" "How can we test our hypothesis?" The laboratory investigation is, of course, the process previously described as the experimentation inquiry procedure.

Interpreting Data

After students have done their library research and reported their findings, the teacher should help them, if possible, to form some conclusions. He may simply ask: "What have we learned here?" Or more specifically: "Does the businessman have any arguments on his side in the pollution question?" The teacher's task in such situations is not to have children form simple answers to complex problems. It is to have them assimilate and classify information so that at least the issues are clear in their minds, and their judgments are based upon facts, not emotion.

For experimental problems, the teacher can help the students to interpret data by asking: "Can we make a chart or graph of our results?" "Should we accept our hypothesis?" "What were some of the weaknesses in our experiment?"

Some Guidelines for Using Oral Questioning Techniques

Above all, the teacher must be familiar with the various types of classroom questions and learn how to use them. But there are also some general guidelines for dealing with oral questioning. Experienced teachers have found the following rules valuable:

1. Most of the questions the teacher asks should be opening questions. Any closing questions should relate to the students' general background.

2. The teacher must accept and reinforce all student responses and attempt to build a warm classroom climate.

3. The teacher must make his behavior as warm as his words. Facial expressions and physical contact often convey more to young children than words do.

4. The teacher must give the students time to answer his questions. Remember that silence following a question does not always mean that nothing is happening. It may mean that thinking is taking place. Students will quickly learn to outwait the teacher who answers his own questions too fast.

Summary

The word *inquiry* in science teaching applies to any procedure where children are involved in problem solving. Inquiry means going beyond the known information to gain new knowledge. There are three major techniques for doing inquiry: the rational approach, the discovery approach, and the experimental approach.

Rational Inquiry is of two types. Type One is employed with primary-grade children and dependent learners such as low achievers, children from low socioeconomic backgrounds, and children with certain exceptionalities. Type One Rational Inquiry features open-ended questions and the use of selected reinforcement.

Type Two Rational Inquiry is used with intermediate-grade students and independent learners. It features the use of open-ended questions, neutral reinforcement, and wait-time following teacher questions and student responses. The proper use of wait-time along with neutral reinforcement during classroom questioning has been shown to have many positive effects both on the quality of student performance during the problem-solving experience and in student attitudes.

In the discovery approach, the children are permitted to manipulate materials and to investigate on their own. In pure discovery lessons, children evolve their own problems and methods of investigation. In guided discovery lessons, the teacher poses questions that lead the children to investigate a common problem.

In the experimental approach, the children formulate and test hypotheses. This approach teaches children to define and control variables in experimental situations, to experiment, and to interpret data, as well as to hypothesize.

There are four common formats for presenting an inquiry lesson. The teacher can present a discrepant event—an activity with an unexpected outcome. He can tell a personal anecdote to introduce a problem. He can stage a demonstration that reveals a problem to be solved. Or he can use charts, graphs, or pictures as invitations to inquiry.

A teacher should know how to pose the three major categories of oral questions. Those categories are: eliciting questions, probing questions, and closure-seeking questions. The success of open classroom discussion and oral problem-solving activities depends largely on the teacher's ability to ask the right kind of questions and to create a warm classroom climate.

Extending Activities

1. Refer to Piaget's theory of the cognitive development of children as described in Chapter 2. Discuss the following questions with your peers.

a. Why is experimentation (manipulation of materials) an important ingredient of learning activities for very young children?

b. Is there an age when children may begin to rely more upon the verbal presentation of authority figures than upon concrete experiences? How may the statements made by authority figures be checked?

2. Write six opening and closing questions. Check to see if others in the class agree with the way you categorize these questions.

3. Give one original example of each of the formats—Demonstration with a Problem, Discrepant Event, Anecdote, and Invitation to Inquiry.

4. Discuss the three categories of oral questions with your peers. Present classroom situations to each other and take turns posing appropriate questions.

Bibliography

Allison, A., and L. Shrigley. "Teaching Children to Ask Operational Questions in Science." *Science Education* 70, no. 1 (January 1986): 61–72.

Borg, W. R., M. L. Kelley, and P. Langer. *Effective Questioning, Elementary Level* (A Far West Laboratory for Educational Research and Development Mini-Course). Beverly Hills, Calif.: Macmillan Educational Services, 1970.

Bredderman, T. "Laboratory Programs for Elementary School Science: A Meta-Analysis of Effects on Learning." *Science Education* 69, no. 4 (July 1985): 577–591.

Cain, S., and J. Evans. *Science: An Involvement Approach to Elementary Science Methods.* Columbus, Ohio: Merrill, 1984.

Cliatt, M., and J. Shaw. "Open Questions, Open Answers." *Science and Children* 23, no. 3 (November/December 1985): 10–13.

Davidson, N. "Small Group Cooperative Learning in Mathematics." *Yearbook of the National Council of Teachers of Mathematics* (1990): 52–61.

Johnson, D., R. Johnson, and F. Holubec. *Circles of Learning: Cooperation in the Classroom.* Edina, Minn.: Interactive Book Co., 1986.

National Science Teachers Association. *Conditions for Good Science Teaching.* Washington, D.C.: National Science Teachers Association, 1984.

National Science Teachers Association. *Safety in the Elementary Science Classroom* (booklet). Washington, D.C.: National Science Teachers Association (1987).

O'Donnell, A. "Learning Concrete Procedures: Effects of Processing Strategies and Cooperative Learning." *Journal of Educational Psychology* 72 (March 1990): 171–177.

Okebukola, P. "The Influence of Preferred Learning Styles on Cooperative Learning in Science." *Science Education* 70, no. 5 (October 1986): 509–518.

Sanders, W., and D. Shepardson. "A Comparison of Concrete and Formal Science Instruction upon Science Achievement and Reasoning Ability of Sixth Grade Students." *Journal of Research in Teaching* 24, no. 1 (January 1987): 39–52.

Slavin, E. Research on "Cooperative Learning: Concensus and Controversy." *Educational Leadership* 47 (January 1990): 52–54.

Tobin, K. "Student Task Involvement and Achievement in Process-Oriented Science Activities." *Science Education* 70, no. 1 (January 1986): 61–72.

Watson, D., and L. Rangel. "Classroom Evaluation of Cooperative Learning." *Educational Digest* (November 1989): 35–37.

Yeany, R., and M. Padilla. "Training Science Teachers to Utilize Better Teaching Strategies: A Research Synthesis." *Journal of Research in Science Teaching* 23 (1985): 85–95.

Teaching for the Process and Content of Science

Look What's in This Chapter

The next step, after becoming familiar with the methods of teaching inquiry science, is to examine how these skills can be integrated into the total science program. In this chapter you'll learn about the primary and integrated process skills children acquire as the result of doing activity-based inquiry science. You'll read about procedures for developing a science curriculum in the discussions of concept mapping and the use of the spiral curriculum. You'll see how inquiry and traditional learning can be integrated through the use of the Inquiry-Concept-Information (I-C-I) sequence. This very important planning/teaching procedure ensures a good marriage between the indirect, problem-solving activities of inquiry and the direct instruction usually associated with a more traditional approach. Issues concerning quality traditional instruction and the selection of science textbooks conclude the chapter.

Those who teach science in the elementary school have two major goals, and they are of equal importance: to help children develop process skills for doing science, and to help them acquire appropriate science content or information. In terms of the procedures and techniques employed for teaching them, these two goals are often contradictory. As stated in Chapter 3, inquiry procedures are necessary if children are to acquire process skills through their science experiences. However, traditional, direct teaching procedures provide the greatest breadth of coverage in a given amount of instructional time and give children exposure to more information on a topic. In this chapter we will show you how to do both with the greatest efficiency—help children to develop the process skills of science and also to acquire the greatest possible exposure to its content. We'll also review some guidelines for implementing direct teaching methods that will ensure that children acquire the greatest understanding of science concepts and facts.

Defining the Primary Process Skills

The skills of science have been variously defined. Perhaps the most widely accepted definitions are those given by the Commission on Science Education of the American Association for the Advancement of Science. Within this system, which formed the basis for the Science—A Process Approach elementary science program, the skills for doing science are categorized into eight primary processes and five integrated processes. The primary processes are generally introduced in kindergarten through grade 3, while the integrated processes are developed by exercises designed for grades 4 through 6. Chart 4–1 names and describes each of the primary process skills. It also lists activities often employed to introduce or illustrate each skill. The activities described are not necessarily from the Science—A Process Approach program, nor do they indicate the complete scope of the process skill.

Using Science Experiences to Foster Process Skills

Inquiry teaching by definition requires pupils to respond at the higher cognitive levels. Examine the techniques of inquiry presented in Chapter 3. Notice the close relationship between the primary process skills and the responses pupils typically make during inquiry sessions. *Inquiry learning tasks almost invariably require the learner to practice one or more of the process skills.*

Observing

The teacher frequently opens inquiry lessons by asking: "What did you see? How does the object feel, taste, smell?" Or he might ask the students to describe some event fully as a prelude to discussion. The children are reminded to differentiate between observations and inferences (Figure 4–1). Often a teacher may ask: "How are these objects the same? How are they different?"

Classifying

The teacher may give the class seashells or other objects to arrange according to some property or properties (Figure 4–2). Multistage classification systems may be built from pictures of animals or plants cut from magazines and pinned to a bulletin board. Such a classification system, built from pictures of a dog, a mouse, a bear, a horse, a chicken, a man, and a monkey, is shown in Figure 4–3.

Communicating

Children develop communicating skills when they are asked to describe objects and events in

Chart 4–1 ▪ Primary Process Skills

Skill	Description	Activities
Observing	Using all the senses to identify and name the properties of objects and events.	Describing properties of objects, systems, and living organisms (texture, color, smell, shape, size, etc.).
Classifying	Categorizing objects according to a predetermined set of properties.	Sorting paper shapes, blocks, animal pictures, leaves, or buttons according to a common property.
Measuring	Developing appropriate units of measurement for length, area, volume, time, weight, etc.	Measuring distances with spans of strings, covering an area with books; counting the marbles that fill a container, learning a standard system of measurement.
Communicating	Compiling information in graphic or pictorial form. Describing objects and events in detail.	Making and interpreting the information from graphs, charts, maps, etc.
Inferring	Suggesting more about a set of conditions than is observed. Differentiating between observations and inferences, changing inferences to accommodate new information.	Inferring that the moisture that collects upon a cold glass comes from the air; inferring the characteristics of an animal from its tracks.
Predicting	From a set of events, predicting a future event. Using graphs to interpolate and extrapolate guesses.	Predicting how long a candle will burn under various sizes of jars; predicting the stopping distance of an object that rolls or slides down an incline from various heights.
Recognizing Space-Time Relations	Describing the position of an object with reference to other objects or to time. Describing changes in the shape and position of an object over a period of time.	Naming and identifying two- and three-dimensional geometric figures; recognizing three-dimensional shapes from their shadows; making statements about the symmetry of objects.
Recognizing Number Relations	Finding the quantitative relationships among data. Using the number line to perform arithmetic operations.	Determining the value of pi by measuring a series of cylinders. Using the number line to add and subtract signed numbers.

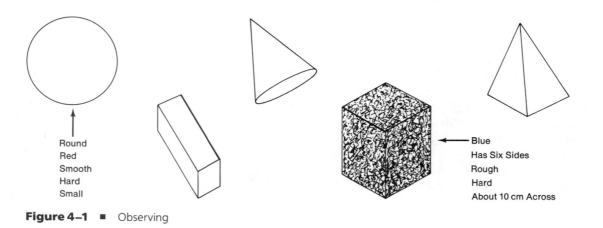

Round
Red
Smooth
Hard
Small

Blue
Has Six Sides
Rough
Hard
About 10 cm Across

Figure 4–1 ▪ Observing

Figure 4–2 ■ How Are the Shells in Each Pile the Same? How Are They Different?

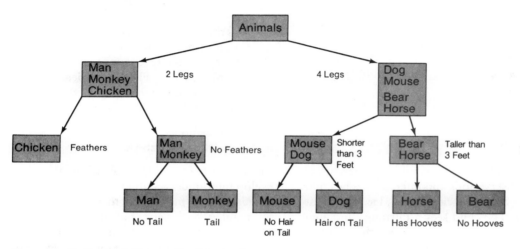

Figure 4–3 ■ A Multistage Classification System

detail. A child's descriptions should be complete enough to enable a second child to identify the object. Communicating skills are also enhanced by having groups of students compile data from an experiment into tables or graphs and report their findings to the rest of the class.

Measuring

Pupils in science have many opportunities to invent their own systems of weights and measures. Scale balances can use fishline sinkers or wash-ers or even water to achieve equilibrium (Figure 4–4). Distances can be measured in sticks or strings or hand spans. Volume can be measured in terms of the number of marbles or beans it takes to fill a container. The basic concepts of measurement may then be developed into established systems of measurement. The habit of measuring precisely will be fostered if the teacher shows that he values this skill and measures precisely as a matter of habit himself. Children can be taught that averaging several measurements is the best way to measure accurately.

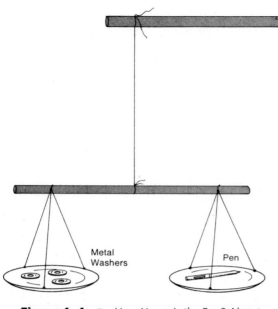

Figure 4–4 ■ How Heavy Is the Pen? About
Three Washers

washers on one side of a scale to counterbalance
one marble on the other side, and nine washers
to counterbalance three marbles, one can predict that six washers will counterbalance two
marbles (interpolation), and twelve washers will
counterbalance four marbles (extrapolation).

Inquiry lessons that require students to
make predictions and test them by experimentation will help to develop this process skill.

Number Relationships

Any science exercise that requires students to
order and compare objects or data according to
some numerical factor helps to develop number
relations skill. Certain kinds of questions elicit
responses that help children to understand number relationships. "How much larger is it?"
"How many times larger than X is Y?" "How
far is it from X to Y?" "How many degrees does
the temperature drop when it goes from $-10°$
Celsius to $-20°$ Celsius?"

Inferring

Teachers should insist that children differentiate
between observations and inferences. The child
observes a clear, colorless liquid. He *infers* that
it is water. The child sees a burning candle go
out beneath a glass jar. He *infers* the cause of
this *observation*. Inferences are guesses, and
making valid inferences on the basis of observation is an essential skill for inquiry learning.
Any inquiry exercise requires the learner to go
beyond the given information to infer new
relationships.

Predicting

Predicting is a highly developed inferring skill.
As employed in elementary school science, predicting normally implies forecasting some future event from a solid base of evidence. For
example, after graphing experimental data (see
Figure 4–5) and finding that it takes three metal

Time-Space Relationships

Teachers do many things that help children to
develop their understanding of time-space relationships. They may teach them to recognize
and name two-dimensional shapes—squares,
rectangles, circles; and three-dimensional
shapes—cubes, prisms, ellipsoids. They may
have them describe their own position in terms
of some reference point, or the positions of other
people or things. "I am in the third row and the
second seat." "The aquarium is below and
about four steps to the right of the flag." The
teacher may demonstrate the symmetry of plane
figures by showing how an axis divides such figures into two parts that are mirror images of
each other (Figure 4–6). Symmetry of solids may
likewise be demonstrated: solid figures are divided by planes rather than axes (Figure 4–7).
Children can be taught to tell time on a clock
and to describe time sequences such as day and
night and the seasons.

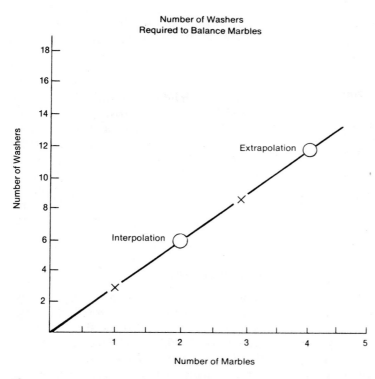

Figure 4–5 ■ Graph of Number of Washers Required to Balance Marbles

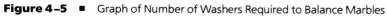

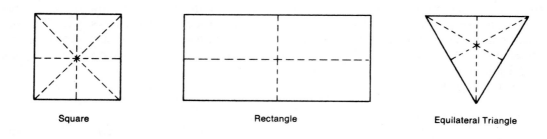

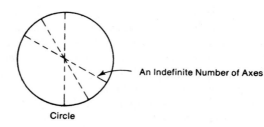

Figure 4–6 ■ Axes of Symmetry

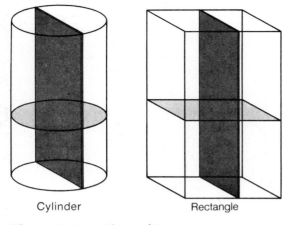

Cylinder   Rectangle

Figure 4–7 ■ Planes of Symmetry

Teaching Science Process Skills to Five- and Six-Year-Old Children

Science experiences for kindergarten and first-grade children emphasize the development of the primary processes and the children's perceptual skills. During these learning activities, children develop their observational skills using their five senses and begin to form concepts of the nature and relationships of the world around them. Some common activities for five- and six-year-old children that are found in various science programs are described below.

Water Play

A large plastic dishpan half-filled with water and a number of smaller containers of various sizes and shapes can provide a group of children with experiences that will aid in their development in several ways. As the children pour the water from container to container, their observations will enhance the growth of Piagetian conservation skills related to volume. Children's free play with water also is believed to be beneficial to the later development of measurement skills. (Some teachers prefer to use sand or rice

rather than water in this type of activity to reduce the problem of cleaning up.)

Stringing Beads

Colored beads purchased in a hobby or craft store and a shoelace will provide opportunities for developing several skill areas. Children learn to recognize colors, shapes, and sizes of the beads as they place them on a shoestring at the direction of the teacher. The children also learn to form sequencing patterns as they duplicate the teacher's completed string of beads or complete a string according to a given sequence of color or shape.

Colored Paper Shapes

Sets of geometric shapes in a variety of colors cut from construction paper provide a number of experiences that are beneficial to children's perceptual and skills development. A teacher may cut a large and small circle, square, rectangle, and triangle from a single color of construction paper. She may duplicate this set in several colors, say, red, green, and blue. With the paper shapes children may learn to recognize colors, to name the geometric shapes, and to classify according to color, shape, and size. They may also create larger, more complex shapes using the basic shapes provided.

Colored Felt Shapes

Activities similar to those performed with paper shapes may be conducted using felt shapes. Shapes may be cut from colored felt cloth, and the same types of learning experiences may be structured. An advantage of the felt shapes is that they will adhere to a flannel board that, held in an upright position, is visible to the children as the teacher gives directions for using the shapes. Many teachers now provide individual flannel boards for children in their classrooms so they can observe the children following directions as they place the felt shapes on their

Observing through tactile experiences.

boards. Flannel boards may be made by gluing a piece of flannel on a cardboard backing and adding a cardboard brace on the back side to support the board in an upright position.

"Feely Bags"

By placing unknown objects in large socks or cloth bags with drawstrings and asking children to describe and attempt to identify the objects, teachers can help children develop their tactile sense. As they handle the unknown objects, children learn words to describe what they feel, such as *smooth, rough, hard, soft,* and so on.

Smell and Taste Activities

Teachers of five- and six-year-old children often collect edible and/or aromatic materials, blindfold a child, and ask the child to identify the substance that she tastes or smells. Rather than

blindfolding the child, some teachers place unknown aromatic materials in separate socks or bags and have the child identify them by smell.

Hearing Activities

Children's ability to discriminate among sounds may be enhanced by having the teacher play notes on a tonette, pitchpipe, piano, or other musical instrument and asking the children to respond to the sounds with the words *louder* or *softer* (intensity), *higher* or *lower* (pitch), or *longer* or *shorter* (duration).

Growing Plants

A milk carton cut off at the top and a small amount of soil provide a child with a proper environment for planting seeds and observing growing plants. The effects of water, fertilizer, sunlight, and temperature on the growth of

Chart 4–2 ▪ Integrated Process Skills

Skill	Description	Example
Formulating Hypotheses	Making a statement that is believed to be true about a whole class of events.	The larger the surface area of a given amount of water, the faster it will evaporate.
Naming Variables	Stating all factors that affect an event.	Amount of water, surface size, humidity, wind, sunlight, temperature, time.
Controlling Variables	Naming the manipulated variable and all variables to be held constant.	Manipulated variable—surface area. Responding variable—volume of water remaining. Wind, humidity, sunlight, temperature, and time held the same for manipulated and control experiments.
Making Operational Definitions	Defining all variables as they are used in the experiment.	Starting amount of water for both manipulated and control experiments—1000 mL; Surface of manipulated water sample—50 cm²; surface of control water sample—100 cm²; wind, humidity, sunlight, and temperature held constant for both manipulated and control experiments. Time is also held the same.
Experimenting	Performing the activity.	Put 1000 mL of water in two rectangular pans, one having a 50 cm² bottom and the other a 100 cm² bottom. Let the two pans sit side by side for one day. Pour the water from each pan into a graduated beaker to find the new volume for each. Repeat for three days.
Interpreting Data	Creating a data table and forming conclusions.	State whether the hypothesis is accepted or rejected. Make any other inferences warranted by the data.
Investigating	Integrating process skills to gather data in discovery learning or by following teacher directions when not employing the formal scientific process.	Manipulate batteries and bulbs to investigate parallel circuits; complete a food web to determine the interrelationships in an ecosystem.

plants may be easily observed. Annual rye grass that germinates in two or three days in warm, moist soil and lima beans that, if soaked in water prior to planting, germinate in about a week, are most often used by the kindergarten teacher for such activities.

Pets and Other Live Animals

Fish, gerbils, rabbits, and other live animals provide young children opportunities for observing and handling experiences. Since animals maintained in a classroom require care over weekends and vacations, many teachers prefer to bring the animals into the classroom on a daily basis. In spite of admitted maintenance problems, many teachers feel that the experiences that children gain from feeding, watering, and caring for animals in the classroom make it worth the trouble. (See Appendix I for detailed information on care and feeding of animals in the classroom.)

Using the Integrated Process Skills

The integrated processes are: formulating hypotheses, making operational definitions, naming and controlling variables, experimenting, and interpreting data. To these integrated process skills, derived from the SAPA Program, we add the skill of investigating, which describes what children do when they are gathering data by the procedure of trial and error, as in discovery, or using structured procedures where no manipulated or responding variable is identified.

The integrated processes may be viewed as combinations of the primary processes and are generally taught to children who have acquired the primary process skills. The integrated processes may be developed through many of the exercises found in elementary science texts. The following lesson employs most of them.

A pendulum is a weight that swings to and fro, suspended from a string. When asked what conditions might be changed to affect the rate at which the pendulum swings, most children will guess: (1) the amount of the weight, (2) the size of the arc, and (3) the length of the string. To their surprise, they will find that only the last answer is correct.

The teacher opens the lesson by showing the children a swinging pendulum (Figure 4–8). After discussing the regular to and fro motion, she says: "If we are going to talk about the pendulum, we must find a name for some of its positions and motions." The pupils then provide names and definitions for the rest position, the length of the pendulum, the size of the swing, and the frequency (number of swings in a given time period). The teacher then says: "I wonder how many swings this pendulum will make in thirty seconds." With the aid of a timer, the class proceeds to count.

The teacher then says, "What can we do to change the number of swings the pendulum makes in thirty seconds?" The children will generally make the guesses listed above. The teacher points out that there are three variables to be

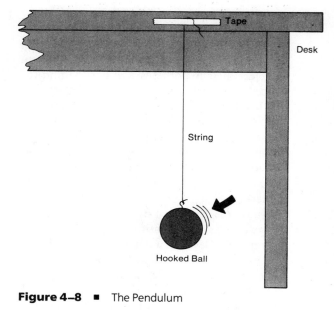

Figure 4–8 ■ The Pendulum

tested. She asks for a hypothesis for the effect of each variable. Examples of acceptable hypotheses would be: "Adding more weight to the pendulum will cause it to make fewer swings in thirty seconds." "Shortening the string will result in more swings in a thirty-second time period." The teacher should define just how big a difference in the number of swings constitutes an increase or decrease in the frequency.

Next, the teacher asks: "How can we test these hypotheses?" The testing may be done as a teacher demonstration or by the pupils working in pairs or small groups. The pupils must be cautioned to test by changing only one variable at a time. That is, if they change the length, they must hold the length of the arc and the weight constant. The goal is to isolate the effect of the single variable upon the pendulum.

Let us review the lesson. The children *formulated hypotheses* when they predicted the effect of each variable. They made *operational definitions* when they defined the parts, positions, and motions of the pendulum and determined the number of swings that would represent a change in frequency. They *controlled* and *manipulated variables* while testing their hypotheses. The whole process of formulating and testing hypotheses by manipulating variables is *experimenting*. The decision to accept or reject their hypotheses was based upon the process of *interpreting data*.

If a teacher gave groups of children string and washers and asked them to find out what they can about pendulums, the skill the children would employ would be *investigating* (if they did not resort to the formality of the experimentation process described in Chapter 3). Data gathering, whether intuitive, as in discovery learning, or structured by the teacher, may be designated as investigating when the students operate at a level that integrates the primary process skills and when they are not performing a formal experiment. See Chart 4–2 for a list of integrated process skills.

There is nothing really new about the process skills. They have always been part of experimental problem solving. (Note the inquiry technique of experimentation, Chapter 3.) What *is* new is the attempt to isolate and define each of the elements of the process. Now you can improve your pupils' ability to deal with problem situations by directing your efforts to developing narrowly defined skills rather than by dealing with the problem-solving process as a whole.

Concept Mapping and the Organization of Science Concepts

In Chapter 2 we described how children observe their environment and subsequently store knowledge at many conceptual levels. A child may think, "That is a tree" (identifying an object as a member of a class of objects). He may think, "Trees shed their leaves in the fall" (an event). He may recognize an object as being a member of a subclass of objects, for example, "This kind of tree keeps its leaves all year." He may conceptualize in terms of processes, such

as photosynthesis, or in terms of characteristics, such as height. Simple concepts, repeatedly observed, come to be accepted as facts of nature.

As the child manipulates and generalizes upon observations and facts, more complex conceptualizations may occur to him. These more comprehensive scientific generalizations are called conceptual schemes. Study the following hierarchal list of science concepts:

Conceptual Scheme:	Life forms on earth are all interdependent.
Concept A:	Animals depend on plants for food.
Concept B:	Plants and animals sustain each other through the oxygen–carbon dioxide cycle.
Subconcept B1:	Animals use oxygen to maintain life processes, and they give off carbon dioxide.
Subconcept B2:	Plants use carbon dioxide to maintain life processes, and they give off oxygen.

Notice that the conceptual scheme is a very broad, unifying statement that encompasses a number of concepts. The science concept, as it is used here, is still somewhat general in nature. It encompasses a number of subconcepts. The subconcept usually deals with relatively narrow relationships. The subconcept is the conceptual level best suited for structuring young children's learning experiences. It can be used to explain many observations and facts, yet it represents a conceptualization that is often narrow enough to be tested. The higher-order concepts and conceptual schemes that are universally accepted are known as principles or laws of science.

It is true that scientific knowledge is expanding at a rapid rate. No child may ever hope to learn all of the facts of science. Consequently, curriculum designers now generally organize science for instruction on the basis of the big ideas—conceptual schemes, concepts, and subconcepts.

Placing Science Concepts in an Elementary Science Program: The Spiral Approach

What do you notice about the following subconcepts of science?

1. Magnets attract some objects.
2. Magnetic effects work through some non-magnetic substances.
3. Like magnetic poles repel; unlike magnetic poles attract.
4. A magnetic field exists about a conductor that is carrying an electric current.

Can you see that the statements imply increasingly more complex ideas? That they likewise imply increasingly more complex methods of testing and demonstrating? That the ideas implied are all related to a single concept: magnetism is a force associated with moving electric charges?

In structuring a science curriculum, you must always answer two questions: When should each subconcept be introduced to the elementary school child? With what methodology? Many science programs use a spiral approach. This involves presenting a single subconcept during each school year, in order of increasing complexity. Thus, one would find subconcept number one, which concerns the discovery of the magnetism phenomenon, presented in the first grade. A popular teaching approach for this subconcept is to have the children test various objects for their attraction to magnets. In the second grade the children would discover subconcept number two by inserting paper, wood, and other substances between the magnet and the magnetic substance. In the third grade the polarity of magnets would be investigated, and in the fourth, electromagnetism would be introduced. The concept of magnetic force would be built up over a period of time. Still within the framework of the spiral approach, more subconcepts would be introduced in succeeding years until the study of magnetism and its interrelationship with electricity had been fully explored.

Elementary science teachers should be aware of the spiral approach if for no other reason than that it will make them feel secure about not trying to teach all of a given concept in one year. In the minds of many curriculum builders, little is gained, and often much is lost, by such saturation methods. It is enough that the teacher should know the children's prior experience with a particular concept and should add one more step to the staircase of knowledge that will lead, finally, to complete understanding.

The work of Piaget is also having an increasing effect on the placement of content in the elementary school science curriculum. Primary-grade programs are now designed to deal with concrete objects and to teach basic skills such as classifying and observing. Topics that encompass the manipulation of ideas are remanded to the intermediate grades or to the junior high school.

Concept Mapping As a Learning Strategy

Recently a teaching strategy has been introduced into science education that utilizes the notion of having students create hierarchies or arrays of concepts. This procedure is called concept mapping. The theoretical foundation for concept mapping is David P. Ausubel's recommendation of the use of advanced organizers. As you recall from Chapter 2, an advanced organizer is a learning activity that illustrates for the student the structure and interrelationships of the content being studied. Helping children to visualize the relationships of learned concepts is also strongly supported by Piagetian theory. Piaget proposed that a learner's assimilation and accommodation of ideas and the development of a cognitive structure may be realized only when the learner understands conceptual relationships. Both theorists advocate the development of types of concept maps, though for somewhat different reasons. Instead of presenting the concept map through a lecture or a study sheet, as advocated by Ausubel, some science educators have advocated having the children independently create it from their examination of the content of the unit. However, at the elementary school level, concept mapping may best be achieved when the teacher provides leadership and guidance for the children. This may be accomplished when concepts are arranged in a spiral curriculum. For example, after a third-grade class has learned such concepts as "Plants use carbon dioxide and give off oxygen as a waste product" and "Animals use oxygen and give off carbon dioxide as a waste product," the teacher would conduct a discussion of the interrelationship of plants and animals in the environment. As the children learn more about plants and animals, the teacher would reintroduce the conceptual scheme that all life forms on earth are interdependent and broaden the concept of synergistic relationships. Frequent discussion of the relationships of learned concepts, accompanied by simple flowcharts on the chalkboard, would satisfy both Ausubelian and Piagetian theorists.

Building a Concept Map for Review and Accommodation of New Concepts

In its simplest form a concept map is an array of related concepts. This type of concept map may be developed simply by asking students to name or state all the things they know of that are related to a topic. For instance, at the conclusion of a unit of study on matter, a fifth-grade teacher might ask her class to name all the ideas or topics that are related to the nature of matter. With some open-ended questioning, the teacher might assist the students in naming the following concepts, which she could then write on the chalkboard in no particular order: matter, atoms, solid, liquid, gas, bonds, ions, heat energy, kinetic energy, electrical forces, electrons, molecular forces, protons, neutrons.

After an acceptable array of ideas has been presented, the teacher might say, "Good, you have shown you know some concepts related to the nature of matter. Can we group any of these ideas together for one reason or another? For instance, I see that electrons, protons and neutrons could go together. Why is that?" The students might respond that the electrons, protons and neutrons are the things atoms are made of, in which case the teacher might circle each of these terms and draw lines connecting them. If the students do not suggest it, the teacher might ask what electrical bonds or forces ionic bonds and molecular bonding have in common, circling each word on the chalkboard (preferably with a different color of chalk), and connecting them with lines. This group she could identify as "forces that hold atoms and molecules together." Heat energy and kinetic energy might be identified as "the energy that tends to cause atoms and molecules to come apart or disassociate." The discussion might continue until the students could form no more conceptual groupings. At that point the teacher could invite the students to discuss the relationships among the conceptual groups. (See Figure 4–9, which demonstrates the concept map created by the class for the topic The Nature of Matter.)

In reviewing the concept map, the teacher noticed that the students did not include covalent bonding, metallic bonding, and electrons, three concepts she considers to be important. If after prompting the students still do not think of one or more of these important concepts, a sixth-grade teacher might ask, "Where would covalent bonding fit?" Or, "Where would electrons fit?" These concepts would then be added to the concept map. Alternative groupings might also be suggested and discussed. This postinstructional development of the concept map helps students more fully develop their personal conceptual framework for the topic they just completed. (Concept maps that are to be used as advanced organizers would usually be constructed primarily by the teacher prior to

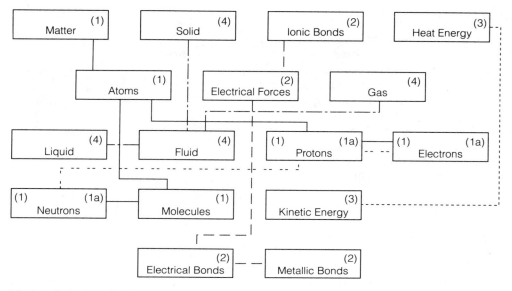

Figure 4–9 ■ The Nature of Matter

beginning the unit, and would be referred to as each new concept was learned.)

Using the I-C-I Sequence to Teach the Process Skills and Content of Science

The makeup of many elementary science textbooks, and common teaching practices, relegate classroom demonstrations to a reinforcing role. The science activity, if done at all, often follows the reading and discussion of the textbook. If inquiry is to take place in the science classroom, this order must be reversed. One cannot structure an inquiry lesson to establish scientific relationships that are based on material the children already know.

The best way to combine textbook material with inquiry training is to employ the sequence: *inquiry-concept-information*. This three-step learning process indicates the order for introducing a unit or chapter of the textbook. First, several activities are chosen from the textbook to be used as vehicles for inquiry lessons. These inquiry lessons may be conducted by any of the three techniques outlined in Chapter 3. Their objective is to establish the major concepts or subconcepts upon which the related textbook material is based. After the children have solved the problems and understand the concepts or subconcepts, the science content in the chapter or in any supplementary materials may be taught to them by one of the several direct teaching procedures described on the following pages.

If he uses inquiry in his classroom, a teacher will find it necessary to maintain control over the textbooks. He will distribute them to the children after the class has completed the inquiry part of the lesson as outlined above. He will then collect and store them after the class has finished reading and discussing the topic at hand. All of the traditional didactic practices—lecture, worksheets, and drill—may be used in the information part of the lesson.

An Example of I-C-I Planning

Suppose that a fourth-grade teacher is about to embark on a new chapter of the science textbook. The chapter is called "Heat and the States of Matter." Upon reading it, the teacher decides that most of the information in it can be related to three subconcepts of science: (1) Many different substances will change their form with the addition of heat. (2) Energy is required to change the state of matter. (3) Molecules of warm liquids move faster than molecules of cold liquids.

The teacher will first conduct three inquiry lessons. To arrive at subconcept number one, he might place some beeswax, some ice, and some solder on a tin plate and heat the plate over a propane torch. (See Figure 4–10.) He would ask such questions as: "What did you see?" and "What can we conclude?" If he knows how to ask opening questions and handle student responses, the children will conclude that many things change state when they are heated and that the temperature at which it happens is different for different things. This exercise is an inquiry lesson using the rational approach. The process skills it develops are observing and inferring.

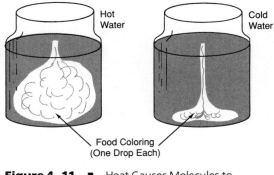

Figure 4–11 ■ Heat Causes Molecules to Move Faster

To arrive at subconcept number two, the teacher might show the class a time and temperature graph. This graph would show that when ice cubes are placed in a beaker and heated over an alcohol burner, their temperature will rise rapidly to 0° Celsius and remain there for a time before starting to rise again. The teacher would ask the students what this means. Using an inquiry technique, he would guide the students to understand that the ice absorbs energy as it changes to water. This exercise opens with an invitation to inquiry and uses the rational approach to obtain the generalization. The process skill it develops is interpretation of data.

To arrive at subconcept number three, the children might be asked to form small groups. Each group of four or five children would be given two bottles, one containing hot and the other cold water. They would be instructed to put one drop of food coloring in each (Figure 4–11). The children would record their observations and make inferences about what they see. The teacher then utilizes the procedures of rational inquiry to discuss their observations and form conclusions and to help the children arrive at the desired concept. This is a discovery lesson. The process skills developed by this lesson are experimenting, observing, and inferring.

Having provided the children with experiences in doing inquiry, having assisted them in

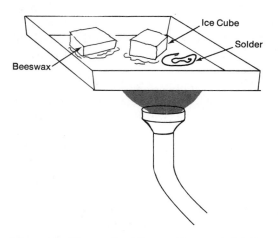

Figure 4–10 ■ Heat Causes Changes in Matter

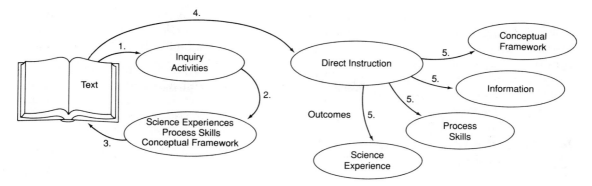

Figure 4–12 ■ The I-C-I Model

acquiring process skills, and having established the three subconcepts relevant to the new chapter, the teacher might now issue the textbooks and give assigned readings. This order is the essence of the I-C-I process. If the subconcepts and the inquiry activities have been properly selected, the children will have a firm conceptual base for their reading and some concrete experiences to relate it to. They may now undertake to learn, through a variety of direct teaching methods, about the states of matter and kinetic motion of molecules as they are related to heat energy. (See Figure 4–12.)

The elementary school teacher who is adept at inquiry techniques may use these techniques to reshape nearly any science lesson so that it will develop one or more of the process skills and help students to create a personal conceptual framework upon which to build an understanding of the facts and content of science.

Advantages of the I-C-I Method

There are several real advantages to employing the Inquiry-Concept-Information sequence with a textbook-based program.

I-C-I Makes Inquiry Possible

The advantages of inquiry science were spelled out in Chapter 3. As you recall, they include maintaining children's curiosity, developing their high-level cognitive skills, developing their positive attitudes toward science, providing concrete experiences for children, developing their problem-solving skills, and others. Through the I-C-I sequence, it is possible to use inquiry teaching methods with a textbook program.

I-C-I Provides Organization for Later Learning

Teaching the more important ideas of a textbook unit through inquiry provides a child with a conceptual framework for later learning activities. The big ideas of the unit serve as *organizers* for sorting and accommodating new information that she acquires through direct means, such as reading, listening, and viewing filmstrips and films. The new information makes sense because it fits with prior experience. The child is able to achieve equilibrium as new ideas mesh with previously assimilated concepts.

I-C-I Helps Slow Readers

Children who have experienced inquiry lessons that deal with the major concepts of a textbook chapter are better equipped to read textual material. Initial inquiry experiences are especially helpful to slow readers who rely heavily upon context clues for understanding as they read. In many cases the very words, phrases, and ideas they are reading have been used in problem-solving discussions during the inquiry lessons. Often they will find pictures and discussions of laboratory exercises that they have already performed or have seen performed. Slow readers gain more from reading the textbook when the I-C-I procedure is followed.

Teaching the Information (Content) of Science

The information (content) of science includes facts, principles, and concepts with all degrees of complexity, not just low-level factual content. The great advantage of the I-C-I procedure is that it permits teaching both the process and content of science from the same textbook. The sequence of the instructional modes is of the greatest importance. The inquiry lessons must be taught first, followed by the content lessons. We now turn to procedures for teaching science content. Research, learning theory, and the experience of veteran teachers all support the importance of following accepted procedures in teaching information directly to children.

Direct Teaching Methods

Common methods for teaching information (content) to children in the elementary school are: lecture, lecture-demonstration, written seatwork, and the use of media, computers, and textbooks. These methods are commonly referred to as procedures of direct teaching. We'll briefly examine each of these activities. (Note: The use of microcomputers in the elementary school science classroom is discussed in some detail in Chapter 8.)

Lecture

Lecture as a method of instruction is used sparingly by teachers in elementary schools. When lecture is used, it is for short periods of time, usually three to five minutes, to explain or clarify some point of information or to give directions. A few guidelines for teaching science information to children by lecture are:

1. Keep it short. Elementary-school-aged children have difficulty understanding and retaining a succession of facts presented to them orally. Use lecture to present only one or two bits of information at a time.

2. Know your information and present it clearly and authoritatively. Planned lectures should be delivered from an outline to ensure the accuracy of the information and instill an air of confidence.

3. Use the "tricks of the trade" of public speaking. Maintain eye contact with the children by looking directly at first one and then another as you speak. Use vocal inflection and intonation to highlight important points and maintain children's interest. Introduce your topic before you give them the information, and summarize at the end of the lecture. (Speech teachers say: Tell them what you are going to tell them; tell them; then tell them what you have told them.)

Lecture-Demonstration

A lecture-demonstration is an activity in which the teacher uses materials to show some aspect of science to children and explain for them what it is they saw and its meaning. Though they both employ materials, the lecture-demonstration is not a form of inquiry. In inquiry the children tell the teacher what they observed and concluded, whereas in the lecture-demonstration the teacher tells the children what they should have seen and its meaning. Sometimes rational inquiry and the lecture-demonstration get mixed together in a lesson. Usually when this happens the inquiry and its benefits to children are short-changed. The lecture-demonstration is a direct method of teaching and explaining information to children. The use of materials often enhances the class's understanding of the concept that is being demonstrated and is considered to have this advantage over the straight lecture. An example of a lecture-demonstration might be:

With a group of children gathered around her, Miss Henry strikes a tuning fork on the heel of her hand and touches the vibrating tuning fork to the surface of a pan of water. (This may also be projected onto a screen by using a glass dish and an overhead projector.) She tells the class, "See how the tuning fork causes waves to spread out in all directions. This is what happens to the air but we can't see the waves. Sound travels in waves through the air just like these waves we see in the water. Now look what happens when we use a tuning fork that vibrates much faster." Miss Henry then strikes a second tuning fork on the heel of her hand and touches it to the water's surface.

Note that in the lecture-demonstration the teacher does all the talking and the children do all the listening. It is an efficient way to present and explain information, but the children are operating intellectually at the knowledge and comprehension levels of the cognitive domain.

Seatwork

Written seatwork is widely used by elementary school teachers as a means of introducing and reinforcing science concepts and information. The seatwork may be structured as simply as teaching vocabulary by having the children select words from a list to fill in blank spaces in a written text. Sometimes the worksheets are in game and puzzle form in an attempt to increase the motivational levels of students. Drill and practice have legitimate places in the elementary classroom when used wisely. Wisely in most science educators' minds means sparingly and limited primarily to use as reinforcement of learned information.

Use of Media

Charts and posters may be used to help the teacher convey information to children with greater clarity than through the spoken word alone. Charts and posters are particularly helpful to teachers who have small aptitude in drawing sketches on the chalkboard to illustrate their lectures. Other popularly employed media in the elementary school classroom are filmstrips, films, and videotapes and disks. Through graphic portrayal and action these media are very effective in demonstrating and teaching science concepts and information. Several suggestions incorporated into the use of "action" media can make their use as teaching tools more effective.

1. Always preview the material before using it in class.
2. Prior to its use, give the children several questions or points of information to consider as they view the material.
3. Ensure that the children consider the use of media an important learning activity by reviewing the information they are to learn and holding them responsible for it. Followup activities may also be assigned that grow naturally from the topic covered by the media presentation.

Teaching with the Textbook

A large part of the money spent by elementary schools on instructional materials for science is invested in textbooks, and textbooks appear to be the primary teaching tool employed by many teachers. A few guidelines may be of value in obtaining the optimum level of instruction and learning from a textbook.

For maximum learning on the entire range of cognitive levels it is necessary that children investigate and explore through the inquiry activities contained in the text. Using the textbook to teach information also requires some thought and planning on the part of the teacher. Experienced teachers find that even when the reading level of the science textbook matches the reading ability of their class there are some things they can do to enhance students' understanding of the content. The teacher may introduce a new chapter in the textbook by asking questions or previewing the new topic, touching on the major concepts. This introduction provides a proper mental set and the motivation for students to read and study the material. It is also helpful for teachers to discuss new vocabulary words that the students will encounter in the chapter, pronouncing them with the class and defining them. This aids understanding as students read the new material. Another common practice that provides purpose for the student is to pose several questions to be answered from the reading. Of course, when inquiry lessons have been taught about the material, most of these concerns have been taken care of.

It is always helpful when, on the day following the reading assignment, the teacher clarifies and reinforces the students' understanding of what they have read. Teachers do this through discussion and through answering students' questions about concepts that are unclear. Those teachers who attend to procedures such as those outlined here, and who do not rely on the students' unaided ability to read the science textbook, will find their students achieve far better understanding of the subject matter.

Many good-quality textbooks contain questions to be answered by the students. Exercises that involve students with answering questions posed in the textbook are of value as a learning experience, but they cannot be relied on to carry effectively the major burden of instruction. To maintain a high level of interest and learning, reading and answering questions from the textbook should be preceded by inquiry lessons and supplemented by lecture, group projects, speakers, media presentations, and other activities.

The deadliest sin of teaching with a textbook is the practice of "reading around the horn," or "taking turns." Since silent reading rates of most students far exceed their oral reading rates, taking turns reading is unproductive for most of the students. Those not reading orally must mark time as they wait for the oral reader to catch up. When students are not en-

gaged in the learning process the teacher finds an increase in discipline problems. The practice of taking turns at reading a textbook orally often results in management problems for the teacher. As an additional consideration regarding the practice, reading experts find there is little relationship between reading comprehension and oral reading skill and that there is relatively little value to the reader in the activity.

It appears that the optimum utilization of the textbook as a learning tool depends on selecting the proper text for the class and teacher, helping the students to read the text through a proper introduction of the concepts and vocabulary, and followup of the reading by discussion and enrichment. A textbook is a valuable tool in the hands of a skilled teacher; it rarely can do a proper job of teaching students all by itself.

Summary

The traditional problem-solving skills have been more specifically defined by the Science—A Process Approach program as process skills. The process skills are: observing, classifying, measuring, communicating, inferring, predicting, and recognizing number and time-space relationships. The activities employed to introduce these skills are similar to those already used by many teachers. Any teacher can teach the primary process skills, often in conjunction with a regular program.

The integrated process skills, except for the skill of investigating, are closely related to the inquiry method of experimentation. This method involves formulating hypotheses, making operational definitions, controlling variables, experimenting, and organizing and interpreting data.

Concept mapping, as it is employed by curriculum designers and teachers who wish to use a concept map as an advanced organizer for instructional purposes, is a hierarchy of concepts that range from the most narrow to the most comprehensive. Concept maps may be constructed by a class *following* the study of a unit or chapter. By listing the concepts covered in the unit or chapter on the chalkboard, drawing lines between related ideas, and discussing the relationships, students review the material learned and restructure their individual conceptual frameworks. This aids each student in assimilating the concepts and information learned.

The teacher who wants to incorporate skill building and inquiry into a science program while retaining the content of the textbook should follow the inquiry-concept-information sequence. Within this sequence, inquiry is used first, to teach both concepts and selected skills. Textbook readings and other didactic practices follow.

A major tool of direct instruction is the lecture. Lectures in the classroom should be planned and delivered with the same techniques and care that go into a successful speech. Lectures should be given from an outline and not read from a text; they should be short, lasting from twenty to thirty minutes; and they should follow a format of preview-presentation-review. The effectiveness of a lecture may be enhanced with the use of media, such as charts, graphs, transparencies, and filmstrips, and by the use of manipulatives or equipment that may be used to demonstrate the concept that is being presented.

The quality of written student reports may be improved by procedures that introduce the assignment as a question or problem to be answered and by providing instruction to the students in the proper procedures for organizing and writing the report. These procedures should be followed regardless of the subject being taught. The use of a textbook as the major tool of instruction is improved through the employment of certain introductory and culminating procedures related to each reading assignment and by supplementing the information in the textbook with enriching lectures and materials. Refrain from the deadly sin of having students take turns reading the textbook aloud in class and remember the importance of a sense of humor in establishing and maintaining a rapport with students.

Extending Activities

1. Examine an elementary school textbook series. List the concepts presented at each grade level for each topic. For example, under the heading Heat Energy, list the concepts that the authors of the series consider appropriate for each grade level. Make similar lists for as many topics as time permits.

2. Devise a lesson that expands upon one of the primary process skill activities cited in Chart 4–1. Describe and discuss your lesson with a group of your peers.

3. You wish to conduct an experiment to investigate the pitch of vibrating string. You have one thick and one thin rubber band, one set of weights, and one ruler.
   a. Name the variables that affect the pitch of a vibrating string.
   b. Formulate hypotheses to be tested.
   c. Describe the method for testing the hypotheses. Be sure to define all terms and to control all variables.
   d. Conduct the experiment.
   e. Interpret the data.

4. Teach a five-minute lesson to a small group of your peers using one of the following techniques: lecture, lecture with media, or lecture with a demonstration. Critique each lesson that is taught using information provided in this chapter.

5. Select a chapter from an elementary science textbook series and construct a lecture outline for a ten- to twenty-minute lecture. Compare and discuss your outline with a peer.

6. Select a chapter from an elementary school science textbook. Construct a concept map as was shown in Figure 4–9, The Nature of Matter.

7. Develop a plan for assigning a written report to students on a topic of your choice. Write out the directions you will provide and an outline of the instruction you will provide to prepare them for the assignment.

Bibliography

Bainer, D. "What to Do When People Disagree: Addressing Ideational Pluralism in Science Classes." *Science Education* 70, no. 2 (April 1985): 173–184.

Berliner, D. C., and B. Rosenshine. *The Acquisition of Knowledge in the Classroom.* Technical Report N-1. San Francisco: Far West Laboratory for Educational Research and Development, 1976.

Esler, W. K. "Putting It All Together: Inquiry, Process, Science Concepts, and the Textbook." *Science Education* 57 (1973): 19–23.

Esler, W. K. "Structuring Inquiry for Classroom Use." *School Science and Mathematics* 70 (May 1970): 454–458.

Esler, W. K., and P. Sciortino. *Teaching Strategies.* Raleigh, N.C.: Contemporary Press, 1990.

Hamrick, L., H. Harty, and C. Ault. "Concept Structure Interrelatedness Competency (ConSic): A Tool for Examining and Promoting Cognitive Structure." *School Science and Mathematics* 87, no. 8 (December 1987): 655–664.

Harty, H., et al. "Gender Influence on Concept Structure Interrelatedness Competence." *Science Education* 71, no. 1 (1987): 105–115.

Hawk, P. "Using Graphic Organizers to Increase Achievement in Middle School Life Science." *Science Education* 70, no. 1 (January 1986): 81–88.

Jackson, R. "Thumbs Up for the Direct Teaching of Thinking Skills." *Educational Leadership* 43, no. 8 (May 1986): 32–36.

Livermore, A. H. "The Process Approach to the AAAS Commission on Science Education." *Journal of Research in Science Teaching* 2, no. 4 (1964): 271–282.

McLeod, R., and B. Hunter. "The Data Base in the Laboratory." *Science and Children* 24, no. 4 (January 1987): 28–30.

Rogan, J. "Conceptual Mapping As a Diagnostic Aid." *School Science and Mathematics* 88, no. 1 (January 1988): 50–59.

Staver, J., and M. Bay. "Analysis of the Conceptual Structure and Reasoning Demands of Elementary Science Texts at the Primary (K–3) Level." *Journal of Research in Science Teaching* 26, no. 4 (1989): 329–349.

Stepans, J., and C. Kuehn. "Children's Conceptions of Weather." *Science and Children* 23, no. 1 (September 1985): 44–47.

Their, H. "Societal Issues and Concerns: A New Emphasis for Science Education." *Science Education* 69, no. 2 (April 1985): 157–164.

Tobin, K. "Validating Teacher Performance Measures Against Student Engagement and Achievement in Middle School Science." *Science Education* 70, no. 5 (October 1986): 539–548.

Wilson, V. "Theory Building and Theory Confirming Observation in Science and Science Education." *Journal of Research in Science Teaching* 24, no. 3 (March 1987): 279–283.

CHAPTER 5

Planning Instruction and Evaluating Student Learning in the I-C-I Science Program

Look What's in This Chapter

Our goals for this chapter are to provide you with the information necessary to write a brief unit plan based upon the I-C-I sequence and to properly evaluate student performance in the science classroom. Sample daily lesson plans for both inquiry and traditional (information) lessons build upon information in the previous chapter to help you to structure the I-C-I unit. Discussions of topics such as writing learning objectives, writing test items, using checklists and rating scales, and making a good fit between the stated objectives and the methods of evaluation will prepare you to evaluate student progress in the science classroom. You also will learn about cautions and procedures that promote safety and positive health practices in an activity-oriented program.

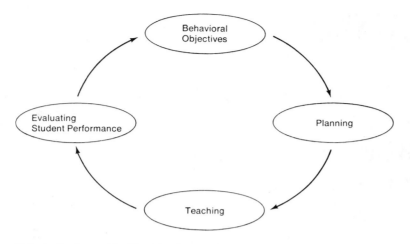

Figure 5–1 ■ The Teaching Process

Two of the most practical skills you can acquire are the ability to make good lesson plans and the ability to evaluate student performance. They are treated together in this chapter. These skills are part of a cyclical process that includes writing educational objectives, planning for instruction, teaching, and evaluating student performance (Figure 5–1). All teachers are involved at some level with this process. But the depth and kind of involvement always depend upon the individual teacher—on her experience, interest, and ability.

The Teacher as a Curriculum Planner

As a curriculum planner, the teacher may operate on one of three levels. The lowest level is that of technician. The technician utilizes prepared materials and a prepared curriculum. She makes a few changes in the program, but attempts to carry out its design to the best of her ability.

The second level is that of manipulator. The manipulator selects those parts of prepared curricula that seem best suited to her own classroom and her students. She may add to, delete from, and change the prepared materials. Her

goal is to adapt them to her own unique situation.

The third level is that of innovator. An innovator appraises the needs and interest of her students and builds her own curriculum to satisfy those needs. The innovator is a truly creative teacher.

Few elementary school teachers can operate at the innovator level in every area. They may still be very fine teachers. Children benefit greatly from the teacher who can do a good job of presenting ideas from a program devised by experts in a given field. A teacher who does not construct her own curriculum is free to concentrate on methods and on the children. Since most beginning teachers operate as technicians or manipulators, we will discuss planning at these lower levels. It will become apparent that even at these levels, operating a good science program takes skill.

Planning for Instruction

Our discussion of planning for instruction will unfold as follows: First, we'll discuss the skills and understanding necessary for writing lesson plans; next, we'll develop a model for writing lesson plans for inquiry lessons and information lessons. We will then proceed to the creation of the I-C-I unit plan. At this point, issues of planning for safety in the science classroom will be explored. When we have established a firm foundation for writing lesson plans and I-C-I units, we will proceed to considerations of evaluating student performance.

Writing Teaching Objectives

Teaching objectives are simply statements of what the teacher expects the students to be able to do following planned instruction. Several examples of teaching objectives are: The children will identify the primary colors; The children will state the generalization "temperature affects the rate at which things dissolve in water"; and the children will demonstrate the ability to read a Celsius thermometer. Notice that there is some variety in the types and levels of expected student performance. Students may be expected to perform in the cognitive, affective, and psychomotor domains. (See Chapter 2 for a review of these domains.)

Choice of Verbs

In specifying desired student behavior in all three of the domains, it is important to choose the right verb. You must know clearly what behavior you want to elicit before you can plan activities designed to elicit it. Use common verbs like these to describe activities at the various levels of each domain.

The Cognitive Domain

Knowledge recall, recite, list, enumerate, fill the blank, etc.

Comprehension match, translate, interpret orally, select the right answer, etc.

Skill (Application, Analysis, Synthesis, Evaluation) solve, construct, describe in writing, analyze, hypothesize, plan and carry out experimentation, etc.

For each of these verbs, simply begin with the phrase "the students will . . . " and follow it with a description of what they are to do. For example: "The students will solve two-digit multiplication problems" or "The children will construct a model of a water atom.''

Each day's lesson plan need not consider every cognitive level. But the teacher should examine his lesson plans every few weeks to make sure that he is not neglecting any one level. Some experts suggest that at least 30 percent of class time be spent in activities that utilize cognitive skills above the comprehension level. Many educators would advocate a much higher percentage.

Affective Objectives

Most teachers readily recognize desirable attitudes in children. Stating them as teaching objectives may encourage the children to believe that such attitudes are worth developing. Perhaps "turning on" a child to a subject and increasing his self-concept may be a more worthwhile goal than those that are concerned with subject matter. Behavioral objectives that concern the affective domain can give the teacher great satisfaction. They can make him see that the attitudinal changes he has worked so hard to achieve for his children are important in their own right. Some examples of affective behavioral objectives are:

Immediate Behaviors

1. The child will turn in all homework assignments for one week.
2. The child will make at least one oral contribution to class discussion each day.
3. The child will exhibit an alert interest during inquiry discussion.
4. The child will actively participate in all manipulative exercises.

Long-Range Behaviors

1. The child will repeat science activities at home.

2. The child will volunteer proposals for science activities in addition to those he does in class.
3. The child will work on independent home projects in science.
4. The child will choose to elect science courses in later school years.
5. The child will state an interest in a science-related vocation.

Psychomotor Objectives

The two levels of the psychomotor domain that are most applicable to science instruction in the elementary school are Level 3, Perceptual Abilities, and Level 5, Skilled Movements. Although all levels of the domain are important to their general development, children's experiences in the elementary school science classroom are most strongly related to the behaviors of these two levels. Some examples of objectives of the two levels of the psychomotor domain follow.

Level 3—Perceptual Abilities
The child will distinguish between two similar geometric shapes.
The child will describe the texture of objects.
The child will copy a simple line drawing.

Level 5—Skilled Movements
The child will pour a liquid from one container to another.
The child will use a platform balance to accurately weigh an object.
The child will use a graduated cylinder to determine the volume of a liquid.

Writing Science Skill Objectives

The skills used in doing science have been defined earlier in Chapter 4 as the primary and integrated processes. The primary process skills, you may remember, are to observe, infer, classify, recognize time/space relationships, measure, predict, and recognize number relations. The integrated processes are to hypothesize, name and control variables, make operational definitions, experiment, and interpret data. You will recall that we added one other skill, investigation. A student is performing the skill of investigating when she or he is using equipment or materials in order to gather data to solve a problem. Investigating requires the student to integrate the use of the primary process skills.

The primary and integrated processes may serve as the verbs for learning objectives for science skills. Some examples of skill objectives are:

The children will observe by tasting various foods and will classify the foods as sweet and sour.

The children will observe an ice cube and will infer that ice turns to water at room temperature.

The children will experiment using a pendulum and will interpret their data to form a generalization concerning the period of a pendulum (the time it takes for the pendulum to make one swing back and forth).

The children will investigate a simple electric circuit and will infer the conditions required to make a light bulb light.

Models for an Inquiry Lesson Plan and for an Information (Traditional) Lesson Plan

The model that will be used in this textbook for writing an inquiry lesson plan contains the elements shown in the two plans on the facing page. Sample lesson plans utilizing both the inquiry model and the information model are presented later in this chapter.

Model for an Inquiry Lesson Plan

Orientation: The grade level or other designation of the target group.

Content Objective: Those things cognitive, affective, and psychomotor that the children are expected to demonstrate following instruction. See the preceding paragraphs.

Skill Objective: The process skills students are to demonstrate in carrying out the planned activity.

Materials: All materials necessary to carry out the planned activity.

Evaluation of Student Performance: All the criteria or evidence that aids in evaluating student performance during the activity. This topic will be discussed later in this chapter.

Procedure:

This portion of the lesson plan includes written statements related to the safety of the children during the activity as well as detailed, step-by-step directions for carrying out the activity. Procedures for inquiry lessons often contain sample questions designed to elicit desired responses from students, statements of desired learning outcomes, such as concepts or generalizations, and any other information helpful to the teacher.

Now that we are familiar with the model of the inquiry lesson plan, let's take a look at the model for writing an information or traditional lesson plan.

Model for an Information Lesson Plan

Orientation: Same as for the Inquiry Lesson Plan.

Content Objective: Same as for the Inquiry Lesson Plan. (Note: No skill objective is required.)

Instructional Technique: Typical traditional instructional techniques are lecture, lecture-demonstration, seatwork, drill, media, and so on.

Materials: Lecture notes, handouts, seatwork, media, and any other equipment or materials necessary to carry out the lesson.

Procedure

Set:

Any preliminary activity designed to gain students' attention and achieve an academic focus—often merely a review of past activities or preview of things to come. *Set* can also be more elaborate or even theatrical, such as reading a science-related poem, playing music on an instrument, and so on.

Activity Outline:

Contains lecture notes, safety precautions, provisions for frequent review, use of media, and so on.

Closure:

Often a review or summary of what has been learned by the students. This may take the form of a teacher lecture, a question-answer review, or even a written review.

Safety in the Elementary School Science Classroom

The materials and equipment used in doing science often cause concern among teachers and administrators responsible for the safety of children. This concern is real but need not become a limiting factor in implementing a hands-on science program if certain precautions and guidelines, presented later in this chapter, are observed.

Planning an I-C-I Unit in a Textbook Science Program

Some Guidelines

In Chapter 4 you read that to ensure that inquiry is taking place it is necessary to teach following the sequence of Inquiry, Concept, Information. Following is an explanation and example of how to plan an I-C-I unit where a textbook is the primary resource and guide.

If he follows a prescribed curriculum, such as a textbook or special program, the teacher need not decide which concepts to teach, in what order, or even, with some programs, how to teach them. Because science programs place varying planning requirements upon teachers, because the amount of innovation varies with individual teachers, and because of the variety of things that are taught as science, it is very difficult to outline a single planning format that will serve for every lesson. There is only one universal requirement. Some kind of planning must take place.

Regardless of the curriculum, a good lesson plan must satisfy certain criteria:

1. The lesson should be part of a developing, articulated master plan.
2. The objectives of the lesson should be clearly stated in behavioral terms.
3. The activities employed to reach the objectives should be clearly defined.
4. Learning outcomes should be evaluated.

Good science teaching is not doing whatever happens. Films, television lessons, student demonstrations, and so forth must all be part of a plan designed to develop an evolving understanding of scientific concepts and skills. The teacher must understand how each lesson will further his long-range goals. If he must prepare or collect teaching materials, he must plan his lessons well in advance and arrange to have necessary supplies on hand. Without advance planning, the lessons will usually degenerate into a day-to-day, unimaginative routine.

Formulating a Unit Plan

One way to organize a long-range plan is to choose the broad topics that are to be covered and to list under each topic the basic concepts that are important to its development. These concepts may be found in textbooks, usually as section headings or listed on the first page of a chapter.

Let us say that you wish to teach a unit on weather to your fourth-grade class. The material you have at your disposal is a textbook that contains a chapter titled "The Weather and You" and a box of miscellaneous items that you have accumulated over a period of months. Since you are a teacher who thinks it important to teach process skills as well as content in science, you decide to structure the weather unit following the I-C-I scheme. Here is what you would do to plan your unit.

First, examine the material in the textbook, looking for the major concepts of weather that are covered in the chapter. You notice that in your textbook, as is the case in most textbooks, there are only a few major ideas presented. Your textbook authors have centered the study of the weather about four of them. You might list those four concepts:

Weather:

1. Water is taken into the air through evaporation. (Evaporation)

2. Water will condense from cold air. (Precipitation)
3. Warm air rises, cool air settles. (Winds, Storms)
4. Weather may be predicted. (Observation)

According to the I-C-I procedure you will develop inquiry lessons that will teach the four selected concepts to your students. Usually, the activities found in the textbook may be adapted to be taught as inquiry lessons. For instance, the first concept, "Water is taken into the air through evaporation," can be taught by restructuring two common, simple activities so they are taught by inquiry procedures as in the following lesson plan:

Lesson Plan ▪ A

Orientation: Grade 4

Content Objective:
1. The children will state orally that water can go into the air, and that
2. Water evaporates faster on a warm, sunny day than on a cloudy day.

Skill Objective: The children will *observe* demonstrations of evaporation and *infer* a generalization from their observations.

Materials: Wet sponge, writing pad, two shallow pans.

Evaluation of Student Performance: Observation of oral responses, sketch.

Procedure

Wipe a wet sponge across the chalkboard. Ask: "What happens to the water?" (It went into the air.) Make two wet marks with the sponge. Fan one mark vigorously with a writing pad. "What happened?" (The mark that was fanned disappeared faster than the mark that was not fanned.) "What could this tell us about how wind might affect the wet ground after a rain shower?" (It will help the water to evaporate faster.)

While the children are watching, carefully measure and pour identical small amounts of water into two identical pans. "What will happen if I put one pan on my desk and one on the window sill in the sunlight?" Let the children guess, and then place the pans as suggested. After several hours, or the next day, look at the pans and ask: "How does sunlight affect the speed with which water evaporates?" (Water evaporates faster in the sunlight.) "What can we say about how much evaporation takes place on a warm, sunny day?" (More water evaporates on a warm, sunny day, than on a cool, cloudy day.) To conclude, instruct the children to draw a sketch that shows evaporation.

The second concept listed as a main idea for the unit, "Water will condense from cold air," can be taught as inquiry with the following lesson plan:

Lesson Plan ■ B

Orientation: Grade 4

Content Objective: The children will state orally that cold air cannot hold as much moisture as warm air.

Skill Objective: The children are required to *observe* condensation and to *infer* a generalization from their observations.

Materials: Two metal cans, warm water, ice water.

Evaluation of Student Performance: Observation of student responses, student sketch.

Procedure

While the children are watching, fill one metal can with warm water and the other metal can with very cold water. After a short wait, ask: "What do we see?" (Water forms on the outside of one can.) "Where does the water come from?" (From the air.) If some students believe the water seeps through the can, add food coloring to the can containing cold water. (The moisture on the outside is clear.) "Why does one can have water on the outside and the other doesn't? Is there a difference in the cans?" If the children do not guess that the wet can contains cold water, permit several children to feel both cans. "What must the cold can do to the warm air around it?" (Cool it.) "What can we say about the ability of cold air to hold water vapor as compared to warm air?" (Cold air cannot hold as much water vapor as warm air.) "What do we see sometimes in the morning because of this?" (Dew.) "What do we call it when a great deal of water vapor collects in the cool air of the sky?" (Clouds.) "Where does the water vapor go when the air gets cold?" (It rains.) To conclude, ask the children to draw a sketch that shows how it rains.

The third concept, "Warm air rises, cold air settles," may be taught as inquiry with a lesson plan such as the following:

Lesson Plan ■ C

Orientation: Grade 4

Content Objective: The children will state orally that warm air rises and cool air moves in to take its place.

Skill Objective: The children are required to *observe* a convection current and to *infer* a generalization from their observations.

Materials: Large glass jar, large candle, index card, piece of paper.

Evaluation of Student Performance: Observation of oral responses, review worksheet.

continued on next page

Procedure

Put a lighted candle in a large glass jar. Twist a piece of newsprint, light it with a match, blow it out, and hold the smoking paper twist over the jar. "What do you see?" (The smoke rises. The candle went out.) Wave the jar in the air to restore the oxygen supply and light the candle again. Partition the jar into two parts by inserting a card alongside the candle, holding it slightly off the bottom of the jar. Again hold a smoking paper twist over the top of the jar. Ask: "What happens now?" (The smoke goes down one side of the jar and up the other.) "Is the candle going out?" (No.) "What is the temperature of the air over the candle?" (Warm, hot.) "How about the air in the other half of the jar?" (Cool, not as hot.) "What can we say about warm air and cool air?" (Warm air rises, cool air settles, sinks.) "How could this explain winds over a hot land area?" (Warm air over the land rises, and cool air sinks to take its place.) Students will complete a review worksheet on the lesson.

Communicating the fourth concept, "Weather may be predicted," may require two lessons, one lesson to teach children to read a thermometer and a second to teach them to organize their weather observations into a chart.

Lesson Plan ■ D

Orientation:	Grade 4
Content Objectives:	1. The children will state a temperature in degrees Celsius by reading from a Celsius thermometer.
	2. Given sample temperatures in degrees Celsius, the children will respond with the proper adjective: hot, warm, average, cool, and cold.
Skill Objective:	The children will *measure* using a Celsius thermometer.
Materials:	Demonstration thermometer with adjustable red ribbon to represent Celsius temperatures, five Celsius thermometers.
Evaluation of Student Performance:	Observation of group activities, review worksheet.

Procedure

Ask the children if they are comfortable. Ask them what a thermometer tells us. Show them room temperature on the demonstration thermometer (22°C). Ask: "How would you feel if the temperature were this high?" while adjusting the height of the red ribbon on the demonstration thermometer. Do this several times. (100°F equals about 38°C; 32°F equals 0°C.)

Have one child fix a temperature on the demonstration thermometer. Have a second child read the temperature from the thermometer. Have a third child describe how he would feel if the air were that temperature. Repeat this several times.

Divide the children into groups. Provide each group with a Celsius thermometer. Direct them to permit each child to read the thermometer. The readings may be varied by having the children hold the bulb on the end of the glass tube. Conclude the lesson with a review worksheet that requires children to "read" temperatures from drawings of a thermometer.

Lesson Plan ▪ E

Orientation: Grade 4

Content Objectives: The children will state that weather can be predicted from observed conditions. (Example: Rain may follow the appearance of dark, puffy clouds.)

Skill Objective: The children will *observe* weather conditions over a period of time and *infer* a relationship from their observations.

Materials: One weekly weather chart, one outdoor Celsius thermometer.

Evaluation of Student Performance: Checklist of student group work performance, group weather chart.

Procedure

"We are going to see how a weatherman does his job. We are going to keep a record of the weather for five days."

Appoint three thermometer readers, three estimators of cloud cover, three students to describe precipitation, and three to describe wind conditions. Each committee will report its findings and record them on the weather chart at 11:00 A.M. each day. Chart 5–1 is a sample weather chart.

At the end of the week ask: "From our data how might we predict rain? What else can we tell from our record of the weather?" Accept all answers that are based upon observation.

Chart 5–1 ▪ Our Weather Chart

		Observations		
	Temperature	Clouds	Precipitation	Wind
MONDAY	22°C	None	None	Breezy
TUESDAY	18°C	Dark, whole sky	Rain	Breezy
WEDNESDAY	20°C	White patches	None	None
THURSDAY				
FRIDAY				

An examination of the lesson plans shown here illustrates how activities that are often performed as teacher demonstrations or ignored altogether may be restructured to become inquiry lessons. One asks questions that involve children in a problem-solving process—questions that help them to utilize their higher-level intellectual processes, to go beyond the given experience and to make inferences and form conclusions. When properly taught, these four plans will form the first two links in the I-C-I process. The children will have participated in inquiry experiences that will help them to develop their abilities with the process skills, and they will now possess a conceptual framework of scientific principles that will be the foundation for understanding all other information they encounter concerning the study of weather.

After the children have mastered the four selected concepts of the weather unit and have reviewed and discussed them thoroughly, they will be ready to undertake learning activities to build on this foundation, to complete the third stage in the I-C-I sequence—acquiring information.

Planning for the Information Stage of the I-C-I Sequence

In Chapter 4 we discussed many of the most common techniques for teaching information. They were: lecture, lecture-demonstration, reading and answering questions from the textbook, reading trade books, seatwork, using media, and others. A daily lesson plan constructed to utilize one or more of these direct teaching techniques differs from the daily lesson plans constructed to teach inquiry lessons. Examine the sample information-stage lesson plan that follows and contrast its procedures with the inquiry stage plans presented earlier.

Let's examine the lesson plan format for the information-stage lesson. The first thing you might notice is the absence of a process skill

Lesson Plan ■ F—Information Stage

Orientation:	Grade 4
Content Objective:	The students will demonstrate a knowledge of the terms and concepts contained in the lecture outline and sound filmstrip, "Weather Systems." (Note: No skill objective is required.)
Instructional Technique:	Lecture, sound filmstrip.
Materials:	Lecture outline, filmstrip and filmstrip projector, study questions, review worksheet, pictures of weatherfronts.
Homework:	Complete review worksheet.
Student Evaluation Procedure:	Oral review, study questions (filmstrip), review worksheet.

Procedure

Set:

Review weather concepts learned from inquiry lessons.

Water can go into the air (evaporation).

Water evaporates faster on a sunny day than on a cloudy day.

Cold air cannot hold as much moisture as warm air can (condensation).

Warm air rises and cooler air moves in to take its place (convection current).

Weather may be predicted.

Activity 1 Outline (Lecture)

Warm front — low pressure, warm air mass, cirrus and stratus clouds.

Cold front — high pressure, colder air, cumulus clouds.

Stationary front — unchanging weather conditions.

Cloud types — cumulus, stratus, cirrus, nimbus, cumulonimbus.

Forms of precipitation—rain, snow, sleet, hail, dew.

Examples and nonexamples—use pictures to illustrate.

Review lecture—question and answer.

continued on next page

Procedure (Filmstrip):

Activity 2 Outline (Filmstrip)

Hand out and introduce "study" questions and filmstrip.

Show filmstrip.

Review "study" questions and discuss.

Questions: What happens when a warm air mass follows a cold air mass? What happens when a cold air mass follows a warm air mass? What are the five most common forms of precipitation?

Closure:

Final review for the total lesson. Hand out review worksheet to be done as homework.

---

objective. It is possible, even quite likely, that during the direct instruction of an information lesson, some children might make inferences or perform some other higher-level cognitive act. However, the acquisition by students of process skills is not an objective of the lesson. It is not necessary to state a skill objective for an information lesson plan. The instructional techniques are defined by one or more of the traditional or direct teaching procedures described in Chapter 4; there is, of course, no inquiry technique necessary. Materials for instruction, including all teaching aids, media, and worksheets, are listed in the lesson plan. You may notice that, because it is a common component of traditional teaching methods, a homework assignment also is presented in the plan. And, as in the inquiry plan, the method of evaluating student progress is described.

There are a number of new terms and teaching techniques associated with the traditional, information lesson teaching that did not appear in the inquiry lesson plan. The term *set* is used to indicate what a teacher does to get the class ready to undertake the new activity. *Set* in the model lesson plan above was a review of the concepts previously learned. *Set* is sometimes also a preview of the day's activity, or something more dramatic, designed to motivate the learner, such as a demonstration of a discrepant event or a riddle, an anecdote, or a story. Set is the most interesting procedure a teacher can invent to begin a lesson given the time, availability of materials, and the teacher's creativity. Set in an inquiry lesson is usually taken care of with the use of manipulative or demonstration materials. If a lecture is to follow set, a reasonably detailed outline of the material to be presented should be a part of the lesson plan. A number of things can be done to make the lecture more understandable and better retained. Explanations of concepts should be carefully structured; they should be specific and unambiguous. Use examples and nonexamples of a concept when possible. For example, water on the outside of a cold soda bottle and on the cold ground in the morning are examples of condensation. Water on the outside of a porous water-filled container is a nonexample. Notice in the information lesson plan that review takes place frequently, both during the lesson and at its conclusion. Frequent review, through either teacher presentation or question and answer sessions, aids understanding and retention of concepts and facts. Closure is a procedure for ending a learning activity by some sort of summarizing or review activity. Try to end each separate learning activity with some sort of closure.

Some teachers tend to spend too little time planning how to teach information lessons in the I-C-I lesson; this is probably because these types of lessons seem traditional and familiar. However, information lessons in science will almost always be more effective and motivating for students when the details of the instruction are considered well beforehand.

Safety Precautions and Guidelines for the Elementary School Science Classroom

1. Avoid using chemicals that are hazardous to children. Children can learn almost any principle of science using chemicals that are safe for them to handle. Chemical events can be demonstrated using vinegar and baking powder, Alka-Seltzer and water, a rusty nail, vinegar and limestone, and others (elementary level textbooks and sourcebooks are replete with such examples). Screen all activities that involve potentially hazardous materials and try to find alternatives for those that are questionable. Never permit children to handle potentially dangerous materials or equipment.

2. Use plastic laboratory vessels, beakers, graduated cylinders, tubing, and so on. Use glass vessels only when necessary, such as when applying heat.

3. Use only dry cells and flashlight-type cells as power sources when studying electricity. Avoid using alkaline batteries, as they generate a large current that causes connecting wires to heat. Never permit children to work with electricity that is plugged into a wall receptacle.

4. Check student health records. Note which of your students are subject to allergic reactions and the nature of their allergies. Note any children who have childhood diabetes or other conditions that may be affected by science activities.

5. Have on hand a first-aid kit to care for any injuries and antiseptic soap for children to scrub their hands with after handling materials that may harbor bacteria.

6. Make sure children are seated a safe distance from any demonstration lesson.

7. Do not store science equipment and materials on open surfaces where children may have unsupervised access.

8. Never permit children to use propane or bunsen burners. Use hot plates, candles, or alcohol burners as heat sources.

9. Have children tie back long hair and loose clothing when working near an open flame. Have a ready water supply and/or sand bucket handy in case of an accident; use the bucket as a receptacle for spent matches.

10. Caution children to refrain from tasting any materials or putting any materials or objects in their mouth, nose, or ears. Remind them also to refrain from rubbing their eyes, lip, or other parts of their face while handling any type of foreign substance.

11. Caution children about potential safety hazards prior to starting an activity. Appoint a safety monitor for each group of students to remind the others of the safety hazards during the activity.

12. Advise students to report all accidents or injuries as soon as possible, no matter how minor.

13. Obtain a copy of any safety codes available for your school or system. Check your room for potential hazards.

14. Do not permit children to transport science materials down a hallway when other students are around; passersby may try to handle the materials.

15. Animals in the classroom present a potential safety problem. Allow children's pets to remain in the classroom for only a short time. In general, permit only the owner or other children familiar with the animal to handle it. Wild animals, chameleons, lizards, toads, and so on should be handled primarily by the teacher. It is best to keep these creatures for only a day or two and then release them in a suitable habitat.

Although this list demonstrates that much care should be exercised when supervising children who are actively involved with science materials and equipment, for the most part it is no more than any prudent adult would do to protect a child in his or her care. Teaching safety rules and respect for materials and equipment is an important part of what we teach in the elementary school.

(Note: Safety on field trips is a special concern and will be dealt with in Chapter 6.)

Evaluating Pupil Performance

Two Ways to Evaluate Pupils Through Testing

Two separate views of evaluating pupil performance exist in today's schools. One viewpoint is to evaluate pupil performance in terms of the performance of other children. Each child is compared to his classmates, or, in the case of standardized tests, to some larger normative group. Grades are sometimes tempered by considerations of a child's ability, but his "mark" is still a result of comparing his performance with his peers. This type of evaluation procedure is called *norm-referenced measurement*. Most grading systems and standardized test data reflect the norm-referenced measurement philosophy.

In the second viewpoint all comparison is avoided. The child is evaluated on his performance as it relates to predetermined goals or objectives. As the child progresses through a program's objectives and performs acceptably on evaluative exercises, a record is maintained of those objectives he has met. The child then has a personal profile sheet indicating the skills and knowledge he has demonstrated. This type of evaluation procedure is called *criterion-referenced measurement*. Science—A Process Approach is the major elementary science program that reflects the criterion-referenced measurement philosophy.

Common Elements

At first glance norm-referenced evaluation tests appear to be very similar to criterion-referenced tests. Both tests are composed of objective test items, mostly of the multiple-choice variety. The test items read about the same and measure the same skills and knowledge. The difference is in how they are used. Each item on a criterion-referenced test is keyed to a program objective or skill. By associating test items to program objective, the teacher may build a profile for the individual child or for her class. For norm-referencing purposes the pupils' performance on any one item is not as important as their total score on the test or subtest. Student scores are recorded as standings, percentiles, grade levels, or other comparative standards. You may recognize that astute teachers have long employed norm-referenced standardized tests as diagnostic tools by personally relating test items with the skills or knowledge for which they serve as criterion measures. A point might be made that the real difference between norm-referenced evaluation and criterion-referenced evaluation is not found principally in the test items or the tests, but in how the tests are used.

Short-Test and Nontest Evaluation Procedures

Few real tests are administered in some classrooms, especially primary-grade classrooms. Many teachers choose to evaluate the progress of their pupils by short tests (quizzes), by their daily work, or by observation. The advantages of such evaluative procedures are that they save classroom time, are generally nonthreatening to the students, and may be used to evaluate complex skills and attitudes.

Frequent but brief evaluations of pupil performance are, in many ways, superior to the infrequent longer test. Quizzes have the added advantage of increasing the motivation of the students on a daily basis.

Using Daily Work to Evaluate Pupil Progress

How can you best know whether a pupil can construct a data sheet, read a thermometer, or use a platform balance? The records turned in by pupils as they complete their science laboratory activities are perhaps the best source of such information. Certain skills and attitudes cannot be measured with test items, but only by examining the product of a pupil who has completed a complex task. We have traditionally been victims of a test-oriented culture, and teachers have shunned all but the test in evaluating progress of pupils. Fortunately, we are now breaking away from this fixation and are recognizing that the satisfactory completion of daily tasks may tell us more about a student than all of the tests he may take.

Evaluating Subject Matter and Skills

You must consider two things when you plan your lessons: the subject matter must be covered, and the learner must develop good cogni-

tive and affective responses. And just as planning involves both considerations, so does the evaluation process.

Forming a Table of Specifications

To make sure that you do consider both things, you might construct a table of specifications like Chart 5–2.

Chart 5–2 refers to the short weather unit described earlier in this chapter. The teaching objectives are found along the top of the table. They are arranged in terms of the cognitive level at which the pupils must operate to achieve them. This prevents the teacher from neglecting any of the three major cognitive levels. Content is listed by topic in the left-hand column of the table. This ensures that no topic will be totally neglected in the evaluation process. The digits in the grid spaces indicate the number of test items used to evaluate each content-objective interface. For example, you may see from Chart 5–2 that two test items are used to evaluate *specific terms (knowledge level)* related to *condensation*. One test item is used to evaluate *condensation* at the *comprehension* level.

Chart 5–2 ▪ Table of Specifications for a Third-Grade Weather Unit

	Objectives				
	Knowledge Items		**Comprehension Items**	**Skill Evaluation**	
Content	**Symbols Specific Terms Facts**		**Relationship of Basic Concept to Weather**	**Reading a Thermometer**	**Making Inferences from Observations**
Making Observations	3	4		Use pupil data sheets to evaluate thermometer reading skills.	Evaluate pupil performance during inquiry sessions (rating scale).
Evaporation	2	2	1		
Condensation	2	2	1		
Wind, Convection Currents	3	3	1		
Total no. of items	10	11	3		
Percent of total	42%	46%	12%		

The teacher would design rating scales to use with this table of specifications to evaluate the attainment of the skill-level objectives. He might also use interpretive test items for the same purpose. For example, to evaluate student ability to make valid inferences from observations, a teacher might provide pictures of weather conditions and ask, "What will the weather be like later this day?" or "What caused this to happen?" Such interpretive questions may be answered orally, or the teacher could construct multiple-choice questions from which the children select the correct response.

All the items contained in a table of specifications need not appear on a single test. Many teachers, especially in the primary grades, prefer to use short exercises or worksheets. Several such worksheets might be formulated from a table of specifications constructed for a single unit of classwork. The table would then serve as a unifying influence. It would ensure a consistent and comprehensive evaluation of pupil performance. A table also permits the teacher to weight the importance of the various objectives for instruction and grading purposes. A table of specifications, then, offers a convenient and concise overview of the unit plan.

Experienced teachers do not always construct a table of specifications for each unit they teach. But, like many other recommended procedures in education, the use of such a table builds positive attitudes toward the teaching process. It makes teachers more aware of the many facets of the human intellect—and better able to deal with each of them. As awareness and attitude mature, the need for formal processes decreases. Beginning teachers usually require the formal process, at least for a time, as they grow with the job. For them, constructing a table of specifications can be a valuable exercise.

Writing Test Items

A test item is a small task selected from a large array of tasks presented to the learner. Its design determines what kind of demand it places on the learner's intellect. A knowledgeable tester can largely determine the test-taker's level of cognitive activity as he or she responds to each item on a test. Certain kinds of test items are associated with fairly specific levels of cognitive activity. (See Chart 5–3.)

Knowledge-Level Items

Tasks requiring only the recall of specific, memorized facts are commonly presented as short-

Chart 5–3 ■ Objective Types of Test Items Related to Levels of Cognitive Activity

Cognitive Level	Class of Test Item	Type of Test Item
Knowledge	Simple Objective	Short Answer Alternate Choice (True-False) Multiple Choice
Comprehension	Intermediate Objective	Matching Multiple Choice Alternate Choice
Application, Analysis, Synthesis, Evaluation, Skill	Complex Objective (Interpretive)	Multiple Choice

answer, true-false, or multiple-choice questions. Short-answer questions are those requiring the student to supply a word or phrase or to list items of information. Some examples of knowledge-level items are:

1. The device used to measure temperature is called a _____ .

2. Name the three major types of clouds. _____, _____, _____ .

3. White, puffy clouds are called cumulus. True-False.

4. What is the freezing point of water on the Celsius thermometer?
   a. 100°
   b. 0°
   c. 32°
   d. 212°

Comprehension-Level Items

Test items that measure the comprehension level of achievement answer the question: Does the student understand what he has memorized? Comprehension is commonly measured with matching, multiple-choice, and short-answer essay questions. Such questions require the student to make judgments about information, to extrapolate new meanings from information, and to classify or pair items of information. Some examples of comprehension-level items are:

1. Match the words that are most closely associated by drawing a line from the word in the left-hand column to the matching word in the right-hand column. One word in the right-hand column is not used.

Cold Front	Cirrus Clouds
Warm Front	Funnel-Shaped Cloud
Thunderstorm	Fog
Tornado	Cumulus Clouds
	Cumulonimbus Clouds

2. A glass tumbler contains ice cubes and water. What is the most probable temperature of the ice-water mixture?

   a. 100°C
   b. 50°C
   c. 25°C
   d. 0°C

3. Write *yes* beside each type of cloud that generally produces rain and *no* beside each type of cloud that generally does not produce rain.
   a. Dark, billowy clouds.
   b. Gray, sheetlike clouds.
   c. High, white clouds.

Examine the questions given above. Compare them with the knowledge-level questions given earlier. Unless you know what learning activities preceded it, you cannot always be sure which category a question belongs in. However, it should be apparent that the knowledge-level questions require the student to recall memorized facts. Question number one above requires him to recognize relationships between pairs of terms. Question number two requires him to consider a fact outside of its familiar context. And question number three requires him to associate a condition with its consequences.

Skill-Level Items

To make evaluation simpler, all cognitive levels above the comprehension level can be grouped together with affective behavior and motor skills. The category so formed is called skill level. Multiple-choice items used to evaluate student responses on the skill level are necessarily more complex than other multiple-choice items. Usually they take the form of a problem presentation followed by three or four plausible solutions. The student must select the best answer. The problem may be presented as an anecdote, a statement, a table of data, or even a picture. To solve it, the students must use such skills as problem solving by formula, interpreting data, formulating hypotheses, and deductive and inductive thinking. Here are several examples of skill-level items:

1. John left home to go to school one morning. When he walked out of the door, he saw the ground was wet. The air felt warm and humid. A large gray cloud covered the sky. What should John conclude?

   a. A warm front is passing through his area.
   b. A cold front is coming.
   c. The barometer will be high.
   d. It will probably rain for only a short time.

2. Below is a list of barometer readings taken one day at hourly intervals:

Time	Barometer Reading
6:00 A.M.	750 mm
7:00 A.M.	750 mm
8:00 A.M.	751 mm
9:00 A.M.	740 mm
10:00 A.M.	735 mm
11:00 A.M.	720 mm
12:00 Noon	710 mm

Answer the following questions using the data provided:

   a. During what hour did the barometer hold steady?
      1. 6:00 to 7:00 A.M.
      2. 7:00 to 8:00 A.M.
      3. 8:00 to 9:00 A.M.
      4. 9:00 to 10:00 A.M.

   b. During what hour did the barometer reading change the most?
      1. 8:00 to 9:00 A.M.
      2. 9:00 to 10:00 A.M.
      3. 10:00 to 11:00 A.M.
      4. 11:00 to 12:00 A.M.

   c. What will the weather be like on the afternoon of the day on which the barometer readings were taken?
      1. Stormy.
      2. Fair.
      3. Snowing.
      4. Foggy.

Figure 5–2 ■

3. What is most likely to be inside the glass tumbler in Figure 5–2?

   a. Hot water.
   b. Warm water.
   c. Ice water.
   d. Air.

Generally speaking, the higher the cognitive level being tested, the harder it is to construct test items. Test items that deal with the higher cognitive levels also tend to be longer and to require more answering time, so that fewer of them can be answered in a given period. For all of these reasons, teachers seldom use them on tests.

Interpretive test items can also be used to evaluate the child's ability to make value judgments. In this case, the child is asked to choose the *best* answer, not the correct answer. See the following example:

1. Select the three variables that may best be used to predict weather:

   a. Wind direction, temperature, humidity.
   b. Cloud type, wind direction, temperature.
   c. Cloud type, barometer reading, temperature change.
   d. Humidity, cloud type, temperature.

The child's answer will depend on the value system he has formed through his experiences with the subject matter. Such questions should never deal with topics that the children have previously discussed. Responses should not depend primarily on memory.

The examples of test items given in this chapter represent some, but not all, of the various items that you can use on tests. The possibilities are limited only by your own imagination.

Rules for Constructing Test Items

In constructing test items, you should follow a few basic rules to ensure clarity. Only when all ambiguity and uncertainty are removed can you be certain that a pupil's score accurately reflects his or her achievement. Here are some rules for constructing the commonest types of objective test items:

Rules for Constructing Multiple-Choice Items

1. Design each item to measure an important learning outcome.
2. Present a single, clearly formulated problem in the *stem* of the item.
3. State the stem of the item in simple, clear language.
4. Put as much of the wording as possible in the stem of the item.
5. State the stem of the item in positive form wherever possible.
6. Underline negative wording whenever it is used in the stem of an item.
7. Make certain that the intended answer is correct or clearly best.
8. Make all alternatives grammatically consistent with the stem of the item and parallel in form.
9. Avoid verbal clues that might enable students to select the correct answer or to eliminate an incorrect alternative.
10. Make the distracters plausible and attractive to the uninformed.
11. Vary the relative length of the correct answers to eliminate length as a clue.
12. Vary the position of the correct answers in a random manner.
13. Make certain each item is independent of the other items in the test.

Rules for Constructing True-False Items

1. Include only one central, significant idea in each statement.
2. Word the statement so precisely that it can be judged unequivocally true or false.
3. Keep the statements short and use simple language.
4. Use negative statements sparingly and avoid double negatives.
5. Avoid giving extraneous clues to the answer.
6. Avoid the use of such words as always, never, sometimes, and usually.

Rules for Constructing Matching Items

1. Include only homogeneous material in each matching item.
2. Keep the list of items short and put the brief responses on the right.
3. Use more or fewer responses than premises, and permit the responses to be used more than once.
4. Specify in the directions the basis for matching and indicate that each response may be used once, more than once, or not at all.

Rules for Constructing Short-Answer Items

1. State the items so that only a single, brief answer is possible.
2. Use direct questions. Use incomplete statements only when the meaning is perfectly clear.
3. The words to be supplied should relate to the main point of the statement.
4. Place the blanks at the end of the statement.

5. Avoid giving extraneous clues to the answer.

Rules for Constructing Essay Test Items

Children should be encouraged to express their thoughts in writing as early as possible. Essay test items may be employed as soon as the children have learned to write sentences. A third-grade student's essay responses may be only one or two sentences long, while a sixth-grader's may run to a paragraph. The teacher's expectations should match the child's writing ability. Some rules for constructing essay test items are:

1. Pose well-defined problems. Do not ask broad, general questions.

2. Be explicit. Indicate exactly what the child is to do.

3. Indicate about how long the answer should be.

4. Bear in mind the elements of the desired response. Know what comprises a good or acceptable response to a question.

Observational Techniques

Teaching objectives that concern skills, work habits, and attitudes do not lend themselves to evaluation by test. They are best evaluated by teacher observation. To obtain reliable evaluations, the teacher must observe systematically and objectively. Ideally, the teacher should define specific desired student behaviors and record his judgment systematically and regularly, using checklists (Chart 5–4) and/or rating scales.

A checklist is used to note the presence or absence of a particular behavior. It is not used to assess the quality of the behavior. A completed class checklist will show not only the deficiencies of individual students, but also those of the class as a whole.

Unlike the checklist, the rating scale (Chart 5–5) does not take yes-or-no, all-or-nothing answers. It indicates whether the desired behavior is observed, but it also assesses the quality of performance. It gives a continuum of qualities of performance for each behavior being rated. The rater's task is to assign the rank on the continuum that best describes the observed behavior. There are normally three to seven possible ratings.

The use of observational techniques to evaluate student performance helps to show the student that those aspects of science not readily evaluated by testing are important nonetheless. If the teacher neglects to evaluate skills, habits, and attitudes, the pupil will assume that these things are not important. The teacher may say what he likes, but students typically believe that only those things he evaluates really matter. To give only lip service to habits, attitudes, and skills is to render them unimportant in the minds of the students.

Chart 5–4 ■ A Sample Checklist for Evaluating Pupil Work Habits

Pupils' Names	Shows Initiative	Uses Time Wisely	Uses Equipment with Care	Is Persistent	Is Dependable	Is Creative
Joe						
Jane						
Susan						
Jill						

Directions: Place a checkmark (√) in those spaces where the student is thought to possess the habit described.

Chart 5–5 ■ A Sample Rating Scale for Evaluating Science Skills

Pupils' Names	Formulates Hypotheses	Plans Experiment	Records Data	Interprets Data	Performs Experimentation

Joe	1 2 3
	   x
		1 2 3
		 x
			1 2 3
			    x
				1 2 3
				   x
					1 2 3
					   x

Jane	1 2 3
	 x
		1 2 3
		 x
			1 2 3
			   x
				1 2 3
				    x
					1 2 3
					    x

Jack	1 2 3
	   x
		1 2 3
		   x
			1 2 3
			 x
				1 2 3
				   x
					1 2 3
					   x

Directions: Rate the pupil on each skill by placing an x in the space that best describes proficiency. 1 = Poor, 2 = Fair, 3 = Good.

Making a Good Fit— Evaluation Items and Behavioral Objectives

Often inconsistency arises in teacher-made tests between the test items and stated behavioral objectives. In many cases, objectives are written as starting points for planning learning activities but are forgotten when test-making time arrives. The starting point for constructing an evaluation instrument for a unit of work is the behavioral objectives for that unit. If behavioral objectives identify what the teacher thinks is important for the pupils to know before they begin the unit, these behaviors should form the basis for postunit evaluation.

Sometimes a behavioral objective specifically spells out its own evaluation item. For instance, let's examine the objectives from Lesson Plan D. They are: *(1) The children will state a temperature in degrees Celsius by reading from a Celsius thermometer. (2) Given sample temperatures in degrees Celsius, the children will respond with the proper adjective: hot, warm, average, cool, cold.* What would you do to directly evaluate pupil performance on these objectives? You could evaluate pupil performance on these objectives by interviewing each child and listening to his oral responses. In most cases, this procedure is too time-consuming for teachers, and pencil-and-paper tests or student data sheets that they maintain over the week period are used for evaluation purposes. Objective 2 might be evaluated with a written test item such as the following:

Write the word hot, warm, average, cool, or cold that best describes the weather condition that would prevail with the following Celsius temperatures:

1. _____ 35°C
2. _____ 0°C
3. _____ 20°C
4. _____ 10°C
5. _____ 30°C
6. _____ −1°C

Does this item correspond to the *intent* of Objective 2?

The content objective of Lesson Plan E of the Weather unit is: *The children will state that weather can be predicted from observed conditions.*

How would you evaluate each child on this objective? Again individual interviews with the children would be the ideal evaluation of student ability to make reasonable inferences about weather changes. But for the teacher who chooses to use a pencil-and-paper evaluation criterion it may look like the following:

For each set of stated weather observations state your prediction regarding any change that is likely to occur in the weather.

Weather Observation
1. Temperature 30°C, large billowy, white clouds changing to dark, billowy, very active clouds.
2. Temperature 20°C at 11:00 A.M. and 23°C at 12:00 A.M., high-altitude white clouds becoming darker and sheetlike.

Predictions
1.

2.

Is this item a proper criterion for a child's ability to make two inferences in predicting weather?

The content objectives of Lesson Plans A, B, and C of the Weather unit are:

1. The children will state orally that water can go into the air and that water evaporates faster on a warm, sunny day than on a cloudy day.

2. The children will state orally that cold air cannot hold as much moisture as warm air can.

3. The children will state orally that warm air rises and cool air moves in to take its place.

It is obvious that the intent of these objectives in specifying an *oral* response relates to the problem solving of the class as a whole during the inquiry lessons. It is probably unrealistic to attempt to have each child offer an oral response to meet the objective. On a paper-and-pencil test one might come close to the intent of the objectives with criteria like the following:

1. Ms. Jones left a wet cloth on a countertop. She returned for it later in the day and it was dry. Where is the most likely place the water from the cloth might have gone?
   a. Into the countertop.
   b. Into the air.
   c. Into the cloth.

A

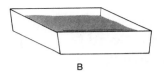

B

The water will evaporate faster from container _____.

Figure 5–3

2. The water will evaporate faster from container _____ in Figure 5–3.

3. The air in Plain City is warm and contains a great deal of water vapor. During the night the temperature drops to 20°C. What would a person likely find outdoors in the morning?
   a. A clear sky.
   b. Hard winds blowing.
   c. Heavy dew on the ground.

In summary, to construct a test for a unit of work, avoid the too common practice of flipping through a book and constructing test items by taking statements out of the text. Instead, begin with the unit objectives and construct test items that measure the criteria that they define. Review the section on constructing a table of specifications to ensure that all objectives and subject matter are adequately covered.

Summary

Most teachers operate as technicians and manipulators of established curricula. That is, they select and employ prepared materials. Most planning, then, involves using prepared materials skillfully.

To plan an I-C-I unit the teacher follows several steps:

1. She selects the big ideas or concepts from the textbook that is being used.

2. She then structures inquiry lessons that permit the development of the selected concepts.

3. She plans to teach the information stage of the I-C-I sequence by structuring direct teaching procedures so that the new ideas presented are related to the children's prior knowledge.

4. Finally, she develops the evaluation instruments and techniques appropriate to the material taught.

Teaching an I-C-I unit requires that the teacher plan for instruction in both the inquiry and the information (content) models. The components of an inquiry lesson plan are: the level of instruction, a content objective, an inquiry objective, a list of all materials required to teach the lesson, the procedures for evaluating student performance, and an outline of the learning activity procedures. Inquiry lesson plans are often characterized by group or individualized instruction wherein students use hands-on manipulative materials and problem-solving processes to arrive at generalizations or concepts of science. The information or content lesson plan has: a grade-level designation, a content objective (no skill objective is necessary), materials or media required to conduct the learning activities, a plan for evaluating student performance, and procedures for conducting the lesson. Some of the components of the procedure section of the information lesson plan are: set (used to gain student attention and motivate them to learn), a lecture outline (if appropriate) that provides for frequent review and summary, the use of examples and nonexamples, the proper use of media, which includes an introduction, a set of study questions, and review, and others. Information lesson plans are characterized typically by lecture, lecture-demonstration, seatwork, drill and practice, use of media, and other procedures.

Learning objectives (teaching objectives, behavioral objectives) are written in each of the three domains: the cognitive, the affective, and the psychomotor. Objectives in the cognitive domain express those things students know and understand and the abilities they have to solve problems and analyze or create written or artistic products. Affective objectives describe the attitudes and values students will acquire as the result of educational experiences, and psychomotor objectives describe physical movements of the body from the most simple (grasping of objects by infants) to the most complex (communicating by pantomime). Clearly stated objectives aid both teachers and students to know those things the students are to learn from instruction.

Student performance may be evaluated in many ways. Tests, both objective and essay types, may be used as either formative or summative instruments. Formative evaluation instruments are used to judge the progress of the individual student in a given task or curriculum. Formative procedures are generally associated with diagnostic and remediation procedures and individualized instruction. Summative evaluation procedures compare students with one another and traditionally result in letter grades and the concepts of passing and failing. In addition to carefully constructed tests wherein the test items closely match the desired learning objectives, there are many other procedures employed in the elementary schools to evaluate student learning. Some of these are observation instruments (rating scales and checklists), homework, seatwork, written reports, participation in learning activities, and others. An evaluation plan that most effectively measures students' performances will over time include a wide variety of these procedures.

Extending Activities

1. a. Select a chapter from an elementary school science textbook. Write the behavioral objectives in the cognitive domain that are appropriate for the chapter.

   b. Make a list of the verbs that might be used to write behavioral objectives for each of the three cognitive levels. Compare lists with your classmates and discuss them.

2. Extend the list of affective behaviors given in this chapter to include as many desirable attitudinal characteristics as you can think of.

3. Use the table of specifications from this chapter as a model to construct one of your own that deals with a different topic of science.

4. Write three examples of different types of simple objective test items (knowledge). Write three examples of intermediate objective test items (comprehension). Construct two complex objective (interpretive) test items. (See Chart 5–3.)

5. Discuss with your peers the advisability of posting a rating scale on the bulletin board that shows the level of performance of each child in the class.

Bibliography

Carter, K. "Test-Wiseness for Teachers and Students." *Educational Measurement: Issues and Practice 5*, no. 4 (Winter 1986): 20–23.

Deming, B. S. "The Performance Approach: Limitations and Alternatives." *Educational Forum* 41, no. 2 (January 1977): 213–220.

Gagné, R., and L. Briggs. *Principles of Instructional Design.* New York: Holt, Rinehart & Winston, 1974.

Gega, P. *Science in Elementary Education*, 5th Ed. New York: Macmillan, 1986.

Hungerford, H., and A. Tomera. *Science Teaching Methods in the Elementary School.* Champaign, Ill.: Stipes Publishing, 1985.

Stiggins, R., N. Conklin, and N. Bridgeford. "Classroom Assessment: A Key to Effective Education." *Educational Measurement: Issues and Practices 5*, no. 2 (Summer 1986): 5–17.

Materials and Resources for Teaching Elementary School Science

Look What's in This Chapter

Every high-quality elementary school science program requires the acquisition, storage, maintenance, and distribution of manipulative laboratory materials. In this chapter you will learn procedures for doing these things. You will also learn to acquire and manage other equipment, materials, and such resources as print media, electronic media including computers and computer software, field trips, and human resources such as community volunteers and speakers. After reading this chapter you will understand how to acquire free and inexpensive materials for science activities and become knowledgeable concerning some special-focus science programs that can enrich your curriculum. Finally, you will learn how to evaluate and select science textbooks for use in your classroom, which is a very important factor in establishing a quality science program for children.

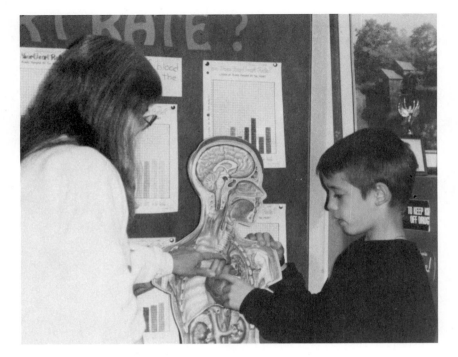

A classroom that is rich in materials and media is an exciting place for children to be.

Sources of Materials for Inquiry-based Science

The I-C-I science classroom brings together the diverse instructional techniques of inquiry or laboratory-based science and the methodologies of direct or traditional teaching. A wide array of materials is available to facilitate these instructional approaches. The common sources of manipulative, laboratory-based elementary school science materials are publishers' kits, general science kits, science supply houses, and readily available materials from home and community. As you contemplate the acquisition, storage, and maintenance of materials for doing hands-on science, you may think the process seems burdensome in terms of the time and effort involved. Many beginning teachers, however, find that the problems of dealing

with manipulative science materials have been greatly exaggerated once they are involved in the process. In fact, many teachers find the time requirements for organizing and conducting inquiry science to be less demanding than the planning needs for traditional instruction, because once they are in place, the materials of hands-on science greatly facilitate classroom instruction. Teachers of operational laboratory-based science programs, for instance, find they are able to spend more instructional time talking with individuals or small groups of students, and they have more time to *enjoy* teaching. Let's take a look at each of the sources of manipulative science materials. (You may wish to scan Appendix A, Selected Commercial Suppliers of Science Materials, and Appendix E, Sources of Materials for Environmental and Energy Education, to become familiar with sources of materials and equipment for teaching science in the elementary school.)

Publishers' Kits

Many science textbook publishers produce programs that include a broad spectrum of instructional materials in addition to the textbook. In some cases these materials include laboratory kits containing materials for conducting the inquiry activities described in the text. These materials are usually packaged in the drawers of a cardboard storage cabinet. The cabinets are portable and easy to carry from classroom to classroom. When more than one class uses the materials in a single kit, the expendable items required for each class may be purchased in a separate package. One problem in using publishers' kits is that the equipment and supplies some publishers offer are not sufficient to service a large class of students working in problem-solving groups. In these instances, the supplies must be supplemented. Some publishers make available children's activity guides in booklet or ditto form. Other materials available from publishers include teacher's guides, review or drill activities, films, filmstrips, videotapes and discs, and Spanish language materials. Teachers whose schools are using a publisher's text may usually obtain from that publisher a teacher's guide and a brochure that provides information about the program; all the teachers need to do is write a letter to the publisher on school stationery. It is always worthwhile for teachers and principals to know about all of the materials that exist to support a science textbook program. (Please see Appendix C for a list of selected elementary school science textbook publishers.)

General Science Kits

The materials in a general science kit are not related to any particular textbook or program, but rather contain materials and supplies common to many. General science kits are available in a great variety of sizes and levels of sophistication, from small boxes to large rolling tables containing a water supply, sinks, and bottled gas outlets. Many kits provide an activities manual, which contains descriptions of demonstration activities to be done using the materials provided.

General science kits are very useful lecture-demonstration or rational inquiry lessons, but they generally do not contain sufficient quantities of items to support a class of students working in problem-solving groups. A kit might contain, for instance, two dry cells, one balance, three beakers, one pair of bar magnets, and so on—not enough of any one piece of equipment to supply five or six working student groups.

Science Supply Houses

Perhaps the least costly way to secure commercially available science supplies is through the catalog purchasing option of a science supply house. Keep in mind, however, that some supply houses require the purchaser to order supplies by the box, gross, or some large quantity. You may be able either to bypass these businesses or to combine orders with other schools.

Ordering from the catalogs of science supply houses can be a baffling ordeal if you do not know very much about science equipment. For instance, you might open a catalog of science materials to several pages that just list test tubes. Test tubes, you find, come in a bewildering array of sizes (described in metric units); they are made of several kinds of glass, and they may or may not have lips. The same thing happens when you turn to wire or flasks or dry cells. Let us pause at this point to look at some common science equipment. The items are described below in the nomenclature used in the supply catalogs. The specifications are suggestions only.

Test Tubes

Select a general purpose test tube with a lip. Choose one made of heat-resistant glass (Pyrex, Kimax). Average dimensions might be a length of 150 millimeters (mm) and a diameter of 15 millimeters (mm).

Flasks

All flasks for general use should be made of heat-resistant glass (Pyrex, Kimax). Flasks commonly come in two shapes: the bulb-shaped Florence flask and the cone-shaped Erlenmeyer flask. Several sizes of flasks are commonly found in elementary schools: 250, 600, and 1000 milliliters (approximately a cup, a pint, and a quart respectively).

Beakers

Beakers may be made of polyethylene material (unbreakable plastic) or glass. Polyethylene beakers cannot be heated over an open flame as can the heat-resistant glass beakers. Beakers are usually purchased in 250-, 600-, and 1000-milliliter sizes.

Stoppers

Many suppliers sell rubber stoppers by the pound in miscellaneous sizes. In such assortments one finds stoppers that are solid, stoppers with a hole, and some with two holes. Two pounds of assorted rubber stoppers generally is enough to supply an elementary school.

Tubing

Tubing is made of glass, rubber, or flexible plastic. Using rubber or plastic tubing removes the necessity of bending, breaking, and fire polishing. All these things must be done with glass tubing. Rubber and plastic tubing are also safer for children to handle. Short pieces of glass tubing may be useful to insert into stoppers. Order tubing with the same outside diameter as the holes in the rubber stoppers. One pound of glass or twenty feet of plastic tubing is usually sufficient.

Dry Cells

Flashlight cells are the only electric power source necessary for teaching elementary science. It is best to avoid buying the more expensive alkaloid and nickel-cadmium cells, for their greater current output can cause small diameter wires to heat excessively. (Buying flashlight cells for elementary school science is one of the rare times where cheaper is better.) Each flashlight cell produces one and one half volts. It may also be convenient to order battery holders that have clips to which wires may be easily attached. Local stores may actually be a cheaper source of cells than the science supply houses. (See Appendix A for a list of selected suppliers of elementary science materials and equipment.)

Miniature Lamps and Lamp Bases (Receptacles)

Miniature lamps should have the same voltage rating as the dry cells that will provide their power supply.

Copper Wire

Copper wire for general use in the elementary classroom should have a gauge number of about 20. Wire of this diameter is flexible and easy for elementary school children to manipulate. While wire of 18 gauge is acceptable, it is stiffer; 22- and 24-gauge wire is also acceptable, but somewhat lighter. (A *decrease* of six gauge numbers indicates an *increase* in the diameter of the wire by a factor of approximately two. That is, 18-gauge wire is twice as thick as 24-gauge wire.) To be reusable, wire ordered for the elementary classroom should be plastic-coated. Wire that is termed *pushback* is preferable; it is simple to bare the ends of this wire to make connections. One pound of wire is generally sufficient for an elementary classroom.

Easily Obtainable Materials from Home, School, and Community

Many science teachers keep a large box containing miscellaneous materials they have gathered from various sources. They "collect everything, throw nothing away." The materials in their "scrounge box" may have come from other teachers, children, parents, businesses, workmen, and others. You can begin to build a useful inventory of miscellaneous materials by inviting your children to bring specified items to school. You can also check around the school cafeteria, lounge, custodial stations, and principal's office for likely items. Remember, too, that most principals have petty cash funds that might be spent locally on inexpensive items. Once you achieve a reputation for being a collector, many people will bring unsolicited materials to you. Some commonly found and useful items are:

glass and plastic containers (gallon food jars make good aquaria and terraria)

aluminum foil, food coloring, foil food pans, film cans

paper plates, soda straws, scrap cardboard and paper (a local printing house usually has an abundance to give away)

candles, thumbtacks, paper clips, magnets taken from hardware

toys and home products, old clocks, wire (ask the telephone installer for some)

balls, balloons, floating toys, corks, rubberbands, miscellaneous wood blocks (from the high school shop class), Pyrex baby bottles (you can heat liquids in them)

modeling clay, wallpaper cleaner, pocket mirrors, flashlights

flashlight cells, flashlight bulbs, and so on

The list of materials you might collect is endless. You will learn which of the materials has immediate purpose. You will also be amazed at the inventiveness of children when they are permitted free access to the materials in the scrounge box.

Organizing Science Supplies

Shoebox Kits

The teacher who teaches science from a publisher's kit or with one of the manipulative science programs has her storage and materials management systems organized for her. This situation is somewhat rare in today's schools. Usually, the teacher builds a program in science using a textbook as her major organizational and resource tool and acquires the manipulative materials needed to teach the science activities over a period of time. Where the teacher develops her own set of materials to teach science, storage may be a major concern.

Whether you teach science as a whole group activity or organize your lessons into centers, the *shoebox kit* concept offers an efficient materials management system. Shoebox kits are boxes of varying sizes containing the materials for doing a specific science activity; see Figure 6–1 for an example. If clearly marked and readily accessible, these kits are very convenient. They are self-contained, complete, and ready for immediate use. The shoebox kit should contain an inventory of its contents on the outside of the box and any instructional task cards or worksheets inside. The shoebox kit used in conjunction with a file folder learning center creates a very efficient materials management system. The major drawbacks to this combination are the time it takes to organize the system and the need to duplicate some materials so that each kit is complete and self-contained.

Central Storage System

A central science storage center and distribution system is the most economical and efficient way to use resources allocated for science in a school. A central storage system reduces the need to duplicate materials for each teacher or grade level and provides an overseer to ensure the integrity of the science supplies throughout the school. Such a system, however, requires the cooperation of teachers, students, and those charged with managing the center to be successful. Communication between the person responsible for the maintenance and storage of science materials in a school and the teachers who use them is essential. Teachers should make the caretaker aware of any broken and missing materials, any new materials that are needed,

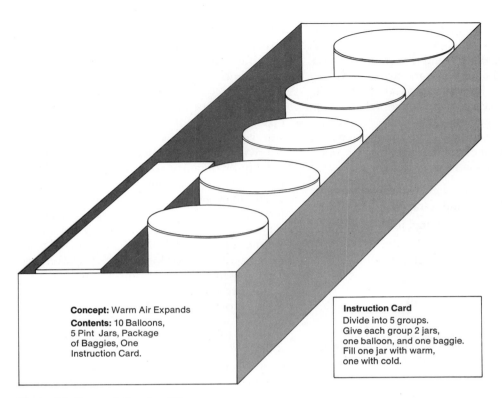

Concept: Warm Air Expands
Contents: 10 Balloons,
5 Pint Jars, Package
of Baggies, One
Instruction Card.

Instruction Card
Divide into 5 groups.
Give each group 2 jars,
one balloon, and one baggie.
Fill one jar with warm,
one with cold.

Figure 6–1 ■ A Shoebox Kit

and any problems related to the storage and distribution system. Because many teachers use the materials from the central storage area, the major responsibility for communicating needs and problems related to the system is theirs. When devising a system for the central storage of science materials and supplies, it's important to keep in mind several considerations: access to the materials, organization of the materials in the storage facility, maintenance of the currency of the science material inventory, and repair, replacement, and resupply of materials and equipment.

Access to the Materials

To best service the needs of teachers, a central storage facility for science materials must be accessible before, during, and after the school day. When teachers must obtain and return materials during specified periods of time, it in-

creases the difficulty of doing hands-on science. The ideal distribution and collection system permits teachers to place an "order" for the materials and have them delivered to their rooms. Older and trusted students may be used for this purpose when an adult, aide, media specialist, or community volunteer is available to supervise the process.

Organization of the Materials

Materials in the science supply center can be organized along any of a number of possible schemes: by grade level (there would be "crossovers," of course), by science topic (electricity, sound, growing things, and so on), by the nature of the materials (glassware, large plastic containers, paper products, and so on), or others. Bins, boxes, and drawers should be clearly labeled to indicate the location of materials. One adult should be responsible for the delivery of

Central storage and distribution offers an efficient method for utilizing science materials.

materials to the classrooms and return of materials to the supply facility.

Maintenance of the Currency of the Science Materials Inventory

Many of the materials found in elementary schools are similar in nature. However, when new programs and activities are added to the curriculum of a school—for instance, a new unit on the metric system—the inventory of the science supply center may need to be upgraded to include metric weights and measuring devices. Again, someone must be in charge of accepting requests for materials from teachers and of scanning newly introduced curricula to provide proper materials for instruction.

Repair, Replacement, and Resupply of Materials and Equipment

The repair and replacement of broken and worn equipment and the resupply of expend-

ables is very important. During the school year and, most important, at year's end, an inventory of the science materials and equipment should be conducted and necessary replacements and repairs made.

Resources for Teaching Science

Free and Inexpensive Materials

Would you believe that hundreds of state and national governmental agencies, business organizations, special interest groups, and others are anxious to provide teachers with free and inexpensive materials that are useful in teaching elementary science? The National Aeronautics and Space Administration (NASA) will mail you beautifully colored posters on a variety of subjects ranging from a space suit to close-up views of the planet Uranus sent back by the Vanguard

The use of media enhances student learning.

space probe. A booklet from the American Petroleum Institute illustrates the origins of natural gas and petroleum and how the reserves of these resources are located and brought to the surface. The National Committee for World Food Day will provide booklets and activity sheets for students that illustrate the hunger problem in various parts of the world. The Brown Swiss Breeders Association will send you colored pictures of twelve different examples of Brown Swiss cattle. The American Coal Foundation will send their "Coal Sample Kit," which contains samples of peat, lignite, and bituminous and anthracite coal.

The possibilities for adding to your classroom materials in this way are virtually endless. Each year, new organizations are added to the list of suppliers and others are removed. Some school libraries have a copy of the book *Elementary Teacher's Guide to Free Curriculum Materials*, published by Educators Progress Service, Inc., 214 Center Street, Randolph, Wisconsin 53956. This publication contains annotated listings of 1,834 different educational items categorized by subject matter. If this comprehensive source of free materials is not available to you, take a look at Appendix D in this text, "Selected Sources of Free and Inexpensive Science Teaching Materials." When writing to suppliers for materials, incidentally, it is advisable to use school stationery if you are a teacher. Many of the suppliers listed in Appendix D will also respond to requests of preservice students; you may want to start a collection of your own teaching materials in this way. Use a postcard, and be sure to identify yourself as a preservice teacher. Although suppliers often prefer to receive requests for specific materials, a blanket request can produce pleasant surprises. Figure 6–2 shows a sample of a postcard request for materials.

Graphic and Audiovisual Media

Some guidelines for using media in the classroom were presented in Chapter 4; you may

```
Dear Sir or Madam:

I am a student in the K-6
teacher education program
at Delta University.
Please send any materials          Hawaiian Sugar Planters
your association has that              Assoc.
are appropriate for                 Public Relations
elementary school                   P.O. Box 1057
students.  Thank you.               Aiea, HI  96701-1057

John Jones
12 Ace Street
Akron, OH  44212
```

Figure 6–2 ■ Sample Postcard Request for Materials

refer to those guidelines as needed. In most school systems, media equipment is owned and controlled by each school. Media centers in many schools house a sometimes extensive collection of filmstrips, overhead transparencies, videotapes, models, posters, and charts. Get to know the media specialist and media collection soon upon your arrival at a school where you will teach or serve an internship. Films, being more expensive than other forms of media, are usually housed in a central location within a school system. Each school should have a catalog of the school system's media center collection of films and other media. Take the time to become familiar with the catalog offerings.

Selecting Graphic Media for Purchase or Use

Graphic media includes all charts, posters, visual aids, and the like. Graphic media by definition must be easily seen by students if they are to be effective tools for instruction. When selecting such media for purchase or use in the classroom, examine them from the point of view of a student who sits in the seat located farthest from the presentation. Are the pictures and writing clearly seen? Charts and posters are often cluttered with too much information, which causes the graphics to be small and difficult for some students to see. A second consideration when selecting graphic media is the vocabulary and clarity of concept development. It is important that these factors match the readiness levels of the students. Finally, consider the attractiveness of the graphics, the use of color, the "freshness," and the creativity of the overall design.

Selecting Audiovisual Media for Purchase or Use

Audiovisual media includes films, sound filmstrips, videotapes, video discs, and so on. Because they are relatively expensive to purchase, audiovisual materials should be previewed prior to purchase if at all possible. We recommend that they also be previewed by the teacher who will use them in the classroom. What factors should be considered when evaluating audiovisual materials? The characteristics of appropriate and quality audiovisuals are much the same as those listed above for graphic media. Making the materials visible to students is usually a controllable problem when using audiovisual equipment, because the equipment can usually be moved around. As with graphic media, the vocabulary and concept development of the information presented is of prime importance—it should match the readiness levels of the students. The medium's initial appeal for students will depend again on the graphics, color, freshness of presentation, and, additionally, the quality of the narration and background music. Today's children are used to viewing media for longer periods of time than children in the past. However, unless the presentation has as much appeal as Sesame Street or the Muppets, viewing times for primary-grade children should be held to about fifteen to twenty minutes.

Selecting Computer Software for the Science Classroom

The various types of computers and their uses in elementary science are discussed in Chapter 8, Individualizing Science/Science for Exceptional Children. It is appropriate here, however, to briefly discuss the selection of software for use in computer-assisted instruction.

The same criteria exist for selecting computer software as pertain to selecting graphic and audiovisual media. The computer medium has features of both—still graphics, vocabulary, concept development, the use of color, and factors related to the artistic nature of the presentation. Additionally, several other factors should be considered. Here are some questions to guide you in selecting software for your classroom. (You may also want to peruse Appendix G, Selected Publishers of Microcomputer Software for Elementary Science.)

1. Will the software operate on the available computers? Different computers from the same manufacturer may not be of the same model and may vary in the random access memory (RAM) available for operating a program. Check the distributor's catalog to see if the desired software is compatible with your equipment.

2. Is the program easy to use? Because most computer programs require students to respond to commands and otherwise interact with them, run through each program to determine whether the directions for those interactions are simple and easy to follow.

3. Is the program flexible in handling student responses? If a student responds correctly to a computer query, the program should go on to new information. If a student responds incorrectly, the program should permit the student to review the previous material and respond again to the missed query.

4. Does the computer program properly motivate students' responses? Computer programs often are designed to reward students' correct responses with combinations of points, sounds, or graphic displays. The program should not reward the student for wrong answers with interesting displays, even if the sounds or graphics are designed to be negative. For example, airplanes being shot down or a clown falling off a ball may indicate an error on the part of the student, but if the displays are loud, colorful, or exciting students may opt to miss questions in order to view the displays.

5. Has the software been reviewed by your school system or some other reliable source? Reviews of software can be found in several magazines: *Classroom ComputerNews, The Computer Teacher, Journal of Courseware Review, Electronic Learning, Science and Children,* and others. Microsoft, a nonprofit clearinghouse for software evaluations, has been formed to review educational software.

Microcomputers — a new medium for learning.

Special-Focus Programs

Some science programs that have a special focus have become popular among some elementary science educators. These programs tend to be somewhat narrow in scope and purpose and provide activities and, in some cases, manipulative materials that may be used to supplement or enrich an ongoing program. Five such special-focus programs are: Project Learning Tree (PLT), Outdoor Biology Instructional Strategies (OBIS), Starlab, Science on a Shoestring (SOS), and the Full Option Science System (FOSS).

Project Learning Tree (PLT)

An environmentally oriented program of The American Forest Institute, PLT consists of eighty-nine learning activities grouped into seven conceptual themes: Environmental Awareness, Diversity of Forest Roles, Cultural Contexts, Societal Perspectives on Issues, Management and Interdependence of Natural Resources, Life Support Systems, and Lifestyles. The titles of some

popular activities are: "Adopt a Tree," "Sounds in City and Forest," "Plant Dyes," "Make Your Own Paper," "School Yard Diversity," and "Make a Fossil." Complete lesson plans are contained in the *Project Learning Tree Supplementary Guide for Grades 1–6*. The guide contains complete lesson plans and appendices listing, among others, addresses for additional information and materials. For information write American Forest Institute, 1619 Massachusetts Ave. N.W., Washington, D.C. 20036.

Outdoor Biology Instructional Strategies (OBIS)

OBIS consists of twenty-seven packets that contain materials for conducting six to nine "quick and easy" outdoor science activities. The materials in the plastic carrying pouch include a leader's survival card and reproducible student materials. All activities can be conducted using everyday items and are appropriate for students eight years and older. Some packet titles are: "Adaptations," "Animal Behavior," "Aquatic

Animal Behavior," "Desert," and "Forest." Also available are OBIS Lawn and Pond Guides and the OBIS Library Edition, which contains ninety-seven individual activities. For a catalog containing OBIS materials write: Delta Education, Inc., P.O. Box M, Nashua, NH 03061.

Starlab

Imagine an accurate, versatile, and portable planetarium available for use by a single elementary school. The Starlab projection surface is an inflatable dome made of nylon-reinforced polymer fabric. Inflated, the dome has a diameter of 16 feet (4.9 meters) and holds up to 30 adults. A simple projection system projects images on the 10.5 foot (3.2 meter) ceiling of the dome, providing a three-dimensional feel for viewers. The night sky may be projected as it appears from any place on earth in a given hour of a given day. Replaceable projection cylinders permit the projection of images of mythological constellations, the earth's surface, plate tectonics, and a biological cell. When deflated and packed up, the polymer dome weighing only 48 pounds (19.1 kilograms) can be folded into a bag that fits easily into an automobile trunk. Starlab provides supplementary instructional materials such as an activity book, a celestial sphere kit, and a Teacher's Sampler for use with the dome/projector equipment. The dome may be quickly erected in any classroom, cafeteria, multipurpose room, or gymnasium. For information concerning Starlab write to: Learning Technologies, Inc., 59 Walden Street, Cambridge, MA 02140.

Science on a Shoestring (SOS)

The focus of Science on a Shoestring is to provide a hands-on science program for K–8 teachers at a very low cost. The activities of SOS may be undertaken by teachers with a minimal background in science, because most of the materials are common to everyday life. The program includes scripted lesson plans that demonstrate how to introduce and carry out each lesson. Sufficient materials are supplied to permit students to work individually, in pairs, or in small groups. SOS activities include investigations in both life and physical science on such topics as: using a microscope, magnetism, electromagnetism, electricity, properties of gases, including air, life cycles and metamorphosis, and simple chemistry. Print materials of SOS include the *Science on a Shoestring* text, *Learning to Use the SOS Microscope Student Guide,* and the *Microscope Teacher's Guide.*

For information about Science on a Shoestring write to: Learning Spectrum, 1390 Westridge Drive, Portola Valley, CA 94025.

Full Option Science System (FOSS)

The Full Option Science System (FOSS) was developed at the Lawrence Hall of Science in Berkeley, California, as a general classroom application of the SAVI/SELPH program developed for use with exceptional children. (See Chapter 8 for more detailed information on the SAVI/SELPH program.) Designed for use in grades 3 through 6, the FOSS program is comprised of sixteen modules divided evenly among the four topics, Scientific Reasoning and Technology, Physical Science, Earth Science, and Life Science. Some typical module titles are: Measurement, Magnetism and Electricity, Landforms, and Environments. There are detailed teacher's guides and student equipment kits that make the hands-on activities easy to teach. The curriculum developers suggest that the program materials may be used to support or enrich an existing program or as the beginning of a new program. The materials of FOSS are distributed by Encyclopaedia Britannica Educational Corp., Chicago, Illinois.

School and Community Resources

There are many resources for teaching science in the school and community not yet mentioned in this chapter. Some additional resources available to teachers are:

School building field trips to investigate energy conservation, heating and air conditioning plants, and so on.

School yard field trips to observe signs of erosion, evidence of animals (worms and worm tracks in mud puddles, birds and bird tracks, live and dead insects, and so on), evidence of plants (trees, shrubs, leaves, detritus, seeds, and so on); to take temperature measurements, make weather observations, study shadows, and much more.

Neighborhood field trips to visit a stream, lake, pond, wooded area or other habitat, to map and record the plants found along the streets and in the yards of the neighborhood, to visit a fire station, and much more. See Chapter 8 for directions for planning and conducting field trips.

Library/media center to have the library specialist show the collection of science trade books and to demonstrate how to locate books of interest. The library specialist may also show the science models that are available for students to explore, as well as point out the science magazines for children, such as *Ranger Rick, Science World,* and *The Curious Naturalist.*

The local museum, which may have exhibits of archeological or scientific interest. It may also have a speakers bureau or a "science in a suitcase" program that sends speakers to schools to demonstrate issues of scientific interest. Of course, if there is a science and technology museum nearby, a field trip would be worthwhile.

School volunteer programs whose members are adults from the community who may be available to speak or demonstrate things of scientific interest.

Medical, dental and business societies, which often have programs for elementary school children.

Incidentally, you should always check out guest speakers and resource volunteers before you invite them to your class. Visit with them in person or talk to them on the telephone to assess the appropriateness of the information they will be presenting and their ability to communicate with children. Obtain the approval of the school principal prior to their classroom visit.

Choosing a Science Textbook

Despite the availability of various federally funded manipulative science projects that grew out of the 1960s, most teachers in today's elementary schools teach science from a textbook. The textbook and the accompanying teacher's guide provide the basic structure, content, and teaching strategies for the science program. These materials determine what a child will learn during science and how the teacher will teach. Clearly, the selection of a science textbook is of great importance.

Below are some questions to ask when considering the adoption of a science textbook:

Will the children for whom the textbook is intended be able to read it with understanding?

Nearly all textbook publishers include readability indexes in their advertising brochures. However, since the readability scales vary widely in their assessment methods, the resulting readability indexes assigned to a textbook series may be ambiguous. Two different readability indexes may vary by more than a whole grade level for the same material. Publishers, of course, might tend to advertise the readability index for their textbook series that is most favorable. It is always wise for teachers to read sample materials from textbooks that are under consideration and add their judgment on the reading level to the publisher's information.

Will the teachers who will be using the textbooks find information to enable them to understand the content and its organization?

Many publishers provide background information to help teachers. To teach with understanding and provide continuity to science lessons, the teacher must be able to follow and appreciate the way the subject matter is structured in the textbook series. If the subject matter is arranged in a unique fashion, there should be an explanation available in the teacher's guide or elsewhere that is sufficiently clear for the average teacher's understanding.

A publisher should provide a scope and sequence chart for the subject matter presented in a textbook series. Few classroom teachers can be expected to pass judgment on the validity of the facts and concepts presented by the authors of the textbooks, but they may make appropriate assessment as to whether the children who will be using the books will be able to comprehend them. A teacher can also examine scope and sequence charts for specific topics that they believe to be current and important, such as energy conservation or ecology.

Does the textbook provide for inquiry or problem solving by the students?

Currently, many publishers claim that their textbook is inquiry oriented and provides for student investigations. Examine the activities provided by the book to see if their claim is valid. Some textbooks ask problem questions that have the trappings of introducing inquiry, but also provide on the same page the answer to the question both in picture form and in boldface print. Most children will look at the pictures in the book and read the answers to the questions before they begin any suggested investigation. This format short-circuits investigation. Children end up attempting to reinforce those conclusions that were presented to them much earlier, much in the fashion of the traditional secondary school science laboratory workbooks. Little inquiry takes place under these conditions, and the children get little practice in performing the science processes.

Are the materials required to perform the manipulative activities in the textbooks spelled out and readily available?

Several of the elementary science textbook publishers provide kits suitable for use with their series. Examine kit samples to determine how easily the materials are incorporated into the program and whether materials are provided in sufficient numbers for student involvement. Problems of price, storage, and resupply of expendable items should also be explored. Textbook series that are not accompanied by a materials kit but suggest the utilization of readily available materials should provide help to the teacher in determining those materials that will be required for a unit. Such information will permit the materials to be acquired prior to when they are needed. Materials are the heart of an inquiry-oriented science program, even one that is organized around a textbook series, and much consideration should be given to all aspects of their acquisition, storage, and use when selecting a textbook series.

Are supplementary materials available for the science program?

Most publishers present to prospective buyers complete educational packages that include, in addition to textbooks, such things as teacher's guides, student manuals, special topic booklets, audiovisuals (films, filmstrips, charts, and so on), materials kits, worksheets, ditto masters, and activity cards appropriate for constructing learning centers and otherwise individualizing instruction. All of these materials should be considered when adopting a science textbook.

Does the textbook provide a balanced treatment of all sexes, races, and cultures?

Science textbooks for today's schools should place both sexes on equal footing as science students. They should represent girls as able and interested students and avoid the stereotype of depicting boys as the dominant doers and thinkers in the science classroom. Women, ethnic and racial minorities, and a variety of cultures should all be fairly represented in the photographs and written references.

A textbook is a tool in the hands of a teacher: the better suited that tool is to the job at hand, the better the chance that a quality product will result. The time and care taken in selecting a textbook can pay off well for years to come.

Summary

Manipulative science materials and media of various types all contribute to quality science teaching in the elementary school. Many textbook publishers distribute laboratory kits, media, and print materials appropriate for use with their programs. The laboratory activities are designed to support an associated textbook. Some school districts find them expensive, and some teachers find the amount of materials insufficient for individual and group work. General science kits are packaged, generic science materials and equipment. Some are simple boxes, and some are elaborate, with rolling tables equipped with sinks and electrical outlets. Although they are very handy for demonstration lessons, general science kits usually do not have materials in the proper quantities to support individual and group science activities. Elementary science programs also use large quantities of common materials found in schools, homes, and communities. One way to utilize locally obtained materials is by creating shoebox kits. A shoebox kit is a self-contained lesson complete with a teacher's lesson guide, which is stored and used intact.

The most efficient system for utilizing science materials in an elementary school is the central storage and distribution system. The central system makes all science materials in a school available to all teachers. Cooperation among the teachers and the person responsible for operating the central storage and distribution system is necessary for it to work effectively. The center must be accessible before, during, and after school hours; the procedure for obtaining and returning materials must be simple. Teachers must make every effort to return materials to the center in the same numbers and condition in which they were obtained. Teachers should communicate in writing any additional needs and any deficiencies in the materials or system.

Graphic, audiovisual and computer software media should be selected with care whether it is for purchase or for use in a classroom. All media should be appropriate for students in terms of vocabulary and conceptual level, and concepts and information should be clearly presented. The graphics must clearly support the concept being developed and be interesting to the students.

Five special-focus science programs suitable for the elementary school are: Project Learning Tree (PLT), an environmentally oriented program; Outdoor Biology Instructional Strategies (OBIS), which provides quick and simple lessons in life science for grades K–6; Starlab, a portable projection observatory for astronomy and other applications; Science on a Shoestring (SOAS), a collection of activities that utilize inexpensive materials and cover both physical and biological sciences for K–8; and the Full Option Science System (FOSS), which offers activities that may be utilized completely independent of each other. These programs are all characterized as being "teacher friendly"—easy to use for those with only minimal knowledge of science. Other often overlooked resources for science teaching are found in the school and community. They center around the media center's collection of trade books, children's science magazines, and science models. The school and school grounds can provide opportunities for field trips, as can the neighborhood adjacent to the school. Other resources for science teaching are: school volunteers with special knowledge and/or exhibits to share, medical, dental, and business societies, the fire station, and others.

In selecting a textbook for elementary school science, teachers should consider whether the reading level is appropriate, whether a teacher's guide is available, whether the text provides for inquiry teaching, whether supplementary materials (student laboratory books, worksheets, media, and so on) are available, and whether the text is free of sexual, racial, and cultural bias.

Extending Activities

1. Write to various science textbook publishers to obtain catalogs, brochures, and any other materials they may wish to send.

2. Use the addresses in Appendix D, Selected Sources of Free and Inexpensive Science Teaching Materials, to solicit materials.

3. Create a shoebox kit using any lesson plan or activity of your choice.

4. Arrange to visit the media center of both a school system and an elementary school. Observe the nature of the materials that are available for teaching science.

5. Walk around the building, grounds, and neighborhood of an elementary school and plan some field trips appropriate to science instruction.

Bibliography

American Forest Institute, Inc. *Project Learning Tree, Supplementary Learning Guide for Grades K Through 6*. Washington, D.C.: American Forest Institute, Inc., 1977.

Cole, P., and G. Mallon. "One Planetarium—To Go." *Science Teacher* 54, no. 3 (1987), reprint.

Schneider, E. R. "How to Choose a Textbook." *Science and Children* 15, no. 2 (October 1977): 30–33.

Smith, B. "Museum of the Rockies Starlab." *Bozeman Daily Chronicle* (December 13, 1988), reprint.

Lab Report, "Starlab Teacher Training." New York Hall of Science (Fall 1985), pamphlet.

For the names and addresses of suppliers and resources for elementary science supplies, please refer to Appendixes A, B, D, E, and G in this text.

Integrating Science with Other Subjects

Look What's in This Chapter

The practice of integrating subject matter in the elementary schools is becoming increasingly popular. Activity-based science is a rich resource that lends itself to integration with all of the other subjects in the elementary school curriculum. After reading this chapter, you will understand the following ideas that deal with the integration of science with other subjects:

science as a reading readiness program

science as a basis for whole-language reading/ language arts programs

activity-based science as it contributes to the development of mathematics skills

the link between social studies and science, especially where technology interfaces with society

art and music and how they may be integrated with science to enrich children's experiences with the natural world

While field testing some of the manipulative science programs for children, researchers found, often quite by accident, that many interesting things happened that they had not designed into the programs. They discovered that in addition to learning the process skills and content of science, the children were also developing skills in other subject matter areas. Some of these accidental findings were listed in Chapter 1, and the list could easily be doubled in length as study after study has revealed even more benefits that accrue to children actively involved with science.

How can it be that the study of one subject can produce so many benefits for children? There is no particular mystery and certainly no magic involved in the answer to this question. The solution is quite simple. Manipulative science activities, especially in the primary-grade levels, are identical to many of the basic skill activities taught in readiness programs, reading programs, mathematics programs, and social studies programs. As curriculum designers of the various subjects discovered those things in science programs that worked with children, they incorporated them into their own curricula until today there is a great overlapping of the actual learning activities of reading, mathematics, and social studies programs with science. Also, science curriculum publishers, seeing the positive effects of their kindergarten and first-grade materials on the development of skills in the other subjects, began to customize their materials and offer them as prereading programs or readiness programs. Ginn's reading readiness program from Science—A Process Approach and Rand McNally's Beginnings program were developed in this way.

Because many of the learning activities and learning outcomes of diverse programs overlap, it is possible to integrate lessons to teach children basic skills in several of the traditional subject areas of the elementary school. A common lament of elementary school teachers is that they don't have enough time to teach all the things they are supposed to teach. Teaching basic skills common to two or more subjects would appear to be at least a partial solution to this problem.

Science and Reading— A Natural Pair

Figure 7–1 contains the Santa Clara Inventory of Developmental Tasks—one of the more popular management systems for preschool and primary-grade general skills (often called prereading or readiness skills). The shaded blocks in the chart represent those developmental skills that are taught in the Science Curriculum Improvement Study or in Science—A Process Approach, two of the most commonly employed manipulative science programs. More than 50 percent of the developmental tasks for prereading skills listed in the Santa Clara Inventory are taught directly with materials and activities of one or both of these science programs, and many of the other tasks may be developed through minor adaptations in the science activities. A number of studies have shown the SAPA and SCIS programs to be very effective for reading readiness.

Science and Common Prereading Skills

An examination of the general categories of prereading skills contained in Chart 7–1 demonstrates the amount of overlap that exists between reading and manipulative science programs. The shaded blocks in Figure 7–1 indicate skills thought to be taught directly by the science programs. Note that the congruency between general prereading skills and manipulative science is fully 90 percent according to the skills chart.

Of course, the context of a skill taught in science may differ from the context of the same skill taught through reading activities. For instance, the cause-and-effect skill (IIIC on Chart 7–1) taught by having children observe the

Name _____ Birthdate _____

School _____ Teacher _____ Grade _____

Scoring:
0—Almost never
1—Some of the time
2—Most of the time

Testing Dates:

C.D.			
L.D.			
A.M.			
A.P.			
V.M.			
V.P.			
V.M.P.			
M.C.			

Conceptual Development

give personal information	assign number value	identify first, last, top, middle, bottom	tell how 2 items are alike	sort objects 2 ways
7-7	8-8	8-9	8-10	8-11

Language Development

perform 3 commands	describe simple objects	relate words and pictures	define words	language usage
6-6	7-8	7-9	7-10	7-11

Auditory Memory

identify common sounds	repeat a sentence	repeat a tapping sequence	repeat 4 numbers	recall story facts	recall 5 numbers
5-5	6-7	6-8	6-9	6-10	6-11

Auditory Perception

locate source of sound	discriminate between com. sounds	match beginning sounds	hear fine diff. between similar words	match rhyming sounds	match ending sounds
4-5	5-7	5-8	5-9	5-10	5-11

Visual Memory

name objects from memory	recall a 3-color sequence	recall 2 items in a sequence	reproduce design from memory	recall 3 items in a sequence	recall 3-part design	recall word forms
3-5	4-6	4-7	4-8	4-9	4-10	4-11

Visual Perception

recall animal pictures	match form objects	match size objects	match size and form on paper	match numbers	match letters	match direction on design	isolate visual images	match words
4-4	3-4	3-5	3-6	3-7	3-8	3-9	3-10	3-11

Visual Motor

match color objects	copy a cross	copy a circle	copy a square	cut with scissors	tie shoes	copy letters	copy a sentence	copy a diamond
3-3	2-4	2-5	2-6	2-7	2-8	2-9	2-10	2-11

Visual Motor Performance

string beads	copy a circle	balance on one foot	use of hands and arms	balance on walking beam	jump rope assisted	jump rope unassisted
2-2	2-3	1-6		1-8	1-10	1-11

Motor Coordination

creep	walk	run	jump	hop	skip			
1-1	1-2	1-3	1-4	1-5	1-7			

follow target with eyes

PRE-SCHOOL	5-5½ YRS.	5½ YRS.	6-6½ YRS.	7 YRS.

Each task scored: 0 1 2

Figure 7–1 ■ Developmental Profile: Santa Clara Inventory of Developmental Tasks (Shaded Blocks Represent Developmental Skills Taught Directly in the Science Curriculum Improvement Study or in Science—A Process Approach)

135

Chart 7–1 ▪ General Categories of Reading Skills

I. Decoding Skills

- A. Symbol to sound association of letters
- B. Word recognition
- C. Grapheme-phoneme relationships
- D. Blends

II. Word-Processing Skills

- A. Syllabication
- B. Accent
- C. Vocabulary
- D. Prefixes, suffixes, root words
- E. Abbreviations, symbols, acronyms
- F. Synonyms, antonyms, homonyms
- G. Content clues

III. Context-Processing Skills

- A. Main idea
- B. Details
- C. Cause/effect
- D. Following directions
- E. Contrasts and comparisons
- F. Predicting outcomes
- G. Conclusions and generalizations
- H. Inferences
- I. Signal words
- J. Critical reading
  1. Reliability
  2. Character traits and actions
- K. Reorganizational skills
  1. *Classifying*
  2. *Sequencing*
  3. *Summarizing*
  4. *Synthesizing*
  5. *Fact and opinion*

IV. Study Skills

- A. Dictionary skills
- B. Library skills
- C. Reference skills
- D. Diagrams
- E. Tables
- F. Graph skills

bounce of various balls dropped from varying heights will not correspond in form with the cause-and-effect skill as it is taught by reading a paragraph or story. Some transfer of the concept would have to be taught to children if they are to respond correctly to test items presented in the format and language of a reading lesson.

The primary advantage of using science activities to teach or reinforce specific reading skills lies in the motivational nature of the manipulative science activity. Instruction worksheets and drill activities that grow naturally from children's experiences with their environment offer a welcome change of pace to such activities that are unrelated to their experiences. On the following pages you will find some examples of ways in which the experiences of children with science materials may be adapted to teach reading and language arts.

Science as a Vocabulary Builder

One of the major strengths of manipulative science programs in teaching reading and language arts skills is the richness of the vocabulary developed by children. Children in manipulative science programs learn new words and their meanings by experiencing them, not by merely reading about them. For instance, how much greater is the understanding of a child of the terms "lighter than" and "heavier than" who has placed numerous objects on a balance and observed the results than it would be had the child simply read the definitions? Similarly, direction words—right, left, up, down, forward, and backward—are more meaningful to a child who has moved an object or himself to commands from his classmates or his teacher. A science program introduces and defines hundreds of words, each with the active involvement of the children. The vocabulary words are not all specialized or scientific, but include direction words, color words, texture words, and many other categories found on the most commonly used vocabulary lists associated with elementary school reading. Elementary school science programs provide a rich resource for helping children develop vocabulary.

Science Experience Stories and the Whole-Language Approach to Teaching Reading/Language Arts

Janice Jones, a first-grade teacher in an inner-city school, was frustrated by her children's lack of response to her reading program. They were making little progress. It was, Janice decided, time to experiment, to try something else.

She noticed that the children showed real interest when she had introduced a science lesson using an aquarium. They talked and listened to one another as they discussed the guppies she had placed in the tank. Gathered about the aquarium, they watched intently, counting the new baby fish and laughing with delight as the guppies came to the surface to feed. Janice decided to capitalize upon the children's interest in the aquarium. As the class discussed their observations, she wrote their statements on the chalkboard.

We have fish.

Fish live in water.

Fish eat food.

Fish swim.

Janice used the children's statements to develop their vocabularies and communication skills. The children began to keep recordbooks. They noted the words: *fish, swim, we, water,* and so on. Janice would read each statement written on the chalkboard to the students and have them "read" them back. She asked questions like "Which statement tells us what we have?" and "Which statement tells us what fish can do?" The children continued to add to their recordbooks throughout the year as they grew bean plants, sorted colored geometric shapes, and performed other activities from the science

program. In June, tests showed that most children in Janice's class were reading at or above grade level.

Janice used the whole-language approach to teaching reading/language arts. She put basal textbooks aside and used the firsthand experiences of children as a springboard for building vocabulary and teaching reading and writing to her class. Ample research evidence supports this approach over traditional reading, writing, and language arts instruction. Whole-language instruction is effective at all grade levels of the elementary school.

Science and Language Arts— A Natural Pair

By the intent of curriculum developers, children involved with manipulative science programs talk a lot. As they respond to the materials and problem situations of the science programs, children exchange ideas with the teacher and their classmates—sometimes in whole-class situations and at other times with a small group of their peers. Thus, they learn to express themselves orally, translating thoughts and events into words and sentences. Manipulative science provides a setting in which language development occurs naturally and without self-consciousness on the part of the children. A teacher may optimize that oral language development in a number of ways.

Involving Children in Verbal Interaction

One method to enhance this development is to involve all children in the verbal interaction that takes place during science lessons. During whole-class activities, the teacher may call on those children who normally do not volunteer to talk. This may be done through unthreatening questions such as: "What do you see here?" or "What are your thoughts on this?" To ensure the participation of all children during group work, a teacher may make the group leader responsible for eliciting participation from all members of the group, or the teacher may join a group and attempt to draw shy youngsters into the verbal interchange.

The Oral Report

The oral report is a second procedure that may be used during science to develop a child's oral language skills. The oral report in a manipulative science program may be different from one generated from a reading assignment. In the science program the child is reporting on something she and others have done. She will be reporting a firsthand experience to her classmates. If the children are not permitted to merely read their report to the class, but are required to tell about their experiences using notes or tables or charts, a unique opportunity for developing a particular set of oral language skills is provided. Since other children have often performed the same activity or are aware of certain acceptable procedures for carrying on the activity, the speaker is responsible for the details contained in his report and may have to defend and explain his actions. Such reporting activities encourage the speaker to do a better job of speaking and require the class to listen well—as they may want to ask questions of the child or group that is reporting to them.

The Written Report

Writing is another major area associated with language arts. Properly taught, science programs cause children to begin writing early, often in preschool and kindergarten, and to continue to write throughout their school years. In the primary grades, children experiencing manipulative science may copy words and sentences written on the chalkboard or label their own simple diagrams and sketches that serve as culminating activities for the science lesson. At about the third-grade level, these assignments may begin to take the form of reports with the children using complete sentences and constructing rudimentary paragraphs. In the inter-

mediate grades, the teacher may begin to demand greater sophistication in the children's reports, calling for the use of diagrams, tables, and graphs.

Example of reports written by children at various levels are shown in Figure 7–2.

Well-written reports in science (or any other subject) do not just happen. The skills of report writing must be taught and developed over a long period of time. The science curriculum provides children with a unique and interesting opportunity to translate details and events of their own experiences into written language, while utilizing tables, diagrams, and graphs as additional methods of communication.

Some language arts skills such as spelling and punctuation appear to be best taught by repetition and drill. These skills may be enhanced, however, by a teacher who emphasizes the importance of proper punctuation and spelling. There is always a question in assigning and grading reports of elementary school children about the extent to which the teacher should demand accuracy in spelling and punctuation. There is a danger that demanding accuracy in grammar and spelling may cause the child to become so preoccupied with these requirements that the child's ability to write his thoughts and experiences will be inhibited. There is no answer for this dilemma. Spelling, punctuation, and form cannot be totally ignored by the teacher interested in teaching children to write well. The proper advice for teaching children to write science reports is the same as it is for many other areas of teaching. Know your children and tailor your demands to their capabilities and achievement levels. Some general guidelines to help children develop their abilities to write well in science are:

1. Let the creative writing come first. Accept a child's initial attempts to communicate and disregard errors in punctuation and spelling.

2. Attend to a single language arts skill at a time (the use of commas, for instance) rather than showing concern for all skills.

Grades K–1

Flower

Grades 2–3

— seed

← Petal

— stem

Plants need sun.
Plants need water.

We planted grass seeds in wet dirt.
The foam cup was on the window sill.
It took three days for a seed to germinate.
In five days our plant was one centimeter tall.

Grades 4–6
Observations

First day	nothing
Second day	nothing
Third day	It shows tiny green spots
Fourth day	The Plants grew taller
Fifth day	The tallest plants were about one centimeter
Sixth day	

Figure 7–2 ■ Possible Written Science Assignments, by Levels

3. Evaluate the content of the report separately from the spelling and punctuation. When you wish to give a grade for grammar and punctuation skills, assign a separate grade for the content of the report. Always stress the positive aspects of the child's report of her science experience.

The communication aspect of a report in science should take precedence over concerns for punctuation and spelling. If a child feels so threatened by the technical requirements of the reporting that he is inhibited from writing, the benefits in language arts and the science goals of the lesson are lost.

A Science-based Whole-Language Approach— Motivating Children to Read

As we have seen, specific skills of reading may be taught and reinforced directly through instructional techniques that utilize activity-based science programs, but perhaps the major benefit to a child's reading proficiency from the use of science as a teaching tool is that the child reads more. It is a nearly universal experience of teachers that children will choose for their own reading pleasure those trade books that relate to topics that are under discussion in the classroom. This is especially true when the children are intimately involved with the subject matter—as is often the case with investigative science. If the assumption that children who read more, independently, and of their own choice, will be better readers has validity, then activity-oriented science can do much to enhance the general reading level of elementary school children.

Science and Mathematics— A Natural Pair

From the time that the earliest humans began to observe, they began to count things in the environment. The natural curiosity that caused them to view their surroundings with great interest, and their penchant for counting things and putting them into categories to better understand them, created the close association of science and mathematics in earlier civilizations. The relationship of science and mathematics seems so close and natural that there have been several attempts to recombine the two disciplines into a unified curriculum. The close relationship between science and mathematics is as evident today as ever, and many concepts and skills of the two subjects may be integrated into a single set of learning activities. You may recall the AIMS Project from Chapter 1. Although AIMS is a collection of activities that utilize sciencelike activities as a vehicle for teaching mathematics skills and not a true integration of the subjects, it is the latest project to catch the attention of science and math educators.

Chart 7–2 lists skills of elementary school mathematics that are also taught by one or more of the manipulative science programs.

The great overlap in science and mathematics in the elementary school is obvious when one looks at such a list of common skills. The opportunities for utilizing science activities to teach the basic skills of mathematics are numerous and are relatively simple to structure.

Science and Mathematics Programs for Kindergarten and First Grade

The Santa Clara Task Inventory presented earlier in this chapter (see Figure 7–1) provides an overview of those tasks and skills thought to be basic for preschool and primary-grade children. The inventory represents a mix of those things that have at various times been classified as math, science, and reading or reading readiness. Because of the interdisciplinary nature of the skills taught very young children, great similarities exist among the curriculum materials provided for this age group in the names of the various disciplines. Primary-grade programs for both mathematics and science in which the use

Chart 7–2 ▪ Skills Taught in Both Science and Mathematics Programs

Numeration:	Comparing, classifying, recognizing patterns, describing positions, making one-to-one correspondences, constructing sets, writing numerals 0–9, recognizing more/less, comparing, using the number line, ordering, recognizing before/after and between, using sets, recognizing larger than/smaller than
Measurement:	Comparing length, comparing objects, measuring liquids, naming days of the week, telling time, measuring and estimating length, recognizing metric units, computing perimeter, computing area, measuring and estimating capacity, naming months, using the calendar, constructing and interpreting bar graphs and line graphs, using abbreviations/symbols, measuring and estimating weight, interpreting tables, using thermometers
Geometry:	Recognizing and drawing shapes (two dimensional), recognizing solid shapes (three dimensional), recognizing component shapes, naming angles, naming polygons, relating parts of circles, recognizing pyramids, describing paths, describing position, recognizing symmetry
Operations:	Performing simple addition, subtraction, multiplication, division, using decimals, using fractions.*

*One program, Science—A Process Approach, teaches the mathematics operations directly to prepare children to record and interpret data from their observations.

of concrete materials is stressed have children string beads, sort colored geometric shapes, utilize feely bags that enable them to identify and describe materials by touch, and do many other things in common. There is little difference in the majority of the physical materials of primary-grade manipulative science and mathematics. Mathematics programs stress counting and reading and writing numerals and number words, while the science programs provide a wide variety of experiences that include experiences with living things, both plant and animal. Many math and science curricula in the primary grades are based on Piaget's theories, and in programs of both subjects children may be found pouring water into variously shaped containers, sequencing materials, ordering materials by size, and generally manipulating concrete objects designed to develop conservation skills.

To restructure a primary-grade manipulative science program to teach the skills of mathematics, a teacher need do little more than stress the counting experiencing of children, introduce activities to teach the reading and writing of number words and numerals, and utilize the programs classifying activities to introduce set theory.

Mathematics—The Tool of Science

When a child observes an object or set of objects, she first sees the properties that describe their quality, such as their color, shape, symmetry, or beauty. Then if she pursues her observations, she will begin to notice the quantitative properties of the objects, such as the number of the objects and their sizes. A child's first impression of size may be to describe an object simply as "big" or "little." Then she may move on to compare them, one with the other—"the red one is bigger than the green one"—and later use her hand or fingers to measure each object. As she matures as a student, her teacher may show her how to use a meterstick to measure the objects. Thus, the skill of observation is developed—enabling the child to gather more meaningful and useful data.

Through the use of materials, a child's ability to observe and to make use of the product of her observations improves. She begins by describing and counting, learns to measure and compare, and then in the upper elementary grades to construct data tables, make graphs, and to interpret them. The development of these mathematics skills is essential to her ability to do the science activities properly. Counting, measuring, comparing, graphing, and interpreting graphs are her tools for making meaningful inferences from her involvement with the materials in her environment. Mathematics is indeed the tool of science.

Let us look at a lesson taught by Mrs. Green to her fifth-grade class to see how she has integrated the children's experiences with "the suffocating candle" science activity with their mathematics program.

To introduce the activity to her class, Mrs. Green inverted a small jar over a lighted candle. The children saw the candle burn brightly for a while, then the flame grew smaller and finally went out. Mrs. Green asked, "I wonder why that happened?" The children responded that perhaps "the air burned out" and "the air was used up." While holding a large jar in the air, Mrs. Green asked, "If you are right in saying that the candle went out because the air was used up, what would happen if I placed this jar over the lighted candle?"

"It would burn longer because there is more air in the jar," the children responded.

"So if your inference is correct that the candle went out because the air was used up, a candle will burn longer in a larger jar than in a smaller jar. How can we set up an experiment to test your inference?" Mrs. Green sat down on the edge of her desk as the children described how they would take jars of various sizes and measure the burning time of a candle that was placed under them. They would then compare the burning times of the candle and the volumes of the jars. Mrs. Green guided the children as they performed the experiment, cautioning them to wave the jars in the air each time they repeated the activity so that they would start with fresh air in their jar. With each group of children measuring its candle's burning time under the jar they had selected, Mrs. Green helped them build a data table (Chart 7–3) and graph from the findings.

As Mrs. Green constructed the graph on the chalkboard she pointed out to the class that (1) the manipulated variable—the variable that

Chart 7–3 ▪ Class Data Table

Team	Jar Volume	Time (seconds)
1	150 mL	28
2	250 mL	34
3	500 mL	51
4	820 mL	57
5	900 mL	59

is purposefully changed—goes on the horizontal line of the graph; (2) the responding variable—the variable that is observed for its change—is placed on the vertical line; (3) the horizontal and vertical lines are numbered in regular intervals; (4) both lines are given a title that tells what the numbers describe and what units are used. With the help of the class, Mrs. Green developed a title for their graph (Figure 7–3).

After their graph was complete, the children decided that the data in it supported their inference. Then Mrs. Green asked, "How long do you think the candle would burn if a jar with a volume of 700 milliliters was placed over it?" The class used the graph to guess that the candle under the 700-milliliter jar would burn for about fifty-four seconds. Mrs. Green told the class they had made a prediction by *interpolating* from the graph, making a guess about data that appears between two known points on their graph. Then Mrs. Green asked the class to make a prediction on how long a candle would burn under a jar with a 1000-milliliter volume. She explained that this was predicting by *extrapolating* from the graph, making a guess about data that appears beyond the known points on a graph.

Mrs. Green felt good as the children returned the materials to the storage boxes and cleaned up the room. This was certainly a better way to teach graphing than plotting the world population over the last 200 years as was suggested in the mathematics book. She planned to have the class do another experiment the following day and construct graphs of their own.

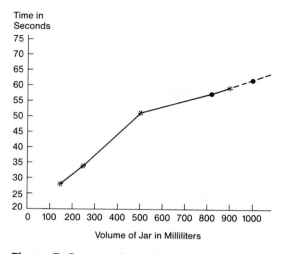

Time in Seconds

Figure 7–3 ■ A Comparison of the Burning Times of Candles Under Jars of Various Volumes

The amount and variety of mathematics skills that Mrs. Green's class used in doing the "suffocating candle" activity is striking. The children measured the volumes of the jars in milliliters, told time by the clock as they observed their candle's burning time, selected a proper scale for the axes of their graph, and wrote the numbers on the scale in even intervals. They also learned to predict by interpolation and extrapolation from a graph. This activity was truly a marriage of mathematics and science.

Using Science Experiments to Teach and Reinforce Basic Mathematics Skills

Any time children count and measure as they observe things happening during their science lessons, they are learning basic mathematics skills. Skill deficiencies in mathematics are common in today's classrooms, and the teacher is often faced with the need to reinforce specific skills. Data from science activities can provide a smooth and reasonable entry to drill exercises for mathematics skills.

Suppose that Mrs. Green had determined that her class needed practice in division. She might have asked her class to find the burning time per milliliter for each candle and jar. From the data table the children would obtain the numbers that represent the jar's volume and the burning time of the candle. They would then divide the time in seconds into the jar's volume in milliliters to find the burning time per milliliter. Mrs. Green could suggest other jar volumes and burning times to provide further practice for the class. Once data tables are established, a teacher can use the data to enhance the mathematics skills of children by asking such questions as "How much larger is jar A than jar B?" or "How many candles could be burned under the 1000-milliliter jar while one candle is burned under the 500-milliliter jar?" Worksheets with drill activities related to the science activity would reinforce the selected mathematics skill. Data from science tables provide meaningful numbers that the imaginative teacher may use to reinforce nearly any basic mathematics skill.

The same caution should be observed in utilizing science activities to teach and reinforce basic mathematics skills as was noted in relation to teaching reading from science activities. Don't fall into the trap of using a little bit of science activity to introduce a lot of mathematics drill activity. The motivational impact of the hands-on science has limitations and will not sustain mathematics drill that has lost its meaning over a long period of time and a series of drill worksheets. It is also important to make sure the *science* concepts generated by a hands-on activity are fully developed and not neglected in the pursuit of mathematics skill development.

Advantages of Using Manipulative Science to Teach Mathematics and Reading

Reading and mathematics are aggregations of skills. Learning activities for these skills are best structured upon children's experiences with the people and things of their environments. When the learning activities appear contrived and outside the experience of the learner, the teacher must depend upon extrinsic reward systems to motivate the children. Though the designers of reading and mathematics programs try mightily to make their materials meaningful and relevant to the lives of children, it is a nearly impossible task to provide daily lessons that fit this description for a majority of children. Motivating children in mathematics and reading programs is a serious problem in today's elementary schools.

Utilizing science activities to teach or reinforce these two skills helps solve the motivation problem and presents other advantages as well. It shifts learning from an extrinsic reward system to an intrinsic one where children are actively involved of their own volition with learning. Using science to teach basic skills also:

1. Enhances the development of Piagetian conservations thought to be an essential prerequisite to learning to read and do mathematics.

2. Aids in concept development of young children. (Indeed, many educators would say such experiences are essential to concept development in children in the Piagetian stage of concrete operations.)

3. Enhances both original learning and the retention of such learning (heightened motivation creates a positive emotional and intellectual state in the child).

Either as an alternative program or to provide a change of pace to basal reading and mathematics programs, manipulative science curricula have great potential.

Science and Social Studies— A Natural Pair

Social studies is the other subject taught in the elementary school that, along with science, possesses its own body of knowledge, skills, and concepts. Since social studies is often taught in a problem-solving mode, it shares with science the distinction of offering children experiences that develop and reinforce higher-level cognitive skills. In today's schools the majority of a child's time is spent in performing drill activities associated with behaviorally based reading and mathematics systems. Often, a properly taught inquiry lesson in social studies with children working in problem-solving groups is a welcome respite from a fare of individualized instruction that to them means completing one worksheet after another over a long period of time.

Social studies skills are commonly divided into two general categories, those for obtaining knowledge and those for processing knowledge. The skills of obtaining knowledge are those associated with reading, listening, and observing. These skills include learning the proper use of the library and media as research tools. The skills for processing knowledge are variously listed as:

1. Map and globe skills (directions, locating positions, scaling, latitude and longitude, inferring from comparing maps).

2. Interpreting pictures, charts, graphs, and tables.

3. Evaluating information (fact, fiction, opinion, source, recognizing propaganda, inferring, and generalizing).

4. Time and chronology (time system, calendar, sequencing events, concept of time span).

5. Problem-solving skills (recognizing and defining a problem, collecting and reviewing data, planning to study a problem, gathering new data, summarizing and drawing conclusions, withholding opinions, changing opinions).

6. Communicating (speaking with accuracy and poise, writing with clarity, constructing graphs, maps, charts, tables, and pictorial material, drama).

7. Group problem solving (role assumption, establishing rules, following rules, sharing ideas, listening, helping seek closure).

Manipulative science programs and problem-based social studies programs share the seven categories of processing knowledge almost in their entirety. The major difference between the two subjects as they are taught in the elementary school is that *usually* problem solving in science involves the interpretation of physical materials and phenomena, and *usually* problem solving in social studies involves the interpretation of stored information and ideas. Both subjects utilize similar types of instruction, such as individual and group interaction in a problem-solving mode.

Integrating Instruction in Science and Social Studies

Where science and technology touch human problems and concerns, we find common ground for the scientist and the social scientist and an area that lends itself to the integration of the two subjects in the elementary school curriculum. The dangers of nuclear power, energy resources, pollution, water treatment plants, the environment, euthanasia, and genetic engineering are a few examples.

A major problem of integrating these co-equal curriculum partners is giving each proper attention and emphasis so that the point of view and activities of one subject do not dominate the union. One solution to this dilemma is to use science activity as one method of gathering data. For when the students understand the science concepts involved with the problem, they will be better able to offer solutions and reasonable courses of action.

For instance, let's consider as a proper vehicle for integrating science and social studies, the problem of a local sewage treatment plant that is dumping improperly treated sewage into the stream that runs through Mr. Young's town.

The problem is defined in Mr. Young's sixth-grade class by the question: "Should the city no longer permit the sewage treatment plant to empty its effluent into Snyder's Creek?"

Mr. Young began the study of the problem by taking his class to Snyder's Creek. While there, the children searched for and recorded the various plants and animals found in and alongside the creek. They put leaves and stems of plants in plastic bags to investigate at a later time. They also took samples of water from the creek. For the next several days the children examined the leaves and plants they had brought back to their classroom and attempted to classify and name them using a field guide. The children also took turns examining the water samples under a microscope, looking for living organisms. One group of children conducted an experiment that used methylene blue and yeast to examine the effect of sewage on the oxygen content of water. As the science experiments drew to a close, Mr. Young discussed with his class the need for more information. From this discussion, study teams were organized to investigate these issues:

1. The cost of improving the sewage treatment plant or building a new one.

2. The effect of organic sewage on aquatic life.

3. The attitudes of the citizens of the town toward the pollution problem caused by the sewage treatment plant.

After the study teams completed their investigations, several days were spent having the teams report their findings to the rest of the class. A letter summarizing the class's investigations was sent to the mayor of the town to culminate the activity.

Mr. Young's integration of social studies and science was designed to maintain the integrity of both disciplines. The science activities were activity based, and the children learned techniques, concepts, and information associated with the subject of freshwater ecology.

Through library research and a survey of public opinion, they gathered further data that helped them to formulate generalizations and to draw conclusions. Reading and language arts skills were enhanced through the children's library research projects and their reports and classroom discussions. During the course of the science experiments, the children learned to measure liquid volume using the metric system. All four of the major subjects were utilized in the project. It was an integration of science, social studies, mathematics, and language arts/reading.

In the integration of science with social science, experimental science activities should be conducted prior to the use of the library as a research tool. When this is done, the science activities can serve to stimulate student interest and to provide data to be added to and clarified by that data gathered through library research. In this way investigations into the principles of science and technology related to the topic under study are made more meaningful. The basic skill subjects can be easily incorporated into any project for they serve as a means of gathering, analyzing, and storing information.

Science and the Arts

Music and visual art activities may become an integral part of a science unit or utilized as concluding or culminating exercises. During music class it is common to teach elementary school children about the pitch and intensity of sounds. The same activities are part of many science programs. During science children can be seen blowing across the tops of bottles filled to varying levels with water or tapping on the sides of water-filled jars to learn about musical pitch. The Elementary Science Study materials offer several units where children make whistles and stringed instruments and learn to make music on them. Since music is the art of creating and listening to pleasant sounds, activities that permit children to become actively involved with music are ideal springboards to learning about the science of sound.

A few suggested activities that may be used to integrate science and music are listed below.

1. Making and learning to play homemade musical instruments. (See Whistles and Strings and Musical Instruments units from Elementary Science Study, McGraw-Hill Book Company.)

2. Having the children state whether a sound is higher or lower in pitch as the teacher plays notes on a piano or other musical instrument.

3. Having the children tell whether sounds are louder or softer as a teacher plays pairs of notes of the same pitch on a piano or other musical instrument.

4. Having the children create and sing songs about science topics.

Example:

The Food Chain
(To the tune of "The Farmer in the Dell")

The mouse eats the seed, the mouse eats the seed.
  Hi ho the dario the mouse eats the seed.

The owl eats the mouse. . . .
The fox eats the owl. . . .
The bear eats the fox. . . .
The man eats the bear. . . .

The mouse needs the seed. . . .
The owl needs the mouse. . . .
The fox needs the owl. . . .
The bear needs the fox. . . .
The man needs the bear. . . .
No animal stands alone. . . .

Other topics that lend themselves to song writing are the water cycle, carbon cycle, and other cycles in nature, pollution, dying lakes and streams, the growth of young animals and flowers.

Some ideas for activities that may be used to integrate science and art are:

1. Having the children mix primary pigment colors to produce the secondary pigment colors.

2. Having the children mix the primary colors of light by shining flashlights (or slide projectors) through colored cellophane filters on a white surface.

3. Having the children make collages from various categories of materials. Examples are leaves, trash found on the playground, pictures of animals, materials of various textures, pictures of alternative energy sources, and so on.

4. Having the children create interpretive drawings related to the science topic under study. Examples are the animal that could best survive in a swamp, on a mountain, in the desert; a space station environment; an animal that is difficult to see even when it is not hiding, and so on.

5. Having the children draw sketches of experimental situations as an aid in reporting their results to others.

6. Having the children create original papier-mâché animals and plants that represent their ideas of how they would exist under certain conditions—on the moon, in a desert, in the ocean, and so on.

7. Having the children create figures from clay.

8. Having the children sculpt using plaster of Paris blocks.

9. Having the children make shell impressions in plaster of Paris and paint them.

10. Having the children arrange and mount butterfly collections.

Ideas for integrating art and music with science are limited only by the imagination of the teacher. The combination of science and the arts provides children the rare opportunity for experiencing the joy of discovering and the satisfaction of creating in a single activity.

Summary

As they currently exist, there is a substantial overlap in the skills and activities that are associated with manipulative science programs and those associated with reading readiness, reading, mathematics, and social studies programs. Science inquiry activities enhance skills in other areas of the curriculum.

Science activities may be used as a basis for teaching specific reading skills and enriching the vocabularies of children. The use of science experience stories may be structured as a total reading program, especially in the primary grades, or to teach and reinforce specific reading skills. Reading skills of intermediate-grade children may also be reinforced by constructing practice exercises and drill activities that utilize their experiences in science. To prepare children to cope with standardized tests, it is necessary to introduce them to practice items in the testing format and teach for the transfer of learning. Through oral and written reports in a manipulative science program, children develop speaking and writing skills. Three rules for grading children's written science reports are:

1. Let the creative writing develop before evaluating grammar and spelling.

2. Grade only one language arts skill at a time.

3. Give a separate grade for the content of the report and the language arts skills.

The great similarity between primary-grade manipulative science and mathematics programs permits the easy substitution of one for the other with some modifications and additions. Mathematics is the tool of science and as such is highly utilized in experimental activities. Specific mathematics skills may be taught to children using their experiences with science materials.

Some advantages in using science to teach basic skills in mathematics and reading/language arts are:

1. Concrete materials of science programs aid the development of Piagetian conservation skills.

2. Concrete materials of science aid in concept development.

3. Manipulative science programs are highly motivating to children and for this reason increase both the amount of learning and its retention.

Social studies and science may best be integrated when both are taught as problem-solving activities. A recommended procedure for integrating the two subjects is to perform the related science investigations first and follow these with any desired library research. Mathematics and reading/language arts may easily be integrated into any problem where science and social studies are utilized.

Numerous activities may be used to integrate science with music and art and provide children with opportunities to develop their creative abilities as a natural outgrowth of their involvement with science.

Extending Activity

Construct a lesson plan for one or more of the following situations:

1. Use a science activity to develop mathematics skills.

2. Use a science activity to develop oral language skills.

3. Use a science activity to develop writing skills.

4. Outline a lesson that integrates science and social studies.

5. Outline a lesson that integrates science and art or music.

6. Write a jingle (song) for the human skeleton or the water cycle.

Bibliography

Baker, G. C. *Planning and Organizing for Multicultural Instruction.* Reading, Mass.: Addison-Wesley, 1983.

Esler, W. K., J. Midgett, and R. C. Bird. "Elementary Science Materials and the Exceptional Child." *Science Education* 61, no. 2 (1977): 181–184.

Fisher, R., and R. L. Fisher. "Reading, Writing, and Science." *Science and Children* 23, no. 1 (September 1985): 23–24.

Luminack, L. "Mr. T Leads the Class: The Language Experience Approach and Science." *Science and Children* 24, no. 5 (February 1987): 41–42.

Petty, C. "Integrating Science and Art." *Science and Children* 23, no. 3 (November/December 1985): 6–9.

Ritz, W. C. "The Effect of Two Instructional Programs (Science—A Process Approach and the Frostig Program for the Development of Visual Perception) on the Attainment of Reading Readiness, Visual Perception and Science Process Skills in Kindergarten Children." Ph.D. dissertation, State University of New York, Buffalo, n.d.

Switzer, T., and B. Voss. "Integrating the Teaching of Science and Social Studies." *School Science and Mathematics* 82 (October 1982): 452–462.

Resource: Modern Curriculum Press, materials to integrate science with language arts, 13906 Prospect Rd., Cleveland, OH 44136.

Individualizing Science/Science for Exceptional Children

Look What's in This Chapter

Instruction in elementary school science may be easily modified for various formats and purposes: for structured, sequential curricula, in the open classroom, and as enrichment experiences for children. You will find a discussion of each of these approaches in this chapter. You will also find instructions for developing and using learning centers that employ the inquiry method of instruction. Other ways of individualizing instruction that you will find discussed are: computer-assisted instruction, the science fair, science for children with special needs such as SLD, EH, EMH, sight-impaired, hearing-impaired, and gifted children. Finally, you will learn how to help integrate children from diverse cultures and racial groups into your science classroom.

Individualizing Instruction in Science

Individualized instruction has become a catchall phrase in education that includes all modes of teaching where the child, either as an individual or as a member of a group, has assumed primary responsibility for carrying on a learning activity. In the science classroom in the elementary school, individualized instruction can be characterized by several distinct modes of operation. These are:

1. The systems approach.
2. The open classroom.
3. Enrichment learning centers.
4. Inquiry centers.

Learning Centers in the Systems Approach Classroom

Any elementary school science program may be transformed into a systems approach mode. To create the materials for a systems approach unit, a teacher:

1. Determines learning objectives.
2. Creates a student performance record form.
3. Structures activity sheets or cards for use by the individual child.
4. Sets evaluation procedures.
5. Gathers appropriate materials for the prescribed learning activities.

To begin work in a center in the systems approach elementary school classroom, the child will go to a set of file folders that have been placed in a convenient location. Each folder contains classroom sets of a single task sheet. At the teacher's direction, the child selects a task sheet from a folder, collects the materials necessary to complete the activities on the task sheet, and goes to a work station where he carries out the prescribed tasks according to simple, clearly written directions. When he has finished his activities and has answered all questions on the task sheet, the student will go to the teacher or to a designated place in the classroom, locate an answer key, and evaluate his work. If it is satisfactory, the child checks the lesson off on an individual student performance record that has his name on it and proceeds to the next task sheet. At his own pace, he works his way through a series of activity sheets in the file folders.

A sample activity sheet from a systems approach program is shown in Figure 8–1.

The procedure described above has each child working independently on the assigned activities, securing materials from a central location, and proceeding to a work station. Such a procedure requires enough materials so that each child has a set. Some alternatives that would reduce the amount of materials required would be to place the materials for a specific activity at a center. There may be enough materials present to accommodate only six or so children. The class will be instructed that when a center is full a child is to select another activity sheet and find the appropriate center that is not at the stated capacity.

To further conserve materials some teachers have the children at a center work in groups, even though each child must complete his or her own task sheet. Some guidelines for preparing activity sheets are discussed later in the chapter.

Learning Centers in the Open Classroom

The open classroom provides for a great deal of freedom that permits children to select from among many learning centers. The open classroom is likely to be ringed with learning centers, at least one of which will be labeled a science center. The activities of the science center are likely to resemble the discovery model of inquiry that was presented in Chapter 3. Here one

Task Sheet One
Observing Change in a System
(For the teacher's use)

Objective: The child will state that one evidence of chemical change is a change in color.

You will need: bottle marked BTB, bottle marked vinegar, a medicine dropper, a soda straw, and a plastic cup half full of water

What to Do:

1. Use the medicine dropper to place five to eight drops of the liquid from the BTB bottle into the cup of water. Stir gently with the dropper as you add the BTB.

2. What color is the water after the BTB is added? _____

3. Use the soda straw to blow your breath into the BTB water. Keep blowing until you see a change.

4. What happened? _____

5. Empty the BTB water into the sink, and gently pour water over the colored liquid in the sink until all color is gone down the drain.

6. Refill your plastic cup of water until it is about half full. Again add five to eight drops of BTB with a medicine dropper stirring gently with the dropper.

7. Using the medicine dropper slowly, add liquid from the bottle marked vinegar.

8. What happened? _____

9. What happened when you blew into the BTB water? _____

    What happened when you added vinegar to the BTB water? _____

    Was there a change? _____

10. What was the evidence of change? _____

11. The BTB, the vinegar, and your breath are all called chemicals, and the change produced when they are mixed together is a chemical change.

12. Write a statement about what you found to be evidence of a chemical change.

THIS TASK SHEET HAS BEEN COMPLETED.
CLEAN ALL THE MATERIALS AND THE CONTAINERS AND PLACE THEM BACK WHERE YOU FOUND THEM.

Now check your answers with the answer sheet for: TASK SHEET ONE. You will find it in the folder marked ANSWER SHEETS. If you answered the questions correctly, put a check mark in the proper space on your Progress Report.

Now take a task sheet from the folder marked TASK SHEET TWO and follow its directions.

Figure 8–1 ▪ Sample Activity Sheet

would find an abundance of manipulative materials, many of them homemade or procured locally. In the operation of the classroom, children may receive guidance in the forms of questions and helpful suggestions as they pursue their investigations. To date, most open classrooms in this country are found at the early primary-grade level.

One science center in an open classroom might focus on a "Sink or Float" activity. In this Sink or Float center are a large plastic basin half full of water and a box containing a wide variety of materials found commonly around the home and school—nuts, bolts, and other items made of metal, wooden blocks and sticks, leather and plastic items, and any other small, water-immersible materials. Hanging from strings above the center are two placards. One asks, "What things sink?" and the other, "What things float?" With no more direction than this, the children are left to explore with the materials and the basin of water. The teacher may visit the center from time to time and might suggest, if it is not already happening, that the children make piles of those things that sink and those things that float. He may also ask the children to float some material that sank or to find a way to sink a material that floated. In this classroom there is no formal evaluation; the teacher satisfies his concerns for the progress of each child by what he observes as they go about their activities in the center. The teacher may sometimes suggest that the children make a drawing or write a sentence about what they did in the center as a culmination to the open-ended, manipulative discovery activities.

Learning Centers for Enrichment

Many teachers choose to use science learning centers to supplement or enrich their ongoing programs. Such enrichment centers take many forms. Some are unstructured "interest centers" containing materials to pique the interest of children. Such centers often contain trade books and other reading materials associated with the topic of the center. At times, science learning centers consist of materials that permit children to perform laboratory activities that they have previously studied in their textbooks. An interest center on the earth or geology might contain a collection of rocks, a filmstrip, and several books that will help the children to identify and classify them. The children may be asked to try the scratch test for mineral hardness by rubbing selected rocks on pieces of glass or a penny. They might place drops of vinegar on limestone and other rocks to see the reaction. But no requirement is made of the children to perform any of the activities, or even to visit the center at all, and no record is maintained as to their performances there. The primary goal of an interest center is to motivate children to want to learn more about the subject.

The Science Inquiry Center

Inquiry as defined earlier in this book is a problem-solving activity that causes a child to extend her thinking beyond the known facts to gain new insights. The inquiry center is a collection of self-directed activities designed to elicit that behavior. Typically, an inquiry center contains materials to be manipulated by the children, directions for that investigation, and open-ended questions to be answered at the end of the inquiry. An inquiry center represents original learning to the child involved with its activities. Inquiry centers differ from many learning centers in today's elementary school classrooms, especially those common to the language arts and reading that serve primarily to reinforce prior learning experiences.

To construct a science inquiry center, select a topic. A sample inquiry center topic might be MAGNETS. Use legal-size manila folders as a backdrop for the center. (These folders also offer a convenient way to store the center.) Cast-off science textbooks and children's magazines are excellent sources of colored pictures to illus-

A science inquiry center on electricity.

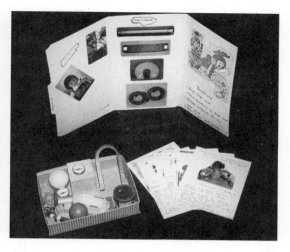

A science inquiry center on magnetism.

trate the activities in the center and to make it more attractive. Of course, line drawings using magic markers will also serve this purpose.

After the topic has been selected, the next step is to decide on the science concepts that you wish to teach. The appropriate concepts may be taken directly from a science textbook and posed as questions. The concept *Some metals are attracted to magnets and some nonmetals are not* may become "What kinds of materials are attracted to magnets?" And the concept *Magnetic fields operate through many materials* may become "Will magnets work through glass?" and "Will magnets work through paper?" After turning the science concepts into simple questions appropriate for the children who will be using the inquiry center, make an activity card for each concept (question).

To understand how the inquiry center works, picture the following equipment on a table at the rear of a third-grade classroom. In a box marked with a large numeral 1 are found a small magnet, an iron nail, an aluminum nail, an iron screw, a brass screw, an iron paper clip, a wood stick, and a penny. Under the box is a stack of worksheets as illustrated in Chart 8–1.

Chart 8–1 ▪ What Do Magnets Attract?

Which of the objects in the bag will stick to the magnet? Write yes beside the name of the object if it sticks to the magnet, and no if it does not.

Objects	Yes or No
Iron (Gray) Nail	(yes)
Aluminum (White) Nail	(no)
Iron (Gray) Screw	(yes)
Brass (Yellow) Screw	(no)
Iron Paper Clip	(yes)
Wood Stick	(no)
Penny	(no)

After trying all the objects in the bag, you may QUIETLY test other objects in the science area with the magnet. What sticks to the magnet?

A second box prominently marked with the numeral 2 contains a small test tube with iron filings inside and assorted other small bottles and jars for use with activity card 2. There is a box of materials for each activity card in the center. The typical number of activity cards in a center is three to five. Over a span of several days, the children are scheduled at the science inquiry center, perhaps during reading time, while the teacher conducts a reading group. The children may work at the center singly, but time limitations usually require that they be scheduled into the center in small groups. The time required to complete the activities will vary. Fifteen- to thirty-minute periods for primary-grade children and thirty- to forty-five minute periods for intermediate-grade children are typical.

Preparing Children to Work at an Inquiry Center

Working independently at an inquiry center is a unique experience for most children. For this reason, the nature of the experience and the teacher's expectations for the children's performance must be spelled out before the children begin. To prepare a class to work at an inquiry center, it may be wise for the teacher to hold a discussion with all the children prior to introducing the first group to the center. A leader may be appointed or other roles assigned for individual children. Through discussion, rules may be formulated that deal with all phases of the children's activities at the center.

For a class's introduction to an inquiry center, the teacher may wish to clarify procedures for using the task cards to complete the center's activities, perhaps actually demonstrating the activities on one of the cards. During the preparation period the teacher should anticipate any safety hazards or activities that might cause problems and discuss them with the children. No thinking college teacher would start a class on a new type of learning experience without thorough preparation, and it is foolish to do less with young children.

Some Hints for Constructing Inquiry Centers

The ultimate test for an inquiry center is that the students achieve desired learning objectives and are able to complete the work independently.

Some questions that you might ask to evaluate the center are:

Were the Directions Clear?

Written directions should be given in a numbered sequence, not in paragraph form. Directional statements should be brief and clear. Avoid wordiness. For young children and problem readers, oral tapes may be employed in directing activities. A generous use of pictures also adds to the clarity of written directions.

Did the Children Know Where to Begin and When They Had Finished?

It may be necessary to print a message for the child or group approaching a new inquiry center to "Begin Here" and in the same way let them know when they have finished the center activities.

Were the Activities Appropriate for the Level of the Children?

Inappropriate leveling often leads to problems in learning-center activities.

Were the Desired Concepts or Skills Developed?

You should have some evidence that the children acquired the concepts or skills the center was to develop. The evidence may be in the form of data sheets, written statements, a quiz, or oral discussion.

Was Provision Made for the Following Group?

Unless you wish to rearrange and resupply the inquiry center after each individual or group has used it, you should provide directions to have the center restored by the group that is finishing its activities.

Were Safety Factors Considered?

Where the use of candles, alcohol burners, or other heat sources is necessary, it is wise to appoint a single responsible child to manipulate the heat source. A second child appointed a "fire marshall" could assume responsibility for the group's safety. The wise selection of materials and reminders of possible dangers can help children avoid accidents at the center.

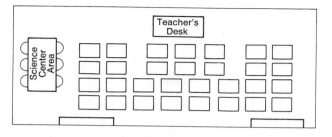

Figure 8–2 ■ Classroom 1: A Beginning

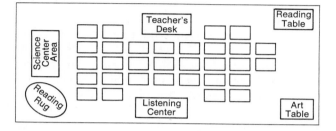

Figure 8–3 ■ Classroom 2: Expanding Learning-Center Activities

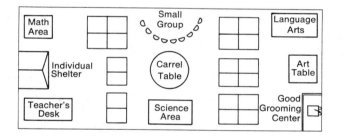

Figure 8–4 ■ Classroom 3: Further Expansion of Learning-Center Activities

Arranging the Classroom for Learning Centers

For those teachers who have never operated with learning centers, the best approach is to move into this mode of classroom operation gradually. It is best to start with a single science center. This will permit learning the "ins and outs" of constructing centers. It will also provide experience for the children in operating in a self-directed learning situation. As confidence and skill in handling learning centers increase, the

teacher may wish to add more learning centers. Examine the three classroom arrangements in Figures 8–2, 8–3, and 8–4. In classroom 1, we see a fairly traditional arrangement of student desks with the addition of a science center area. In classroom 2, other centers have been added. The desks have been squeezed more into the center of the room with learning centers located about the periphery. In classroom 3, we find an arrangement suitable for the teacher who uses teaching centers a large part of the school day. In this classroom, the children's desks are pushed together into clusters to gain additional space, and learning centers now occupy a greater share of the floor space. In classroom 3, there is a learning center for each subject area in the curriculum, plus a flexible carrel table and an area for small group instruction. It is also possible that as learning-center areas are developed, some of the children's desks may be removed from the classroom.

Learning Centers and I-C-I

As you may recall from Chapter 4, I-C-I stands for the learning sequence of inquiry, concept, and information. The sequence is designed to permit inquiry and the acquisition of process skills by the children while using a textbook-based science program. Learning centers are entirely compatible with the I-C-I plan, just so long as the proper sequencing of learning activities is observed. First the children should be permitted to work through self-directing inquiry lessons at an inquiry center and then pursue learning activities to obtain information in an information center. An information center might use programmed materials, film loops, filmstrips, films, slides, magazines, and books.

Computers in the Elementary School

Computers are the latest of a long history of technologies that have affected the elementary school program. Beginning with the abacus, and progressing through the printing press, still and film projectors, television, and calculators, and culminating now with personal computers combined with laser disk applications, technology is a vital force in shaping instruction. However, though the possibilities are seemingly endless and exciting for utilizing computers in science instruction in the elementary school, in practice teachers are faced with some facts that limit the impact of the new technology.

Currently, even in more progressive school systems, the ratio of computers to children in the elementary school is about one computer per twenty children. Distributed about the classrooms, this is about one and a half computers per teacher unit. In schools where the computers are placed in a computer laboratory that is shared by all the children in the school, the individual child's access to a computer is limited. It is felt by some educators that if computers are to be used as a general instructional tool, the ratio of computers to children will need to be at least one computer per five children.

Space is a second limiting factor in the use of computers as a general tool for instruction in the elementary school. Many classrooms are too small to house six or more computers along with all of the furniture and other instructional centers that normally exist. And many elementary schools do not have four or five classrooms to devote exclusively to computer laboratory facilities. Even if computers become smaller and less costly, the problem of space will still be a problem that will have to be solved to make a computer available to elementary school children for extended periods of time on a regular basis.

Other factors that are currently limiting the use of computers in the elementary classroom are: the unfamiliarity of many teachers with computers; the limited and inappropriate software available in the schools; the reliance of many educators on textbooks and paper-and-pencil learning activities; and a lack of awareness of the many possibilities that computer technology has for providing efficient and reasonably priced instruction for children.

Many of the problems that have served to limit the use of computers are rapidly being reduced. Hardware is becoming smaller and cheaper and the quality and variety of software is increasing rapidly. The use of interactive video/computers is adding new dimensions to the instructional sophistication of the medium. Where the future will take us in the utilization of computer technology in elementary school

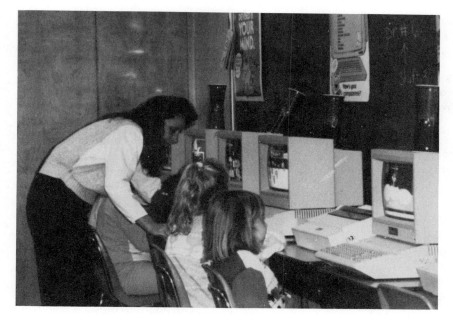

Availability of appropriate software is a must for an effective microcomputer laboratory.

science is an interesting question. We will have to wait to know the answer.

Using Computers to Teach Science in the Elementary School Classroom

While some authorities suggest that elementary schools place computers in laboratories for maximum utilization by students, this is not happening in most schools. Typically the computers that are available are located in the classrooms, usually one or two computers per room. As computers become more numerous and each classroom has five or six of them for student use, this deployment in individual classrooms will make the machines more accessible to more children. For now though, most teachers must plan to use only one or two computers in their classroom, sometimes sharing them with other teachers. Some ways that teachers are utilizing a single computer in their classroom are:

1. Remediation: Students who need drill and practice on vocabulary or concepts may work independently or in small groups with a computer.

2. Enrichment: Students who complete their assignments may work at the computer to enrich and broaden their knowledge of science.

3. As a learning center: All students in a class may be scheduled to use a computer that is set up as a learning center.

4. As part of an interest center: An interest center on animals, for instance, may contain a computer activity in which children work through a tutorial program on animal skeletons. The rest of the center would be comprised of manipulative materials, books, audio tapes, filmstrips, and so on.

5. As a whole-class learning activity, which utilizes a computer in conjunction with a video disc player.

For each of these suggested activities, it is possible for children to work in groups of two or three and still benefit from the computer.

Types of Software Programs Available for Science Instruction

Tutorials

A well-designed tutorial program uses graphics and instructional statements to teach terms and concepts. Most have interactive features that ask questions and permit the learner to respond by using the keyboard.

Drill and Practice

The most effective drill and practice programs use games to make learning more palatable for the student. Most are interactive and some involve branching to provide instruction where student weaknesses show up. Some programs also maintain a record of student achievement.

Problem Solving

Some computer programs use graphics to challenge students' higher-thinking skills. Some, for example, use two- and three-dimensional mazes that require the child to find a path to a desired destination. Another very common form of problem-solving activities found in computer programs is simulations where students are confronted with a problem and asked to make selections from menus of possible choices. The program will then show them the consequences of each choice. For example, the rabbit that elects to "run out of the woods" may get eaten by a hawk that is circling the clearing. Some software also simulates actual science experiments, and the learner sees via graphic display the results of the choices he or she makes from menus of possible actions. Computer simulation is a rather safe way to mix the wrong substances—the explosion can then be watched on the video screen.

Computer-Driven Video Discs

The number of video discs on the market suitable for teaching science has risen steadily in the last several years until today there are over 600. A video disc consists of thousands of images that may be accessed as single frame "stills" or in an action mode. Video discs may be utilized at three levels. The least sophisticated video disc system consists of a disc, a disc player, and a remote control pad. The visuals are stored as stills or as moving videos that can be turned on and off and adjusted in speed by using the remote pad. With this system there is little interaction between the teacher and children.

At the next higher level of sophistication is a system that has an internal computer that controls the order or sequence of the visual images. At this level of operation the player may access the video images in any preprogrammed order as stills or moving videos. There is, however, little chance for the users to interact directly with the video player.

By using an external microcomputer connected to the video disc player and a software program, students and teachers may directly control the display on the video screen that is taken from the video disc. This permits a teacher to customize the presentation and utilize a wide range of video images in still moving forms in a single lesson. For the most part, video disc players found in the elementary school classrooms today are at the first or second level of sophistication; third-level systems generally are confined to business applications. However, as equipment and discs become cheaper, the computer-driven video disc will surely find its way into the elementary school.

Laboratory Instrumentation Programs

Computer programs that utilize data generated by sensing probes to provide data tables, graphs, and charts are not very common but do exist. The digital readout thermometer now in common use in both homes and hospitals is an example of one such sensing device. Other attributes commonly recorded by such computers are light intensity, time, and motion. The displays on the monitor screens are not simulations but actual data from an experimental procedure.

Complete Science Programs

Some software distributors offer complete science programs comprised of program disks, teachers' guides, laboratory activities (real ones), and student worksheets. Some of these programs are designed to maintain a record of the progress of each student in the class. At this point, though, there has been little experience with such computer-based science programs and there are many questions that need to be explored about the effects of such programs on different levels and types of learners.

Software for Teachers

Among the programs commonly available for teachers are: word processing, which makes the task of writing documents and reports easier; gradebook programs, which average grades and print out the results; test-construction programs, which are modified word processing programs that help teachers write, modify, and change the order of items on tests; and crossword puzzle construction programs, which automatically produce puzzles when responses are entered into the program.

The Science Fair

There is a heightened interest in science fairs in the elementary school. As an awareness grows of the importance of teaching science at the elementary school level, the proliferation of science fairs is seen by many teachers as a demonstration to the public of the school's interest in the subject. The science fair provides a vehicle for promoting the involvement of parents and the community in the education of children. There are several positive outcomes for children who participate in science fairs, especially those who undertake projects in which experimentation and the scientific method are emphasized. Science fairs provide students the opportunity to work at their own pace on a project of their choosing. In carrying out the activities of the inquiry-based science fair project, the students experience the feel of doing science in the same way scientists work. In structuring and carrying out their data gathering, the pupils learn to apply the processes of inquiry. In developing a presentation of the results of their research, the pupils must apply many of the communicating skills that they have been taught in science, mathematics, and language arts.

The Nature of the Science Fair Project

Science fair projects at the elementary level may be classified as being descriptive projects or as research-oriented collections. Descriptive projects are those for which children typically draw sketches or diagrams and build replicas and models. These projects generally require a relatively small investment in time and effort. Though they have some value in teaching and reinforcing science concepts, they often represent only a modest level of pupil motivation. Collections, when properly done, are a step up from descriptive projects in terms of the learning outcomes. Some common collections are leaves, flowers, rocks and minerals, insects, butterflies, and others. For the greatest impact on student learning, collections should be displayed in an orderly manner, such as mounted on boards and labeled with the name of the specimen and some relevant information about it. In addition to the scientific knowledge students acquire from making collections, they also develop some observing and classification skills.

The research-based project, though requiring a great deal more time and energy from teachers and children, yields a great deal more in terms of the development of children's skills,

Sixth-grade science fair projects.

school children is originality or creativity. Young children are not at a stage in their experience with science to create novel topics for investigation. Their energies may be better spent in developing a plan for and carrying on experimentation with common phenomena. They may look for ideas in their own science textbooks, in trade books found in the school library, or in science-related publications, such as those of the National Geographic Society, the Wildlife Federation, or the Time/Life Publishing Company. Developing process skills acquired by carrying on research should take precedence over the requirement of originality.

Getting Started

There are several advantages to prescribing *group* projects for the science fair. A group of three children sharing ideas and tasks provides mutual support and helps maintain a high level of interest in the project. Group projects require fewer materials, less supervision, and less space for display. Fewer projects make judging of the science fair easier. Often the quality of supervised group projects is higher than that of individual projects. Many teachers require each student to maintain individual logs or record books while participating in a group. Maintenance of individual logs requires each student to participate in the group effort and to maintain a high level of interest in the long-term project.

Once a group has chosen a project or topic, the first step in the inquiry process is to formulate a question related to the topic that is worthy of investigation. A group of students interested in plants might ask, "What is the effect of colored light on plant growth?" or "What household materials make fertilizers?" A group interested in electricity might ask, "How can we make an electromagnet stronger or weaker?" or "How can we connect light bulbs to a battery so that the greatest number of bulbs will light?" The students may also formulate hypotheses related to the same problems, such as, "Plants will

attitudes, and knowledge. For this reason we will emphasize the long-term, research-based project in our discussions as the most appropriate for the elementary school pupil.

Finding and Developing Projects

The most difficult step in the science fair project is deciding on a topic and developing procedures for carrying on the investigation. One of the most overrated criteria for selecting and judging science fair projects of elementary

Group projects are an effective means for individualizing instruction.

grow better in red light than in any other color," or "Putting more turns on wire on an electromagnet will make it stronger." A research problem may begin with either a question or a hypothesis.

The second stage of structuring a group science fair project is to formulate a plan for testing one or more variables. The teacher may remind the students that only one experimental variable may be tested at a time by purposefully manipulating a second variable and controlling all other variables so they do not affect the results of the experiment. For the problem with the electromagnets (How can we make an electromagnet stronger or weaker?) the strength of the electromagnet would be the experimental or responding variable and the number of turns of wire around the iron core might be the manipulated variable. The strength of the electromagnet could be defined by the number of paper clips that might be suspended chain fashion from its pole. All other variables, such as the size of the wire, the number of batteries in series, the number of batteries in parallel, the size of the core,

the material of the core, and so forth, would be held constant. Other variables may also be tested in turn as time and materials permit.

After several weeks, as students begin to accumulate data from their research activities, it would be well to provide some instruction for the class in the construction and maintenance of data tables and graphs. A data table usually contains a heading and data that represent the relationship of the manipulated and dependent variables. (See the section "Mathematics—The Tool of Science" in Chapter 7 for examples of a data table and line graph.) For our tests on the strength of an electromagnet, there would be pairs of numbers representing (1) the number of turns and (2) the number of paper clips suspended.

On our graph, the number of turns of wire wrapped around the iron core would be represented on the horizontal axis and labeled Turns of Wire. The number of paper clips suspended from the electromagnet would be represented on the vertical axis and labeled Number of Suspended Paper Clips. A line graph would be constructed using the pairs of related data. Knowing how to construct a data table and line graph will help the pupils in interpreting their data and planning the actual presentation of their project.

Some teachers require their pupils to prepare a report on related background information to accompany their science fair project. Students prepare these reports by searching out and reading material in such resources as encyclopedias and trade books. Background reports are usually brief, often containing only one or two pages of text, but they are thought to help the children to acquire some understanding of the science concepts that are related to their project.

Prizes are sometimes awarded science fair projects more on the basis of elaborate displays or other factors than on the quality of the research. One way to reduce the chances of this occurring is to limit the size of the backdrops and the area that may be permitted on the display tables at fair time. Size restrictions will permit the energy of the participants to be concentrated where it should be—on the research and reporting activity. This will reduce competition to create large and impressive displays.

Judging the Science Fair

Judges for elementary school science fairs may be obtained from among parents, junior and senior high school science teachers, and college professors. For ease of judging, it is best to have the projects arranged in categories according to grade levels and/or areas of science, such as life science, earth science, or physical science. Judges should be provided with forms that spell out the criteria to be used for making judgments about the students' projects. The criteria should reflect the intent or philosophy of the school or those responsible for organizing the science fair. One example of criteria for judging an elementary school science fair is presented in Chart 8–2.

For greater objectivity, several judges should review and assign points to each project,

Chart 8–2 ■ Project Judging Form

Research Techniques	
Design of the research	20
Thoroughness of the research	20
Interpretation of results	20

Quality of Presentation	
Neatness, esthetic appeal	10
Clarity of presentation	20
Originality/creativeness of project	10
	100

and their results should be pooled in some fashion.

Arranging a Science Fair

Below are listed some details and decisions that are necessary to consider when arranging a science fair for a single school:

1. Formulate rules, such as size of the projects, use of animal experiments, use of electrical outlets, the nature of student research logs and background papers, size and nature of groups permitted to work on a project, etc.
2. Set deadlines for finishing the projects.
3. Devise entry forms to accompany each project on display.
4. Devise judging forms.
5. Arrange for judges several months in advance.
6. Arrange for space and tables for the fair. Schedule with the principal and custodian.
7. Publicize the fair to the public and other teachers. Newsletters are normally available in many schools.
8. Optional: Prepare a science fair program, listing all projects and participants.
9. Have pictures taken of the projects. Slides

Chart 8–3 ▪ A Classroom Teacher's Operational Plan for Participation in a School Science Fair

	Week													
	1	2	3	4	5	6	7	8	9	10	11	12	13	14
Draft rules criteria for judging	X													
Introduce science fair project to students		X												
Exploration for project ideas		X	X											
Formulation of hypotheses/ questions/begin planning			X	X										
Outline of plan due				X										
Begin weekly or biweekly check of logs, recordbooks					X									
Data gathering by groups					X	X	X	X	X	X	X	X	X	
Instruction on constructing graphs, data tables, charts, etc.									X	X				
Background reading			X	X	X	X	X	X	X	X	X	X	X	
Finishing and constructing presentation											X	X		
Science fair day													X	
After-the-fair details														X

and picture displays can be a source of ideas for future projects.

10. After the fair: Arrange for students to claim projects. Arrange for tables and other equipment to be returned. Publicize results of the fair judging. Send thank-you notes to judges and other volunteers.

The operational plan shown in Chart 8–3 may help a teacher in planning and assisting students to participate in a school science fair.

To create a Classroom Teacher's Operational Plan for Participation in a School Science Fair, list all the organizational and student activities required to conduct a science fair in the left-hand column and create a weekly time grid as in the chart. For each activity place an X in the week(s) during which the activity is to be conducted. The completed grid provides a quick visual reference for the teacher involved in the ongoing process of carrying out a science fair in her school or classroom.

Some Problems with Science Fairs

Because prizes and ribbons are often awarded, science fair projects may arouse a sense of competition among students and parents. Hurt feelings among students may be avoided by awarding ribbons to many, if not all, projects in a sort of everyone-is-a-winner atmosphere. Through class discussions and reinforcement of the individual student's self-esteem, teachers can do much to reduce the negative aspects of the competitiveness of the science fair. When teachers take time over the course of weeks or months prior to the science fair to hold class discussions and confer with individuals concerning projects, the influence of parents who would be overly ambitious in helping their children is diminished.

Some schools and teachers prefer to hold science days or weeks in which children display collections and projects, speakers are invited to talk on science-related subjects, and the schoolrooms and hallways are decorated with science posters. Events such as a science day reduce feelings of competition and yet are strongly motivational to many students.

Field Trips

When they are well planned and thoughtfully conducted, field trips may be very valuable experiences for children. The simplest field trip to arrange is one conducted on the school campus. Students may explore the heating and air conditioning plants, look for ways to conserve energy, or examine the building for health and safety problems. Outside on the school grounds, students may collect leaf and seed specimens, look for signs of animal life or soil erosion, observe the sky and clouds, explore shadows and sounds, and more. As in any other lesson, on-campus field trips should be well planned to maximize student learning. Teachers should set predetermined goals and objectives and make them known to the children. With so many

things to do and see, children may easily be distracted; it is helpful if they have an exploration guide who provides them with specific things to look for and questions to answer. Much teaching and learning may take place during the trip as teachers gather students into groups to discuss observations. A post–field trip discussion often creates further understanding for the children.

Off-Campus Field Trips

Trips to off-campus sites such as a zoo, museum, stream, lake or pond, natural habitat, dairy, water treatment plant, fire station, or other science-related location require greater planning and management than do on-campus field trips. Transportation, lunches and snacks, chaperones, money to cover the costs of the trip, communication with parents, coordination with the principal and other teachers, pretrip and posttrip learning activities are some of the details that must be planned. When more than one class is involved, the requirements for coordination are increased. Although preparing for a half- or full-day field trip off campus can be demanding and time-consuming, the experiences can be very rewarding for students and teachers alike. Trips that prove to be most effective can be taken year after year. Familiarity and a good filing system make the task of planning for such trips easier the second and third years.

Selecting Field Trips

Field trips should contribute to the ongoing school curriculum. They are much less effective when they bear no relation to students' studies. Field trip sites should be safe for students and adults. Each destination should be of interest to the children and appropriate to their age levels. Where there is machinery, animals, or any other potential dangers, precautions should be taken to ensure the safety of all concerned. Many schools and/or school systems have identified approved sites to visit. Check the school administration to see if your school participates in this kind of field trip approvals.

Planning the Educational Experience

Learning experiences prior to a field trip make students' on-site experiences much more valuable. Prior to a trip to the zoo, for instance, a class should learn about the animals they will see. Before taking a trip to collect seeds and leaves from a woods environment, children should learn something about seeds and leaves so they may readily locate them and appreciate their function and structure. Many teachers prefer to supply students with an observation/question worksheet, which they fill in while on a field trip. This gives structure and meaning to the experience. On a long bus ride to and from a field trip site children may work on learning activities that are appropriate for the trip. Crossword puzzles, games, and connect-the-dots activities are examples of such tasks. The day after a field trip also provides an important opportunity for students to organize and reorganize information and concepts. This can be done through class discussion, working with collected materials, writing, and drawing pictures about their experiences.

Some Thoughts on Planning and Taking Field Trips

Even where school policy does not require it, transportation to and from field trip sites should be by bus, not by private cars. Buses are safer and eliminate the chance for drivers of private vehicles to get lost.

Chaperones, who may be teachers, aides, parents, or volunteers, should be provided in a ratio of one chaperone for every ten children at an inside or closed site. The ratio should be one chaperone to every five children when visiting zoos, parks, and other open-space sites. Each adult should be assigned to be responsible for specific children. Having color-coded name tags for each group makes identification much easier. Some schools have distinguishable t-shirts, which are worn on off-campus field trips.

Many schools have policies that assure all children access to field trips regardless of their ability to pay for the costs. You may want to establish student fees that are 25 percent higher than cost to cover those students who cannot pay. Some parents will willingly contribute for additional children if given the opportunity.

Clear communication with parents is vital. Inform them of departure and return times and locations and provide a local telephone number of a teacher, principal, or parent who will act as a communication center should the return of the group be delayed. Other details to include in a letter are costs, a permission form requiring a parent signature, and possibly a student pledge of conduct. Please see Figure 8–5 for a sample letter to parents informing them of a field trip, and Figure 8–6 for a sample of a final letter to parents.

Teaching Science to Exceptional Children

Today federal law mandates that all handicapped children be taught in "the least restrictive environment." Children classified as educationally mentally handicapped (EMH), as emotionally handicapped (EH), as having specific learning disabilities (SLD), and as having sight and hearing impairments may be spending at least part of the school day in the normal classroom. The classroom teacher in most cases is responsible for designing and carrying out an individual educational plan (IEP) for each handicapped child in her class. Because of its freedom from reading requirements, manipulative science programs can play an important role in providing meaningful learning experiences for such children. A great deal can be done to adapt current laboratory science programs to meet the needs of those children who can be mainstreamed, i.e., who are able to spend at least a portion of the school day in a regular classroom.

Dear Parents:

We have reserved a chartered bus for a trip to Gatorland on
_____. The total cost per passenger will be $8.00. This
includes transportation to and from school, the tickets for admission,
and lunch. Please understand that if your child for some reason cannot
go, money cannot be refunded.

If you prefer paying by check, please make it payable to
_____ Elementary School. A receipt will be sent home with
your child. Because some of our students cannot afford to make this
trip, we would appreciate receiving any donation you care to make to
fund these students.

No child may go without the signed permission slip. Please send the
permission slip and the money at the same time. The DEADLINE FOR
SENDING THE PERMISSION SLIP AND MONEY IS (usually 1 week prior to the
trip). We must have ample time to prepare for the trip, and to reserve
our time. If you have any questions, please call your child's teacher.
This trip will be completed within the school day; you need not make
special arrangements to pick up your child.

Sincerely,

SECOND GRADE TEACHERS

We (I) give permission for ____(student name)____ to go with his/her
class to Gatorland on _____. I understand that if the student
has paid for the trip and cannot go, the money will not be refunded.
IF A SITUATION WARRANTS, I ALSO GIVE MY PERMISSION FOR ANY MEDICAL
TREATMENT FOR MY CHILD.

_____
Signature of parent/guardian

Figure 8–5 ■ Sample Field Trip Letter to Parents

Dear Parents:

This is the final letter of information regarding our field trip to Gatorland.

1. Be sure your child is at school on time. We plan to depart about 9:00 A.M. and return before dismissal time.

2. NO MONEY is to be taken on this trip. There will not be an occasion to purchase anything. TEACHERS WILL NOT BE RESPONSIBLE FOR MONEY LOST OR STOLEN.

3. CLOTHING
   A. The weather will probably be quite warm, so please dress children accordingly. A ____(school)____ T-shirt would be most appropriate attire, as it will be extremely helpful in keeping our group together. Jeans and casual shoes (tennis shoes—not sandals) will allow students to participate fully in the learning activities.
   B. Please check your child's attire to see that it conforms to the standards appropriate for students of _____ Elementary School.

4. It is most important that your child gets to bed early the night before the trip. See that he/she gets up early enough to have time for a good breakfast. PLEASE DO NOT SEND YOUR CHILD IF HE/SHE FEELS ILL IN ANY WAY.

5. We would greatly appreciate your having a serious talk with your child pointing out how important it is for him/her to follow these rules:
   A. Stay with the adult who has been assigned to his/her group.
   B. Listen to the guide as he/she lectures or points out things of interest.
   C. Do not touch anything that is designated as "hands off."
   D. Do not run, lag behind, wander away, go to the restroom, or get water.
   E. Obey, at all times, not only the teachers, but any adult in charge.
   F. Come immediately when the whistle is blown or when an adult in charge calls. Having to wait each time for just a few may cause us all to miss seeing many things.
   G. If there is an emergency and the child must suddenly leave the group, he/she is to notify someone in the group to go directly to the teacher to report this.

____(school)____ Elementary students have a history of good conduct. We feel this is largely due to the cooperation and preparation of parents and teachers. We are counting on you to help this to be a successful, happy learning event.

Sincerely,

SECOND GRADE TEACHERS

Figure 8–6 ■ Final Letter Regarding Field Trip

Specific Learning-Disabled and Educationally Mentally Handicapped Children and Science

Numerous studies have been conducted indicating that EMH and SLD children can benefit from manipulative science. (A bibliography of curriculum and research writings related to educating handicapped children is updated annually by NSTA, Washington, DC 20009.) Materials can be adapted and activities structured so that these children can work with materials independently or in small groups and benefit from the interaction. In various studies it has been found that handicapped children involved with manipulative science activities develop Piagetian conservations, learn science concepts, and improve in general achievement.

At Ball State University, many of the units of the Elementary Science Study program have been successfully tried in classrooms with various categories of exceptional children. A teacher's guide is available that provides research information, summaries of research experiences with exceptional children from kindergarten through high school, and some suggestions for instituting each of the units. The teacher's guide divides the ESS units into three groups. The perceptual group includes such activities as Tangrams and Attribute Games. These activities appear to be best suited to develop students' perceptual and thinking skills. The psychomotor group includes such units as Batteries and Bulbs, Sink or Float, and Clay Boats and requires a great deal of student manipulation. A third general category exists for those units that do not fit into the perceptual and psychomotor categories. Research indicates that the units in the psychomotor group appear to be better suited for young (kindergarten through grade 5) learners while the perceptual group produces desirable benefits for the junior and senior high school students.

Manipulative science materials have also been successfully employed to teach reading and language arts to EMH students in the middle and junior high schools. Following many years of failure in traditional reading programs, most upper elementary and junior high school students have developed a great deal of anxiety that appears to block learning in reading activities structured in the usual mode. Science activities can provide an alternative that may reduce the reading-connected anxieties of the ten- to sixteen-year-old students and permit them to make gains in acquiring reading and problem-solving skills.

In one instance, a "mystery powders" activity from Science—A Process Approach was used by Jeanice Midgett of the University of Central Florida to promote reading and problem-solving skills among children in an EMH classroom. In this activity students added water, vinegar, and iodine solution to baking soda, baking powder, cornstarch, and talc. Small groups of students experimented with the simple manipulative science materials. During the activity, vocabulary words were introduced and discussed with the group members. The students found that remembering science terminology, locating materials, and following directions were requirements for participating in the experiment. Initially, the instructors perceived this as a potential anxiety-producing requirement. Surprisingly, however, these requirements provided positive affective responses due to the high interest level of the students.

After the completion of the science activities and a whole-class discussion, the language experience approach was used as a component of a remedial reading strategy. A summary of the activity and of the results was organized and dictated sometimes to one student who wrote on the board while the others copied the material on paper, and at other times into a cassette to be typed later on a ditto for duplication and distribution.

The written record of the science activity was used the following day to check the students' retention of the content and their skill in outlining the sequence of events and locating information. Time and words read correctly were charted on individual record forms. The improvement in reading and the attending skills was noticeable and encouraging.

Using science activities as an alternative reading program appears to have two major benefits: the science activities give the students a genuine purpose for reading, and the activities provide highly motivating experiences suitable for introducing reading activities. Such procedures also produce other benefits: group problem solving, social skills, and the skills of observing, recording, and communicating data.

Many teachers have found some guidelines to be of help in directing the science activities of SLD and EMH children. For example:

1. Exceptional children require more structure than regular children. For instance, open-ended directions, such as "See all you can find out about how different liquids form drops," are troublesome to these children. Such directions should be replaced by specific directions, such as: "Use the dropper to put one drop of water on a piece of waxed paper. Now put a drop of glycerine beside it. Which drop is flatter? Which drop is wider?"

2. Work periods for exceptional children should be short and confined to a single task. Relationships among separate operations are not always easily seen and too many different tasks may cause confusion.

3. EMH and SLD children may require direct instruction by the teacher at the conclusion of a lesson to imprint the meaning of what they have learned in their minds. Since retention among these children is a problem, a review of the major vocabulary and concepts learned from a lesson should be repeated and reviewed the following day.

With proper structure a class of EMH and SLD students can benefit greatly from manipulative science activities, and one or two of these exceptional children in a classroom can function along with the regular students if the teacher watches over their interaction with their classmates and intercedes occasionally to explain and direct them.

Sight- and Hearing-Impaired Children and Science

Normal children learn about their environments from all of their senses. Children with sight or hearing impairments suffer from a deficit of stimulation and learning from these two very important senses. Those children who have lived with their handicap from birth or for any appreciable period of time prior to starting to school have had far fewer experiences on which to base their learning than normal children. And without attention to the continued sensory deprivation fostered by their handicap, the gap between the handicapped and normal students will increase each year. To help children with sight and hearing impairments to grow and learn at an optimum rate it is necessary to increase the stimulation to the senses that are operational.

For children with sight problems, it is necessary to provide a maximum amount of tactile, hearing, smelling, and tasting activities to compensate for the loss of sight. For instance, a sight-impaired child can learn about the metric system by feeling a meter stick and comparing other objects in the environment with the length of the stick. Though such children cannot read from the meter stick, they can develop the concept of that unit of measure. The decimeter and centimeter may be taught in the same manner. The concepts of *heavy* and *light* may be taught by feeling, lifting, and comparing items. Other materials may be classified by smell and texture. Even the position of the sun at various times of the day may be recognized by sightless children when they feel its warm rays on their bodies. As they learn more about their environment through their operating senses and the information provided by the teacher, their confidence and feelings of safety increase.

Children with hearing impairments obtain most of the information about their environment through their eyes. This important sense is reinforced with the stimuli of other operating senses. The major task of teachers who have children with hearing impairments in their classrooms is to provide them with directions and information concerning ongoing science activities. The major means of communicating with hearing-impaired children is through hand language and through written materials. Severely sight-impaired children are taught to read braille. Children with hearing problems gather a great deal of information from seeing the facial expressions and reading the lips of a speaker. Place children with hearing problems in seats where they are able to see your face as you give directions and provide information. Children with sight and hearing impairments are especially dependent upon experiences with the materials of their environment to help them develop their ability to function at a level close to their potential.

The SAVI/SELPH Science Program

The SAVI/SELPH program was initially developed by the Lawrence Hall of Science in Berkeley, California, as a program for sight-impaired children in grades 2 through 10, but it was found to be effective with children who possessed other disabilities as well, including the physically handicapped (orthopedically handicapped), hearing impaired, and children with learning disabilities. The program consists of nine modules of enrichment activities suitable for use in special education classrooms and in mainstream classrooms that contain handicapped students. The address of the Lawrence Hall of Science is University of California, Berkeley, CA 94720.

The Emotionally Handicapped Student

Emotionally handicapped students (EH students) operate best in a class where the rules are clearly defined and the environment is highly structured. Try to generously reward EH children for all appropriate behaviors with verbal praise, stars, candy, or other signs of approval. It is best to try to ignore inappropriate behaviors of these children as much as possible. Be controlled and consistent in your reactions to students; do not challenge or berate them. The best way to help EH students in your classroom is to be sensitive to their behaviors and intervene to redirect them before conflict arises.

Gifted Children and Science

Giftedness is an exceptionality among children that many educators feel has been too long neglected. One of the problems that may have caused uncertainty in dealing with this type of student is identification—who is a gifted student; how can we recognize her? The U.S. Office of Education defines giftedness as the following: "Gifted and talented children are those . . . who by virtue of outstanding abilities are capable of high performance. These children . . . require differentiated educational experiences, programs and/or services beyond those normally provided by the regular school program in order to realize their potential contribution to self and society." Another definition is that giftedness is the result of the interaction of three traits—above-average ability, task commitment, and creativity. Gifted and talented children are those who possess or are capable of developing this composite set of traits.

Currently, federal guidelines provide for identification in only one of the three categories listed here, that of above average ability as defined by individual intelligence tests. Many children in programs for the gifted may be presumed to possess the other two unmeasured traits as well. However, high intelligence is no guarantee of a child's commitment to learning or an indicator of creative ability. Therefore, in addition to providing appropriate learning programs for truly gifted children, teachers are faced with the challenge of developing positive motivation and fostering creativity among some of them.

The following learning environments have

been successfully employed in creating programs for the gifted.

Open-Ended Experimentation

Manipulative materials in the hands of a gifted student often result in extensive learning and skill development. This is especially true where meaningful problems are defined and the child sets out on his own to find solutions or form opinions. It must not be assumed that students, no matter how gifted, will automatically know and use good scientific processes in carrying out experiments. It may be necessary to point out that measurements must be carefully made and manipulations meticulously controlled. Reading technical and semitechnical literature, trade books, textbooks, and journals may provide depth to what gifted children learn from experimental studies.

Open-Ended Problem Solving

The solutions to some problems often give way to data collected in library research and surveys. These problems, often socially oriented, provide the opportunity for gifted children to investigate real life problems and to interact with the community outside the school setting. For instance, problems involving the location of nuclear power plants might lead a group of gifted children to acquire a great deal of information on nuclear power generation and to make a survey of student and/or adult opinion on the subject.

Nature Camps

Nature study at outdoor camps provides valuable experiences for all children, but by virtue of their superior ability, gifted children may gain a great deal from such activities. Specially designed programs with much detailed information and demanding investigations are possible with gifted children and interaction over long periods of time with other gifted children can have a positive effect in arousing a child's curiosity and creating an exciting learning atmosphere.

Community Internships

In a few instances elementary school children have been permitted to spend a day, or several days, in a research facility or a high-technology manufacturing plant. Their experiences with adult scientists and technicians serve to motivate gifted children toward careers in science and in return have given the adult community a new awareness of the high ability of some of the children in our schools. Tours and interning experiences in the community are valuable resources when developing a program for gifted students. When children cannot visit in the community, invite adult experts into the school as resource speakers and consultants to the class's ongoing research projects.

Multicultural Science Instruction

In many parts of the country, children in our schools are undergoing a multicultural experience the level of which has not been seen since the wave of immigration that took place at the beginning of the twentieth century. In the past two decades there has been a major influx of people from the Far East and from Caribbean and Central American nations. These new citizens have often been the victims of wars and economic deprivation and view the United States as a place that will provide a better life for themselves and their families. They come to our shores with their own languages and cultures as did the European immigrants ninety years ago. The schools are again playing a major role in integrating the children of these new citizens into our society.

Teachers must help the children to overcome language difficulties and the effects of dramatic changes in culture and to adjust to their multicultural environment. They may do this by promoting concepts of the worth of each individual and the acceptance of the culture that each represents. (Just as importantly, they must attempt to cultivate the same values in the American children in their classroom. Children from diverse cultures must learn of their own responsibility for maintaining their native culture in the context of the national culture of their adopted land. The goal of integration of children from multicultural backgrounds into their new surroundings may be implemented in a number of ways in the general curriculum and during science instruction. For example:

Bulletin Boards	Pictorial displays must include pictures that portray diversity.
Seating Arrangements	Students should have the freedom to sit where they would like, but caution must be taken to avoid racist and sexist seating patterns.
Audiovisual Aids	Books, films, filmstrips, slides, charts, and all other forms of audiovisual aids must be multicultural.
Resource People	Deliberate attempts must be made to ensure the inclusion of minorities and women as resource people in nontraditional roles.
Field Trips	Field trips should be planned so as to expose students to forms of diversity that they might not otherwise have the opportunity to experience.
Holidays	No student should be discriminated against for observing religious holidays and/or for not participating in those observed by the school.

Science Activities

1. Have the children bring in pictures of animals cut from magazines, arrange the pictures in groups, and discuss the similarities and differences among the animals. Use the pictures of wild animals to discuss the relationships of the environments in which the animals live and their characteristics, showing that form and function are related. Follow up this activity by having the children bring to class pictures of people from various cultures. Discuss how the dress and physical characteristics of these people are related to the environments of their native countries. Try to show how each people developed their unique culture.

2. Diversity among living things may also be demonstrated by examining the structures of various plants. Discuss how the plants are at the same time both different and alike. Pond water animals may also be observed and described as to their general appearance and function (movement, eating habits, excretory habits, and so on) and the observational data used to demonstrate similarities and differences among living things.

In each of these activities the teacher, in order to help children develop healthy attitudes about themselves and those from other cultures, should stress the values of being unique and cooperating with others who are different.

Summary

Science in the elementary school may be organized for individualized instruction using the systems approach, the open classroom approach, enrichment learning centers, or inquiry centers.

The systems approach to science instruction is highly structured, utilizing specific learning objectives, self-directing, self-checking learning activities, and an individual student progress checklist. Children working in a systems approach program may work individually or as a member of a group.

The open classroom approach is most commonly employed in the lower primary grades. In the open classroom, children may work in groups or as individuals exploring and investigating those materials that interest them at a center. With this format there are no specific learning objectives and no formal evaluation techniques.

Enrichment learning centers are primarily motivational and informational in nature. These centers may contain trade books, magazines, and other media in addition to objects to be viewed and/or manipulated.

Inquiry centers are designed to utilize the inquiry mode in an independent learning situation. In an inquiry center a child or group of children perform operations with materials and generalize upon their experience. Thus, they develop skills of problem solving along with appropriate science concepts.

Computers are rapidly invading elementary school classrooms as a tool for individualizing instruction in science and other subjects. To use computers as a tool for teaching science a teacher needs to be aware of the types of software available and how to select among the various programs offered.

The use of video discs is a new technology that is just beginning to find use in the elementary schools. Video discs provide the possibility of "freezing" images to display still pictures as well as utilizing the live-action effect of video. When coupled with computers, video discs have enhanced capabilities for producing imagery and educational experiences. The latter use of the video disc appears to be somewhere in the future for elementary schools.

Many children with exceptionalities are now found in normal classrooms. Learning-disabled and mentally retarded children can benefit from appropriately structured science activities that stress involvement with manipulative materials. Hearing-impaired and sight-impaired children should be exposed to science materials that utilize those senses that are operational. Gifted children require special programs that may include experimentation with materials, exploring problems through research

and survey, nature study, and involvement with scientists and technicians in the community.

A new wave of immigration has once again made our schools places of great cultural variety. Teachers are faced with the responsibility for helping children from diverse cultures fit into their classes and for teaching the children in their classes to accept the differences they observe in other children. Often the classroom teacher must help children of immigrant parents to overcome language barriers. One way teachers can provide for cultural differences is to make sure all materials and media used in the classroom represent a variety of cultures. Teachers may also use community resource volunteers, bulletin boards, and the holidays of other nations and cultures to provide the children with a broad international viewpoint. Science activities may be useful in demonstrating the similarities and differences among the plants and animals that live on the earth and that differences in physical attributes and customs are to be accepted as natural events.

When carefully selected and organized, field trips have great potential for enriching elementary school students' learning experiences. There are two distinct categories of field trips, those that take place on the school grounds and those that are off campus. For both categories, student learning will be enhanced when plans are made to provide appropriate pre-trip, in-trip, and post-trip activities. Off-campus field trips create added responsibilities for teachers in that they must provide for the safety of the children and adults present, arrange for transportation, communicate to parents about the trip, and handle the financial arrangements required. Both on-campus and off-campus field trips require that a sufficient number of adults are present to chaperone the students—at least one adult for each ten children in an inside, controlled environment and at least one adult for each five students in an outdoor environment. Field trips should be selected to support the ongoing curriculum; taking field trips as an isolated event should be avoided. Many school systems have a list of approved field trips, and teachers should be cautioned to secure permission from the school administration for all field trips as the first step in the planning process.

Extending Activities

1. Construct an inquiry center according to the directions in the text. You may select a lesson plan from Section Two and use the activities from the plan to build your center. This may be done as a small-group project.

2. Visit a computer supply store. Ask to see a demonstration of any computers that are appropriate for use in the elementary school classroom. Ask for a catalog of available software that is suitable for elementary school science instruction. Collect any advertising literature that is available. If there is no store located in your area, obtain the address of computer suppliers from your local library and write seeking information on their products.

3. Choose a problem-centered science fair project and organize a class science fair. Have the fair judged and award ribbons or prizes.

4. Select an activity from anyplace in this textbook or elsewhere and make a shoebox kit. Place all the materials and an activity card in the box with an index containing a list of materials taped to the outside of the box.

Bibliography

Abruscarg, J. *Children, Computers, and Science Teaching.* Englewood Cliffs, N.J.: Prentice-Hall, 1986.

Artwood, K., and B. Didham. "Teacher Perceptions of Mainstreaming in an Inquiry Oriented Elementary Science Program." *Science Education* 69, no. 5 (October 1985): 619–624.

Ball, D. W. *ESS Special Education Teacher's Guide.* New York: Webster Division, McGraw-Hill, 1978.

Blume, S. "Science Investigations." *Science and Children* 23, no. 2 (October 1985): 19.

Cartwright, W. *Educating Exceptional Learners.* Belmont, Calif.: Wadsworth, 1981.

Coble, C., and G. McCall. "Centering on Fossils and Dinosaurs." *Science and Children* 24, no. 2 (October 1986): 28–30.

Esler, W. "Fun and Gains with Science." *School Science and Mathematics* 79, no. 8 (1979): 637–640.

Fuller, K. "Beyond Drill and Practice: Using Computers to Teach Classification." *Science and Children* 23, no. 6 (March 1986): 20–22; no. 8 (May 1986): 16–19.

Kartoaka, J., and J. Patton. "Teaching Exceptional Learners: An Integrated Approach." *Science and Children* 27, no. 1 (September 1989): 48–51.

Litchfield, B. "Slipping a Disk in the Classroom: the Latest in Video Technology." *Science and Children* 28, no. 1 (September 1990): 16–21.

McNay, M. "The Need to Explore, Nonexperimental Science Fair Projects." *Science and Children* 23, no. 2 (October 1985): 17–18.

Mokros, J., and R. Tinker. "The Impact of Microcomputer-Based Lab on Children's Ability to Interpret Graphs." *Journal of Research in Science Teaching* 24, no. 4 (April 1987): 369–384.

Pinchas, J. "Current Potential Uses of Micro Computers in Science Education." *Computers in Mathematics and Science Teaching* 5 (1985–86): 18–28.

Renzulli, J. S. "What Makes Giftedness: A Reexamination of the Definition." *Science and Children* 16, no. 6 (March 1979): 14–15.

Reynolds, K. "How to Use the Software Evaluation Form." *Science and Children* 23, no. 1 (September 1985): 19, 20.

Reynolds, K., E. Walton, and T. Logue. "Software Evaluation Form." *Science and Children* 23, no. 1 (September 1985): 18.

Science and Children. "Software Review." (A regular department feature of each issue of *Science and Children,* from 1987 on.)

VanDeman, B., and P. Parfitt. "The Nuts and Bolts of Science Fairs." *Science and Children* 23, no. 2 (October 1985): 14.

Teaching Children to Solve Problems of Science, Technology, and Society

Look What's in This Chapter

In this chapter we'll discuss important information to assist you in teaching children to solve problems outside of the discipline of science that are of a more personal or societal nature. Many problems that are appropriate for all levels of the elementary school will be covered, as well as the skills, attitudes, and values that children develop through experience with general problem-solving activities. We'll discuss how to incorporate general problem solving into a science curriculum. Two decision-making procedures described in the chapter will help you to guide children in this difficult task. A detailed example on the topic of "Global Warming" will help illustrate the procedures for engaging children in a lengthy, comprehensive problem-solving project.

Fourth-grade students gather data for problem-solving.

Science, Technology, and the Human Experience

Scientific knowledge, in all its applications, permits humans to control the environment in which they exist. They can stay warm when the climate is cold and stay cool when the climate is warm. They can produce food by cultivating crops and raising livestock and deliver it to population centers by train and truck. In the developed regions of the world, inhabitants are protected from disease through medical inoculations and treatment. They travel great distances by automobile, train, and airplane. They wear clothing made from synthetics and processed natural fibers and build tremendous structures in which they live and on which they drive their many vehicles. But science has another effect on our environment, too. Every day, each inhabitant of the developed countries, in living his or her normal life, causes damage to the environment in which he or she lives. Each of us, by turning on the electric light in the morning, eating a bowl of cereal and milk, spraying deodorant on our bodies, riding the

bus to work, buying a nylon blouse, or viewing television programs in the evening, is causing changes in the closed system we call planet Earth. With the rapidly increasing population of our planet, many concerns have become real problems and, some believe, major crises. A growing number of science educators believe we should recognize and have our students study problems related to the interface of science, technology, and human existence as early as in the elementary school grades. The problems appropriate for study in these grades are of two kinds, those occurring in the school and community, and those of more universal concern. Let's look at the first kind, next.

Problems Appropriate for Study in the Elementary School

General problem solving for grades K–3 is usually limited to simple problems that exist in the children's immediate environment. An example is: "The classroom is too messy. What can we do to change this?" Sometimes teachers enlist the aid of students to help a classmate do a better job of following the rules: "How can we help Robert to stay in his seat or control his talking?" A teacher may also ask, "How can we find out which animal is the most popular pet in our class?" or "I wonder what the favorite television program of our class is. How can we find out?" A very common problem-solving experience for primary-grade children begins with the teacher asking, "What are some rules we should follow as we work in our science groups?" or "Where can we find some information on caring for gerbils?" General problem solving occurs in the primary grades any time the teacher solicits from students suggestions for making a change or collecting some information.

Most of the suggestions presented above for introducing general problem-solving activities at the K–3 levels also would be appropriate to use at the intermediate grade levels. However, the problems generally would be expanded to include more than the students' own class. The teacher might challenge her class, "So we agree the cafeteria is too messy and noisy. What can we do to change this?" The class might formulate a plan and submit it to the principal for consideration. Intermediate-grade children may attempt to find a solution to many problems that involve collecting data through opinion polls, such as, "What do the students at Liberty School think about the use of drugs in our school?" or "Which candidate will win the presidential election?" Intermediate-grade students can also investigate problems of pollution at a local park or pond or stream.

The Relationship Between General Problem-Solving Skills and the Science Processes

Scientific inquiry, as it has been discussed in the earlier chapters of this textbook, is a form of problem solving that has as its educational goals the development of all process skills and the acquisition of scientific knowledge and conceptual understanding of the natural world. The process

skills such as observing, classifying, inferring, formulating hypotheses, designing and carrying out experiments, and interpreting data provide a firm foundation for young learners to begin to acquire the skills and attitudes of general problem solving.

The goals for general problem-solving learning activities in the elementary school are the acquisition of general problem-solving skills (sometimes called critical thinking skills) and a positive attitude. Armed with these, individuals are prepared to confront in a rational way problems and decisions that everyone living in our modern-day society must face. Science educators strive, through the development of general problem-solving skills, to prepare young learners to deal rationally with real-life issues that are somehow related to the field of science and technology. The skills developed by children in their science classes that enable them to form opinions and make rational decisions about personal and societal issues will carry over to other areas of their lives.

In using the science processes, we teach children to search for the solution, concept, or generalization that explains a phenomenon of the natural world. In using the general problem-solving skills, we attempt to help children to approach all problems, personal and societal, in a rational way and to form a "best solution" or "best course of action" for a problem. To pursue solutions for problems of a general nature, students must add additional intellectual and academic skills to the science process skills. Children must practice solving life problems to acquire proficiency just as they must practice the process skills to achieve proficiency. Let us take a look at the specific skills involved in general problem solving.

Categorizing General Problem-Solving Skills

As we stated, general problem-solving skills overlap with science process skills in terms of their basic form. General problem-solving skills

Chart 9–1 ■ General Problem-Solving Skills

Fluency of Ideas: This is the ability to think of many ideas concerning a given situation, for example, some uses for a wire coat hanger, brick, or other common object, a variety of solutions for a problem, and so on.

Flexibility of Thought: This is the ability to originate various possibilities or solutions for a situation and adjust ideas as new information is presented.

Literary Research Skills: These are the skills required to locate, synthesize, and organize information in print media. These include the use of the library card catalog, note taking, summarizing information, and so on.

Discriminating Between Relevant and Irrelevant Information: This is the ability to recognize information as essential or helpful for solving a problem, for example, whether the size of an animal close to extinction is a factor in determining its importance to the ecosystem.

Recognizing Fact and Opinion: This is when a person utilizes only that information determined to be factual in nature, checks authenticity of facts, and discards information not verified.

Recognizing Cause and Effect Relationships: This is the ability to relate events with the cause(s) of the events, for example, gravity causes objects to fall to earth, and fertilizer runoff from farmland and homes increases plant growth in lakes.

Defining a Problem: This refers to setting parameters on a problem by using very specific language to describe that problem, for example, "water runoff from a city landfill is polluting a stream called Clear Creek."

Constructing Problem Questions: This means writing questions that provide a clear focus for pursuing an investigation, for example, "Is drainage from the city landfill causing pollution of Clear Creek?"

Defining Sources of Information for Solving a Problem: This means finding out where the most helpful information can be obtained, for example, from county topographic maps and by testing water draining from the landfill into Clear Creek and water taken from Clear Creek.

Collecting Data: This refers to performing assigned data collection activities, for example, testing water samples and writing an analysis; obtaining and analyzing topographic maps to determine the direction of water drainage and writing a report; taking and having developed pictures of the landfill drainage area and pollution in Clear Creek; collecting information from the city library regarding the history of the problem.

Interpreting Data: In our example, this means answering the question "Is drainage from the city landfill polluting Clear Creek?" (A procedure for analyzing data and arriving at a "best" answer—the "force field" procedure—will be introduced later in this chapter.)

Proposing Solutions: An example of a proposed solution is: The city may close the landfill or build holding ponds between the landfill and Clear Creek that cause the drainage water to percolate through the earth before entering the creek. Students should consider the benefits, cost, and risks of each of their solutions.

---

also overlap with other areas of the curriculum, such as language arts and social studies. You may recognize some of them from the discussion that follows. (See Chart 9–1 for a summary of general problem-solving skills.)

The general problem-solving skills listed in Chart 9–1 represent those that are most commonly associated with problem solving in the elementary school. The first two skills, fluency of ideas and flexibility of thought, are skills that are intellectually basic to many types of problem-solving situations and creative activities. They may be developed apart from any formal problem-solving procedures by having children, individually or in groups, orally or in writing, list uses for common objects or ways to empty water from a barrel, move a heavy box from the floor to the table, or order four colored cubes. You may also have children state possible solutions for a hypothetical problem or dilemma such as finding a book on the stars or selecting the one toy they would have if they could have just one. The total *number* of responses generated by the students represents their fluency of thought, and the number of *quality* responses represents the flexibility of thought. The teacher will judge which of the responses are original and of unusual quality for her or his group of students.

The last ten general problem-solving skills listed in Chart 9–1 are related to procedures for solving problems in a structured way. You will see later in the chapter that the degree to which each of these ten problem-solving skills is uti-

Children engaged in group problem-solving develop desirable skills and attitudes.

lized will vary with the nature of the problem to be solved and the learning objectives of the lesson. For instance, not nearly as much time would be spent on each general problem-solving skill by a first-grade class determining the favorite pet of the children in the class as by a sixth-grade class investigating the issue associated with the city's closing of a children's playground.

Helping Children Develop the Attitudes of the Rational Problem Solver

Teachers help children to develop the proper attitudes of the rational problem solver by their own behaviors as well as through their instruction. Children can best acquire a rational spirit through observing these behaviors in teachers and other adults and through teachers' efforts to explain these attitudes and point out instances when the children are violating them.

Some commonly accepted attitudes of rational problem solving follow. The rational problem solver

maintains his or her objectivity, is free from preconceptions.

considers all points of view, is open minded.

considers all possible solutions to a problem.

maintains a rational spirit free from prejudice, searches for solutions based on facts.

Children should strive to maintain these attitudes in all facets of their school experiences.

The skills and attitudes of general problem solving are by definition appropriate for seeking solutions and making decisions in all facets of a person's life. In science and technology their application is particularly useful, because the interface of science and technology with our society is fast becoming of paramount importance to the survival of the human race.

Learning activities for developing general problem-solving skills need not be comprehensive in nature. As was true with teaching science process skills, lessons may be problems arising from "targets of opportunity," which are those planned or unplanned instances when problems to be solved appear in the ongoing curriculum. Targets of opportunity arise each day in the normal course of delivering instruction to children.

There are, of course, some specialized, general problem-solving kits and programs on the market today. In some instances, teachers take time out of the school day to do the exercises provided by these materials, and the activities have no relationship to the ongoing curriculum. They are taught completely out of context. This type of problem-solving program, once popular, is now found less frequently in the classroom, because, as we stated earlier, research indicates there is little transfer of skills and knowledge from these specialized program activities to the lives of the students. One fact is abundantly clear in the teaching of problem-solving skills: problem-solving skills are best taught in conjunction with the ongoing curriculum. For this reason, the notion of taking advantage of targets of opportunity is important.

Classroom gardens help children understand problems of food production.

Universal Problems of Science, Technology, and Society

The problems generated by the application of science and technology in our society are numerous and may be found at all educational levels. We will divide these problems into four categories: (1) problems related to the human condition, (2) problems related to improving the earth's environment, (3) protecting wildlife and wildlife habitat, and (4) setting limits on the applications of technology.

Problems Related to Improving the Human Condition
world hunger, overpopulation, widespread disease, lack of housing, and others

Problems Related to Improving the Earth's Environment
atmospheric pollution, including the related topics of smokestack emissions, tailpipe emissions from vehicles, acid rain; protecting the ozone layer; solid and human waste disposal; water pollution, including concerns for ground water, rivers, streams, and lakes; toxic waste disposal; ocean pollution from human and industrial wastes; oil spills; dangers of nuclear power plants and resulting radioactive waste; ocean freighter dumping; global warming; saving the tropical rain forests; and others

Protecting Wildlife and Wildlife Habitat
saving endangered species such as whales, elephants, rhinoceros, and the spotted owl; protecting habitats from industrial, housing, and agricultural development; saving the tropical rain forests; and others

Setting Limits on the Applications of Technology
test-tube babies, surrogate motherhood, genetic intervention in human reproduction, transplants of vital organs in humans, the right to die with dignity, and others

Global or large-scale environmental problems such as global warming, the loss of the ozone layer, and saving whales from extinction are fairly abstract concepts for young learners, because solutions to such problems appear to be far beyond students' power to make an impact. School- or community-based problems are likely to have more relevance to students' lives and offer more opportunities for making decisions and forming solutions.

Examining Values in Science-related Societal Issues

All problems that relate to the interface of humans with science and technology introduce issues of human values. Whether the issue is controlling world population, reducing the impact of urban development on the environment, protecting an endangered species of animal or plant, or setting limits on economic support for organ transplants in humans, there are always fundamental issues of human values involved in the decision-making process. What is our society's obligation to feed starving children in Ethiopia? Should a greater effort have been made to save the dusky sparrow from extinction? Should families in China be limited to one child per couple in order to control the fast-growing population? Should German manufacturers bear the cost of installing pollution-control equipment to reduce acid rain in Sweden? The answer to each of these values-loaded questions depends upon the cultural, religious, and philosophical backgrounds, and often the economic interests, of the individuals involved. The answer to the question "Should the destruction of the Amazon rain forests be stopped?" would be different coming from a Brazilian farmer who will, for the first time in his life, own some farmland, than it would coming from a climatologist living in London who is concerned with global warming. The needs and values of the two individuals are quite different. Compromise will be necessary to achieve a solution for the issues involved. More and more frequently in the United States, issues arise that challenge the values of business people, environmentalists, politicians, and ordinary citizens. Let us examine a fairly common scenario, determine the values involved, and suggest a solution or solutions:

Sam is the president of the Bulldozer Development and Construction Company. Sam has spent more than a year completing all the necessary governmental requirements for building houses on eighty acres of forested land. He has also borrowed a large sum of money from the bank to pay for building the roads and sewers that must be built prior to starting the house construction. Ten families have signed contracts and made down payments to have homes built in Sam's new project. On the day the bulldozers begin to clear away trees and brush, making a path for the new roads, two members of the Audubon Society discover a pair of bald eagles nesting in a tall tree right in the middle of the property. Since the bald eagle is on the endangered species list in their state, the Audubon Society asks the government to halt the development of the property.

What do you think the Environmental Protection Agency should do? What is the basic value issue here? We can formulate a value statement as follows:

Value Statement: The possible procreation of one or two bald eagle chicks has priority over the economic interests of the developer and the families who are having homes constructed.

What is your judgment? Should the construction be halted? Should a dollar amount be put on the lives of the bald eagle chicks? In other words, if the cost exceeds a set amount, should the construction be permitted to proceed? For many of these issues, a law has been enacted or a precedent has been established that guides all parallel situations that arise later. This example was based on a real situation that arose in Florida, where construction was halted for nearly eight months until the bald eagle chicks could hatch and develop.

In the field of medicine, many issues arise for which there is little law or precedent to guide those who are charged with making decisions. One example that received national attention revolved around using material from the umbilical cord of a newborn baby for a bone marrow transplant for an older sister. The sister, then sixteen years old and suffering from leukemia,

Students involved in independent group problem-solving develop skills for living in a complex society.

had little success in being genetically matched with a bone marrow donor through normal medical channels. Because it appeared that their daughter's only chance for survival depended on a successful bone marrow procedure, the parents, then in their early forties, decided to have a baby that could supply the needed transplant materials. This situation received much media attention, and created many questions concerning the ethics of having a baby expressly for the purpose of supplying donor tissue. What do you think? Should this be permitted to proceed, or should authorities intervene in the process, stopping it? Can you state the value issue?

Value Statement: Babies (or fetuses) should be created for the express purpose of providing materials for therapeutic procedures for others.

What are your feelings about this value issue? This issue is likely to become an important topic many times in the future, because other medical uses for fetal tissue have been discovered, such as brain implants as therapy for Alzheimer's disease.

When presenting students with issues for consideration in which the underlying values

are not clear, it is useful to help them establish a value statement and discuss it thoroughly prior to proceeding with problem-solving procedures. Students will discover that values may vary with the ethnic and religious experiences of the discussants and their relative economic or personal backgrounds.

Planning and Conducting In-School, Science-Based General Problem-Solving Activities

Every time a classroom teacher asks her class, "How can we best organize ourselves to do the experiment?" or "What are some rules we should follow when we go on the field trip tomorrow?" she is requiring the students to use general problem-solving skills. Thinking skills of fluency and flexibility are brought into play when students are asked to name all the vehicles that have two wheels or when they contemplate the fact that the mystery powder they were thinking was baking soda was really something else. Elementary-grade students exercise problem-solving skills when the teacher asks them to make decisions concerning the nutritional value of their lunches or to formulate a plan for presenting to the rest of the class group data and findings from a science experiment. Directly related to science and technology are opinion or preference polls related to issues such as pollution or energy use in the school building or on the school grounds.

Making Decisions and Formulating Solutions in General Problem Solving

Very often closure in an inquiry science lesson occurs when the students arrive at the single concept or generalization of science that explains their observations. In general problem-solving activities, there often is no one best solution for a problem; there is only a solution that is judged best in light of all known information. Two methods are commonly used to organize information and facilitate decision making in problem-solving situations—the force field method and the costs/benefits/risks method.

The Force Field Method

In this method of decision making, the decision makers list the arguments for accepting a particular course of action in one column and the arguments against accepting a particular course of action in another. For example, a third-grade class, after discussing the value of a field trip to a dairy, organized their decision-making process in this way:

Forces For Making the Trip	*Forces Against Making the Trip*
Some things were interesting such as making ice cream.	It was too far, a long bus ride.
The people were nice;	We missed our P.E. time.

they told us things and answered questions.	It cost our parents money.
It is good to know about the things we eat, milk, cottage cheese and ice cream.	The floor was slippery, someone could fall and get hurt.
It was fun to see the cows.	We had to eat peanut butter and jelly sandwiches.

After making and discussing this list, the teacher might ask, "What do you think? Should we take other children on this field trip to the dairy?" It should be pointed out that the quality of the items in each list is much more important than the number of items. Permit the children to discuss their decisions thoroughly. Stress the importance of using all the information available to make decisions.

The Costs/Benefits/Risks Method

The costs/benefits/risks (CBR) method is commonly used when considering issues of the environment, for in these issues there are economic costs to be borne, benefits to be derived, and risks to be taken by society. When the costs and benefits of a particular decision or course of action are not known to elementary school children, their importance to the decision-making process should be made known to them. In the course of considering a solution to the problem of preventing runoff of drainage water from the city landfill, the organization of the CBR decision-making data may have looked like this:

Costs

Money to build the retention ponds

Loss of land to the landfill

Possible purchase of land for a new landfill

Benefits

Reduced health risks from Clear Creek

Improved environment for fish and wildlife along Clear Creek

Increased recreational opportunities along Clear Creek

Risks

Retention ponds may be a safety and health hazard.

Loss of land to retention ponds could cause the shutdown of the landfill many years sooner than expected.

Flash floods could occur in periods of heavy rainfall, dumping highly concentrated pollutants into the creek.

In utilizing the CBR model for decision making, the realities of pollution control and ecological planning are brought home to the students. Can the town afford to clean up Clear Creek? Will the townspeople be willing to pay new taxes for this purpose? Will those who live downstream from the retention ponds be willing to risk flash floods? Problems at the interface of science, technology, and society are complex, affecting many people with different interests and beliefs. What appear to be simple truths often are not, and compromise is required from all concerned.

Procedures for Conducting Comprehensive Problem-Solving Activities

You have already read how it is possible to informally teach many skills of general problem solving by taking advantage of "targets of opportunity" for problem solving in the ongoing curriculum. Following are some procedures and suggestions for conducting the more comprehensive or formal processes of general problem solving.

Selecting and Defining the Problem

The basic requirement of an issue or problem selected for study by elementary school children is that it provide students with opportunities for developing and using the general problem-solving skills. Learning activities that primarily serve to heighten the awareness of students about a problem and lack the structure of the problem-solving process will not do. Having students pick up the trash on a playground or write and present a skit about global warming have value, but they are not problem-solving activities. An activity must include formulating a hypothesis or problem question, gathering and organizing data, and conducting a decision-making or solution-forming process. Through participating in structuring the problem, developing the investigative procedures, and formulating a decision, plan, or solution, students will learn the process of general problem solving.

Formulating the Problem Question

The parameters of a problem should be set prior to proceeding with the study. The best way to set problem parameters is by constructing a problem question.

Many problem-solving activities begin with the query "Is there a problem?" If the initial investigation reveals the problem exists, the next question is," What can we do to solve it or make it better?" For instance, you may want to start the problem-solving process with open questions such as: "Is littering a problem in our school?" or "Is the illegal use of drugs a problem in our school?" or "Is there a need for a park and playground in our neighborhood?" The problem-solving process that grows out of such queries will serve to determine the existence, nature, and extent of a problem. A companion question for each problem situation might be: "If littering is a problem in our school, what can we do to reduce it?" "If use of illegal drugs is a problem in our school, what can we do to reduce it?" "If there is a need for a park/playground in our neighborhood, what can we do to cause them to be built?" The answers to these questions obviously call for the development of plans for actions to be taken. The students will learn that the start of the rational process of problem solving is to establish a knowledge base about the problem, to not rely entirely upon untested information.

Determining Sources of Information

If we consider the problem questions related to the illegal use of drugs in the school setting, we can observe how sources of information to a problem are established. You may recall the problem questions were: "Is the illegal use of drugs a problem in our school?" and "If the use of illegal drugs is a problem in our school, what can we do to reduce it?" Generally the information obtained from a source is related to both questions and a single list will serve both.

Sources of Information

1. Conduct a survey among the fourth-, fifth-, and sixth-grade students to assess their attitudes and use of illegal drugs.
2. Invite experts on drug abuse from the community to inform the class concerning the nature of illegal drugs and pattern of their use: a police officer, physician, drug treatment counselor, and so on.
3. Conduct a search in the school library and in the public library for print and other media containing information related to drug abuse.
4. Contact agencies involved with drug abuse prevention programs to acquire information on actions that help prevent student drug use.
5. Contact agencies involved with drug abuse treatment to obtain information concerning ways to help students stop using drugs.

Structuring the Procedures for Collecting Data

A class might not use all of the sources named to collect data. The amount of time available, the importance of the potential data, and the abilities of the students can influence the actual selection of data sources to be tapped. In this case the teacher might decide to have the whole class involved with the construction, administration, and evaluation of a survey instrument. The teacher might also assign the whole class to conduct library research to answer specific, nar-

rowly defined questions such as "What is cocaine, marijuana, 'crack,' and amphetamines?" or "What are other schools doing about drug abuse among their students?" Committees might be appointed to write letters soliciting visits by police officers, drug prevention experts, and drug treatment experts. A committee of students might help the teacher locate media, films, video tapes, and so forth that would provide information appropriate to the project. The teacher can easily control the scope and depth of the study by setting limits on the research assignments.

Interpreting Data

A number of activities may be used to organize, analyze, and interpret data. Some suggestions follow.

1. Working in groups, students might tally the results of a survey and group the results to form a single data set.
2. During a class discussion, a summary report might be outlined and the student assigned to write their own final report.
3. The teacher could make an overhead transparency showing the important findings of the survey.
4. Following the presentation of each guest speaker or media presentation, the class might summarize the important information presented.
5. Students could be assigned to prepare a large chart that displays these summaries. After all data have been collected and processed, the teacher would one day write the problem question "Is the use of illegal drugs a problem in our school?" on the chalkboard. Under the question the teacher would write the words YES or NO with a vertical line drawn between them. The teacher would then ask, "What evidence do we have that the answer to this question is yes? No?" Student statements would be listed under the proper heading. Finally a consensus decision would be sought to

A problem-solving group prepares a presentation of their solution to a problem. Problem-solving activities accent the integration of the school curriculum.

Example of a Formal Problem-Solving Project: Global Warming

Global warming is a complex problem that involves broader issues such as air pollution, energy sources, and world population. Basically, global warming describes a situation wherein gases that are given off by the burning of fossil fuels and that remain in the atmosphere absorb some of the heat energy that is normally radiated into space from the earth's surface. Many believe that the retention of this heat energy will increase the mean temperature of the lower levels of the earth's atmosphere. This phenomenon is sometimes called the "greenhouse effect," because it is the same set of conditions that occur when sunlight passes through the glass cover of a greenhouse and the heat is trapped inside.

What do scientists know about the greenhouse effect and global warming? Seventy-eight percent of the energy used by humans is derived from their burning of fossil fuels. The remaining 22 percent comes from hydroelectric, wind, solar, and nuclear power, and from alternative fuels such as methyl and ethyl alcohol. Many chemical components and combustion products such as heavy metals, and the oxides of carbon, sulfur, and nitrogen, are emitted into the atmosphere when fossil fuels are burned. The major gaseous product emitted from the combustion of natural gas, petroleum products (such as gasoline, fuel oil, butane, and propane), coal, and wood is carbon dioxide (CO_2). Researchers estimate that in 1980 more than five trillion tons of carbon dioxide entered the earth's atmosphere in this way. The major sources of CO_2 are the internal combustion engines of cars, trucks, and buses, and the smokestacks of industry and electric generating plants. The industrialized regions of the world, chiefly North America, Western and Eastern Europe and Russia, account for nearly 80 percent of fossil fuel emissions and the rest of the world for about 20

answer the question. If the answer to the problem question is yes the teacher might then write the second problem question on the chalkboard: "What can we do to reduce the use of illegal drugs in our school?" Suggestions for a plan of action would be listed and decisions made as to which of those to carry out.

Of course, problem-solving projects such as this one, which have potential to generate public notice and provoke strong reactions, must have the blessings of the principal before they are started. The teacher should keep the principal informed of the progress and scope of the project as it develops. Any problem-solving project should support the goals of the school and the school system. At times the final resolution of school-based, problem-solving projects may take the form of a written or live presentation before the school system administration and school board.

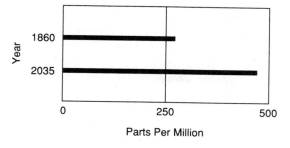

Figure 9–1 ■ The Projected Growth of CO_2 in the Atmosphere

percent. However, as the Third World countries become industrialized, their share of fossil fuel pollutants added to the world total is increasing dramatically.

Cause-and-Effect Relationships

It is estimated that the amount of carbon dioxide in the atmosphere has increased by 20 percent since human beings first appeared on earth. Scientists, using the world's largest and fastest computers, have developed several models of climatic change that estimate the temperature increase in that period to be in the range of 3 to 7 degrees Fahrenheit, or 1 to 3 degrees Celsius. At first glance this increment does not appear to be alarming. But when you consider that the estimated increase in the earth's mean temperature in the next century (3 to 5 degrees F) will be ten to fifty times the rate of increase that has occurred since the last ice age, the problem takes on a different perspective. (See Figure 9–1.) Climatologists warn that the mean or average increase of a few degrees can have a disproportionate impact on particular regions of the earth. In some locations the regional temperature increase may be as much as ten or twenty degrees, seriously affecting the rainfall, and in some cases turning fertile farmland into desert. Some climatologists attribute a very hot, dry summer in 1988, which engulfed the plains states of the United States and drastically re-

duced crop yields, as the beginning of the global warming phenomenon.

An increase in world temperatures also poses a threat to the existence of cities along the coastlines of continents by setting up conditions that could melt polar ice and raise the levels of the oceans. In the minds of some experts, cities such as New York, London, and Los Angeles one day will be required to spend billions of dollars to hold back the rising oceans—either that, or they will perhaps be abandoned or moved inland. Global warming is a serious and real problem that is now gaining the attention of politicians and world leaders.

Solutions to the Problem

The simplest solution for stopping progression of the greenhouse effect and reducing global warming is to stop using fossil fuels as a source of energy. This action would largely eliminate the emission of fossil fuels into the atmosphere. However, currently about 88 percent of the world's energy is generated from fossil fuels, and only 12 percent comes from alternative fuel sources. Much research and development must be accomplished before any combination of alternatives to fossil fuels as the world's primary energy source may be realized. Let us examine some of the options.

Nuclear Energy

Nuclear energy currently supplies about 5 percent of the world's total energy needs. In this technology, heat energy produced by the breaking up, or fission, of atoms of uranium or plutonium is used to create steam, which powers electric generators. In spite of problems posed by threat of nuclear accidents and disposal of nuclear wastes, many feel that nuclear energy is the most viable alternative to fossil fuels and that it can reliably produce energy on a large scale. A new technology, hydrogen fusion, wherein heat is produced by joining together hydrogen atoms, may become possible but is still a long time off in the future.

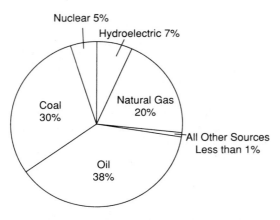

Figure 9–2 ■ The World's Major Energy Sources

Hydroelectric Power

Hydroelectric power currently supplies about 7 percent of the world's energy needs. Hydroelectric power is derived by directing the flow of water that has been impounded by a dam over the turbines of an electric generator. While hydroelectric power is a clean, desirable energy source, it has limitations relating to availability, and the construction of dams has a negative impact on the environment.

The world's major energy sources are shown in Figure 9–2. Some lesser sources are discussed below.

Solar Electric Cells

Solar electric cells currently supply a negligible percentage of the world's energy needs. Thin slices of silicon and other crystals are exposed to the direct rays of sunlight and yield small amounts of electricity. The electric currents of many such cells may be stored in batteries to be used as a power source. While the efficiency of solar cells has been greatly enhanced in recent years, most experts view solar electricity as a supplementary energy source, not as a practical source for producing energy in large amounts.

Solar Water Heat

Solar water heat also currently supplies a negligible percentage of the world's total energy needs. The direct rays of the sun are used to heat water stored in a container or moving through a pipe. Although this energy source has become commonplace in many homes and in businesses as a supplementary energy source, it has limitations related to climate and reliability. One large-scale experiment wherein five acres of movable mirrors reflected sunlight upon a water tower was considered a success, but no commercial application has been made of this technology.

Wind Energy

Wind energy also currently supplies a negligible percentage of the world's energy needs. In regions of the world where the wind is fairly constant, it is used to drive large propellers which in turn power machinery and electric generators. Electricity produced by wind-driven generators has proved to be a valuable source of energy in some coastal regions of the world, supplying 10 to 15 percent of the electrical energy needs. However, its use is regional and it has some problems of reliability.

Geothermal Energy

Geothermal energy also currently supplies a negligible percentage of the world's energy needs. An unlimited supply of heat energy resides deep in the earth's crust, caused by the compression of the rocks and minerals by the forces of gravity. To date, attempts to harness this energy pool have used hot water, which is pressurized and forced to the surface as in geysers and hot springs. Problems in utilizing geothermal energy stem from the relatively small number of natural sources of steam or very hot water—sources that often are isolated from large population centers. An additional problem is the minerals that are deposited in the pipes and tanks of the generating system, making the maintenance of the operation very expensive.

Biomass Energy

Some small efforts have been made to utilize methane gas that is naturally emitted from cattle and pig manure. However, because methane produces CO_2 when it burns, its use would not be a solution to the global warming problem. A more promising use of biomass is the production of alcohols produced from corn and other grains for use as fuels. Several distributors of gasoline in the United States are offering gasohol, a mixture of 10 percent ethyl alcohol and 90 percent gasoline. Although its use is now negligible in relation to the world's energy needs, alcohol is viewed by many as a viable partial solution to the shortage of fossil fuels. And since its major combustion product is water, alcohol fuel does not contribute to the global warming problem. The use of grains for the production of fuels also promises to create a profitable market for the farmers of the Midwest.

Tides and Ocean Currents

Because they are constantly in motion, the earth's oceans would appear to be a possible source of kinetic energy that might be harnessed to produce electricity. At this point only one sizable electrical generating plant that uses ocean tides or currents exists. The French have harnessed tidal energy of a small river in which the current flows upstream, powering electrical generators during the incoming tide and downstream back into the ocean on the outgoing tide. To provide a constant source of energy, a large amount of water is stored behind a dam through electrical generators during the period of receding and low tide.

Nuclear energy, although a significant alternative to fossil fuels, presents problems of safety, which were dramatized by the events of Three Mile Island in the United States and by Chernobyl in Russia. If these extremely serious problems can be overcome, nuclear power bears the greatest promise of all alternative sources for producing large amounts of electrical energy. The United States currently produces slightly more than 20 percent of its electricity and France more than 75 percent from nuclear energy. On the average, industrialized nations of the world use nuclear generation for about 20 percent of their electrical power. Other alternative energy sources—hydroelectric, solar, wind, and tidal energy—have limitations of availability, reliability, and production capacity. Biomass energy sources (producing energy by utilizing organic matter) bears some promise in the production of alcohol from corn and other grain, but the costs of production and use have so far limited this alternative.

As the cost and availability of petroleum increase and the efficiency of the carbon dioxide-free energy sources improve, their use will become much more common, especially for the generation of electrical energy. Experts are also looking into the increased use of ethyl and methyl alcohol, which produce water as their primary combustion product, to replace gasoline and diesel fuel for use in ground transportation vehicles.

Increased Operating Efficiency

Another thrust in engineering and technology that will help to reduce the amount of emissions generated into the atmosphere is the improvement of the efficiency of the internal combustion engine and of industrial and electrical power-generating plants. Increased efficiency of operation will not solve the emissions problem, but it will greatly reduce it. Automobiles, for instance, now use 30 percent less fuel than did their counterparts just twenty years ago. Unfortunately, the increased number of vehicles in use has just about wiped out these benefits. Currently, higher fuel taxes and costs and increased availability of public transportation appear to be working to reduce Americans' dependence on their personal automobiles, something that is already true in Europe and the rest of the world.

Maintaining Our Forests and Oceans

Less direct in their impact but no less important to alleviating the global warming

Chart 9–2 ■ Global Warming: Causes and Effects

Cause	Effect
Emission of CO_2 from the combustion of fossil fuels accumulates in the earth's atmosphere.	Absorption of heat reflected from the earth's surface increases the atmospheric temperature; CO_2 causes the "greenhouse effect."
Contributing factors	*Impact on the Atmosphere*
Third World industrial development	Greater need for energy; more fossil fuels burned; more CO_2 emissions
World population increase	Increase in need for energy; increased use of fuels
Planet deforestation. Ocean pollution	Loss of CO_2-regulating plant life; increase in net CO_2 in air. Loss of one-celled, CO_2-regulating organisms; net increase in CO_2 in atmosphere

phenomenon are the efforts of conservationists to stop the destruction of the world's forests and to reduce the pollution of the oceans. Plants use carbon dioxide (CO_2) for photosynthesis; diatomaceous (one-celled) organisms living near the surface of the oceans extract carbon dioxide from the water and use it in the manufacture of their limestone "skeletons." The loss of millions of acres of forest area over the last several centuries and the growing pollution of the oceans, which threatens the existence of the one-celled organisms that live in them, pose a serious threat to the earth's natural mechanism for regulating the carbon dioxide content of the atmosphere. Solutions to these problems would involve ef-

forts to reforest the planet and reduce the amount of pollutants that are flowing into the oceans through the rivers that empty into them.

Chart 9–2 summarizes the causes and effects of global warming.

Constructing a Plan to Study the Problem of Global Warming

Start a problem-solving project on the topic of global warming with the following two lessons. Additional activities follow the lesson plans.

Lesson Plan ▪ Introductory Activity 1

Orientation: Intermediate grades

Concept: Global warming is caused by the greenhouse effect, whereby gases in the atmosphere absorb some of the heat energy normally radiated into space from the earth's surface, increasing the temperature of the lower levels of the atmosphere.

Content Objective: Students will state that some transparent materials permit the sun's energy to pass through, but reflect heat energy; this creates a region of greater heat concentration.

Skill Orientation: The students will observe, create data tables, and interpret data.

Materials: Two cardboard boxes, sheets of foam insulation or wooden boxes, one pane of glass about 70 cm square, two thermometers.

Evaluation: Participation in problem-solving activities, data tables, written data interpretation.

Procedure

From cardboard, wood, sheets of foam insulation, and other suitable material, construct two topless boxes, shaped like cubes, about 70 cm wide on each side. Tape a thermometer to the bottom of each box close to one side so that temperatures may be read easily. Cover the open top of one of the boxes with a pane of glass and tape the glass to the sides of the box with masking tape. Place both boxes in the sunlight so the sun's rays do not shine directly upon the thermometers. (This is best accomplished by doing the activity in the morning or afternoon rather than noontime.) Have the students, in small groups, read the two thermometers at the beginning of the experiment and at ten-minute intervals for half an hour. Have selected students or the recorder of each group write their data in a table drawn on the chalkboard. Ask, "What do the data tell us?" "In which box was the temperature higher?" "What happened when the sunlight struck the glass plate; did some solar energy pass through the glass?" "What kind of energy does sunlight create when it strikes a surface on earth?" "What could have held the heat energy in the covered box?" "Can someone tell me what caused the temperature to be higher in the glass-covered box?" The temperature of the air in the box covered by the glass will be higher, because the glass reflects heat energy that strikes it back into the box. This is the greenhouse effect. This is what some pollutant gases, especially carbon dioxide, do to cause the temperature of the atmosphere to be higher where they exist.

Direct each student or group to construct a data table and write a brief description of the activity, including an explanation of the observed data.

Lesson Plan ▪ Introductory Activity 2

Concept: Carbon dioxide (CO_2) is a colorless, odorless gas; it is produced by the body and exhaled during breathing.

Content Objective: Students will state the properties of CO_2.

continued on next page

Skill Objective:	Students will observe and make inferences; they will demonstrate fluency and flexibility of thought by associating CO_2 production from the body and CO_2 production from the burning of fossil fuels.
Materials:	Baking powder, a small sheet of aluminum foil or a foil pan, one large candle, a quart glass jar, matches, a sink or a bucket of water.
Evaluation:	Student will give oral responses.

Procedure

Put three heaping teaspoons of baking powder into the glass jar. Pour about ten milliliters of water into the jar on top of the baking powder. Place an index card or the jar lid loosely over the mouth of the jar. (See Figure 9–3A.) Ask, "What is happening?" (The powder is fizzing. There is some kind of chemical reaction.) "What is being given off?" (Some kind of gas.) State the reaction time it took to be completed. (Note: Use less water or baking powder to shorten the time of the reaction.) Ask, "What can you say about the gas that was produced?" (You can't see it. It is colorless.) Pass the jar close to some students' faces, warning them against inhaling deeply, and ask, "Can you smell anything?" Most students will agree there is no distinct odor.) Now light a candle, let it drip on a small sheet of aluminum foil, then place the base of the candle on the drippings and hold it upright as the base hardens.

Carefully tilt the glass jar to a near horizontal position with the mouth just above the burning candle, making sure no water pours from the mouth of the jar, as in Figure 9–3B. The CO_2 will pour from the jar and snuff out the candle flame. Ask the students, "What happened?" and "What could have put out the flame?" (It must have been the gas that was produced.) "What can we say about the gas?" (It puts out fires, and because it poured downward onto the flame it must be heavier than air.) "What can we say about the gas that was produced by the reaction of water and the white powder?" (It is colorless, odorless, heavier than air, and does not burn.)

You may now disclose the nature of the powder and the name of the gas. You may tell students that when the gas is present in the earth's atmosphere in sufficient amounts, it can cause the earth's temperature to rise. This is called global warming.

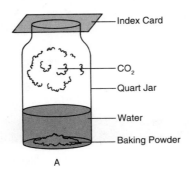

A

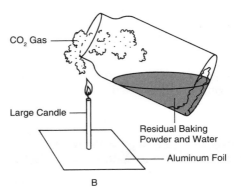

B

Figure 9–3 ■ Carbon Dioxide Generator

continued on next page

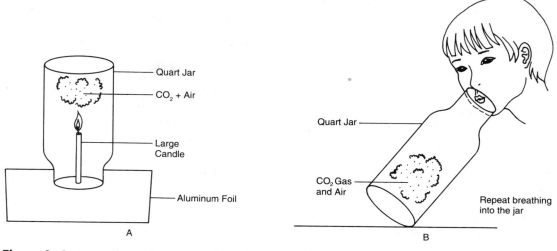

Figure 9–4 ■ Producing Concentrated CO_2 from Breathing

Optional Activity

Place a large candle upright on a piece of aluminum foil or a foil pan by setting it in melted wax. With the candle burning, place the quart jar upside down over the candle. (See Figure 9–4A.) Observe the length of time the candle stays lit. Rinse the jar in a sink or bucket of water, dry it out with a cloth or paper towel, and, holding the jar upright, breathe repeatedly into the jar, making a loose seal around the mouth of the jar with your hands as in Figure 9–4B. (Caution: You may begin to get lightheaded.) Now place the jar again in an inverted position over the burning candle and observe the length of time the candle burns. Ask, "What did we see?" (The burning time was less when we breathed into the jar.) "What gas do we give off when we breathe?" (Carbon dioxide.) Help students to see that carbon dioxide is essentially colorless and odorless and does not support combustion. Remind them that you held the jar upright without a cover after you breathed in it, and the carbon dioxide stayed in the jar. "What are some sources of carbon dioxide in nature?" (People's and animals' breathing—they burn sugar in the body and give off carbon dioxide. Also: burning wood, gasoline, coal, and other fuels.)

Project Plan Outline: Global Warming

Following is a sample project plan outline for carrying out the problem-solving project on the topic of global warming.

Activity 1

Conduct the introductory lesson. Using open-ended questioning, help students to understand the analogy that the earth is a large greenhouse and the polluted atmosphere, especially the carbon dioxide given off by fossil fuels, a window reflecting heat energy back to earth. You may conduct Lesson Plan 2 or the optional activity as you acquaint students with some properties of CO_2. Challenge the students to accept the task of investigating the global warming problem and offering possible solutions. Provide a brief reading or lecture on the general nature of the global warming problem. Assign students to locate in the library, magazine, newspaper, or other source at least one article on the topic of global warming and to make notes on the information provided.

Activity 2

Discuss what students have learned from their assignment on global warming. Following a discussion, write a problem statement or question offered by the class on the chalkboard that defines the problem of global warming. Also list on the chalkboard the causes and effects of the problem. Then have students generate preliminary or established solutions to the problem. Such solutions should center around the reduced use of fossil fuels, the increased use of alternative fuels by the people of the world, and perhaps the effects of growing populations in Third World countries. Select the small number of solutions that appear to hold the most promise. Define the parameters of the investigation. Suggest that students think about which of the possible solutions they would like to investigate. Note: Any of the alternative fuels or the world population could easily be used as a problem-solving topic in its own right.

Activity 3

Organize the students into investigative teams and assign each group a topic for study, for example, nuclear energy, hydroelectric power, world population, and so on. Permit time for each group to organize and plan for its own investigative activities. Each group should also create a list of resources where they are likely to find materials on their topic. The teacher may offer suggestions and guidance.

Activity 4

Provide students with access to the school library and the assistance of library personnel; also make available any materials you have gathered from other sources. Instruct each

group to offer a solution to the problem and to estimate its effect—little help, moderate help, or perhaps great help in solving the problem of global warming. Have each group list the benefits of their solution by writing general statements about the cost of the solution (such as very costly or not very costly) and the risks generated by their solution (such as effects upon the environment, dangers to populations, possible economic impacts, and so on.)

Activity 5

Permit as many work sessions as the problem warrants and time allows. Spending time for students to engage in group problem-solving activities under the supervision of a teacher has many educational benefits. When children are assigned a problem to investigate and are required to perform the investigation independently, outside of class, and report their solutions, many of the same benefits are not realized and many of the problem-solving skills are not developed.

Activity 6

Provide the groups with a format for reporting and discussing group findings. Some common formats are: group oral reports using charts and other media, a panel consisting of one or two members from each group who report the results of the investigations, or a colloquia, wherein a panel may present the findings of the groups and all members of the class may ask questions or offer information or ideas at any time during the proceedings.

Activity 7

The students will report the results of their investigations.

Activity 8

It is time for the class to develop a single, composite solution and/or action plan for dealing with the problems of global warming. The teacher may conduct a discussion and list on the board those things that are agreed on by the class members. A completed report consisting of a problem statement, discussion/explanation of the problem, possible solutions with benefits, consideration of costs and risks, and an overall conclusion should be compiled by the students. If possible, the class report should be bound and each student given a copy.

These activities suggest only a few of the procedures that could be developed to enhance the study of global warming. The most important ingredient is organization. In a well-organized activity, students learn ways to investigate problems and make decisions that reflect reason and study. It is important for teachers at the outset to set some limits and articulate their expectations. Students work better when they are told, "I am expecting about a one-page report" or "The oral group report should be only about twenty minutes long." Obviously the sophistication of the investigations and the problem-solving efforts will vary with the ages and abilities of the students.

Summary

In our efforts to control our environment, provide food, shelter, and clothing, and pursue recreation, we greatly impact the earth's environment. The effects of society upon the earth's ecology as well as our increased ability to extend life and genetically alter plant, animal, and even human forms create many problems that require solutions and decisions if we are to survive on this planet. A few examples of our most pressing issues are: global warming, acid rain, extinction of plant and animal species, human organ transplants, and genetic engineering. In elementary school science, the larger problems of humankind may be considered, but some teachers prefer to teach problem-solving skills by introducing problems related to the class-

room, school, or community. Making decisions regarding investigative procedures, setting guidelines for student behavior during science class, and cleaning up a classroom, cafeteria, or playground by reducing litter are examples of such problems. Intermediate-grade students may become involved with community-wide problems such as environmental issues and public elections.

The primary and integrated processes of science are a good foundation for students just beginning to enter into general problem solving, because many of the skills and attitudes are overlapping. General problem-solving skills include some basic intellectual skills such as fluency and flexibility of ideas, literary research skills such as using a library, note taking, writing summaries of readings, and others. Closely associated with the literary skills are those of distinguishing between fact and opinion, recognizing cause-and-effect relationships, and recognizing relevant and irrelevant information. A comprehensive problem-solving process requires students to know how to define a problem, write appropriate problem questions, locate information necessary to study the problem, organize and analyze data and form conclusions, make decisions, and recommend solutions.

The force field procedure for decision making requires students to make lists of forces that influence the decision for and against a particular action and then analyze the two lists. The cost/benefit/risk procedure for decision making requires making lists under each of the three headings. A decision is made after a careful analysis of the three arrays of information.

Extending Activities

1. Outline a plan for teaching four of the following five problem-solving projects.

   a. Primary grade level—Topic: Caring for animals in the classroom.

b. Intermediate grade level—Topic: Exploring students' use of and attitude toward illegal drugs.

c. Intermediate grade level—Topic: Improving the safety of students at school and when coming from and going to school.

d. Intermediate grade level—Topic: Saving the manatee, an endangered species.

e. Any hypothetical problem situation.

2. Create several hypothetical "force fields" with suitable statements supporting a particular decision and opposing the decision that are appropriate for teaching the decision-making process to fifth-grade students.

3. Describe one situation for the study of each subject—science, mathematics, social studies, and language arts—where problem solving could be introduced as a "target of opportunity."

Bibliography

Abell, S. "The Problem Solving Muse." *Science and Children* 28, no. 27 (October 1990): 27–29.

Aikenhead, G. "Collective Decision Making in the Social Context of Science." *Science Education* 6, no. 4 (July 1985): 453–476.

Bainer, D. "What to Do When People Disagree: Addressing Ideational Pluralism in Science Classes." *Science Education* 70, no. 4 (April 1985): 173–184.

Bybee, R., and R. Bonnstetter. "Implementing the Science—Technology—Society Theme in Science Education: Perceptions of Science Teachers." *School Science and Mathematics* 87, no. 2 (February 1987): 144–152.

Carr, J., P. Epping, and P. Nonether. "Learning by Solving Real Problems." *Middle School Journal* (February 1986): 14–16.

De Bono, E. "The Direct Teaching of Thinking Skills." *Phi Delta Kappa* 64, no. 10 (1983): 703–708.

Environmental Conservation, 15, no. 2 (summer 1988). Printed in Switzerland: provides European viewpoint of environmental problems.

Esler, W. K., and P. Sciortino. *Teaching Strategies*, 2nd Edition. Raleigh, N.C.: Contemporary Press, 1990.

4RS Project, *A Solid Waste Management Curriculum for Florida's Schools, 4th–5th Grades*. Florida Department of Education, Recycling Awareness Program.

Marzano, R., and D. Arrendo. "A Framework for Teaching Thinking." *Educational Leadership* 43, no. 8 (May 1986): 20–22.

National Science Teachers Association. *Directory of Energy Education*. Washington, D.C.: National Science Teachers Association, 1987.

Pizzinai, E., S. Abell, and J. Vander de Wilt. "Scrape, Scrape, Scrape, Problem Solving in the Lunchroom." *Science and Children* 24, no. 67 (1987): 14–15, 43.

Project Wild, Western Regional Environmental Council, Boulder, Col., 1983.

Rubba, P. "Perspectives on Science—Technology—Society Instruction." *School Science and Mathematics* 87, no. 3 (March 1987): 181–186.

Sternberg, R. "Teaching Critical Thinking, Part I: Are We Making a Critical Mistake?" *Phi Delta Kappa* 67, no. 3 (November 1985): 194–198.

Swartz, R. "Restructuring Curriculum for Critical Thinking." *Educational Leadership* 43, no. 8 (May 1986): 43–44.

Their, H. "Societal Issues and Concerns: A New Emphasis for Science Education." *Science Education* 69, no. 2 (April 1985): 157–164.

White, R. "The Great Climate Debate." *Scientific American* 263, no. 1 (July 1990): 36–43.

Scientific American, 263, no. 3 (September 1990). (Entire issue devoted to energy and related topics of global warming, acid rain, alternative fuels, and so on.)

"It will always do to change for the better."
—THOMSON

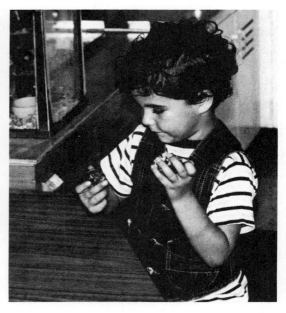

". . . man knows nothing truly that he has not learned from experience."
—WIELAND

T ▪ W ▪ O

Units of Study for Elementary School Science

Section Two is comprised of eighteen units of study in elementary school science. Each unit (or chapter) covers an important topic of natural science or technology. The four chapters in Part A, "Investigating Living Things," cover plant and animal life, ecological relationships, and the human body. The nine chapters in Part B, "Understanding Physical Science," cover various aspects of physical science, from the basic properties of heat and matter to the origins and development of aviation.

Each chapter is structured around a conceptual framework that defines the important concepts and subconcepts for that topic, followed by explanation and discussion of each concept and subconcept. One or more inquiry lesson plans are presented that can be used to introduce a specific concept to elementary school students. Taken as a whole, Section Two can serve as a basic science curriculum for the elementary school.

To complete the I-C-I sequence of instruction introduced in Chapter 4, teachers will need to introduce materials and activities for the information stage (direct instruction). Because print and electronic media and other resources vary greatly among school settings, and because a wide range of direct instructional activities may be used, plans for teaching the information stage are best developed by individual teachers.

Lesson Plans

Each lesson plan that appears in Section Two is designed to introduce and develop a *specific* concept or subconcept; with but two exceptions there is at least one inquiry lesson plan for each concept or subconcept presented in the chapter. Each lesson plan is designated as being appropriate for primary or intermediate levels of instruction. The plans may be modified to better suit the needs of a particular classroom, and many may be used across a wide range of grade levels. Since inquiry instruction results in children's acquisition of knowledge and science skills, each lesson plan contains both a content objective and a skill objective. Each lesson plan lists the materials required for the planned activities, methods for evaluating student performance, and detailed procedures for carrying out the instruction.

The instructional units of Section Two allow for considerable flexibility as to their application. Teachers who wish to may present the entire unit with the assurance that they have introduced most of the concepts and subconcepts commonly included in elementary school science textbooks. Or, a teacher may select one or more of the inquiry lessons to introduce or supplement a textbook program. As we stated in Chapter 8, "Individualizing Science/Science for Exceptional Children," many of the lesson plans from Section Two may be easily restructured to create inquiry learning centers.

Content Coverage

The eighteen chapters in Section Two cover all of the topics traditionally taught in elementary school science and technology. The technique we employ—presenting a brief discussion of each concept or subconcept of science as it is introduced—is intended to aid the reader by making the information available exactly where it is needed. This removes the necessity for reading many pages of material in search of the background information required for teaching a single lesson. However, the cumulative discussions of all the concepts provides coverage of the broad range of the natural sciences and technology. We have tried to stress the conceptual development of science while minimizing the use of unnecessary terminology and quantitative relationships.

In summary, Section Two is more than a collection of miscellaneous lesson plans and more than a source for inquiry teaching activities. It is an elementary school science curriculum, a resource for science content, and a model for teaching both science content and process skills to elementary school students. We hope you will find it useful.

Investigating Living Things

"Childhood and genius have the same master-
organ in common—inquisitiveness."

—BULWER

CHAPTER 10

Investigating Plant Life

Look What's in This Chapter

In this chapter we'll discuss important concepts and subconcepts related to the study of plant life, and we'll introduce lesson plans that are designed to teach these concepts and subconcepts to children.

Concept 1 Matter may be classified as living or nonliving.

Concept 2 Plants may be grouped into families.

   Subconcept 2–1 The plant kingdom may be divided into two separate categories: vascular plants and nonvascular plants.

   Subconcept 2–2 Vascular plants may be grouped into several classifications.

Concept 3 Plants reproduce offspring in many ways.

Concept 4 Plants carry on a variety of life processes.

Concept 5 Bacteria are important members of the Monera kingdom.

How do you feel when you look at a field of wildflowers or a marshy glen? Many untrained observers view a bucolic setting with apathy, seeing only a monotonous panorama of grass, bushes, and trees. To a trained observer, the same scene may be highly exciting, motivating him to search out new organisms and ecological relationships. Why don't more people share the pleasure of the trained observer? To do so, they must become aware of the similarities and differences among living things.

The five following concepts concern plant life. Understanding them may help you share the enthusiasm of others for the world of plants.

Concepts

1. Matter may be classified as living or nonliving.
2. Plants may be grouped into families.
3. Plants reproduce offspring in many ways.
4. Plants carry on a variety of life processes.
5. Bacteria are important members of the Monera kingdom.

Each of the five concepts is discussed below. The lesson plans that accompany each concept suggest activities appropriate for presenting that concept to elementary school children.

Concept 1

Matter may be classified as living or nonliving.

Discussion

Living things are different from nonliving things in some very important ways. Living things have self-directed powers to move, grow, reproduce, respond to stimuli. Nonliving things may be made to move by man or by forces of nature, but they do not move of their own will. Rocks may aggregate material and appear to grow, as do stalagtites and stalagmites in caves, but these are not processes that may be originated and, to any degree, controlled by these objects. Objects may be reproduced by man, but only living things create offspring that grow predictably into the images of the parents. Living things respond to stimuli, as evidenced by plant tropisms and by the reactions of animals with central nervous systems. Plant stems turn toward the sunlight, and their roots grow toward water. Even simple animals react to outside stimuli when they retreat from heat and to internal stimuli when they "eat." Living things also possess internal structures and systems that serve special purposes in carrying on the processes associated with life. For instance, the nucleus of a one-celled organism is necessary for reproduction, the chlorophyl-containing leaves of plants are necessary for producing plant growth, and the muscles of animals are necessary for movement. Living things may be identified through these special attributes that only they possess.

Lesson Plan ■ A

Orientation:	K–5
Content Objective:	The children will state that matter may be classified as living or nonliving.
Skill Objective:	The children will *observe* and *classify* living and nonliving matter.
Materials:	Clear plastic shoebox-size containers, sand plants such as grasses, ferns, and so on, several small animals such as crickets, turtles, or chameleons, several small rocks and plastic flowers, rubber or plastic animals.
Evaluation:	Students' oral responses, student performance worksheet.

continued on next page

Procedure

Give each group of children a plastic container and a cupful of sand. Instruct them to make a level layer of sand in the container (terrarium). Next, give each group a cupful of potting soil and have them make a layer on top of the sand. Then have them plant several living plants, such as a sprig of grass and small ferns. Have them also plant several plastic flowers or other plants. Instruct the students or an adult to water all the plants. Place one or more small live animals, such as crickets or turtles, in the terrarium, along with at least one rock and one plastic animal such as a toy turtle or lizard.

Place a lid or cover over the terrarium.

Permit the children to observe the terrarium for several days. Permit them to touch the objects in the container carefully. Permit them to feed the animals and to discuss their experiences among themselves and as a class. After they have had time to explore the terrarium, ask: Can you name something in the terrarium that is living? Why do you think it is a living thing? Can you name one thing in the terrarium that is not living? Why do you think it is not living? Make separate lists on the chalkboard of all things the students identify as living or nonliving. Help them to summarize those attributes that living things possess that nonliving things do not. Examples: Living things can move by themselves to eat and avoid danger; they take in food and/or water. (The leaves of live plants are moist when crushed.) Living things respond to stimuli. (Lizards, crickets, and turtles move to avoid a poking finger or pencil; plants grow toward the sunlight.) If you wish you may add to the children's list of attributes of living things by demonstrating or discussing that living things also reproduce and grow without help from people. To conclude the lesson, hold up several living and nonliving objects and have the students write the appropriate word, *living* or *nonliving*, beside the pictures of the objects on a worksheet that you provide. Collect the worksheets.

Concept 2

Plants may be grouped into families.

Discussion

One of the goals of all human intellectual activity is to group information for better understanding and retrieval. This is the rationale for dictionaries, encyclopedias, and supermarket shelves. Categorizing data according to patterns of common properties makes it much easier for people to deal with large numbers of facts and items that would otherwise be incomprehensible. Biologists long ago recognized the advantages of classifying the countless thousands of living plants into groups, each group of plants possessing similar characteristics.

The broadest classification of matter is made by placing it in one of two categories—living and nonliving. Living matter may be classified as *plant, animal, protistan, fungus,* or *moneran.* (See Figure 10–1.) Protistans are simple forms of plant and animal life. The first four of these classifications will be discussed in this chapter. The fifth classification, animals, will be the focus of Chapter 11.

The Plant Classification

The following are some common but not universal characteristics of plants:

1. Plants lack general mobility; they are generally fixed in place.

2. Plants generally possess the ability to produce structure and sugars from water, carbon dioxide, and other raw materials.

3. Plants may reproduce in a variety of ways, both sexual and asexual.

Though all plants share some common characteristics, they also differ in very real ways. One of these is structure. This difference in structure is the basis of the two major groupings of plants.

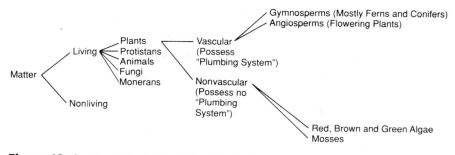

Figure 10–1 ■ A Simple Plant Classification System

Subconcept 2–1

The plant kingdom may be divided into two separate categories, vascular plants and nonvascular plants.

Discussion

The *vascular* plants contain a system of tubes extending through their roots, stems, and leaves. Through this system, water and dissolved substances may be carried throughout the plant. The *capillary action* that occurs within the vascular tubes permits the plants that grow on the land to provide nutrients to upper stems and branches that may be several hundred feet high. The vascular plumbing system is so necessary to plant growth and survival that one might guess that any plant over three feet tall is a vascular plant.

When the average person thinks of plants, he is generally considering vascular plants. This group contains all of the trees, grasses, ferns, weeds, and flowers that make up most of the landscape. *Nonvascular* plants do exist in great abundance, but they are not so conspicuous as the vascular varieties.

Mosses and *liverworts* are common nonvascular plants. They may be found growing in moist areas on soil or on other vegetation.

Aquatic plants are comprised almost entirely of *algae*. Algae are nonvascular, but they sometimes grow very big; some species are nearly 150 feet long. In these plants, food and waste are transported directly by the water that surrounds them. Most school children are familiar with the yellow and green algae found in small lakes, ponds, and aquaria. Though many algae thrive primarily in oceans, lakes, and streams, others are found in polar snowbanks and deserts where they may lie dormant for years.

Lichens are found over much of the earth's surface. A lichen is not really a single plant, but a combination of fungi and algae. The fungi provide the base for the organism and help to maintain a moist environment. The tiny algae provide the food for both life forms. This is called a *mutualistic* relationship.

The Fungi Classification

Fungi as a kingdom include mushrooms, molds, mildew, rust, and smut. Many types of fungi may be found growing on decaying vegetation in the woods, and other forms exist as parasites on living plants. All fungi possess these characteristics:

1. They have no vascular structure.
2. They reproduce, at least partly, by means of spores.
3. They lack chlorophyl and therefore the ability to produce their own food.

The Monera and Protista Classifications

The Monera kingdom is made up of microscopic organisms that include bacteria, viruses, blue-green algae, and other less well-known forms. The Protista kingdom is made up of unicellular algae, protozoans (one-celled animals), and some other intermediate forms.

Lesson Plan ▪ B

Orientation: Grades K–3.

Content Objective: The children will demonstrate their recognition of properties of objects by placing the objects that possess common properties into sets.

Skill Objective: The children are required to *observe* properties of objects, to *classify* objects, and to *communicate* orally in the classroom.

Materials: An assortment of seashells or nuts or buttons.

Evaluation: Students' verbal interaction, seat work, and sketches.

Procedure

Give each child an assortment of shells or nuts or buttons. Tell the class that you will give them some instructions later, but until then they may quietly do as they please with the objects on their desks. Allow time for many of the children to group the objects according to some characteristic such as size, shape, or color. Then walk around the room asking individual children why they arranged the objects as they did. Clarify their responses and encourage further grouping. After the children have had time to regroup the objects by several characteristics, you may call the class to attention and ask individual children how they grouped the objects. List on the board the various properties that they suggest.

If the children are still interested, ask them to choose one grouping of the objects, put the other groupings aside, and try to divide the single group according to other properties. After they have done this, ask individual children to describe single objects according to the properties by which they have grouped them. For example: "This is a large, white button," or "This is a blue button with four holes." Explain to the class that they are observing properties of objects and classifying the objects according to the observed properties.

Lesson Plan ▪ C

Orientation: Grades 3–6.

Content Objective: The children will state the characteristics of vascular and nonvascular plants and describe the habitat in which each may be found.

Skill Objective: The children are required to *observe* properties of plant specimens, to *classify* the plant as vascular or nonvascular, and to *communicate* orally in the classroom.

Materials: Specimens of vascular and nonvascular plants to be gathered on a field trip or brought to school by the children.

Evaluation: Students' verbal interaction, student group problem-solving skills.

continued on next page

Procedure

If a wooded area is nearby, take the children for a walk to gather some specimens for examination. Try to locate and gather specimens of toadstools, mushrooms, and other fungi, along with twigs, weeds, and ferns. Ask each child to return to the classroom with one specimen. Back in the classroom, ask the children to examine the specimens with hand lenses and classify them as vascular or nonvascular. Ask each child to describe the kind of environment in which his plant specimen was found. Discuss with the class what the various plants require in order to grow. Point out the difference in size between vascular and nonvascular plants.

If there is no wooded area close to the school, the children may bring specimens from home and describe to the class the habitat in which each was found.

Lesson Plan ■ D

Orientation:	Grades 2–6.
Content Objective:	The children will state that liquids in plants are transported through vertical tubes.
Skill Objective:	The children are required to *observe* the changes in the appearance of the celery and to *infer* from their observations.
Materials:	A bunch of celery or six flowers such as geraniums, six glass tumblers, food coloring.
Evaluation:	Students' verbal interaction, student group problem-solving skills.

Procedure

Divide the class into small groups. Say to each group: "Add food coloring to a tumbler of water. Place a stalk of celery that has had the bottom inch of its length freshly cut off in the colored water. We will leave it in the tumbler overnight or as long as it takes." Then have the children examine the leaves of the celery for evidence of color. Cut each group's celery stalk in cross sections and have the children examine them. They may compare the cross sections taken from the celery that was immersed in colored water to those taken from the other celery. Ask the students to state how the coloring was transported to the upper part of the celery stalk. (See Figure 10–2.)

Optional Supplement: Touch the bottom of a blotter or cotton cloth to the water. Ask the children: "What do we observe?" (The water creeps up the blotter or rag.) "How is this like the celery stalk?" (The

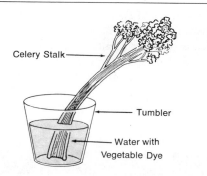

Figure 10–2 ■ How Liquids Are Transported in Plants

water crept up the tubes of the celery, too.) "How do you suppose water is supplied to the tops of tall trees?" (Through tubes that run from the tree's roots to its upper branches.)

Subconcept 2–2

Vascular plants may be grouped into several classifications.

Discussion

We have seen that all plants may be classified as being vascular or nonvascular. Let us examine the vascular plants further. Over 200,000 kinds of vascular plants have been identified. About 95 percent of these plants bear *flowers* and make up a classification called *angiosperms*.

Botanists consider flowers to be short branches that bear specialized leaves. Flowers are the center of the plant's reproductive activity. The flower is generally made up of green, leaflike structures on the underside called *sepals*, the leaflike and colorful *petals*, the pollen-producing *stamens*, and the pollen-receiving *pistil* that is found in the center of the structure (Figure 10–3). The seeds of reproduction develop in an *ovary* at the base of the pistil.

The survival of a species often depends upon the efficiency of its seed dispersal mechanisms. In some plants, such as the peach, plum, and tomato, the ovary walls thicken to form fleshy fruits. The seeds of such plants are often dispersed by passing through the digestive tracts of animals. Seeds of other plants, as nonfleshy fruits, are often dispersed by the wind. Notable examples are the maple seed and the dandelion. Seeds of still other plants, such as the cocklebur,

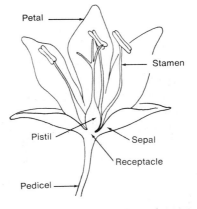

Figure 10–3 ■ A Flower's Parts

are dispersed by attaching themselves to passing animals. The touch-me-not seeds are flung from the pod when it dries and splits.

The class of vascular plants called *gymnosperms* includes the common *evergreens—pines, firs,* and *spruces*—as well as some deciduous trees and shrubs. Seeds of gymnosperms are not contained in flower structures. Rather, they grow upon the upper surface of flat, exposed scales that are usually formed into *cones*. Nearly all of the approximately 600 species of gymnosperms are trees and shrubs. The oldest living plants that exist on earth are gymnosperms. They include the sequoia and bristle-cone pine trees of the western United States.

Other species of vascular plants are *ferns, club mosses,* and *horsetails.*

Lesson Plan ■ E

Orientation:	Grades 4–6.
Content Objective:	The children will classify plant specimens according to a demonstrated two-stage classification.
Skill Objective:	The children are required to *classify* plant specimens according to a predetermined classification system.

continued on next page

Materials:	Six sets of the following plant specimens: flowers (or fruit), pine cones, fern branches, tree bark that bears moss on its surface, tree bark that bears fungi on its surface.
Evaluation:	Student group problem-solving skills, seat work, and sketches.

Procedure

Collect five or six sets of specimens that include the following: flowers (or fruit, such as apples or oranges), pine or spruce cones, fern branches, pieces of tree bark that have moss on their surfaces, and twigs or pieces of bark with fungi growing on them (mushrooms, toadstools, molds, and so on).

Attach each specimen to a numbered card. All like specimens will have the same number (all flowers are numbered 1, all fungi 2, and so on). There should be one set of specimens for each row of students and enough specimens so that each child has one. Duplications are allowable.

Place the following classifications on the board:

Vascular	Nonvascular
Angiosperms	Mosses
Gymnosperms	Fungi
Ferns	

Discuss thoroughly the characteristics of each group of plants. The description may be left on the board if the teacher so desires. One set of specimens is to be distributed to each row of children. They are to write on a sheet of paper the number of the specimen, whether it is vascular or nonvascular, the name that identifies the specimen. Allow one minute for identifying each specimen. Each child must then, upon signal, pass his specimen to the person in front of him, receive his new specimen, and repeat the process.

Concept 3

Plants reproduce offspring in many ways.

Discussion

All living things must eventually die. If no new organisms were produced, life would disappear from the earth. Plants may reproduce their own kind through both *asexual* (one parent) and *sexual* (two parents) reproduction.

Asexual Reproduction

Asexual or vegetative reproduction is common among garden and household plants. New potato plants spring from the eyes of parent potatoes. Strawberry plants multiply where roots form on runners that grow from the parent plant. Ivy takes root along its stem. Cuttings from many woody plants may be rooted in moist sand. Each of these instances illustrates a form of asexual reproduction called vegetative regeneration.

Fission and *budding* are asexual reproductive processes common to one-celled organisms wherein the organism splits into two equal parts or develops and sheds an organism in its own image.

Some plants, notably ferns and many fungi, produce specialized structures for reproduction called *spores*. When a spore case breaks open, thousands of tiny spores, each consisting of a single, thick-walled cell, pour forth and are spread over great distances by wind and water currents. Upon reaching favorable conditions, a spore will develop into a new organism.

Sexual Reproduction

Sexual reproduction begins with the union of two specialized cells called *gametes*. This union is called *fertilization*. A cell formed by the union of two gametes is a *zygote*. For a single-celled species, the zygote is the new organism. Sometimes a zygote will remain dormant for months or even years before developing into a mature plant. In other species the zygote develops into an *embryo*, which may remain dormant for long periods of time. Under the proper conditions, the embryo will grow into an adult plant. Sexual reproduction in plants is associated with flowering, seed-bearing angiosperms.

In flowering plants, *stamens* produce the male gametes, called *pollen*, and the *pistil* produces the female gametes, called *ovules*. When a pollen grain finds its way down the pollen tube and unites with the female gamete, a plant embryo will develop. Other cell divisions occur that provide a buildup of food material for the embryo. The wall of the ovary may thicken and form a fruit that encloses the embryo-bearing seeds, or the seeds may be ejected to be carried about until they come to rest in an environment favorable to growth.

Lesson Plan ■ F

Orientation:	Grades K–4.
Content Objective:	After manipulating soaked and unsoaked lima beans, the children will describe the similarities and differences between the two. The children will state that a "baby plant" exists in each bean.
Skill Objective:	The children are required to *observe* the beans carefully and to *infer* from their observations.
Materials:	Thirty lima beans soaked in water overnight and thirty unsoaked lima beans.
Evaluation:	Students' verbal interaction, student group problem-solving skills, laboratory worksheets, log, and reports.

Procedure

Soak about thirty lima beans in water overnight. Give each child one soaked and one dry lima bean to observe. Tell the class: "One of the beans was soaked in water while the other was not. What differences do you observe between the beans?" (One is fatter, darker colored, and softer.) Show the children how to separate the two halves of the soaked bean by inserting a fingernail along its rounded edge. After the children have had time to examine the inside of the beans, ask: "What can we see now?" (A tiny plant, some soft, mushy stuff, and a covering.) "What may seeds be used for?" (To grow new plants.) Have the children draw a sketch of the opened bean seed.

Lesson Plan ■ G

Orientation:	Grades 3–6.
Content Objective:	The children will design and carry out an experiment that defines the effect of various variables upon the germination of seeds.

continued on next page

Skill Objective:	The students are required to exercise the skills of *Formulating Hypotheses, Controlling and Manipulating Variables, Experimenting,* and *Interpreting Data.*
Materials:	Bean seeds or other seeds, soil, six milk cartons, a glass tumbler, blotter paper.
Evaluation:	Students' verbal interaction, student group problem-solving skills, laboratory worksheets, log, and reports.

Procedure

Develop with the class the idea that seeds produce new plants when they are placed in the right set of conditions. "I wonder if we can guess what conditions are best for the beans to grow into plants?" The children respond that water and heat, or sun, are necessary. (Naming variables.) Ask the children to predict whether a plant can grow downward instead of up and whether a seed will sprout in the dark. (Formulating hypotheses.) List the children's statements on the board:

1. Beans require water to sprout.
2. Beans require heat to sprout.
3. Beans require light to sprout.
4. Bean plants will grow upward and bean roots downward, regardless of the position of the seed.

Include any other hypotheses that the children propose.

Discuss with the children means of testing their hypotheses. Following are some suggested procedures. (Controlling variables.) (1) Plant several beans in each of two milk cartons. Water one carton, draining off the excess water each day, and do not water the other. Place both cartons side by side on a window sill. (2) Plant several beans in each of two milk cartons. Water each carton. Place one carton in a dark, warm place and the second in a refrigerator at home or at school. Compare the seeds after sprouts have appeared in the carton placed in the warm, dark place. (3) Line two tumblers with blotter or construction paper. Insert several seeds in each tumbler between the paper and the glass. Fill each tumbler about one-third

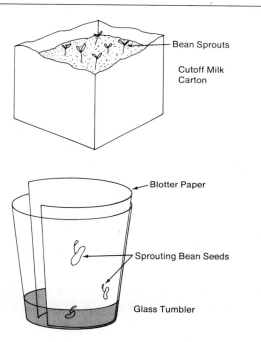

Figure 10—4 ■ Germination of Seeds

full of water, swirling it about to wet the paper thoroughly. (See Figure 10—4.) After about a week, observe that the roots always grow down and the sprout up. Have the students draw and describe the experiment daily in a log.

As the experiments are concluded, discuss the results with the class. Ask them to examine some of the beans that have produced large sprouts and roots. Ask: "Where did the food for the new plants come from?" (From the soft, mushy material of the bean seed.)

Lesson Plan ■ H

Orientation: Pre-K–K.

Content Objective: The children will state that all apples of the same variety contain seeds: the seeds vary in number, size, and appearance.

Skill Objective: The children will *observe* an apple and *communicate* their discoveries.

Materials: Paper towels, one apple of the same variety per child, one serrated plastic knife per child.

Evaluation: Observation of student manipulations and verbal interaction.

Procedure:

Close to snack time disperse an apple to each child in the class. Ask the children to refrain from eating them. Have individual children describe their apples (color, texture, shape, and so on). Using a serrated plastic knife, cut an apple in half so that one or more seeds are exposed. Ask the children to describe what is inside an apple. Now hand a paper towel and plastic knife to each child, and ask the children to cut their apples apart, and to find and save all the seeds. After the children have done this, ask them, "Are all the seeds the same inside your apple?" (The seeds will vary in appearance.) Ask them to describe the seeds. Ask the children to count the seeds and have some of them report the number of seeds they found to the class. (The number of seeds will vary among the apples.) Review the activity with the children; then permit them to eat the rest of their apples. Have the children turn in the apple seeds, do not permit them to eat the seeds. You can repeat this activity with oranges, cherries, plums, cucumbers, squash, and other fruits and vegetables.

Lesson Plan ■ I

Orientation: Pre-K–2.

Content Objective: The children will describe how seeds germinate and grow.

Skill Objective: The children will *observe* plants grow and will *interpret* pictures of growing plants.

Materials: Bean, corn and radish seeds, three foam cups or similar containers per group of children, potting soil, paper towels, one small cardboard box per group, water, camera, and film.

Evaluation: Observation of group work, verbal interaction.

Procedure

Demonstrate for the children how to plant radish seeds by pouring potting soil in a foam cup or other container until it is half full, sprinkling a few radish seeds over the surface of the soil, and adding about one-half centimeter of soil to cover the seeds. Then carefully sprinkle water on the soil until it is soaked.

continued on next page

Put the children in groups of four to eight each and supervise them as each group plants its own radish seeds. (You may wish to have each group also plant corn, bean, or other seeds in separate containers.) Place the germination cup of each group on a window sill or table that is sunny throughout the day. Designate each group's cup by writing a number on it with a marker. Using a camera (preferably a Polaroid) and colored film, take a picture of each group's cup. Have the children examine their cups each day that follows and discuss their observations. Start taking a picture of each cup each day as soon as any plant begins to appear through the soil. (You will find the approximate germination time for a seed on the seed packet.) Have the children water the plants every two or three days after you test the soil to be sure the soil is neither too wet nor too dry. Continue the observations, picture taking, and discussions of the plants for eight to ten days. Arrange the pictures in order on a bulletin board or other appropriate place. Prior to terminating the activity, review the proceedings with the children, asking them to describe the germination and growth of their plants. Ask, "How long did the seeds take to germinate?" "What parts of a plant grow?" You may want to pull one or two of the plants to examine their root systems after five days and ten days.

Lesson Plan ■ J

Orientation:	Pre-K–2.
Content Objective:	The children will state that many kinds of seeds are found in nature.
Skill Objective:	The children will *observe* seeds as they exist in nature and will *classify* them according to their properties.
Materials:	Small paper or plastic bags, magnifying glasses.
Evaluation:	Observation of student group problem-solving skills, verbal interactions, and sketches.

Procedure

Note: This activity is best conducted in the fall season, when plant seeds are most prolific.

Show children and/or describe the seeds of plants such as grasses, trees, weeds, flowers, and so on. Tell them they are going on a search for seeds in the schoolyard. Provide each child or group of children with a paper or plastic bag, and take them outside on the school grounds. It may be best to take them first to a weedy patch or flowering hedge, where seeds may be found on the plants or on the ground under them. Permit the children to discover the seeds, collect several, and place them in their bags. Then instruct them to continue to find and save as many other types of seeds as they can. Return to the classroom, pass out magnifying glasses if they are available, and permit the children to examine the seeds they have found. Ask them, "How many different seeds did you find?" "Hold up your largest seed; your smallest." "Put all the seeds that are alike in separate piles." Children who are old enough to draw a sketch of one or more seeds may be asked to do so.

Orientation: Grades K—4.

Content Objective: The children will state that plants may reproduce from roots, stems, or leaves.

Skill Objective: The children are required to *observe* reproductive processes and to *classify* the plants according to their reproductive process.

Materials: Sweet potato; wide-mouthed jar; toothpicks; philodendron, geranium, or coleus plant; glass tumbler; African violet or begonia plant, sand.

Evaluation: Students' verbal interaction, laboratory worksheets, log, and reports.

Procedure

Tell the children that they are going to learn if plants can reproduce in other ways than from seeds. Have the children help set up the experiments wherever possible.

From Roots: Place a large sweet potato, narrow end down, in a wide-mouthed glass jar (Figure 10—5). Fill the jar with water so that the lower one-third of the sweet potato is submerged. Place the jar in a warm place, add water when necessary, and the potato will produce a large vining plant.

Cut the top inch from a carrot, beet, or turnip, leaving the foliage attached to the severed piece. Allow the cuttings to remain in a shallow dish of water until roots appear.

From Stems: Place a stem from a philodendron, geranium, or coleus plant in a tumbler of water (Figure 10—5). Keep the tumbler out of the direct sunlight, and a root system will develop on the stem.

From Leaves: African violet and begonia leaves will produce new plants if several of the veins are cut cross-wise with a razor blade and the leaf is pressed into moist, warm sand. In two or three weeks, with regular watering, small roots will have grown from the cuts in the veins. These will be followed by stems.

Other plant parts that produce new plants are rhizomes (iris roots), tubers (seed potatoes), shoots (strawberries and ivy), and bulbs (tulips and narcissus). Discuss with the children why it is important that

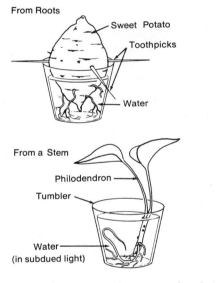

Figure 10–5 ▪ Plants Reproduce in Many Ways

plants can reproduce in a variety of ways. Since they cannot control their environment or move to more favorable locations as animals do, plants must survive by adapting their reproductive process to the conditions in which they exist. Have the students draw a sketch of one or more examples of asexual reproduction and label the components of the system—for example, carrot, dish, water, roots, and so on.

Lesson Plan ▪ L

Orientation: Grades 4–6.

Content Objective: The children will structure and carry out an experiment to determine the effect of certain variables on the growth of mold.

Skill Objective: The students are required to *name* and *control variables, experiment,* and *interpret data.*

Materials: Moldy orange, bread, or cheese; bread that does not contain a mold inhibitor; eight shallow dishes.

Evaluation: Students' verbal interaction, student group problem-solving skills, laboratory worksheets, log, and reports.

Procedure

Show the class a moldy orange or piece of bread or cheese. Ask the class: "Does anyone know what this is?" (Mold.) "I wonder what sort of conditions molds thrive under?" (Accept the opinions of the students.) Establish with the class that they are going to grow mold specimens and that mold spores are found all around us. A piece of bread that is touched to a dusty surface will pick up the spores. Under the proper conditions the spores will develop into mold. Ask the class: "In what sort of conditions can we test the growth of mold?" (Wet, dry, cold, warm, light, dark, and so on.) (Naming variables.) Establish with the class all possible combinations of the three variables to be tested and the conditions for testing. (Controlling variables.)

Variables	Conditions for Testing
1. Wet, cold, light	
2. Wet, cold, dark	(Wet bread in refrigerator)
3. Wet, warm, light	(Wet bread in plastic dish in sunlight)
4. Wet, warm, dark	(Wet bread in covered dish)
5. Dry, cold, light	
6. Dry, cold, dark	(Dry bread in refrigerator)
7. Dry, warm, light	(Dry bread in plastic dish in sunlight)

Suggest that some students may wish to find a way to test for mold growth with conditions 1 and 5 although these are more difficult to establish.

Assign individuals or groups to test the growth of molds under the various conditions and to maintain a daily log, including sketches of their experiment. After three or four days, have the children show their specimens and discuss the results. (Interpreting data.) Have the children examine the mold with a magnifying glass to view threads and spore cases.

Concept 4

Plants carry on a variety of life processes.

Discussion

Although the evidence is less dramatic, plants carry on most of the same vital life processes as do animals. In addition, they may conduct one process that is unique to the plant kingdom—photosynthesis. Plants that possess the ability to manufacture sugars and starches from water and carbon dioxide feed all the other organisms of the world. Plants without this ability and all animal life depend upon them for survival. All foodstuffs must ultimately come from a plant that is carrying on the process of photosynthesis.

Photosynthesis

Plants that contain chlorophyl are capable of producing sugars from carbon dioxide and water. The chlorophyl acts as a catalyst and in the presence of sunlight helps the two compounds to combine chemically. Some of the simple sugars are then converted to fats and proteins. These are stored in the stems and roots of the plant. Oxygen is a by-product of the photosynthesis process.

Other Processes

The rate at which water evaporates from a plant (*transpiration*) is controlled by the size of openings (*stomata*) on the underside of its leaves. Plants must take in oxygen, and release carbon dioxide and water vapor, through the stomata as they carry on their life processes. This is called *respiration. Digestion, assimilation,* and growth processes occur in plants as nutrients are dissolved and transported to the growth areas by the sap. Plants reproduce themselves in a variety of ways.

Tropisms

Plants respond to external stimuli. The movement of a plant in response to a stimulus is called a tropism. Plants grow toward the light (phototropism); plant roots grow down and plant stems grow up in response to gravity (geotropism); roots grow toward water (hydrotropism) and respond to heat (thermotropism), touch (thigmotropism), and the chemical content of the soil (chemotropism).

Lesson Plan ■ M

Orientation:	Grades 4–6.
Content Objective:	The children will state that healthy plants (1) exchange gases with the atmosphere, (2) must have sunlight on their leaves, (3) produce oxygen, and (4) give off water vapor.
Skill Objective:	For each activity the students are required to *experiment* by following a set of directions, to *observe* the results of their experimental conditions, and to *infer* from their observations.
Materials:	Three geranium plants, Vaseline, aluminum foil, aquarium, elodea, glass funnel, test tube, plastic bag.
Evaluation:	Students' verbal interaction, student group problem-solving skills, laboratory worksheets, log, and reports.

Procedure

Tell the class that they are going to set up some controlled conditions with green plants and make inferences concerning their observations. Divide the class into four experimental groups. Charge each group with setting up the experimental situation and recording their observations. The entire class may observe all experiments and discuss and make inferences concerning them. Have the students draw a sketch of each experiment and describe the result in writing.

continued on next page

Group A: Coat the top and bottom of one or two leaves of a healthy geranium plant with Vaseline. Keep the plant in a sunny location. The students will observe that the Vaseline-covered leaves will turn yellow. They should infer, among other things, that no gases could enter or leave the stomata, and therefore there was no carbon dioxide available for the process of photosynthesis.

Group B: Cover one or two leaves of a healthy geranium plant with aluminum foil. After several days the students will observe that the leaf is turning yellow. They should infer that no sunlight was available for the photosynthesis process.

Group C: Put a water plant such as elodea in an aquarium filled with water. Invert a glass or plastic funnel over the plant and a test tube filled with water over the stem of the funnel. (See Figure 10–6.) Set the system in the sun for several days. The students will observe bubbles of gas displacing the water in the test tube. When most of the water has been displaced, remove the test tube and insert a lit match or glowing wood splint. The students will see the match or splint burn or glow brightly. If they cannot guess from this test that the gas is oxygen, tell them. The students should infer that oxygen is given off by plants.

Group D: Cover a live geranium plant with a plastic bag and tie the bag securely about the pot (Figure 10–7). Inflate a second plastic bag by waving it through the air and tying off the open end. Place both the plant and the empty plastic bag in the sunlight for several hours. The students should observe that water droplets form on the inside of the plastic bag that covers the plant, but not in the empty plastic bag. They should infer that a live plant gives off water vapor.

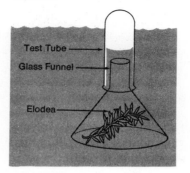

Figure 10–6 ■ Plants Give Off Oxygen

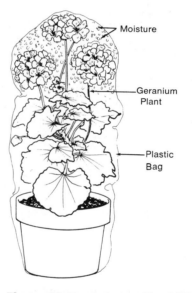

Figure 10–7 ■ Leaves Give Off Water

Lesson Plan ■ N

Orientation: Grades K–6.

Content Objective: The children will state that plants are sensitive to the effects of gravity and sunlight.

Skill Objective: The students are required to carefully *observe* the effects of gravity and sunlight upon plants and to *infer* a generalization concerning the effect of the two variables.

continued on next page

Materials:	Bean seeds, a glass tumbler, cup, blotter paper, milk carton, soil, shoebox.
Evaluation:	Students' verbal interaction, student group problem-solving skills, laboratory worksheets, log, and reports.

Procedure

Permit groups of children to carry out each of these activities. Sprout some lima beans in a glass tumbler, as in Lesson Plan F in this chapter. After the sprouts and roots are well defined, turn the seeds in several directions. After several days the children should observe that the roots are again growing downward, and the stems are again growing upward. They should infer that the plants are sensitive to the force of gravity. (Do not expect K–3 students to use the term *gravity*.)

Also plant several lima bean seeds in a soil-filled cup. Place the cup in a shoebox that has only a single, one-inch opening cut near the center on one side (Figure 10–8). After the beans have sprouted, have the children observe them briefly for several days. Then turn the plants completely around and continue to observe them. The students should see that the plants

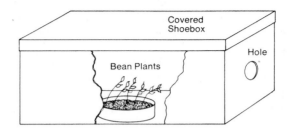

Figure 10–8 ■ Plants Grow Toward Light

grow toward the opening, and when turned around, they will reverse their direction of growth back toward the opening. Students should infer that the plants are sensitive to light and grow toward a light source. Students should maintain a log of their observations and conclusions.

Concept 5

Bacteria are important members of the Monera kingdom.

Discussion

Bacteria are one-celled organisms, members of the Monera kingdom, and structurally related to blue-green algae. They are very simple in structure, being composed of a thin cell wall enclosing a mass of living protoplasm. They have no well-organized nucleus or other internal structures. Ten thousand large bacteria placed side by side would form a line just one inch long. These tiny organisms are found everywhere—in air, water, food, soil, and living matter.

How Bacteria Affect Other Living Things

Bacteria are most commonly associated with disease. However, only a small percentage of bacteria are known to be harmful (*pathogenic*) to man. Many forms of bacteria have no effect on man while some forms are quite beneficial. Bacteria help to break down animal wastes and dead vegetation and thereby provide chemicals to generate other living things. Bacteria are used to produce fermented foodstuffs, such as sauerkraut, vinegar, and cheese. Bacteria are essential to linen production, curing tobacco, and tanning animal hides. Bacteria residing in certain plants called *legumes* fix nitrogen from the air to produce protein.

How Bacteria Carry on Life Processes

Bacteria are mobile. They move with the aid of whiplike *flagella* that extend from the cell body. A bacteria cell reproduces by the simple process of dividing into two cells upon reaching maturity. In this way a single cell may produce millions of cells within a period of hours after entering a favorable environment. Bacteria ingest food and expel wastes through their cell walls.

The Forms of Bacteria

Bacteria cells are found in three main shapes: coccus forms (round), bacillus forms (rod-shaped), and spirillum forms (spiral-shaped). Round and rod-shaped bacteria join to form colonies that are classified as follows:

1. Diplococcus—pairs of round cells or two-celled filaments.

2. Staphylococcus—clusters of round cells.

3. Streptococcus—strings or chains of round cells.

4. Streptobacillus—strings or chains of rod-shaped cells.

Spiral-shaped bacteria seldom join to form colonies.

Lesson Plan ■ O

Orientation:	Grades 4–6.
Content Objective:	The children will describe the effects of household chemicals on the growth of bacteria.
Skill Objective:	The students are required to *experiment* by establishing the controlled conditions for the cultures, to *observe* the specimens, and to *infer* from their observations.
Materials:	Nutrient agar, pan, fifteen petri dishes (or saucers covered with Saran wrap), common household chemicals.
Evaluation:	Students' verbal interaction, student group problem-solving skills, laboratory worksheets, log, and reports.

Procedure

The teacher should prepare specimens as follows: Boil a pint of water and add five tablespoonfuls of nutrient agar to it. (A nutrient solution may also be prepared by boiling a potato in water and adding one-quarter teaspoon of baking soda.) Pour the nutrient solution into petri dishes or other suitable containers. Close off and seal with cellophane tape one dish to use as a control. Sneeze or expectorate into three petri dishes that contain the nutrient solution.

These cultures will be used to test the effect of different variables on bacterial growth. You might spray Lysol in one culture, put a drop of iodine in another, and a drop of tap water in the third. Seal all petri dishes with cellophane tape. Have the children observe the cultures regularly for about a week. Instruct the students to keep notebooks in which they maintain a detailed record of their observations. At the conclusion of the observation period, have the students discuss their observations and write their conclusions in their notebooks. The teacher should dispose of all specimen petri dishes in an incinerator.

Summary

Living things may be classified as plants, animals, protistans, fungi, or monerans. We may consider plants to be those organisms that lack general mobility, produce food and structure from water and carbon dioxide, and reproduce in a variety of ways.

Plants may be generally classified as having vascular systems or nonvascular systems (algae, mosses, fungi). Vascular plants include all flowering species (angiosperms), evergreens (gymnosperms), ferns, club mosses, and horsetails.

Plants may reproduce by asexual, vegetative means—as from stems, leaves, tubers, rhizomes, shoots, or spores. Or they may reproduce sexually from seeds. In sexual reproduction, two specialized cells called gametes combine to form a zygote. The zygote, in turn, grows into an embryo and eventually becomes an adult plant.

Plants carry on many life processes. Some of the more important ones are photosynthesis, reproduction, respiration, digestion, transpiration, and excretion. Plants respond to external stimuli with movements called tropisms.

Bacteria are one-celled organisms of the monera family. Some are pathogenic (harmful) to man, but many are harmless and many others are beneficial. Bacteria are mobile and carry on such life processes as ingestion, digestion, reproduction, and excretion. Bacterial cells exist in three recognizable forms—round (coccus), rod-shaped (bacillus), and threadlike spirals (spirillum).

CHAPTER 11

Investigating Animal Life

Look What's in This Chapter

In this chapter we'll discuss some important concepts and subconcepts related to the study of animal life, and we'll introduce lesson plans that are designed to teach these concepts and subconcepts to children.

Concept 1 Animals may be grouped according to their structure.

Subconcept 1–1 The animal kingdom is commonly divided into two major categories: vertebrates and invertebrates.

Concept 2 Animals reproduce principally by sexual means.

Concept 3 Animals carry on a variety of life processes.

Concept 4 Animals and plants have many similar characteristics.

Nearly one million different kinds of animals have been identified. They are as diverse in size and complexity as sponges and elephants, jelly-fish and whales. There are animals with a hundred legs, six legs, or no legs; animals protected by skin, scales, or shells. Animals may have four-chambered hearts, two-chambered hearts, or no hearts at all. They may be found attached to the ocean floor or soaring miles above the earth. Because it is so tremendously diverse in size, habitat, structure, and function, the animal world requires a system of classification to be understood.

Concept 1

Animals may be grouped according to their structure.

Discussion

Though animals are often widely dissimilar, they are also alike in many ways. It is these similarities of structure and function that enable man to classify them.

Subconcept 1–1

The animal kingdom is commonly divided into two major categories: vertebrates and invertebrates.

Discussion

Vertebrates

Vertebrates are what we generally think of as the higher animals. All vertebrates have certain common characteristics. The major one is the presence of a *notochord* in the early stages of development. This notochord develops into a backbone in nearly all vertebrates. Vertebrates possess *internal skeletons* to which a covering of muscle and other tissue is attached. In general, vertebrates are also bilaterally symmetrical and possess two pairs of appendages attached at the shoulder and hip.

All vertebrates belong to the *phylum* of animals called Chordata. The phylum is the largest category of the classification system of biology. Phyla are subdivided succeedingly into *classes, orders, families, genera, species,* and *varieties.* As one goes down the ladder of classification, the similarities among members of a group become progressively more striking than the differences. Examine Chart 11–1. Notice that at each stage from kingdom to species you are adding more specifications to describe the animal. The categories become narrower and more specific, and the animals within the group are more and more similar.

The common *classes* of vertebrates, with some examples of each class, are:

1. Chondrichthyes—sharks, sawfish. About 600 species.
2. Osteichthyes—bony fishes. About 20,000 species.
3. Amphibia—salamanders, frogs. About 2,800 species.
4. Reptilia—snakes, alligators, turtles. About 7,000 species.
5. Aves—birds. About 8,600 species.
6. Mammalia—classified by *order* (selected samples only):
   a. Marsupialia—kangaroos, opossums.
   b. Chiroptera—bats.
   c. Primates—monkeys, gorillas, man.
   d. Rodentia—rabbits, mice.
   e. Carnivora—dogs, cats.

Invertebrates

While one phylum includes all of the vertebrates, there are nineteen phyla of invertebrate animals. The names and characteristics of some of the more common invertebrate phyla are:

Protozoa—Tiny, one-celled animals that exist individually or in colonies. Examples: amoeba, paramecium, euglena. About 16,000 species.

Porifera—The simplest of the multicelled animals; have two layers of cells making up the walls of a tubelike body; the walls of the body

Chart 11–1 ■ The Classification of an Animal Species

The Eastern Red Squirrel	
Kingdom (Animalia)	All animals.
Phylum (Chordata)	Animals with backbones.
Class (Mammalia)	Animals with backbones and milk glands.
Order (Rodentia)	Animals with backbones, milk glands, and long, sharp incisor teeth.
Family (Sciuridae)	Animals with backbones, milk glands, long, sharp incisor teeth, and bushy tails.
Genus (*Tamiasciurus*)	Animals with backbones, milk glands, long, sharp incisor teeth, and bushy tails; and that climb trees.
Species (*Tamiasciurus hudsonicus*)	Animals with backbones, milk glands, long, sharp incisor teeth, and long, bushy tails; and that climb trees and have brown fur on their backs and white fur on their underparts.

contain many openings or pores. Examples: sponges. About 4,200 species.

Coelenterata—Simple, two-layered, hollow bodies with an opening on one end surrounded by tentacles; some possess stinging cells. Examples: jellyfish, hydra, coral. About 9,200 species.

Platyhelminthes—Unsegmented flatworms; bodies consist of three cell layers; possess rudimentary nervous and digestive systems; some are parasites. Examples: tapeworm, planarian, fluke. About 6,000 species.

Nematoda—Unsegmented roundworms; bodies are often long and thin with an opening at each end; possess a definite digestive system; some are parasitic. About 6,000 species.

Annelida—Mostly segmented roundworms; possess well-defined nervous system, digestive system. Examples: earthworm, leech. About 6,500 species.

Echinodermata—Marine animals; possess internal limy skeletons that are often spined; possess radial symmetry. Examples: starfish, sea urchin, sand dollar. About 5,000 species.

Mollusca—Shellfish and snails; usually possess soft, unsegmented bodies with exterior shells made of lime; well-developed nervous, digestive, and circulatory systems. Examples: oyster, clam, snail, octopus. About 70,000 species.

Arthropoda—Animals having segmented bodies with distinct regions; possess hard, jointed exoskeleton; they are bilaterally symmetrical with pairs of movable, jointed appendages. Examples: lobster, crab, crayfish, spider, insects. About 750,000 species.

Lesson Plan ■ A

Orientation:	Pre-K–2.
Content Objective:	The children will state that pets (animals) have many common characteristics and needs.
Skill Objective:	The children will *observe* the behaviors and characteristics of animal pets.
Materials:	Children's pets.
Evaluation:	Observation of students' verbal interaction.

continued on next page

Procedure:

Ask the children to talk about the pets they have at home. Ask them to tell the other children the name of their pet, what kind of animal it is, how it looks, feels, and acts, and so on. Decide on three or four pets of different kinds. (Good choices for study include dogs, cats, goldfish, gerbils, toads, snakes, rabbits, and others. Avoid soliciting for large animals and those that require special care and equipment.) Contact the children's parents and arrange for the pets to be brought to school on "pet day" and taken home after school. Ask each parent to supply directions for the care of the pet and food that the pet is used to eating. (Remember to ask whether the pet may be handled only by their child or by all the children.) All pets should have a cage or box to house them during the day. On pet day, permit each of the three or four children who are the pet owners to show their pet and to tell the class what it eats and drinks, some nice or funny things the pet does, and what must be done to take care of it (feeding, watering, cleaning up its wastes, grooming, treating for fleas and other parasites, providing medical treatment, and so on). While the pets are being shown, ask questions of the other children such as: "Do all dogs have long hair like Rex?" and "What do snakes eat?" Permit the other children to tell how they take care of their pets at home. Use your judgment about which pets the other children may touch, considering the welfare of both the children and the pet. After all the pets have been observed, ask questions such as: "What things do all or most pets require to be healthy?" The children should name food, water, removing wastes given off by the pet, general cleanliness of its surroundings, exercise, love and attention, and others. Ask the children to compare the needs of the animals with one another and with humans. Remind them that animals, according to scientists, have similar needs and characteristics to those of humans.

Lesson Plan ■ B

Orientation:	Pre-K–2.
Content Objective:	The children will describe how to care for classroom pets, the different behaviors of classroom pets, the things that classroom pets eat and do not eat, and the movements and sounds of classroom pets.
Skill Objective:	The children will *observe* and *communicate* about classroom pets; they will develop positive attitudes concerning the care and maintenance of pets.
Materials:	Camera (Polaroid preferred), film, one or more classroom pets, suitable habitat to keep the pet(s), necessary food, water and other materials to maintain the pet.
Evaluation:	Children's group problem-solving skills, verbal interactions, attitudes toward and care of animals.

Procedure:

Please see Appendix I for information on the care and feeding of classroom pets.

Activity 1—What are pets? Ask the children to describe the pets they have at home. Ask them how they feel about their pet(s). Show pictures of common pets—dogs, cats, canaries, and others. The children should understand that pets are animals we love and take care of.

continued on next page

Activity 2—There are many kinds of pets: If possible, show pictures of pets that are found less often in homes, such as hamsters, gerbils, snakes, chameleons, rabbits, rats and mice, and others. Discuss the fact that many people prefer different types of animals as pets, but that all pets must receive proper care.

Activity 3—Introducing classroom pet(s) to the children: Discuss the things that are necessary in caring for the pet: feeding, watering, cleaning the pet's cage or habitat, making sure the temperature is controlled, making sure no one mishandles the pet, and others. Form five groups of children, and make each group responsible for caring for the pet one day of the week. Show them how to give the pet food and water and how to clean the cage. If the children are permitted to hold the pet, make reasonable rules for handling it. Generally it is not a good idea to allow the children to remove a pet from its cage without being supervised by an adult.

Activity 4—Investigating the pet's behaviors: Set an alarm clock for ten, twelve, and two o'clock (or some other array of times during the school day). Every time the alarm sounds, have the children observe the pet and discuss its behaviors. Take a picture at each observation. Because some animals are nocturnal, cover the cage or habitat with a lightproof covering on one or two days and continue to make the regular observations by lifting the cover. Arrange each day's pictures

in order on a bulletin board. At the end of a week, hold up the pictures and discuss the activities of the pet at different times of the day.

Activity 5—What does the pet eat? Feed the pet at the same time each day, providing a commercial or standard food the pet likes to eat. Some animals such as snakes do not eat each day; amend this activity to suit their feeding habits. After about a week, try to substitute other foods, such as lettuce, carrots, cereals, and so on (make certain the foods you choose will not be harmful to the animal's digestive system). Take a picture of the pet's acceptance or rejection of the food. If the pet rejects the trial food for thirty minutes or so, provide it with the standard food. After several days of experimenting with different foods, show the pictures and have the children decide whether their pet liked to eat each food.

Activity 6—Mimicking a pet's movements and sounds (if appropriate): Ask the children if they ever heard their pet make a sound. Ask them to make the sound themselves. You may extend the activity by asking them to make the sounds of other pets they have heard. Then ask the children to show the class how the classroom pet moves. Permit several children to demonstrate, and have perhaps the whole class demonstrate together. Ask the children to show how other pets move; repeat the activity several times.

Lesson Plan ■ C

Orientation:	Grades K–4.
Content Objective:	The children will place pictures of animals in groups having similar characteristics. The children will give reasons for their choices.
Skill Objective:	The children are required to *classify* the animal pictures according to some set of characteristics and to *communicate* reasons for their choices.
Materials:	Pictures of a wide variety of animals.
Evaluation:	Students' verbal interaction, student group problem-solving skills, seat work, and sketches.

continued on next page

Procedure

Ask each child to bring to school one picture of some animal. The teacher should point out that animals include worms and insects as well as pets and other domestic varieties. One day, before the children arrive, divide a large bulletin board into four sections with a picture of one animal in each section. The pictures should represent a diverse array of animal characteristics. Examples might be a horse, a fish, a snake, and an insect. Ask the children, one by one, to thumbtack their picture to the section of the bulletin board where the animal is most like their own. As each child adds his own picture to the display, ask the class: "Why do you suppose Johnny put his picture there? Might it also be placed in another group?" In this way the class may classify their animal pictures into four groups and discuss the characteristics of the animals in each group.

If the teacher wishes to extend the classification lesson, he may choose any one of the four groups of pictures and ask the children: "Could we divide these pictures in any other way? Do some seem to go together more than others? Are some more alike than they are like the others?" While discussing the characteristics of the individual animals, have the class divide one group of pictures into two or more groups. Sometimes a single animal will comprise its own group. The classification process may continue as long as the nature of the animals represented lends itself to further grouping. As the class forms groups of pictures, the teacher may ask various members of the class to print labels that describe the characteristics of each group. Give the children a worksheet that contains pictures of animals. Have them color animals with like characteristics the same color.

Lesson Plan ▪ D

Orientation:	Grades K–4.
Content Objective:	The children will correctly name those objects and animals that possess symmetry.
Skill Objective:	The children will correctly *identify* objects, animals, and replicas of animals that possess symmetry.
Materials:	Worksheet containing simple sketches of animals, animal toys.
Evaluation:	Students' verbal interaction, seat work, and sketches.

Procedure

Draw several regular geometric shapes on the chalkboard, such as a circle, square, and rectangle. Draw a line through each figure so that it is divided into two congruent parts. Ask the children: "What does the line do to the figure each time?" (Divides it into two equal parts.) Tell the children that if, by drawing one line, a figure can be divided into two equal parts that look just the same, the figure is *symmetrical* and the line is called a line of *symmetry*. Draw several more shapes on the board and invite the children to draw lines of symmetry on them.

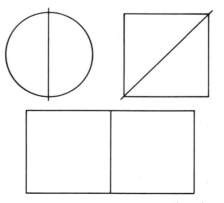

continued on next page

Now show a toy animal. "Can animals be symmetrical? Can we draw a line somehow that divides the animal into two parts that look the same?" Permit children to come forward and trace a line on the toy animal. Do this with several toy animals.

Pass out a worksheet containing line drawings of animals that show a front, back, or top view. Ask the children to draw lines of symmetry on the pictures so as to divide each animal into two parts that look the same. Note: Try to include drawings of one or two animals that are not symmetrical, such as a fighting conch. Tell the children that knowing about symmetry will help them to describe animals and tell how they are different or alike.

Lesson Plan ■ E

Orientation: Grades 4–6.

Content Objective: The children will sketch and describe various plant and animal forms found in pond water.

Skill Objective: The children are required to *observe* the organisms in pond water and to *communicate* their observations to others verbally and by drawing.

Materials: Jar of pond water, raw rice or boiled wheat seeds, depression slides, microscope or microprojector.

Evaluation: Student group problem-solving skills, seat work, and sketches.

Procedure

Collect water from a ditch or pond. Try to include in your collection some submerged leaves, floating leaves, and bottom mud. Back in your classroom, add a few raw rice grains or boiled wheat seeds to the water and store in a cool spot. Cover the container loosely with aluminum foil. Prepare slides of the pond water by placing a drop of the water on slides and covering them with cover plates. Have the students examine the organisms in the pond water, either by individually viewing the slides through a microscope of at least 100 power or by viewing the organisms through a microprojector. Instruct the children to try to find as many different kinds of organisms as possible. They may sketch and describe each life form they discover.

In pond water specimens, one may commonly expect to find amoebae, paramecia, vorticellae, and forms of protozoans (Figure 11–1).

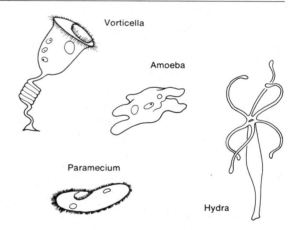

Figure 11–1 ■ Pond Water Organisms

Concept 2

Animals reproduce principally by sexual means.

Discussion

Asexual Reproduction

Some simple animals reproduce by the asexual processes of fission and budding. During fission, the nucleus of a mature cell splits (mitosis) into two parts, each portion forming the nucleus of a new cell. This form of reproduction is common to the *amoeba, paramecium,* and other single-celled animals. Some simple *protozoans,* notably the *hydra,* reproduce by budding. During this process, a small bud forms on the animal, breaks off, and develops into an adult organism.

Sexual Reproduction

Most animals reproduce sexually. Sexual reproduction requires the production of sex cells or *gametes.* Most of the animals that reproduce sexually have specialized organs, the *gonads,* which produce gametes. *Testes* are the gonads of the male animal; they produce the gametes called *sperm. Ovaries* are the gonads of the female animal; they produce the gametes called *ova* (singular: *ovum*). Ova are usually quite large; they contain nourishment for the developing new organism. Sperm are usually small and highly mobile, with long, whiplike tails that propel them along.

Variation from Sexual Reproduction

Organisms that are produced asexually by fission and budding are exact replicas of the parent organism. Except for rare, accidental rearrangements of nuclear matter by cosmic rays or other radiations, each succeeding generation is exactly like the one that preceded it. Thus, asexual reproduction produces no variety within a species. This is not true of sexual reproduction. The material that one gamete supplies to the union is not the same as that supplied by the other gamete. Each offspring of a sexual reproductive process is a unique organism, differing in some ways from all other members of its species. As will be shown in Chapter 12, this variation is highly important because each succeeding generation must cope with a changing environment. The variety of genetic types in a population is an important factor in the evolution of life forms.

Fertilization and Growth of the New Offspring

In most animals there are two sexes, *male* and *female.* Males are defined as sperm producers and females as ova producers. Reproduction occurs when a male sperm enters the cell wall of a female ovum and unites with it. For this union to occur, the sperm and ovum must be ejected into the same environment simultaneously. In some animals, notably fishes, the reproductive process occurs when both male and female gametes are simultaneously deposited in the water. In land animals, *internal fertilization* is nearly always the rule. In this process, male sperm are deposited in the tract through which the ovum must pass to reach the outside of the female's body. With internal fertilization, the union of the gametes is likelier to occur.

After the female cell has been fertilized, the new organism (zygote) undergoes a series of rapid cell divisions. With continued cell division, differentiated tissues are produced, each having a special appearance and unique function. A zygote may develop internally in a female womb, as in *placental* animals, or externally, as with the *egg-producing* animals.

Lesson Plan ■ F

Orientation: Grades 4–6.

Content Objective: The children will sketch and describe the hatching and development of brine shrimp eggs.

Skill Objective: The children are required to *observe* carefully the brine shrimp larvae and to *communicate* their observations verbally and by drawings.

Materials: Brine shrimp eggs, gallon jar, rock salt, heavy paper, flat pan, depression slide, microscope or microprojector.

Evaluation: Students' verbal interaction, seat work, and sketches.

Procedure

Brine shrimp eggs may be purchased at many aquarium supply shops. They may be hatched in the following manner. Add four tablespoons of rock salt to one gallon of water. Pour the solution into a wide, flat pan and add one-half to one teaspoon of dried brine shrimp eggs. If available, an aerator should be used or placed in the brine solution. Brine solution should be kept at room temperature. Cover the pan with heavy paper or cardboard that has a one-half inch hole at one end. As the larvae (Figure 11–2) hatch out of the eggs, they are attracted to the light coming through the hole. The developing larvae may be examined under a microscope after a drop of the salt-water solution has been placed in a depression slide. Ask the students to sketch the various stages of larval devel-

Figure 11–2 ■ Brine Shrimp Larva

opment. Discuss the process of the reproduction of brine shrimp.

Lesson Plan ■ G

Orientation: Grades 4–6.

Content Objective: The children will sketch and write a description of the metamorphosis of a fruit fly.

Skill Objective: The students are required to *observe* carefully the stages of the fruit fly's development and to *communicate* their observations verbally and by drawings.

Materials: Banana, yeast, six jars, hand lens.

Evaluation: Students' verbal interaction, student group problem-solving skills, laboratory worksheets, log, and reports.

continued on next page

Procedure

Dissolve a package of yeast in one-half cup of water. Dip a piece of ripe banana into the yeast suspension. Place pieces of the banana, along with strips of paper towel, in several open bottles or jars and set the containers outside until the fruit flies are attracted to lay their eggs. (Fruit flies may also be purchased from biological supply houses and introduced directly into the containers.) Have the children examine the fruit fly eggs with a hand lens. The eggs are white with two filaments attached at one end. Larvae will hatch within a day. After a time, pupae form and then tiny adults. Ask the students to observe the metamorphosis of the fruit fly carefully and to draw and describe what they observe.

Lesson Plan ■ H

Orientation:	Grades 3–6.
Content Objective:	The children will sketch and describe orally the metamorphosis of a praying mantis.
Skill Objective:	The children are required to *observe* carefully the specimen and to *communicate* verbally and by drawing.
Materials:	Foamy egg masses of the praying mantis, gathered locally or purchased from a biological supply house.
Evaluation:	Students' verbal interaction, student group problem-solving skills, seat work, and sketches.

Procedure

Dark, foamy egg masses of the praying mantis may be found on the stems of weeds and bushes. If the children find and bring to school several specimens of praying mantis eggs, they may be put in a protected place and watched until they hatch in early spring. If they observe carefully, the children will see the three-stage metamorphosis—egg, nymph, adult—of the praying mantis.

Lesson Plan ■ I

Orientation:	Grades 3–6.
Content Objective:	The children will sketch and describe orally the development of the chicken embryo.
Skill Objective:	The children are required to *observe* carefully the stages of development of chicken embryos and to *communicate* their observations to others.
Materials:	One dozen fertilized chicken eggs, egg incubator, ten saucers.
Evaluation:	Students' verbal interaction, student group problem-solving skills, seat work, and sketches.

continued on next page

Procedure

You may purchase fertilized chicken eggs from a hatchery and keep them in an incubator for the twenty-one-day incubation period. Or you may prefer to purchase fertilized eggs in various stages of development. To understand how the chicken embryo develops, the children should examine an egg two days after fertilization and each four days thereafter. Open each egg carefully and place it in a saucer. Each child should examine the developing embryo and sketch his observations. The teacher may direct a discussion of the developing features of the embryo at each successive stage. Eggs not reaching maturity should be disposed of. All hatchlings should be placed in an environment where they may receive care.

Concept 3

Animals carry on a variety of life processes.

Discussion

In addition to reproduction, all animals, regardless of their size or complexity, carry on certain other life processes.

1. They *ingest, digest,* and *assimilate* food.
2. They exchange gases with the atmosphere (*respiration*).
3. They give off solid and liquid wastes (*excretion*).
4. They create chemical substances (*secretion*).
5. They react to their environment (*sensitivity*).
6. They move about in their environment (*motility*).

Ingestion, Digestion, and Assimilation

All life forms require a constant source of energy to grow and to repair damage to their structure. This energy is supplied by chemicals taken into the body as food. Animals depend totally upon the energy supplied to them by plant life. During photosynthesis and other processes, plants fix the energy from the sun into the chemical bonds of sugars, starches, and simple proteins. This energy is later released within the animal as chemical and heat energy. Taking food into the body is called *ingestion*. The process whereby food is broken down to simpler chemical forms, or altered in some other way to make it usable by the organism, is called *digestion. Assimilation* occurs within individual animal cells when food is converted to energy or living matter.

Respiration

The chemical process whereby food is converted to energy is *oxidation*. During oxidation, oxygen is combined with the food, breaking it down and setting energy free. Oxidation creates certain waste products, chiefly carbon dioxide. Animals must receive a constant supply of oxygen, and they must continue to eliminate gaseous waste products. When an organism exchanges gases with the atmosphere, the process is called *respiration*.

Complex animals have specialized tissues and organs to carry on the process of respiration. During any respiratory process, oxygen and carbon dioxide must pass through the cell walls from regions of greater concentration to regions of lesser concentration. The gills of fish and the lungs of land animals are the specialized tissues wherein oxygen from the surrounding environment is separated from the oxygen-starved cells of the blood only by thin cell membranes. In these same tissues the waste gas, carbon dioxide, contained in the blood is separated from the outside environment by only the same few thicknesses of cells. The gases are exchanged by diffusion, oxygen dispersing into the living organism and carbon dioxide into the environment.

Excretion

Waste products are constantly formed as an animal carries out its life processes. If the animal does not eliminate these wastes, they will interfere with the proper function of the organism and act as poisons. Elimination of wastes in higher animals is carried out by means of the lungs, skin, intestines, and kidneys. The process also occurs in lower animals even though there may be no special eliminative organs.

Secretion

Animals require many special substances to carry on their activities. When these substances are not found in the food ingested by the animal, its body must manufacture them. Special tissues and organs secrete chemicals required for special purposes. Examples of such secretions are digestive juices and hormones.

Sensitivity

Even simple forms of life react to the conditions of their environment. One-celled animals are attracted to light and repelled by certain chemicals. Many animals have specialized tissues and organs that are sensitive to certain energy forms. Nerve endings in the skin permit an animal to react to pressure and heat. Certain other nerves are sensitive to light, others to slight variations in atmospheric pressure. The ability to react to the environment is a decided advantage in the struggle for survival.

Motility

Animal life is distinguished from most plant life by the ability to move about at will. Motility helps organisms to adapt to their environment. Unlike plants, animals can leave an undesirable habitat. When food or water is scarce, animals can move about to search for a new source of supply. When danger threatens their existence, animals can run away. Motility helps preserve animal species by enabling the males and females to seek each other out.

Lesson Plan ▪ J

Orientation:	Grades K–3.
Content Objective:	The children will state that a fish will respond to stimuli.
Skill Objective:	The children will *investigate, observe* their investigation, and *infer* that fish do respond to stimuli.
Materials:	Six quart jars, six fish (guppies or goldfish), six marbles, several flashlights, fish food.
Evaluation:	Students' verbal interaction, student group problem-solving skills, seat work, and sketches.

Procedure

Stand in front of the darkened classroom with a flashlight. Shine the flashlight at several children and ask: "Why did you look away from the light?" (It hurt our eyes. It was too bright.) Point out that the children were responding to a stimulus. The light is the stimulus.

Now tell the children to put their heads on their desks. Tell them that when they hear music they should lift their heads. Hum or blow on a pitchpipe. "Why did you raise your heads? What was the stimulus?" Ask: "Will other, more simple animals respond to a stimulus? Let us see."

Divide the children into groups of five or six. Pro-

continued on next page

vide each group with a quart jar containing a fish. Tell the children to observe how the fish responds to the stimuli of tapping on the jar close to the fish, shining the light directly on the fish, dropping a marble close to the fish, and putting a pinch of fish food in the jar.

Have each group record their observations.

After each group has completed the experiment, discuss whether the fish responded to stimuli. In each case ask: "What was the stimulus? How did the fish respond?"

Lesson Plan ■ K

Orientation:	Grades 4–6.
Content Objective:	The children will structure and carry out experimentation to determine the effects of selected variables upon the life process of the brine shrimp.
Skill Objective:	The children are required to *control variables* as they construct their experiment, to *observe* the effects of their experimental variables, and to *communicate* by maintaining a written logbook.
Materials:	Brine shrimp eggs, gallon jar, rock salt, heavy paper, ten flat pans, other materials required by each experimental group as they pursue their problem.
Evaluation:	Students' verbal interaction, student group problem-solving skills, laboratory worksheets, log, and reports.

Procedure

Hatch the brine shrimp eggs by the process described in Lesson Plan F. The larval and adult brine shrimp may be dipped off from around the hole in the paper and used by the students in their investigation. Let all the students observe the forms of the developing brine shrimp as described in Lesson Plan F. Suggest that they find out everything they can about these little animals by observing them and changing their environments. Some conditions the students might decide to test are:

1. Varying the salinity of the water.
2. What and how the fish eat.
3. Sensitivity to amount of light.
4. Sensitivity to heat.

Help the students to structure the conditions so they are observing the effects of a single variable. Encourage them to maintain a logbook that describes what they did, what they saw, and what they conclude.

Concept 4

Animals and plants have many similar characteristics.

Discussion

All living things have some common characteristics not shared by nonliving things. For instance, living things have a characteristic form and size, and all living things develop in predictable ways. All living things have a definite life span. And very significantly, living things reproduce offspring in their own image.

As one reads about the life processes of plants and animals, one is struck by other similarities. Plants and animals function alike in many ways. All life forms, plant and animal, require nourishment. All life forms must give off waste products. Both plants and animals absorb and assimilate chemical materials for building protoplasm and providing energy. These functions are performed in various ways by the various plant and animal forms, but the similarities are nonetheless striking.

The difference between plants and animals is often one of the prevalence with which a particular life process occurs. Plants reproduce in a variety of ways, both sexual and asexual, while animal reproduction is almost entirely sexual.

Very few plants can move about freely while most animals possess this ability. The single process that most clearly differentiates plants from animals is photosynthesis. Most organisms that are classed as plants possess chlorophyl and can produce food material from carbon dioxide, oxygen, and water. Most animals do not have this ability.

Upon reflection, it might be said that although the diversity of life processes appears endless, *living things are more alike than they are different.*

Lesson Plan ▪ L

Orientation:	Grades 4–6.
Content Objective:	The children will correctly fill in a chart of plant and animal characteristics and conclude that plants and animals have many similar characteristics.
Skill Objective:	The children are required to *classify* information.
Materials:	Chart 11–2 on the chalkboard or on individual worksheets.
Evaluation:	Students' verbal interaction, student group problem-solving skills, seat work, and sketches.

Procedure

Provide each child with a copy of Chart 11–2. Individually or as a group, the chart should be filled in to the best of the students' abilities. After the chart is filled, ask: "In what ways are plants and animals similar? In what ways are plants and animals different?" And finally, "What can we say about the characteristics of plants and animals?" (Plants and animals have many similar characteristics.)

continued on next page

Chart 11–2 ■ Plant and Animal Characteristics

Characteristic	Degree to Which the Characteristic Is Found in	
	Animals	Plants
Photosynthesis		
Sexual Reproduction		
Asexual Reproduction		
Skeleton		
Digestion		
Respiration		
Motility (Movement)		
Sensitivity		
Conclusions:		

Summary

Nearly one million different animals have been classified according to their structure. Most of the higher forms are vertebrates. Vertebrate animals nearly always have a backbone and an internal skeleton. Invertebrate animals do not have backbones. This large group includes a tremendous variety of forms: paramecia, sponges, jellyfish, flatworms and roundworms, starfish, oysters, crabs, and houseflies—to name only a few.

Although several classes of animals reproduce asexually by fission or budding, most animals reproduce sexually. Sexual reproduction involves the union of two unlike cells, a sperm and an ovum. The adult animal develops from this union by fission. The joining together of cells from different animals to form a new animal produces variety in the offspring. This variety aids the species in its struggle for survival.

Animals carry on the life processes of ingestion, digestion, assimilation, respiration, excretion, secretion, sensitivity, motility, and reproduction. Plants also carry on most of these processes. The similarities between plant and animal functions are striking. The major differences between plant life and animal life are that most plants produce their own food, while animals do not; plants are usually stationary, while animals are mobile; plants reproduce in a variety of ways, both sexually and asexually, while animals almost always reproduce sexually.

CHAPTER 12

Investigating Ecological Relationships

Look What's in This Chapter

In this chapter we'll discuss some important concepts and subconcepts related to the study of ecology, and we'll introduce lesson plans that are designed to teach these concepts and subconcepts to children.

Concept 1   Life forms undergo constant change.

> Subconcept 1–1   Animal and plant populations are constantly changing due to heredity.

> Subconcept 1–2   Animals and plants adapt to their environment by nonrandom selection.

> Subconcept 1–3   Dispersal is a means of adapting to the environment.

> Subconcept 1–4   Animal and plant communities may change over a long period of time.

Concept 2 All living things in a community are dependent upon each other.

Subconcept 2–1 There is diversity among living things.

Subconcept 2–2 Some living things are directly dependent upon other living things.

Subconcept 2–3 Food webs illustrate the interdependence of life forms in a community.

Subconcept 2–4 Food pyramids illustrate the quantitative relationship of food chains.

Subconcept 2–5 Plants and animals exhibit interdependence through the cycling of chemicals.

Ecology deals with the relations between living organisms and their environment. The activities of the myriad living things within a defined region are so interwoven with one another, and with the conditions of their environment, that the interrelationships almost defy description. However, certain principles may be stated. Living populations and their environments change constantly. Populations adapt to changing environments. Environments resist population increases. And organisms change gradually over long periods of time to produce drastically new and different life forms.

The interdependence of living things is exemplified very dramatically by the *parasitic* and *symbiotic* relationships that exist in nature. Less obvious, but highly significant, are the *dependent* relationships exhibited in *food chains*, the *oxygen–carbon dioxide cycle*, the *water cycle*, the *calcium cycle*, and others.

Concept 1

Life forms undergo constant change.

Discussion

Nearly one million different animals and approximately the same number of plants have been identified. Of course, there are many similarities among these plants and animals. But what accounts for their diversity? Why do so many different forms of life exist? A discussion of the following subconcepts sheds some light upon these questions.

Subconcept 1–1

Animal and plant populations are constantly changing due to heredity.

Discussion

The process of sexual reproduction creates a new organism that differs in some ways from each of its parents. Sexual reproduction is common to most animals and many of the higher plants. Hence the phenomenon of gradual, generation-by-generation change.

Inheritance

The basic building blocks of living matter are cells. Each cell contains, among other things, a *nucleus*. The nucleus consists of genetic material called *chromosomes*. When a body cell splits, all the chromosomes divide in half. Each half of the long, rodlike chromosome chain then regenerates itself to form a complete set of chromosomes. Next, the cell completely splits to form two new cells. However, when sex cells (sperm and ova) are formed, each takes with it only one-half of a chromosome chain. When a sperm and an ovum unite, a whole body cell is formed. Half of its chromosomes come from the sperm and half from the ovum. *Thus, each parent contributes one-half of the genetic material that determines the attributes of the offspring.* From each new union, a unique individual is formed, whose characteristics are the result of chance encounter.

Complex living things have countless characteristics. Each is determined by one or more specific *genes*. Genes are small, chemical units that make up the chromosomes. When gametes unite, as we have just seen, each gamete contributes one-half of each pair of genes. There are three ways in which the halves may combine to determine a given characteristic. For example, if two "tall" genes are combined, the offspring will probably be tall. If two "short" genes combine, the offspring will probably be short. And if one "tall" and one "short" gene combine, the offspring will probably be middle-sized. Human skin color, hair color, posture, the number of fingers and toes, even the tendency to contract certain diseases are determined by the chance union of specific genes.

Lesson Plan ■ A

Orientation:	Grades 4–6.
Content Objective:	After constructing a distribution chart, the children will state that the inherited characteristics of tallness and shortness are the result of chance and that organisms may change from generation to generation.
Skill Objective:	The children are required to *experiment* by manipulating chips and to *infer* the application of this exercise to the principle of random selection.
Materials:	Plastic chips (any two colors) and a chart like Chart 12–1 for each group.
Evaluation:	Students' verbal interaction, student group problem-solving skills, laboratory worksheets, log, and reports.

Procedure

Provide each group of children with two plastic chips of different colors, say, red and blue. Have the children mark each chip with a *T* (tall) on one side and an *S* (short) on the other. Have each group toss their two chips in the air and record on their chart how the chips fall. For instance, if both the red chip and the blue chip fall with the T-side up, place one mark in space 1. Have each group toss their two chips at least ten times and record its findings. Draw a big chart on the board, ask each group for the results of its activity, and place the totals in the appropriate places on the master chart. Ask the class: "In how many instances did we find a TT pair?" "In how many instances did we find an SS pair?" "In how many instances did we find a TS or ST pair?" "If the red chips represent male genes for tall

Chart 12–1 ■ Random Distribution

Red Chip		Blue Chip	
		T	S
	T	1. ℕℕ	2. ℕℕ
	S	3. ℕℕ	4. ℕℕ

and short, how many different combinations can we have?" "According to our study, what are the chances that an organism would acquire each combination?" "Can we see how organisms might change from generation to generation?" "What would happen if female organisms preferred to mate with tall male organisms? With short organisms?"

Subconcept 1–2

Animals and plants adapt to their environment by nonrandom selection.

Discussion

Barring external factors, a population that began with a particular proportion of some characteristic would tend to retain that proportion. But in nature, external factors are constantly at work. They encourage the selection of traits needed to survive. In animals, traits commonly thought to affect the survival of a species are size, strength, speed, coloration, and intelligence.

To understand nonrandom selection, imagine a species of insect some of whose members are green while others are white. Which do you think are likeliest to survive in a pasture full of birds? Or consider a deer population in a cold, snow-covered environment. They have eaten all the leaves and bark off the trees and underbrush. The only browse left is high up on the trees. Which deer is likely to survive, the tall one or the short one? The nature of populations is not determined solely by genetic factors. It is influenced greatly by environmental forces as well.

Plant life is also affected by the principle of nonrandom selection. Plants of the same species may have short roots or long roots, many leaves or few leaves. The ones with short roots will perish more readily in a drought, and the ones with many leaves will attract browsing animals. Those with long roots or few leaves will survive.

Adaptation is said to have occurred when a plant or animal possesses characteristics that help it to survive in a particular environment. When the population of green and white insects in the pasture described above changes so that the majority of the insects are green, adaptation has taken place. The insect is now, by virtue of its coloration, better able to survive in its environment. Adaptation will produce tall deer in deep snow belts and long-rooted plants in dry climates. Of course, adaptation is not planned and carried out by animals and plants themselves. It occurs because the environment places a stress upon the species. The individuals whose characteristics enable them to meet this stress survive.

Lesson Plan ■ B

Orientation:	Grades 4–6.
Content Objective:	The children will state that environmental factors affect the characteristics of plants and animals that live in an area.
Skill Objective:	The children are required to *investigate* (by analogy) and to *interpret their data by inferring* the relationship of their game to the principle of natural selection.
Materials:	Thirty green paper squares, fifteen white paper squares, a box marked Green Insects containing twenty-four "Survivor" cards and eight "Eaten by Birds" cards, a box marked White Insects containing twenty-four "Eaten by Birds" cards and eight "Survivor" cards.
Evaluation:	Students' verbal interaction, student group problem-solving skills, laboratory worksheets, log, and reports.

Procedure

Give each member of half of the class a green paper square and each member of the other half a white paper square. Tell them they are insects in a pasture. In two boxes marked "Green Insects" and "White Insects," place cards on which you have written "Eaten by Birds" or "Survivor." For the green insects there should be a ratio of three "Survivor" cards for each "Eaten by Birds" card. The ratio of cards for the white insects should be three "Eaten by Birds" cards for each

"Survivor" card. Mix the cards thoroughly in each box and permit each "insect" to draw a card from the appropriate box. Record the number of surviving insects of each color on a chart on the chalkboard.

Now redistribute "Green Insect" and "White Insect" squares to the entire class in the same ratio of green to white survivors; that is, give out three "Green Insect" squares for each "White Insect" square. Reshuffle the "Survivor" and "Eaten by Birds" cards.

continued on next page

These should remain in the same ratio. Again permit the children to draw a card from the appropriate box. Record the number of survivors of the second generation. Continue the game until the last "White Insect" has been "Eaten by Birds." Then discuss the results of the game by asking the following questions: "Why did we make the game so that the white insects were eaten more often than the green insects?" "What happens to animals or plants that are not well adapted to their environment?" "In what environment would a white insect survive best?" "How do the spots on a leopard and the stripes on a tiger help them to survive?" Ask students for other examples of how the characteristics of animals help or hinder their survival.

Chart 12–2 ▪ Nonrandom Distribution

	Number at the Start	Survivors of First Generation	Survivors of Second Generation	Survivors of Third Generation
Green Insect	15	12	9	?
White Insect	15	4	2	?

Note: These numbers are hypothetical.

Lesson Plan ▪ C

Orientation:	Grades 3–6.
Content Objective:	The children will state that characteristics such as color help determine the nature of the animal population in a given place.
Skill Objective:	The children are required to *experiment* (by analogy) and to *infer* the relationship of their data to the principle of adaptation.
Materials:	String, 100 each of red-headed, yellow-headed, and green-headed straight pins or colored toothpicks.
Evaluation:	Students' verbal interaction, seat work, and sketches.

Procedure

Enclose a patch of green grass about ten feet square with string. Within this area, stick colored toothpicks or pins into the ground. Use about 100 each of red, yellow, and green. Tell the children they are "pick-eater" birds, and they are to find as many picks as they can in some time period, say, ten minutes. At the end of the allotted time, return with the class to the classroom. Have each child turn in his toothpicks and report the number of each color he has found. The children should locate more red and yellow toothpicks than green toothpicks. After the total number of toothpicks has been reported and recorded, ask such questions as: "Which color was easiest to find?" "Which color was most difficult to find?" "More toothpicks of which color remain in the grass?" "If toothpicks were alive and produced little toothpicks of their same color, which color of toothpick would be most prevalent?" "What are some other characteristics besides color that determine which plants and animals survive? How?" Have the students draw a wild animal of their choice and describe how it survives.

Lesson Plan ▪ D

Orientation:	Grades 1–5.
Content Objective:	The children will draw animals in an environment and tell how each animal is adapted to that environment.
Skill Objective:	The students are required to *infer* the suitability of an animal to an environment and to *communicate* their inferences to others.
Materials:	Paper and crayons.
Evaluation:	Students' verbal interaction, seat work, and sketches.

Procedure

Tell the children about a new island that has been made in a river. The island has only one tree and no grass on it. Ask the children to make a crayon drawing of the island. After most of the class has completed their drawings, tell the children to put some animals on the island. Caution them to remember that their animals must first be able to get to the island, to eat and sleep there, and to hide from enemies. Tell them to draw pictures of two animals that might live on the island. When they have finished, have each child display his drawing and tell what the animals are. The class may discuss where the animals would stay and where they would find their food.

Subconcept 1–3

Dispersal is a means of adapting to the environment.

Discussion

We have seen how nonrandom selection will alter the nature of an animal or plant species. Though changing color is a very obvious form of adaptation, almost any characteristic of a species may be altered over a long period of time by a differentiated survival pattern.

The reproductive processes of animals and plants are usually more than sufficient to perpetuate the species. Under favorable conditions each new generation has more members than the last. Since each organism must have a certain amount of space and food to sustain it, overpopulation places stresses upon the ecosystem. The inhabitants must now *compete* for the space and resources of their habitat. Those organisms best suited to an environment will tend to survive in greater numbers. Tall plants, for instance, will shade out short plants, and thistles may tend to survive plants that are more palatable to animals. Because it is mobile, animal life often meets the stress of competition by moving to new areas. As they move into new territory, animals continue to overpopulate. And when the competition for food and space resumes, some of the members move to still other areas. This results in the dispersal of the species. Dispersal is often enhanced by the aggressive behavior of parents toward offspring and toward certain members of their own generation.

Though plant life cannot disperse of its own will, dispersal nonetheless occurs. Seeds and pollen are carried by the wind or by animals to new territory. If the conditions of the new area are favorable, the plant will survive and grow and reproduce. In this way, plants are distributed over large areas that will support their survival.

Over a long period of time, plants or animals that began as a single species and have been dispersed into drastically different environments may evolve quite different characteristics.

Imagine a flowering plant that disperses from a fertile river valley into the desert. The climate becomes drier as the plant advances from the valley. The members of the species that survive would have a longer root system and fewer leaves to give off water vapor to the air. The appearance of the desert plants might alter drastically. A new species altogether might be formed. Changes that take place over long periods of time as a species adapts to its environment are called *evolutionary changes*, and the process is called *evolution*.

Lesson Plan ▪ E

Orientation:	Grades 3–6.
Content Objective:	The children will state that competition is a factor in causing the dispersal of animals and plants.
Skill Objective:	The students are required to *investigate* (by analogy) and to *infer* the relationship of their data to the principle of competition among animals.
Materials:	Wrapped candy.
Evaluation:	Students' verbal interaction, student group problem-solving skills, seat work, and sketches.

Procedure

Take the children out on the playground. Have the girls form a large circle with all the boys in the center. Tell the boys you have some wrapped candies (caramels, for instance) that you are going to toss in the air. Each boy may have what he can find. Tell the boys they may not eat the candies yet. Toss the candies, and let the boys scramble for them. Repeat the process with the girls in the center of a ring of boys.

Back in the classroom, list all of the children's names on the chalkboard and write the number of candies each possesses. Ask the children: "Why did some of you get candy and not others? Why did some get more than others? Suppose that candy was the only thing you had to eat. How would that affect your behavior?" Have the students write a paragraph describing how competition among wild animals affects their existence.

Lesson Plan ▪ F

Orientation:	Grades 3–6.
Content Objective:	The children will state that competition for food and shelter forces plants and animals to disperse to other environments.
Skill Objective:	The students are required to *experiment* (by analogy) and to *infer* the relationship of their data to the principle of competition among animals.
Materials:	Three chalkboard erasers, fifteen ditto sheets containing tic-tac-toe grids, cards reading "A Dead Squirrel" and "Moved to the Seashore."
Evaluation:	Students' verbal interaction, student group problem-solving skills.

continued on next page

Procedure

Set the stage for the activity by telling the children that they are all squirrels in a beautiful, but small, valley. There is not room or food enough for all of them. Some of them must move to other areas—some to the mountains and some to the desert. To determine where each of the squirrels will live, organize a series of three-member eraser races. The winner of each race will go to a section of the room called *Valley*, the second-place finisher to a section called *Mountains*, and the third-place finisher to a section called *Desert*.

To begin the competition, place three children at the back of the room at a starting line. Each child is to balance an eraser on his head and at the signal "go" is to walk (not run) to the front of the room, touch the wall, and return to the starting line. Upon completing the race, each student should go to the section of the room determined by his finishing position. The teacher will act as judge for each race.

Next, remind the class that they are squirrels in a new habitat and that they must compete with the other squirrels in that habitat. Each habitat will support only five (or some other number) squirrels. Pair off the children in each group and supply each pair with a ditto master containing several tic-tac-toe grids. Each pair of children will play all the games on the sheet. The player who wins the most games is the survivor. In case of a tie, both "squirrels" are survivors. The losers of the tic-tac-toe competition will draw from a pile of cards on which is written either "A Dead Squirrel," or "Moved to the Seashore." Those students who draw "Dead Squirrel" cards should return to their seats and rest their heads on their arms. Those students who draw "Moved to the Seashore" cards may pair off and begin another competition of tic-tac-toe. You may stop the game at any time after most of the children have completed the first tic-tac-toe competition.

Discuss the exercise with the class by asking such questions as: "What do animals do when their habitat becomes too crowded?" "How is it decided which animals will die and which will survive?" "What conditions other than crowding might cause squirrels or other animals to move to other areas?" "Would the animals that moved to the desert live like the animals that moved to the mountains? How might their lives be different?" "Would the animals that survive in the desert look exactly like the animals that survive in the mountains?"

Stress the point that competition among wildlife often results in dispersal out of an original habitat to habitats with different conditions. Animals that survive under the new conditions may be different in some ways from those in the original habitat.

Subconcept 1—4

Animals and plant communities may change over a long period of time (succession).

Discussion

Over long periods of time, the earth's crust changes. Low-lying swamp may be elevated to form mountains and plateaus. Higher elevations may subside to be submerged under water. As glaciers advance, a temperate climate may become polar. When such changes occur in the topography and climate of a region, it follows that the plants and animals of the region must also change. Aquatic plants and animals will disappear as swamp is elevated to form a dry-land habitat. New life forms will appear that are better suited to the new environment. If the dry land is resubmerged in water, the plants and animals will change once more. Changes in the nature of a biotic community occurring over a long period of time that are due to changes of geography are termed *succession*. Evidence of succession is found in the records left by fossils in sedimentary rocks. Examples of rapid succession may be seen where land is submerged under water by dams or rockslides, but most succession occurs gradually. Often it takes millions of years.

Succession may also occur within a region that has a fairly stable climate. When a new island is formed by volcanic activity or by the buildup of coral, repopulation begins almost immediately. Birds come to rest upon the newly emerged land. They may bring seeds and spores of plants and deposit them. Plant life may also be washed ashore by the ocean tides. Such succession, known as *primary succession*, pro-ceeds slowly. *Secondary succession*, which occurs upon cultivated or burned-over land, proceeds much faster. There are surviving seeds, spores, and damaged plants within the region, and these elements also move in quickly from surrounding areas.

Lesson Plan ▪ G

Orientation:	Grades 3–6.
Content Objective:	The children will state that succession occurs less rapidly in a baked, sterile soil sample than in an unbaked soil sample.
Skill Objective:	The students are required to *observe* the soil samples over a period of time and to *infer* reasonable explanations for their observations. They will also *communicate* by maintaining a notebook.
Materials:	Rich field soil, large aluminum foil pans, baking oven.
Evaluation:	Students' verbal interaction, student group problem-solving skills, laboratory worksheets, log, and reports.

Procedure

Collect two samples of rich field soil in large aluminum foil pans (Figure 12–1). Punch several holes in the bottom of each pan for drainage. Bake one of the soil samples for two hours at 450°F. After cooling, place the baked (sterile) soil and the natural soil where they will get direct sunlight and precipitation. Have the children observe the samples regularly and maintain a notebook that describes the amount and appearance of the plant and animal life they find in each sample. Discuss the fact that succession occurs more rapidly in "live" soil. The children might conclude that the difference is due to the presence of seeds and pollen in the live soil.

Baked (Sterile) Soil Sample

Unbaked Soil Sample

Figure 12–1 ▪ Succession in Soil Samples

Lesson Plan ▪ H

Orientation: Grades 3–6.

Content Objective: The children will state that succession occurs less rapidly in boiled pond water alone than in boiled pond water to which plant material and mud have been added.

Skill Objective: The students are required to *observe* the pond water samples over a long period of time, to *communicate* orally and by keeping a notebook, and to *infer* reasonable explanations for their observations.

Materials: A gallon jar of pond water, two large jars, a large pan for boiling, pond plants and mud, depression slides, a microscope.

Evaluation: Students' verbal interaction, student group problem-solving skills, laboratory worksheets, log, and reports.

Procedure

Sterilize one gallon of pond water by boiling it. Put half of the sterilized water in each of two large glass jars. Into one of the jars drop several leaves and stems of aquatic plants and a small amount of mud from a pond (Figure 12–2). Cover the jars with cheesecloth, or loosely with aluminum foil, and place them where they receive strong, but not direct, sunlight. Have the children observe the jars closely for about a month and describe the difference in the appearance of the two specimens. After at least one month of observation, place drops of water from each jar in depression slides and have the class examine them under a microscope. Instruct the students to record their observations and to write down their conclusions. They should observe many more microscopic life forms in the "live" water than in the sterile water.

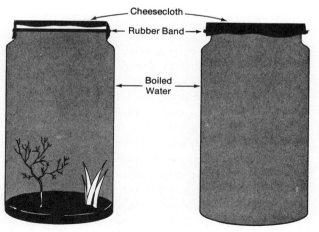

Plants and Mud from a Pond

Figure 12–2 ▪ Succession in Water

ɔncept 2

All living things in a community are dependent upon each other.

Subconcept 2–1

There is diversity among living things.

Discussion

A biotic community includes all the things that live in a given region. Most people are aware of large, conspicuous plants and animals such as trees and deer. But few people have discovered the less conspicuous forms of life that exist all around them. How many people notice or observe carefully the movements of ants or the flight of bees or the presence of lichen on a tree? Learn to observe your environment carefully if you want to understand and appreciate the diversity of living things.

Lesson Plan ▪ I

Orientation:	Grades K–6.
Content Objective:	The children will state that there are many different plants and animals around them.
Skill Objective:	The children are required to *observe* plant and animal life, to *communicate* their observations verbally to others, and to *infer* that there is diversity among living things.
Materials:	Plant or animal specimens gathered by the children.
Evaluation:	Students' verbal interaction, student group problem-solving skills, seat work, and sketches.

Procedure

Before taking the children on a tour of the playground or a nearby field or woods, brief them about the differences between living and nonliving things. Living things include any objects that have lived previously. Instruct each child to return to the room with one small sample of a living thing. You may mention examples of a leaf, a twig, or an insect shell.

Take the class outside. You might point out some of the differences among trees, shrubs, grass, and weeds. You might ask the children to notice how tall or short the different plants are, the shape of their leaves, whether or not they have flowers, and so forth. At least once on the trip, seat the children on the ground and ask them to look around them for small animals—insects, worms, and so on. Warn them not to pick up any of the animals, but merely to point it out to their neighbors. Then have each child select a living thing to take back to the classroom.

After returning to the classroom, have a few of the children bring their specimens to the front of the room and display them. The class may discuss where the specimens were found and what they are. The teacher may conclude by asking the children: "How many things did we see today?" "What can we say about the number of different things that live around us?" Have the students title a blank sheet of paper "Diversity of Living Things" and draw line sketches of four of the specimens they collected.

Orientation: Grades 3–6.

Content Objective: The children will state that plant and animal populations may be estimated by sampling and that many different organisms exist in the environment.

Skill Objective: Students are required to *observe* by sampling from a large population, to *communicate* their observations verbally to others, and to *infer* that there is diversity in living things.

Materials: Ten wire coat hangers fashioned into circles, pencil and paper.

Evaluation: Students' verbal interaction, student group problem-solving skills, seat work, and sketches.

Procedure

Fashion ten or twelve hoops from wire coat hangers. Provide each group of two or three children with a hoop and take them to a nearby field or vacant lot. Have each group throw its hoop into the air, go where it lands, and carefully count and describe all the living and nonliving things within the hoop (Figure 12–3). The students should keep a careful record of their observations. If they find anything they cannot name, they should make a rough sketch of it. Each group should repeat the counting process several times in different parts of the field, identifying and enumerating each of the living and nonliving things. Back in the classroom, have some of the students present their findings. The teacher may conclude the experience by asking such questions as: "Do you feel we know fairly well what kinds of living and nonliving things are in the field?" "Since we didn't observe every bit of the field, how can we say this? Can we guess?" "How many different things did we find?" "What might we say about the variety of things in our environment?"

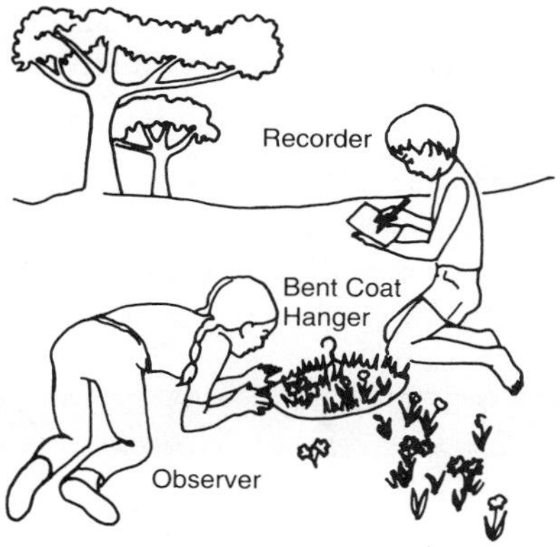

Figure 12–3 ▪ Sampling Large Populations

Subconcept 2–2

Some living things are directly dependent upon other living things.

Discussion

Each living thing has some effect on all other living things in a community. Herbivorous animals obviously depend on plants for survival. Some of the relationships among living things are less direct, but they are nonetheless important. Rabbits may use abandoned groundhog burrows for homes. Bluebirds take up residence in holes cut out of tree trunks by woodpeckers. The pollen of a flowering weed may be spread by a passing animal. The alligator may dig large holes in mudbanks that then hold water for aquatic life. Plants and animals touch each other's lives in many indirect—as well as direct—ways.

Predators

Organisms that kill and consume animals are called *predators*. Hawks consume rabbits and mice. Birds eat worms and insects. A Venus'-flytrap captures and digests insects. Many forms of life, particularly animal life, are predators.

Parasites

Organisms that obtain their food directly from other living organisms are called *parasites*. Fungi live upon the trunks and roots of trees. Ticks and fleas survive on the bodies of hairy mammals. Microorganisms live in the digestive tracts of all larger animals. Leeches suck the blood of some. Parasitic plants and animals depend for their survival on the food produced by a *host* organism.

Commensalism

In some relationships between two living things, one organism benefits while the other is largely unaffected. Such a relationship is termed *commensalism*. The remora and the shark is a common example. The remora attaches itself to the body of the shark by suction discs. The shark gains nothing from this relationship, but the remora obtains both mobility and bits of the shark's food.

Mutualism

Sometimes two organisms live together in a relationship that benefits both. This is called *mutualism*. It is demonstrated by *lichens*—small plants found on rocks and trees. Lichens have no roots, stems, or leaves, but are actually composed of two different plants, algae and fungi. The algae, having chlorophyl, produce the food for the plant while the fungi provide protection and moisture for the algae. A mutualistic relationship also exists between the hippopotamus and a small bird. The bird enters the hippopotamus's mouth to eat any leeches attached inside.

Lesson Plan ■ K

Orientation:	Grades 3–6.
Content Objective:	The children will state that fungus is a parasite that lives off a host. They will describe the fungus in detail.
Skill Objective:	The children are required to *observe* fungus specimens and to *infer* the relationship of the fungus and its host.
Materials:	Specimens of plant bark having fungus growing on them, six magnifying glasses.
Evaluation:	Students' verbal interaction, student group problem-solving skills, seat work, and sketches.

Procedure

Bring to class, or have the children bring to class, small limbs and twigs that have a white fungus growing on them. Have the children examine the fungus with magnifying glasses. Ask the children to describe the relationship between the twig and the fungus. Ask: "Which plant provides support for the other?" "From the color of the fungus, would you guess it possesses chlorophyll?" (Older children may test for the presence of starches and sugars in the fungus.) "Where does the fungus obtain its food?" "What would you say is the relationship of the bark and the fungus?"

Chart 12–3 ▪ Marine Environment Food Chain

Producer	Primary Consumer	Secondary Consumer	Tertiary Consumer	Scavengers
Algae	Fish	Sharks	Man	Crabs
Diatoms	Fish	Eels		Bottom Fish
		Large Fish		

Chart 12–4 ▪ Woods Environment Food Chain

Producers	Primary Consumers	Secondary Consumers	Scavengers
Trees–Leaves	Birds	Man	Birds
Bushes–Berries	Mice	Foxes	
	Insects	Birds	
		Cats	

Subconcept 2–3

Food webs, chains, and pyramids illustrate the interdependence of life forms in a community.

Discussion

Animals may be classified according to how they secure their food. All green plants may be classified as *producers* because they manufacture their own food from chemicals in their environment. Animals that eat plants (herbivores or vegetarians) are called *primary consumers*. Animals that eat primary consumers (carnivores or flesh eaters) are called *secondary consumers*. Animals that eat both producers and primary consumers are called *omnivores*. Humans are omnivores; they eat both vegetable matter and flesh. Some animals eat dead organisms. These animals are called *scavengers*. Charts 12–3 and 12–4 illustrate sample food webs for two different environments.

These charts depict simple relationships. Food chains are actually more complex. Some animals are omnivorous and therefore might be listed as both primary and secondary consumers. Some birds, such as crows, act as both scavengers and primary consumers. The interrelationships of the producers, consumers, and scavengers in a community form a complicated web rather than a simple chain.

Figure 12–4 shows the relationships of the Woods Environment in greater detail. The arrows are directed from the food source to the consumer. Can you see why it is more valid to speak of food webs than food chains?

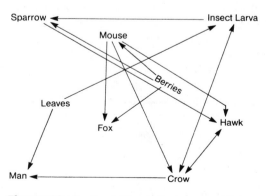

Figure 12–4 ▪ A Woods Environment Web

Examine Figure 12–4. What would happen if you removed the berries from the community? How many other life forms would be either directly or indirectly affected? Obviously no life form, plant or animal, exists in isolation. All are bound together in a web of dependency. Stress placed on one living thing is stress placed on all living things.

Lesson Plan ▪ L

Orientation:	Grades 3–6.
Content Objective:	On completing one or more food web games, the children will state that living things are interdependent.
Skill Objective:	The children are required to *infer* the results of changing an aspect of the environment on the relationships among living things.
Materials:	Chalkboard and/or worksheets.
Evaluation:	Students' verbal interaction, student group problem-solving skills.

Procedure

Write on the chalkboard the names of various plants and animals inside rectangles as shown:

Divide the class into two groups, A and B. Have one member of Group A draw a line from some substance that is eaten to something that eats it. Then have a member of Group B do the same. Continue until all possible lines have been drawn from one box to another. The group that draws the last line wins the game. Each group may challenge the line drawn by the opposing group. If a line is challenged, the child who drew it should be permitted to explain his reason for doing so. The teacher acts as a judge to settle any disagreements.

When the game is over, ask the class to examine the food web they have created. Ask such questions as: "What would happen if there were no more corn? What other things would be affected?" The teacher

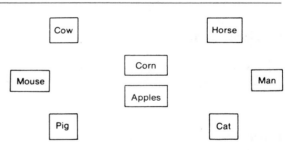

should stress the interdependence of living things. The game may be repeated, using other communities of plant and animal life. An example of another community is: grass, shrubs, grasshoppers, rabbits, caterpillars, frogs, snakes, hawks, and vultures.

The web of life game may be played by pairs or individuals or as a competition between small groups of children. When it is played this way, the teacher distributes the block diagrams on ditto masters.

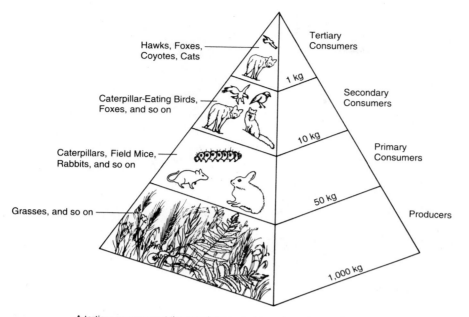

Hawks, Foxes,
Coyotes, Cats

Tertiary
Consumers

1 kg

Secondary
Consumers

Caterpillar-Eating Birds,
Foxes, and so on

10 kg

Primary
Consumers

Caterpillars, Field Mice,
Rabbits, and so on

50 kg

Grasses, and so on

Producers

1,000 kg

A tertiary consumer at the top of the pyramid requires a successively greater expenditure
of food mass and energy from the levels that support it.

Figure 12–5 ■ A Food or Energy Pyramid of a Grassy Field Habitat

Subconcept 2–4

Food pyramids illustrate the quantitative relationship of food chains.

Discussion

Food webs and food chains demonstrate the complex interrelationships that exist among plants and animals in ecosystems; that is, they indicate how organisms depend on one another as food sources necessary for sustaining life. However, food webs and chains do not demonstrate *how much* of each component is required—the quantitative aspect of the relationship. For instance, in the food chain of a grassy field (which includes grass, caterpillars, birds, and hawks), the whole chain depends on the amount of grass that exists. This is because the grassy plants must not only provide food for the caterpillars and other animals that eat it, but also must produce an excess that provides the seeds which permit the plants to reproduce. And, of course, there must be enough caterpillars to sustain the moth population and enough birds to sustain their population in addition to providing food for the other forms of life not shown on the pyramid in Figure 12–5 that depend on them. Thus, a thousand kilograms of grass might be able to sustain only fifty kilograms of caterpillars, and fifty kilograms of caterpillars might sustain only ten kilograms of caterpillar-eating birds, and only one kilogram of hawks. Thus, one ton of grass might sustain only a single hawk in the food pyramid. This example shows that a very large amount of plant matter must be available to support the consumers in any food chain. In our earlier example of a marine food chain, perhaps thousands of

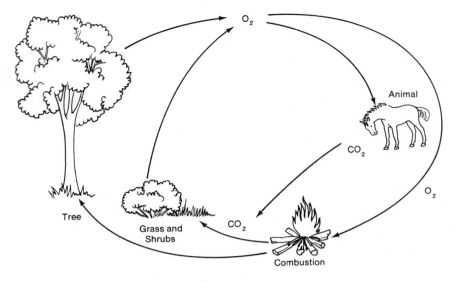

Figure 12–6 ■ The CO_2–O_2 Cycle

kilograms of algae would be consumed to eventually produce a single codfish that is eventually consumed by man.

Ecologists and conservationists are concerned by the pyramidal relationship in the food chains of humans. There is a tremendous amount of energy lost when people eat meat from cattle that are fed corn and other grains. Were people to eat the grains directly, many more humans might be fed from a given grain crop, and much less pollution might be generated were cattle not raised in large numbers for food. The food pyramid is a valuable tool in examining world hunger and pollution problems.

Subconcept 2–5

Plants and animals exhibit interdependence through the cycling of chemicals.

Discussion

The earth is like a huge spaceship hurtling through the hostile environment of space. The ship has aboard it only a limited amount of life-sustaining raw materials. These must support all living things for as long as possible. Chemicals of the earth's crust are used over and over again as an organism is born, lives, dies, and decomposes. A *cycle* is the process whereby chemicals become part of an organism and its life processes and are finally returned to a condition where they may be used again. The recycling of available raw materials has maintained life on earth for millions of years.

The CO_2–O_2 Cycle

Animals use oxygen to burn food inside their bodies. One of the products of this oxidation process is carbon dioxide, CO_2. Wood, coal, and gas fires also release CO_2. Plants absorb CO_2 and combine it with other chemicals to form carbohydrates and other plant material. Oxygen is released from plants as a by-product of this process. The CO_2–O_2 cycle (Figure 12–6) maintains a supply of these necessary chemicals for both plants and animals. It is an important process.

The Calcium Cycle

Rainwater leaches calcium from rock layers. Plants and animals absorb calcium compounds along with the water they imbibe. When dead plant and animal matter decomposes, some calcium is recycled directly to other plants and animals while some is absorbed by surface water and carried to lakes and oceans. Marine animals utilize calcium from the water to form their skeletons and shells. When they die, the skeletons and shells settle to the bottom of the ocean or lake. There they are covered with mud and form rock. Calcium is also deposited as rock layers when salt lakes dry up. During a period of geological upheaval, the former lake or ocean bottom is raised and exposed to the erosive effects of rainwater. Lakes formed by the mineral-rich runoff water are then subjected to the effects of the evaporating process. Thus, the calcium cycle (Figure 12–7) continues to operate.

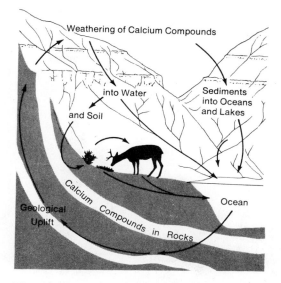

Figure 12–7 ■ The Calcium Cycle

The Nitrogen Cycle

The atmosphere is nearly 80 percent nitrogen. Ordinarily these nitrogen molecules are very stable and do not readily combine with other elements. However, there are two mechanisms that fix nitrogen atoms with oxygen and other atoms. One such mechanism is lightning. The other is the nitrogen-fixing bacteria found in the roots of some plants. Other types of bacteria break down nitrogen compounds and return the nitrogen to the atmosphere.

Within this large nitrogen cycle (Figure 12–8), a smaller cycling of nitrogen compounds occurs. Plants assimilate nitrogen compounds from the soil. These nitrogen-bearing plants are consumed by animals and become part of their body structure. When an animal dies, bacteria help to decompose the body. This releases nitrogen compounds to the soil where growing plants use them again. Since life cannot continue unless nitrogen compounds are available, the nitrogen cycles are extremely important.

The Carbon Cycle

Because all molecules of living matter contain carbon, it is vital that carbon compounds be continually available for carrying on life pro-

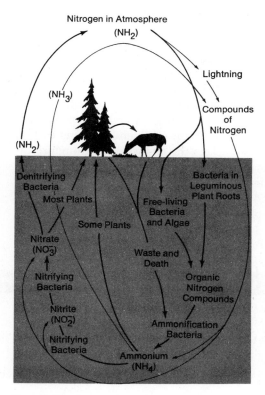

Figure 12–8 ■ The Nitrogen Cycle

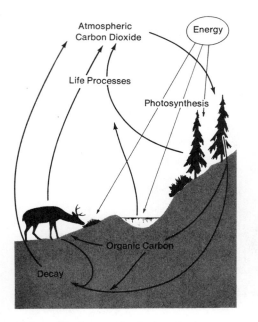

Figure 12–9 ▪ The Carbon Cycle

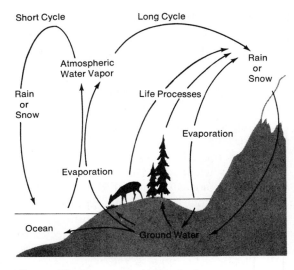

Figure 12–10 ▪ The Water Cycle

The Water Cycle

Everyone knows that living things need water. Through evaporation, huge amounts of water are transferred from lakes and oceans to the atmosphere. The water returns to the earth as precipitation. Plants absorb water to carry on their life processes and return water vapor to the atmosphere through transpiration. Animals imbibe water directly as well as through eating moisture-laden plants. Animals also give off water vapor through their skin and respiratory systems. The available supply of water is constantly being recycled to support life, as shown in Figure 12–10.

cesses. The carbon cycle (Figure 12–9) begins with photosynthesis. All green plants absorb carbon dioxide from the atmosphere. They use it as a raw material for manufacturing sugars, starches, and cellulose. Animals consume and assimilate the plant products, releasing carbon dioxide back to the atmosphere through respiration. The decay of both plant and animal structures also returns carbon dioxide to the atmosphere. Here it is ready to be used again in the photosynthesis process.

Lesson Plan ▪ M

Orientation:	Grades 3–6.
Content Objective:	The children will state that the water and CO_2 cycles are typical of other cycles found in nature.
Skill Objective:	The children are required to *observe* the interactions and *infer* from their observations.

continued on next page

Materials:	Hotplate, two Pyrex beakers or bowls, water, ice, limestone or seashells, vinegar, or weak HCl solution.
Evaluation:	Verbal interaction, problem-solving activities, sketches of water and CO_2 cycles.

Procedure

With the class watching, place a medium-size seashell in a jar and pour white vinegar or diluted HCl solution into the jar until the seashell is covered. Put a lid on the jar and place it so that all the children can observe the interaction taking place. (A second, untreated seashell about the same size as the one in the jar may also be displayed.) While the students are observing this activity, place a beaker of water on a hotplate and bring the water to a boil. Now, divert the students' attention and do the following: Hold a second beaker or jar containing ice water and ice cubes. Hold the jar low over the boiling water so that the steam condenses on the outer surface and eventually falls off in droplets. Ask: "What do you see?" "What is happening here?" (Water evaporates into the air, forms or condenses on the cold jar, and drops off into the boiling water.) "Is this like any other thing you see happen with water?" (It is like water evaporating into the air and returning to the earth as rain.) "Where does the rain come from? Where do the clouds come from? Is it possible for the same water to fall as rain more than once?" Tell the children we call the repeated process of evaporation and precipitation a *water cycle*.

Now say, "There are other cycles in nature. Let's examine another one of them." Hold up the jar containing the seashell and also hold up the second, untreated shell. Ask the children to describe what has happened to the shell in the jar: "If some of the shell is gone, dissolved, where must it be?" (In the liquid in the jar.) "Where do shells come from?" (The ocean.) Tell the children that seashells are made of a substance called calcium, as are their bones. "Where might the animals obtain calcium to build their shells?" (From the ocean water.) Tell the children the solution in the jar is a mild acid and then ask, "Under what conditions may a shell return to the water?" (When it dissolves in an acid solution.) "Describe a cycle that may occur in nature that causes calcium to be formed as shells and returned to the water." (Animals take calcium from the seawater to form shells and the shells can redissolve back into the water to be used again.) Tell the class this is called a *calcium cycle*. Ask them to draw the water and/or the calcium cycle as it occurs in nature.

Lesson Plan ■ N

Orientation:	Grades 3–6.
Content Objective:	The children will indicate an understanding of the various cycles that occur in nature.
Skill Objective:	The children are required to *infer* from a set of hypothetical conditions.
Materials:	None.
Evaluation:	Students' verbal interaction, problem-solving activities, sketches of the various cycles.

continued on next page

Procedure

Organize the class into groups. After discussing the various life-sustaining cycles in nature, ask the groups to discuss such hypothetical questions as: "What would happen if all nitrogen-fixing bacteria were to vanish from the earth?" "What would happen if the process of condensation stopped?" "What would happen if the life processes of animals returned some chemical other than carbon dioxide to the atmosphere?" "What would happen if all calcium remained buried in the rock layers of the earth?" Have each group prepare a written response to each question and present them to the class.

Summary

Plants and animals undergo constant change. Sexual reproduction processes produce variety among organisms. The organisms that are best suited to cope with the stresses of their environment thrive while those less suited perish. Thus, a constant sorting-out occurs, and over a long period of time the nature of the organism changes. The organism is then said to have adapted to its environment.

Another method of adaptation is dispersal. A plant that cannot compete in one environment may thrive in another. Animals move from one geographic location to another as the competition for food and space increases. In their new environments the members of a species may undergo adaptive changes. Differences among the members of a species develop in response to the demands of different habitats.

When environments themselves change due to geomorphic activity, succession may occur. That is, a series of changes in the biotic community may occur in the same location over a long period of time.

One of the major concepts of ecology today is that all living things are interdependent. Parasitism and mutualism are obvious dependent relationships. Food chains and webs are not so readily observed and understood. Producers of food, primary, secondary, and tertiary consumers, and scavengers are all related in a web of interdependence. Any one organism in the chain affects many others.

Chemicals are recycled in nature. Some common examples are the carbon cycle, the calcium cycle, the nitrogen cycle, the carbon dioxide–oxygen cycle, and the water cycle. All of these chemicals are used by animals and plants; recycling enables them to be used over and over again.

CHAPTER 13

Investigating the Human Body

Look What's in This Chapter

In this chapter we'll discuss some important concepts and subconcepts related to the study of the human body, and we'll present lesson plans that are designed to teach these concepts and subconcepts to children.

Concept 1 The human body carries on life processes.

> Subconcept 1–1 The human body must take in and digest food.
>
> Subconcept 1–2 The human body must give off waste products.
>
> Subconcept 1–3 Movement of the human body is made possible by the skeleton and muscles.
>
> Subconcept 1–4 The human body takes in oxygen and gives off carbon dioxide.
>
> Subconcept 1–5 The human body responds to stimuli.
>
> Subconcept 1–6 Humans reproduce.

Subconcept 1–7 The circulatory system is the transportation system of the body.

Concept 2 The use or abuse of drugs and other chemicals may be harmful to the body.

Humans are unique animals. Never has a single species so dominated the environment as we do now. We are the first organism that can alter its environment on a large scale rather than adapting to conditions as we find them. How are we similar to other animals? How are we unique? The answers to these two questions lie in the characteristics and processes of the human body.

Concept 1

The human body carries on life processes.

Discussion

It was pointed out earlier that all living organisms carry on certain life processes. How they do so, with what special cells and tissues, differentiates them one from another. The human body is particularly complex. It has many specialized cells, tissues, and organs. Each performs one or more activities directed toward maintaining the well-being of the organism as a whole. The life processes of the human body are summarized in the following subconcepts.

Subconcept 1–1

The human body must take in and digest food.

Discussion

Body cells are constantly being worn away by friction (hair, skin) and destroyed by injury and disease. New cells must be formed in order for a body to grow. Certain chemicals are required to regulate the functioning of body tissues. The

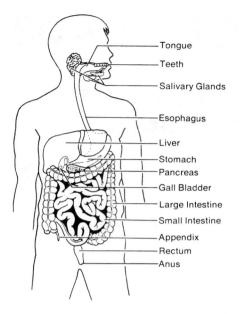

Figure 13–1 ▪ The Human Digestive System

muscle structure requires chemical energy to produce motion. For all of these reasons the human body must take in, break down, and utilize food.

The Digestive System

The cells of the body cannot utilize most foods in their natural form. The molecular structures are too large and complex. They must be reduced to smaller, more simple forms before the individual body cells can use them. The digestive system (Figure 13–1) breaks up unusable, complex food molecules into usable forms and passes them on to the circulatory system, which carries them to the body cells. This transformation of food materials is carried out by both mechanical and chemical means.

The mechanical breakdown of food is accomplished chiefly in the mouth. *Mastication* is accomplished by the grinding action of teeth. Of course, the more finely food is broken down by mechanical means, the more efficient are the chemical processes that further break down the large food molecules. Besides breaking down the food material into smaller units, complete mastication enables the food to mix more thoroughly with the digestive chemicals known as *enzymes*.

The chemical breakdown of food molecules is accomplished throughout the digestive tract. During mastication, *saliva* is mixed with the food material. Saliva contains enzymes that convert starch molecules to simple sugars. This conversion continues as the saliva-impregnated food passes through the *pharynx* (throat) and the *esophagus* into the *stomach*. In the stomach, additional enzymes secreted in the stomach walls are mixed with the food material by the churning action of the stomach muscles. Stomach enzymes and hydrochloric acid break down complex protein molecules into smaller, usable molecules, and starches into sugars.

Most digestion occurs in the *small intestine*. The small intestine is a one-inch tube over twenty feet long connected to the stomach. Certain digestive enzymes are produced in the walls of the small intestine. These are mixed with the now liquefied food. In addition, juices from the *pancreas* (pancreatic juice) and the *liver (bile)* flow into the small intestine. These enzymes attack fat substances primarily, breaking them into tiny globules that can be transported through the circulatory system to the body cells. Nutrients pass through small, blood-rich protrusions in the intestinal wall (*villi*) to get into the circulatory system.

The food material in the small intestine, now robbed of most of its useful nutrients, passes into the large intestine, a tube about five feet long. Here much of the water from the near-liquid substance is absorbed back into the body. The solid waste material (*feces*) then passes through the lower intestine (*rectum*) and out through an opening (*anus*).

Lesson Plan ■ A

Orientation:	Pre-K–2.
Content Objective:	Children will state that vegetables are good snack foods.
Skill Objective:	Children will *experiment* and *observe* using the sense of taste.
Materials:	Small carrots, celery, cabbage, cucumber, and other vegetables, plastic knives with serrated edges, paper towels, paper napkins.
Evaluation:	Observation of student group work and verbal interaction.

Procedure

Show the children a bunch of carrots, a bunch of celery, a cucumber, a small head of cabbage or cauliflower, some cherry tomatoes, or other vegetables. Ask the children to identify each vegetable and describe its color, shape, and other attributes. Tell the children they are going to make their snack for snack time. Give each child a paper napkin, paper towel, a plastic knife with a serrated edge, and a carrot. (If the carrots are too thick for the children to cut, you may wish to cut them lengthwise before distributing them.) Direct the children to cut the carrots into sections and place the pieces on a napkin. Do the same with two other vegetables, making whatever preliminary preparations are necessary. After the children have completed cutting up the vegetables, permit them to eat them as a snack. Explain to them that experts who study foods believe that vegetables are more healthful than traditional snack foods such as candy, cake, cookies, potato chips, corn chips, and

continued on next page

such. Explain that vegetables contain things that their bodies need and that too much sugar, which is often found in sweets, is harmful.

You may repeat this activity using fresh fruits such as apples, pears, cherries, bananas, and others. Reinforce the idea that vegetables and fruits are more healthful snacks than sweets and foods cooked in oil. You may also wish to repeat the activity demonstrating that certain cakes, such as angel food, as well as bran muffins, and cookies that are cereal-based and without icing are more healthful than those containing a great deal of sugar.

Lesson Plan ▪ B

Orientation:	Pre-K–2.
Content Objective:	The children will state that cream contains fat.
Skill Objective:	The children will *investigate* and *observe* fat being separated from cream.
Materials:	Six pint-size glass or clear jars with screw top lids, three pints of whipping cream, plastic spoons, soda crackers or bread, a saucer.
Evaluation:	Observation of children's group skills, verbal interaction.

Procedure

Show the children a container of milk or cream or a picture of the same. Ask them what is in these containers and where milk comes from. (You may wish to show them pictures of milking cows and discuss them.) Tell them that today they will discover something about milk.

Divide the class into groups of four to six children each and supply each group with a jar half full of whipping cream. Tell them that the cream comes from milk. Make sure the lid is securely tightened on each jar, and instruct the children to take turns shaking the jar vigorously. After several minutes, tell the children to set the jar in the middle of their table and observe it for a while. Have them describe what they see. There should be small clumps of butter floating on the top of the liquid. Now have them shake the jars again for several minutes and again observe them. You may then collect the jars from the groups, remove the lids, and scoop the "butter" from the surface of the liquid, placing it on a saucer. Permit the children to rub a small drop of the "butter" between their fingers. Ask them what it feels like. Tell them this is the substance commonly called butter. You may wish to spread a bit of the butter on saltine crackers (the salt on the cracker will serve to flavor the butter so that it tastes more like the commercial product.) You may then explain that butter is a fat and doctors who study food believe that too much fat in a person's diet is unhealthy, although small amounts of fat are not harmful. Explain that some people use margarine, which contains vegetable fat rather than animal fat, instead of butter.

Note: It is important to refrain from overstating the harmful effects of fats in nutrition so that children will not be afraid to eat all fats.

Lesson Plan ▪ C

Orientation: Pre-K—2.

Content Objective: Children will state that their bodies grow over time.

Skill Objective: The children will *observe* the imprints of their hands or other parts of their bodies and *recognize* the body parts and the growth that occurs (space/time relations).

Materials: Plaster of paris or modeling clay, small (approximately 6-inch-square) shallow aluminum baking pans, a roll of butcher paper, crayons or markers, a large mixing bowl, a spoon, Vaseline, hand lotion.

Evaluation: Plaster of paris or clay imprints, body imprints, students' verbal interaction.

Procedure

This activity should be done early in the school year. Mix plaster of paris in a large bowl according to the directions on the package and cover with a wet cloth. Discuss with the children ways to describe how big their bodies and body parts are. They may compare the sizes of their bodies and their hands and feet with other children. They may make a mark on the wall to describe their heights, or compare themselves with objects in the room. Be sure to point out to the children that being large or small is not in and of itself important—that all children and adults are different and every kind of body is fine. Tell them that what is interesting is not just what size they currently are, but the rate at which they are growing.

For each child, spread a layer of Vaseline on the inside of a shallow, square baking pan. Add and smooth out a layer of plaster of paris about one and one half inches thick. Have each child rub hand lotion over one hand, press the hand down on the plaster of paris, hold it still for a brief moment, and remove it. (You may wish to have each child make a cast of both hands in the same mold.) Let the casts set overnight and then remove them from the pans. You may permit the children to paint their hand imprint with tempera paint. Have the teacher or students write their names on each casting, along with the day's date. Place the casts on a shelf where students may see them. Permit them to examine their own hand casts and those of others. Discuss with the children what things they can do with their hands, and ask what would happen if their hands were just like their feet, or if they had no hands at all.

In the Spring—perhaps in May—repeat this activity and display the students' old hand casts alongside the fresh ones. Have them describe the changes in their hands that occurred over the intervening months. Discuss with them the terms *growth* and *growing*.

Note: This activity may also be done using modeling clay or wallpaper cleaner. You may also wish to conduct the following activity: Tear off several pieces of butcher paper, which are slightly longer than the height of the tallest child. Have each child lie on his or her side on a piece of the butcher paper. Using a marker or crayon, trace the outline of the child's entire body. Put the name of the child on the back of her or his body outline. Tape the body outlines to the wall and have the children guess which body outline belongs to each child. Again, you may wish to discuss the fact that differences exist among all individuals and one type or shape of body is not preferable to any other. Roll up the body outlines after displaying them for a while and save them.

Orientation: Grades 3–6.

Content Objective: The children will describe the tests for starches, sugars, and fats.

Skill Objective: The students will *experiment* by following a set of directions while testing for nutrients, *observe* carefully the results of their experiments, and *communicate* by maintaining a written record of their work.

Materials: Cornstarch, potato, bread, soda cracker, egg white, cheese, paper plates, tincture of iodine, apple juice, corn syrup, onion, Benedict's solution, twenty test tubes, six test tube holders, six candles or alcohol burners, brown wrapping paper.

Evaluation: Students' verbal interaction, student group problem-solving skills, laboratory worksheets, log, and reports.

Procedure

The following are tests for certain food nutrients. Have the students maintain a notebook in which they record their observations of the tests. Tell them that they will use the tests for later investigations.

Activity 1 — Test for starches: Divide the children into groups of four or five. Have each group place the following items on a paper plate: cornstarch, potato, bread, soda cracker, egg white, and cheese (Figure 13–2). Have them label each item by writing on the paper plate. (Other common food items may be substituted for those listed above.) Now pass among the groups and place a drop of tincture of iodine on each food item. Ask the children to observe the color of the iodine before and after it is added to the food and to record their observations. Direct the students to decide which items have something in common. Those that turn black or blue black contain starch. Ask the class: "What is the test for starch?" (Add tincture of iodine. Foods that contain starch will turn black.)

Activity 2 — Test for sugars: Have each group of children place a small amount of the following food materials in separate test tubes: apple juice, corn syrup, soda cracker, onion. Put several drops of Benedict's solution in each test tube. Tell each group to heat the test tubes over a flame (candle or alcohol burner), as in Figure 13–3, and to observe and record their find-

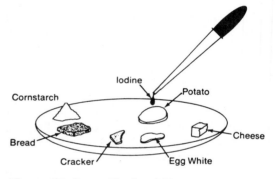

Cornstarch

Iodine

Potato

Bread

Cheese

Cracker

Egg White

Figure 13–2 ■ The Starch Test

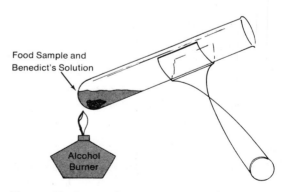

Food Sample and Benedict's Solution

Alcohol Burner

Figure 13–3 ■ The Sugar Test

continued on next page

ings. Direct the class to decide which items have something in common. Those that turn yellow and brick red contain simple sugars. Ask the class: "What is the test for simple sugars?" (Add Benedict's solution and heat. Food that contains simple sugars will turn yellowish, then red.) Note: Clinitest paper that may be purchased locally at a drugstore may be used for this activity.

Activity 3 — Test for fats: Have each child in each group feel a number of food substances and then rub his fingers together. If they feel oily and slippery there may be a fat present. Each group of children may then rub each food substance on a piece of brown wrapping paper. Direct them to hold the paper up to the light. The paper appears translucent where a fatty substance is rubbed on it. Some food substances that may be tested are margarine, bacon, lettuce, nuts, and soda crackers. Ask the class: "What is the test for fats?" (Rub the food on brown paper and see if the paper becomes translucent.)

Lesson Plan ■ E

Orientation:	Grades 4–6.
Content Objective:	The children will state that chewing soda crackers (mixing them with saliva) causes starch to be broken down into sugar.
Skill Objective:	The children are required to *experiment* by conducting tests for nutrients on chewed soda crackers, to *observe* the results of their experiment, and to *interpret* the data they have acquired.
Materials:	Soda crackers, eighteen test tubes, tincture of iodine, Benedict's solution, six candles or alcohol burners, brown wrapping paper.
Evaluation:	Students' verbal interaction, student group problem-solving skills, laboratory worksheets, log, and reports.

Procedure

Remind the class that they have conducted several food tests on soda crackers. Have them search their notes to confirm what they found out about soda crackers (soda crackers yielded a positive test for starch and negative tests for sugars and fats). Ask the class: "How can we find out what, if anything, will happen to soda crackers when we chew them?" The students should suggest chewing some soda crackers and then testing the chewed material for each of the three nutrients.

Give one member of each group of students a soda cracker and tell her to chew it thoroughly. After the cracker has been chewed for one minute, have the chewer take it out of her mouth and place a portion of it in each of three test tubes. Each group should test for the presence of sugar, starch, and fat with the appropriate procedure. Note: The moisture in the salivated cracker may cause a brown paper to become temporarily translucent. Suggest that the experimenters put the paper aside and observe it after several minutes have passed.

Discuss the results of the investigation with the class by asking: "Which tests were positive?" (Sugar test, starch test.) "The chewed cracker contained which nutrients?" (Starch, sugar.) "What must happen as we chew a cracker?" (Starch is converted to sugar.)

Orientation:	Grades 3–6.
Content Objective:	The children will state that proteins are broken down by acids.
Skill Objective:	The children will carefully *observe* the changes that take place with protein immersed in an acid and *infer* from their observations.
Materials:	One bottle of Coke or dilute hydrochloric acid, cooked lean beef.
Evaluation:	Students' verbal interaction, student group problem-solving skills.

Procedure

Place small bits of cooked lean beef in a bottle containing Coke or dilute hydrochloric acid and cap the bottle (Figure 13–4). Have the children observe the contents for one week. The children should conclude through class discussion that acids (carbonated beverages contain carbonic acid) affect meat. They may be led to infer that acids in the digestive tract serve to break down meat protein.

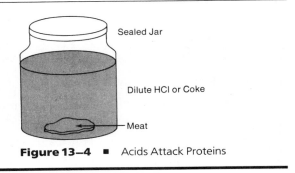

Figure 13–4 ■ Acids Attack Proteins

Subconcept 1–2

The human body must give off waste products.

Discussion

Waste products of the body are any materials produced by the body that are not usable. It has been demonstrated that the solid waste product of the digestive process (feces) is removed via the rectum and anus. The life processes of individual body cells form other waste products. These too must be removed from the body; otherwise, they interfere with the normal functioning of the cells and poison the system.

The oxidation of sugars, starches, and fats produces *carbon dioxide* and *water vapor*. The carbon dioxide and some water vapor are re-moved from the body by the *lungs* during respiration. The remaining water vapor is removed by the kidneys. When body tissue breaks down, it gives off *nitrogen compounds* such as *ammonia*, as well as some mineral salts. The kidneys remove these waste products from the blood tissue.

Materials removed from the blood by the kidneys are stored as *urine* in the *urinary bladder* and are subsequently expelled from the body.

The skin also serves as an excretory organ. Excess salts and water are expelled from sweat glands through the pores of the skin as perspiration. The cooling effect of the evaporating perspiration also helps to regulate body temperature.

Lesson Plan ■ G

Orientation: Grades 1–6.

Content Objective: The children will state that exhaled breath contains carbon dioxide.

Skill Objective: The children are required to investigate by blowing into a bottle of bromo-thymol-blue (BTB), to *observe* the change in the indicator, and to infer that their breath contains carbon dioxide.

Materials: Six glasses, BTB, thirty soda straws.

Evaluation: Students' verbal interaction, student group problem-solving skills.

Procedure

Divide the children into groups of three to five. Provide each group with a glass half full of BTB solution and several soda straws. Instruct several of the children in each group to blow through a straw into the BTB solution, as in Figure 13–5. Children are to observe carefully and record their observations. Ask: "What did you see?" (The BTB turned from blue to yellow to clear.) Tell the children that this effect upon BTB is the test for carbon dioxide. Then ask: "What is in the air we exhale?" (Carbon dioxide.)

Figure 13–5 ■ BTB Turns Yellow in the Presence of Carbon Dioxide

Lesson Plan ■ H

Orientation: Grades 3–6.

Content Objective: The children will state that carbon dioxide interferes with body functions and must be excreted.

Skill Objectives: The children are required to *observe* changes as a candle goes out and BTB turns yellow in an inverted tumbler and to *infer* that carbon dioxide may interfere with combustion.

Materials: One large jar, one candle, bromo-thymol-blue solution.

Evaluation: Students' verbal interaction, student group problem-solving skills.

continued on next page

Procedure

Place several drops of BTB on the sides of a large jar and on the table next to a burning candle. Place the jar over the burning candle. After the candle goes out, ask several of the class members to examine the drops of BTB. Ask the observers: "What did you see?" (The BTB turned yellow.) "What does this mean?" (There was carbon dioxide present.) "What happened to the candle?" (It went out.) "What factors could have caused the candle to go out?" (Lack of oxygen. Excess of carbon dioxide.) "Since our body burns food like the candle, what does this tell us our body must have for good functioning?" (The body must have a supply of oxygen and a way to remove carbon dioxide.)

Lesson Plan ▪ I

Orientation:	Grades 3–6.
Content Objective:	The children will state the manner in which solid, liquid, and gaseous waste products are excreted from the body.
Skill Objective:	The children are required to *observe* by taste and sight and to *communicate* information by compiling a chart.
Materials:	Chalkboard, chalk (or worksheets).
Evaluation:	Students' verbal interaction, student group problem-solving skills.

Procedure

Following some vigorous activity, direct the children to touch the backs of their wrists to their tongues. Ask them to describe the taste.

Ask: "What materials are excreted through the skin?" (Salt and water.)

Provide several children with mirrors. Ask them to breathe on the mirror and describe what they observe. (It fogs over. Moisture collects on it.) "From this exercise and from blowing into limewater, what do we know about waste products given off by breathing?" (Water and carbon dioxide are given off.) Ask the children to complete a chart like Chart 13–1.

Chart 13–1 ▪ Body Excretions

	Given off by	Given off as
SOLIDS:		
Salts	Skin, Kidneys	Perspiration, Urine
Food Wastes	Rectum	Feces
Nitrogen Compounds	Kidneys	Urine
LIQUIDS:		
Water	Skin, Kidneys, Lungs	Perspiration, Urine, Vapor
GAS:		
Carbon Dioxide	Lungs	Gas

Subconcept 1–3

Movement of the human body is made possible by the skeleton and muscles.

Discussion

The skeleton gives the human body its shape, protects the *central nervous system (brain* and *spinal cord)*, and provides a rigid structure for the attachment of *voluntary muscles*. There are over 200 bones in the skeleton. They may be classified into four categories by virtue of their general shape and functions. The *skull* is a hollow case that provides protection for the brain. The *spinal column* is composed of thirty-three separate vertebrae that serve to protect the spinal cord and are sources of attachment for many of the major muscles of the body. The *ribs* are flat bones that form the chest cavity. There are twelve pairs of ribs. All twelve pairs are joined to the spinal column, while the seven upper pairs are joined to the breastbone or sternum as well. The ribs serve as attaching points for the muscles that expand and contract the rib cage in the process of breathing. The arms and legs with their accompanying digits are known as the *extremities*. They enable man to move about at will and give him the power to perform useful tasks. It is in the extremities that the association of the skeletal and muscular systems is most dramatic.

Some involuntary muscles such as those found in the digestive tract and the rib cage are smooth and unstriated. The heart, however, is a striated involuntary muscle. Involuntary muscles control the circulation of blood, the movement of food through the body, and breathing. These functions are ordinarily considered to be involuntary—that is, they are not controlled by the will.

Voluntary muscles are long and round. They are bundled together by connective tissue. These large muscles of the body may be contracted at will. Voluntary muscles, in conjunction with the rigid skeletal system, enable man to move about and to do work.

Most skeletal muscles have their *origin* in one bone and their *insertion* in a second, often adjoining bone. Since bones are joined together by a movable joint, a *contraction* (shortening) of the muscle causes one or both bones to move. The contraction of the front upper arm muscle (*biceps brachii*), for instance, raises the forearm. The origins of the biceps brachii are in the shoulder region of the upper arm bone, and the insertion is in one of the bones of the forearm.

The largest muscles of the skeletal-muscular system originate in the hip region and are inserted at the knee region. The contraction of these muscles enables you to raise your knee toward your chest, partially rotate your leg, bend over, and straighten up.

Muscles must work in pairs in order to produce movement in two directions at the same skeletal joint. Since muscles can only contract and relax, they can exert a force in only one direction. By contracting the biceps of the upper arm, the forearm can be raised against a force, as when lifting a weight held in the hand. The force of gravity will cause the forearm to return to its pendent position when the biceps muscle is relaxed. To pull downward against resistance, the arm must rely upon the muscle at the back of the upper arm, the triceps brachii. With the biceps relaxed, the contracting triceps, which has points of attachment at the back of the shoulder and forearm, will exert a force to extend the forearm downward. In this way the triceps and biceps of the upper arm work as a pair, the biceps flexing to move the forearm inward or upward at the elbow, and the triceps contracting to extend the forearm to align with the upper arm. All muscles, whether they tend to flex, extend, or rotate the skeletal structure, must work as opposing pairs to control body motion.

Orientation:	Grades 3–6.
Content Objective:	The children will state that muscles work in pairs in opposition to each other.
Skill Objective:	The children are required to *observe* carefully an analogous experiment and to *infer* that the relationship demonstrated by the analogy demonstrates that muscles work in pairs.
Materials:	Two-foot length of dowel rod, six-foot clothesline, one milk bottle.
Evaluation:	Students' verbal interaction, student group problem-solving skills.

Procedure

Tie a two-foot dowel rod or pointer at the center of a six-foot rope. Ask for two volunteers. Have each child grasp one end of the rope so that the dowel is hanging downward as in Figure 13–6. Their task is to insert the end of the dowel rod in the opening of a bottle that you place on the floor about halfway between them. After several pairs of children have tried the exercise, ask: "Why was it so difficult to place the rod in the bottle?" (You couldn't push, you could only pull. You had to work together. One person could move the rod only in one direction.) "If we use this analogy to describe how muscles of the body work, what might we say about how muscles produce movement?" (Muscles work in pairs. Muscles can only pull, not push.)

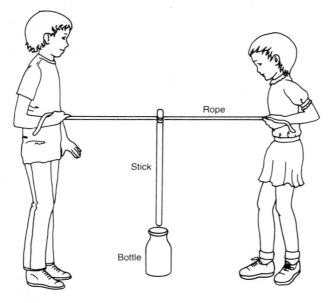

Rope

Stick

Bottle

Figure 13–6 ■ An Analogy: Muscles Work in Pairs

Lesson Plan ▪ K

Orientation: Grades K–4.

Content Objective: The children will state that the hardness of bones is due to the presence of minerals, mostly calcium.

Skill Objective: The children are required to *observe* bones before and after they are soaked in vinegar and to *infer* from their observations that bones contain both animal and mineral matter.

Materials: Six chicken thigh bones, one large jar, vinegar.

Evaluation: Students' verbal interaction, student group problem-solving skills.

Procedure

Pass around several chicken thigh bones. Permit each child to examine one. Place the bones in a jar containing vinegar and leave them for about one week. (One bone may be placed in an empty jar for later comparison.) Wash the bones off and have the class handle the bones again. Ask the class: "What is the difference between the bones now and before they were soaked in vinegar?" (They are not stiff now. They may be easily bent.) Establish that the vinegar is a weak acid and has acted upon the calcium compounds in the bone. Bone is made up of both animal and mineral matter. You may also want to ask: "Babies' bones are soft and flexible when they are born. What do you think occurs as they grow older?" (Calcium salts are deposited in the bone.) "Why is it important for children to eat foods containing calcium?" (Calcium is necessary for bone formation.)

Lesson Plan ▪ L

Orientation: Grades 4–6.

Content Objective: The children will describe the muscles that contract to produce various body movements.

Skill Objective: The children are required to *observe* by sight and touch the muscles that contract to produce body movements and to *infer* that muscles work in opposing pairs.

Materials: Worksheets.

Evaluation: Students' verbal interaction, student group problem-solving skills, seat work, and sketches.

Procedure

Pair off the class by sex, boys paired with boys and girls with girls. Present each pair with the following directions for observing their muscle structures:

1. Examine the back of your hand as you wiggle your fingers. What do you see? (Tendons are moving.) Grasp your right forearm with your left hand and wiggle your fingers. What do you feel? (Movement in the

continued on next page

forearm.) Continue to wiggle your fingers vigorously for several minutes. What part of your body seems to become tired? (The forearm.) Where are the muscles that control the movement of your fingers located? (In the forearm.)

2. While seated at your desk, turn the palm of your left hand up and press vigorously upward against the desk top with your fingers. Feel your straining arm with your free hand. How does each of the following muscles feel? Forearm top (hard); forearm bottom (hard); upper arm front (hard); upper arm back (soft). Which muscles appear to be contracting in this exercise? (All except the back of the upper arm.) Now turn your hand over, rest the fingernails against the desk top, and press down vigorously. How does each of the parts of the arm feel? Forearm top (soft); forearm bottom (hard); upper arm front (soft); upper arm back (hard).

3. Stand up and bend over forward from the hips. Feel your body with your hands. Which muscles appear to be contracting to support the weight of your upper body? Are the stomach muscles contracting? (The lower back muscles are contracting. The stomach muscles are relaxed.)

4. Hook the toes of one foot under your partner's desk. Exert a force upward with your leg. Feel your upper leg before and after you exert the force. Describe the position of the muscles that appear to be contracting. Which muscles appear to be comparatively relaxed? (The top thigh muscles are contracting; the bottom thigh muscles are comparatively relaxed.)

5. Bend one knee. Put the foot of the other leg behind the heel of the leg with the bent knee. Now force strongly backward. Which muscles of the thigh appear to be contracting? (The bottom thigh muscles.) Which appear to be relaxed? (The top thigh muscles.)

6. Press vigorously from various positions against a wall or other immovable object. Try to determine the location of muscles that are contracting to provide the force in each instance.

Discuss the children's observations.

Subconcept 1–4

The human body takes in oxygen and gives off carbon dioxide.

Discussion

The major function of animal respiration is to take in oxygen and give off carbon dioxide. When muscular action forces the rib cage up and out, and a large, sheetlike tissue called the *diaphragm* down, the increase in volume permits the lung tissue to expand. As the lung expands, the air pressure inside is reduced. Outside air rushes into the lung, bringing with it a supply of fresh oxygen. When the muscles of the rib cage and diaphragm relax, the volume of the chest cavity is reduced. This creates a pressure on the lungs, forcing air out. This expelled air has a relatively high concentration of carbon dioxide. Thus, the mechanical act of breathing supplies fresh oxygen to the lungs and removes excess carbon dioxide.

Air enters the human body through the *nose* and *mouth*, passes into the *trachea* (windpipe), through the *larynx* (voice box), and into a pair of tubes called *bronchi*. In the region of the lungs, the bronchial tubes begin branching into smaller and smaller passages. These terminate in tiny sacs of lung tissue called *alveoli*. The oxygen–carbon dioxide exchange takes place through the thin walls of the alveoli, which are filled with blood capillaries. The red blood cells carry oxygen and carbon dioxide. They exchange carbon dioxide for oxygen in the lungs, and they carry the oxygen through the circulatory system to the billions of individual body cells. The body cells remove the oxygen from the red corpuscles and deposit carbon dioxide in its place. Then this waste product is returned to the lungs for removal from the body. Blood plasma also transports gases between the lungs and body cells.

Lesson Plan ■ M

Orientation: Grades 3–6.

Content Objective: The children will state that lung capacity may be measured by displacing water in a container.

Skill Objective: The children are required to *experiment* to determine their lung capacities, to *communicate* by constructing a chart or graph, and to *infer* from their data.

Materials: Four plastic quart bottles, four pans, four rulers, one dozen soda straws.

Evaluation: Students' verbal interaction, student group problem-solving skills, laboratory worksheets, log, and reports.

Procedure

Divide the class into groups of four. Provide each group with a plastic quart bottle, a pan, a ruler, a large container of water, and several soda straws. Instruct the class: "Your problem is to measure the lung capacity of each member of your group. Find out how much air each person's lungs can hold." (See Figure 13–7.)

After a time, if no child suggests it, mention that filling the plastic bottle and the pan with water may be helpful. After another time you may ask: "What happens when we invert a bottle of water with an index card or a hand over its mouth, and place the mouth of the inverted bottle in a pan half full of water? Try it." (The water stays up in the bottle.) "Now do you have any ideas about measuring lung capacity?" Continue to guide the discovery lesson until the children decide to mark a scale on the side of their bottles and in this way compare each person's ability to blow air

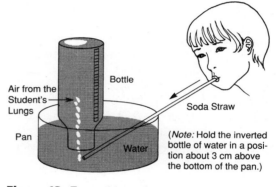

Figure 13–7 ■ Measuring Lung Capacity

into the bottle with only one deep breath, using a soda straw. Ask the children to keep a record of their data. Make a chart or graph comparing girls and boys.

Subconcept 1–5

The human body responds to stimuli (sensitivity).

Discussion

Primitive, one-celled plants and animals respond to such stimuli as light and electric shock. Complex plants respond to a variety of stimuli, such as light, gravity, and water. Complex animals have highly developed systems for sensing and reacting to conditions in their environments. We are one of the most sensitive animals; our special sensory organs are extensions of a highly developed central nervous system. We have five senses: sight, hearing, touch, taste, and smell.

Sight

Like most other animals, we have nerve endings in our eyes that are sensitive to certain frequencies of the electromagnetic spectrum. This narrow band of frequencies is called *light energy*. (See Chapter 16.) Light energy enters the eye through a transparent cover called the *cornea*, passes through an adjustable opening (*pupil*), and strikes nerve endings located in the tissue *(retina)* in the back of the inside eyeball. The nerve endings in the retina are activated by certain frequencies of light to transmit electrical impulses through the *optic nerve* to the brain. These nerve impulses are interpreted as sight.

According to the most popular theory, color vision is achieved by the intermixing of electrical signals from three groups of specialized nerve endings located in the retina. One group of nerve endings is sensitive to red light frequencies, one to blue frequencies, and one to green frequencies. All other colors are produced by a mixture of nerve impulses from these specialized groups of nerves. The same principle of mixing the three primary colors of light to produce other colors is employed in color television.

Hearing

The sense of hearing depends on a highly specialized organ, the ear. The ear receives mechanical energy, usually as the result of slight variations in atmospheric pressure. This energy is transmitted through the eardrum and a series of bones to a liquid-filled chamber where the pressure variations cause special nerve endings to generate electrical impulses. From nerve endings in the liquid-filled chamber, the electrical impulses are transmitted to the brain. (See Chapter 19 for a more complete treatment of sound and hearing.)

Touch

Nerve endings located in the skin are sensitive to pressure and temperature. Some regions of the body are richer in nerve endings than others and are thus more sensitive. The fingertips, for instance, are more sensitive than the back of the hand. Electrical signals are transmitted from the sensory nerves to the brain or the spinal cord. When the neural signal is received by the spinal cord, the result is an *involuntary* (reflex) reaction. When it is received by the brain, the result is a controlled, *voluntary* reaction to the stimulus.

Taste

The tongue has several small regions that are sensitive to taste. In these regions are clusters of nerve endings called taste buds. There are only four primary taste sensations: sweet, sour, salty, and bitter. There are likewise four types of taste buds, each sensitive to a particular kind of chemical. The sensation of taste combines the various reactions of each type of taste bud with the sensation of smell.

Smell

Nerve endings located in the nose are sensitive to certain chemicals in the air. Impulses from these nerve endings are transmitted to the brain where they are interpreted as smells. Much of what we think of as our sense of taste is really our sense of smell.

The Nervous System

Nerve cells (neurons) are composed of a cell body, containing the nucleus and most of the cytoplasm, and nerve fibers that branch out from the cell body. Most of the nerve fibers are short. These are called *dendrites*. One of the nerve fibers of each cell is usually very long. This is the *axon*. The axon carries impulses over great distances throughout the body.

The cell bodies of most nerve cells are located in the brain and spinal cord. Receptors, located at the ends of the axons, carry impulses to the cell body. There the signal passes through dendrites to the axon of an *associative nerve cell*. These nerve cells are usually located close to the spinal column. The neural message is processed in the association center and directed through motor nerves to the muscles of the body without going to the brain. This is called a *reflex action*. Thus, in a reflex action the neural signal is transmitted to the spinal cord via a sensory neuron, across an associative neuron, and then, via a motor neuron, immediately back to the muscles in the region from which the signal was generated. Through this mechanism we can react almost instantly to an unpleasant stimulus.

The mechanics of the brain are complex and little understood. The *cerebrum*, which is the largest part of the brain, is the center for thinking, memory, reasoning, and imagination. The cerebrum processes messages from the sense organs and controls the voluntary muscles used to respond to outside stimuli. Below and behind the cerebrum is the much smaller *cerebellum*. The cerebellum helps to coordinate complex muscle movements and helps the body to maintain its balance. The *medulla* is located at the top of the spine. The medulla controls involuntary muscle activities, such as the heartbeat, breathing, and peristalsis.

Lesson Plan ■ N

Orientation:	Pre-K—2.
Content Objective:	The children will name the five senses—sight, hearing, taste, smell, and touch—and tell how they help us to live.
Skill Objective:	The children will use all five senses to observe.
Materials:	Activity 1—Sight: Miscellaneous objects from the classroom.
	Activity 2—Hearing: Pencils, tape or record of the sounds of objects, player.
	Activity 3—Smell: Six plastic photographic film cans with "mystery" odors in them.
	Activity 4—Taste: At least one foam or paper cup with an opaque lid for each group. An assortment of common liquids such as fruit juices or soda. One soda straw for each child.
	Activity 5—Touch: One set of textured objects per group: silk cloth, wool cloth, sandpaper, a glass tumbler, a piece of unfinished wood, and others. Five paper bags (with the top gathered and secured by a rubber band), which permit children to push their hands into the bag. Inside the bag will be common "mystery" objects.
Evaluation:	Observation of group activities, classroom verbal interaction.

Procedure

This lesson plan contains suggested activities for observing with all five senses.

Activity 1 — Sight: Have each student describe a classmate, including height, hair color, clothing, and so on. Then have them reveal the name of the student they described. Discuss the term *sight*. Place three common classroom objects on a table. Ask the students to name them. Ask them which of their senses allows them to identify the objects. Add two other objects. Have the children close their eyes. Remove one object from the table. Permit the children to open their eyes and ask them what object is missing. Ask what sense allows them to know this. You may repeat this activity removing two objects from the set at a time.

continued on next page

Activity 2—Hearing: Have the children close their eyes and put their heads on their desks. Tell them to raise their heads when they hear their names spoken. Then, varying your voice from soft to loud and high to low, say each child's name. Ask how they knew when to raise their head. Explain that this is the sense of hearing. Then ask the children to take a pencil in hand, holding it by the pointed end. Tell them to tap on their desks with their pencils in the same way you tap on yours. Tap once and say, "Now." The children should tap once. Then tap three quick times and say, "Now." Then vary the rhythm of your taps, making them increasingly complex. Again ask the class how they knew what to tap. (It is through their sense of hearing.) As an optional or extending activity, you may play tapes or records of sounds such as a dog barking, bell ringing, train whistle, auto passing by, and so on. These tapes and records are commonly available in schools or may be made by the teacher. Have the students identify the sources of the sounds.

Activity 3—Smell: Place a small amount of some common substances in small, opaque containers such as plastic photographic film cans, and tape a piece of thin cloth or gauze over the opening. Some suggested substances are pine-scented deodorizer, a ripe banana, apple, orange, fingernail polish remover, and gasoline. Give one can to each group of children and ask them to pass the cans around and try to identify what is in them. After each group identifies a "mystery" odor, ask the class how the group was able to identify what was in the can. After all "mystery" odors have been identified, pass the cans among the groups and see if they agree with the first group. Talk about the importance of the sense of smell.

Activity 4—Taste: Pass out soda straws (one straw per child). Provide each group of children with a foam or paper cup that has an opaque lid and is numbered 1 through 4 on the lid. Cup #1 should contain apple juice, cup #2 grape juice, cup #3 orange juice, and cup #4 7-Up. (If enough cups are available, you may wish to provide each child with a cup. In this case, all cups within a *group* would contain the same liquid.)

Ask each group to sip the liquids through their straws and identify each one. If all children in a group do not agree on the identity of the mystery liquids, accept each response. After the groups have identified the liquids, ask them what sense permitted them to do this. Discuss the importance of the sense of taste. Where there are disagreements among the members of a group, have children from other groups taste the liquid and give an opinion. Finally, identify the liquid(s) that each group tasted. If supplies are sufficient, permit the children to have a glass of one or more of the juices.

Activity 5—Touch: Provide each group with a set of miscellaneous textured materials such as silk cloth, wool cloth, sandpaper, a smooth glass tumbler, a piece of unfinished wood, a piece of aluminum foil, or others. Give each group time to feel all the materials, and then ask them to describe how each material feels. Emphasize texture-related words such as *smooth, rough, soft, hard*, and so on. Ask the children what sense they were using to describe the objects. Next, pass out the paper bags that contain the "mystery" objects to be identified by touch. The top of each paper bag should be closed with a rubber band that may be stretched so that a child may insert his or her hand into the bag without seeing the contents. Pass the bags among the groups, asking children to identify the contents by using their sense of touch. When the children have had time to feel the mystery objects, pull them one by one from the bags and show them to the rest of the class. Review all five senses with the class.

Lesson Plan ■ O

Orientation: Grades 3–6.

Content Objective: The children will state that overstimulating the sight nerves will cause them to temporarily lose their capacity for transmitting sight stimuli.

Skill Objective: The children are required to *observe* carefully the aftereffect of prolonged stimulation of the sight nerves.

Materials: Flashlight, colored cellophane, white paper.

Evaluation: Students' verbal interaction, student group problem-solving skills.

Procedure

Darken the room. Cover a flashlight with red cellophane and shine the light so that a red spot is formed on a white surface. Ask the children to stare intently at the light for two minutes. At the end of the two minutes turn off the flashlight and instruct the class to continue to stare at the place where the red spot was. Ask them what they see. (A blue-green spot.) Repeat the exercise with a blue and a green filter if they are available. (In each case the aftereffect of staring at a colored light spot is seeing a spot that is the complement of the original color.) This exercise will also work with black figures and white figures. The image will be reversed in the aftereffect: white becomes black and black becomes white. Discuss the idea with the class that overstimulating a nerve center will cause it to become fatigued and to shut down temporarily.

Lesson Plan ■ P

Orientation: Grades 4–6.

Content Objective: The children will state that the senses may be fooled.

Skill Objective: The children are required to *observe* carefully.

Materials: Drawings of optical illusions.

Evaluation: Students' verbal interaction, student group problem-solving skills.

Procedure

Show the children drawings of Figure 13–8. Ask them: "Which line is longer, A or B?" "Which circle is larger, A or B?" Let the children measure each of the figures and discover that the pairs of lines and circles are each the same size. Ask the children: "What can we say about what we sometimes see?" (Our eyes can be fooled. We must be careful observers.)

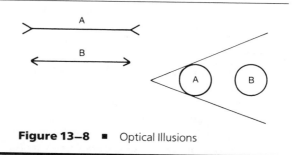

Figure 13–8 ■ Optical Illusions

Orientation:	Grades 5–6.
Content Objective:	The children will name the parts of the body that are most sensitive and least sensitive to touch.
Skill Objective:	The children are required to *measure* distances between pressure points on the body and to *infer* which parts of the body are most sensitive to touch.
Materials:	Dull pencils, rulers.
Evaluation:	Students' verbal interaction, student group problem-solving skills, laboratory worksheets, log, and reports.

Procedure

Divide the class into groups of three. Appoint one member of each group to be the measurer-recorder, one to be the investigator, and one to be the subject. Using two fairly dull pencils with the points held closely together, the investigator is to gently touch the subject's back. Repeat, moving the pencils farther and farther apart. The subject is to tell the instant he can feel two separate points of pressure. The measurer-recorder will measure the distance between the pencil points and record it. With the subject's eyes closed, repeat the same procedure on other parts of the body—the forearm, the leg, the palm of the hand, or the fingertips. During discussion, ask the class which part of the body is best able to distinguish the different pressures. Which is least able?

Lesson Plan ▪ R

Orientation:	Grades 3–6.
Content Objective:	The children will locate the regions of taste on a sketch of a tongue.
Skill Objective:	The children are required to *observe* the taste of various substances and to locate on the sketch of a tongue where particular taste buds are located.
Materials:	One box of cotton buds, small containers of salt water, sugar water, and vinegar solution, sketches of the tongue.
Evaluation:	Students' verbal interaction, student group problem-solving skills, laboratory worksheets, log, and reports.

Procedure

Pair off the students. Each student should have several cotton buds, and each pair of students should have small containers of salt water, sugar water, and dilute vinegar. Direct the children to dip the cotton buds into the solutions and lightly touch different regions of the tongue. Each pair of students should draw a sketch of the tongue and locate the various taste centers on it, as in Figure 13–9.

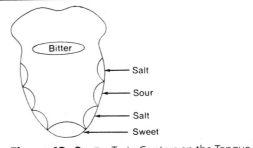

Figure 13–9 ▪ Taste Centers on the Tongue

Lesson Plan ▪ S

Orientation: Grades K–3.

Content Objective: The children will state that the senses of smell and sight, as well as taste, help us to identify foods.

Skill Objective: The children are required to *observe,* using the senses of taste, smell, and sight.

Materials: Common food substances such as raw potato, apple, turnip, pear, and onion; six blindfolds.

Evaluation: Students' verbal interaction, student group problem-solving skills, laboratory worksheets, log, and reports.

Procedure

Out of view of the children, have slices of the various food substances prepared. Blindfold six children and seat them facing the class. Tell each child to hold his nose tightly while he chews and swallows a food sample you will place in his mouth. After each child has swallowed a bit of one of the foods, ask him to write or say what it was. Repeat the procedure with several foods. (Not many foods will be identified by taste alone.)

Permit each child in the experimental group to taste the same foods while not holding his nose. Ask them to name each food orally or in writing. (Some of the foods will be correctly named.)

Remove the blindfolds and repeat the food-tasting procedure. Ask the children to name the foods. (All of the foods should be named using this procedure.)

Ask the children: "What did we find out about tasting things? Can we easily identify foods by taste alone?" (No. The senses of smell and sight help us to identify foods.)

Lesson Plan ▪ T

Orientation: Grades K–3.

Content Objective: The children will say that all senses may be used to describe an object.

Skill Objective: The children are required to *observe,* using the senses of taste, smell, touch, sight, and hearing.

Materials: One candy mint or Lifesaver candy for each child.

Evaluation: Students' verbal interaction.

Procedure

Give each child a Lifesaver or candy mint. Tell them not to eat the mint for a while since they will be doing something with it. Ask these questions: "Tell me something about the object in your hand that you learned by using your eyes." (It is round, flat, white, and so on.)

"Now tell me something about the object that you learned by using your ears." (It makes no noise. When I scrape it, it sounds funny. When I drop it on the desk, it clicks.) "Now tell me something about the object that you learned by using your nose." (It has no smell. It smells like . . . , and so on.) "Now tell me how the

continued on next page

object feels." (It is sticky. It has a low place in it. It is rough around the outside.) "Now tell me something about how the object tastes." (It is sweet. It tastes like . . .) "How many ways can we tell about things? What senses may we use to describe things?" (Sight, hearing, smell, touch, taste.)

Subconcept 1–6

Humans reproduce.

Discussion

Humans reproduce sexually. In sexual reproduction, the female periodically produces an egg (*female gamete, ovum*) that travels through a tube (*fallopian tube*) to the *womb (uterus)*. If the ovum is not fertilized by a male *gamete (sperm)*, it passes from the uterus through the *vagina*, along with the blood-rich lining that had accumulated upon the *uterine wall*. If the ovum is fertilized in the uterus, the fertilized egg (*zygote*) attaches itself to the uterine wall and the embryo grows through a series of *cell fissions*. As the embryo develops, tissues are formed of different kinds of cells. Nourishment is supplied the growing *fetus* through the *umbilical cord* that is attached to a vascular tissue (*placenta*) of the mother and to the abdominal region of the fetus. When fully developed, the baby is expelled through an enlarged vaginal opening.

Subconcept 1–7

The circulatory system is the transportation system of the body.

Discussion

The circulatory system performs many vitally necessary functions. It carries food and oxygen to each of the billions of body cells. It removes waste products that each of the body cells generates. It contains special chemicals that fight disease. It contains special cells that migrate among the body cells and engulf foreign matter such as bacteria. It contains other cells that promote clotting where a blood vessel is broken or cut. It helps to regulate body temperature by distributing heat generated in the body cells. Blood plasma contains a ready supply of water for maintaining proper cell function, and it removes excess water that accumulates among the cells. Clearly, the circulatory system is vital to the proper maintenance of the body.

The Blood

There are about six quarts of blood in the average human body. The blood is made up primarily of *plasma*, which is mostly water with some dissolved salts and other disease-fighting chemicals (antitoxins, antibodies). Cellular material in the blood consists of *red corpuscles*, *white corpuscles*, and *platelets*. By far the most numerous are the red cells. These cells contain an iron compound called *hemoglobin* that serves as a carrier for oxygen and carbon dioxide. White corpuscles are large cells, variously shaped. Many migrate among the tiny capillaries that supply body cells with nutrients. The function of the white corpuscles is to destroy foreign cells that find their way into the body. Platelets release a chemical that clots the blood at the point of a wound. They are small, irregularly shaped cells.

The Heart and Circulatory System

The heart is the pump that circulates blood throughout the body. It is a muscular organ containing four separate chambers. As it comes from the body, blood enters the upper right-hand chamber (*auricle*). As this auricle contracts, the blood is forced into the lower right-hand chamber (*ventricle*). As the right ventricle contracts, the blood is forced out of the heart via the *pulmonary artery* to the lungs. The blood circulates through the tiny vessels of the lungs (*capillaries*), exchanging carbon dioxide for oxygen. Then the oxygen-rich blood returns to the heart via the *pulmonary vein* to the upper left-hand chamber (ventricle), and subsequently through a large artery (*aorta*), to be carried to all parts of the body. *Arteries* carry blood away from the heart. They become smaller and smaller as they branch throughout the body. Blood seeps through tiny passages among the body cells (*capillaries*), and the blood plasma engulfs the living body-cell walls. While seeping among the cells, the plasma gives off food and oxygen and takes on waste products. The blood returns to the heart via a system of tubes called *veins*.

The lungs remove the gaseous waste products from the blood. The kidneys remove excess salts and nitrogen compounds. The liver and spleen filter off bacteria and worn-out blood cells. Thus, the blood is continually cleansed as it circulates through the body.

The pulse is caused by the opening and closing of valves that separate the upper and lower chambers of the heart and close off the opening of the aorta. The valves are loose flaps of tissue that permit blood to flow in one direction but seal off and obstruct its flow in the other direction. Blood can flow from the auricles to the ventricles and from the left ventricle into the aorta, but the heart valves prevent it from flowing in the opposite direction.

Lesson Plan ▪ U

Orientation:	Grades 4–6.
Content Objective:	The children will state that exercise increases the rate of heartbeat.
Skill Objective:	The children will *observe* the changes in their own heartbeat that are produced under various conditions of stress.
Materials:	A clock with a sweep second hand.
Evaluation:	Students' verbal interaction.

Procedure

Help each child to locate and feel her pulse by pressing the forefinger of her right hand against the inside of her left wrist. After each child has located her pulse, tell them that each individual is going to count the number of heartbeats that occur in thirty seconds. When all the children are ready, signal: "Start counting. Go." At the end of thirty seconds, signal: "Stop. Stop counting." Each child will write down the number of heartbeats she counted in the thirty-second interval and multiply by two. This will yield the number of heartbeats that would occur in one minute. (The children should not be alarmed if their heartbeat is very slow, say, forty-five beats per minute, or as fast as ninety beats per minute. The rate of seventy-two beats per minute is only an average; it is not an optimum functioning rate.)

Direct the children to do some vigorous exercise, such as jumping jacks or rapid toe-touching, for two minutes, and then to count their pulse rates again. Discuss the significance of the differences in the heart rates before and after exercise.

Wait five minutes and have each child check her pulse again. Ask: "Has your pulse returned to normal? What can we say about how the nature of the body activity affects the heart rate?" (The heart rate increases with body activity and returns to normal when the activity stops.)

Concept 2

The use or abuse of drugs and other chemicals may be harmful to the body.

Discussion

The widespread use and abuse of drugs and other harmful chemicals has been well documented and publicized in the newspapers and on the radios and television sets of this country. Researchers estimate that more than 12 million persons are addicted to alcohol and 3 million to heroin and/or cocaine. Countless others are seriously affected by the use and abuse of a wide array of chemicals not included in the list of "hard-core" drugs, including PCP (phencyclidine), LSD (lysergic acid diethylamide), and prescription medicines such as sleeping pills, tranquilizers, and painkillers. Tobacco in any form must also be included in the group of substances that are addicting and harmful to the body. On a more exotic note, human beings are even known to inhale volatile substances such as airplane glue, gasoline, and common solvents such as benzene, carbon tetrachloride, and turpentine. Chemical abuse takes many forms and affects many different populations.

Drug Abuse in the Elementary School

What was once thought to be a problem of the adult population and secondary schools has found its way into the elementary schools. And although drug abuse often occurs in inner cities and in other low-socioeconomic neighborhoods where children see and participate in drug trafficking, the drug problem is not confined to these environments. Students experiment with and are addicted to drugs in all types of schools, including those in the middle- and upper-class environments. It is a problem that elementary school teachers and administrators are being forced to confront.

Why Do Young Children Use Drugs?

In general, children of elementary school age use drugs for many of the same reasons their parents and other adults use them:

Drugs make them feel good. The primary reason most people use drugs is that they like the feeling they get when they take them. The euphoria or "high" associated with drugs has led countless young people to graduate from experimentation and occasional use to addiction.

They live in a "chemical society." Alcohol, tobacco, tranquilizers, pain medicines, and the many other substances used in their homes on a daily basis to help lose weight, relieve distress, and provide a sense of euphoria are so common to the experiences of young children that they see no harm in them. There may be reason to be grateful that many more children do not use drugs, given their prevalence in our society.

Peer pressure. Children are very susceptible to the pressures exerted by their peers to "go along with the crowd"—to experiment with tobacco, alcohol, and other drugs. Teachers can help students stand up to these pressures and reject those things that are potentially harmful to them. Children who have a healthy self-concept and value system have a much better chance of keeping themselves drug-free.

Curiosity. Children are naturally curious and like to try things that they see others using. That is why the use and abuse of drugs is often evident among several members of a family.

The Effect of Drugs Upon the Body

Drugs of abuse act primarily upon the central nervous system to produce euphoria. When used in excess, they may cause serious and permanent damage to the system, which, of course, includes the brain. (Please refer to Chapter 2 in this text for information about the physiology and functioning of the brain.) Some of the more serious effects are loss of memory, a lessening of the ability to think and reason, and changes in personality. Some chemicals, notably alcohol and tobacco, inflict serious damage over time on vital organs other than the central nervous system, such as the lungs, heart, liver, and kidneys. However, the most serious dysfunctions that result from heavy drug use are indirect in nature, that is, they are caused by inattention to those things that maintain the body in a healthy condition. In many cases, drug users do not eat or sleep for long periods of time or attend to normal body hygiene. The need for the drug becomes the overpowering drive in their lives. Dependence upon drugs appears to exist at several levels of use. The recreational user has little or no dependence upon the chemical and suffers little from its absence. Few drug users maintain themselves at this level, although it most likely is the intention of nearly all when they first began their association with drugs.

A second level of drug dependence is habituation. People who have a drug habit continue to function fairly normally in their daily lives. They go to school or work, maintain healthy social relationships and health habits. However, the habituated person suffers from both psychological and physical withdrawal symptoms when the drug is withheld. Withdrawal symptoms include headaches, nausea, uncontrolled muscle movements, tremors, sweating, and depression. Physiologists believe these withdrawal symptoms result when the cells of the nervous system and other vital organs lose some of their ability to function as they adjust to the absence of the chemicals that have been common in their fluids. At the highest state of drug dependence, addiction, the person lives primarily to relieve the misery caused by the absence of the drug in his or her system. As described above, the true drug addict's general physical condition deteriorates due to neglect.

An Overview of the Drugs of Choice of Drug Abusers

Drugs that are abused in our society may be classified according to the laws of society as legal or illegal. Legal drugs are those that can be obtained in drug stores and supermarkets as over-the-counter drugs or those prescribed by a doctor. When misused, that is, when not taken for the intended purpose or when taken in quantities exceeding the prescribed dosage, legal drugs may be just as harmful as illegal drugs; a person may do as much damage to his or her body with alcohol, tobacco, tranquilizers, and prescription painkillers as he can with illegally purchased heroin and cocaine. Legally distributed drugs are a bit safer to use because they are generally free from harmful contaminants often found in "street drugs." Alcohol and tobacco are, of course, legal for adults to purchase and use, but illegal when sold to minors.

Classifying Drugs of Abuse

Drugs or chemicals act upon the central nervous system either to enhance the transmission of nerve impulses or to impede them. Therefore, most drugs of abuse may be classified as *stimulants* (uppers) or *depressants* (downers). Since the most dramatic result of some drugs is the production of hallucinations, a third category, the hallucinogens, is sometimes added to the classification system. It should be pointed out that prolonged and heavy abuse of nearly any drug, along with the neglect of bodily needs, may result in hallucinations, but the drugs categorized as hallucinogens produce them as the inevitable and dramatic result of their use. Following is a summary of stimulant drugs and the effects they have upon the body.

Stimulant Drugs

Amphetamines

Amphetamines, including methamphetamine or "speed," are prescribed by doctors for weight-loss programs or as antidepressants. Chemically, amphetamines are related to the neurohormone acetylcholine, which is produced by the adrenal gland and excreted as adrenaline to produce the "fight or flight" syndrome. The most notable characteristic of a person who has taken the drug amphetamine is a state of exaggerated alertness and increased activity. Persons high on amphetamines have an intoxicated feeling and require little sleep, sometimes staying awake for several days in a row. During these "binges" they eat little and drink few liquids. Prolonged use of amphetamines may produce hallucinations and feelings of paranoia. An additional danger to the methamphetamine user is the perceived "superman" phenomenon wherein he may feel himself to be invincible and jump from great heights or attempt to stop automobiles by stepping in front of them.

Cocaine

Cocaine is an alkaloid or natural chemical that is extracted from the coca plant, which is grown principally in the Andes Mountain region of northern South America—Peru and Bolivia. Cocaine is a pure white powder (sometimes called "snow") that is taken orally, sniffed up the nose, or injected into a vein with a needle. "Crack cocaine" or "ice" is a crystalline form of cocaine that is often smoked. The drug quickly produces effects of heightened energy and animation followed by depression when the effects wear off. "Crack" is a popular form of cocaine because it is relatively cheap compared to the powdered form and because the onset of the euphoric effects after use is nearly immediate, although short-lived. In the 1960s and 1970s, wealthy people, who were the principal users, believed that cocaine, being a natural alkaloid, was not addictive. We now know that this notion was unfounded and that cocaine is in fact a highly addictive drug.

Nicotine

Nicotine is the stimulant drug found in tobacco. The drug produces a mild stimulation following use and is addictive. Nicotine causes an increase in the user's blood pressure and heart rate, and long-term use has deleterious effects upon the heart. The dangers of prolonged use of tobacco in regard to lung and other cancers are well publicized in this country.

Caffeine

Caffeine, a mildly stimulating drug, is found in many beverages, especially coffee, tea, and soft drinks. Overuse of caffeine may affect sleep habits and appetite.

Hallucinogens

Most hallucinogens are stimulant drugs that tend to produce hallucinations.

LSD

Lysergic acid diethylamide is perhaps the most potent hallucinogen; with most users, only a few milligrams can produce visions. Discovered by a Swiss drug manufacturer, LSD has no known medical uses today. Unfortunately, the chemical can be fairly easily produced in illegal and clandestine laboratories. LSD produces in the user kaleidoscope visions in vivid colors, which are often beautiful and sometimes very frightening. Some users claim these visions often appear as "flashbacks" many months or even years after the last use of the drug. Long-term users also frequently suffer permanent mental health problems in the form of psychosis.

Peyote

The peyote cactus grows in the desert southwestern United States and contains the alkaloid mescaline. A bitter tea made from this low-growing plant has a long history of use by the American Indians, especially in their religious ceremonies. Its use by the Native American Church is still legal and common on some Indian reservations. Mescaline is a fairly mild hallucinogen; its bitter taste serves to limit its use in the illegal drug trade.

PCP

An animal tranquilizer, PCP (or phencyclidine) is making a comeback as a recreational drug after a period of diminished popularity. PCP can be easily manufactured in illegal laboratories, and its easy availability and low price account for its popularity. PCP produces hallucinations and often results in serious and permanent psychoses when used heavily over a substantial period of time. Cases have been reported where abstinence after prolonged use produces withdrawal symptoms in users, and it therefore is considered to produce both physical and psychological dependence.

Mushrooms

A few mushrooms that grow in fields and pastures of many parts of the United States contain alkaloids that are mildly hallucinogenic. Because some wild mushrooms are poisonous to humans, a few accidental deaths have occurred when individuals seeking a drug high have mistakenly chewed or drunk a tea made from the wrong mushrooms. The hallucinogenic mushroom has had a limited but romantic attraction as a natural alkaloid.

Marijuana

Marijuana is the most frequently used illegal drug in the United States. This plant, *cannabis sativa,* grows wild in many midwestern and southeastern states. It was once grown for the long fibers that were used to make hemp rope and a rough cloth. *Cannabis sativa* contains about thirty different alkaloids, principally in the leaves and flowers, which have psychedelic effects upon humans. When the resin from the cannabis plant is harvested, the crystalline substance is known as hashish or "hash." The most prominent alkaloid of the cannabis plant is THC, tetrahydrocannabinol. Because of the variety of alkaloids that may be present and because of differences in the body chemistry of users, it is difficult to classify marijuana as a stimulant or a depressant; it has been found to exhibit both properties in different persons at different times. In most people, marijuana has a slightly depressant, mellowing effect. Marijuana is mildly addictive and, like most drugs, the more an individual uses it, the more is required to achieve the same effect. This is due to buildup in tolerance by the body. Prolonged use

by smoking the plant leaf carries significant danger of lung cancer, which results from the carcinogens created by the smoking process.

In the early years of its popularity in the 1960s, most marijuana was smuggled into this country from the islands of the West Indies and from South America. However, today much of the illicit supply is grown clandestinely in fields and forests throughout the United States.

Depressant Drugs

As we stated earlier, drugs that are classified as depressants tend to reduce the activity of portions of the central nervous system. Some of the most commonly abused depressant drugs are discussed below.

Barbiturates

The family of drugs known as barbiturates was originally developed in the form of sleeping powders or pills. The most common of the barbiturates are phenobarbital, Seconal, Tuinal, and Nembutal. The most outstanding effect of these drugs is to produce euphoria and sleep. With the use of barbiturates the heart rate slows, blood pressure drops, and the user becomes less animated. (Again, in some users barbiturates cause effects much like those of stimulants. The reason for this rare phenomenon is not known.) All barbiturates are habit forming and addictive. Overdoses may result in death, either by design (suicides) or accident. The combination of barbiturates and alcohol, both depressant drugs, is particularly dangerous.

Narcotics

Narcotic drugs are derived from certain species of the poppy plant. When cuts are made on the sides of developed seed pods, a white resin is exuded, which hardens and is called opium. From opium, morphine, heroin and codeine are derived. Opiates are depressants to the central nervous system and have long been used in medicine to control pain. Morphine is the narcotic drug most commonly used in medicine today, but like all of the opiate drugs, it is highly addictive. Heroin was developed in the late nineteenth century and introduced into medicine to replace morphine in the belief that it was less addicting. Sadly, this was not the case and heroin has become the drug of choice for large numbers of hard-core drug users. Heroin is sold in powdered form and may be sniffed through the nose or "tasted" by letting it dissolve on the tongue. Hard-core users melt the powder by holding a match under a spoonful of the drug and injecting the resulting liquid into a vein. Heroin is highly addictive, and abstinence results in severe withdrawal symptoms, making it very difficult for most users to "kick the habit." The constant search for a "fix" of this expensive drug debilitates users, who are nearly entirely dysfunctional in carrying out everyday activities. Especially in inner-city environments, even elementary-school-age youth are known to use heroin.

A whole array of synthetic narcotics such as Percodan, Quaalude, and Dilaudid are now on the medical market and are sought after by drug abusers.

Tranquilizers

Valium, Librium, and Librax are but several of a whole array of mood-modifying drugs prescribed by doctors to patients suffering from stress. Possessing less potency than the barbiturates or narcotics, tranquilizers were first thought to be nonaddicting; however, this assertion has proved false. Because of the many prescriptions written for them and because they are easily accessible through illicit trade, tranquilizers are easily available and widely abused. When taken as prescribed, tranquilizers produce a feeling of relaxation and well-being. When abused they may produce euphoria and a drunken stupor. Abstinence by the user results in withdrawal symptoms.

Thorazine and chlorpromazine are major tranquilizers used to calm patients suffering from various psychoses. PCP, phencyclidine, is a tranquilizer used by veterinarians on large animals. All of these are abused by some individuals.

Alcohol

Ethyl alcohol or ethanol is an intoxicant chemical that results from the fermentation of sugars and carbohydrates. It is found in beer, wine, and distilled products such as whisky, rum, and vodka. Alcohol is a depressant drug that is highly addictive to many individuals. In terms of sheer numbers, alcoholism is the greatest drug problem that exists or perhaps has ever existed. Drinking fermented fruits and grains has been a socially acceptable practice since biblical times. The presence of alcohol appears to be a requirement at many types of social functions; it is commonly available in the majority of homes in any community. Its ubiquitous nature is the essence of the problem: Social drinking for many persons is a path to addiction, an addiction that is difficult to end.

Alcohol intoxication is commonly known and recognized. A moderate user may enjoy a mild euphoria and a feeling of well-being. Heavy drinking may lead to unconsciousness and death. It is most common for the addiction to progress and grow more severe over a long period of time as the alcoholic neglects his or her body and the drug affects the liver, stomach, heart, and other organs.

Many elementary-school-age children have access to alcoholic beverages and some experiment with them. Certainly this drug should be high on the agenda for any drug abuse program aimed at children in this age group.

Volatile Solvents

Preadolescents often do not understand the dangers of "sniffing," a game in which the participants try to get high by inhaling the fumes of airplane glue, nail polish remover, gasoline, auto tail pipe emissions, and others. The outcome may be brain damage or death, both of which have been recorded many times over the past several decades. Fumes from volatile solvents depress the central nervous system and deprive the body of oxygen by blocking the gaseous exchange process of the lungs. Deaths have occurred when users of these substances place some in a paper or plastic bag and put the bag over their head to inhale the fumes; they pass out and suffocate. Because elementary-school-age children have easy access to many solvents and because this practice is popular among the young, the dangers of inhalation of volatile solvents should be included in any drug abuse program.

Figure 13–10 summarizes the addictiveness and effects of abuse of some commonly abused drugs.

Drug Abuse Education

Part of any effective drug abuse education program must be to provide information about drugs, their effects upon the body, and the dangers of abusing them. Research shows, however, that providing children with information about drugs is not sufficient for causing children to resist future drug use: An effective drug abuse prevention program must include information combined with *values education* that provides children with the will to live their lives drug-free. The effective drug prevention program must make it more fashionable to say *no* to drugs than to participate in their use. The common "wisdom" among students must be that they are in charge of their own bodies and futures and that they will not be led by peer pressure to do harm to themselves. To accomplish this very difficult goal it is often necessary to institute a schoolwide or communitywide action program of drug prevention education. Several of the following school- and community-based activities have been incorporated into Project DARE (Drug Abuse Resistance Education) and into the Just Say No Program sponsored by law enforcement organizations and other community agencies across the country.

Schoolwide Activities

Resource Volunteer Speakers—Many agencies and organizations will supply speakers, often trained and experienced, to speak to school-wide assemblies or individual classes on the topic of drug abuse. Some examples are law enforcement officers, local and county medical associations, Alcoholics Anonymous and other volunteer rehabilitation organizations, and the American Heart Association, the American Lung Association, and other health-related associations.

Community Partners—Enlist the support of local businesses and service organizations such as Rotary or Kiwanis in conducting a drug abuse prevention program. Community partners sometimes provide financial support for field trips, t-shirts, and other supplies. By lending their support, community partners lend credibility to drug abuse prevention projects in the minds of the students, community, and media.

Drug Awareness Day—Provide children with a t-shirt, cap, ribbon, balloon, or homemade "badge" that they wear to show they support the right to refuse to take part in drug use.

Poster and/or Essay Contest—Individuals and classes submit posters and/or essays that depict drug abuse resistance themes. Display all the posters and have the best essays read during an assembly or over the public address system.

Classroom Activities

Review information in Chapter 9, "Teaching Children to Solve Problems of Science, Technology, and Society," for ideas for organizing values education lessons. Following are some suggestions you might consider.

Conduct a survey to ascertain student attitudes and practices related to drug use.

Have students investigate the drug abuse problem and make suggestions for improvement at the school level.

Have students write and act out a drama, television show, or radio show that demonstrates how a student who has the courage can resist joining his or her friends in using drugs.

Hand out a paper on which has been drawn the outline of a shield such as those used by the

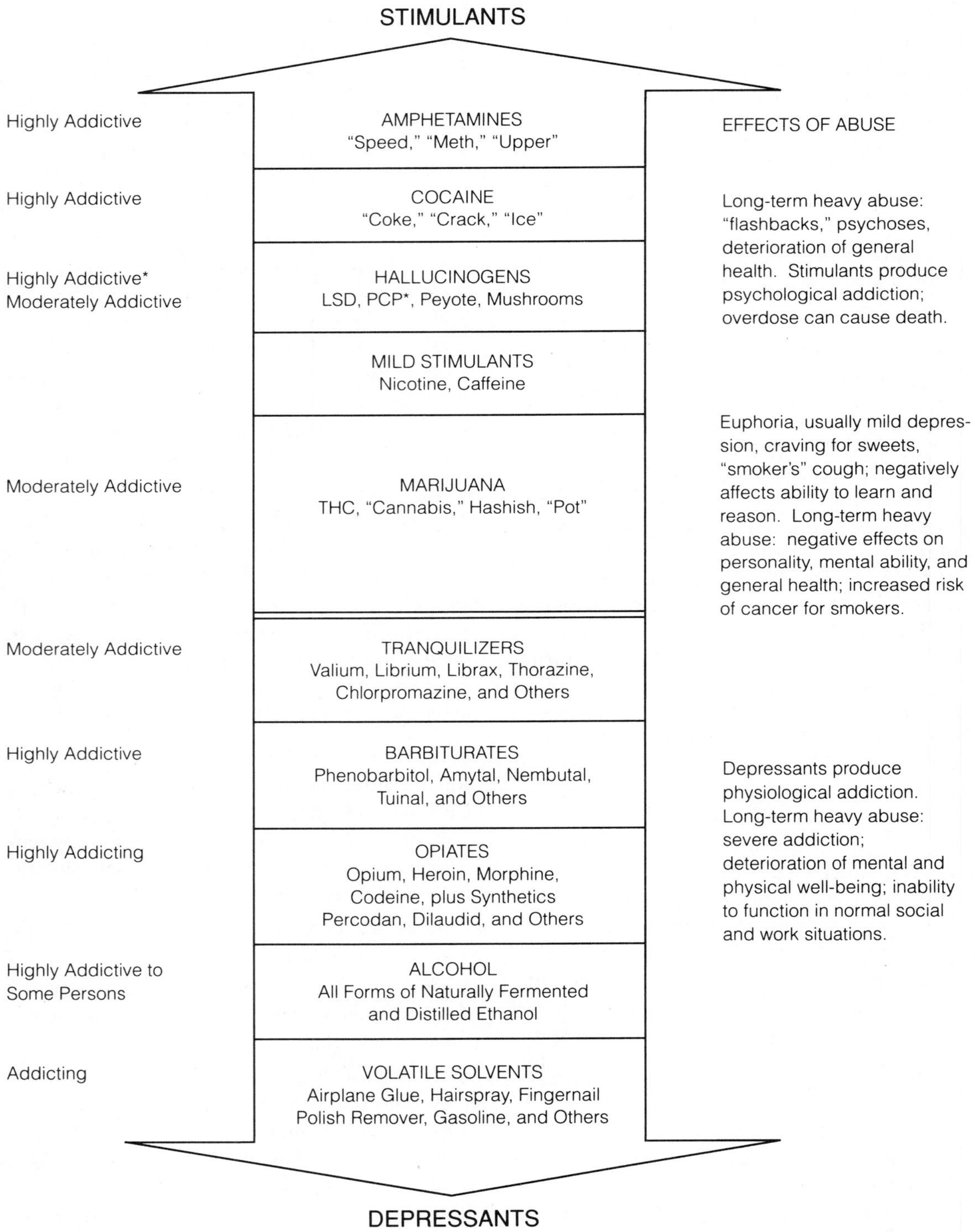

STIMULANTS

Highly Addictive	AMPHETAMINES "Speed," "Meth," "Upper"	EFFECTS OF ABUSE
Highly Addictive	COCAINE "Coke," "Crack," "Ice"	Long-term heavy abuse: "flashbacks," psychoses, deterioration of general health. Stimulants produce
Highly Addictive* Moderately Addictive	HALLUCINOGENS LSD, PCP*, Peyote, Mushrooms	psychological addiction; overdose can cause death.
	MILD STIMULANTS Nicotine, Caffeine	
Moderately Addictive	MARIJUANA THC, "Cannabis," Hashish, "Pot"	Euphoria, usually mild depres- sion, craving for sweets, "smoker's" cough; negatively affects ability to learn and reason. Long-term heavy abuse: negative effects on personality, mental ability, and general health; increased risk of cancer for smokers.
Moderately Addictive	TRANQUILIZERS Valium, Librium, Librax, Thorazine, Chlorpromazine, and Others	
Highly Addictive	BARBITURATES Phenobarbitol, Amytal, Nembutal, Tuinal, and Others	Depressants produce physiological addiction. Long-term heavy abuse:
Highly Addicting	OPIATES Opium, Heroin, Morphine, Codeine, plus Synthetics Percodan, Dilaudid, and Others	severe addiction; deterioration of mental and physical well-being; inability to function in normal social and work situations.
Highly Addictive to Some Persons	ALCOHOL All Forms of Naturally Fermented and Distilled Ethanol	
Addicting	VOLATILE SOLVENTS Airplane Glue, Hairspray, Fingernail Polish Remover, Gasoline, and Others	

DEPRESSANTS

Figure 13–10 ■ Common Drugs of Abuse

knights of medieval Europe. Instruct children to use crayons or paints to create their own shield, showing at least four things about themselves that make them proud.

Have each student finish the sentence: "I like myself because . . ."

Summary

The human body carries on the same basic life processes as other living things. The common life processes are ingestion, digestion, assimilation, excretion, motility, respiration, sensitivity, reproduction, and circulation.

Common Life Processes

Ingestion, Digestion, and Assimilation

To grow, the body must continuously create new body cells and replace cells that wear out and die. It must also continually expend energy to maintain its functions. For these reasons the body must continually ingest, digest, and assimilate food. Food is taken into the mouth where it is masticated and mixed with digestive enzymes. It then passes into the stomach where it is further churned to a liquid state and where more enzymes are added. Complex food molecules are broken down into simpler molecules in the mouth, stomach, and small intestine. Dissolved nutrients are absorbed into the blood through the walls of the small intestine and are carried to the body cells.

Excretion

Solid wastes are removed from the digestive tract through the large intestine, rectum, and anus. Gaseous waste products (primarily carbon dioxide) and some water vapor are removed from the body through the lungs. The kidneys remove excess salts, nitrogen compounds, and water from the blood, and these wastes pass from the body as urine. Sweat glands excrete water and dissolved salts.

Movement

The human body moves by muscles attached to a skeletal system. Voluntary muscles permit us to move about and do work. Involuntary muscles produce autonomous body functions such as breathing and peristalsis. Voluntary muscles work in pairs to produce controlled body motion.

Respiration

When the rib cage expands and the diaphragm is stretched downward, air rushes into the lungs. When relaxed muscles permit the rib cage and diaphragm to return to normal, air is forced out of the lungs. During the breathing process, carbon dioxide and water vapor are given off, and oxygen is absorbed into the blood tissue.

Sensitivity

The body has five senses—sight, hearing, touch, taste, and smell. Through the senses, we are made aware of the conditions of our environment. Each sense has its own special nerve receptors and brain center where stimuli are interpreted and acted upon. The body of a nerve cell usually resides in the brain or spinal cord, with long fibers extending to other points in the body. Stimuli travel through the receptor nerves to associative nerve cells that pass them on to motor nerve cells. The work of the associative nerve cell may be very simple (reflex action) or very complex (reasoned activity).

Reproduction

Humans reproduce sexually. In this process, male sex cells unite with female sex cells to produce a body cell. The body cell divides repeatedly within the mother's uterus to form the embryo that develops into the offspring.

Circulation

The circulatory system is the transportation system of the body. Blood circulating through arteries, capillaries, and veins carries nutrients to the millions of body cells and removes waste products. Blood plasma contains special cells and antibodies that fight disease. Blood is circulated throughout the body by the pumping action of the heart. The heart forces blood to the lungs, from which it returns cleansed of carbon dioxide and with a fresh supply of oxygen. Contractions of the heart muscle then force blood out through the arteries to all parts of the body. There it performs its supply and waste-removal functions.

Drug Use and Abuse

Elementary-school-aged children are increasingly exposed to the selling and use of drugs, both legal and illegal. Most experts agree that drug abuse prevention programs must begin in the elementary schools if they are to be successful.

Mind-altering drugs act upon the central nervous system, the brain, and major neural pathways. Their effects are to either enhance the ability of the central nervous system (CNS) to transmit electrical impulses or diminish the transmission ability. Those drugs that enhance neural efficiency are called stimulants; those that reduce the efficiency are called depressants.

Drug abuse education programs in the elementary school should include both the presentation of information concerning the nature and effects of mood-altering drugs and activities that strengthen the self-concepts of the students and their resolve to reject the use of such chemicals.

Understanding Physical Science

"Nature is [humankind's] teacher. She unfolds
her treasures to their search."

A. B. STREET

CHAPTER 14

Atoms and Molecules — The Building Blocks of Matter

Look What's in This Chapter

In this chapter we'll discuss some important concepts and subconcepts related to the study of atoms and molecules, and we'll introduce lesson plans that are designed to teach these concepts and subconcepts to children.

Concept 1   Models help us to understand the atom.

Concept 2   Matter has electrical properties.

Concept 3   Atoms are made of tiny, electrically charged particles.

Concept 4   All atoms are made of the same building blocks.

Concept 5   Atoms join together to form molecules.

 Subconcept 5–1   Electrons cause chemical reactions.

 Subconcept 5–2   A few kinds of atoms form many different molecules.

Concept 6 Molecules are attracted to one another by electrical forces.

Concept 7 Substances possess different physical properties.

How much do we really know about atoms? Textbooks often take great pains to emphasize that atoms are impossible to see or photograph even with the electron microscope. The following pages of the textbook are then usually filled with drawings and diagrams showing the makeup of the atom and the arrangement of its parts in intricate detail. How can this be? How is it that we have never seen an atom, yet can give a detailed description of its nature and structure? The answer is that we use models.

Chapter 1 described the process of model building in science with an amended parable of the Three Blind Men of India. Each blind man guessed at the nature of an elephant by feeling one of its parts. The illustration went on to describe how a better and better mental image of the elephant was obtained as the three blind men gathered more and more data and restructured their model accordingly.

Scientists, too, are often "blind." We cannot "see" the edge of the universe or a neutron star. Certainly we cannot say that we have "seen" inside an atom. How, then, can we trust the diagrams and descriptions presented in textbooks? What are these diagrams based on? Let us see.

The History of the Atomic Model

The history of science is a history of the search for the primary building block of matter. Many scientists feel that when we discover the elementary particle from which all the universe is constructed, the mysteries of nature will unfold before our eyes.

The philosophers of ancient Greece believed that all matter was composed of tiny, indestructible particles called atoms. These atoms, they

believed, were joined together by hooks and barbs on their surfaces. This promising beginning of atomic theory was forgotten during eighteen centuries following the birth of Christ. During this time another theory of the nature of matter was popular. This theory, devised by the Greek Aristotle and accepted by the Catholic Church, held that all matter was made of *four elements—earth, air, fire,* and *water.* Thus, the promising atomic model of the ancient Greeks was supplanted by the now-discredited *model of four primary elements.* Aristotle's model withstood many tests of observation and intellectual argument. However, gradually more and more information was acquired, and Aristotle's theory was abandoned.

Speculation on the nature of matter was removed from the realm of pure philosophy with the work of the *alchemists.* Attempting to turn base metals into gold, these medieval chemists conducted the *first experiments* with chemicals, *described the properties* of many substances, and devised *systems of symbols* to represent the substances with which they worked. The systematic labors of the alchemists blossomed into the achievements of sixteenth-, seventeenth-, and eighteenth-century chemistry and led to what is now known to have been the forerunner of modern atomic theory.

Concept 1

Models help us to understand the atom.

Discussion

Every child knows that atoms are too small to see. How, then, can scientists say what they look like? What kind of evidence did they use to arrive at the modern conceptual model of the atom?

Suppose you are a scientist. You know that when hydrogen and oxygen combine to form water, they always combine so that there are

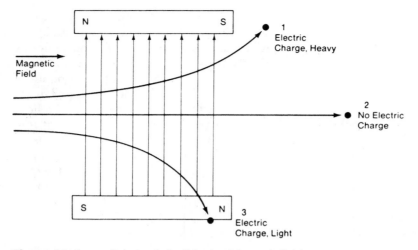

Figure 14–1 ▪ Subatomic Particles in a Magnetic Field

eight parts by weight of oxygen for one part of hydrogen. Whether the amounts are small or large, this ratio always holds. Likewise, sulfur and oxygen combine in a weight ratio of two to one to form sulfur dioxide. Suppose you know that *all known substances combine in small, whole-number ratios* to form compounds. What might you surmise about the nature of matter? Might you not guess that matter is made up of small building blocks that join together in various combinations like bricks to form new substances?

Eighteenth- and nineteenth-century chemists, continuing the work of the alchemists, found that elements always combine in small, whole-number ratios by weight. From there, it was a natural intuitive leap to surmise that small, discrete units of matter join together (and come apart) during chemical reactions. These small discrete units were called *atoms*.

While some scientists were rediscovering the atom, others were noticing that the atom gave off particles still smaller than itself. The existence of these *subatomic particles* was proven by their effects on *photographic plates* and by the trails they left as they passed through *clouds of vapor*. Next, it was noticed that as subatomic particles passed through magnetic fields, their paths were bent or curved (Figure 14–1). The magnetic field exerted an effect upon the particles. From variations in this effect, the weight, charge, and other characteristics of the particles were determined. Heavy particles did not change direction as fast as light particles; positive charges bent in one direction and negative charges in another while uncharged particles did not bend at all.

The next question was: "What is the atom's structure?" To answer this one, imagine again that you are a scientist. You have some radioactive material such as radium. The material gives off particles that, from the way they behave in the presence of a magnet, you believe to be very heavy, heavier than some whole atoms.

You place a piece of heavy metal foil in the path of the radiating particles, as in Figure 14–2. Most of the particles pass directly through the foil. It has little or no effect on them. But occasionally you observe a very spectacular thing: one of the heavy particles is bounced back

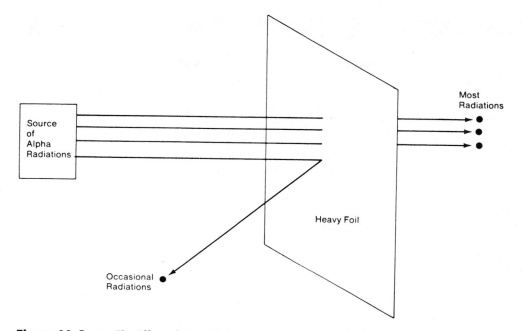

Figure 14–2 ■ The Effect of Metal Foil on Moving Subatomic Particles

or deflected! What would you think? Almost all the heavy particles went straight through the foil, but once in a while one was deflected.

The scientist who saw this phenomenon thought that because the tiny subatomic particles could pass through apparently solid materials with very little difficulty, the atoms composing these materials must be made up mostly of empty space. The occasional particle that rebounded from the solid material was believed to have struck a dense, heavy part of the atom—the part where most of its mass was concentrated. So it was from evidence obtained by beaming subatomic particles at sheets of metal foil and observing the effect that the modern concept of atomic structure grew. Atoms are thought to consist of a tiny, dense nucleus surrounded by a great deal of space. The space around the nucleus is thought to be occupied by electrons.

The evidence of the structure of atoms is all *indirect*. Scientists can only observe the effects of the atom and of subatomic particles and from this evidence conceptualize a model showing how the atom would look if we could see it. The more new evidence they gain, the more their understanding increases, and the more they can refine the model they have built.

Orientation:	Grades 1–6.
Content Objective:	The children will state that the nature and identity of unseen objects may be inferred.
Skill Objective:	From evidence gained through manipulating "mystery boxes," the children are required to *infer* the properties and identity of unseen objects.
Materials:	Six small boxes, each containing one or two common objects, the contents of no two boxes being the same. Suggestions: coins, marbles, small ball, pencil, Lifesaver candies, and so on.
Evaluation:	Students' verbal interaction.

Procedure

Divide the class into six groups. Provide each group of children with a numbered box containing one or two common objects. Tell the children they may shake and tilt the box, but may not look inside. Permit each group to handle their box for several minutes and then write down their best guess as to what is inside. Example: box 1, marble. On signal, the boxes should be passed around so that each group handles all six boxes.

To conclude the exercise, write the numbers 1 through 6 on the chalkboard. Ask each group to write their inferences for each box under the proper heading. After reviewing the responses, dramatically reveal the contents of each box. Ask: "Can we sometimes describe an object without seeing it? Our guesses are called inferences." Explain that scientists sometimes make inferences about things they cannot see, such as the inside of the earth, quasars, and atoms.

Concept 2

Matter has electrical properties.

Discussion

Many materials, when rubbed together, produce static electricity. Hair becomes unmanageable when combed, a sweater crackles when taken off, and a person receives a shock when reaching for a doorknob. Static electricity is evidence that matter is made up of, or at least contains, tiny, electrically charged particles. These particles exert forces upon one another. The concept of electrical forces in nature is very important because it is these forces that hold all matter together, particle to particle, atom to atom, and molecule to molecule. (See Chapter 18 for a more complete discussion of static electricity.)

Lesson Plan ■ B

Orientation: Grades 1–6.

Content Objective: The children will state that rubbing some things produces static electricity and that electrically charged objects exert forces on each other.

Skill Objective: The children will *experiment* by manipulating materials, *observe* the effects of static electricity, and *infer* that static electricity exerts a force.

Materials: Six combs, bits of paper, wool cloth or fur, balloons.

Evaluation: Students' verbal interaction.

Procedure

Divide the class into groups, and provide each group with a comb, bits of paper, string, and several balloons (Figure 14–3). Help the children to blow up their balloons if necessary. Rub one balloon on some child's hair or sweater and ask if the children think the balloon will stick to the wall. Then say: "I wonder why the balloon stuck to the wall. There must be a force to hold it there." Direct the children to find as many ways as they can to create similar forces. Some activities you might suggest are: rubbing the comb through a child's hair or on a sweater and observing the reaction of bits of paper held near the comb; rubbing two balloons on hair or wool to see how they interact; suspending a balloon on a string and bringing a second "rubbed" balloon close to it.

In these activities, the children will be observing the effects of the forces exerted by charged particles (electrons) that were removed from wool atoms and deposited on the comb and balloons. To conclude the lesson, ask: "What did we observe?" (Rubbing the objects with wool caused them to attract or repel one another.) "We were putting electric charges on the comb and balloons. Where did they come from?" (The charges came from the hair and the wool.) "Is there electricity in hair? In wool?" (Yes.) "Do charged objects have to be touching to exert forces upon one another?" (No. Electric charges attract and repel at a distance.)

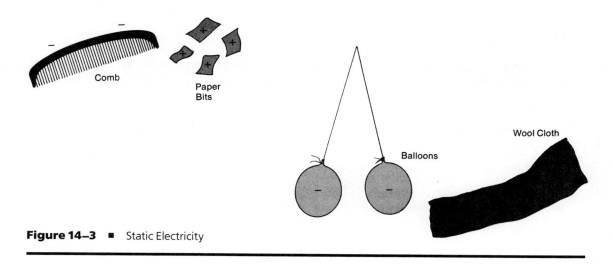

Figure 14–3 ■ Static Electricity

Concept 3

Atoms are made of tiny, electrically charged particles.

Discussion

The nucleus of an atom is composed of many kinds of particles. Nuclear physicists have identified nearly fifty different kinds of matter as products of the breakup of atomic nuclei. Since at this point the complex atomic nucleus is little understood, no attempt is usually made to teach it to young children. A convenient atomic model for elementary school science has an atomic nucleus that is composed of only two kinds of particles—*protons* and *neutrons* (Figure 14–4). Both are heavy particles. Protons possess a positive electrical charge; the neutron is thought to possess both positive and negative charges and to be electrically neutral. The *nucleus is very tiny*. It occupies only one-ten-thousandth of the diameter of the atom.

In the accepted atomic model for elementary school use, electrons move about the tiny, dense nucleus like a swarm of angry bees about a hive. The electrons are negatively charged, light, and fast moving. Because they move fast, a few electrons can occupy a large space.

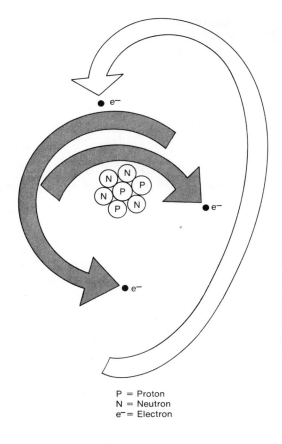

P = Proton
N = Neutron
e⁻ = Electron

Figure 14–4 ■ Schematic Diagram of an Atom

Lesson Plan ■ C

Orientation:	Grades 4–6.
Content Objective:	The children will state that an atom is composed mostly of space and that it has a tiny nucleus with one or more fast-moving electrons orbiting around it.
Skill Objective:	The children are required to *observe* a model of an atom in order to develop proper *spatial relationships* concerning atomic structure.
Materials:	Two one-inch spheres: marbles, balls, and so on.
Evaluation:	Students' verbal interaction.

continued on next page

Procedure

Take the children outdoors. Let one child hold a one-inch sphere or paper circle, as in Figure 14–5. Starting from this child, pace off 135 large (three-foot) steps. Hold up a second one-inch sphere. Explain the analogy. One tiny sphere represents the nucleus of an atom, and the other an electron moving about the nucleus. Emphasize that the tiny electron, because of its rapid movement, occupies all the space in a large sphere that has a radius equal to the distance shown and that the nucleus is at the center. Emphasize that the model is three dimensional. The electron flies all about the nucleus at high speed. Ask: "What is an atom chiefly made of?" (Space.) "What do you think would be the chances of a bee flying through our atom without striking the nucleus?" (A bee is not likely to strike the nucleus.) "What might this tell us about the chances of a small particle striking a nucleus as it passes through a hydrogen atom?" (The chances are poor that a particle would strike the nucleus.)

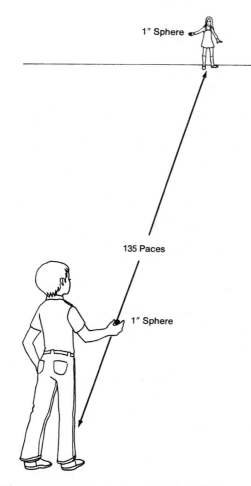

1" Sphere

135 Paces

1" Sphere

Figure 14–5 ■ Outdoor Model of a Hydrogen Atom

Orientation:	Grades 4–6.
Content Objective:	The children will state that electrons in atoms occupy a great deal of space by virtue of their motion.
Skill Objective:	The children are required to *observe* a model of an atom and to *infer* the transfer of the *spatial relations* of the model to the atom.
Materials:	One bicycle wheel, soda straw.
Evaluation:	Students' verbal interaction.

Procedure

Show the children a spoked wheel (Figure 14–6). Ask them what fraction of the space the spokes occupy. Spin the wheel and have the children attempt to poke a soda straw through the spokes. Ask: "What happened?" (The soda straw won't go through.) "Why not?" (The spokes stop it.) "But if the spokes occupy only a small fraction of the space within the wheel, how can they stop the straw?" (The spokes are moving.) "How might this be like the atom?" (The electrons of the atom are moving and occupy space.)

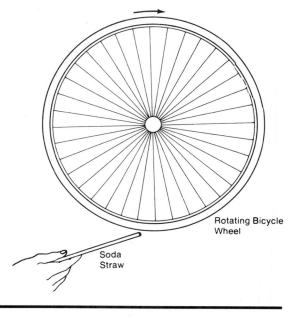

Rotating Bicycle Wheel

Soda Straw

Figure 14–6 ▪ Wheel Spokes Occupy Space

Concept 4

All atoms are made of the same building blocks.

Discussion

Hydrogen is the lightest element. It has the simplest atom of all the elements. The hydrogen atom consists of a single proton for a nucleus and a single electron swarming about the proton. The next lightest element is *helium*. The nucleus of a helium atom has two protons and two neutrons. There are two electrons swarming about the nucleus. *Lithium*, the next heaviest atom, has three protons and three neutrons in the nucleus and three electrons swarming about the nucleus. And so it goes. By adding more protons and neutrons to the nucleus and more electrons to swarm about the nucleus, new and different atoms are formed. The number of protons contained in the nucleus of an atom is called its *atomic number. Ninety-two different*

Chart 14-1 ■ The Makeup of the Atoms of Five Common Elements

Atomic No.	Element	Protons	Electrons	Neutrons	Atomic Mass No.
1	Hydrogen	1	1	0	1
2	Helium	2	2	2	4
3	Lithium	3	3	3	6
29	Copper	29	29	34	63
92	Uranium	92	92	146	238

atoms occur commonly in nature, with atomic numbers ranging from one for hydrogen to ninety-two for uranium. Since each kind of atom is characteristic of a particular element, ninety-two elements occur in nature.

The number of *protons* and *electrons* in a complete atom is always the same. The number of neutrons in atoms of an element may vary but it is always at least equal to the number of protons. (An exception is most hydrogen atoms, which have no neutrons.) Because the number of neutrons in atoms may vary, atoms of the same element may weigh slightly different amounts. Each form of the atom containing a different number of neutrons is called an *isotope*. All elements exist in more than one *isotopic form*.

It is important to remember that though the atoms of the various elements differ from each other in weight and other physical properties, they are all made of the same building blocks— electrons, protons, and neutrons. *The only difference between the structures of any two atoms is the number of particles that join together to form them.*

Chart 14-1 provides some information for the commonest isotopes of five elements.

Atomic Mass

You will remember that protons are heavy particles. The proton is used as the basic unit of *atomic mass*. A proton has a mass of one unit. The mass of the electron is so small that it is ignored in discussions of atomic mass. The combined mass of *all* electrons in the heaviest atom, uranium, is only about one-twentieth of a mass unit. The approximate mass of any atom is equal to the sum of the number of protons and neutrons.

In Chart 14-1 note that:

1. The atomic number of an element is the same as the number of its protons.

2. There is an equal number of protons and electrons in every atom.

3. The atomic mass of an atom is the sum of the numbers of protons and neutrons.

4. With the exception of hydrogen, the number of neutrons always equals or exceeds the number of protons in an atom.

Lesson Plan ■ E

Orientation:	Grades 5–6.
Content Objective:	By completing Styrofoam atomic models, the children will indicate the proper positions of electrons, protons, and neutrons in the atoms.

continued on next page

Skill Objective:	The children must *manipulate materials* and show an awareness of the *spatial* and *number* relationships that exist among parts of atoms.
Materials:	One-inch Styrofoam balls, two-inch Styrofoam balls, watercolor paints or food coloring, glue, toothpicks or soda straws.
Evaluation:	Students' verbal interaction, student models.

Procedure

Paint or dip Styrofoam balls according to some color scheme, such as:

Protons—one-inch balls—blue

Neutrons—one-inch balls—white

Electrons—two-inch balls—red

Have the children glue the blue balls (protons) and white balls (neutrons) together to form the nucleus of each atom. Red balls (electrons) may be added to the nucleus by using toothpicks or soda straws. The number of particles for each atom may be obtained from Lesson Plan F and given to the children. Display the atomic models by hanging them from strings around the room. See how many of the atoms the children can identify by naming elements with which they are associated.

Lesson Plan ■ F

Orientation:	Grades 5–6.
Content Objective:	The children will successfully complete a chart that illustrates the relationships among atomic number, mass number, and numbers of protons, electrons, and neutrons in atoms.
Skill Objective:	The children are required to *infer* missing data from a chart by utilizing the data that is present.
Materials:	Copies of Chart 14–2.
Evaluation:	Students' verbal interaction, seat work, and sketches.

Procedure

Discuss the relationships among atomic number, atomic mass, and the numbers of protons, electrons, and neutrons that exist in atoms. Then present individuals or groups with copies of Chart 14–2 with the spaces above the rules blank. Ask the children to complete the chart and to be prepared to tell how they arrived at their answers.

Remember in completing and discussing the chart:

1. Atomic number, number of protons, and number of electrons are always equal.

2. The number of neutrons may be found by subtracting the number of protons from the atomic mass number.

3. The atomic mass number may be found by adding the numbers of protons and neutrons together.

continued on next page

Chart 14–2 ▪ A Chart of Atomic Particle Relationships

Element	Atomic Number	No. of Protons	No. of Neutrons	No. of Electrons	Atomic Mass No.
A	1	1	0	(1)	(1)
B	2	2	2	2	4
C	3	(3)	4	(3)	(7)
D	(6)	6	6	(6)	(12)
E	8	(8)	(8)	(8)	16
F	(19)	(19)	20	(19)	(39)
G	(26)	26	30	(26)	(56)
H	67	(67)	98	(67)	(165)
I	92	(92)	(146)	(92)	238

Concept 5

Atoms join together to form molecules.

Discussion

We have seen that matter has electrical properties and that these electrical properties cause charged particles to exert forces on one another. Negatively charged electrons attract positively charged protons. This is the force that holds an atom together. But what kind of force causes one atom to join with other atoms?

If *atoms* did not join together to form *molecules*, the whole universe would be invisible, or rather would cease to exist as we know it. Since atoms are so small, everything we can see or touch must be made of many atoms that have joined together. Iron atoms join with oxygen atoms from the atmosphere to form iron oxide molecules. Hydrogen atoms combine with oxygen atoms to form water molecules. In some cases the combining process may be reversed, and the atoms are pulled apart, becoming elements again. Iron oxide molecules can again become iron and oxygen atoms, and water molecules can again become hydrogen and oxygen atoms. What kind of forces hold atom to atom? You might have guessed: electrical forces.

Where Are the Electrons?

You may recall that the electrons in the atom are light and fast-moving negative charges that swarm about the nucleus. If you could see the parts of an atom, you could hardly make sense out of their speedy and complex motion. However, they do appear to arrange themselves about the nucleus in predictable ways. Their arrangement is based on the energy they possess. The lower-energy electrons are closer to the nucleus, and the higher-energy electrons are farther away. The *first energy level* closest to the nucleus can contain a *maximum of two electrons*. The *second energy level* can contain *eight*. The *third energy level* will at first contain *eight*, though this number does increase in larger atoms. The atomic diagrams in Figure 14–7 show some arrangements of electrons in an atom. We say that an electron ring is complete when it contains the maximum number of electrons possible. Remember: for the first three levels this is two, eight, and eight. How many of the *electron shells* in Figure 14–7 are complete?

How do we know when atoms are joining together or separating—that is, when a *chemical reaction* is taking place? Sometimes the color of the substances changes. Sometimes heat is absorbed from the surrounding materials. Often heat and light are given off, or particles may come out of a solution as a gas or a *precipitate*. All of these are evidence that atoms are joining together or separating.

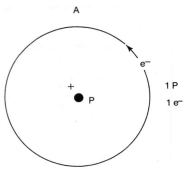

A

1 P

1 e⁻

Hydrogen

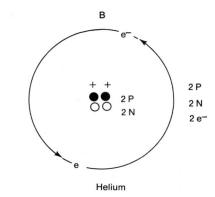

B

2 P
2 N

2 P
2 N
2 e⁻

Helium

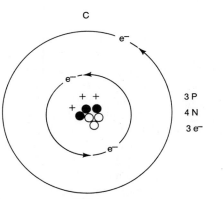

C

3 P
4 N
3 e⁻

Lithium

P = Proton
N = Neutron
e⁻= Electron

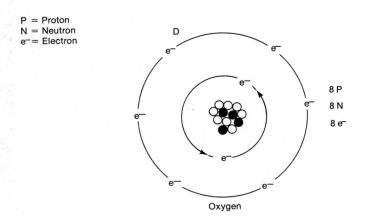

D

8 P
8 N
8 e⁻

Oxygen

Figure 14–7 ■ Atomic Diagrams

Lesson Plan ■ G

Orientation: Grades 4–6.

Content Objective: The children will draw atomic diagrams showing the arrangements of electrons, protons, and neutrons in the atoms having the atomic numbers one through ten.

Skill Objective: Using certain guidelines, the children are required to *infer* the arrangement of the parts of atoms having atomic numbers one through ten.

Materials: Copies of Chart 14–3, drawing paper, crayons or Magic Markers.

Evaluation: Students' verbal interaction, seat work, and sketches.

Procedure

Provide each child, or group of children, with a copy of Chart 14–3, drawing paper, and a crayon or Magic Marker. Direct them to draw a schematic or ring diagram showing the arrangements of the parts of the atoms listed. In discussing the results of the exercise, ask: "Which atoms have completed outer electron shells?" "How many electrons does each atom require to complete its outer shell?"

Chart 14–3 ■ Makeup of Atoms with Atomic Numbers One Through Ten

Element	Protons	Neutrons	Electrons
Hydrogen	1	0	1
Helium	2	2	2
Lithium	3	4	3
Beryllium	4	5	4
Boron	5	5	5
Carbon	6	6	6
Nitrogen	7	7	7
Oxygen	8	8	8
Fluorine	9	10	9
Neon	10	10	10

Lesson Plan ■ H

Orientation: Grades 3–6.

Content Objective: The children will correctly identify those conditions that produce a chemical change.

Skill Objective: The children are required to *investigate, observe* evidence of chemical reactions, and to *interpret data* by stating whether a chemical reaction took place.

Materials: Baking soda, vinegar, litmus paper, lemon juice, matches, test tubes, limewater, table salt, paraffin (candle sections), wooden-handled spoons, eyedroppers, cups or small jars.

Evaluation: Students' verbal interaction, student group problem-solving skills, laboratory worksheets, log, and reports. *continued on next page*

Procedure

Divide the class into groups. Provide each group with a copy of Chart 14–4, with the answers under Observation and Conclusion omitted and with the materials required for investigation. Have each group report the results of their experiments. Emphasize that where chemical reactions took place, atoms were joining together and separating.

Chart 14–4 ▪ Experiments to Determine Evidence of Chemical Reaction

Materials and Action	Observation	Conclusion
1. Add 3 drops of vinegar to a half teaspoon of baking soda.	*Fizzing, gas produced*	*Chemical reaction*
2. Dip a strip of blue litmus paper in lemon juice.	*Blue litmus turns red, color changes*	*Chemical reaction*
3. Light a match.	*Heat and light given off*	*Chemical reaction*
4. On a paper, mix one teaspoon each of soda and salt.	*No observable change*	*No chemical reaction*
5. Hold a candle section in a teaspoon over a flame.	*Candle melted, no heat, light, gas, color change*	*Physical change only*
6. Blow through a soda straw into a test tube of limewater.	*Clear liquid turned milky, a precipitate formed*	*Chemical reaction*

Subconcept 5–1

Electrons cause chemical reactions.

Discussion

Electrical attraction causes one atom to join with another atom. It does this in three major ways: by ionic bonding, covalent bonding, and metallic bonding.

Ionic Bonding

The atomic diagrams in the preceding exercises show that some given number of electrons is required to fill the various energy levels of each atom. Atoms are most stable chemically when all energy levels that contain electrons are completely filled. If this is true, what happens if an atom has only one or two electrons in a ring that requires eight electrons for stability? Obviously it might tend to lose those one or two electrons. And what happens to an atom that has six or seven electrons in a ring that requires eight for stability? It might tend to gain one or two electrons.

The atoms of those elements called *metals* tend to lose one, two, or three of the electrons in their outermost energy levels. Atoms of *nonmetals* tend to gain electrons in their outermost energy levels because they have nearly completed levels of five, six, or seven electrons. (See Chart 14–5 for a partial list of metals and nonmetals.) When atoms that tend to lose electrons easily are near atoms that tend to gain them easily, an exchange takes place. For example, when a sodium atom (metal) is near a chlorine atom (nonmetal), the sodium atom will lose an electron and the chlorine atom will gain an electron. The loss of an electron gives the sodium atom a plus charge. (Remember that it originally had an equal number of negative and positive charges.) The chlorine becomes negatively charged with the addition of an electron. Since unlike charges attract, the two atoms,

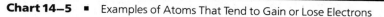

Chart 14—5 ▪ Examples of Atoms That Tend to Gain or Lose Electrons

Metals		Nonmetals	
Tend to Lose 1 Electron	**Tend to Lose 2 Electrons**	**Tend to Gain 1 Electron**	**Tend to Gain 2 Electrons**
Lithium	Beryllium	Fluorine	Oxygen
Sodium	Magnesium	Chlorine	Sulfur
Potassium	Calcium	Bromine	
	Zinc	Iodine	

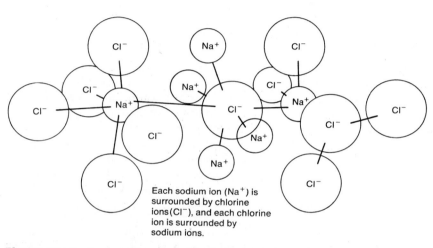

Each sodium ion (Na$^+$) is surrounded by chlorine ions (Cl$^-$), and each chlorine ion is surrounded by sodium ions.

Figure 14—8 ▪ Ionic Structure of Sodium Chloride

now called *ions* (Figure 14–8), are joined by the electrical force. In this way crystals of common table salt are formed. This is called ionic bonding.

Covalent Bonding

Atoms whose outer energy level is about half filled usually share electrons with other atoms rather than gain or lose them. For example, hydrogen has one electron in its first energy level, which is complete with two electrons. Suppose that two hydrogen atoms are located next to an oxygen atom (oxygen will accept or share two electrons). The two hydrogen atoms will each share their single electron with the oxygen atom. The shared electrons will sometimes be found in the region of the hydrogen atom and sometimes in the region of the oxygen atom (Figure 14–9). The migration of the electrons

Chart 14—6 ▪ Examples of Atoms That Commonly Share Electrons

Number of Electrons Shared	Elements
1	Hydrogen
2	Oxygen
3	Boron, Aluminum
4	Carbon, Silicon
5	Nitrogen, Phosphorus

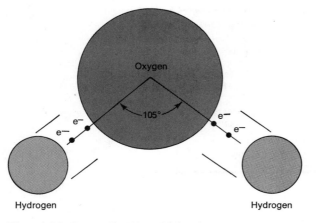

Figure 14—9 ■ The Water Molecule

causes a shifting of the electric charge. When this shifting creates unlike charges in neighboring regions of the two atoms, the unlike charges will cause the atoms to join. This is called *covalent bonding*.

Metallic Bonding

When many metal atoms come together, the electrons in their outer energy levels—which

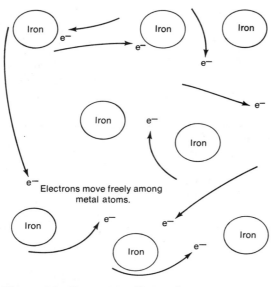

Electrons move freely among metal atoms.

Figure 14—10 ■ Metallic Bonding

are held only loosely—migrate relatively freely about in the substance formed (Figure 14–10). As the electrons move about, some tiny regions of the metal gain extra electrons and are negatively charged. Other regions, having lost some electrons momentarily, are positively charged. These differences in charge bind the metal atoms together. This is called *metallic bonding*.

Getting Some Terminology Straight

An *atom* is the simplest building block of an *element*. If the atom is somehow torn apart or changes the number of its particles, it is no longer an atom of the same element. All of the atoms of an element have the same numbers of protons and electrons. When substances are mixed together without any chemical reaction (heat, light, color change, and so on), the result is called a *mixture*. The constituent parts of a mixture retain their own properties and may be separated by physical means. Examples are salt and pepper or flour and soda. When a chemical reaction takes place between two or more substances, a *compound* is formed. The basic building block of the compound is the *molecule*. For example, the union of hydrogen and oxygen forms a water molecule. The union of oxygen and iron forms iron oxide or rust. The information in Chart 14–7 summarizes the relationships among these various terms.

Chart 14–7 ▪ Elements, Mixtures, and Compounds

	Element	Mixture	Compound
Description	Made of one kind of atom	Two or more substances, chemically uncombined	Made of two or more kinds of atoms, chemically combined
Basic Unit	Atom	Atoms or molecules	Molecules
Comment	All pieces look the same when subdivided	May be separated into two or more substances by mechanical means	May be separated into elements only by chemical means

Lesson Plan ▪ I

Orientation:	Grades 4–6.
Content Objective:	The children will state that iron and sulfur comprise a mixture before they react chemically and a compound after they react chemically.
Skill Objective:	The children are required to *observe* a chemical change and to help structure tests of *hypotheses* concerning the nature of the constituent materials.
Materials:	Iron filings, sulfur, test tube, Bunsen burner (propane torch), magnet.
Evaluation:	Students' verbal interaction, student group problem-solving skills, seat work, sketches, laboratory worksheets, log, and reports.

Procedure

Mix two parts by weight of iron filings with one part by weight of sulfur. Place about half the mixture in a test tube or some other heat-resistant receptacle (Figure 14–11) and heat with a Bunsen burner or propane torch until the mixture begins to glow with a reddish light. Watch as the red glow spreads throughout the mixture. Ask the children: "Did a chemical reaction take place?" (Yes.) "What evidence do we have of a chemical reaction?" (Heat and light were given off. The appearance of the mixture changed.) "Have the physical properties of the iron and sulfur changed?" (Yes. The sulfur is no longer yellow. The iron has lost most of its magnetic properties.) At this point, ask how a magnet might be used to test the difference between the magnetic properties of the iron-sulfur mixture and those of the iron sulfide compound. The children

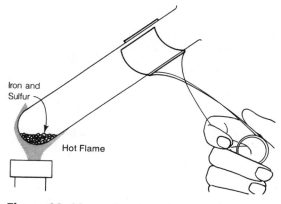

Iron and Sulfur

Hot Flame

Figure 14–11 ▪ Forming a Compound

might suggest placing a magnet close to each. The iron filings in the mixture will be attracted to the magnet. The iron in the compound will not be attracted.

Orientation: Grades 4–6.

Content Objective: The children will state that mixtures may be separated by mechanical means.

Skill Objective: The children will *investigate* as they attempt to separate the constituents of various substances.

Materials: Kidney beans, navy beans, iron filings, sand, sugar, magnets, water, glass tumblers, magnifying glasses.

Evaluation: Students' verbal interaction, student group problem-solving skills, laboratory worksheets, log, and reports.

Procedure

Divide the class into groups. Provide each group with the following mixtures: navy and kidney beans; sand and iron filings; sand and sugar. Tell the groups to separate, if they can, the materials that make up each mixture. Tell them that they may use the things they find on the work table or anything else they may find in the room. On the work table place the following items: bar or horseshoe magnets, glass tumblers, magnifying glasses. Permit the children to attempt to solve the problems on their own.

Possible methods of separation are:

Kidney and navy beans—manual separation.

Iron filings and sand—using a magnet to extract the iron filings.

Sugar and sand—putting the mixture in water and pouring off the dissolved sugar.

Discuss with the class why the materials that they worked with were mixtures and not compounds.

Lesson Plan ▪ K

Orientation: Grades 4–6.

Content Objective: The children will state that compounds may be broken apart chemically into elements.

Skill Objective: The children are required to *observe* the changes that occur in a chemical reaction and to *infer* that a compound has been reduced to form two elements.

Materials: A large test tube, one-half test tube of mercuric oxide, propane torch.

Evaluation: Students' verbal interaction.

Procedure

Show the children a test tube half full of mercuric oxide. Tell them the name of the compound and write the formula on the board: HgO. Ask the children to describe the mercuric oxide. (It is a red powder.) Heat the test tube and contents vigorously over a propane

continued on next page

torch for about five minutes. Ask the children to carefully observe the contents of the test tube. (Droplets of mercury have formed near the mouth of the test tube. The powder has turned black.) Now ask: "Where did the mercury come from?" (From the decomposition of the mercuric oxide.) "What can we say about molecules when they are heated?" (Some molecules break apart when heated.) *Caution:* Do not permit children to handle the drops of mercury found in the test tube.

Lesson Plan ■ L

Orientation:	Grades 4–6.
Content Objective:	The children will state that sugar will decompose when heated; that it will form water vapor and a black residue (carbon).
Skill Objective:	The children are required to *experiment* and to *observe* changes in the properties of sugar as it is heated; they must then *infer* that the sugar decomposed into two simpler products.
Materials:	Six hot plates, six metal pans, sugar, six glass tumblers.
Evaluation:	Students' verbal interaction, written report.

Procedure

Gather together a hot plate, a tin pan, some sugar, and a glass tumbler. Put a teaspoonful of sugar into the tin pan and heat it vigorously. Hold a tumbler inverted over the sugar, as in Figure 14–12. Ask the class to describe:

1. The sugar before heating.
2. The sugar during heating.
3. The sugar after heating.
4. What collects on the inside of the tumbler.

Ask the class such questions as: "How did the sugar change?" "What appeared to collect in the tumbler? Where did this substance come from?" "What happened to the sugar compound?" Have the students write a paragraph describing what they saw and what they learned about how substances decompose.

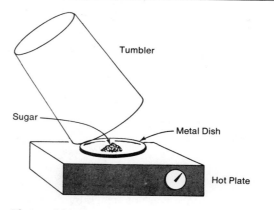

Figure 14–12 ■ Molecules Break Up When Heated

Orientation:	Grades 3–6.
Content Objective:	The children will state that there are spaces between molecules.
Skill Objective:	The children will *investigate*, carefully *observe* as photographic fixer is added to water, and *infer* that there are spaces between molecules.
Materials:	A box of photographic fixer or chili saltpeter, twelve test tubes, two dozen rubber bands, twelve plastic spoons, twelve metric rulers.
Evaluation:	Students' verbal interaction, seat work, and sketches.

Procedure

Divide the class into groups. Have each group fill a test tube two-thirds full of water and place a rubber band on the test tube to mark the water level. Then have them place a second rubber band on the test tube about two millimeters above the first. Tell the children to add the photographic fixer or chili saltpeter to their test tube, carefully counting the number of even spoonfuls that are required to raise the water level to the second rubber band. Ask: "How many spoonfuls of fixer did it take to raise the water level in the test tube two millimeters?" "Where did all of the fixer go when it was added to the water?" (The fixer ions must have gone into the spaces between the water molecules.)

Subconcept 5–2

A few kinds of atoms form many different molecules.

Discussion

Look around. Are you not struck by the seemingly infinite variety of substances you see? Although ninety-two different kinds of atoms exist in nature, most familiar substances are composed of only about thirty-five common elements. How can just thirty-five different building blocks make up so many different substances? The answer is that atoms can combine in many different ways.

Oxygen (a gas) may combine with nitrogen (a gas) in the following ways: N_2O (two atoms of nitrogen, one atom of oxygen); NO (one atom of nitrogen, one atom of oxygen); NO_2 (one nitrogen, two oxygens); NO_3 (one nitrogen, three oxygens); and N_2O_5 (two nitrogens, five oxygens). Thus, two gaseous elements can form five distinctly different compounds. Now consider molecules that are composed of three atoms or five atoms—of a hundred or two hundred atoms. How many ways could such molecules be formed? Remember that rearranging the order of any two atoms in a molecule can change the nature and identity of the molecule. When you realize that molecules are composed of anywhere from two to several hundred atoms, the number of possible combinations becomes staggering. And the molecules themselves may combine in nearly limitless ways to create substances. No wonder there are so many substances in our environment!

Orientation:　　　　　Grades 4–6.

Content Objective:　　The children will state that a few atoms form many kinds of molecules.

Skill Objective:　　　The children are required to *experiment* by manipulating materials and to *infer* how their discoveries relate to the construction of molecules.

Materials:　　　　　Six sets of the following: two ⅛" stove bolts, two ⅛" carriage bolts, two 2" lengths of ⅛" threaded rod, five ⅛" washers, five hexagon ⅛" nuts, and five square nuts.

Evaluation:　　　　Students' verbal interaction, student group problem-solving skills, laboratory worksheets, log, and report.

Procedure

Provide each child or group of children with the following materials: two ⅛" stove bolts, two ⅛" carriage bolts, two 2" lengths of ⅛" threaded rod, five ⅛" washers, five hexagon ⅛" nuts, and five square ⅛" nuts (Figure 14–13). Ask each child (group) to put the nuts, washers, bolts, and rods together in as many ways as possible. Ask the children to draw a rough sketch of each assembly.

When the children have had ample time to explore the many different combinations, ask each child (group): "How many ways did you find to put the parts together?" (Listen to several of the reports.) "How many different pieces do we have?" (Five.) "What can

continued on next page

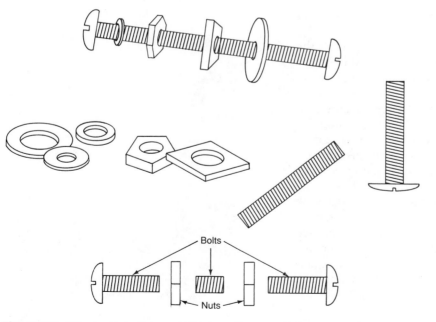

Figure 14–13 ▪ Nuts, Bolts, and Washers Illustrate the Variety of Molecular Structures

we say about how many ways there are to put together the five pieces?" (There are many ways to put together the five pieces.) "What if these five pieces represented five kinds of atoms? What could we say about the number of ways the atoms might be joined?" (Five atoms might be joined together in many different ways.) "How might we say this in terms of atoms and molecules?" (Atoms may join together in many ways to form molecules. A small number of atoms can form many different molecules.)

Concept 6

Molecules are attracted to one another by electrical forces.

Discussion

Trees, grass, rocks, people, and nearly everything else in our environment are composed of molecules. Molecules, in turn, are formed by the joining together of atoms. By definition atoms are electrically neutral—they contain equal numbers of protons and electrons. It follows that molecules, composed of atoms, are also electrically neutral. What holds molecules together? What forces keep molecules fixed in place among other molecules?

The secret to this apparent anomaly is the uneven distribution of charges within molecules. When an oxygen atom joins with two hydrogen atoms to form a water molecule, it shares a pair of electrons with each of them. However, the sharing is not equal. The oxygen atom retains a greater share of the electron pairs than do the hydrogen atoms. The uneven distribution of charges has the effect of creating poles of opposite electrical force in regions of the molecule. The oxygen end of the molecule has a weak negative charge. The hydrogen atoms have a weak positive charge. Where they are located close to other molecules that have an uneven distribution of charges, electrical forces interact. Positive areas of one molecule are attracted to negative areas of other molecules (Figure 14–14). The uneven distribution of electric charges is the primary cause of attraction between molecules.

Concept 7

Substances possess different physical properties.

Discussion

Because they are made up of different combinations of atoms, substances possess different physical properties. Some of the properties are hardness, lustre, state (solid, liquid, gas), conductivity (ability to conduct heat or electricity), malleability (ability of solids to be shaped or drawn into a wire), index of refraction (ability to bend light waves), density (weight or mass per unit volume), and many others. The various physical properties define the appearance and

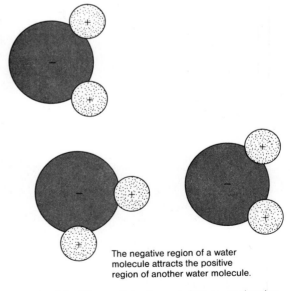

The negative region of a water molecule attracts the positive region of another water molecule.

Figure 14–14 ■ Polar Forces of Water Molecules

attributes of substances that permit their identification and application to technology. One of the most commonly recognized and useful properties of substances is density.

Density

Substances vary in their weight or mass per unit volume. A bushel of rocks weighs more than a bushel of feathers. Therefore, we say that rocks have a greater density than feathers. If the bushel of rocks weighs 100 pounds, its density may be expressed as 100 pounds per bushel. If the bushel of feathers weighs 1 pound, its density is expressed as 1 pound per bushel. One cubic foot of water weighs about 64 pounds. The density of water is then 64 pounds per cubic foot. In metric mass units, the density of water is 1 gram per cubic centimeter.

Bouyancy

Substances that are more dense than water sink when placed in water. Conversely, substances that are less dense than water float. The force that is exerted upon an object that is immersed or floating in water is called the bouyant force (Figure 14–15). Even objects that are more dense than water and therefore sink in water have bouyant forces acting upon them. You know that you can easily lift and support a friend while swimming. That is because the bouyant force exerted by the water is doing much of the lifting. The actual amount of the

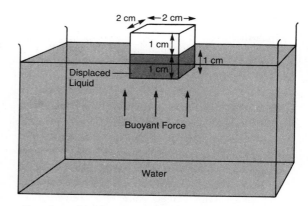

- The volume of the displaced water is 4 cm³ (2 cm x 2 cm x 1 cm).
- The "weight" of 1 cm³ of water is 1 gram.
- The buoyant force is equal to 4 grams.

Figure 14–15 ▪ Bouyant Force Acting Upon a Floating Wooden Cube

bouyant force is equal to the weight of the water that is displaced by the person's body; that is, if the person's body occupies two cubic feet of space (and when submerged, displaces two cubic feet of water) the bouyant force would be 2 × 64 pounds (the density of water), or 128 pounds. To support a friend who weighs 130 pounds, you would have to exert only 2 pounds of lift. Archimedes, an ancient Greek scientist, expressed the principle governing bouyant force this way: "The bouyant force exerted upon a body immersed or floating in a liquid is equal to the weight of the liquid displaced."

Lesson Plan ▪ O

Orientation:	Pre-K–2.
Content Objective:	The children will state that lighter objects float and heavier objects sink when placed in water.
Skill Objective:	The children will *investigate* and *observe* objects immersed in water.
Materials:	A water table or large basins of water, miscellaneous metal, wooden, and plastic objects such as wood blocks, paper clips, foam blocks, metal nuts or washers, coins, plastic toys, and others, aluminum foil.
Evaluation:	Observation of group problem-solving skills and students' verbal interaction.

continued on next page

Procedure

Activity 1—Place the large basins of water and the miscellaneous objects in a work area. Organize the class into groups and provide the children with water-repellent aprons. Allow them some free time for discovery with the materials. After a group discovers that some things sink and some float, ask the children to make two piles, one for each category of object. As the children continue to test materials, ask them, "What kinds of things sink in water? Float?" "How can you make a floating object sink?" "How can we make a sinking object float?"

Activity 2—Give each group of children a 10-cm square of aluminum foil. Ask them to find a way to make the foil float in water. The children may utilize their prior experiences and place the foil on top of a floating object such as a sheet of plastic foam. Accept all these efforts before asking them to find a way to make the piece of aluminum foil float without using any other object or material. If the children are unable to solve this in a reasonable amount of time, show them a "canoe" or "boat" made from a piece of foil. Ask them to make their own canoe or boat. Provide each group with small objects such as paper clips or washers, and have them determine how many their boat will support. If time permits have them construct alternative designs for their boats.

As a follow-up activity, you may wish to have the children draw or color a sketch of sink or float activities.

Summary

All matter is made up of tiny, electrically charged particles. These particles join together to form atoms. Atoms have a tiny, heavy nucleus thought to be composed of neutrons and protons. Whirling about this tiny bit of mass at a high rate of velocity are electrons. These electrons, by virtue of their great speed, occupy a relatively large volume. All atoms of an element have the same number of protons and electrons. Atoms of different elements vary only in the number of atomic particles present.

Atoms join together to form molecules. The forces that hold the atoms together are electrical in nature. Atomic bonding occurs when atoms exchange electrons (ionic bonding), share electrons (covalent bonding), or free electrons to move about in the substance (metallic bonding).

Molecules join together because the unequal distribution of electrons within the molecules creates regions of positive and negative electrical forces. These forces are mutually attractive.

Bouyancy is the force exerted by a liquid on an object that is floating or immersed in the liquid. Archimedes's principle states that the bouyant force acting upon an object floating or immersed in a liquid is equal to the weight of the displaced liquid. Objects more dense than water will sink when placed in water and objects less dense will float.

CHAPTER 15

Heat and Matter

Look What's in This Chapter

In this chapter we'll discuss some important concepts and subconcepts related to the study of heat and matter, and we'll introduce lesson plans that are designed to teach these concepts and subconcepts to children.

Concept 1 Atoms and molecules are held together by electrical forces.

Concept 2 Molecules move.

   Subconcept 2–1 Heat causes molecules to move.

Concept 3 Heat affects the state of matter.

Concept 4 Heat energy is transferred by conduction, convection, and radiation.

Concept 5 Heat and temperature are related.

Matter is often composed of tiny particles called molecules that are composed of even smaller, elementary particles called atoms. When substances absorb heat and other forms of energy, the atoms that compose the substances are affected in two basic ways. Their electrons react to the absorption of energy, as we will see in Chapter 16. And their *kinetic energy*, or energy of motion, increases. The relationship between heat energy and the motion of molecules is the subject of this chapter.

The state of matter—whether a substance exists as a *solid*, a *liquid*, or a *gas*—is determined by two things. One is the strength of the electrical forces of attraction that exist among its molecules or atoms. The other is the energy of movement that its molecules or atoms possess, which tends to cause them to tear away from one another.

Concept 1

Atoms and molecules are held together by electrical forces. (See also Chapter 14.)

Discussion

The commonly accepted model of atomic theory provides three principal mechanisms to explain how atoms are held together. In each case the particles are bonded by electrical forces. The three forces are ionic forces, polar forces, and metallic forces.

Ionic Forces

In Chapter 14 we discussed how atoms may gain or lose electrons. Atoms that gain an extra electron are negatively charged. Atoms that lose an electron are positively charged. Since unlike electrical charges attract each other, an attractive force will exist between such atoms. Such electrically charged atoms are called ions, and the force between them is called an ionic bond. Table salt, sodium chloride, is a common substance composed of ions.

Polar Forces

When atoms join together to form molecules, the electrons of the atoms are sometimes unevenly distributed throughout the molecule. When this happens, different regions of the molecule will possess slight positive and negative charges. In the water molecule, for instance, more electrons will tend to reside around the oxygen atom than around the hydrogen atoms. The water molecule is said to be slightly polar, with the portion in the region of the oxygen atom possessing a slight negative charge, and the regions around each of the hydrogen atoms possessing a slight positive charge. The regions of unlike charge on two adjacent water molecules will attract each other.

Metallic Forces

Metal atoms have one or more loosely held electrons in their outer energy level. When packed closely together, they lose these loosely held electrons, which are then free to migrate among the atoms. Tiny regions of matter become momentarily charged as the electrons become more dense in some areas and less dense in others. This exchange of electrons provides the force that holds metal atoms together. The atoms of any sample of pure metal or metal alloy are held together by such metallic bonds.

Concept 2

Molecules move.

Discussion

The molecules that make up a substance are not normally at rest. They exhibit several kinds of movement. When held in place by electrical forces, a molecule will expand and contract and also vibrate about a fixed position. When not held firmly in place by electrical forces, a molecule will move freely among other molecules. This energy of movement is termed *kinetic energy*.

Subconcept 2–1

Heat causes molecules to move.

Discussion

As the molecules that compose a substance absorb heat energy, their movement will increase. Molecules that are fixed in a *solid substance* will pulsate rapidly as they expand and contract in size and will also vibrate back and forth about a fixed position. Physical evidence of this increase in movement is the almost universal expansion of solids when heated.

Molecules of *gases* will decrease their rate of movement as they lose heat energy. Evidence of this phenomenon is the decreased pressure on the walls of a closed container of gas as it is cooled. A gas at 0° Celsius will lose 1/273 of its volume with every one-degree drop in temperature. As the temperature continues to drop below 0° Celsius, the volume of the gas will continue to decrease until the gas turns to a liquid or solid form. As the temperature of the liquid or solid continues to drop, the activity of the atoms and molecules that make up the substance will diminish until the substance reaches a temperature of −273° Celsius when the particles will have lost all of their kinetic energy. This temperature, −273° Celsius, is theoretically the coldest a gas can attain—the temperature at which it has absolutely no heat left. This temperature is called absolute zero.

Molecules of liquids will increase their rate of movement as they absorb heat energy. Visible evidence of this mechanism is the increase in a liquid's evaporation rate with the addition of heat energy.

Lesson Plan ■ A

Orientation:	Grades 5–6.
Content Objective:	The children will state that metals will expand when heated; that atoms increase their movement when heated.
Skill Objective:	The children are required to *investigate* by heating metal rods and to *infer* the cause of their *observations*.
Materials:	Twelve small roller bearings or cylindrical toothpicks, six two-foot boards, six metal cylinders about ¼" in diameter, twelve paper pointers, glue or tape.
Evaluation:	Students' verbal interaction, student group problem-solving skills, laboratory worksheets, log, and reports.

Procedure

Divide the class into groups, and provide each group with the following directions: Place two metal or wood cylinders parallel to each other on blocks of wood about one foot apart. Lay a long metal bar or cylinder of metal across the two rollers. Glue or tape a paper pointer on the end of one or both rollers and note carefully the position of the pointer. Heat the center of the rod between the wood blocks with an alcohol burner or a large candle (Figure 15–1).

After each group has performed this activity, ask: "What did we observe?" (The pointer moved.) "In which direction did the pointer move?" (Children indicate the direction.) "What does this mean?" (The

continued on next page

metal bar expanded and caused the rollers to move.) "What must be happening to the atoms where the bar is heated? Do they take up more room or less room than when the bar was cool?" (More room.) "If the atoms are not free to move over one another in the rod, what kind of movement must be taking place?" (They might be vibrating in place.)

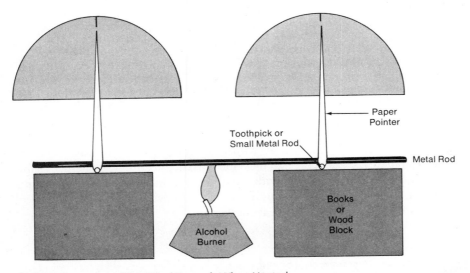

Figure 15–1 ■ A Metal Rod Expands When Heated

Lesson Plan ■ B

Orientation:	Grades 5–6.
Content Objective:	The children will state that metals will expand at different rates when heated.
Skill Objective:	The children are required to *hypothesize* concerning the expansion of metal rods, to *control variables* as they experiment, and to *interpret* the data that they gather.
Materials:	Twelve small roller bearings or cylindrical toothpicks, six two-foot boards, twelve paper pointers, six metal wires or cylinders of two different metals (brass, copper, iron, and so on).
Evaluation:	Students' verbal interaction, student group problem-solving skills, laboratory worksheets, log, and reports.

Procedure

You may extend Lesson Plan A by asking: "Do all metals expand at the same rate? How could you test this?" Permit each group of children to formulate hypotheses concerning the expansion of metal rods. Have them suggest tests for their hypotheses. One test would be to heat rods made of several different met-

continued on next page

als. In each case remind them to carefully mark on a card the position of the arrow indicator before and after three minutes of heating with a burner. The data so gathered may be used to compare expansion rates directly—the metal that causes the greatest rotation expands the most. The result of the experimentation will indicate that metals expand at different rates. Allow the students to communicate their findings to the rest of the class. The class should discuss the experimental procedures and compare data.

Lesson Plan ■ C

Orientation:	Grades 4–6.
Content Objective:	The children will state that molecules of a warm gas move faster and are farther apart than molecules of a cold gas.
Skill Objective:	The children are required to *observe* the expansion of a heated balloon and to *infer* a generalization from their observations.
Materials:	Two large balloons, an insulated cooler, ice.
Evaluation:	Students' verbal interaction, seat work, and sketches.

Procedure

Blow up two balloons to about one-half their capacities and have the children note that you have tied the ends of both tightly. Place one balloon on a heat vent or in the sunlight. Place the other balloon in an ice chest with ice. (See Figure 15–2.) (*Note:* Some teachers may prefer to heat one balloon in a hot water bath.) After five to ten minutes, ask the children: "What do we observe about the balloons?" (One is larger.) "Is there *more* air in the balloon than before?" (No.) "What can we say about the air in the larger balloon compared to the air in the smaller balloon?" (It is warmer. It takes up more room.)

You may wish to stop at this point with primary-grade children or with some groups of intermediate-grade children. To proceed with other groups, ask:

continued on next page

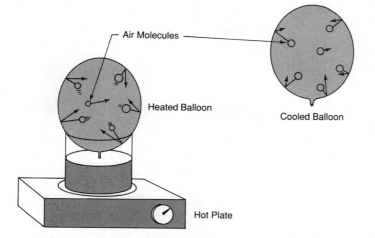

Figure 15–2 ■ Molecules of Warm Air Move Faster Than Molecules of Cold Air

"How can the same number of air molecules take up more space? How can they keep the balloon this large?" (There must be a greater distance between the molecules.) "If we think of the air molecules as moving freely about inside the balloon, what do you think their speed would be compared to the ones in the smaller balloon?" (They would have to move faster.) "What can we say about molecules of a warm gas?" (Molecules of a warm gas are farther apart and move faster than molecules of a cool gas.) You may wish to emphasize that the molecules do *not* expand appreciably when heated. The increase in the size of the balloon is due to the greater average distance between the molecules. Have the children draw a balloon containing warm air and a balloon containing cooler air on the same paper.

Lesson Plan ▪ D

Orientation:	Grades 4–6.
Content Objective:	The children will state that molecules in hot water move faster than molecules in cold water.
Skill Objective:	The children are required to *observe* the diffusion of food coloring in liquids of different temperatures and to *infer* a generalization from their observations.
Materials:	Two glass bottles, food coloring, hot and cold water. *Note:* The cold water must be at refrigerator temperature.
Evaluation:	Students' verbal interaction, seat work, and sketches.

Procedure

Fill one bottle with hot water and one with very cold water. Carefully add a drop of food coloring to each bottle (Figure 15–3). Ask the children: "What is happening?" (The coloring in the hot water is mixing faster than the coloring in the cold water.) Some teachers may wish to stop here with the generalization: "Coloring diffuses more rapidly in warm water than in cold water." With more advanced classes, the teacher may continue: "Remember that the water and the coloring are both composed of molecules. What can we say about the molecules in the hot water?" (The molecules in the hot water are moving faster.) You may want to discuss the mechanism whereby the food coloring is scattered throughout the water bottles. According to the popularly accepted model, the water molecules are moving freely about and bumping the food coloring molecules, causing them to disperse in the water.

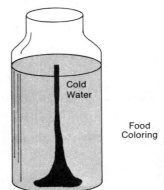

Figure 15–3 ▪ Molecules of Hot Water Move Faster Than Molecules of Cold Water

Write the concept on the chalkboard and have the children copy it on a sheet of paper.

Concept 3

Heat affects the state of matter.

Discussion

The interaction of forces among the molecules of a sample of water will illustrate the basic tenets of the *kinetic molecular theory.*

Picture the individual water molecules of an ice cube that has been placed in a deep-freeze at a temperature of 0° *Fahrenheit.* Each molecule is fixed firmly in place, but is vibrating to and fro in all directions about its central position. The kinetic energy (movement) of the molecules is not great enough to allow the molecules to escape their confinement.

Now the ice cube is removed from the deep-freeze and heat is applied to it. A person with supermicroscopic vision might see something like this taking place. As the ice cube gains heat energy and its temperature rises toward the *freezing point* (32°F), the molecules vibrate with more and more energy about their fixed positions. When its temperature reaches 32°F, chains of molecules gain enough movement to break free and move about. Some liquid (water) begins to form. As more heat is added, all the fixed water molecules are freed, and the entire substance becomes a *liquid* with a temperature of approximately 32°F (0° Celsius). As heat continues to be added, the temperature rises to between 32°F and 40°F. Now the superobserver sees long chains of molecules swimming freely but sluggishly about one another. At this point the molecules comprising the chains are still attracted to one another, and occasionally several might weld together momentarily, only to vibrate apart again as their kinetic energy continues to increase.

As the temperature of the liquid climbs toward 40°F, the energy of the individual molecules increases and the long chains begin to break up until at some higher temperature each molecule in the liquid is free from its neighbor. The *electric forces* are still present between individual molecules, but the kinetic energy of the particles is so great that they pass by one another without becoming attached.

If the water is heated still more, the motion of the molecules increases until at a *temperature of 212°F*, the kinetic energy of the individual molecules is so much greater than the attractive forces between molecules that the molecules are completely free of one another. They move about as a gas at a very high rate of speed. *Steam* has been formed. If a temperature of 212°F (100° Celsius) is required to change water to steam, how might one explain the fact that evaporation appears to occur at much lower temperatures?

Figure 15–4 illustrates the phases of water.

Evaporation

Picture in your mind the activity of water molecules moving freely about in a beaker of water. You must not suppose that all of these countless molecules possess exactly the same amount of energy. Though there is an average amount of kinetic energy each molecule may be thought to possess, some individual molecules are moving relatively slowly while others are rushing about at a much higher speed. As they move, molecules collide with other molecules. A few molecules may be bumped in such a way as to gain sufficient energy to overcome the forces binding them to their neighbors. This permits them to fly off into the air. The more heat energy available to the molecules, the greater the chance that some of them will acquire enough motion to leave the liquid. Thus, all other things being equal, the evaporation rate of a liquid is related to the temperature. The higher the temperature, the greater the number of molecules flying off. At the boiling point (212°F or 100°C), the rate at which molecules are leaving the liquid (and thereby removing energy from the liquid) is great enough to maintain a fairly constant temperature in the liquid. At the boiling point, the kinetic energy of most of the molecules is almost enough to permit them to disassociate from their neighbors. The addition of just a little heat will result in rapid evaporation.

Ice

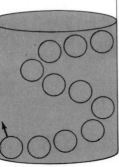

Melting
Point

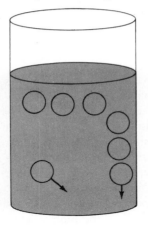

Liquid
(Greatest Density)

0°F (−17.5°C)
Molecules Vibrating
in Place

32°F (0°C)
Some Molecules
Fixed in Place,
Some Molecules
in Moving Chains

40°F (4°C)
Some Molecules
in Moving Chains,
Some Molecules
Moving Individually

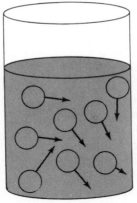

Liquid

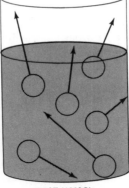

Boiling Point

40°-212°F (4°-100°C)
All Molecules
Moving Freely

212°F (100°C)
Molecules Rapidly
Escaping from
the Liquid

Figure 15–4 ■ Phases of Water

Lesson Plan ■ E

Orientation:	Pre-K—2.
Content Objective:	The children will describe the properties of water and ice.
Skill Objective:	The children will *investigate* and *observe* the properties of water and ice.
Materials:	Assorted paper, foam, and plastic containers such as small drinking cups, medicine cups, party favor cups, margarine tubs or basins of water, and waterproof aprons. You will also need six small aluminum pie plates, some fruit juice, and a drinking cup for each child. A hot plate is optional.
Evaluation:	Observation of group work, students' verbal interaction.

Procedure

Activity 1—Place the water tubs and containers on a table or counter. Organize the class into groups. Have the children put on waterproof aprons and allow them to have some time for free discovery. As the children explore with the water and containers, listen to their verbal interaction. Ask questions such as, "I wonder how many of the medicine cups it would take to fill the drinking cup?" or, "Do all the tall containers hold more water than the shorter ones?" The children will pour the water from one container to another, observing the properties of water. You may also ask, "I wonder which container will hold the most water?" (or "the least water?"). You can also instruct the children to "Pour about one half of the water from the margarine tub" or "Fill the pitcher half full." Have the children describe how water looks, feels, tastes, and smells, and how it sounds as it is poured or splashed.

Activity 2—With a marking pen, write on small paper drinking cups *Group 1*, *Group 2*, and so on, so that each group of children has its own cup. Have the children fill their cups full of water. Place the cups on a small tray or piece of board and put them in the freezer of a refrigerator. Add six or eight extra unmarked cups of water. Permit them to stay in the freezer overnight. The following day, give each group a small aluminum pie pan and its cup of frozen water. Make sure the children understand that the ice they have in their cups is the water they placed in the freezer earlier. Have the children examine the cup of ice for a few minutes,

describing it to one another and contrasting it with the water. When possible, have the children turn the cups upside down, permitting the ice to fall from the cups into the pie pans. Have them observe the ice for a few minutes while you place some cups of ice on pie plates and set them in different locations: in the freezer, in the refrigerator, on a table out of the sun, on a table in the sun, and so on. If a hot plate is available, turn it to the low setting and place a cup of ice in a pie pan that rests on its surface. Permit the children to examine the ice samples located about the room. After ten minutes, take the ice from the freezer and refrigerator and let the children examine it. The children should observe that ice is frozen water, and when ice melts, water is formed; that ice is cold, and that although water may be different temperatures, it is always warmer than ice. The children may also observe that ice will melt faster when the sun shines on it and when it is on the hot plate—that heat makes ice melt faster. They should also observe that ice kept in cold places such as a freezer or refrigerator melts very slowly or not at all.

Activity 3—At snack time pour juice kept at room temperature into the children's drinking cups and add one or two ice cubes. Have the children let the juice sit for a few minutes before drinking it. You may ask, "How does ice affect juice?" "What happens to the ice?" "Where did the water from the ice go?" "Did the water become warmer than the ice?"

Orientation: Grades 4–6.

Content Objective: The children will state that heat is required to change ice to water, to change the state of matter from solid to liquid.

Skill Objective: The children are required to *observe* the changing temperatures of an ice-water mixture, to *communicate* by constructing a graph, and to *interpret* the energy relationships presented in the graph.

Materials: Hot plate, Pyrex or ceramic pan, large Celsius thermometers, ice.

Evaluation: Students' verbal interaction, laboratory worksheets, log, and reports.

Procedure

Fill a Pyrex or ceramic pan about half full of ice cubes, as in Figure 15–5. Place a thermometer deep among the ice cubes and allow it to remain for several minutes. Record the temperature. With the thermometer

continued on next page

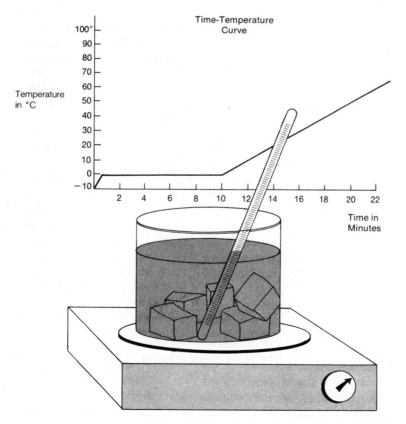

Figure 15–5 ▪ Change of State

remaining in the pan, heat the pan *slowly*. Select one child to read the thermometer periodically. The children should record the temperature at regular time intervals, say, two minutes. Stir the ice cube–water mixture constantly to ensure a uniform heat distribution throughout the mixture. After all the ice is melted, have the children enter their data on a graph with the time on the horizontal axis and the temperature on the vertical axis. (See Figure 15–5.)

After the children have constructed their graphs, ask: "In view of the fact that heat was constantly added to the ice-water mixture, what do you see that is peculiar about the graph?" (There is a flat place where the temperature did not increase.) "What was the temperature that remained steady for so long?" (0°C.) "What might have been happening here?" (The heat energy was being used to change ice to water. It requires heat to change ice to water.)

Lesson Plan ■ G

Orientation:	Grades K–3.
Content Objective:	The children will state that evaporating liquids take heat from their surroundings, that evaporation is a cooling process.
Skill Objective:	The children are required to *observe* by feeling the cooling effect of evaporation and to *infer* a generalization from their observations.
Materials:	Alcohol, eyedropper, wet cloth.
Evaluation:	Students' verbal interaction.

Procedure

Pass among the children and put a drop of alcohol in the palm of each child's hand. Ask: "What do you observe?" (The alcohol disappears. It feels cool.) "Where did the liquid go?" (Into the air. It evaporated.)

Now pass among the children and dab the backs of their hands with a wet cloth. Ask: "What do you observe now?" (The water disappears. It feels cool.) "Where did the water go?" (Into the air. It evaporated.) "What might we say about evaporation and tempera-ture?" (When a liquid evaporates, it makes the things around it cool.)

With young children the lesson might end here, with some generalizing statements about getting cold when our bodies are wet. With older children (grades 4–6), you might continue: "If our hands felt cool, would this mean that the evaporating liquid was taking away heat or adding heat?" (Taking away heat.) "What can we say about heat and evaporation?" (Evaporation takes heat from its surroundings. It takes heat to allow liquids to evaporate.)

Concept 4

Heat energy is transferred by conduction, convection, and radiation.

Discussion

Heat energy is transferred in solids by means of *conduction*. Conduction occurs when each atom or molecule of a substance absorbs heat energy and subsequently passes it on to all those neighboring atoms or molecules that possess less heat energy. Thus, *heat is distributed from the region of greater concentration to the region of lesser concentration.*

Heat energy is transferred in liquids and gases (fluids) by *convection*. When a local region of a fluid is heated, the molecules of that region gain kinetic energy, and the average distance between the molecules in that region increases. The heated fluid thus becomes less dense than the surrounding cooler fluid. The warmer fluid rises and the cooler fluid moves in to replace it. This causes a movement in the substance called a *convection current*.

Heat energy is transferred through a vacuum by *radiation*. Heat is a form of radiant energy as are light energy and radio waves. It may be radiated over long distances through a vacuum or over shorter distances through the earth's atmosphere. Radiant energy generally travels in a straight path. It may be absorbed by the material that it strikes.

Lesson Plan ■ H

Orientation:	Grades 3–6.
Content Objective:	The children will describe conditions that permit the transfer of heat.
Skill Objective:	The children are required to *investigate* by trial and error and to *observe* the effects of their experimentation.
Materials:	Six jars, ice cubes, miscellaneous materials such as newspapers, aluminum foil, rags, and so on.
Evaluation:	Students' verbal interaction, seat work, and sketches.

Procedure

Tell the children that they are about to have an ice-cube race. The object of the race is to prevent an ice cube from melting. They are free to use any materials or apparatus that they find in the classroom. (Previously place some small sheets of aluminum foil, newspapers, and rags on a counter.)

Give each group of three or four children an ice cube in a glass jar and say: "Go, the race is on." Observe as the children attempt to prevent their ice cubes from melting. After about ten minutes, stop the race.

Declare a winner by measuring the amount of melt water each team has in its jar. The team with the least water wins.

Let some of the unsuccessful teams describe what they did to prevent their ice cubes from melting. Discuss with the class the reasons for their failure. Examine the winning team's procedure. Discuss the winning team's procedure in terms of the three methods of heat transfer—conduction, convection, and radiation. Have them complete a worksheet that evaluates their understanding of the three terms.

Lesson Plan ■ I

Orientation:	Grades 2–5.
Content Objective:	The children will state that heat moves through a metal rod from an area of higher concentration to an area of lower concentration.
Skill Objective:	The children are required to *observe* the conduction of heat through a metal rod and to *infer* a generalization from their observations.
Materials:	Metal wire or rod, candle or burner, paraffin, wooden clothespin.
Evaluation:	Students' verbal interaction. *continued on next page*

Procedure

Carefully place drops of melted paraffin from a burning candle about two inches apart along a metal wire or rod. Heat one end of the rod with a large candle or alcohol burner, holding the other end with a wooden clothespin, as in Figure 15–6. Ask the children: "What is happening?" (The wax droplets are melting and dropping off one by one in succession, starting from the heated end of the metal rod.) "What does this indicate?" (The heat travels through the rod from the heated end to the opposite end—from where the rod is hottest to where it is coolest.)

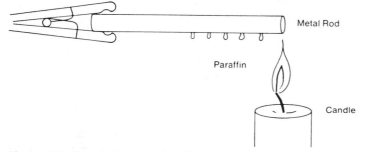

Figure 15–6 ▪ Heat Travels by Conduction

Lesson Plan ▪ J

Orientation:	Grades 2–6.
Content Objective:	The children will state that some metals conduct heat better than others.
Skill Objective:	The children are required to *hypothesize* about the ability of different metals to conduct heat, to *control variables* as they *experiment*, and to *interpret* the data obtained.
Materials:	Rods of various metals, all of equal diameter, large candles or other heat sources, clock, paraffin, wooden clothespins.
Evaluation:	Students' verbal interaction, student group problem-solving skills, laboratory worksheets, log, and reports.

Procedure

To extend Lesson Plan I, ask: "Do all metals conduct heat equally well? How can we find out?" Divide the class into groups. Have each group formulate hypotheses concerning the rate at which rods of various metals conduct heat. Have them suggest procedures for testing their hypotheses. Remind them to define and control variables and to keep accurate records of their findings. Have each group report their results to the rest of the class. Draw some general conclusions from the data of the class as a whole.

The most obvious procedure for testing the hypothesis that metals conduct at different rates is to repeat Lesson Plan I using various metals and to *time* the melting of the wax droplets for each metal. Some variables that should be considered are: type of metal, diameter of metal rods, distance of the flame from the paraffin, constancy of the flame.

Orientation: Grades 4–6.

Content Objective: The children will state that when air is heated it rises, forming a convection current.

Skill Objective: The children are required to *observe* and to *infer* a generalization from their observations.

Materials: Hot plate, sheet of plastic food wrap, ruler, tape.

Evaluation: Students' verbal interaction, seat work, and sketches.

Procedure

Turn on an electric hot plate and permit it to warm up for several minutes. While the hot plate is heating, ask the children: "What happens to the air that touches the hot plate? Where does it go? Anyplace?" Tear off a twelve- to fourteen-inch sheet of plastic food wrap from a roll. As the children watch, tape the sheet of plastic wrap to a ruler or meterstick and hang it beside the hot plate, taking care not to let the plastic come into contact with the hot plate element. Ask: "What happens? What do you see?" (The plastic wrap flaps toward the burner and is carried upward by the rising air.) "What is causing the plastic wrap to move like this?" (The air near the hot plate is rising and carrying the plastic wrap with it.) "What happens to air when it is heated?" (It rises.) "We saw what happened when the plastic wrap was held alongside the hot plate. How is the air rising over the hot plate replaced? (Air from around the hot plate moves toward the hot plate to take the place of the hot air that is rising above it.) The children should summarize that when warm air rises cooler air moves in to take its place. Tell the class that this movement of air is called a convection current. Have them draw a convection current that occurs over an asphalt parking lot on a hot, sunny day.

Orientation: Grades 2–6.

Content Objective: The children will state that when warm water lies under cold water, the warm water rises and the cold water moves in to take its place, forming a convection current.

Skill Objective: The children are required to *observe* the mixing of hot and cold water and to *infer* a generalization from their observations.

Materials: Four small-mouthed bottles, hot water, cold water, food coloring, stiff index card.

Evaluation: Students' verbal interaction.

continued on next page

Procedure

Fill two bottles with hot water and two bottles with cold water. In one bottle of hot water and one bottle of cold water, place a few drops of food coloring. Place a doubled index card over the mouth of the remaining bottle of clear hot water, invert it, and place it over the bottle of colored cold water, as in Figure 15–7. Repeat, inverting the remaining bottle of clear cold water over the bottle of colored hot water. Remove the index cards and observe. Ask: "What is happening?" (The liquids in one pair of bottles mix and the liquids in the other pair do not.) "Can anyone guess why this happens? You may ask questions in order to obtain facts with which to work." If the children cannot establish the temperature relationships by questioning, let them discover them by feeling the bottles. "Now what do we know happened?" (The warm water rose into the cold water, but the cold water did not rise into the warm water.) "What might we conclude from this activity?" (Warm water rises.) "And what must have happened to the cold water when the warm water rose into the top bottle?" (The cold water fell into the lower bottle. Warm water rises and cold water moves in to take its place.)

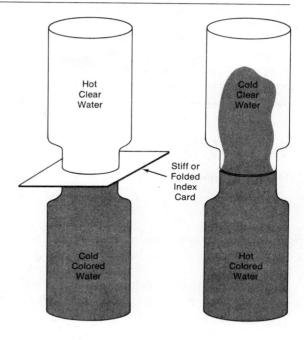

Figure 15–7 ■ Heat Travels by Convection Currents in a Liquid

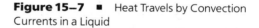

Lesson Plan ■ M

Orientation: Grades 3–6.

Content Objective: The children will state that heat energy is transferred by radiation.

Skill Objective: The children are required to *observe* heat being transferred by radiation and to *infer* a generalization from their observations.

Materials: An electric lamp.

Evaluation: Students' verbal interaction.

Procedure

Turn on an incandescent lamp for twenty to thirty seconds. Permit the children to feel the lamp bulb. Ask: "What do you feel?" (The bulb is warm.) "Where

did the heat come from?" (From the wire in the bulb [filament].) "How did it get to the glass from the filament?" At this point you may wish to explain that a

continued on next page

light bulb contains only a bit of inert gas—that inside the glass is a vacuum. "Could the heat have been transported by conduction from the wire to the glass? By convection?" (No.) "How could the heat have been transported?" (By radiation.) The children may also observe that heat is transferred away from the bulb through the air. Ask: "Could this heat be traveling by conduction?" (No. Air is not a solid.) "By convection currents?" (Maybe, but the heat may be felt *under* the bulb. Since warm air rises, it must not be by convection currents.) "How is the heat transferred through the air?" (By radiation.)

Concept 5

Heat and temperature are related.

Discussion

The terms *heat* and *temperature* are often confused; many people think they are synonymous. This is not true. The following three definitions should clarify the relationship between heat and temperature.

Heat

Heat is a form of radiant energy. Common sources of heat are the sun, the interior of the earth, chemical reactions (combustion), friction, electricity, and nuclear energy.

Calorie

The calorie is a unit of measurement. It measures the *amount* of heat energy a substance possesses or transfers. One calorie of heat energy will raise the temperature of one gram of water one degree Celsius.

Temperature

Temperature is an *indirect* measure of the rate at which a substance gives off heat energy. It is *not* a measure of the amount of heat energy a substance possesses. Temperatures are measured with a thermometer. The thermometer absorbs the heat from the substance being measured. Thus, it is really measuring the rate at which the substance is giving off heat energy.

Substances Absorb Heat Energy

The absorption of heat energy affects the temperature of different substances differently. Water, for instance, is a good absorber of heat. When water is heated, its temperature will rise more slowly than that of, say, a metal block. Two substances having different temperatures may thus possess identical amounts of heat energy. Or two substances having the same temperature may possess different amounts of heat energy. It is simply a case of one substance being better able to retain heat energy than another.

Lesson Plan ■ N

Orientation:	Grades 4–6.
Content Objective:	The children will state that the same amount of heat energy will produce different temperatures in different substances.
Skill Objective:	The children are required to *observe* the effect of heating upon two different substances and to *infer* that the same amount of heat may produce different temperatures in different substances.

continued on next page

Materials: Pyrex container, water, pot holder or glue, a 100-gram metal weight, alcohol burner or large candle.

Evaluation: Students' verbal interaction, seat work, and sketches.

Procedure

Place 100 milliliters (about 100 grams) of water in a Pyrex beaker. Place the beaker over an open flame for one or two minutes. Ask several children to test the temperature of the water by touching it, or if the class can read a thermometer, they may take the temperature of the water. Now heat a 100-gram metal weight over the same flame for an identical period of time. (See Figure 15–8.) Ask the children: "How many of you would want to feel the metal weight?" (Of course, no child should be permitted to touch the hot metal.) You might demonstrate the temperature of the metal by dropping several drops of water on it. "Which is hotter, the metal weight or the water?" (The metal weight.) "Although we lost some heat during the heating of the substances, could we say that each substance received approximately the same amount of heat?" (Yes.) "What might we say happened in our experiment?" (The same amount of heat caused the metal to become hotter than the water.) "What can we say about heat and temperature?" (The same amount of heat may produce different temperatures in different substances.) Have the children write a statement expressing what they learned about various substances' abilities to absorb heat.

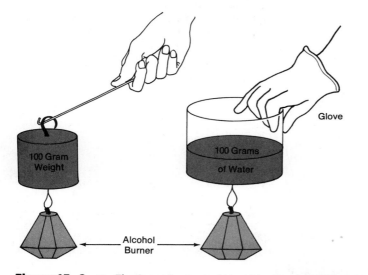

Figure 15–8 ■ The Same Amount of Heat May Result in Different Temperatures

Orientation:	Grades 5–6.
Content Objective:	The children will state that the same amount of heat will produce different temperatures in different substances.
Skill Objective:	The children are required to *experiment*, to *communicate* by constructing a graph, and to *interpret* the data from the graph.
Materials:	Twelve Pyrex beakers, balance, glycerine, water, six thermometers, six tripods, six alcohol burners, a timer.
Evaluation:	Students' verbal interaction, student group problem-solving skills, laboratory worksheets, log, and reports.

Procedure

Divide the class into groups of five or six students. Provide each group with the following set of directions: Place identical beakers on each side of a balance. Fill one beaker half full of water. Add glycerine to the other beaker until the beakers of water and glycerine balance. Place a thermometer in the beaker of water. Note the time and the temperature of the water. Place the beaker on a tripod stand over an al-cohol burner flame. Stir the water continuously. Note and record the temperature of the water each minute for fifteen minutes. Repeat the same procedure with the beaker of glycerine. Make a chart of your data. Put the time on the horizontal axis and the temperature on the vertical axis. Label one line *water* and the other line *glycerine*. What can you conclude from this data? (See Figures 15–9 and 15–10.)

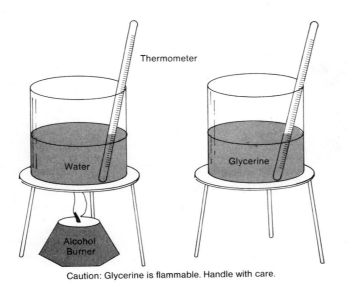

Thermometer

Water

Glycerine

Alcohol Burner

Caution: Glycerine is flammable. Handle with care.

Figure 15–9 ▪ The Same Amount of Heat Produces Different Temperatures in Water and Glycerine

continued on next page

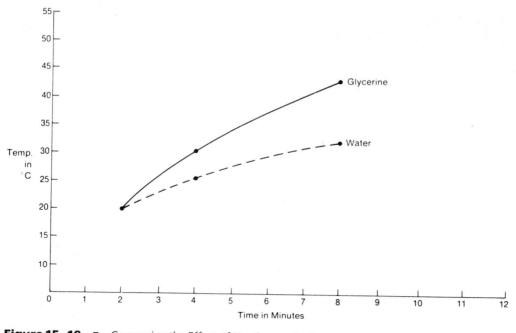

Figure 15–10 ■ Comparing the Effect of Heating on the Temperature of Water and Glycerine

Summary

The atoms and molecules that make up substances are held together by three different kinds of electrical forces: ionic, polar, and metallic. These molecules and atoms also possess kinetic energy, the energy of movement. Whether a substance is a solid, a liquid, or a gas depends upon the relationship that exists between the electrical bonding forces and the stress placed on the bonds by the kinetic energy of the particles. A substance will be solid when the bonding forces are strong enough to withstand the stresses created by the movement of the molecules and hold them fixed firmly in place. A substance will be liquid when the average motion of the molecules is great enough to cause the particles to move from fixed positions and to slip over one another freely. A substance will be gaseous when the average kinetic energy of the molecules is great enough to overcome the effects of the electrical attraction so that the molecules move about independently.

Heat energy is transferred through solids by conduction and through fluids (liquids and gases) primarily by convection. Radiation occurs when the heat energy is given off by a source. The radiated energy travels through space and through some matter in the same way as light energy and radio waves do.

Heat is a form of energy. A calorie is a unit of heat energy. Temperature is an expression of the rate at which a substance gives off heat energy.

Heating affects the temperature of different substances differently. Some substances are able to absorb and retain heat energy better than others. For example, the temperature of a block of metal will rise faster, given the same amount of heat, than the temperature of water. This is because water retains heat energy better than metal does.

CHAPTER 16

Light

Look What's in This Chapter

In this chapter we'll discuss some important concepts and subconcepts related to the study of light energy, and we'll introduce lesson plans that are designed to teach these concepts and subconcepts to children.

Concept 1 Atoms absorb energy.

Concept 2 Electrons emit energy.

Concept 3 The energy of the light family travels in waves.

Concept 4 The light family has many members.

Concept 5 Light energy may be seen.

    Subconcept 5–1 White light may be separated into colors.

Concept 6 Light has wave properties.

    Subconcept 6–1 Light may be reflected.

    Subconcept 6–2 Light may be refracted.

    Subconcept 6–3 Objects may be magnified.

Have you ever wondered what causes the light that comes from a burning fire? Why the sun shines? How a radio operates? Some of the most mysterious phenomena in nature are those related to light energy. Let us see what we can learn about these phenomena.

Concept 1

Atoms absorb energy.

Discussion

When substances are exposed to various types of energy—such as heat and light—some of the energy is absorbed by the atoms composing the substances. The absorption of energy causes the atoms to change in two major ways. The atom may increase its physical motion, that is, it may move around or vibrate in place with a greater vigor. This affects the physical state of the substance as we saw in Chapter 15. A second change occurs when individual electrons within an atom absorb heat or light energy. This interaction of energy and electrons is the source of the light family.

You recall that electrons are tiny, charged particles moving about the atomic nucleus at a high rate of speed and that the electron's distance from the nucleus is determined by the amount of energy it possesses. When an electron absorbs heat or light (or other) energy, it moves farther from the nucleus and revolves about the nucleus in a higher energy level. The electron is then said to be in an unstable, excited state.

Lesson Plan ■ A

Orientation:	Grades 2–6.
Content Objective:	The children will state that substances absorb energy.
Skill Objective:	The children are required to *observe* a substance absorbing heat and to *infer* a generalization from their observations.
Materials:	Alcohol burner, paper, matches, wire screen.
Evaluation:	Students' verbal interaction.

Procedure

Light an alcohol burner. Ask the children: "What would happen if you held a piece of paper over the top of the flame?" (It would burn, catch fire.) Demonstrate this. Then place a piece of wire screen in the flame and have one of the children hold a piece of paper over the screen. Ask: "Now can we hold a piece of paper over the flame?" (Yes.) "Where is the heat going?" (Into the screen.) "What evidence do we have that the screen is absorbing the heat?" (It changed color.) At this point you might put a drop of water on the screen. The effect of the heat on the water is further evidence that the screen absorbed heat. Objects other than a screen may be used to show that atoms absorb energy from their surroundings. A container of water, for instance, would serve the same purpose. (See Figure 16–1.)

continued on next page

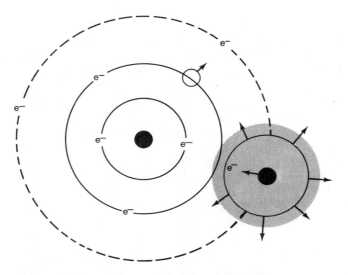

Figure 16–1 ■ Electrons Absorb and Give Off Energy

Concept 2

Electrons emit energy.

Discussion

Excited electrons usually retain their excess energy for only a very short time before they give it up and return to a more stable energy level. And as they fall back into their more stable level, they give off a pulse of energy. Depending on the frequency of the pulse, this energy takes various forms. Some of the best known are radio waves, heat energy, light energy, and X rays. These energy forms are known as the light family.

Lesson Plan ■ B

Orientation:	Grades 3–6.
Content Objective:	The children will state that an object may emit heat and several colors of light energy when heated.
Skill Objective:	The children are required to *observe* the energy radiated from a heated object and to *infer* from their observations.
Materials:	Wooden clothespin, iron wire or small nail, propane torch, matches.
Evaluation:	Students' verbal interaction, seat work, and sketches.

Procedure

Heat a fine wire or a small nail in a flame. (*Caution:* Hold the iron wire or nail with a clothespin so you do not burn yourself.) After the nail has become hot, but *before* it turns red, hold it in the air and ask the children: "What kind of energy is the nail giving off?"

continued on next page

(Heat energy.) Drop water on the nail to demonstrate that heat energy is being emitted by the iron atoms.

Now heat the nail in a flame until it is red. Hold the nail in the air and ask: "What forms of energy are being given off now?" (Heat and light energy.) You may add that some electrons in the iron atoms are emitting heat energy while others are emitting light energy (Figure 16–2). "What can we say about the kinds of energy a heated object may emit?" (A heated object may emit several kinds of energy.) Now heat the nail until it becomes cherry red to white. Ask: "What happens to the color of light that is being emitted as the temperature is increased?" (As the temperature is increased, the color of light changes from red to whitish.) Ask the students to write down the concept that was demonstrated by the activity.

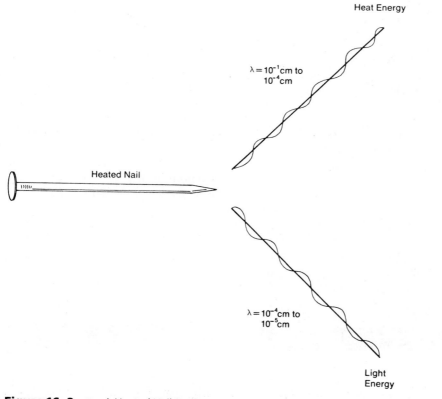

Heat Energy

$\lambda = 10^{-1}$cm to 10^{-4}cm

Heated Nail

$\lambda = 10^{-4}$cm to 10^{-5}cm

Light Energy

Figure 16–2 ■ A Heated Nail Radiates Heat and Light Energy

Concept 3

The energy of the light family travels in waves.

Discussion

We have seen that every time an excited electron falls back to a stable position, a pulse of energy is given off. What is this energy composed of? What is its nature?

Do you recall what happens when two electrically charged objects are brought close to each other? Or when two magnetic objects are held close together? A force is exerted in each case. Since the electrical and magnetic objects

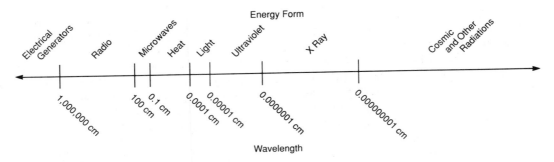

Figure 16–3 ■ The Electromagnetic Spectrum

need not be touching in order to interact, there must be a region around each object where forces can be exerted. If both electrical and magnetic forces are present in the same region, an *electromagnetic force field* is said to exist. This is the kind of energy that is given off by excited electrons. It consists of pulses of both electrical and magnetic force fields. These pulses are called *electromagnetic waves*. These waves affect the electrical charges with which they come into contact.

Every time an excited electron falls back to a stable condition, a pulse of electromagnetic energy is given off. If this happens rapidly, the pulses of energy will be close together as they travel through the air or through space. If the pulses of energy are emitted at a slower rate, they will be farther apart. It is just like making ripples with your finger in a pond. If you tap your finger rapidly in one place, the waves that spread out in concentric circles will be close together. If you tap your finger slowly, the waves will be farther apart. The distance between the waves is called a *wavelength*, and the number of waves that pass by a point in space in one unit of time is called the *frequency* of the waves. Obviously, as the frequency of the waves increases, the distance between the waves must decrease.

The analogy of water waves applies equally to electromagnetic waves. They, too, vary in frequency and wavelength (Figure 16–3).

Lesson Plan ■ C

Orientation:	Grades 4–6.
Content Objective:	The children will state the following properties of waves: waves expand in circles from the source; waves rebound from a surface; waves pass through each other; waves are close together when the water is tapped rapidly and farther apart when it is tapped slowly.
Skill Objective:	The children will *investigate*, list *observations*, and *infer* the relationship of water waves to light waves.
Materials:	Six pans or deep paper dishes or paper plates, water, six pieces of chalk or blocks of wood.
Evaluation:	Students' group problem-solving skills, laboratory worksheets, log, and reports.

continued on next page

Procedure

Provide groups of three or four children with a shallow pan filled about one-half inch deep with water. (Deep paper plates will do for this purpose.) Ask: "When you touch the water with your finger, what happens?" (A wave spreads out through the water.) Appoint a recorder for each group and say: "Now here is what I would like you to do. Write down as many things as you can about water waves. List everything that you actually see."

Allow the children ample time to make their observations. While the children are working, you may pass among them and ask such questions as: "Do waves pass through each other? What happens where waves meet?" Later you may wish to suggest that the children place something in their dish to serve as a barrier (a pencil, chalk, heavy paper, and so on) and observe what happens when the waves strike the barrier.

To conclude the lesson, have the recorder from each group report one interesting observation to the class. The observations should be written on the chalkboard so that the children can see them. Now say: "Let's see how many things that happen to water waves also happen to light." Some of the observations should be:

1. Waves expand in circles from the source.
2. Waves rebound when they strike a surface.
3. Waves pass through each other.
4. Waves are higher when the water is tapped harder. (The intensity of light is related to the energy available.)
5. Waves are closer together when the water is tapped rapidly. (The color of light is related to its frequency.)

This is a good time to clarify the concepts of wavelength (the distance between waves) and frequency (the number of waves that pass a point in a given time interval).

Extending the analogy, some classes may predict some properties of light that are not readily observable. Examples of such predictions are: light waves interfere with one another where they meet, and light bends around corners. From the group data, list all the characteristics of waves that were demonstrated in the activity.

Concept 4

The light family has many members.

Discussion

Radio, heat, light, and X rays are all members of the light family. They all consist of pulses of electromagnetic energy. The only essential difference among them is the frequency of their pulses, or the wavelength between pulses.

Radio waves have a low frequency, in the range of several hundred thousand waves per second. The wavelength of common broadcast radio waves may be measured in yards or meters. Heat waves have wavelengths measurable in hundredths of a centimeter. The wavelengths of visible light measure several ten-thousandths of a centimeter. The high-frequency waves, such as ultraviolet rays, X rays, and cosmic rays, have wavelengths that measure tiny fractions of millionths of a centimeter. Humans can *see* light waves and *feel* heat waves. Radio waves are defined as those wavelengths normally utilized in electronic systems. (*Note:* You do not *hear* radio waves. The radio waves are converted to sound waves by a radio.)

No exact wavelengths separate the adjacent portions of the electromagnetic spectrum. Rather, they constitute general areas of a continuum of wavelengths or frequencies of electromagnetic energy. All of the energies of the light family travel through a vacuum at the incredible speed of 186,000 miles or 300,000 kilometers per second.

Orientation:	Grades 3–6.
Content Objective:	The children will state that light and heat have many similar properties.
Skill Objective:	The children are required to *classify* information concerning heat and light energy and to *infer* that they are similar.
Materials:	Chalkboard and chalk.
Evaluation:	Students' verbal interaction, seat work, and sketches.

Procedure

Begin by asking the class: "What two kinds of electro-magnetic energy can we detect with our senses?" (Heat energy and light energy.) "Let's list the ways in which they are the same and the ways in which they are different." The two lists that evolve might look like this:

Heat and Light

How They Are the Same
They both travel through the air.
They both travel through a vacuum.
They can both be reflected from shiny surfaces.
They can both be aimed (by shaped reflectors such as flashlights or electric heating elements).
They both cause things to heat up.
They both burn our skin.
They both come from light bulbs.
They are usually found together.

How They Are Different
Light is seen, heat is felt.
Heat is used to cook. (Could we cook with light?)

When the lists are completed, ask the children: "What can we say about how heat and light are the same and how they are different?" (They are the same in many ways. They are different mostly in how we feel them.) Point out that heat and light are both forms of electromagnetic energy, and microwaves are radio waves. How can we use this force of energy? Have the students draw an electromagnetic spectrum with the energy forms light, heat, and radio waves. Show them Figure 16–3 if necessary.

Lesson Plan ▪ E

Orientation:	Grades K–4.
Content Objective:	The children will state that light energy may be converted to heat energy.
Skill Objective:	The children are required to *observe* as light energy is focused on a paper and to *infer* that light energy is converted to heat energy.
Materials:	Hand lens, sunshine, a piece of paper.
Evaluation:	Students' verbal interaction.

continued on next page

Procedure

After the class is familiar with the general concept of electromagnetic energy, you may use the following activity to reinforce the idea that various energies are convertible.

Hold a lens over a small piece of paper that has been placed on a glass dish so that sunlight passes through the lens onto the paper. Adjust the lens by moving it closer to or farther from the paper until the light on the paper is converged to a small, intense dot. The paper will turn dark and burst into flames (Figure 16–4). Ask: "What did we see?" (The light formed a small dot on the paper and the paper started to burn.) "What kind of energy struck the paper?" (Light.) "What kind of energy do we associate with burning?" (Heat.) "What happened to the energy here?" (Light energy was converted to heat energy.) "Where did the change take place?" (In the paper.)

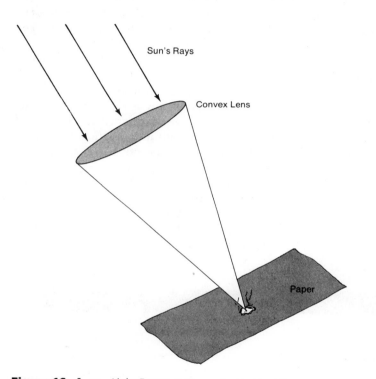

Figure 16–4 ■ Light Energy Is Converted to Heat Energy

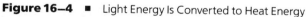

Concept 5

Light energy may be seen.

Discussion

The human body is sensitive to several kinds of stimuli in nature. We can hear through a special organ, the ear. We can smell through a special organ, the nose. Specialized nerve endings in our tongue permit us to taste, and we feel through nerves in the skin. The eye is a specialized organ that permits us to see.

The nerve endings in the eye are sensitive to a very narrow range of frequencies of electromag-

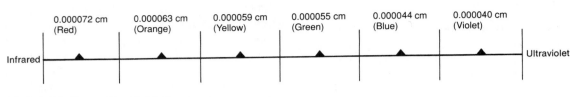

Median Wavelength

| 0.000072 cm (Red) | 0.000063 cm (Orange) | 0.000059 cm (Yellow) | 0.000055 cm (Green) | 0.000044 cm (Blue) | 0.000040 cm (Violet) |

Infrared — Ultraviolet

Figure 16–5 ▪ The Visible Spectrum

netic energy. This narrow range of frequencies is called light. The wavelength of light varies only 3/10,000 of a centimeter between the shortest waves and the longest waves. The shortest light waves measure 4/10,000 of a centimeter. The longest measure 7/10,000 of a centimeter.

Subconcept 5–1

White light may be separated into colors.

Discussion

White light contains all of the colors of the visible spectrum: red, orange, yellow, green, blue, indigo, and violet. The only difference among these colors is their wavelengths. Red has the longest wavelength and violet the shortest. The other colors have wavelengths that fall between these two. (See Figure 16–5.)

All wavelengths of light travel at the same speed in a vacuum: 186,000 miles per second. However, this is not true outside a vacuum. Light travels more slowly in air than in a vacuum, and more slowly yet in water, glass, and other transparent substances. What is more, all wavelengths of light do not travel at the same speed outside a vacuum, but slower or faster depending on the individual frequencies. Because the different wavelengths of light slow down by different amounts as they enter a glass prism, the light will emerge on the other side of the prism separated into its component colors.

Lesson Plan ▪ F

Orientation:	Pre-K–2.
Content Objective:	The children will describe how looking through colored cellophane filters changes the view; how looking through magnifying glasses changes the view; and how sunlight is reflected off shiny surfaces.
Skill Objective:	The children will *investigate, observe,* and make *inferences.*
Materials:	Forty cardboard or plastic frames for photographic slides, sheets of colored cellophane, including red, green, and blue, scissors, cellophane tape, small magnifying glasses, miscellaneous objects such as leaves, seeds, nuts, pieces of cloth, paper, wood, and so on, ten 3″ × 5″ mirrors or pieces of shiny metal.
Evaluation:	Group problem-solving skills, students' verbal interaction.

continued on next page

Procedure

Activity 1—Looking at the world through colored filters: Obtain about forty frames from old 35 mm (or larger) slides, a variety of colors of cellophane sheets, and cellophane tape. To make colored light filters, cut the sheets of colored cellophane into appropriate-sized pieces and mount on the slide frames with tape. Give each group of three to five children a set of all available colors of the colored light filters. Permit them to explore with the various colors. Ask the children to share the filters so that all the members of each group may have access to all the light filter colors. This is a good opportunity to teach or reinforce the names of the colors by asking a child to name the filter color that he is using. If the child does not know, tell him which color he is looking through. Try to stress the colors red, green, and blue. After the children have had ample time to explore, ask them to lay aside all the filters except the red, the blue, and the green ones. Now show them how to place one filter over another and look through the two colors at once. Permit them to try all the combinations of the red, green, and blue filters. At the end of the allotted time have the groups, if they have not already done so, look through all three at once. Ask them such questions as: "What was your favorite filter color to look through?" "What color did you see when you looked through the red filter? the blue filter? the green filter?" "What color of light was getting into your eye with the red, the blue, and the green?" "What did you see when you combined the red and green filters?" and so on. It is not advisable at this time to attempt to teach the children that red, green, and blue are the primary colors of light.

Activity 2—Looking at the world through magnifying glasses: For each group of children collect a box of miscellaneous objects such as seeds, bits of cloth, pieces of wood, paper, and others, and one magnifying glass per child. Permit the children free time to examine the materials with the magnifying glasses. You might also suggest that they examine their own fingernails, the skin on the back of their hands, and their own clothing. Walk among the children asking them what they see and what a magnifying glass does to help them see things. The children might examine

materials for fifteen to twenty minutes at a time for several days. After they are done, ask them "What did you find the most interesting?" "What was the biggest surprise?"

Activity 3—Taking a magnificent look at the classroom and school: Provide each child with a magnifying glass and permit the children to examine their surroundings in the classroom and school. In the classroom the children may freely examine the bulletin boards, the teacher's desk, their own desks, the window blinds, books, art materials, science materials, and other interesting things. Following their exploration, discuss with them the things they saw. Ask them what they saw that was most interesting and what thing surprised them the most.

Activity 4—Magnifying the great outdoors: Provide each child with a plastic bag and a magnifying glass. Take the children outside to the school yard. First direct them to examine the school building and the sidewalks. Then take the children to an area where there is grass, bushes, trees, and other plants. Permit them to examine the leaves, seeds, blooms, branches, and trunks of the growing things. If there are insects, caterpillars, or other living things on the plants, warn the children that they should not touch them without the teacher's permission. Encourage them, however, to examine any stationary animal life with their magnifying glasses. If there is time, you may want to have them place a pinch of sand or soil, a few different leaves, and other small objects of interest in their plastic bags to examine when they return to the classroom. When they return to the classroom, discuss the events of the field trip. Help the children describe what they saw through their magnifying glasses. If they later examine materials from their collection bags, discuss those experiences also.

Activity 5—Looking at light reflections in mirrors: On a day when the sun is shining through the classroom windows, close the blinds or drapes except for a two-foot opening in the middle. Give each child or group of children a small metal mirror. Have them "aim" their mirrors at the sunlight coming in the window and see

continued on next page

what occurs. (Some children will have to move to the center of the room to participate.) The reflections from their mirrors will appear on the ceiling and walls. Permit them to freely examine the reflected light for a few minutes. Then say, "I want you to make your light spot shine on the corner over there," and point to the corner of the room where the front wall and window wall meet. See if the children can do this. Help any that cannot adjust their mirrors until their reflected light is in the desired location. Repeat this for other points in the room. Let pairs of individual children or groups play tag, with one reflection "chasing" another. After sev-

eral minutes, stop this activity and open the blinds. Discuss the activity with the children. Tell them the light was reflected from the mirrors. The mirrors caused the sunlight to change directions.

You may permit the children to examine themselves in the mirrors. They may also place a book, pencil, crayon, or other common objects close in front of them on the table, hold the mirror beyond the object, and examine it in the mirror. The children may also hold the mirror over the top of objects and examine them from this angle. Discuss with them what mirrors do and how they make things look.

Lesson Plan ■ G

Orientation:	Grades 3–6.
Content Objective:	The children will state that white light may be separated into colors; that opaque objects absorb some colors and reflect others; and that transparent objects may absorb some colors and permit others to pass through.
Skill Objective:	The children are required to *investigate* by manipulating materials and to *infer* some generalizations from their observations.
Materials:	Sunlight or artificial light sources, six prisms, squares of assorted colors of construction paper, squares of assorted colors of cellophane.
Evaluation:	Students' group problem-solving skills, laboratory worksheets, log, and reports.

Procedure

Divide the class into groups. Ask the entire class to observe as you project sunlight through a triangular prism, onto a white wall or a white piece of paper. If sunlight is not available, an incandescent source of light such as a slide projector may be used. Ask the children: "What colors can we identify?" (The colors of the spectrum.) Now say: "I wonder what each group can find out about light with the materials I will give you."

Provide each group with a prism, squares of assorted colors of construction paper, and colored cellophane. Let the groups begin to discover on their own. If necessary, guide them to project the light pass-

ing through the triangular prism onto screens of variously colored paper. Ask: "What colors can we see?" (Colors of the spectrum minus some of the colors.) "Why?" (The paper screen will reflect some of the colors of the spectrum and absorb others.) Also guide the children to project the light spectrum through transparent filters of various colors and then through the prism, onto a white screen (Figure 16–6). Ask: "What colors do we see?" (Colors of the spectrum minus some of the colors.) "Why?" (The filter absorbs some colors and transmits others.) Have each group write a paragraph stating what they learned about how different colors of light are reflected and absorbed and pass through various substances.

continued on next page

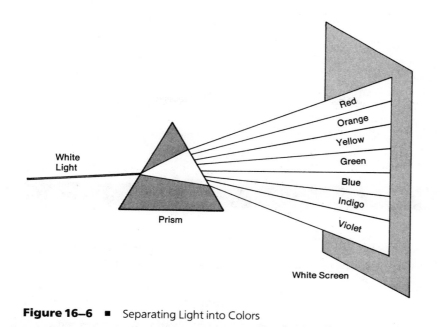

Figure 16—6 ■ Separating Light into Colors

Concept 6

Light has wave properties.

Discussion

An early scientific argument concerning the nature of light centered about its composition. Was light composed of waves or of tiny particles? It appeared to possess the properties of both. Light could be reflected from a surface much like a ball bouncing off a wall, yet it would spread out in all directions after passing through a tiny opening, just as a water wave would. Today we believe that light has properties of *both* the particle and the wave.

Light exhibits its wave properties in several easily demonstrated ways:

1. Light spreads out uniformly from a source.
2. Light may be reflected.
3. Light may be refracted or bent.

Review Lesson Plan C for a lesson that deals with the wave properties of light.

Subconcept 6—1

Light may be reflected.

Discussion

How do you know what your friend looks like? How do you know the color of your shoes? The only way we can see things that do not produce their own light is through *reflection*. Reflection occurs when light strikes a surface and bounces off. Some materials, such as mirrors and shiny metals, reflect nearly all of the light that strikes them. Other materials reflect almost none of the light, but rather absorb all of the energy. In general, shiny or white objects are good reflectors while black objects are poor reflectors.

Colors of Objects

Why might a friend's sweater look red and his jeans look blue? Since he is standing in the same light, why do they not look the same? The colors of objects that are not light sources depend upon the colors they *reflect*. Red objects reflect red wavelengths of light and absorb all others. Blue objects reflect blue wavelengths and absorb all others. As for your friend, his sweater is reflecting red wavelengths of light and his jeans blue ones. *Dyes* are chemicals that absorb particular wavelengths of light and reflect others.

Lesson Plan ▪ H

Orientation:	Grades K–4.
Content Objective:	The children will state that some materials reflect light better than others do; shiny and light materials reflect better than rough and dark ones do.
Skill Objective:	The children are required to *observe* light reflections from materials and to *infer* a generalization from their observations.
Materials:	A flashlight, two pieces of aluminum foil, one smooth and one roughened by crumpling, pieces of white paper, brown paper, and black paper.
Evaluation:	Students' verbal interaction, seat work, and sketches.

Procedure

Darken the room. Shine a flashlight on a sheet of aluminum foil. Ask: "What do you see?" (The light reflects onto the wall, ceiling.) "Now watch carefully as I shine the light on each of these other materials." Shine the light successively on the rough-textured foil, the white paper, brown paper, and black paper. Ask: "Do you notice anything about the reflection?" Shine the light on the materials again if necessary. The children should say that the smooth shiny surface reflected better than the crumpled shiny surface and that the lighter colors reflected more light than the darker colors. If materials are available, permit the children to explore reflections on their own or in groups. Have them write how each material reflects light.

Lesson Plan ■ I

Orientation: Grades K–4.

Content Objective: The children will state that light will pass through some materials better than it will through others; they will correctly define transparent, translucent, and opaque.

Skill Objective: The children will *observe* how light passes through various materials and *infer* a generalization from their observations.

Materials: A flashlight, a piece of glass or clear plastic, various thicknesses of paper, a piece of cardboard.

Evaluation: Students' verbal interaction, seat work, and sketches.

Procedure

Direct a flashlight toward the class and ask: "What do you see?" (A light from a flashlight.) "Watch carefully as I cover the flashlight with various materials." Then cover the flashlight successively with the clear glass or plastic, the papers of various thicknesses, and the cardboard. Ask: "Did you notice anything about the light?" (The most light came through the glass; no light came through the cardboard.) "What might we say about the ability of materials to pass light?" (Some materials pass light better than others.) You may now say: "We call materials that pass no light *opaque*, materials that pass some light but not all *translucent*, and materials that pass all light *transparent*."

Lesson Plan ■ J

Orientation: Grades 4–6.

Content Objective: The children will state that reflected light strikes and leaves a mirror at the same angle.

Skill Objective: The children are required to *observe* light reflecting from a mirror and to *infer* a relationship from their observations.

Materials: Large, flat mirror, flashlight, chalk.

Evaluation: Students' verbal interaction, seat work, and sketches.

Procedure

Lay a large flat mirror on a table or the floor. Darken the classroom. Holding a flashlight at about waist level, ask the children: "If I direct the light at the mirror, what will happen?" (It will be reflected.) "Where on the opposite wall do you think the light will strike?" Allow one child to point to the place on the wall where she thinks the light will strike. Turn on the flashlight, direct the beam to the mirror, and ask, "Was that a good guess?" Mark on the wall the spot where the center of the light struck. Label the mark "waist." Now ask: "Where do you think the light will strike if I hold the flashlight down by my knee and shine it on the

continued on next page

mirror?" Let the children predict where the light will be reflected on the wall. Demonstrate with the flashlight held at various heights and label the spots on the wall "waist," "knee," "head," and so on.

After a number of reflections have been demonstrated, ask: "What can we say about how light is reflected from a mirror?" (It bounces off the mirror in the same way as it hits the mirror.) "Can we talk about angles? What can we say about the angle at which the light strikes and the angle at which it leaves the mirror?" (They are the same. The light leaves the mirror at the same angle that it struck it.) (See Figure 16–7.) Ask the children to draw pictures illustrating the light being reflected from several angles.

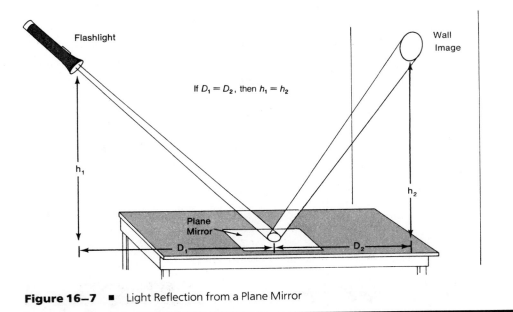

Figure 16–7 ■ Light Reflection from a Plane Mirror

Subconcept 6–2

Light may be refracted.

Discussion

Light energy moves in wave fronts just like water waves. Light energy travels at slightly different speeds in different transparent substances. The speed with which a substance permits light to pass through it is identified by a property called *optical density*. Light passes fastest through a vacuum and more slowly through air, water, glass, and diamond, in that order.

When a wave front passes at an angle from one medium into a second medium of a different optical density, refraction occurs. Figure 16–8 shows that a portion of the wave front enters the glass before the rest. The portion of the wave that is in the glass is moving more slowly than the rest of the wave front, which is still in the air. Like a roller skater dragging one skate to slow down, the wave front turns in the direction of the slower movement. Once the whole wave is inside the glass plate, its motion is again uniform, but the entire front is now traveling in a slightly different direction. This change of direction is the result of refraction.

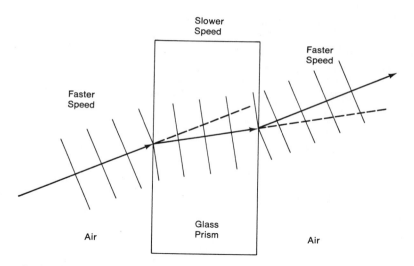

Figure 16–8 ■ Refraction of Light at Air-Glass Boundary

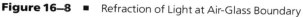

Lesson Plan ■ K

Orientation:	Grades 3–6.
Content Objective:	The children will state that light bends as it leaves water and enters air, that light is refracted as it passes from water to air.
Skill Objective:	The children are required to *observe* the apparent motion of a coin as it is covered with water and to *infer* the reason for the apparent motion.
Materials:	Aquarium, coin, water, stick or pointer.
Evaluation:	Students' verbal interaction, seat work, and sketches.

Procedure

First ask: "How do we see things?" (Light is reflected from objects to our eyes.) Place a coin in the bottom of an aquarium (Figure 16–9). Place a child so that he cannot see the coin over the edge of the aquarium. Add water a little at a time until the child can see the coin. Ask the child to describe what happens. Ask:

"Why can Ben see the coin now over the edge of the aquarium?" (The light reflecting from the coin is bent [refracted] toward Ben's eye.) Now insert a stick or pointer into the water. Ask: "What do you see?" (The stick is "broken.") "Where?" (Where the air and water meet.) "Does the stick look normal in the water? In the air?" (Yes.) "Where does the light bend?" (Where the

continued on next page

water and air meet.) "When we look at fish in a stream, are they farther away or closer than they appear?" (They are closer than they appear.) "Why?" (The light is bent as it leaves the water.) Have several children attempt to "spear" the coin from an angle. Permit the children to immerse the stick into the water at several angles from a vertical to a horizontal position; have them describe what they observe.

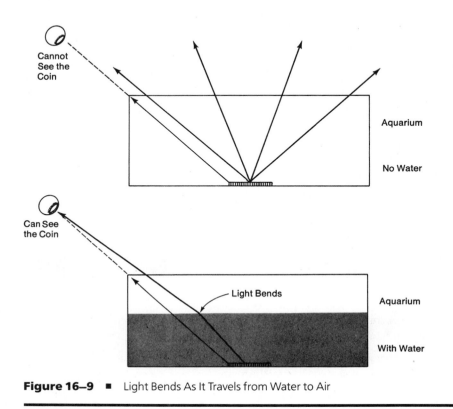

Figure 16–9 ▪ Light Bends As It Travels from Water to Air

Subconcept 6–3

Objects may be magnified.

Discussion

A wave front that is emerging into air from a curved, transparent substance of higher optical density (a water drop, for instance) will be refracted as in Figure 16–10. The portion of the wave front emerging from the curved surface into the air at A will gain speed as it enters the air. This will cause the wave front to turn toward the observer. This bending of the wave front is also occurring at point B. The waves from points A and B converge toward the observer. The observer perceives the light as traveling in straight lines and projects the size of the letter as though the light originated at points C and D. Thus, the letter appears to be larger. Magnification has occurred.

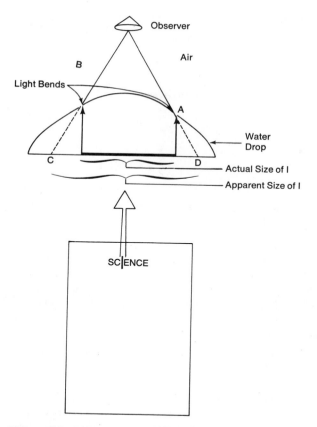

Observer

Air

B

Light Bends

A

Water Drop

C   D

Actual Size of I

Apparent Size of I

SCIENCE

Figure 16–10 ▪ Magnification by a Water Drop

Lesson Plan ▪ L

Orientation:	Grades K–5.
Content Objective:	The children will state that objects viewed through curved glass or water surfaces will be magnified.
Skill Objective:	The children are required to *observe* the effect of curved glass and water surfaces upon light and to *infer* a relationship between the nature of the surfaces and magnification.
Materials:	A dropper, pieces of a printed page of good quality paper (a magazine will do), a quart jar, shallow glass baking dish.
Evaluation:	Students' verbal interaction, seat work, and sketches.

continued on next page

Procedure

Place a printed page of good quality paper on each child's desk. With a dropper, put a drop of water on a single letter of the printed page. Ask: "How does the writing look through the water drop?" (The letter under the drop is larger.) "What is the shape of the top surface of a water drop?" (It is rounded [convex].)

Fill a jar with water. Put a printed paper behind the jar of water as in Figure 16–11. Ask: "What do you see?" (The writing behind the jar of water is larger.) "What is the shape of the surface of the jar?" (It is curved, convex.) "What can we say about viewing things through convex transparent objects?" (They are magnified by such objects.)

Ask: "Will objects be magnified when they are viewed from directly above a flat, transparent surface? Let's find out." Fill a shallow glass baking dish one inch deep with water. Place the dish on top of a page of printed matter. Ask: "What do you see?" (The letters appear about the same.) "Does a flat surface mag-

Figure 16–11 ■ Magnification by a Curved, Water-filled Jar

nify?" (No.) "Are light rays bent when they pass through a flat, transparent substance at right angles to the surface?" (No.) Let the children explore magnification with different sized jars and hand lenses (if they are available). Ask them to sketch an object before and after it is magnified.

Summary

The fast-moving, orbiting electrons within an atom may absorb energy such as heat and light. When they do, they move to a higher energy level in an excited state. After a usually short time, the excited electron gives up the extra energy and falls back to its normal condition. The energy is given up by the electron in the form of electromagnetic radiations. One kind of electromagnetic energy is light. Light energy will: (1) disperse uniformly in a uniform medium, (2) reflect at the surface of a medium, (3) refract at the surface of a medium, (4) interfere with light energy from other sources, (5) diffract, or bend, around corners. These characteristics of light may be explained in terms of its wave properties.

Magnetism

Look What's in This Chapter

In this chapter we'll discuss some important concepts and subconcepts related to the study of magnetism, and we'll present lesson plans that are designed to teach these concepts and subconcepts to children.

Concept 1   Magnetism is a property of moving electrons.

> Subconcept 1–1   Each electron in every atom is a tiny magnet.
>
> Subconcept 1–2   Some materials are magnetic.
>
> Subconcept 1–3   Unlike poles of magnets attract; like poles repel.
>
> Subconcept 1–4   Electric currents have magnetic fields.
>
> Subconcept 1–5   The earth has a magnetic field.

For many children, discovering magnetism is a memorable event. They watch in fascination as objects jump to the magnet or are propelled spinning away from it. The objects have not touched the magnet. The magic has occurred at a distance. The antics of magnets and magnetic substances inspire children to ask the question that many teachers fear most—Why? Why does the tack jump to the magnet? Why is a magnet repelled by a second magnet? Teachers fear why questions when they have no ready answers and feel that they should. But should they? Should a teacher be able to answer all why questions?

Mystery Forces

There exist in nature certain forces that defy explanation. We do not know why they interact with matter or with each other. *Magnetic force* is one of them. We know quite a lot about the forces magnetic fields exert in various situations. The direction of the force on specific materials is predictable as is the extent of the force. But we do not know why it acts as it does, or even why it exists in the first place. One might as well ask why the universe itself exists, or why matter exists in the form of electrons, protons, and neutrons. The answer to why questions concerning the origin or nature of the properties of magnetic fields is: "No one can say. All we know is that they do exist. We know how they act under many conditions. But we cannot say why they exist, or why they act as they do."

Other well-known, but inexplicable, forces that require the same approach are *gravitational forces, electric field forces*, and *nuclear forces*. Why are the planets attracted to the sun? Why does the earth exert a force on us? Why do charged balloons repel each other? What is the force that holds together the nuclei of atoms? All of these questions must be dealt with in the same way. We know *how* these forces act, but we do not know *why* they act that way.

Magnetism and electricity are so related that they cannot be studied separately. To reduce the study of each to the simplest possible considerations, and to avoid confusion, each is treated in a separate chapter. However, the properties of electricity will necessarily be mentioned in this discussion of magnetism, just as the properties of magnetism are mentioned again in Chapter 18. Once you have digested the content of each chapter, you may wish to review both topics. The two halves should then come together to form a more understandable whole.

Concept 1

Magnetism is a property of moving electrons.

Subconcept 1–1

Each electron in every atom is a tiny magnet.

Discussion

Magnetism appears to be a property of an electric charge in motion. That is, every moving electron has a magnetic field around it. It is a tiny magnet. Electrons in atoms have two distinct motions: they rotate upon their own axes and they orbit about the nucleus of the atom (Figure 17–1). Atoms derive a magnetic effect from the orbiting motions of electrons about the nucleus. Additionally, the rotation of each individual electron on its axis provides each electron with its own individual magnetic field. This raises a question. If all electrons in atoms have magnetic fields about them, why are not all atoms magnets? Why, indeed, are not all substances magnetic?

The electrons of most elements exist in pairs. The two members of a pair of electrons are thought to be spinning in opposite directions. The orientation of their magnetic fields is such that they oppose each other. That is, the two magnets pull in opposite directions, and thus their forces are canceled out.

The magnetic fields of the individual electrons orbiting about the nuclei of atoms are oriented in all directions, with no particular pattern. The net effect is that no external magnetic field is detectable. *The cancellation effects associated with the pairing of atoms according to their spin and the randomness of their orbiting motion account for the fact that most substances in nature possess little or no external magnetic field.*

Subconcept 1–2

Some materials are magnetic.

Discussion

To possess a magnetic field a substance must meet two requirements: some of its atoms must possess unpaired electrons, giving each atom strong magnetic properties, and the magnetic fields of some atoms must be so aligned that the magnetic effects are not canceled out. The theory of magnetic domains appears to account for both of these factors.

The Theory of Magnetic Domains

The atoms of three elements possess electrons with unpaired spins. These elements are *iron, nickel,* and *cobalt.* A bar of these metallic elements is composed of small microscopic regions called *domains* (Figure 17–2). Within these domains, all of the magnetic fields of individual atoms are aligned. This in effect makes *each domain a tiny, strong magnet.* To make an entire sample of a substance magnetic, the trick appears to be to align the domains so that their magnetic effects add together.

In nature the alignment of atoms and domains appears to have been accomplished in *lodestone.* Lodestone, an iron-carrying volcanic rock, had its domains aligned under the influence of the earth's magnetic field as the substance cooled from a molten state. Likewise temporary or permanent magnets may be artificially made from iron and iron alloys by subjecting them to magnetic fields. Under the in-

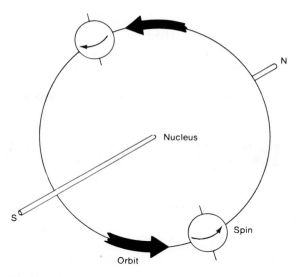

Figure 17–1 ■ Motions of Electrons Create Magnetic Fields

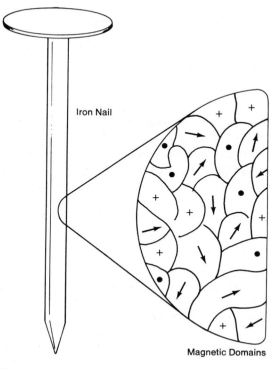

Figure 17–2 ■ Magnetic Domains

fluence of strong magnetic fields, the domains within the metals align themselves in the same direction as the external magnetic field. Soft iron is relatively easy to magnetize, but because of the weak bonds between domains and the kinetic energy of their atoms, it quickly loses its magnetic properties. Steel (a mixture of iron and other elements) requires a very strong magnetic field to align its domains. However, once aligned, steel magnets retain their properties for a long time.

Lesson Plan ■ A

Orientation: Pre-K–2.

Content Objective: The children will describe various kinds of magnets, how magnets interact with one another, how they are used in everyday life, and what they attract.

Skill Objective: The children will *investigate* and *observe* how magnets interact with one another and with other materials; they will *identify* magnets and materials as magnetic or nonmagnetic.

Materials: Magnets of many shapes (bar, horse shoe, U-shaped, ring, rod, disc, and miscellaneous shaped) and materials (iron, steel, nickel, ceramic, rubberlike plastic). (It is not necessary to have *all* these types of magnets.) Also: paper clips, string, short dowel rods, construction paper, two small boxes for each group of students, and miscellaneous materials to test for magnetism.

Evaluation: Students' group problem-solving skills, students' verbal interaction.

Procedure:

Activity 1—Magnets come in various shapes, sizes, and materials: For each group, pass out about ten magnets of three or four different types, including ceramic or refrigerator magnets. Give the children time for free play so that they can discover the ways in which magnets interact with one another. After they have had sufficient time to explore, ask them how the magnets affected one another. ("Sometimes they pushed apart and sometimes they pulled together." "They stick together.")

Activity 2—Magnets may be identified by shape and by what they are made of: Permit the children to explore with all of the available magnets by passing them out among the groups and arranging periodic exchanges of magnets between groups. Give the children time to explore all of the magnets. Ask them to put magnets that seem the same in piles. Discuss the magnets, holding up one at a time and asking, "What is the shape of this magnet?" "How strong is it?" "What might we call it?" "What is this magnet made of?" Provide the names of the more common shapes of magnets such as the bar magnet, horseshoe magnet, U-magnet, and others. Do not be concerned that the children remember all the names.

Activity 3—Magnets attract and repel one another: If Lego or other construction blocks are available, make as many cars and/or trains as possible. If toy vehicles are available, you may use them also. Using tape or a rubber band, attach a strong bar magnet to each car or train. Provide each group with two of the vehicles. Permit them to experiment with them, watching them repel and attract from a number of directions and from a number of distances. Discuss with the children what they observed about how magnets attract and repel one another.

continued on next page

If you have ring magnets, pass out at least two to each group—preferably three or more. Instruct the children to hold a pencil upright and stack the ring magnets on it. They will observe that, depending upon the way each ring is oriented, that is, which side of the ring is turned up, the rings will repel or attract their neighbors in the stack. Again discuss with the children how the forces of magnets act upon one another.

Activity 4—Some magnets are stronger than others, and magnets are stronger at the ends (poles): Provide the children with an ample supply of paper clips and several types and sizes of magnets. Have them see how many paper clips they can pick up with each magnet. If necessary help them count the paper clips. Now suggest they make "chains" of paper clips by hanging them one at a time from the magnets. Compare the strength of the magnets. They will be surprised to discover that the size of a magnet does not necessarily determine its strength. Discuss what part of each magnet picked up the most paper clips. If the children do not remember, permit them to explore further. They will find that magnets are stronger at the ends (poles) and weakest in the middle.

Activity 5—Some materials are attracted to magnets and some are not: Give each group of children a collection of miscellaneous objects, some of which are magnetic and some not. Also provide each group with a box marked *Yes* and one marked *No*. Ask the children to test all the materials provided and place them in the appropriate box—the *Yes* box if they are magnetic and the *No* box if they are not. If the materials to be tested vary among the groups, have them exchange with one another and test various sets. After the testing has been completed, pick up the materials from the *Yes* box one by one. See if the children can name the objects and tell what they are made of. Do the same for the *No* box. The children will find that the materials in the *Yes* box are metals, mostly iron or steel. (Avoid including ceramic and plastic magnets in the materials; children should realize that iron and steel are the common materials that are naturally magnetic.)

Activity 6—Testing the magnetic properties of objects in the classroom: Provide each small group (two or three students) with a magnet. Ask them to test different objects and surfaces in the classroom to see if they are magnetic. Tell them to test carefully and try to remember which objects and surfaces are magnetic. Permit the children to move about the classroom, touching objects and surfaces with their magnet. Move about among the groups of children, showing them to test the various materials that make up parts of an object. For instance, they should test the metal part and the wooden part of a desk separately. After the children have had ample time to make their tests, ask them to be seated and discuss what they discovered. Check any disagreements by rechecking all questionable objects. See if they can describe the kinds of things that are magnetic (iron) and nonmagnetic (wood, cloth, and other nonmetallic things).

Activity 7—A magnet's force can work through some materials: Provide each group of students with several magnets and some 10 cm square pieces of paper and paperboard of different thicknesses, a piece of wooden board, two baby-food jars (one two-thirds full of water), and several paper clips. Hold up a magnet to which a paper square is attached by the force of the magnet holding a paper clip on the underside. Ask the children to test to see what types of materials, when placed beween a magnet and an object, allow a magnet to still work. Circulate among the groups, asking questions and encouraging the children to try each thickness of paper and to stack the paper and then try with the increased thickness. Suggest that the children put a paper clip in the baby-food jar and see if they can move it with a magnet held on the outside of the glass. Suggest also, if they do not think of it, that they place a paper clip in the bottom of the jar filled with water and see if it is attracted to a magnet that is lowered toward it through the water. Discuss the activities with the children. They should see that magnets can work through many different materials.

Orientation: Grades 3–6.

Content Objective: The children will state that forces are added together when they pull in the same direction; that when the magnetic forces of iron atoms pull together, the iron becomes a magnet.

Skill Objective: The children are required to *observe* an analogy of magnetic forces interacting and to *infer* the relationship of the analogy and magnetic substances.

Materials: Five-foot length of clothesline.

Evaluation: Students' verbal interaction, student group problem-solving skills.

Procedure

Have one child hold the end of a five- or six-foot length of clothesline. Place three children at the opposite end of the clothesline and direct them to pull against one another. Ask the children: "How do all of these three forces affect the child on the opposite end of the clothesline?" (The child on the opposite end of the line is not greatly affected by the forces.) Now direct the three children to pull in the same direction against the single child on the opposite end of the clothesline.

Ask: "Now how do the forces exerted by the three children affect the single child?" (He is pulled along by the forces exerted by the three children.) "How is this like aligning the atoms in a magnetic substance in order to form a magnet?" (As long as the magnetic fields of the atoms are pulling against each other, no magnetic force is exerted by the substance; but when the magnetic fields of the atoms pull together in the same direction, the substance becomes a magnet.)

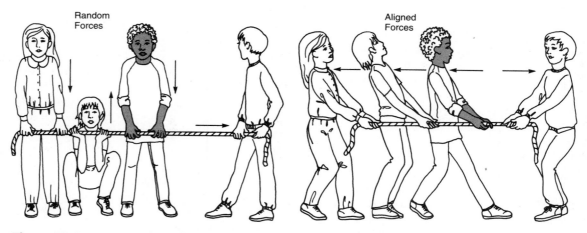

Figure 17–3 ▪ An Analogy of Aligning Magnetic Domains to Make a Magnet

Lesson Plan ▪ C

Orientation: Grades 4–6.

Content Objective: The children will state that stroking a needle with a magnet causes the needle to become magnetic; that the magnetic domains within the needle are aligned by the influence of the magnet.

Skill Objective: The children will *observe* the making of a magnet and *infer* the cause of their observation according to a preconceived model.

Materials: A large darning needle, a strong magnet, iron tacks or filings.

Evaluation: Students' verbal interaction.

Procedure

Show the children that a large darning needle will not attract iron tacks or iron filings. Stroke the needle with either end of a strong bar magnet. The strokes should be in one direction along the length of the needle. Now ask the children to observe as the needle is again brought close to the iron tacks or iron filings. Ask: "What is happening now?" (The tacks [filings] are attracted to the needle.) "We may say that the needle is acting as what?" (A magnet.) With more advanced children who will know of the domain theory of magnetism, ask: "How was stroking the needle with a magnet like the analogy of the children pulling the rope?" (The magnetic fields of the bar magnet caused some of the domains that make up the needle to align themselves so that their magnetic fields pulled together.)

You may continue with advanced students: "Let us see what happens when we heat the needle." After stroking the needle again several times with a bar magnet and demonstrating its magnetic properties to the class, heat the needle in the flame of a candle. After cooling the needle again, touch some iron tacks or filings. Ask: "What happened to the needle?" (It lost its magnetic properties.) "How does heating affect the alignment of the magnetic domains?" (The domains lose their alignment. Their arrangement becomes random again.)

Lesson Plan ▪ D

Orientation: Grades K–3.

Content Objective: The children will state that needles may be made into magnets and that heating magnets causes them to lose their magnetism.

Skill Objective: The children are required to *experiment* by following directions, to *communicate* by writing a report, and to make *inferences* from their observations.

Materials: Six strong bar or horseshoe magnets, six large darning needles, one large candle or alcohol burner, iron filings or carpet tacks, a clothespin.

Evaluation: Students' verbal interactions, student group problem-solving skills, written report.

continued on next page

Procedure

Divide the class into groups. Provide each group with a large darning needle, a bar or horseshoe magnet, and some carpet tacks. Give each group the following directions and have them work independently.

1. Touch the needle to the tacks. What happens?

2. Stroke the magnet along the length of the needle at least ten times.

3. Now touch the needle to the tacks. What happens? Why?

4. Stroke your needle again with the same pole of the magnet. Take the needle to me. I will hold it by a clothespin and heat it in a candle flame. Let it cool. Again touch the tacks. What happens? Explain.

5. Can you make the needle into a magnet again? Can you make it lose its magnetism without heating it?

6. Write or copy a report describing what your group did and the results.

Lesson Plan ■ E

Orientation:	Grades K–3.
Content Objective:	The children will describe or sketch the pattern of iron filings about several arrangements of permanent magnets.
Skill Objective:	The children are required to *experiment* by following directions and to *communicate* by sketching and *describing* the results of their activities.
Materials:	Twelve bar magnets, six horseshoe magnets (the number of magnets required may be reduced by sharing), cardboard, iron filings.
Evaluation:	Students' verbal interaction, student group problem-solving skills, seat work, and sketches.

Procedure

Have the children lay a sheet of heavy paper or cardboard on a single bar magnet and sprinkle iron filings liberally on the cardboard. They should tap the cardboard and observe the pattern that the iron filings form. (See Figure 17–4.) Direct the children to sketch the pattern of the iron filings.

Ask: "Where do most of the magnetic lines of force appear to be concentrated?" (At the poles [ends] of the magnet.) "Where is a magnet the strongest?" (At the poles.)

Now give the children another bar magnet and a horseshoe magnet and have them repeat the procedure. Ask: "What is the appearance of the magnetic lines of force in the region between two unlike poles?" (The lines of force appear to run from one pole to another.) "How do unlike poles affect each other?" (They attract.) "What is the appearance of the magnetic lines of force in the region between two like poles?" (The lines of force do not meet, but curve away from each other.) "How do like poles affect each other?" (They repel.) Have the children draw sketches of the lines of force that occur about a single bar magnet, two bar magnets with opposite poles adjacent to one another, and two bar magnets with like poles adjacent to one another.

continued on next page

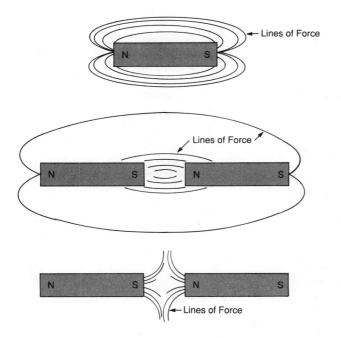

Figure 17–4 ▪ Magnetic Fields Around Permanent Magnets

Orientation:	Grades K–3.
Content Objective:	The child will orally describe the three-dimensional force fields observed and will make a sketch of them.
Skill Objective:	The children will *investigate* following directions and will *communicate* by describing or sketching their *observations.*
Materials:	A cooking oil–iron-filing magnetic force field detector.
Evaluation:	Students' group problem-solving skills, seat work, and sketches.

Procedure

Divide the children into groups. Provide each group with a cooking oil–iron-filing magnetic field detector (see Figure 17–5) and a variety of magnets, bar magnets, horseshoe magnets, ring magnets, or others. Direct the groups to experiment by holding the various magnets close to the magnetic field detector and moving them around in different positions. For instance, have the children hold the magnets on opposite sides of the detector and at right angles to one another. Each child should sketch the magnetic fields he observes in

continued on next page

the detector. Discuss the children's observations by asking questions such as: "Which part of the bar (horseshoe, ring) magnet produced the strongest field?" "How far from the detector could each magnet be held and still have an effect on the iron filings?" To use the oil–iron-filing magnetic field detector, students should invert it and shake it until the iron filings are suspended uniformly in the oil.

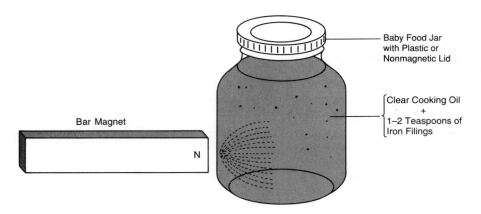

Bar Magnet

N

Baby Food Jar with Plastic or Nonmagnetic Lid

Clear Cooking Oil + 1–2 Teaspoons of Iron Filings

To Use: Turn the magnetic field detector upside down and shake vigorously. Bring any magnetized object close to the jar.

Note: A demonstration model of the magnetic force field detector may be made from a pint or quart plastic or glass jar, and increased amounts of cooking oil and iron filings.

Figure 17–5 ■ Magnetic Force Field Detector

Lesson Plan ■ G

Orientation:	Grades K–3.
Content Objective:	The children will name several materials that are magnetic and several that are not magnetic.
Skill Objective:	The children are required to *investigate* by manipulating materials and to *classify* materials by their magnetic properties.
Materials:	Six envelopes containing an assortment of objects such as: iron tack, copper tack, paper clip, rubber band, string, rubber eraser; six magnets; worksheet.
Evaluation:	Students' group problem-solving skills, laboratory worksheets, log, and reports.

continued on next page

Procedure

Give each child or group of children a magnet and an assortment of common objects such as an iron tack, a copper tack, a paper clip, a rubber band, a piece of string, a rubber eraser, and so on. Permit each child to test the materials with a magnet and record the results under the proper heading on a worksheet labeled Yes–No (Figure 17–6). Ask the children: "What sorts of objects are not attracted by magnets?" (Erasers, copper tacks, rubber bands, string, and so on.) "What sort of objects are attracted by magnets?" (Some paper clips, some tacks, some nails [some metals].) "Are all metals attracted by magnets?" (No.) Allow the children to test objects in the classroom for magnetic properties and add them to their checklists.

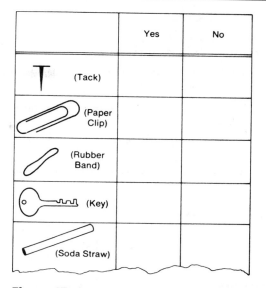

	Yes	No
(Tack)		
(Paper Clip)		
(Rubber Band)		
(Key)		
(Soda Straw)		

Figure 17–6 ■ A Checklist of Things Magnets Pick Up

Lesson Plan ■ H

Orientation:	Grades K–4.
Content Objective:	The children will state that magnets will work through some substances such as water, paper, and glass.
Skill Objective:	The children are required to *hypothesize* concerning the property of materials that permits a magnetic field to pass through them, to *experiment* by manipulating materials, to *communicate* by writing a report, and to *infer* a generalization from their data.
Materials:	Six bar or horseshoe magnets, cardboard, paper, tacks, iron filings, glass dish, and any other materials that individual groups require.
Evaluation:	Students' group problem-solving skills, laboratory worksheets, log, and reports.

Procedure

Ask the children: "Will magnets work through things that do not make magnets, such as glass, paper, or water?" (Children will offer some guesses.) "How can we find out?" Let the children suggest ways to test whether a magnet will attract through nonmagnetic substances. Some suggested procedures are:

continued on next page

1. See if tacks that are immersed in a glass or pan full of water can be moved by a magnet.

2. See if tacks can be moved through a piece of cardboard placed between the tacks and the magnet.

3. See if tacks can be moved through a glass plate placed between the tacks and the magnet.

Divide the class into groups and permit them to carry out the suggested activities.

For more advanced students, you may suggest that they test the number of thicknesses of paper through which a bar magnet will attract a paper clip. Students may also measure the distance at which a magnet and various objects interact. They may suggest other substances to test for the property of permitting a magnetic field to act through them. Permit the children to pursue individual or group plans for testing the properties of magnets. Ask each group to write a report describing their activities. The report should include: what we did; what we saw; what we think.

Subconcept 1–3

Unlike poles of magnets attract; like poles repel.

Discussion

Humans are not ordinarily sensitive to the presence of a magnetic field. That is, we have no sensory organs that permit us to detect magnetism as we have to detect heat and light energies. Magnetic fields are known to exist only by their effect upon other magnetic fields. Thus, a compass, which is a small magnet, may be used to determine the presence and orientation of the earth's or other magnetic fields. The nature of magnetism has been defined experimentally by the manner in which one magnetic field acts upon another. This involves a trial-and-error process of creating various conditions of magnetic interaction and observing the results.

The two ends of a magnet are called its *poles*. Either pole of one magnet will interact differently with each pole of a second magnet. It will attract one end of the second magnet, but it will repel the other end. Thus, the two poles of a magnet may be classified according to the way they interact with a *test pole*. Suppose that an experimenter marks the poles of two bar magnets according to whether they attract or repel a test pole. He then notes the interaction of the two bar magnets with each other. He observes that the poles of the two magnets that were attracted to the test pole repel each other. Also, the poles of the two magnets that were repelled by the test pole repel each other. However, the poles that were attracted to the test pole attract the poles that were repelled. The experimenter thus concludes that the two poles are different in nature. Like poles repel each other. Unlike poles attract each other.

Lesson Plan ■ I

Orientation:	Grades 3–6.
Content Objective:	The children will state that like poles of magnets repel each other, but unlike poles of magnets attract each other.
Skill Objective:	The children are required to *investigate* by manipulating materials and to *infer* relationships among their observations.

continued on next page

Materials: Eighteen bar magnets with the pole markings taped over, string, pencils or crayons.

Evaluation: Students' verbal interaction, students' group problem-solving skills, laboratory worksheets.

Procedure

This activity may be performed by individuals or small groups. Each group should be supplied with three unmarked bar magnets, or bar magnets with the markings taped over. Instruct the children that one end of one bar magnet will be used to test the properties of the other two bar magnets. Have the children mark either end of this bar magnet with the words *test pole*. Tell them to mark the ends of the other two bar magnets A for "attracted to the test pole" or R for "repelled by the test pole." (See Figure 17–7.) When they have marked the poles of the magnets, instruct the children to find out what they can about the magnets. Ideally, they will discover that the R poles repel each other, the A poles repel each other, and both pairs of R and A poles attract each other. Have the children describe what they observed. Ask: "If we consider the poles marked A as being like poles, and the poles marked R as being like poles, what can we say about the poles of a magnet?" (Like poles repel each other.) "If we say that A and R poles are unlike poles, what can we conclude?" (Unlike poles attract each other.) Provide the students with a worksheet showing pairs of magnets in various positions and have them mark each pair as *attracting* or *repelling*.

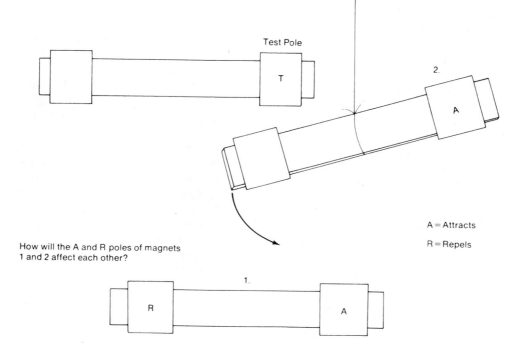

How will the A and R poles of magnets 1 and 2 affect each other?

A = Attracts

R = Repels

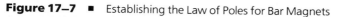

Figure 17–7 ■ Establishing the Law of Poles for Bar Magnets

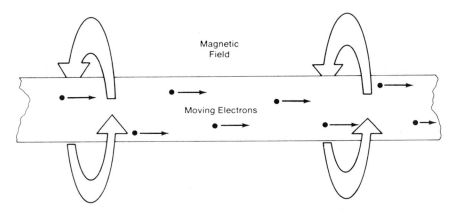

Figure 17–8 ▪ Moving Electrons Produce a Magnetic Field Around a Wire

Subconcept 1–4

Electric currents have magnetic fields.

Discussion

The concept upon which this entire chapter is based is that magnetism is a property of moving electrons. Since an electric current is comprised of many electrons moving through a conductor, it follows that an electric current should generate a magnetic field about the conducting wire. This is, in fact, the case, as Figure 17–8 illustrates. The region surrounding a straight current-bearing conductor does possess a magnetic field.

When the straight conductor is made into a coil, the magnetic effects in the center of the coil become stronger. The magnetic field is more concentrated in the center of the coil. A bar of soft iron placed in the center of a conducting coil will become magnetized. The magnetic field of the current-bearing wire forces some of the magnetic domains of the soft iron core into alignment, and the core becomes a magnet. The combined magnetic effect of the iron core and the current-bearing wire is strong. When the electric current is discontinued in the wire, the domains of the soft iron core again become randomly arranged, and the magnetic properties are lost. This situation is called *temporary magnetism* and the device is called an *electromagnet*.

Permanent magnets may be made by inserting bars of hard *iron alloys*, usually containing nickel, into the center of a current-bearing coil. The forces between the domains of the metal bars, and the magnetic field of the current-bearing conductor, must both be much stronger to produce permanent rather than temporary magnets. Once the domains of the nickel-iron alloy have been aligned, they tend to remain in alignment under normal conditions. Thus, the magnets produced in this manner are more or less permanent. The major enemies of permanent magnets in the classroom are heating and rough handling.

Lesson Plan ▪ J

Orientation: Grades 3–6.

Content Objective: The children will state that current flowing through a wire produces a magnetic field and that a wire shaped into a coil has a stronger magnetic field than a straight wire.

Skill Objective: The children are required to *investigate* by manipulating materials and to *infer* some conclusions from their observations.

Materials: Six flashlight cells or dry cells, six two-foot lengths of insulated bell wire, twelve compasses.

Evaluation: Students' group problem-solving skills, laboratory worksheets, log, and reports.

Procedure

Divide the class into small groups. Provide each group with a dry cell, a two-foot length of insulated bell wire, and several compasses. (See Figure 17–9.) Give the following directions orally or in writing: "Connect one bared end of the wire to one post of the dry cell. Place the compass close to the wire. Now *briefly* touch the other post with the other bared end of the wire. (*Hint:* Remind the children to connect the second end of the wire for only short periods so that the wire will not become hot and the batteries won't be drained.) What do you observe? Find out all you can about how a wire carrying an electric current affects a compass."

Things the Children May Discover:

1. When the second end of the wire is touched to the dry cell post, the compass needle jumps.

2. The compass needle always comes to rest so that it is at right angles to the wire.

3. The compass needle points in one direction when it is on top of the wire and in the opposite direction when it is beneath the wire.

4. A compass needle is deflected each time both bare ends of a wire coil are connected to a dry cell.

5. When the ends of the wires are switched on the dry cell posts, the compass needle points in the opposite direction.

   If no child makes a loop of the wire, show them how to wrap ten to fifteen turns about several fingers so that a two-inch coil is formed. Direct the groups to

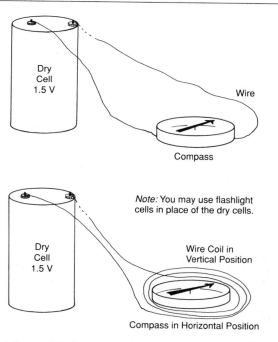

Figure 17–9 ▪ An Electric Current Affects a Compass

find out what they can about how the coil now affects the compass.

Conclude the lesson by having the groups report their observations. The following summarizing questions may be asked: "What did we find out?" (Children list observations.) "What happens when both

continued on next page

bared ends of the wire are touching the separate posts of the dry cell?" (A current flows through the wire. The compass needle moves.) "Do you think that there might be a relationship between an electric current and magnetism?" (Yes, a wire that is conducting an electric current has a magnetic field around it.)

Lesson Plan ■ K

Orientation: Grades 3–6.

Content Objective: The children will state that the factors affecting the strength of an electromagnet are: the number of turns of wire, the nature of the core, and the nature of the power supply (batteries).

Skill Objective: The children are required to *hypothesize* concerning the strength of electromagnets, to *control variables* as they *experiment*, and to *interpret* data as they accept or reject their hypotheses.

Materials: A dozen flashlight cells or dry cells, six two-foot lengths of insulated bell wire, six nails, tacks or paper clips.

Evaluation: Students' group problem-solving skills, laboratory worksheets, log, and reports.

Procedure

Show the children that a nail or some other soft iron object will not attract tacks. Connect a coil of fifteen to twenty turns of wire to a dry cell. Show that the magnetic field produced is not strong enough to attract tacks either. Now wrap fifteen to twenty turns of wire about the nail, as in Figure 17–10. Connect the ends of the wire to the terminals of the dry cell, and pick up as many tacks as possible with the apparatus. Ask: "Why, if the nail and coil alone did not attract the tacks, does the combination of the wire coil and the nail attract the tacks?" (The electricity makes a magnet out of the nail. The magnetic domains of the nail are aligned and thereby magnetized by the magnetic field of the current-bearing coil.)

To teach problem-solving techniques, you might continue this exercise by asking: "What are some things (variables) that would affect the strength of an electromagnet? How could we make it stronger or weaker?" The children should guess such factors as the number of turns of wire, the number of batteries (strength of the electric current), and the kinds of material used as the core of the electromagnet. Record all hypotheses in complete statements, such as: "The more turns of the coil, the more tacks the electromag-

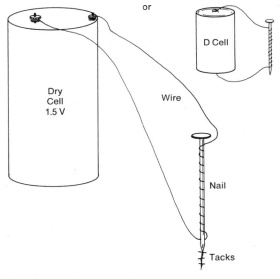

Figure 17–10 ■ An Electromagnet

net will pick up in a string. The number of tacks that may be picked up in a string is used to define the strength of the electromagnet." Have groups of children test each hypothesis, record their observations, and state any conclusions.

continued on next page

A word of explanation may be appropriate concerning the procedure for connecting dry cells. When cells are connected as in Figure 17–11, they are said to be in series. If all cells are strong, this method of joining will create an appreciably greater current in the electromagnet because the voltages of the separate 1.5 volt cells are added to create a 4.5 volt force on the electrons in the system. When the cells are connected as in Figure 17–12, they are said to be in parallel. This method will increase the current only slightly. Cells in parallel voltages are not added together, and the total voltage of the system remains 1.5 volts.

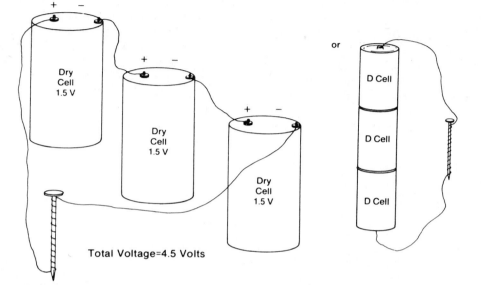

Figure 17–11 ■ An Electromagnet with Three Dry Cells in Series

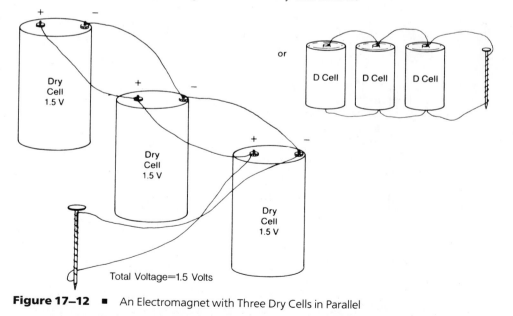

Figure 17–12 ■ An Electromagnet with Three Dry Cells in Parallel

Subconcept 1–5

The earth has a magnetic field.

Discussion

The earth is like a huge, but weak, bar magnet. Any magnets located close to the earth will tend to point in approximately the same direction—toward the north pole. This is the phenomenon behind the compass. A compass is a tiny magnet that is free to swing about on an axis. Due to the presence of the earth's magnetic field, the tiny compass magnet will always align itself in a north-south direction. The north-seeking pole of the compass will always point in the general direction of north.

The origin of the magnetic forces that permeate the earth and surrounding space is a matter of speculation. In keeping with the basic concept that magnetism is a property of a moving electric charge, the most accepted hypothesis rests upon the notion of a fluid earth core. This large, iron-nickel core is thought to be a very hot, dense fluid due to the pressure of the rock layers that lie on top of it and the force of gravity. Currents of fluid, metallic matter churning slowly in the earth's deep interior provide electric charges with motion. This results in the phenomenon of the magnetic field (Figure 17–13).

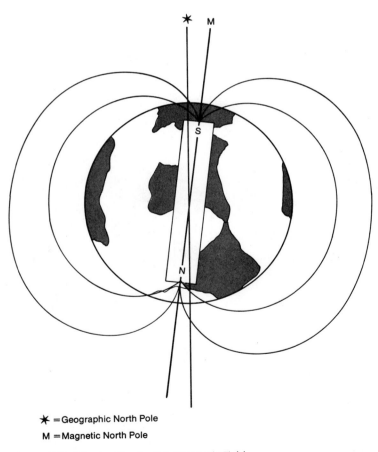

✴ = Geographic North Pole

M = Magnetic North Pole

Figure 17–13 ■ The Earth's Magnetic Field

Evidence gained from orbiting satellites has shown that the regular pattern of the earth's magnetic field is greatly distorted by the effects of the showers of electrical particles that emanate from the surface of the sun. These showers are sometimes termed solar winds. The solar winds do not appear to appreciably affect the magnetic field close to the earth's surface.

The Earth's Shifting Magnetic Field

Geologists have discovered an interesting thing by examining deposits in the natural magnet, lodestone, at different depths in the earth's crust. You remember that lodestone is formed when molten rock consisting partly of iron atoms is spewed forth from volcanoes. As the lava cools and solidifies, some of the iron atoms have their magnetic fields aligned by the weak magnetic field of the earth. In this way the lodestone becomes a magnet whose magnetic field is aligned with the earth's magnetic field. Scientists theorize that the currents occurring in the iron-nickel core change pathways as their magnetic fields affect one another. Over thousands of years, forces build up that cause a sudden "flipping" of the earth's field. The magnetic north pole of the earth has resided in several locations other than its current one, including one point in the middle of the Pacific Ocean. When geologists find magnetic rock layers that have their magnetic poles oriented toward the Pacific Ocean, they assume that the rocks were formed during the time period when the Pacific Ocean was the location of magnetic north. This permits them to determine the ages of the rocks and the fossils they contain.

Lesson Plan ▪ L

Orientation:	Grades 2–6.
Content Objective:	The children will state that magnetized needles placed in floating corks will all point in the same direction; that the earth has a magnetic field.
Skill Objective:	The children are required to *investigate* by manipulating materials and to *infer* a generalization from their observations.
Materials:	Twenty to thirty sewing needles, twenty to thirty corks, six shallow pans, water, detergent, six strong bar or horseshoe magnets.
Evaluation:	Students' group problem-solving skills, seat work, and sketches.

Procedure

Divide the class into groups of five or six. Instruct each group to pierce several small corks with one sewing needle each, as in Figure 17–14. Ask them to float the corks in a glass baking dish filled with water. (*Note:* Since iron vessels are magnetic, they should *not* be used for this exercise. Aluminum or paper pans are acceptable.) A few drops of detergent in each pan will reduce surface tension and allow the corks to rotate freely. After each group has had a chance to observe the results of their work, ask: "Do the needles appear to align themselves in any one particular direction?" (No, they seem to point randomly in all directions.) Instruct each group to remove the needles from the corks, stroke them vigorously eight or ten times with a bar magnet, and replace them in the corks. Ask the children: "Now do the needles appear to be pointing in the same general direction?" (Yes.) "If I told you that each needle was now a tiny magnet, what could we

continued on next page

conclude?" (The needles are being aligned by a magnetic field.) "If we make sure that there are no magnets around, and if I tell you the same thing would happen any place on earth, what could we conclude is the origin of the magnetic field?" (The earth is the origin of the magnetic field.) Have the children make a sketch showing the needle/cork system aligning itself in the water.

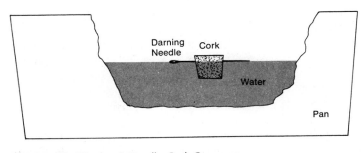

Figure 17–14 ■ A Needle-Cork Compass

Summary

Magnetism is a property of an electric charge in motion. Electrons moving within atoms impart magnetic properties to the whole atom. In the atoms of some elements, such as iron, nickel, and cobalt, the magnetic forces created by the moving electrons do not cancel each other out. Such substances have strong magnetic properties.

Permanent magnets are created when the magnetic fields of tiny domains of magnetic substances are aligned by an external magnetic field. The magnet is permanent if the bonding forces that hold the individual domains in place are strong enough to withstand the thermal agitation of the atoms. Temporary magnetism occurs when the domains of a soft iron bar are aligned by a magnetic field. Objects made of soft iron lose their magnetic properties rapidly due to the activity of individual atoms and the relatively weak forces that hold the magnetic domains together.

Electromagnets are temporary magnets composed of a current-bearing conductor wrapped around a soft iron bar. The domains of the soft iron bar are aligned by the magnetic field of the electric current.

The earth has a magnetic field. This is thought to be due to currents of iron and nickel in its central core.

Electricity

Look What's in This Chapter

In this chapter we'll discuss some important concepts and subconcepts related to the study of electricity, and we'll present lesson plans that are designed to teach these concepts and subconcepts to children.

Concept 1 Static electricity is an excess or lack of electrons.

>   Subconcept 1–1 Unlike electric charges attract and like charges repel.

Concept 2 Electric current is the movement of electrons through a conductor.

>   Subconcept 2–1 Chemicals may produce electricity.

>   Subconcept 2–2 Magnetism may produce electricity.

>   Subconcept 2–3 Heat and light may produce electricity.

Subconcept 2–4 The voltage, resistance, and current of an electric circuit are all interrelated.

Subconcept 2–5 Electricity may flow in series or parallel circuits.

Concept 3 Electricity produces heat, light, motion, and chemical activity.

The study of electricity is neglected in the elementary school. This situation is often due to lack of information, but it is sometimes the result of real fears on the teacher's part. As a teacher, you should be concerned for the safety of the children in your classroom. But your concern should be for real, not imaginary, dangers. *No lesson suggested in this chapter is dangerous to the teacher or the children.* You may teach these experiments confident that the safety factor has been considered. *Never permit your students to investigate electricity that comes from wall plugs. Use flashlight cells or dry cells as the source of current.*

Concept 1

Static electricity is an excess or lack of electrons.

Discussion

Normally, all atoms are electrically neutral. Each atom has the same number of negative electrons and positive protons. Protons reside in the nucleus of the atom and are rarely transported. Electrons are found whirling about the nucleus at high speed. They may be removed from the atom by friction (Figure 18–1).

The presence of excess electrons on the surface of a substance produces a negative charge. The lack of electrons results in a positive charge. This is because there is an excess of protons in atoms that have lost electrons.

Note: Lesson Plan B of Chapter 26 describes a discovery lesson that deals with the nature of static electricity.

Subconcept 1–1

Unlike electric charges attract and like charges repel.

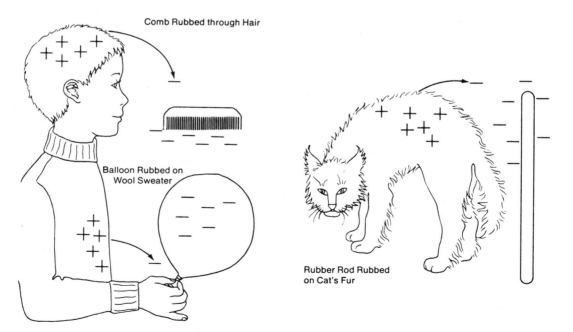

Figure 18–1 ■ Electrons Are Removed by Friction

Discussion

Two bodies each possessing excess electrons (negative charge) will repel each other. So will two bodies each lacking electrons (positive charge). It is the nature of electric force fields that similar force fields will tend to move away from each other. Thus, static charges will be found distributed evenly over the surface of a spherical object as the electrons arrange themselves as far apart as possible.

Lesson Plan ▪ A

Orientation:	Grades K–6.
Content Objective:	The children will state that static electricity is caused by friction when electrons are removed by rubbing; that like charges repel, unlike charges attract.
Skill Objective:	The children will *investigate* by manipulating a homemade electroscope and make *inferences* from their *observations*.
Materials:	Thirty pith balls or puffed wheat kernels, silk thread, tape, eight combs.
Evaluation:	Students' verbal interaction, laboratory worksheets, log, and reports.

Procedure

Simple electroscopes may be made by inserting a thread through a pith ball or even a kernel of puffed wheat, as in Figure 18–2. The string may be taped to the edge of a table or desk as in the figure. Static charges may be applied to the electroscope from a hard rubber rod or a comb that has been rubbed with a wool cloth. Two pith balls suspended side by side from strings will provide the children with the opportunity to make many interesting observations. Some sample observations might be:

1. An uncharged pith ball is attracted to the charged comb.
2. After touching the comb, the pith ball is repelled.
3. Two charged pith balls repel each other.

   With an electroscope (either single or double) for each group of children, permit the groups to experiment and discover. For each activity they perform, ask each group to record:

1. What we did.
2. What we observed.
3. What we think.

Discuss the results after the children have had ample time to experiment.

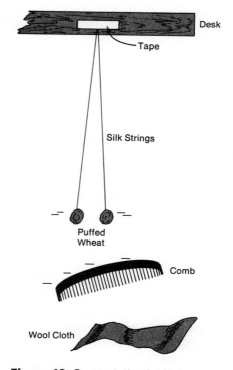

Figure 18–2 ▪ A Simple Electroscope

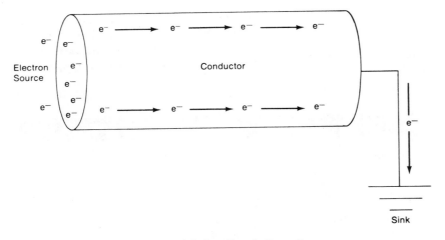

Figure 18–3 ▪ A Simple Model of an Electric Current

Concept 2

Electric current is the movement of electrons through a conductor.

Discussion

In Chapters 14 and 16 we saw that metals are composed of atoms about which electrons migrate fairly freely. Normally, the electrons move about the atoms at random. However, under certain conditions, some of the free electrons may be made to migrate in the same general direction. When this happens—when electrons within a conductor are migrating in the same direction—an electric current is said to be flowing in the conductor.

In a copper wire, some electrons will move freely and randomly among the copper atoms making up the wire. But suppose, as in Figure 18–3, that in some way many electrons are brought close to one end of the wire. Repulsive forces will be exerted upon the electrons in the wire. The electrons in the wire will tend to migrate away from the area of electron concentration. If a path is provided on the other end of the copper wire, permitting the electrons to move to an area that absorbs them (the earth is such a sink for electrons), electrons will continue to migrate along the wire. The movement is away from the source of electrons. The movement of electrons through the wire constitutes an electric current.

Chart 18–1 ▪ Electromotive Series

Element	Voltage
Lithium	−2.96
Potassium	2.92
Calcium	2.76
Sodium	2.71
Magnesium	2.40
Aluminum	1.70
Zinc	0.76
Iron	0.44
Cadmium	0.40
Nickel	0.23
Tin	0.14
Lead	0.13
Hydrogen	0.00
Copper	+0.35
Mercury	0.80
Silver	0.80
Gold	1.36

To produce an electric current requires a source of electrons, a conducting path, and a place for the electrons to go—a ground or sink. We will examine several conditions where enough electrons are made available to produce a useful current. These methods utilize chemical, magnetic, heat, and light energies.

Subconcept 2–1

Chemicals may produce electricity.

Discussion

The tendency to yield electrons varies from one metal to another. The electromotive series (see Chart 18–1) lists the metals in descending order, according to this tendency. Lithium, at the top of the series, releases its single outer level electron most readily. Zinc releases its two electrons somewhat less readily, and silver its two electrons even less readily than zinc. When any two metals are connected by a wire and immersed in an electrolyte (a conducting liquid), electrons will flow through the wire *from* the metal that is higher in the electromotive series *to* the metal that is lower. This principle is the basis for the construction of dry cells, voltaic cells, lead storage cells, flashlight cells, and other common portable methods of producing electric current. The electrolytes used in storage batteries are commonly acids such as sulfuric acid. However, common salts such as table salt or ammonium chloride will also work in an electric cell.

Lesson Plan ■ B

Orientation:	Grades 4–6.
Content Objective:	The children will describe orally and/or sketch a cell that will produce electricity.
Skill Objective:	The children are required to *investigate* by making an electric cell, to *observe* the effects of the cell, and to *infer* a generalization from their data.
Materials:	Six copper plates or six zinc plates with a minimum surface area of eight to ten square inches; six wide-mouthed jars; dilute hydrochloric acid or saturated solutions of table salt or ammonium chloride; six two-foot lengths of bell wire; six small compasses; plates of lead, aluminum, or other metals; steel wool or sandpaper.
Evaluation:	Students' group problem-solving skills, laboratory worksheets, log, and reports.

Procedure

Divide the class into groups. Provide each group with the following instructions: Polish a copper plate and a zinc plate with sandpaper or steel wool. Make a one-inch loop of ten to fifteen turns of the bell wire. Connect the ends of the wire to the two metal plates. Immerse the metal plates in a bath of dilute hydrochloric acid or a saturated table salt or ammonium chloride solution as in the diagram. (You may copy Figure 18–4 on the chalkboard.)

As the class is working, ask: "What evidence do we see that something is happening in the jar?" (Bubbles are forming on the copper plate.) "If I tell

continued on next page

you that an electric current produces a magnetic field around the conducting wire, what could we use to detect a magnetic field around the conducting wire?" (A compass.) Have them place a small compass in the wire loops and see if the needle is deflected. Ask: "Was the compass needle affected?" You may direct the groups to raise and lower one of the metal plates in the electrolyte as you question them. (Yes, the compass needle is affected.) "What does this indicate about electrons in the wire?" (The electrons are flowing through the wire.) "Would other metals produce an electric current under the same conditions? Try it and find out." Each group may experiment with plates of aluminum, lead, and other available metals. They may also test a number of available salts and acids to determine their ability to conduct electric currents. (*Note:* Maximum deflection of the compass needle will occur when the wire loops are above and below the compass, not when the loops are around the sides of the compass.) Direct each group to write a brief report of what they did, what they observed, and what they think they have learned.

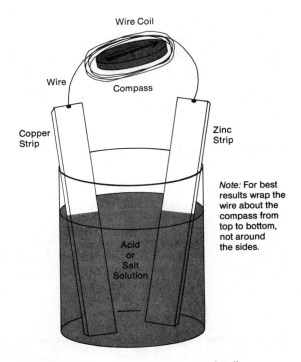

Figure 18—4 ■ An Electrochemical Cell

Lesson Plan ■ C

Orientation:	Grades 3–6.
Content Objective:	The children will accurately describe the construction of a dry cell.
Skill Objective:	The children are required to carefully *observe* the construction of a dry cell and *infer* the functions of its parts.
Materials:	Several flashlight cells or dry cells cut in half longitudinally.
Evaluation:	Students' verbal interaction, seat work, and sketches.

Procedure

Saw several nonalkaline dry cells and/or flashlight cells in halves lengthwise. Permit the children to examine the longitudinal cross sections and state which portion of the cell supplies the electrons and which portion accepts the electrons (Figure 18–5). (The zinc case supplies electrons and the center carbon rod accepts the electrons.) Have the children sketch and label their cells.

continued on next page

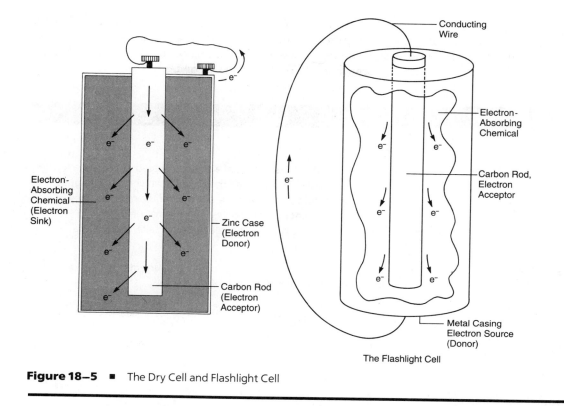

Figure 18–5 ■ The Dry Cell and Flashlight Cell

Conducting Wire

Electron-Absorbing Chemical (Electron Sink)

Zinc Case (Electron Donor)

Carbon Rod (Electron Acceptor)

Electron-Absorbing Chemical

Carbon Rod, Electron Acceptor

Metal Casing Electron Source (Donor)

The Flashlight Cell

Subconcept 2–2

Magnetism may produce electricity.

Discussion

Each electron in an atom is a tiny magnet and will tend to align itself with an external magnetic field. When the external magnetic field changes in direction or magnitude, force is exerted upon the electrons. In metals that are subjected to a changing magnetic field, the electrons that are only loosely held by atoms will tend to migrate in the direction that reduces the stress placed upon them. Since metals tend to have an abundance of loosely held electrons moving about among their atoms, a changing magnetic field will result in a flow of electrons within the metal. When a current is caused to flow in a conductor by means of a fluctuating magnetic field, the process is called *electromagnetic induction*. Commonly coils of copper wire are rotated within a magnetic field to produce an electric current.

Commercial Generators

The commercial electricity used in homes, businesses, and industries is produced by generators. A generator is any device that permits a magnet to be rotated rapidly inside a coil of copper wire and so produce an electric current. The motion of the generators is produced by a variety of means—water power; steam engines that burn oil, gas, or coal; nuclear power, wind power, and so on. In most commercial generators the electrons flow in one direction through the copper wires during one-half of a rotation and in the opposite direction during the other half of the rotation. This produces *alternating current* (AC) as opposed to current that flows always in the same direction, called *direct current* (DC). In most commercial distribution systems, the direction of the current changes sixty times per second.

Lesson Plan ■ D

Orientation:	Grades 5–6.
Content Objective:	The children will state that the strength of a current created by passing a magnet through a coil of wire is affected by the speed at which the magnet moves, the number of coils of wire, and the strength of the magnet. They may also note that a current is created only when the magnet is moving and that the direction of the compass needle deflection alternates as the magnet is inserted and removed.
Skill Objective:	The children are required to *investigate* by inducing a current in a wire coil and to *infer* some relationships from their *observations*.
Materials:	Twelve two-foot lengths of bell wire, twelve tissue tubes, six strong horseshoe magnets, six small compasses.
Evaluation:	Students' group problem-solving skills, laboratory worksheets, log, and reports.

Procedure

Divide the class into small groups. Provide each group with two two-foot lengths of insulated bell wire, a 5 cm long section of tissue tube, a strong magnet, and a compass. Direct each group to wrap twenty-five to thirty turns of wire about a tissue tube. Secure the wire to the tube with tape. Have them connect this coil to a second coil of the same size and place a small compass in the center of the second coil as in Figure 18–6. After all groups have assembled the apparatus, say: "Rapidly insert the magnet into the coil that has no compass and observe the effect upon the compass in the second coil." Then say, "*Rapidly* remove the magnet from the coil." Record all of your observations. *For best results, jerk the magnet abruptly in and out of the wire coil.*

The children may list such observations as:

1. When the magnet is rapidly inserted into the coil, the compass needle moves in a given direction.

2. The faster the magnet is moved, the more it affects the compass needle.

continued on next page

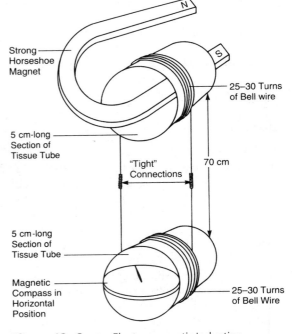

Strong Horseshoe Magnet

25–30 Turns of Bell wire

5 cm-long Section of Tissue Tube

"Tight" Connections

70 cm

5 cm-long Section of Tissue Tube

Magnetic Compass in Horizontal Position

25–30 Turns of Bell Wire

Figure 18–6 ■ Electromagnetic Induction

3. The compass needle moves in one direction when the magnet is quickly removed from the coil and in the opposite direction when the magnet is put into the coil.

4. The needle is deflected only when the magnet is moving, not when it is at rest.

The children may infer:

1. A magnet moving through a wire coil causes a current to flow in the coil.

2. The strength of the current is related to the speed at which the magnet moves.

3. The direction of the current changes with the direction in which the magnet moves.

Subconcept 2–3

Heat and light may produce electricity.

Discussion

The atoms of the metal oxides of potassium and cesium contain electrons that, when struck by

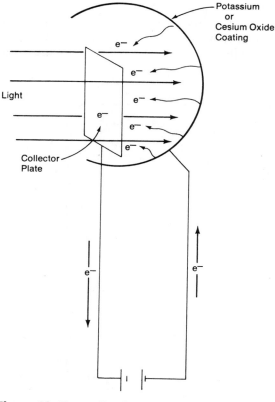

Figure 18–7 ■ The Photocell

light energy, become excited and jump from the surface of the materials. A *photoelectric cell* may be constructed by placing the electron-yielding substance in a vacuum and providing a place for the excited electrons to go, as in Figure 18–7. The stronger the light source, the more electrons will be given off by the photosensitive coating of the cell. Much of this same process takes place in the electronic tubes of radio and television sets. In these applications, the electron-yielding materials are heated. The energy so provided causes electrons to be emitted from the surface of the material, as in Figure 18–8. This process is known as *thermionic emission*.

A *thermocouple* is a device in which two wires of unlike metals are joined and heat is applied to the junction. Electrons will migrate from one metal to the other to produce a small current.

Subconcept 2–4

The voltage, resistance, and current of an electric circuit are all interrelated.

Discussion

We may think of an electric circuit as a path provided by a conductor that enables electrons to leave a source of energy (generator, battery, and so on) and travel through the conductor to an electron sink or an acceptor of electrons. (See Concept 2, this chapter, and Figure 18–3.) Any time a region with excess electrons is joined by a conductor to a region with fewer electrons, the electrons will flow from the region of higher

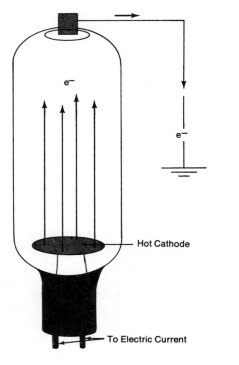

Figure 18–8 ■ A Simple Radio Tube

concentration to the region of lower concentration. The magnitude of the current in a circuit is defined by the number of electrons that flow through the circuit in a given period of time. The unit used to express the number of electrons passing by a given point in a conductor is the *ampere*. One ampere of current represents a tremendously large number of electrons per second, on the order of six followed by eighteen zeros.

Voltage is the force or pressure exerted upon the electrons in the conductor, as illustrated in Figure 18–9. The magnitude of the voltage depends on the difference in the concentration of electrons at opposite ends of the conductor. This difference in concentration affects the number of electrons that move and the energy that they expend as they pass through the circuit. The unit used to express the pressure on the electrons in a conductor, or the energy that they expend in the circuit, is the *volt*.

The *resistance* of a circuit is the opposition to the flow of current in the circuit. The atoms of different materials vary in the ease with

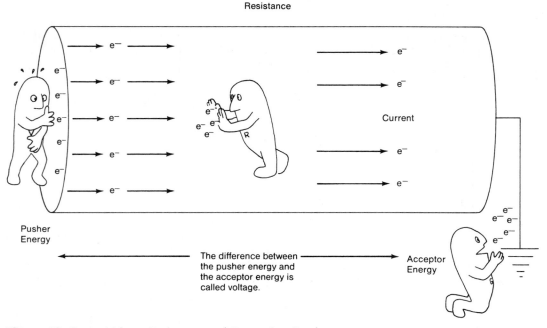

Figure 18–9 ■ Voltage, Resistance, and Current in a Conductor

which they permit their electrons to migrate. Atoms of high-resistance materials hold on to their outer electrons more strongly than do atoms of low-resistance materials. Thus, even with identical voltages, materials vary in the number of electrons they will pass among their atoms. The unit that defines the opposition to the flow of current in a circuit is the *ohm*.

To summarize the relationships that exist among voltage, resistance, and current: the magnitude of the current in a conductor is directly related to the voltage (current will increase when voltage increases); current is inversely related to the resistance (current will decrease when resistance increases). These factors are summarized in the formula $I = \dfrac{V}{R}$ where V equals voltage, I equals current, and R equals resistance. This is known as *Ohm's law*.

The Water System Analogy of the Electric Circuit

Often, for simplicity's sake, electric circuits are compared to a water system. A *water pump* is analogous to the *generator* in that the former produces water pressure and the latter electrical pressure. The pipes of the water system represent *conducting wires* in our electric circuit. Just as the size of the water pipes affects the amount of water that flows through a system, so the size of conducting wires affects the number of electrons that flow through the electric circuit. The constricting effect of the pipes or wires that oppose the flow of water or electricity is termed *resistance*. The amount of water that flows through the water system depends on the pressure exerted by the pump and the resistance offered by the pipes. Likewise, in the electric circuit the number of electrons (current) that flow through an electric circuit depends on the pressure (volts) exerted by the generator and the resistance (ohms) offered by the wires.

How does the flow of water in a water system react to a change in pressure? A change in the size of the pipe? Try Ohm's law on the water system. It should work. The analogy of the water system is useful for understanding the often mystifying effects of current electricity.

Lesson Plan ▪ E

Orientation: Grades 4–6.

Content Objective: The children will correctly match parts and terms of a water system with the analogous parts and terms of an electric circuit and will correctly answer questions concerned with the relationships of current, voltage, and resistance.

Skill Objective: From a water model the children are required to *infer* relationships that exist within an electric circuit.

Materials: Copies of Chart 18–2.

Evaluation: Students' verbal interaction, seat work, and sketches.

Procedure

Provide the children with copies of Chart 18–2 with the answers blanked out.

continued on next page

Chart 18–2 ▪ Electricity Worksheet

A water system is often used as an analogy for an electric circuit. Can you match the parts and terms of the water system to the corresponding parts and terms of the electric circuit by drawing a line between them?

Water System	*Electric Circuit*
pressure pump	resistance
pipe	amperes
water	volts
pressure	generator
gallons/minute	voltage
size of pipe	wire
pounds of pressure	electricity

Fill in the following blanks with electrical terms:

1. When the water pressure increases, the flow of water increases, and when the (voltage) increases, the (current) increases.

2. Small water pipes and clogged water pipes oppose the flow of water just as small (wires) oppose the flow of (electricity). The opposition to the flow of current is measured in (ohms).

3. The rate of flow of water is measured in gallons per minute, and the rate of flow of electricity, called (current), is measured in (amperes).

4. The pressure of water is measured in pounds per square inch, and the pressure of electricity, called (voltage), is measured in (volts).

Fill in the following blanks with the words *increase* or *decrease*.

1. An increase in voltage causes a(n) (increase) in current with no change in resistance.

2. An increase in resistance causes a(n) (decrease) in current with no change in voltage.

Subconcept 2–5

Electricity may flow in series or parallel circuits.

Discussion

When electrons follow a single path from their source to their destination, it is called a *series circuit*. When more than one path is provided for the passage of electrons, the electrons divide themselves among the separate conductors, and current flows in each of the paths. This is called a *parallel circuit*.

Some characteristics of series and parallel circuits are summarized in Chart 18–3.

Let us use Figures 18–10 and 18–11 to examine the variables summarized above.

Continuity of the Circuit

An electric lamp (light bulb) is simply a wire called a filament encased in a glass envelope containing very little oxygen. For a light bulb to burn, a current must pass through its filament. As the electrons pass through the filament of the bulb, this special wire (usually made of tungsten metal) will heat up and give off heat and light energy. If the filament is broken, or if for any other reason the current cannot pass through, the bulb will not light.

Look at Figure 18–10. This circuit provides only one path for current to flow through. The electron must pass through *every bulb*. A break in any one bulb shuts off the current for all other bulbs. Now trace the diagram of the parallel circuit, Figure 18–11. Do you see that a break in

Chart 18–3 ■ Characteristics of Series and Parallel Circuits

Variable	Series Circuit	Parallel Circuit
1. Continuity of the circuit	One light goes out, all go out.	One light goes out, the rest remain lighted.
2. Brightness of lights	Bulbs become dimmer as lights are added.	Bulbs remain the same brightness as more are added (with adequate source of power).
3. Current	Current is reduced with the addition of bulbs.	Current is increased with the addition of bulbs.
4. Resistance	Total resistance is increased with addition of bulbs.	Total resistance is decreased with the addition of bulbs.
5. Path of current	All current follows the same path.	The total current is divided among several paths.
6. Voltage	The voltage of the power source is divided among all bulbs.	All bulbs have the same voltage, which is equal to the voltage of the power source.

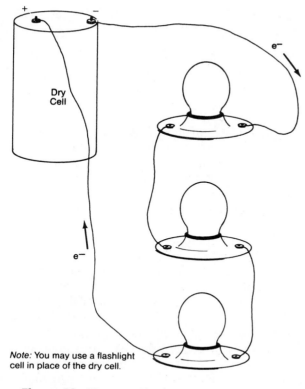

Note: You may use a flashlight cell in place of the dry cell.

Figure 18–10 ■ A Simple Series Circuit

the filament of one bulb will shut off that bulb *only*? All other bulbs will still receive electrons and pass them through. These bulbs will remain in operation.

Amount of Resistance

Where an electric current must pass through a high-resistance material, such as the filament of a light bulb, the number of electrons that pass through is reduced. In a series circuit the current must pass through all resistors. Therefore, adding a resistor, such as an additional light bulb, increases the total resistance of the circuit.

In the parallel circuit just the reverse is true. When an additional resistor is added, this provides a new path for electrons. The number of electrons that flow through the new resistor *adds* to the number already passing through the established resistors. The total current in the circuit is thereby increased even though the current through each of the established resistors remains the same. Since the current was increased, according to Ohm's law the resistance must have been reduced. Adding resistors in parallel *decreases* the total resistance to the flow of electricity.

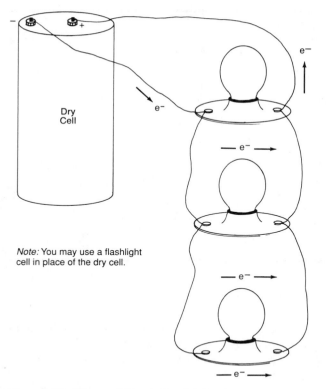

Dry
Cell

Note: You may use a flashlight
cell in place of the dry cell.

Figure 18–11 ■ A Simple Parallel Circuit

Brightness of Bulbs

In a circuit the brightness of the bulbs depends on the amount of current flowing through them. We have just seen how the total resistance of a series circuit increases with the addition of resistors. A greater resistance means a reduced current flow and dimmer light bulbs.

In parallel circuits the addition of a resistor should not affect the brightness of the bulbs. An exception occurs when a parallel circuit is powered by a limited source of power, such as a weak dry cell. The available electrons flowing out of the cell will be divided among all the bulbs and the bulbs may grow dimmer.

Magnitude of Current

The current in a series circuit is the same at any point in the circuit. The addition of a resis-

tor any place in the circuit adds to the total resistance of the circuit and reduces the current that flows through it.

In parallel circuits the addition of a bulb provides a new path for the flow of electricity and adds to the total current of the circuit.

Voltage

The total voltage available to a circuit is determined by the source of power—a generator, a battery, and so on. The voltage is an expression of the energy that is available from the source. In a series circuit, the voltage of the power source is divided among the resistors. In a sample series circuit that has three bulbs of equal wattage and a six-volt battery as a power source, each bulb would account for two volts of power or energy. If a fourth bulb is added to the series circuit, each bulb in the circuit will then receive one-fourth of the available voltage, or 1.5 volts.

In parallel circuits, each of the bulbs has available the full voltage of the power source.

Three bulbs in a parallel circuit with a six-volt power source each have the full six volts of power. If a fourth bulb were added in parallel, each bulb would still have six volts of available power.

Lesson Plan ▪ F

Orientation:	Part A, Grades 1–3; Parts A and B, Grades 1–6.
Content Objective:	The children will draw a sketch of the circuitry—both in series and parallel—that will cause one lamp to glow; two lamps to glow; three lamps to glow.
Skill Objective:	The children are required to *investigate* by manipulating batteries and bulbs and to *communicate* by sketching the circuits that they discover.
Materials:	Twelve flashlight cells, eighteen 1.5-volt lamps, forty to fifty short pieces of bell wire.
Evaluation:	Students' group problem-solving skills, seat work, and sketches, laboratory worksheets, log, and reports.

Procedure[1]

Part A—Divide the class into groups. Give each group a dry cell, a miniature 1.5-volt lamp (bulb), and several pieces of insulated bell wire. Direct them to try to make the lamp light up. As each group succeeds, give them an additional lamp. Direct them to make both lamps light up at once. If any groups succeed in lighting two lamps, give them a third lamp. Nearly all the children who succeed in making three lamps light up at once will do so by constructing a simple series circuit as shown in Figure 18–10. Provide a sketch of a flashlight cell, and ask the children to draw a bulb and wire so the bulb will light.

Part B—As you move among the groups of children, ask those groups who have succeeded in constructing a series circuit: "When one bulb is unscrewed or disconnected, what happens to the other two bulbs?" (They go out.) "Can you find a way

to join the three bulbs together so that when one bulb is unscrewed, the other two remain lighted?" When the children succeed in solving this task, they will have constructed a simple parallel circuit as shown in Figure 18–11.

More advanced children may be asked to solve the additional problems posed by the following questions: "How does the addition of more bulbs affect the brightness of the lighted bulbs in a series circuit? Why?" (The lighted bulbs become dimmer with the addition of more bulbs. In a series circuit all the current must pass through each bulb, thereby increasing the resistance of the circuit to the flow of electrons.) "How does the addition of more bulbs affect the brightness of the lighted bulbs in a parallel circuit? Why?" (The brightness of the lighted bulbs is not affected by the addition of more bulbs in parallel. Each identical bulb in parallel carries the same amount of current regardless of the number of bulbs that are added.)

Ask the children to draw sketches of their circuits. Ask some children to sketch their circuits on the chalkboard to conclude the activity.

---

[1]The activities described in this plan are time-consuming and may take several days to complete on a discovery basis.

Concept 3

Electricity produces heat, light, motion, and chemical activity.

Discussion

Electrons in electrical conductors sometimes yield energy in the forms of heat and light. Thus, two very practical applications of electrical energy are the production of these two forms.

Heat energy and light energy are given off from a conducting wire when the motion of the electrons that are being forced through the wire is opposed by the wire's natural resistance. The opposition causes the electrons to give up energy to their surroundings. When the production of heat or light is desired, as in heating elements, stoves, and incandescent bulbs, high-resistance iron, tungsten, or nichrome wires are used in the circuit.

Motion

Each moving electron produces a magnetic field about itself. Many electrons moving through a conductor will produce a strong magnetic field about the conductor. (See Chapter 17.) The magnetic field about a conductor may repel and/or attract other magnetic substances, thereby causing them to move. This is the basis for the construction of electric motors.

Chemical Activity

Metal atoms often lose one or two electrons to nonmetallic atoms in the formation of salts. Metal atoms are then said to be metal ions. Metal ions may again become atoms with the replacement of the lost electrons. Metal atoms may be deposited from a salt solution upon the surface of a substance that provides the needed electrons. This is the basis for the electrolytic or electroplating cell.

Lesson Plan ■ G

Orientation:	Grades K–6.
Content Objective:	The children will state that electricity produces heat and light.
Skill Objective:	The children are required to *observe* the changes in a conductor as electricity begins to flow through it and to *infer* a conclusion from their observation.
Materials:	A hot plate, electric lamp, electric heater, other electrical appliances that yield heat and light.
Evaluation:	Students' verbal interaction.

Procedure

Before plugging in a hot plate, ask the children: "What is coming out of the wall plug?" (Electricity.) "What is electricity?" (The movement of electrons.) Now permit one child to place his hand close to the hot plate as it is plugged in. Ask: "What kind of energy comes first from the electric current?" (Heat energy.) "Now do we see any change in the wires of the hot plate?" (They are becoming red.) "What kind of energy is this?" (Light energy.) "What can we say about the kinds of energy given off by electricity?" (Electricity produces both heat and light energy.)

You may demonstrate other appliances that use electricity to produce heat and light energy. Allow the children to examine the exposed elements to see how they are different from copper wires.

Lesson Plan ▪ H

Orientation:	Grades K–6.
Content Objective:	The children will state that electricity produces magnetic effects that may be used to produce motion, as in electric motors.
Skill Objective:	The children will *observe* the motion produced by an electromagnet and *infer* a generalization from their observations.
Materials:	A bar magnet, nail, two-foot length of bell wire, dry cell, St. Louis motor if available.
Evaluation:	Students' verbal interaction.

Procedure

Suspend a bar magnet by its center from a string. Construct an electromagnet by wrapping ten to fifteen turns of insulated wire about a nail and attaching the ends of the wire to a dry cell, as in Figure 18–12. Ask the children: "What will happen when we bring the nail close to the bar magnet?" (The bar magnet will be attracted or repelled.) Show the children how the bar magnet may be made to rotate by directing its motion with the electromagnet. Then permit several children to experiment with the apparatus. Ask the children: "What may we say is happening here?" (The electromagnet is attracting and/or repelling the bar magnet, causing it to move.) "What common device uses electric energy to create movement?" (The electric motor.)

Some of the children may wish to construct their own simple electric motors. Instructions for making such projects are provided in many elementary science source books.

continued on next page

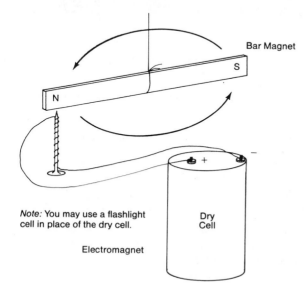

Note: You may use a flashlight cell in place of the dry cell.

Bar Magnet

S

N

Electromagnet

Dry Cell

Figure 18–12 ▪ Electric Current Produces Motion

The children may also be permitted to examine a St. Louis motor (Figure 18–13), if one is available, and trace the flow of current through the armature. Direct their attention to the split-ring (or D-ring) commutator that is located above the armature on the same axle. The commutator serves to change the direction in which the current flows through the armature. This change of direction shifts the magnetic polarity of the armature. This permits the armature to continue to rotate and not come to rest in the magnetic field of the bar magnet.

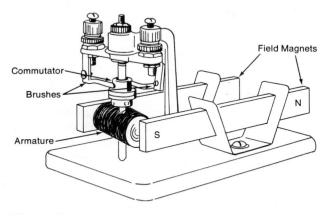

Figure 18–13 ■ The St. Louis Motor

Lesson Plan ■ I

Orientation:	Grades 4–6.
Content Objective:	The children will state that copper may be plated upon a carbon rod by an electric current.
Skill Objective:	The children are required to *observe* an electrolytic cell and to *infer* from their observations.
Materials:	One wide-mouthed jar, one carbon rod, one copper rod, copper sulfate, one large dry cell.
Evaluation:	Students' verbal interaction, students' group problem-solving skills, laboratory worksheets, log, and reports.

Procedure

Assemble an electrolytic cell as in Figure 18–14 by placing a carbon rod and a copper rod in a copper sulfate solution. Connect the outside (negative) terminal of the dry cell to the carbon rod, and the center (positive) terminal of the dry cell to the copper rod. Tell the children what you are doing and what the different materials are. After about two minutes, ask the children: "What do we see on the carbon rod?"

continued on next page

(Some copper is showing on the carbon rod.) "Where did the copper atoms on the carbon rod come from?" (The copper atoms must have come from the copper sulfate solution as electrons were supplied to the copper ions in the solution.) "Will we run out of copper ions if we permit the cell to continue to operate?" (No. Copper ions are probably going into the solution from the copper rod at the same rate as they are being plated on the carbon rod.) "If we reverse the wires so that electrons are supplied to the copper rod, what will happen?" (The copper will be removed from the carbon rod and be plated on the copper rod.) Reverse the wires on the two rods, wait for about two minutes. The copper will disappear from the carbon rod, and a "mush" of copper will be plated on the copper rod. Ask the students to write a report that states what they observed and what they learned or think.

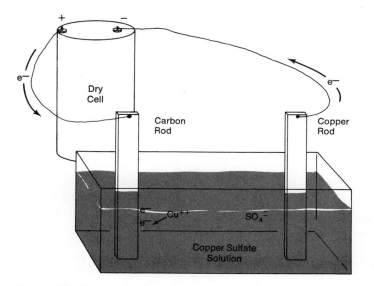

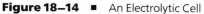

Figure 18–14 ■ An Electrolytic Cell

Lesson Plan ■ J

Orientation: Grades 5–6.

Content Objective: The children will state that copper is plated upon a carbon rod by an electric current.

Skill Objective: The children are required to *investigate* by following directions, to *observe* carefully, to *infer* conclusions, and to *communicate* their observations.

Materials: Six carbon rods, six copper rods, six wide-mouthed jars, copper sulfate, six dry cells, twelve pieces of bell wire.

Evaluation: Students' verbal interaction, students' group problem-solving skills, student model.

continued on next page

Procedure

Divide the class into groups. Provide each group with a carbon rod (the center rods of old dry cells will do), a plate of copper, a jar or beaker two-thirds full of copper sulfate, a dry cell, and two pieces of insulated bell wire. Instruct each group to construct an electrolytic cell as in Figure 18–14. Permit the groups to proceed with the following directions:

1. Examine the carbon rod each minute for five minutes. Describe what you see. Examine the copper plate. Describe its appearance.

2. After five minutes, reverse the wires on the posts of the cell. Examine the carbon rod and the copper plate each minute for five minutes. Describe what you see.

3. If you continued to put copper on the carbon rod, would you eventually run out of copper atoms? Explain.

Conclude the exercise with a discussion of the activities.

Summary

Static electricity is normally caused by excess electrons residing on the surface of some object. Current electricity is the movement of electrons through a conducting medium. Sources of electrons that may be used to produce a current are chemical action, electromagnetic induction, photoelectric effects, thermionic emission, and the thermocouple.

The relationship of voltage, resistance, and current in an electric circuit is expressed in the formula $I = \dfrac{V}{R}$. Current equals the voltage divided by resistance. Electrons in a circuit may follow a single path in a series circuit or multiple paths in a parallel circuit.

Electrical energy is rendered useful to us when it is converted to heat energy, light energy, kinetic energy (with magnetic forces), and chemical energy (electroplating).

Sound

Look What's in This Chapter

In this chapter we'll discuss some important concepts and subconcepts related to the study of sound, and we'll present lesson plans that are designed to teach these concepts and subconcepts to children.

Concept 1 Sound has pitch, quality, and intensity.

Concept 2 The source of all sound is a vibrating object.

Concept 3 Sound travels through many substances.

Concept 4 Sound has wave properties.

Subconcept 4–1 Sound spreads out in all directions from a source.

Subconcept 4–2 Sound waves will echo from a surface.

Subconcept 4–3 Sound waves will bend around corners.

Subconcept 4–4 Sound waves may join together.

Subconcept 4–5 Music is pleasant sound.

Concept 1

Sound has pitch, quality, and intensity.

Discussion

Often the elementary school teacher must help children develop their ability to perceive physical phenomena properly before they can deal successfully with science activities. For example, loudness is often confused in a child's mind with pitch—the highness or lowness of sounds. Also, many children cannot recognize that sounds are identical in pitch if they are different in quality. That is, they cannot hear that a foghorn and a bell are producing sounds of the same pitch although they sound different. Therefore, asking children to match sounds by pitch is often a dubious foundation for an exercise unless they have some training in this skill. Before beginning a unit on sound, you may wish to give the children experience in distinguishing pitch (highness), intensity (loudness), and quality (the mixture of overtones that gives a sound source its distinguishing characteristics).

Lesson Plan ■ A

Orientation:	Grades K–3.
Content Objective:	The children will state that the pitch of sound is how high or low it is, intensity is how loud or soft it is, and quality is what enables us to tell one sound source from another.
Skill Objective:	The children are required to *observe* by listening and to *communicate* their observations.
Materials:	A bell, a whistle, a tonette, a flutophone, a xylophone, or other simple musical instruments.
Evaluation:	Students' verbal interaction.

Procedure

Activity A—Distinguishing the quality of sound: Direct the children to close their eyes and lay their heads on their desks. Ask them to guess the sources of the sounds they will hear. You may use a variety of materials to produce sounds (bells, a dropped textbook, a whistle, and so on). Finish the exercise by playing the same note on any two musical instruments, such as a tonette and a xylophone. After the children have identified the two instruments, ask: "The same musical note was played on each instrument. I wonder how we could tell the difference?" Establish that the quality of sound from different sources is different even when the note played is the same. This perception may be reinforced by sounding notes on various instruments and having the children say whether the notes are the same or different.

Activity B—Distinguishing the pitch of sound: With a musical instrument such as a xylophone, tonette, or ukelele screened from the view of the class, ask the children to distinguish between notes of various pitch. Start the exercise with pairs of notes that differ widely in pitch, and work toward pairs of notes that differ very little. Strike one note and ask the children to re-

continued on next page

spond "higher" or "lower" to the second note. Then play notes of different pitch on two different instruments and have them attempt to state which note is higher in pitch.

Activity C—Distinguishing differences in pitch from differences in intensity of sounds: Continue activity B by playing the same note on an instrument first loudly, then softly. Ask the children which sound is higher in pitch. After they have learned to distinguish pitch from loudness, vary the sounds by playing notes of different pitch with different intensities. Finally, mix together sounds from two different instruments while varying the pitch and the intensity. Continue to ask the children to identify the highest and lowest sounds. Review and give examples of the terms *quality, pitch,* and *intensity.*

Concept 2

The source of all sound is a vibrating object.

Discussion

When an object such as a strip of metal is displaced as in Figure 19–1 to position A and released, it will move forward, sweeping the air before it to form a compression wave that emanates from position C. Upon reaching position C, the metal strip will return through the equilibrium point B to point A, to begin another sweep. As a result, a series of compression waves are generated at C that have the same wave frequency as the frequency of the vibrating object. The distance between the compression waves is called a wavelength. The size of the wavelength depends on how fast the generating object vibrates and how fast the wave moves through the air. The frequency is the number of waves that pass a given point in a given time. It is usually

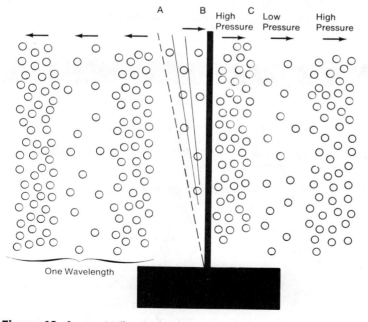

Figure 19–1 ▪ A Vibrating Rod Produces Sound Waves in the Air

expressed as the number of vibrations per second.

We call sound those pressure waves that the human ear can detect. The human ear (Figure 19–2) can interpret frequencies ranging between 16 and nearly 20,000 vibrations per second. Frequencies above the 20,000 vps range are termed ultrasonic.

Along with this thousandfold frequency range, the human ear has other remarkable characteristics. It is so sensitive that it can nearly hear the vibrations of molecules of air. It is sensitive to energies of magnitudes less than 0.0000000000000016 watt per square centimeter. This intensity (loudness) level is less than one-billionth that of normal speech. Humans can also distinguish one complex sound among many other sounds—a single instrument in a symphony orchestra or a friend's voice among the voices of a group. To perform a comparable task the eye would have to be able to separate light into dozens of individual hues and identify specific wavelengths.

In hearing, compression waves strike the eardrum. These cause the eardrum to vibrate. The vibrations of the eardrum travel via a series

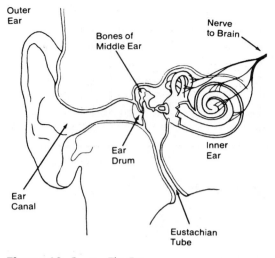

Figure 19–2 ■ The Ear

of three small bones to a fluid-filled chamber called the semicircular canal. Here the auditory nerve receives the vibrations and transmits them via nerve impulses to the brain. The brain then interprets the nerve signals. Thus, the brain interprets a series of small differences in pressure that impinge upon the eardrum.

Lesson Plan ■ B

Orientation:	Grades K–5.
Content Objective:	The children will state that sound is produced by vibrating objects.
Skill Objective:	The children are required to *observe* by listening to sound sources and to *infer* a generalization from their observations.
Materials:	Toy drum, coins or rice grains, large rubber band, tuning fork, glass tumbler, ruler.
Evaluation:	Students' verbal interaction.

Procedure

Show the children a series of sound-producing objects (Figure 19–3) such as:

1. A toy drum with several coins or rice grains resting on the drumhead.

2. A vibrating rubber band.

3. A vibrating tuning fork touching a water surface.

4. A ruler held in place on a desk and extending about two-thirds of its length over the edge of the desk.

continued on next page

Ask: "What do all of these objects have in common?" (They all make noise. They are all moving.) "If we say that an object moving back and forth rapidly is a vibrating object, what could we say about vibrating objects and sound?" (Sound is produced by vibrating objects.)

You may continue by asking: "Is our voice pro- duced by a vibrating object? Let us see." Direct the children to place their hands upon their throats and hum. Ask: "What do you feel?" (A vibration.) "Is there a vibrating object in our throat that makes the sound of our voice?" (Yes.) Ask again, "What did we learn today?" (Sounds are produced by vibrating objects.)

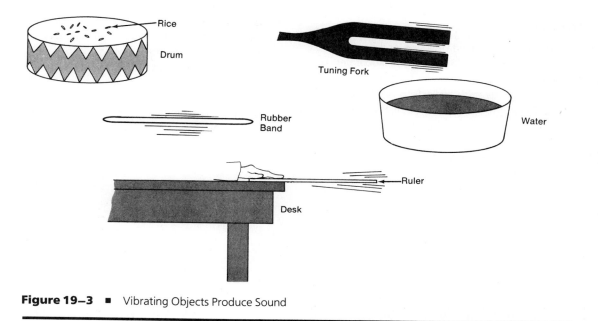

Figure 19–3 ■ Vibrating Objects Produce Sound

Concept 3

Sound travels through many substances.

Discussion

Because sound energy is kinetic energy (energy of motion, matter), it must have a physical me- dium through which to pass. When molecules (or atoms) in an elastic substance are disturbed, they pass on the disturbance to the molecules adjoining them. These disturbed molecules pass on the disturbance to their neighbors and so on until the energy of the disturbance is transmit- ted through the medium. This is how sound is transmitted through solids, liquids, and gases.

Lesson Plan ■ C

Orientation:	Grades 5–6.
Content Objective:	The children will state that sound travels as a disturbance from one molecule to another.

continued on next page

Skill Objective:	The children are required to *observe* a disturbance passing through a substance and to *infer* the relationship of the model to sound waves moving through a substance.
Materials:	Chalkboard eraser.
Evaluation:	Students' verbal interaction.

Procedure

Line up four children side by side and shoulder to shoulder as in Figure 19–4. Place a chalkboard eraser on the head of the child at one end of the line. Each child should gently push against his or her neighbor, thereby showing the transmission of the movement along the line. The eraser falling from the head of the end child is evidence that the disturbance that began on the opposite end of the line has reached that child.

Ask the children: "Did I push on John (the child with the eraser)? On his head?" (No.) "Then how could I disturb him?" (You pushed on —, who pushed —, who pushed —, and so on.) Apply this analogy to sound waves. "When I talk, do the molecules of air from my mouth rush to your ear so that you hear?" (No. The molecules from your mouth bump against the molecules next to them and this bumping is carried molecule by molecule to our ears.)

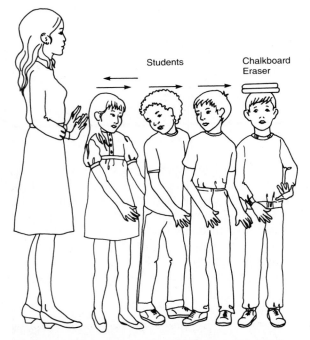

Teacher

Students

Chalkboard Eraser

Did the teacher cause the eraser to fall from the child's head?

Did the teacher touch the eraser?

Figure 19–4 ■ A Disturbance Passes Through a Medium

Orientation:	Grades K–4.
Content Objective:	The children will state that sound travels through many substances.
Skill Objective:	The children are required to *observe* sound pass through various substances and to *infer* a generalization from their observations.
Materials:	Small jar containing a bell immersed in water.
Evaluation:	Students' verbal interaction.

Procedure

Ask the children: "How does the sound of my voice reach your ears? What does it travel through?" (The air.) "Can sound pass through other substances? Let us see." Direct the children to perform the following series of listening activities. "Lay your head down with one ear on your desk. Close your eyes so that you cannot see. When I tap on your desk, raise your head." Pass among the children tapping on desks. "Hold your science book to your ear and close your eyes. When I tap on your book, lay it on your desk." Tap the books. Now say: "I am holding a jar that contains a bell immersed in water. As I pass among you, raise your hand if you hear the bell ring." *Note:* Hold the jar close to the students' ears and jerk the string up and down. (See Figure 19–5.)

After performing the activities, ask the children: "How did the sound get to your ears in each instance?" (Through the desk top; through the book; through the water, glass, and air.) "What can we say about the number of things sound will pass through?" (Sound will pass through many things [substances].) You may wish to have the students suggest other materials to use to see if sound will travel through them.

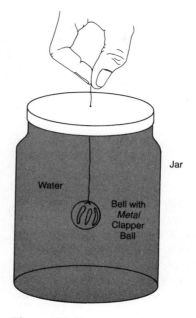

Jar

Water

Bell with *Metal Clapper Ball*

Figure 19–5 ■ Sound Travels Through Water

Concept 4

Sound has wave properties.

Discussion

The wave properties of heat and light were discussed in Chapters 15 and 16. Sound also has wave properties. However, the nature of sound and its energy differs from that of electromagnetic radiations. The energy of sound is kinetic energy, the energy of moving matter. Electromagnetic energy is associated with electric and magnetic fields. The transportation of sound energy requires a physical medium—solid, liquid,

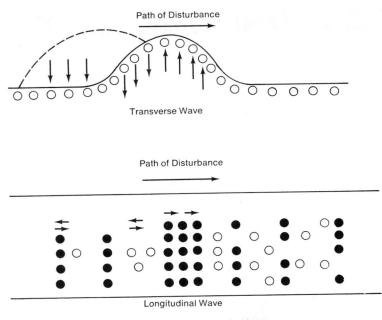

Figure 19–6 ■ Transverse and Longitudinal Waves

or gas—through which a wave can pass. Electromagnetic energy can travel through a vacuum. Electromagnetic waves are *transverse* waves. That is, the disturbance moves at right angles to the path of the wave, much as it does in a water wave. A sound wave is a *longitudinal* wave or compression wave. That is, the disturbance of particles moves in the same direction as the path of the wave. (See Figure 19–6.)

Because sound energy exhibits wave properties, it spreads out uniformly from the source, reflects or echoes off solids, exhibits interference where two waves meet, and will bend around corners.

Note: At this point, you may wish to use Lesson Plan C of Chapter 16, a discovery exercise dealing with the properties of waves.

Lesson Plan ■ E

Orientation:	Grades 4–6.
Content Objective:	The children will acceptably describe a transverse and a longitudinal wave in terms of their respective motions.
Skill Objective:	The children are required to *observe* models of transverse and longitudinal waves and to *infer* their relationship to sound.
Materials:	Six-foot clothesline, ribbon, Slinky toy.
Evaluation:	Students' verbal interaction, seat work, and sketches.

continued on next page

Procedure

Tie a brightly colored ribbon about midway on a five- or six-foot rope. Tie one end of the rope to a desk or door knob. Instruct a child to send a single pulse down the rope by rapidly raising and lowering the free end. Tell the class: "Children, watch the piece of ribbon carefully as the wave passes along the rope." Let the helper make a series of single pulses with short pauses in between. "In which direction did the disturbance or wave in the rope travel?" (Along the length of the rope.) "In which direction did the ribbon move?" (The ribbon moved up and down.) "This kind of wave is called a transverse wave. Can you describe the nature of a transverse wave?" (A transverse wave is when the disturbance or wave travels at right angles to the movement of the rope [medium].)

"Now we will see a different kind of a wave." Tie a ribbon securely to a spiral of a Slinky about one-fourth of the way along its length. Have two children stand five or six feet apart, holding the ends of the Slinky (Figure 19–7). Direct the child closest to the ribbon to gather together six or eight coils and then release them all together suddenly. Tell the children to watch the ribbon carefully as the disturbance passes through the Slinky. Ask: "What was the direction of the disturbance or wave?" (Along the path of the Slinky.) "Describe the motion of the coil to which the ribbon was tied." (The ribbon moved back and forth along the length of the Slinky.) "How was this different from the movement of the disturbance through the rope?" (The ribbon moved up and down across the path of the wave in the rope and back and forth along

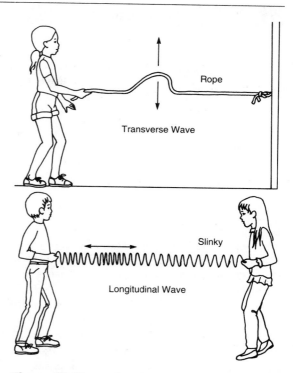

Figure 19–7 ■ Creating Transverse and Longitudinal Waves

the path of the wave in the Slinky.) "The movement of the wave through the Slinky is like a sound wave. This is called a longitudinal wave." You may wish to give the students a worksheet that requires them to identify longitudinal and transverse waves.

Subconcept 4–1

Sound spreads out in all directions from a source.

Discussion

Just as a pebble dropped into the center of a still pond will cause a circular water wave to expand in all directions on the surface, so will a disturbance in the air cause a sound wave to expand in the air. Only, a sound wave expands not in just two dimensions, like the wave on the surface of the pond, but in three dimensions, like an expanding globe-shaped balloon. Sound waves are disturbances that spread out uniformly in all directions from the source of the sound. Listening observers should be able to hear a sound that comes from a nondirectional source (a source that does not use a megaphone or a barrier to aim the sound in a certain direction)—regardless of their positions.

Orientation:	Grades K–3.
Content Objective:	The children will state that sound usually spreads out in all directions from a source, but that it may be aimed.
Skill Objective:	The children will *observe* sound from various positions in relation to the source and *infer* a generalization from their observations.
Materials:	Bell or tuning fork, posterboard or construction paper.
Evaluation:	Students' verbal interaction.

Procedure

Direct the children to close their eyes. Standing in the center of the room, ring a bell or sound a tuning fork. Ask: "Who heard the sound? What do you think it was?" (All of the children will raise their hands and identify the sound.) Continue by saying: "My, all of you heard the sound. In what directions can we say the sound traveled?" (In all directions.) "What directions did we not test?" (Above the sound and below it.) "How could we test these two directions?" The class may suggest placing observers standing on chairs and kneeling on the floor. With these observers in place, make a sound again. "Now, how many heard it?" (Everybody.) "What might we say about how sound travels?" (Sound travels in all directions from a source.)

You may continue by asking: "Are there any times when sound doesn't travel equally well in all direc-

tions?" If there is no response, ask the children why they cup their hands about their mouths when they shout across the playground. Then say: "Let's see if we can cause sound to go better in one direction than in others." Make a megaphone from a piece of construction paper or posterboard by rolling it into a cone and stapling it. Say a word softly without the megaphone. Then, with the megaphone held to your lips, repeat the word several times, aiming the megaphone at different sections of the room. Ask: "Did you notice any difference in the sound with and without the megaphone?" (Yes. The sound was louder with the megaphone.) "Can we cause sound to go mostly in one direction?" (Yes.) Conclude the lesson by reviewing the idea that sound normally spreads out in all directions from a source, but may be made to travel mostly in one direction.

Subconcept 4–2

Sound waves will echo from a surface.

Discussion

Many children have heard echoes. Echoes graphically demonstrate the ability of sound waves to bounce off hard or nonabsorbing surfaces. Since sound travels at a speed of approximately 1100 feet per second in air, the energy of the rebounding wave is often mixed with, and distorted by, other sound waves where distances are small. The effect this has upon speech may be demonstrated in large rooms and auditoriums. Echoes that mix with the original sounds in such situations often give a vibrating quality to the voice of a singer or speaker. Such echoes are known as reverberations. Delayed reverberations may cause a speaker's words to be garbled and unintelligible. The Bible tells of the Tower of Babel, where even the words of wise men were distorted and incomprehensible. Chances are the sun-baked clay walls of the structure reflected the speakers' voices and the resulting reverberations caused the speech to become garbled. Even today unintelligible speech is known as babbling.

We can use echoes to estimate distance. A shout that returns with a one-second delay indicates that the sound has traveled about 1100 feet. Since the sound must travel to the surface and return, the echoing surface must be about 500 feet away. To estimate the distance to any echo-producing surface, count the number of seconds that elapse between the sound and the echo and multiply this number by 500 or 550.

Lesson Plan ■ G

Orientation:	Grades K–5.
Content Objective:	The children will state that sound waves will echo from a surface.
Skill Objective:	The children will *observe* by listening to echoes and *infer* the relationship between the nature of a surface and its ability to produce echoes.
Materials:	Two whistles.
Evaluation:	Students' verbal interaction, laboratory worksheets, log, and reports.

Procedure

Take the children outdoors. Let one child walk away from the group into the middle of the playground and blow a whistle. Tell the children to try to remember the sound. Have a second child stand about five feet from an *inside corner* of the school building and blow a second whistle. Ask the children to describe the difference between the two sounds. (The sound from the whistle close to the building was the louder.) "I wonder why this is so?" (The sound was bounced off the building and reflected to our ears along with the original sound of the whistle.) Continue by asking: "What is the nature of the surface that the sound echoed from?" (Hard, brick, block, and so on.) "Do you think that the nature of the surface might affect the amount of echo that it allows?" Return to the classroom and ask the children to point out the materials that might help reduce echoes in the room. (Plastered walls, acoustical ceiling tile, bulletin boards, and other resilient materials absorb sound and help to reduce echoes.) Have the students write a paragraph describing how echoes are formed; have them give some examples of echoes they have experienced.

Subconcept 4–3

Sound waves will bend around corners.

Discussion

One property of waves is that they will diffract or bend around corners. This is an obvious property of sound.

Orientation:	Grades K–5.
Content Objective:	The children will state that sound waves will bend around corners.
Skill Objective:	The children are required to *observe* classmates responding to sounds from around corners and to *infer* a generalization from their observations.
Materials:	None.
Evaluation:	Students' verbal interaction.

Procedure

Take the children outdoors. Place three children around the corner of the school building. Offer them a suitable reward if they can return to the group when their names are called out. Stand with the class. Have various children, one at a time, loudly call out the names of the three children taking part in the experiment. After they have responded to the calls, ask them: "How did you know when to return?" (We each heard our name.) "Class, how could they hear? They were around the corner." (Sound goes around a corner.) Have the children give other examples of sound bending around corners.

Subconcept 4–4

Sound waves may join together.

Discussion

Sound waves join together or combine. Sometimes the sound becomes louder as a result. Sometimes the result is that the sound is destroyed.

Remember that a vibrating object produces a series of compression waves that travel through the atmosphere. If a second object is vibrating in the same atmosphere, its compressions (regions of high pressure) and rarefactions (regions of low pressure) combine with those of the first vibrating object. The result is a greater compression or rarefaction and a *louder sound*. The waves are said to be adding together *constructively*. This is called *constructive interference*.

Now suppose that the compression waves of one vibrating object are combining with the rarefactions of a second vibrating object. The high pressure and the low pressure combine to create normal pressure. In other words, the atmosphere is not disturbed. Consequently, there will be *no sound*, or at least the intensity of sound will be reduced. When waves combine so as to reduce the intensity of the sound, it is termed *destructive interference*.

We have probably all sat in auditoriums where there were dead spots of sound. These occur where destructive interference reduces the intensity of the sound to a very low level.

Figure 19–8 illustrates a popular demonstration of the interference of sound waves in a closed tube. Examine the figure carefully as you read the following explanation.

A compression wave is broadcast downward by the tuning fork at position A. The compression wave must travel down the length of the tube, strike the water surface, and rebound to join the compression wave being broadcast upward at C. In this way the effects of the waves are added together, and the listener observes an increase in the loudness of the

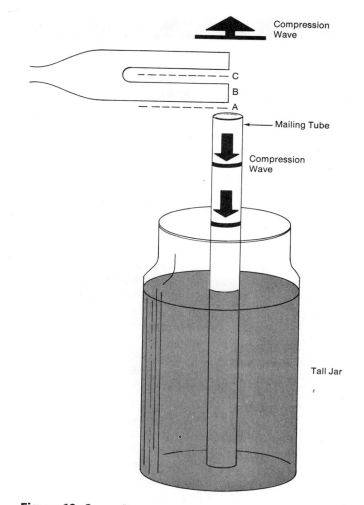

Figure 19—8 ■ Resonance in a Closed Tube

sound. To achieve the proper combination of the upward waves and the rebounding waves, the length of the air column in the tube must approximate one-fourth the wavelength of the sound frequency.

Chart 19—1 lists the approximate lengths of closed tube that will produce constructive interference for three frequencies of sound. In musical instruments such as organs, constructive interference is called resonance. Organ pipes work like the closed tube in Figure 19—8.

Chart 19—1 ■ The Approximate Wavelengths and Lengths of Closed Resonating Tubes for Three Frequencies of Tuning Forks

Frequency of the Tuning Fork	Approximate Wavelength	Approximate Length of the Closed Tube
G 384 vps	36″	9″
A 427 vps	31″	7.5″
C 512 vps	25″	6″

Lesson Plan ▪ I

Orientation: Grades 4–6.

Content Objective: The children will state that the length of a closed tube may be adjusted to produce resonance; that the higher the frequency of a tuning fork, the shorter the closed tube must be to produce resonance.

Skill Objective: The children are required to *investigate* by manipulating materials and to *infer* relationships from their observations.

Materials: Six wide-mouthed gallon jars; water; six heavy mailing tubes; six tuning forks, G, A, and C; six rubber strikers; rulers.

Evaluation: Students' group problem-solving skills, seat work, sketches, laboratory worksheets, log, and reports.

Procedure

Divide the class into groups. Instruct each group to fill a gallon jar with water to a depth of at least twelve inches. They should then insert the end of a cylindrical tube (mailing tube, towel roll) into the water. Tell them to strike a tuning fork upon a soft object (a cork or the heel of a hand) and hold it over the opening of the tube. (*Note:* Tuning forks of higher frequencies, such as G, 384 vps; A, 427 vps; and C, 512 vps have the best wavelengths for this exercise. If tuning forks of lower frequency are used, the depth of the water and the length of the tube must be increased.) The students should raise and lower the tube and the tuning fork so that the length of the air column inside the tube changes. Tell them to raise their hands when they observe anything unexpected happening. When each group has responded, ask: "What difference in the sound did you hear?" (The sound became louder.)

If tuning forks of several frequencies are available, ask the students to measure the length of the air col-

umn above the water at the moment that the sound is intensified. See if they can establish a relationship between the length of the air column and the frequency of the tuning fork. (The higher the frequency of the tuning fork, the shorter the air column required for resonance.)

With a group of bright children you might discuss the exercise by asking: "I wonder why the sound appeared to be louder?" (The sound rebounding from the water combined with the sound from the tuning fork.) "Why did the sound appear louder at only one particular time as you raised and lowered the tube?" (The length of the tube had to be just right so that the waves that were reflected from the water in the tube joined the waves that the tuning fork was making in such a way that they would add together.) Have the students write an explanation of sound resonance from a closed tube.

Subconcept 4–5

Music is pleasant sound.

Discussion

Musical tones are produced by matter that vibrates regularly. Sound produced by irregular vibrations is termed noise. Vocal and instrumental music results from the vibrations of vocal cords, strings, lips, air columns, stretched skins, reeds, and so forth.

Musical *chords* are made up of any three notes that have vibrating frequencies in ratios of four, five, and six. This combination of frequencies is pleasant to the ear. The *diatonic scale* is made up of three major chords. This scale has seventy notes. The *tempered scale*, which is used in tuning and playing musical instruments, grew out of an attempt to reduce this scale of strict ratios of sound frequencies to some manageable number of notes. The notes and frequencies of one octave of the tempered scale are listed in Chart 19–2. Because the tempered scale reduces the number of notes in each octave from seventy to twelve, some tuning forks whose frequencies are marked with the diatonic scale may differ slightly from the frequencies of the tempered scale.

Musical instruments depend upon various sources of vibrations. Percussion instruments are usually solid vibrating objects (drumskins, wooden sticks, gourds). Woodwinds depend upon vibrating reeds and resonating air columns (saxophones, clarinets). Brass instruments depend upon vibrating lips and tongues and resonating air columns (trumpets, trombones). Stringed instruments (guitars, violins), of course, depend on the vibrations of strings to produce musical sounds.

Chart 19–2 ▪ Notes of the Equal-Tempered Scale

Note	Frequency (vps)	Note	Frequency (vps)
C	256	G	383.6
C#, Db	271.2	G#, Ab	406.4
D	287.3	A	430.5
D#, Eb	304.4	A#, Bb	456.1
E	322.5	B	483.3
F	341.7	C	512
F#, Gb	362		

Lesson Plan ▪ J

Orientation:	Grades 2–6.
Content Objective:	The children will name the variables that affect the frequency of a vibrating rubber band or string: thickness, length, and tension.
Skill Objective:	The children are required to *investigate* by manipulating rubber bands and to *infer* the relationship of their observations to musical instruments.
Materials:	Ten thick rubber bands, ten thin rubber bands.
Evaluation:	Students' group problem-solving skills, laboratory worksheets, log, and reports.

Procedure

Divide the class into groups of two or three. Provide each group with two rubber bands, one thin and one thick. Tell the children to see how many ways they can make the two rubber bands sound different. After five to ten minutes, ask them to help you to list these things on the chalkboard. They may list such factors as thickness, length, tension (how hard it is stretched), and some miscellaneous factors related to the way the rubber band is held and plucked.

Ask: "How can we test if the thickness affects the pitch?" (Pull the thick and the thin rubber bands with about the same force and hold them at about the same length.) "How about the tension?" (Pull on a rubber band, first gently, then hard. Pinch off about the same length in each case, pluck the rubber band and compare.) "How can we test for the effect of length on the pitch?" (Pull on a rubber band and listen to it vibrate. Pinch off about one-half the length, maintaining about the same amount of tension, and listen to it vibrate.)

You might show the class a stringed instrument and ask: "How do we get different sounds from this instrument?" (The strings are different thicknesses;

continued on next page

the strings are made shorter by holding them with the hand; the strings are made tighter by adjusting the tension knobs.) Have the students write a report that states what they did, what they observed, and what they think about sounds and vibrating rubber bands or strings.

Lesson Plan ▪ K

Orientation:	Grades K–3.
Content Objective:	The children will state that the length of a vibrating air column determines its pitch.
Skill Objective:	The children are required to *observe* by listening to the musical notes of vibrating air columns and to *infer* the relationship between the musical pitch and the length of the air column.
Materials:	Six soft-drink bottles, water.
Evaluation:	Students' verbal interaction.

Procedure

The pitch of a vibrating air column is determined by its length. Line up four to six soft-drink bottles in a row, and add varying amounts of water as in Figure 19–9. Blow across the tops of the bottles. Try to tune the resonating air columns as closely as possible to the musical scale. Ask the class: "What appears to determine the pitch of the sound that comes from any one bottle?" (The length of the air column in the bottle.) *Note: Focus the attention of the class upon the length of the air column, not the amount of water.* "Can you think of any musical instruments that employ this method of producing sound?" (Organs, whistles, trombones, ocarinas, and so forth.) If possible, you might demonstrate any available instruments that produce sounds by varying the lengths of vibrating air columns.

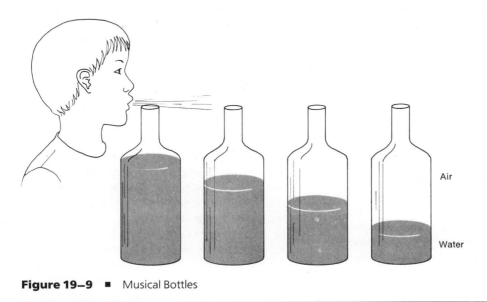

Air

Water

Figure 19–9 ▪ Musical Bottles

Summary

Vibrating bodies disturb the substance in which they are vibrating. The disturbances travel through the substance, transferring energy away from the vibrating object. Vibrations that occur between 16 and 20,000 times per second may be detected by the human ear if the waves possess even a small amount of energy. The detection and interpretation of the energy of vibration by the human ear and brain is known as hearing, and the vibrations are called sound.

Sound is generally described in terms of its loudness (intensity), pitch (frequency), and quality (the number and combinations of vibrations). Sound possesses wave properties. It will be transmitted in all directions from a source; it will rebound from a reflecting surface (echoes); it will bend around corners; and sound waves will interfere with one another (causing dead spots in auditoriums, for instance).

Musical sounds occur when regular patterns of vibrations reach the ear. The regular pattern of the waves makes such sounds pleasant to hear.

CHAPTER 20

Using Energy to Do Work: Simple Machines

Look What's in This Chapter

In this chapter we'll discuss some important concepts and subconcepts related to the study of energy and simple machines, and we'll present lesson plans that are designed to teach these concepts and subconcepts to children.

Concept 1 The sun's energy produces light, heat, and motion on the earth.

Concept 2 The sun is the earth's energy source.

Concept 3 Machines make energy useful.

Subconcept 3–1 The work output of a machine will equal the work input under ideal conditions.

Subconcept 3–2 Machines may multiply force.

Subconcept 3–3 Machines may increase movement.

Subconcept 3–4 Machines lose energy through friction.

Subconcept 3–5 Some friction is useful.

Concept 4 Forces may produce a change in motion.

Concept 1

The sun's energy produces light, heat, and motion on the earth.

Discussion

Aside from communication, our greatest need is for useful motion. We need motion to transport food and materials to processing and manufacturing facilities, and finished products to consumers. We need motion to produce electricity and other energy forms. Much of our technology consists of methods for producing and transforming useful motion.

Lesson Plan ■ A

Orientation:	Grades 3–6.
Content Objective:	The children will state that the sun is a source of energy.
Skill Objective:	The children are required to construct simple solar collectors and use a Celsius thermometer to record temperatures.
Materials:	Three large aluminum pie pans, one small aluminum pie pan, can of black spray paint, graduated cylinder, plastic food wrap, four foam cups, Celsius thermometer.
Evaluation:	Students' verbal interaction, sketches, report, students' group problem-solving skills, report with sketch.

Procedure

Place one small and two large aluminum pie pans on a newspaper and paint them black. Permit the paint to dry. Pour 100 milliliters of water from the same container into each of the painted pie pans and one large unpainted pie pan. Cover one large and one small painted pan with clear plastic food wrap. You should now have four pans, each containing 100 mL of water: one large pan, unpainted and uncovered; one large pan, painted and uncovered; one large pan, painted and covered; and one small pan, painted and covered.

Place the pans on piles of newspapers in the sunlight for about twenty minutes. Carefully pour the water from each pan into a foam cup and have the children use a Celsius thermometer to find the temperature of each. After the temperatures of the water samples have been recorded, ask: "What did we find out?" "What set of conditions created the hottest water?" "What set of conditions was least effective?" "If you were to build a solar hot water heater, how would you do it?" Have the students write a plan and draw a sketch for a simple solar water heater.

Lesson Plan ■ B

Orientation:	Grades 2–6.
Content Objective:	The children will state that the sun is a source of energy.
Skill Objective:	The children are required to *observe* and *infer.*

continued on next page

Materials: One hot dog, cardboard boxes, aluminum foil, coat hanger, thumbtack, string, pencil, two small nuts and bolts, rubber cement.

Evaluation: Students' verbal interaction, sketches, reports.

Procedure

Construct a solar cooker using the directions in Figure 20–1. Discuss with the students ways that solar energy can be used as an alternate energy source. Have them write a brief paragraph discussing at least one idea.

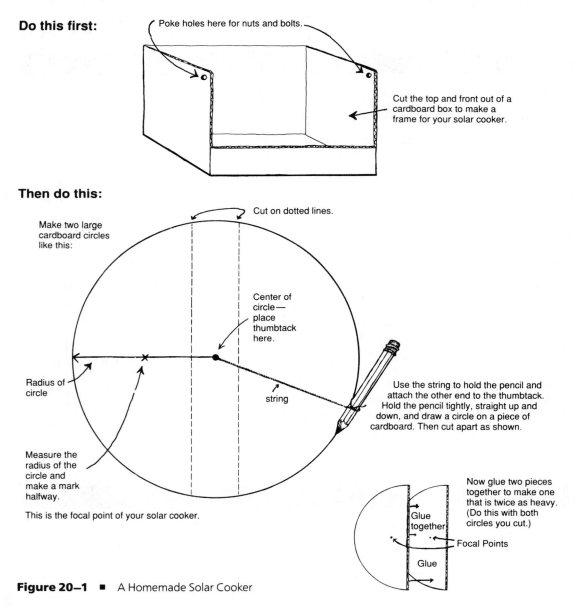

Do this first:

Poke holes here for nuts and bolts.

Cut the top and front out of a cardboard box to make a frame for your solar cooker.

Then do this:

Cut on dotted lines.

Make two large cardboard circles like this:

Center of circle — place thumbtack here.

Radius of circle

string

Use the string to hold the pencil and attach the other end to the thumbtack. Hold the pencil tightly, straight up and down, and draw a circle on a piece of cardboard. Then cut apart as shown.

Measure the radius of the circle and make a mark halfway.

This is the focal point of your solar cooker.

Now glue two pieces together to make one that is twice as heavy. (Do this with both circles you cut.)

Glue together

Focal Points

Glue

Figure 20–1 ■ A Homemade Solar Cooker

Now put the two curved pieces together like this:

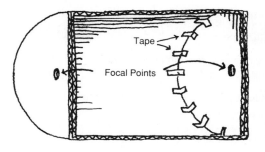

Tape

Focal Points

Cover <u>all</u> of inside with aluminum foil.

Tape another piece of cardboard to the curved edges of the two half-circles you glued together.

The width of the piece of cardboard should be slightly less than the width of the box you cut to make a frame.

Then cover the inside of this piece with the aluminum foil — use rubber cement.

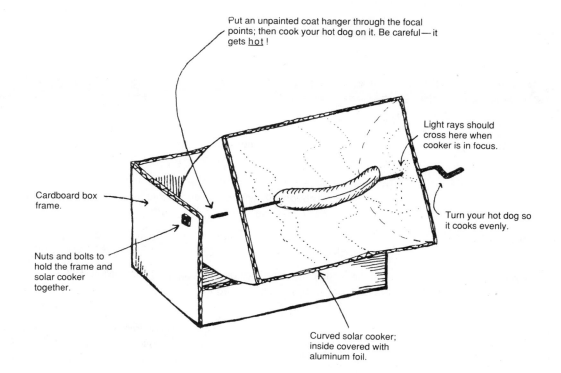

Put an unpainted coat hanger through the focal points; then cook your hot dog on it. Be careful — it gets <u>hot</u>!

Light rays should cross here when cooker is in focus.

Cardboard box frame.

Nuts and bolts to hold the frame and solar cooker together.

Turn your hot dog so it cooks evenly.

Curved solar cooker; inside covered with aluminum foil.

Adjust the cooker so that you can see the sun's rays cross on the focal points. How long does it take to cook a hot dog?

Lesson Plan ▪ C

Orientation: Grades K–5.

Content Objective: The children will name five methods of producing useful motion.

Skill Objective: The children are required to *communicate* by naming and by drawing methods of producing useful motion.

Materials: Pictures of windmills, water wheels, draught animals, people pulling or pushing things, paper and crayons.

Evaluation: Students' verbal interaction, seat work, and sketches.

Procedure

Show the children pictures of humans pushing or pulling things, draught animals pushing or pulling things, waterfalls, water currents, gasoline engines, and steam engines. Then ask: "In what ways is useful motion important to people?" (To get people places, to bring food and other necessary things to people, to make electricity, and so on.)

Conclude the lesson by asking the children to draw a picture showing useful motion being produced.

Lesson Plan ▪ D

Orientation: Grades 3–5.

Content Objective: The children will name four methods of making a pinwheel rotate and name a machine that uses each of these to produce motion.

Skill Objective: The children are required to *investigate* by manipulating a pinwheel, to *communicate* through written records, and to *infer* a relationship between the pinwheel and a machine.

Materials: Paper, scissors, straight pins (or ready-made pinwheels), candle, large pan, glass tumbler, water.

Evaluation: Students' verbal interaction, students' group problem-solving skills, laboratory worksheets, log, and reports.

Procedure

Provide each group of children with a pinwheel or have them construct one as in Figure 20–2. If no running water is available in the classroom, provide each group with a paper cup full of water. A single large candle may be lit beside the teacher's desk. Direct the students to make the pinwheel move in as many ways as they can.

Each group of children should write a description of each method used to turn the pinwheel. They should also name a machine that uses this method to produce motion.

After the children have had ample time to experiment, have them list their activities on the chalkboard in two columns, such as:

continued on next page

Ways We Produced Motion in the Pinwheel	Machines That Use This Method
1. We blew on it.	1. Windmill, gas turbine
2. We poured water over it.	2. Waterwheel, water turbine
3. We spun it with our fingers.	3. Hand tools
4. We held it over a candle.	4. Gas turbine
5. We held it before a fan. (We fanned it.)	5. Windmill, gas turbine
6. We moved it rapidly through the air.	6. Windmill, gas turbine

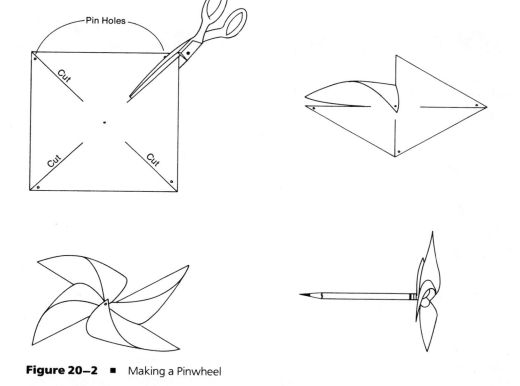

Figure 20–2 ■ Making a Pinwheel

Concept 2

The sun is the earth's energy source.

Discussion

In a primeval swamp huge ferns grow rapidly. They gather energy from the sun and store it in their leaves and stems. The ferns are buried under mud and soil. The mud and soil form layers of rock, and the ferns are pressed into coal. Millions of years pass by before a man digs up the coal and burns it to heat his home, thus releasing the sun's energy that was stored in the plants for so long. The coal may also be burned to operate a steam engine. The steam engine may drive an electric generator that produces electricity to operate light bulbs, toasters, and electric motors. The original energy from the sun has been transformed many times, but the sun still remains the ultimate source of all of the energy forms illustrated above. Except for nuclear and geothermal energy, no common forms of useful energy would exist on the earth except for the energy obtained from the sun. Because the energy of the sun is generated by nuclear reactions deep within its mass, almost all useful energy on the earth may be said to come ultimately from nuclear reactions.

Gravity may cause water to run downhill and so drive water wheels and turbines, but most of the water got uphill in the first place by absorbing the sun's heat energy, evaporating, and coming to earth as precipitation. Gravity can produce useful energy, as when it makes vehicles roll down an incline, but the sun is still the earth's one great energy source.

Lesson Plan ■ E

Orientation:	Grades 5–6.
Content Objective:	The children will state that the sun is the source of energy for producing motion.
Skill Objective:	The children are required to trace energy forms to their origins and to *infer* a generalization from their data.
Materials:	None.
Evaluation:	Students' verbal interaction, report.

Procedure

Ask the children to trace the energy of some common motions back to its origin.

Example 1: Motion caused by animal or human muscle energy comes from food energy, which comes from plants, which come from the sun.

Example 2: Motion at windmills comes from wind, which is caused by the sun heating the earth's atmosphere.

Example 3: Motion of water wheels comes from moving water. The water flows from higher to lower levels because of gravity. The water has energy because it was caused to evaporate by the sun and was carried up to the clouds, where it fell as rain.

The teacher may conclude the lesson by asking: "What did we find was the ultimate source of energy for each of the motions?" (The sun.) Ask the children to trace the energy of another type of motion, such as a steam engine, in a brief paragraph.

Concept 3

Machines make energy useful.

Discussion

Since we depend upon useful motion for our way of life, we build machines that enable us to move things. Machines are built that can:

1. Multiply the rate of motion.
2. Change the direction of motion.
3. Multiply the force exerted.
4. Convert one energy form to another energy form.

A complex machine may perform several of these operations. For instructional purposes it is convenient to concentrate on *simple machines* such as the *lever*, the *pulley*, the *wheel and axle*, and the *inclined plane*.

Some terms used in the study of machines are:

Work

The product of a force exerted on an object and the distance through which it moves. A girl pushes with a force of twenty pounds on a heavy box and succeeds in moving it a distance of ten feet. The work done is found by multiplying twenty pounds by ten feet and equals 200 foot-pounds.

Energy

The ability to do work. Any form of energy may be transformed by machines to motion or work. Therefore, any energy form may be expressed in terms of the work that it would do if it were so transformed and produced motion. The energy the girl exerted in the previous example would have been 200 foot-pounds if we disregard any energy lost in the process of pushing the box.

Effort

The force applied to a machine, for instance, the force that one applies to a lever or a pulley rope.

Resistance

The force opposing motion in a simple machine, for instance, the weight to be lifted by a lever or pulley.

Input

The work (force times distance) applied to a machine.

Output

The work (force times distance) produced by a machine.

Efficiency

The work output of a machine compared to the work input. In an ideal machine the efficiency is one to one, or 100 percent. Because of heat and other energy losses, machines do not achieve this ideal figure. An electric motor, for instance, is thought to be about 60 percent efficient. Some steam engines are only 20 to 30 percent efficient. Work output is, therefore, always less than work input, and machines are never 100 percent efficient.

Mechanical Advantage

An expression of the multiplication of force by a machine; the ratio of the resistance overcome to the effort applied. Example: A boy applies a ten-pound force on a lever and moves a 100-pound rock. The mechanical advantage is ten to one.

Lesson Plan ■ F

Orientation:	Pre-K—1.
Content Objective:	The children will describe the shape, characteristics, and applications of the wheel.
Skill Objective:	The children will visually and tactilely *observe* the characteristics of wheels and draw *inferences* about applications that may be made to everyday use.
Materials:	A collection of objects that contains examples of wheels and nonwheels. Wheels may be represented by wooden or plastic checkers, coins, wheels from broken toys or from Lego or other construction sets, thread spools, plastic cylindrical vials, and others. Objects that are considered nonwheels

continued on next page

may be any shape that is not a disc (circular with flat sides). Some examples are spheres of all sizes, wooden logic blocks, centimeter cubes, and others. The nonwheel objects should clearly *not* possess characteristics of a wheel. Also: one small colored box labeled "Wheels" and a second box of another color labeled "No Wheels"; large paper bags with rubber bands to be used as "feeling bags"; objects with wheels found in the classroom, school and school grounds; Lego or other construction toy set that contains wheels, toy cars, or trains; a collection of pictures showing several means of transportation, some that have wheels and some that do not have wheels.

Evaluation:　　　Children's group problem-solving skills, children's verbal interactions, and experimentation.

Procedure

Activity 1—Getting acquainted with wheels: Place a collection of wheel-shaped and non-wheel-shaped objects on a table for each group of children. Permit time for free play with the materials. As the children manipulate the objects, observe those who are making some of the objects roll (the discs, balls, cylinders, and so forth). Ask them to place all the objects that *will* roll on one side of the table and those that will not roll on the other. After they have done this, remove all the objects that will not roll. Keep the objects that roll for Activity 2.

Activity 2—Separating wheels and spheres: Place all the objects that the children discovered rolled in Activity 1 on a table in the front of the room. Hold up a sphere or ball and a disc-shaped object such as a checker. Roll each one on the table and permit one child to catch them before they fall to the floor. Tell the children we call one object a ball or sphere and the other a wheel because of their shapes. Ask them to describe the difference in the way the balls and the discs roll. Have them describe the differences in the shapes of the balls and the wheels. Pass out several balls and wheels to each group of children and permit them to roll each of them for a while. Then tell them you would like them to place all the balls on one side of their table and all the wheels on another. Have one child from each group bring the balls and another bring the wheels to the front of the room. Put a colored box with "Wheels" written on it and a colored box with "No Wheels" written on it on a desk or table in front of the room. Ask the class to verify the selec-

tion of each object as it is placed in the "Wheels" box or the "No Wheels" box. Cylindrically shaped objects should be included with the disc-shaped objects as wheels.

Activity 3—Feeling for wheels: For each small group (two to four children), provide a large paper bag containing eight or ten objects, at least half of which are wheel-shaped. The top of the bag should be gathered with a rubber band so that the children cannot see inside but can insert their hands into it. Ask the children one at a time to insert a hand into the bag and pull out a wheel-shaped object. Tell them that not all things in the bag are wheel-shaped. Pass the bag among the group until all wheel-shaped objects have been removed. Put the objects back into the bag, exchange bags with another group, and repeat the procedure. While the children are selecting the objects using their sense of touch, move among them to determine if any child is having a problem doing this. Give such children a wheel-shaped object and permit them to hold it in their hand and thoroughly feel it. If the children still cannot select a wheel by feeling, do not press them.

Activity 4—Discovering how wheels are used by people: Tell the children that they have been finding out about wheels, and now they will discover the many ways wheels can be useful. Provide each group with toys that have wheels and axles. Ask the children what holds the wheel to the car, and why the wheels do not fall over, as did the wheels they rolled. When they

continued on next page

describe the rod or fastener that holds the wheels to the cars, tell them it is called an axle. Permit them to roll the toy cars to one another to see how the wheel and axle work together to allow the cars to roll.

Fill a plastic quart milk bottle with sand or water and tape the lid securely in place. Fasten a rubber band to the handle of the milk bottle and have a child attempt to pull it along the table top while holding the rubber band. (*Note:* You may add or delete sand so that the rubber band selected is strong enough to pull the bottle along the table's surface.) Ask the children what happens to the rubber band. (It stretches.) Now place the milk bottle on a toy car, truck, or train and attach the same rubber band to the vehicle. Have the same child pull the vehicle and bottle with the rubber band. Ask the class what happened this time to the rubber band. Ask the child who pulled both systems what the difference was in doing this. Ask them why they think we use vehicles with wheels. (The wheels allow us to move things while using less force.)

Activity 5—Searching for wheels in the school and school yard: Have the children look around the classroom and find things that have wheels. There may be toys, such as wagons and scooters, and movable tables and carts. Ask the children why these things have wheels. Discuss each one. Then take the children on a walk through the school in search of other wheels. They may find dollies and carts used by custodians,

carts that hold film projectors or other media, rolling tables in the cafeteria, waste-paper holders, trash cans, and other items. Again, discuss each one of them, asking the children why they have wheels and how the wheels help to make it easier to perform a task. Finally, take the children outdoors onto the parking lot and driveway. There they will see automobiles, vans, and trucks. Discuss the different vehicles and the advantages and disadvantages of each. Again ask the children how wheels help people to do things. Perhaps there will be a bicycle rack, a delivery truck, a motorcycle, or school bus. Ask the children to count the wheels and tell why some vehicles have more wheels than others.

Activity 6—Finding that some means of transportation have wheels and some do not: You will need an array of pictures showing various forms of transportation. In addition to cars, buses, trains, motorcycles, and airplanes, all of which have wheels, there should be pictures of small and large boats, canoes, seaplanes, packhorses, sleds, and skis, which do not employ wheels. As you show each picture, ask the children if this means of transportation has wheels. Have a child come to the front of the room and point out the wheels on the picture. After looking at all of the pictures, discuss with the children how some means of transportation have wheels and some do not.

Subconcept 3–1

The work output of a machine will equal the work input only under ideal conditions.

Discussion

We have many reasons for building and using machines. One purpose we *cannot* accomplish in building a machine is a gain of *work* output over the *work* input. The total energy output of a machine can never exceed the energy applied. In a machine that is 100 percent efficient—that is, one in which there are no energy losses due to friction, heat loss, and so on—the output will exactly equal the input. Most machines, however, are less than 100 percent efficient. Energy is lost in their operation. Thus, the input exceeds the output.

Orientation:	Grades 5–6.
Content Objective:	The children will state that energy is lost as a machine does work.
Skill Objective:	The children are required to *observe* a simple machine in operation and to draw *inferences* about energy relationships.
Materials:	Chair, six- to eight-foot board, wood block (fulcrum).
Evaluation:	Students' verbal interaction, reports.

Procedure

Instruct a big child to stand on a chair or stool. Ask the class: "Does Carol possess more energy than the rest of us?" (Yes.) "Why?" (Because she is higher. It required energy to climb up on the chair.) "How can we show that Carol can do work because of her position?" After receiving suggestions from the children, place a large block under the center of a long board as in Figure 20–3. Have a smaller child stand on one end of the

board. Ask Carol to step on the opposite end of the board. Ask: "What happened?" (Mike was raised from the floor.) "Did Carol do work in raising Mike?" (Yes.) "Where is the energy that Carol had before she stepped off the chair?" (Mike has it [some of it].) "Does Mike now possess as much potential energy as Carol did before she stepped on the board?" (No. Mike is as high, but he weighs less. Mike could not raise Carol.)

continued on next page

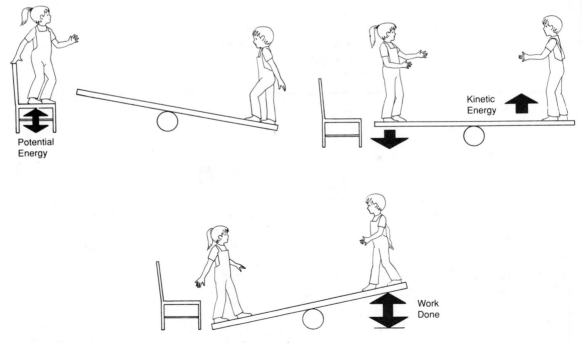

Figure 20–3 ■ Potential Energy Can Produce Work

"Where could the energy that was lost have gone?" (The potential energy of Carol's position was converted to kinetic energy of motion as she stepped on the board. When the board struck the floor, it produced a sound that took some of the energy. Some small amount of heat energy was also produced by the compression of molecules of the system.) "What can we say about energy and machines?" (Machines lose energy when they do work.) Ask the children to write a brief description of at least one other situation that demonstrates that energy is lost in the use of machines.

Subconcept 3—2

Machines may multiply force.

Discussion

The most common use of simple machines is probably to increase the force that is exerted upon a resistance. Machines vary in the way in which this is achieved, but one rule is universal for all machines. The work output may not exceed the work input, and *a gain in output force must necessarily mean a loss of output movement* compared to the input movement.

Lesson Plan ■ H	
Orientation:	Grades 1—6.
Content Objective:	The children will state that a lever may be used to lift heavy objects.
Skill Objective:	The children will *observe* others using a lever and *infer* a generalization concerning levers.
Materials:	Six-foot board; block (fulcrum).
Evaluation:	Students' verbal interaction, seat work, and sketches.

Procedure

Ask the class: "Do you think you can lift my desk?" (With older children you may wish to add "with me sitting on it?") "Come and try." After some of the boys and girls have tried to lift the desk, show the class a long board and ask: "Can we lift the desk using this board?" Allow volunteers the opportunity to construct a lever. If they do not succeed, show them how as in Figure 20—4. After several children have lifted the desk, say: "You could not exert enough force to lift the desk by yourselves. How did the board help you?" (It allowed us to exert a greater force on the desk.) Permit the children to place the block that serves as the fulcrum in several positions. See if they can discover that the closer the block is to the desk, the easier it is to lift the desk. Be sure to emphasize that the lever is *not increasing the work* they are able to do, but *only* the amount of *force* they can exert. Ask the children to write a description of the activity and state what they learned about levers and other simple machines.

continued on next page

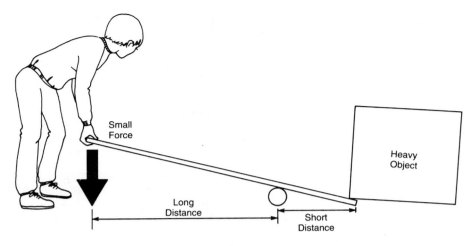

Small
Force

Heavy
Object

Long
Distance

Short
Distance

Figure 20—4 ■ Using a Lever to Increase Force

Lesson Plan ■ I

Orientation:	Grades 1—6.
Content Objective:	The children will state that an inclined plane may be used to lift heavy objects.
Skill Objective:	The children will *hypothesize* on ways to move heavy objects, *observe* an object being moved up an incline, and *infer* a generalization from their observations.
Materials:	Six-foot boards, large box, stool.
Evaluation:	Students' verbal interaction, sketch, report.

Procedure

Fill a large box with miscellaneous articles until a child cannot lift it but can slide it across the floor. Tell the children that you would like to have the box on top of a stool but cannot lift it. Ask them to find a way to place the box on the stool. Place a long wooden board in full view of the class. The children may suggest using the board as a lever or as an inclined plane. After a time, if the children do not succeed in devising an inclined plane with the board and the stool, show them how. Permit several of the children to push the box up the incline as in Figure 20—5. Ask: "What will an incline permit us to do?" (An incline helps us to raise heavy objects.) Ask the children to draw a sketch of an inclined plane and state how inclined planes aid people in doing work.

continued on next page

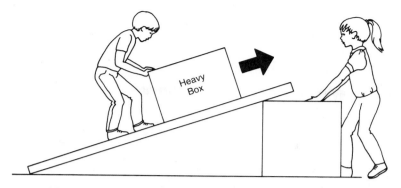

Figure 20–5 ■ Using an Inclined Plane to Raise a Heavy Object

Lesson Plan ■ J

Orientation: Grades 4–6.

Content Objective: The children will state that an inclined plane may be used to multiply force and that the amount of force required to move an object up an incline is related to the angle of the incline.

Skill Objective: The children are required to *hypothesize* about the relationship between force and the angle of an inclined plane, to *make operational definitions*, to *control variables*, to *experiment* by manipulating objects on an inclined plane, and to *interpret data*.

Materials: Six boards 2" × 4" × 12", six boards 1" × 6" × 4', six screw eyes, six spring balances, textbooks.

Evaluation: Students' verbal interaction, students' group problem-solving skills, seat work, and sketches, laboratory worksheets, log, and reports.

Procedure

Put a screw eye in a foot-long two-by-four board. Ask one student to find the weight of the board using a spring balance. Record his data on the chalkboard. Now direct the student to find the force required to pull the board up an incline that is formed by resting one end of a four-foot board on several books. (See Figure 20–6.) Record his data on the chalkboard underneath the weight data. Ask the class: "Does it require more force to lift the board directly upward or to raise its height by pulling it up an incline?" (It requires more force to lift it.) "Does the angle of the incline affect the force required to pull the board up its length? How can we find out?" At this point you may permit the children to investigate the problem as a group activity. Each group would require a 2" × 4" × 12" board, a longer board, a spring balance, and some books. However, if you wish to use this exercise to develop the skills of experimenting, data collection, organization, and interpretation, you may proceed as follows:

continued on next page

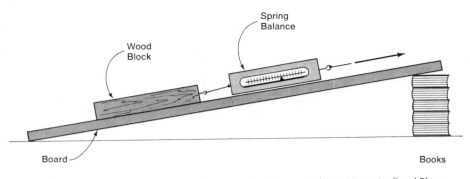

Figure 20–6 ▪ Measuring Forces Necessary to Move an Object Up an Inclined Plane

The students may suggest trying different numbers of books or other uniform objects under the incline and finding the force necessary to pull the board along the incline in each case. They may make a data sheet like Chart 20–1 showing their findings. They may also construct a graph like Figure 20–7 showing the relationship between the number of books (angle of incline) and the force required to move the block.

To conclude the lesson, ask: "What might we conclude from our data?" (The more books there are [the greater the angle of incline], the more force is required to pull the block.) "We can raise a weight with less force through the use of an inclined plane, but what are we giving up?" (The weight must move over a greater distance.)

Chart 20–1 ▪ Data Sheet for Testing the Inclined Plane (Example)

Trial	No. of Books	Force
1	2	200 g
2	2	200 g
3	4	350 g
4	4	360 g

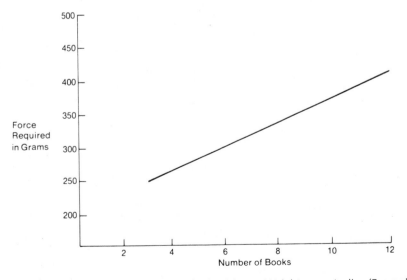

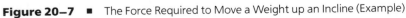

Figure 20–7 ▪ The Force Required to Move a Weight up an Incline (Example)

Orientation: Grades 4—6.

Content Objective: The children will state that pulley systems may be used to increase a force.

Skill Objective: The children are required to *investigate* with pulley systems and to *infer* a generalization from their data.

Materials: For each group of children—two single pulleys and one double pulley, a strong spring balance 0–1000 grams, one-kilogram weight, a stand from which to suspend the pulley systems (in place of a stand, a dowel rod or meter stick may be placed on the seats of two chairs and the pulley systems may be suspended from the rod or meter stick).

Evaluation: Students' verbal interaction, students' group problem-solving skills, seat work and sketches, laboratory worksheets, log, and reports.

Procedure

Provide each group of children with the materials listed above and a worksheet that contains the diagrams in Figure 20–8. Instruct the children to use a 1000-gram (1-kilogram) weight as a load and a spring balance to find the force necessary to move the load at a slow, uniform rate for each pulley system. Have them record their results. Ask these questions: "What was the force required to move the load (one-kilogram weight) for pulley system number 1?" (About 1000 grams.) "Was there any increase in the load that was lifted as compared to the force?" (No. The force exerted and the load were the same." What about pulley system number 2?" (The force was only about 500 grams.) "Was the force multiplied?" (Yes. The load was about twice the force that was applied.) "How about pulley system number three?" (The force was about 500 grams for pulley system number 3. The load was twice as great as the force.) "Pulley system number 4?" (The force was about 250 grams. The load was about four times as great as the force.) "What can pulley systems do?" (They can be used to move loads that are greater than the force applied.)

continued on next page

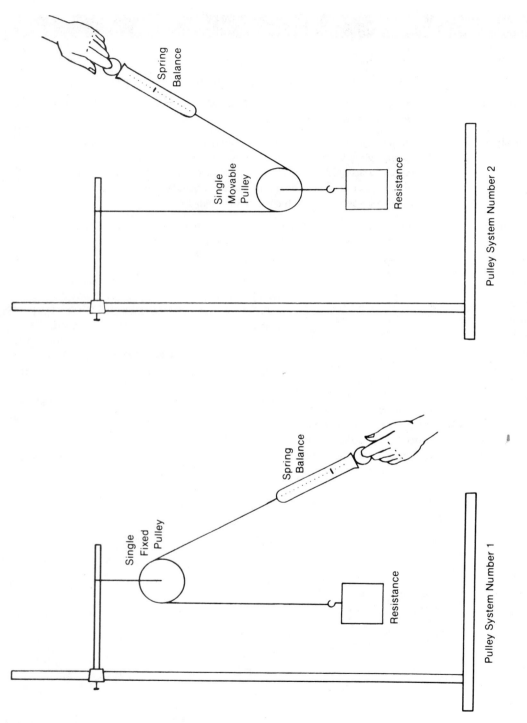

Figure 20–8 ■ Pulley Systems

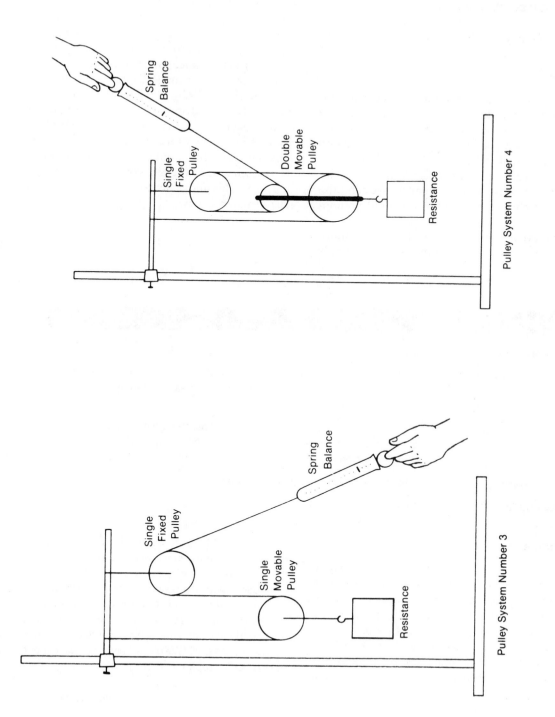

Spring Balance

Double Movable Pulley

Single Fixed Pulley

Resistance

Pulley System Number 4

Single Fixed Pulley

Spring Balance

Single Movable Pulley

Resistance

Pulley System Number 3

Subconcept 3–3

Machines may increase movement.

Discussion

Usually, we think of machines as devices that multiply force. They help us to exert great force and lift heavy objects. But occasionally machines are designed to multiply movement—to convert a small movement of a large effort to a larger movement of a smaller resistance. With machines that multiply movement, we can raise objects higher or faster than we could without them.

Picture a lever that is constructed to multiply movement. Such a lever may be made simply by placing the fulcrum close to the effort. As the effort moves a little bit, it will raise the resistance a great deal. We have gained movement. But what is lost? Remember that the input work (effort × effort distance) must equal output work (resistance × resistance distance) in our machine. Since the distance the resistance moves is greater than the distance the effort moves, the effort must be larger than the resistance. We lose force. There is less force produced than is put into the lever. To summarize: a gain in movement from a machine is accompanied by a loss of force. This movement-force relationship is true of all machines.

Lesson Plan ■ L

Orientation:	Grades 2–6.
Content Objective:	The children will state that a machine may be used to gain an increase in movement, but that an increase in movement means a greater force must be used.
Skill Objective:	The children are required to *hypothesize* about the construction of a lever to gain movement, to *observe* a lever, and to *infer* a generalization from their observations.
Materials:	A three-foot board, a block (fulcrum), a book.
Evaluation:	Students' verbal interaction.

Procedure

Place a book or other object on the end of a two- to three-foot board as in Figure 20–9. Ask the children: "How can I raise the book easily?" (Put a fulcrum under the board. Use the board as a lever.) Do as the children suggest. Illustrate the use of the lever to raise the book. Then ask: "Can I use this lever to raise the book higher than the starting position of the effort? Raise your hand when you think you know." Permit several of the children to show that the book will move higher when the fulcrum is placed close to the end of the lever where the effort is applied. Ask: "What did you notice about the position of the fulcrum and the effort you had to apply?" (The closer the fulcrum was to the effort, the greater the effort had to be to raise the book.) "So what did we gain and what did we give up with our lever?" (We gained height or movement, but we had to apply more force.)

continued on next page

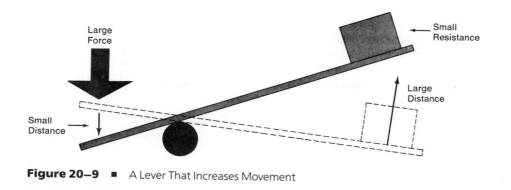

Small
Resistance

Large
Force

Large
Distance

Small
Distance

Figure 20–9 ▪ A Lever That Increases Movement

Subconcept 3–4

Machines lose energy through friction.

Discussion

When two objects are rubbed together, some of the atoms or molecules that make up the exposed surfaces are torn from their positions. The energy that binds these particles to the parent material is given up as heat energy. Thus, when any two objects are rubbed together, small fragments of material are torn away, and the surrounding area becomes warm or hot. The force that opposes the motion and yields heat energy is called friction.

In order to reduce friction, one must prevent the surfaces of two moving materials from making direct contact as they slide over each other. This is commonly accomplished with thin films of oil or graphite that are placed between the contacting surfaces. An alternative is to use roller or ball bearings that allow one material to roll over a second rather than to slide over it.

Lesson Plan ▪ M

Orientation:	Grades K–6.
Content Objective:	The children will state that rubbing things together produces friction and that oil or soap may be used to reduce friction.
Skill Objective:	The children are required to *experiment* by rubbing surfaces together, to *observe* by feeling the results of the rubbing, and to *infer* conclusions from their observations.
Materials:	Twelve blocks of wood, six pieces of sandpaper, dishwashing detergent or cooking oil.
Evaluation:	Students' verbal interaction, reports.

continued on next page

Procedure

Have the children rub their hands together and describe the sensation. (The hands become warm.) Have the children rub a block of wood with sandpaper, feel the block of wood, and describe the sensation. (The block of wood becomes warm.) Have the children rub two blocks of wood together vigorously, feel the surfaces, and comment upon the sensation. (Both blocks of wood become warm.)

Now squirt some dishwashing detergent (or oil) on one child's hands and ask him to rub his hands together. Ask: "Do your hands feel the same as when you rubbed them together without the detergent?" (No, they are slippery. They did not become warm.) You may also squirt detergent upon the surfaces of the two wood blocks and ask a child to rub them together (Figure 20–10). Ask: "Does the same thing happen with the detergent on the surfaces as without it?" (No. No heat is produced.) "What else might we use to reduce friction other than detergent?" (Oil, waxed paper, and so on.) Have the students copy a statement about friction.

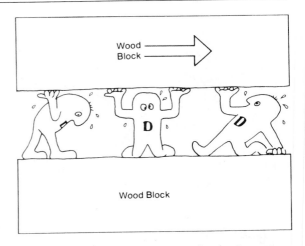

Figure 20–10 ■ Detergent Molecules Separate Moving Surfaces, Reducing Friction

Subconcept 3–5

Some friction is useful.

Discussion

Many types of movement depend upon friction. Automobile tires push against the road surface, causing the automobile to move. People are enabled to walk or run by the friction of their feet on the ground. Machinery is driven by belts and clutches that depend upon the friction of one material moving over another. These and other examples illustrate our dependence upon friction to produce useful motion.

Lesson Plan ■ N

Orientation:	Grades 1–4.
Content Objective:	The children will state that some friction is useful in doing work.
Skill Objective:	The children are required to *hypothesize* concerning the effect of waxed paper upon friction, to *observe* a set of conditions where friction is reduced, and to *infer* a generalization.
Materials:	A sheet of waxed paper.
Evaluation:	Students' verbal interaction, reports.

continued on next page

Procedure

Position one child in front of the room. Tell her to push against the wall. Direct the class to observe her feet. Ask the class: "What is happening with Carol's feet?" (They are pushing against the floor.) "I wonder what would happen if Carol stood on a piece of waxed paper and pushed against the wall?" Accept suggestions from the class. Then place Carol upon a sheet of waxed paper and tell her to push against the wall as in Figure 20–11. "What happens when Carol pushes against the wall while standing on waxed paper?" (Her feet slide on the floor.) "Can Carol exert as much force upon the wall while standing on the waxed paper as she could while standing on the floor?" (No.) Now say: "Carol, I want you to do some work for me. Will you please push my desk over here?" Have Carol stand on the waxed paper and attempt to push the desk. Ask: "Is friction necessary sometimes?" (Yes.) "What might happen if there were no friction?" (We couldn't walk, write on chalkboard, move things, and so on. It would be better for sled riding, skating, and so on.)

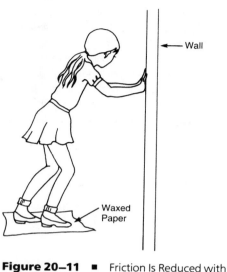

Figure 20–11 ■ Friction Is Reduced with Waxed Paper

Lesson Plan ■ O

Orientation:	Grades 3–6.
Content Objective:	The children will state that the size of the surface does not affect the amount of friction; that the force that presses the surfaces together does affect the amount of friction.
Skill Objective:	The children are required to *hypothesize* concerning variables that affect friction, to *control variables* as they experiment, to *communicate* by writing a laboratory report, and to *interpret* the data gained from their experiments.
Materials:	Six boards 2" × 4" × 12", six screw eyes or hooks, string, six spring balances.
Evaluation:	Students' verbal interaction, students' group problem-solving skills, laboratory worksheets, log, reports.

Procedure

Divide the class into groups. Give each group a 2" × 4" × 12" board with a hook in the end, a string, and a spring balance. Provide each group with the following set of questions and directions. "Do you think it will

continued on next page

require more force to pull the board along at a uniform velocity if it is lying on the four-inch surface or on the two-inch surface? Write a hypothesis that expresses your best prediction." "How can you test your hypothesis? How many trials should you make?" (Pull the board along in each position. At least three trials for each position.) "Write a description of your experiment. Include your hypothesis, procedure, results, and conclusions." "What do you conclude about your hypothesis?" (The force is independent of the surface area.) "What effect do you think adding weight to the wood block will have upon the force of friction? Write a hypothesis that expresses your best prediction." "How can you test your prediction? How many trials should you make?" (Lay some object such as a book on the wood block in each position and pull the block along. At least three trials for each position.) "Write a description of your experiment. Include your hypothesis, procedure, results, and conclusions." "What do you conclude about your hypothesis?" (The weight of an object affects the amount of friction it exerts as it slides over a surface.)

Concept 4

Forces may produce a change in motion.

Discussion

Many elementary science books contain some mention of the laws of motion as formulated by Sir Isaac Newton. In essence these laws are:

1. a. An object at rest will remain at rest unless acted upon by some outside force.
    b. An object in motion will continue in motion in a *straight line* and at a constant velocity unless acted upon by some outside force.
2. a. The acceleration (change in velocity) of an object is directly related to the force exerted upon the object.
    b. The acceleration (change in velocity) of an object is inversely related to the mass of the object.
3. For every action there is an equal and opposite reaction.

The First Law of Motion

The first law of motion is fairly obvious. Unless a force acts upon it, an object will remain stationary or move in a straight line. The implications of this law are sometimes overlooked, however. Any time an object is moving *not in a straight line*, or is speeding up or slowing down, some force or forces must be acting upon it. To realize this is the first step toward identifying the forces involved. Since everything on earth is affected by the earth's gravitational attraction and the friction and pressure of the atmosphere, most of our experience is with objects that have forces acting upon them.

The Second Law of Motion

The more force one exerts upon an object, the faster the object changes its velocity. The velocity may increase (acceleration) or decrease (deceleration). Force exerted upon an object of large mass will result in less acceleration than the same force exerted upon an object of small mass. These two factors, the size of the force and the amount of mass, determine the rate of acceleration of an object.

The Third Law of Motion

No force may be exerted upon any body that does not affect a second body. In terms of observable matter, this means that every change in the motion of one body produces a change in the motion of, or at least a stress upon, some other body. A man pushes upon a wall, and the wall pushes upon the man. A man's hand pushes against a thrown ball, and the ball pushes against the hand. For every action there is an equal and opposite reaction.

Orientation: Grades 5–6.

Content Objective: The children will state that the forces acting upon an object that is being whirled on the end of a string are gravity and the pull of the string; that when the string is released the force of gravity alone acts to change the straight line motion of the moving object. (Note that this ignores the effect of air friction.)

Skill Objective: The children are required to *observe* forces and changes in forces acting upon a moving object.

Materials: Chalkboard eraser, string.

Evaluation: Students' verbal interaction, reports.

Procedure

To analyze the forces acting upon a moving object, tie a chalkboard eraser to a two-foot length of string and whirl the string steadily about your head. Then let the string go. Ask the class: "What happened? Describe the path of the eraser." (First the eraser traveled in circles, then it flew off in a straight line.) "When the eraser was whirling steadily around my head, what forces were acting upon it?" (Gravity, the string pulled on it.) "In which direction does gravity pull?" (Down.) "Was this force important in determining the path of the eraser?" (No.) "What force is left?" (The pull of the string.) "What happened when I let go of the string?"

(The eraser flew off in a straight line.) "What can we say from our observations about the path of a moving object when no forces are acting upon it?" (The object will move in a straight path.) "We have been neglecting gravity here. What effect did gravity have upon the eraser?" (The force of gravity caused the eraser to fall toward the floor.) The teacher may release the whirling eraser at various speeds to show the effect of gravity. "What can we conclude about our observations?" (That an object will continue to move in a straight line when no force is acting upon it.) Have the students draw a sketch of the exercise and write what they learned.

Summary

We have invented many machines to help us do work. All the energy we use must ultimately come from one of the force fields of nature—gravitation fields, electrical fields, magnetic fields, or nuclear forces. Most machines are designed to produce useful motion and to multiply force. The amount of work plus the energy that comes out of a machine always equals the amount of work plus the energy that is put into the machine. Work cannot be multiplied—only movement or force. Simple machines such as levers, inclined planes, wheels and axles, and pulleys can be used to illustrate these relationships.

Friction is a force that opposes motion. When two surfaces are rubbed together, chemical bonds between atoms and molecules are broken, and heat is produced. Thus, friction may cause machines to wear out and to overheat.

Many motions depend upon friction as one body pushes against another. This occurs, for instance, in running and walking. The belt and clutch drives on various machines illustrate another useful form of friction. Here energy is transferred from one moving part of the machine to another by the friction of the connecting materials upon the parts.

The laws of motion are:

1. An object at rest will remain at rest, and an object in motion will remain in motion at a constant velocity and in a straight line unless acted upon by an outside force.

2. The acceleration of an object is directly related to the force exerted upon it and inversely related to the mass of the object.

3. For every action there is an equal and opposite reaction.

Extending Activities

Chapter 9 deals with many of the important issues facing our society as we move from an industrially oriented economy toward an electronic-information-oriented, high-technology-based economy. Children may be involved with the major issues in a variety of ways. Group research projects on specific issues provide information and experience with processes useful for dealing with societal problems. After the children have gathered information concerning an issue, the teacher may organize culminating activities, such as written and oral project reports, debates where children utilize gathered information, general discussions of issues, or action projects, such as writing or visiting responsible authorities.

Suggested Topics for Investigation

1. Effects on people of the emerging high-technology society (homes, jobs, leisure, and so on).

2. The use of robots in the home and industry (robotics).

3. The use of nuclear energy as a weapon of war.

4. The use of technology to relieve world hunger.

CHAPTER 21

Flight: From Kitty Hawk to the Space Shuttle

Look What's in This Chapter

In this chapter we'll discuss some important concepts and subconcepts related to the study of flight, and we'll present lesson plans that are designed to teach these concepts and subconcepts to children.

Concept 1 Air moving at different speeds over surfaces creates regions with different air pressures.

> Subconcept 1–1 The lift provided by the wing of an airplane is produced both by moving air pushing on its underside and fast moving air flowing over the top surface.

Concept 2 The movement of an airplane in flight is the result of the interaction of four forces: thrust, drag, lift, and weight.

Concept 3 The direction of the flight of an airplane is controlled through the use of movable surfaces on the wings and tail.

Concept 4 Spaceships follow the laws of nature.

> Subconcept 4–1 Rocket power must be used to propel vehicles outside the earth's atmosphere.

Concept 5 The space program has achieved success in many areas of science and technology.

Aviation has come a long way in eighty-plus years. Think of it! It was about eighty-nine years ago that Orville Wright on a cold December day was lifted by a primitive airplane ten feet above the sands of Kitty Hawk, North Carolina, and carried about 120 feet along the sandy beach. Later that same afternoon Orville's brother, Wilbur, climbed into the tiny open craft and was carried aloft for a distance of 852 feet. Orville's flight lasted about twelve seconds and Wilbur's fifty-nine seconds.

Today the Concorde supersonic jetliner can fly nonstop from Florida to France, a distance of more than 7,000 miles, in about two and a half hours. By refueling in flight, modern military aircraft can fly around the world. Some airplanes can attain speeds of nearly 2,000 miles per hour and fly at heights exceeding 50,000 feet. And all of this progress in flight has occurred during one human lifespan.

Airplanes are designed to fly in the earth's atmosphere. To fly outside the earth's atmosphere, humans have designed rocket-powered spacecraft that can leave the gaseous envelope that surrounds the earth and fly outside it. Rocket-powered spacecraft have carried men to the moon and cameras and other equipment far out into the solar system to explore the planets. Some spacecraft have left the solar system to cruise through the universe forever. Since the first rockets used for transportation and scientific exploration were launched in the 1950s, the advance of this technology has been even more spectacular than that of the airplane.

In thirty years we have witnessed the first astronaut being fired aloft in a rocketship to land downrange in the Atlantic Ocean, American and Russian astronauts circling the earth in various spacecraft, American astronauts landing on the moon, and unmanned spacecraft sending back to the earth clear and spectacular pictures of the outer planets. And now with each mission of the space shuttle, we see the latest advances in flight technology becoming commonplace. The shuttle is a rocket that first flies like a plane, soaring beyond the atmosphere; then is driven along by a rocket; and finally returns to earth, gliding through the atmosphere like a glider or airplane.

Concept 1

Air moving at different speeds creates regions with different air pressures.

Subconcept 1–1

The lift provided by the wing of an airplane is produced both by moving air pushing on its underside and fast-moving air flowing over the top surface.

Discussion

An object that is stationary in the still air is surrounded by gases of uniform density, and the forces exerted on its surface are also uniform. When the same object is placed in a sea of moving gases (a wind), the forces exerted on the surfaces exposed to the wind are greater than those on the leeward side. The unequal forces created by moving gases can move sailboats over the water, blow leaves from trees, and indeed at times uproot trees. We will see that such a force exerted on the underside of the wing of an airplane can also help keep the aircraft in the air.

Unequal forces may also be created on an object in a second fashion, illustrated by the movement of air over the wing of an airplane. As may be seen in Figure 21–1, the air that strikes the leading edge of the wing is separated

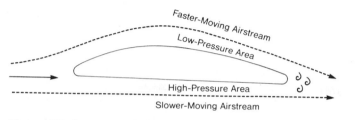

Figure 21–1 ■ An Airplane Wing in an Airstream

as part of the flow is directed beneath the wing and a second portion is directed to flow over the top of the wing. Since the wings of most airplanes are designed so they are tilted upward at an angle to the direction of the flight of the aircraft, the air flowing underneath strikes the bottom of the wing and exerts a force against it much as when the wind blows against the side of a building. Meanwhile the air that flows over the top of the wing must follow a curved surface that has been built into the wing's structure. The air flows freely over the curved wing surface and rejoins the air from below at the rear of the wing. The air flowing over the top surface must flow faster and farther than the air under the wing, and therefore a low air pressure zone develops on the wing's top surface. The difference in the air pressure under and over the wing is small, perhaps on the order of one pound per square inch of surface or less. However, even a small wing that is six feet wide and fifteen feet long has a surface area of nearly 13,000 square inches (15 feet × 6 feet × 144 square inches per square foot = 12,960 square inches). This means that an average force difference of just one pound per square inch will create a force difference of nearly six tons. The total lift created as air passes over an airplane wing is the sum of the force created by air piling up against the bottom of the wing and the force resulting from the difference in the air pressure beneath and above the wing.

Lesson Plan ■ A

Orientation: Grades 3–6.

Content Objective: The children will state the conditions that define when an object is considered to be flying.

Skill Objective: The children will *investigate* and *infer* from their *observations*.

Materials: Various types of paper (heavy and lightweight ditto paper, newspaper, large index cards, and so on), cellophane tape, paper clips, tape measure or measuring sticks.

Evaluation: Students' verbal interaction, students' group problem-solving skills.

Procedure

Divide the class into groups of five or six. In front of each group place pieces of paper having a variety of sizes and weights. While in front of the class, drop a sheet of paper and let it flutter to the floor. Say, "See my paper airplane, doesn't it fly nicely?" Then hold a discussion to define flight so that the class will be able

continued on next page

to distinguish between objects in flight and objects that are simply falling, floating, or hurtling through the air. Some definitions may be: The object is in flight when:

1. It travels a long distance from a small push.

2. It makes consistent or predictable maneuvers in the air.

3. It can go up when thrown down.

4. It can make a reasonable soft landing.

5. It is heavier than air.

In the discussion help the children to differentiate between the movement of light objects, such as balloons, dandelion seeds, and thrown projectiles, and such objects as airplanes, sailplanes, and hang gliders that meet the definitions stated above.

Following the discussion of flight, tell the class that they are to create from the paper before them one object that can fly. Tell them there will be a contest to determine which group's airplane can fly the farthest (greatest distance) and the longest (stay in the air the greatest time). Give the class fifteen to twenty minutes to create paper airplanes and test them (Figure 21–2). Students may create any design using the paper provided. They may attach paper clips and/or tape to change the flight characteristics of their planes. Some rules that may help reduce the noise and confusion are: each group is to work on only one airplane at a time, one person from each group is to test-fly each design, and all flight tests are to be made in a designated area. At some point call the experimentation to a halt and begin the competitive test flights.

Distance. Permit one student from each group to launch their airplane in a specified direction. The

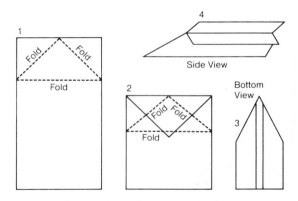

Figure 21–2 ■ Making a Paper Airplane

point at which the airplane touches the ground may be marked by leaving the airplane in place. You may wish to allow several flights for each group and use the best one. Measurement with a tape or measuring stick may be necessary if two competing airplanes do not land close to one another.

Time in Flight. At the signal "5, 4, 3, 2, 1, go!" all airplanes will be launched simultaneously. The airplane that touches the ground last wins. A second or third elimination flight may be necessary to determine the winner.

After the competition the class may discuss the activity. Ask: "What things appeared to make the airplane fly farther? Stay in the air longer?" Which type of paper appeared to be best for constructing the airplane?" Concepts of weight, symmetry, balance (center of gravity), and some terms such as wings, body (fuselage), rudder, and keel may be discussed.

Lesson Plan ■ B

Orientation:	Grades 3–6.
Content Objective:	The children will state that air moving over a curved surface produces a low pressure above the surface.
Skill Objective:	The students will *investigate* and *infer* from their *observations*.

continued on next page

| **Materials:** | An 8 cm × 15 cm sheet of paper. |
| **Evaluation:** | Students' verbal interaction, seat work, and sketches. |

Procedure

Provide each child with an 8 cm × 15 cm sheet of paper. Demonstrate how to hold the paper by the thumb and forefinger and blow gently across the curved surface (see Figure 21–3). As the children blow air gently across the paper, ask, "What is happening to the loose end of the paper?" (The loose end of the paper lifts gently upward toward the moving airstream.) Then ask, "Why is the paper moving *toward* the airstream that is passing over it?" Guide the children to discover that the air pressure above the paper must be reduced by the moving stream and the paper must be forced upward by the higher air pressure on the bottom of the paper. Ask, "What can we say is the shape of the surface of the paper as it is held in your fingers?" "What happens to the air pressure caused by a stream of air moving over a curved surface?" The students should conclude that a stream of air moving

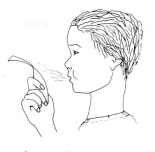

A stream of air will lift the end of a strip of paper because of the Bernoulli effect.

Figure 21–3 ■ Lift Created by an Airstream

over a curved surface will create a low pressure on the surface of the curved object. Have the children draw a sketch of the activity and label the areas of high and low pressure.

Lesson Plan ■ C

Orientation:	Grades 4–6.
Content Objective:	The students will state that air moving over a curved surface will create a low pressure.
Skill Objective:	The children will *investigate, observe,* and make *inferences* from their observations.
Materials:	Ping-Pong ball, string, cellophane tape, large soda straw.
Evaluation:	Students' verbal interaction, sketch.

Procedure

Divide the class into groups of five children. Give each group the materials listed above. Tell them to use the cellophane tape to attach the string to the Ping-Pong ball, as illustrated in Figure 21–4. The string may then be attached to the side of a table or desk so that the Ping-Pong ball hangs freely. The children should blow through the straw for a time, directing the airstream at and around the ball. If after a while the children have not discovered that by blowing the air through the straw alongside the Ping-Pong ball causes the ball to move toward the airstream, suggest that they try this. Ask them, "What force must be pushing the ball toward the moving air?" Remind them through questioning that the Ping-Pong ball has a curved surface

continued on next page

and the air is moving over it. You may remind them of the activity and the concept developed in Lesson Plan B.

The students should conclude that the airstream directed alongside the Ping-Pong ball produces a region of low air pressure and that the higher air pressure on the opposite side of the ball pushes it in the direction of the airstream (low pressure). "What does this show again about curved surfaces with airstreams moving over them?" The teacher may then draw a sketch (or use a prepared poster or photograph) of the cross section of an airplane wing to show the students how the top of the wing is curved, causing air moving over the wing's surface to create a low pressure on the upper surface. The higher pressure on the underside of the wing working against the lower pressure on the upper side of the wing provides the lift that permits airplanes to fly through the atmosphere. Have the chil-

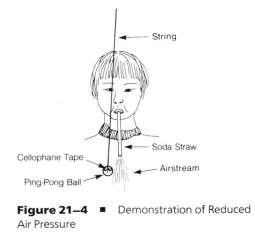

Figure 21–4 ▪ Demonstration of Reduced Air Pressure

dren draw a sketch of an airplane wing, showing the air current flowing under and over it.

Concept 2

The movement of an airplane in flight is the result of the interaction of four forces: thrust, drag, lift, and weight.

Discussion

The engines on an airplane propel it forward through the air, whether it is powered by a propeller or a jet engine. A propeller is shaped so that it pushes against the air in much the same way that the propeller of a boat pushes against the water and thus produces forward motion. A jet engine ejects hot expanding gases at a high velocity, and the reaction to the force of the high-speed stream of hot gases moves the plane forward. The engines provide the *thrust* that moves the airplane through the air.

As any object moves through the atmosphere, a resistance to its movement is created by the air pushing on its surface. The resistance produced by the atmosphere pushing against its surface as an airplane flies through the air is called the *drag*. The drag acts in opposition to

the thrust and tends to slow the airplane down as it moves along.

As described earlier in this chapter, an airplane is able to stay in the air above the ground because of the *lift* created as the atmosphere passes over the curved wing surfaces, producing a low pressure. The wings of most airplanes have their front, or leading, edges tilted upward. The air blowing against the bottom of the wing provides additional *lift* that tends to push the aircraft upward.

The force of gravity acts on an airplane, constantly pulling it toward the earth. This force is the *weight* of the plane. For an airplane to fly, the lift created by the wings must be greater than the force of gravity or the weight of the airplane.

The four forces that interact on an airplane in flight (thrust, drag, lift, and weight) are all interdependent. An increase in thrust will move a plane faster through the atmosphere but, as the plane's speed increases, the friction of the air on the plane's surfaces also increases, tending to slow it down. And any time the weight of an airplane and its contents increases, it will require more lift from the wing surfaces to rise into the air and remain in flight. The lift may be increased by increasing the velocity with which the air flows over the wing's surfaces, and this is accomplished by speeding up the engine and increasing the thrust. An airplane in level constant flight has achieved a balance among the forces of thrust, drag, lift, and weight.

Lesson Plan ■ D

Orientation: Grades 5–6.

Content Objective: The children will describe the interaction of the forces—thrust, drag, lift, and weight—that act on an airplane in flight.

Skill Objective: The children will *infer* relationships among opposing forces.

Materials: A diagram of the forces acting on an airplane in flight.

Evaluation: Students' verbal interaction, sketch.

Procedure

Put a diagram of the forces acting on an airplane in flight (Figure 21–5) on the chalkboard. (A large diagram on a piece of posterboard would also serve the purpose.) Ask, "Using the chart, can you tell me what force holds an airplane in the air? Pulls it to the earth? Causes it to move forward through the air? Resists its movement through the air and tends to slow it down?" After the students have identified the forces, ask, "What would happen to a plane if the thrust were reduced?" (The airplane would slow down and the lift would be reduced.) "What is the advantage of reducing the drag on an airplane?" "How is this done?" (With less drag the same thrust would produce more speed. Drag can be reduced through streamlining the design of the airplane's surface and by cleaning and polishing it.) "What would happen if the lift of an airplane's wings were increased? Are there any ideas of how this might be accomplished?" (The airplane could lift more weight at any given speed. The lift might be increased by making the wings bigger or

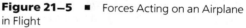

Figure 21–5 ■ Forces Acting on an Airplane in Flight

curving them more. *Note:* This is true only up to a point. Considerations of weight and air turbulence pose limitations on size and curvature of the wings.) "How may the thrust be increased?" (Bigger, more powerful engines. Reduce the drag to take maximum advantage of the available thrust.) Help the students conclude that the four forces on an airplane—thrust, drag, lift, and weight—are all interrelated. Have them draw a sketch of an airplane in flight and label the four forces acting upon it.

Concept 3

The direction of the flight of an airplane is controlled through the use of movable surfaces on the wings and tail.

Discussion

Airplanes may be controlled in flight. The direction of an airplane in flight may be controlled through the use of movable surfaces on the tail surfaces (elevators and rudder) and on the wings (ailerons and flaps, or spoilers). The rudder located on the vertical stabilizer may be deflected right or left. When deflected to the left (see Figure 21–6), the rudder provides a surface on which the passing air pushes, moving the tail of the plane to the right. This orients the nose of the plane to the left, and the craft will move in this new direction. Turning the rudder to the right will cause the reverse situation, with the tail moved to the left and the nose of the airplane and its direction of flight reoriented to the right. Thus, the direction of flight of a plane, right or left, is accomplished by forces acting on the rudder.

The rear surfaces of the horizontal stabilizers located on the tail of the airplane are movable and are called elevators. When the elevators are turned upward into the airstream, the tail of the plane is pushed downward, turning the nose of the plane upward. With an increase in power, this position will cause the craft to climb. Conversely, when the elevators are turned downward, the air striking them will move the tail upward, pointing the nose downward, and the plane will glide or dive toward the earth. Thus, the upward or downward orientation of the flight of an airplane is controlled by the elevators located on its horizontal stabilizers, and both flat right and left turns and upward and downward orientation are controlled through the rudder and elevators located on the tail of the plane.

To bank an airplane and turn (perform a bank turn), the pilot must raise one wing, caus-

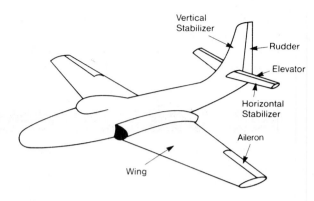

Figure 21–6 ■ The Parts of an Airplane

ing the other to drop, while using the rudder to push the tail around in the desired direction. The simultaneous raising of one aileron and lowering of the other is accomplished with a single movement of the control stick. The airstream pushing against the raised aileron on one wing pushes that wing downward, and the airstream pushing against the lowered aileron on the other wing pushes that wing upward. The rudder located on the vertical stabilizer is controlled by foot pressure placed on foot pedals. To make a banked turn, the pilot must tilt the control stick to one side by hand while placing pressure on the proper rudder control pedal. A *left* bank requires a *leftward* movement of the aileron control stick and pressure on the *left* rudder pedal. The opposite is true to execute a right bank.

Lesson Plan ■ E

Orientation:	Grades 5–6.
Content Objective:	The children will state that the up-and-down direction of an airplane's flight may be controlled with the elevators, and the right and left direction of an airplane's flight may be controlled with the use of the rudder.
Skill Objective:	The children will *observe* and *infer* from their observations. They will record their observations.

continued on next page

Materials: Model paper airplane with adjustable tail control surfaces (rudder and elevators), 5" × 8" index cards, thin soda straws, cellophane tape, thin copper wire (#20 or #22 gauge), scissors, paper clips.

Evaluation: Students' verbal interaction, students' group problem-solving skills, laboratory worksheets, log, and reports.

Procedure

Divide the class into groups of five or six. Provide them with directions for constructing an experimental model airplane as illustrated in Figure 21–7.

1. Fold a 5" × 8" index card lengthwise along its center.

2. Use scissors to cut the outline of an airplane fuselage (body) from the folded card. (You may wish to provide a template that the children can use to trace the outline of the fuselage.)

3. Tape a 2" piece of a small-diameter soda straw or plastic tubing in a vertical position about 2½" to 3" from the nose.

4. Tape a 2" piece of thin copper wire to the inside surface of the rudder along the fold.

5. Fold the index card along the seam and tape the edges together.

6. To make the horizontal stabilizers and elevators, cut a 4" × 4" square from a second index card and fold it along the center line of the 4" axis so that it forms a doubled 2" × 4" rectangle.

7. Tape a 2" piece of small-diameter copper wire on the inside of the folded rectangle. Tape the edges of the folded card together.

8. Take the fuselage section previously made and cut a 2" horizontal slot about ¼" from the bottom below the rudder surface. Insert the horizontal stabilizers and elevators and tape them to the tail of the fuselage, adjusting as needed so the inserted surface is at right angles to the fuselage.

9. Cut slots on the horizontal stabilizer surfaces on each side of the fuselage (rudder) to form freely moving elevators. Also cut into the vertical stabilizer as needed to form a freely moving rudder.

10. Lay the model airplane (without wings) flat on your finger and find the position in which it bal-

A. Index Card

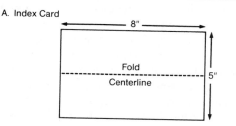

B. Fuselage

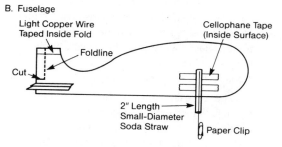

C. Horizontal Stabilizers—Elevators (Top View)

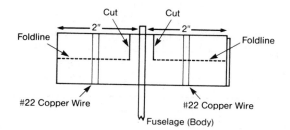

Figure 21–7 ■ The Rudder and Elevators as Control Surfaces

ances without support. On the balancing line about 1" from the bottom of the fuselage, use a sharp object to pierce a hole through the fuselage and insert a short (about 1½") section of small-diameter soda straw or plastic tubing. Tape the soda straw section to the fuselage.

continued on next page

The children should now have the experimental airplane (without wings) that is illustrated in Figure 21–7.

Direct the groups of children to perform the following activities using their experimental model airplanes:

1. Turn the rudder to one side, say, the right. (The wire stiffener in the rudder should maintain it in the desired position.) Have the groups suspend their airplanes by pinning a straightened paper clip into the soda straw that projects vertically downward from the fuselage. Have the children blow a gentle stream of air at the nose of the airplane and observe what happens. (The nose of the airplane turns toward the side of the airplane that has the rudder protruding. The tail of the model is pushed away, causing the nose to rotate toward the side from which the rudder protrudes.) Have them repeat the activity, turning the rudder in the opposite direction. Have the students record their observations.

2. Now have the children straighten the rudder so that it is aligned with the fuselage. They should bend each of the elevators downward so their surfaces protrude below the horizontal stabilizers. Have them place the straightened paper clip into the horizontal piece of soda straw and, using a finger if necessary to help balance the model, gently blow toward its nose. (The moving airstream should strike the lowered elevator surfaces, forcing the nose of the model upward.) Have the children move the elevators to a raised

position and repeat the activity. (The nose of the model is forced downward.)

Permit the groups of children time to freely experiment with their models, adjusting the rudder and elevator surfaces and blowing gently on the nose of the models. Then ask, "What have we found from this activity?" and "How can the direction of the flight of an airplane be controlled?" The students should state that the rudder may be used to control the airplane's side-to-side directions and the elevators may be used to control the airplane's upward and downward motions.

Note: This activity may be extended by building wings with movable ailerons and attaching them to the fuselage. A soda straw may then be inserted into the nose of the fuselage to act as an axis of rotation when a long wire is inserted. With one aileron elevated and the second depressed, have the students press a finger gently against the tail to hold it in place and blow directly at the nose of the plane: the fuselage should rotate about the wire. However, the proper balance and attachment of the wings is difficult to attain and this extension of the lesson can be very time-consuming.

Power for Flight

The speed of a plane is controlled in level flight through the manipulation of the throttle, speeding up the engine or slowing it down. An airplane's speed is also affected by its altitude; it will speed up while descending and slow down while climbing.

Airplanes are powered by a variety of fuel-burning engines. The piston-driven internal-combustion engine rotates a propeller that

pushes against the atmosphere and moves the craft forward. This engine is in design very similar to the gasoline-powered engine used in the automobile. As may be seen in Figure 21–8, gasoline is drawn into each cylinder of the engine as the piston moves downward and then is compressed and ignited by a spark from a spark plug. This controlled explosion in a confined space forces the piston downward, and as it returns it exhausts the burned gases through a valve. Thus, the strokes of a four-cycle piston

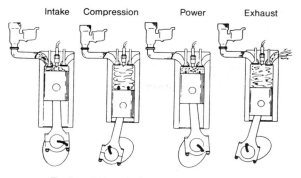

Intake   Compression   Power   Exhaust

The four strokes of a four-stroke-cycle engine
are intake, compression, power, and exhaust.

Figure 21–8 ■ The Four-Stroke Piston Engine

engine, in order of their functions, are: intake, compression, power, and exhaust (see Figure 21–8). The up-and-down motion of the piston is converted to rotary motion by a crankshaft. This motion is used to drive the airplane's propeller.

The gas turbine operates much like the steam engine. Fuels such as gasoline or, more commonly, kerosene are ignited in a combustion chamber, and the hot gases are directed to flow over the blades of a rotating turbine, giving power to the turbine. The rotational motion of the turbine is utilized to drive auxiliary equipment such as electric generators and large propellers (see Figure 21–9).

The jet engine has become increasingly popular for all but small aircraft. The jet engine looks much like a turbine engine, but instead of using the stream of hot gases to turn a turbine, the engine provides propulsion simply by ejecting the gases from the rear.

Concept 4

Spaceships follow the laws of nature.

Discussion

The laws of mechanics do not differentiate between bodies that occur naturally in space and bodies that we place there. Whether a body is confined to the earth, is a satellite, or moves freely through space depends on the relationship between two quantities—gravitational force and the body's inertia. When gravitational force exceeds inertia, a body will remain on the earth. When inertia exceeds gravitational force, the body will move freely into space. When the two are in a state of balance (equilibrium), the body will become a satellite orbiting the earth.

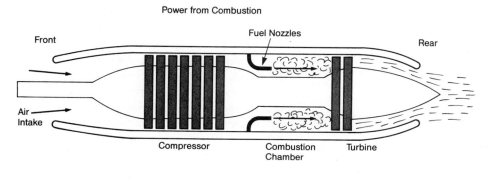

Power from Combustion

Front   Rear

Fuel Nozzles

Air
Intake

Compressor   Combustion   Turbine
                   Chamber

Cross section of a gas turbine. The shaft may be
used to drive a propeller or an electric generator.

Figure 21–9 ■ The Gas Turbine

A satellite's position in relation to the earth depends solely on its speed. Satellites of all sizes, shapes, and masses would maintain the same orbital distance from the earth if they were traveling at the same velocity. The moon is a satellite of the earth. It follows that an artificial satellite of any dimensions to maintain the same orbiting distance as the moon must attain the same speed through space. Chart 21–1 relates height above earth, velocity, and the time required to make a single orbit.

Chart 21–1 ▪ Height, Velocity, and Time of Orbit of Selected Earth Satellites

Height Above Earth (miles)	Velocity (ft/sec)	Time for Each Orbit
0	25,900	84 minutes
100	25,600	88 minutes
400	24,700	98 minutes
1,000	23,100	118 minutes
23,000	10,060	1 day
230,000 (Moon)	3,360	27days

Lesson Plan ▪ F

Orientation: Grades 5–6.

Content Objective: The children will answer objective questions that deal with a satellite's velocity and radius of orbit.

Skill Objective: The children must *infer* relationships between the velocities of artificial satellites and their orbiting distances.

Materials: A worksheet containing the information in Chart 21–1.

Evaluation: Students' verbal interaction, reports.

Procedure

Supply the class with copies of Chart 21–1. Discuss such questions as: "Why cannot a satellite orbit at zero feet above the earth?" (Obstructions, uneven terrain, and so on.) "Could a satellite orbit at ten miles above the ground? This is above the tallest mountain." (No. Heat and drag caused by the earth's atmosphere make this impossible. The satellite would slow down and/or burn up.) "If you wanted to put a satellite in orbit so that it would stay above one spot on the earth below, what velocity would you have the satellite attain?" (A velocity of 10,060 feet per second. At this velocity the time for one orbit is one day. This means the satellite would travel above one spot on the earth as the earth revolved below.) "Do we have any satellites that have an orbit like this?" (Yes. The communications satellites such as *Telstar* are parked in what are called stationary orbits above one spot on the earth. Radio signals are broadcast to *Telstar*, which rebroadcasts the signals back to earth. This enables the signals to span huge distances.) "What is the moon's approximate velocity through space?" (Approximately 3,360 feet per second. This must be true since the time of the moon's orbit is approximately twenty-seven days.) *Note:* The escape velocity of a rocket from earth is generally accepted to be around 26,000 feet per second. Have the children write a statement describing the relationship between the velocity of a satellite and its distance and time of orbit above the earth.

Orientation:	Grades 4–6.
Content Objective:	The children will state that the single factor that determines whether a projectile goes into orbit is its velocity.
Skill Objective:	The children are required to *observe* a model of an earth–satellite system and to *infer* the transfer of the expressed relationship to the actual bodies.
Materials:	Chalk and chalkboard.
Evaluation:	Students' verbal interaction, report.

Procedure

Draw a sketch similar to Figure 21–10 on the board. Explain that it represents an exaggeration of what happens when a boy throws a ball. Ask the children: "What happens when you throw a ball harder and harder?" (It goes faster and farther.) "In which instance did the boy throw the ball the least hard?" (When it fell at A.) "What happened as he threw the ball with more and more velocity?" (It went farther and farther.) "What is happening at D when he threw the ball so that it traveled very, very fast?" (The ball is going all the way around the earth. It is going into orbit.) Remind the class that what caused the ball to orbit was the increase in velocity. Have the children write a statement on what they learned about objects in orbit.

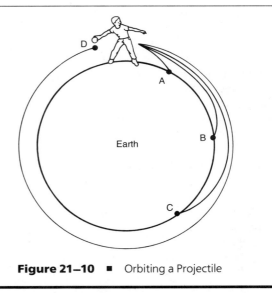

Figure 21–10 ▪ Orbiting a Projectile

Subconcept 4–1

Rocket power must be used to propel vehicles outside the earth's atmosphere.

Discussion

Rocket power has proved to be the only feasible solution to the problem of transporting people and vehicles beyond the earth's atmosphere. Combustion engines, such as the piston engine and the jet engine, can operate only on atmospheric oxygen. *Rocket engines* carry their own oxygen supply and can therefore operate beyond the atmosphere. The fact that they carry oxygen as well as fuel poses problems of weight control for the rocket designer. Each pound of fuel adds to the total weight of the vehicle and to the thrust required to accelerate it to the desired velocity.

Artificial satellites and other spacecraft are not new concepts. But only as recently as 1957–1958 were the first earth satellites launched. Even the idea of a voyage to the moon is not new. It was talked about nearly 2,000 years ago. But in 1961, President John F. Kennedy set the goal of putting an American on the moon within a decade; and in 1969 it happened. Accomplishing a task of such incredible proportions required almost every kind of resource American technology could bring to bear and cost many billions of dollars. Behind the crew were the efforts and skills of hundreds of thousands of scientists and engineers, experts in management and finance, technicians, and laborers. Since we are today a living part of perhaps the most exciting adventure on which we have embarked in history, it is appropriate for each of us to have an understanding of the history and promise of the new aerospace technology.

The dramatic "giant step for mankind" made by astronaut Neil Armstrong when he stepped on the moon brought to a climax centuries of speculation and dreaming by numerous philosophers and writers. Early in Western history, poets and storytellers roamed the Mediterranean world, spinning tales about moon journeys. It was a Greek master of satire named Lucian who first put a moon voyage into written form in the second century A.D. In "True History" Lucian deliberately spoofed these widespread tales as he told of a trip to the moon wherein a ship was propelled to the satellite by a huge waterspout.

In 1865 Jules Verne wrote *De la Terre à la Lune (From the Earth to the Moon)*. Verne's ideas were planted a number of years later in the mind of a Russian scientist, K. E. Tsiolkovskiy, who laid the foundation of modern rocket dynamics.

Science fiction writers and fans got another boost, albeit unintentionally, when Dr. Robert H. Goddard published his serious work *A Means of Reaching Very High Altitudes* in 1919. Much to the dismay of Dr. Goddard, called the father of American rocketry, his ideas were snatched up by the Sunday supplement writers and interpreted to mean moon journeys were at hand.

Rockets as Weapons of War

In the thirteenth century, the Chinese hitched a tube of primitive gunpowder to an arrow and created an effective rocket weapon to defend Beijing against the Mongols. Some time in 1500 a Chinese named Wan Hoo devised a chair with two kites and forty-seven gunpowder rockets on the back. The rockets were duly ignited, presumably with punk. Whatever orbit Wan Hoo achieved in the ensuing fireworks certainly was his last one, and human space flight went into eclipse until the 1960s.

Our national anthem speaks of "the rocket's red glare" at Fort McHenry in the War of 1812. Those were British rockets, fired in an unsuccessful attempt to reduce the American fortress at Baltimore. They had been devised by Sir William Congreve about a dozen years earlier, and many thousands of them were fired during that war.

In 1923, Germany's Dr. Hermann Oberth, then a student, wrote the American Dr. Goddard for information on rocket flight and later published his own work, "The Rocket into Interplanetary Space." Two unfortunate things happened thereafter. The United States virtually ignored the possibilities of long-distance rocketry, and Nazi Germany did not. So it happened that in the early 1940s during World War II, London found itself under attack by 200-mile-range V-2 missiles, arching 60 miles high across the English Channel at 3,500 miles per hour. The V-2 rockets came too late to affect the outcome of the war, and the United States was alerted to a new and urgent field of rocketry to provide the vehicles of the future, both for weapons and as a means of propelling spaceships.

The early Chinese "fire arrows," the British Congreves, and even our familiar Fourth of July skyrockets have certain things in common. One, they are basically tubes of gunpowder, or liquid fuels, lighted at the bottom to make them go in the opposite direction. Two, they are similar in principle to military and space booster rockets such as Atlas, Titan, Minuteman, Polaris, and Saturn, as well as the Space Shuttle. In each case, some kind of fuel is burned in an oxidant. Together fuel and oxidant are called propellents. Great amounts of hot gases are suddenly created, resulting in very high pressures in the combustion chambers in which they are burned. In the combustion chambers of a rocket, these gases try to expand equally in all directions, pressing upward and downward with equal pressure. The same pounds-per-square-inch pressure is exerted against the top of the combustion chamber as against the bottom. At the bottom, however, there is a relatively small opening in the chamber, called the throat. Below this is the exhaust nozzle, flaring out like a bell. Once through the throat, the expanding gases continue pushing in all directions, pushing out against the widening sides of the nozzle. As a given volume of gas reaches the skirt of the nozzle, it is spread out over a much greater area than at the throat. Hence, the pressure per square inch on the skirt is less than within the combustion chamber. Nevertheless, the sum of all the internal pressures acting on the combustion chamber and nozzle skirt in a forward or up direction is more than the sum of all the pressures acting in a rearward direction. It is this net difference that makes the rocket engine and the vehicle attached to it fly.

Rocket Staging

A rocket-powered vehicle must be as light as possible for best efficiency, and designers have therefore adopted the concept of staging. The fuel capsules and engines of each stage are jettisoned after their fuel has been consumed, thus reducing the mass of the vehicle. When the mass is reduced, the remaining rocket engines require less thrust to propel the vehicle to the desired velocity. Most rockets used to place satellites in orbit or to propel vehicles to the moon and planets are multiple staged. A huge, first-stage booster engine drops away after lifting the rocket beyond the upper reaches of the atmosphere and provides it with a velocity of several thousand miles per hour. A second stage generally provides the velocity required for orbiting the satellite. A third stage may be used to adjust the orbit of the vehicle or to propel it into space.

Today's rockets are enormous. Saturn V rockets used to propel the Apollo astronauts to the moon stand as tall as a thirty-six-story building, weigh more than a navy destroyer, and produce 1.5 million pounds of thrust (Figure 21–11).

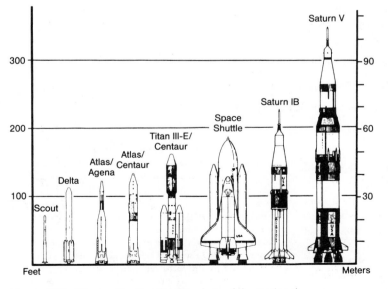

Figure 21–11 ■ The Family of Rockets of the National Aeronautics and Space Administration (NASA)

Lesson Plan ▪ H

Orientation:	Grades K–4.
Content Objective:	The children will state that a balloon may be propelled by escaping air and a rocket may be propelled by escaping gases.
Skill Objective:	The children are required to *observe* free-flying balloons and to *infer* the causes of their motion.
Materials:	Six balloons of various sizes.
Evaluation:	Students' verbal interaction, sketch.

Procedure

Distribute six balloons of varying size throughout the classroom. Ask the children to blow up the balloons and hold them until you tell them what to do. Then say: "When I say go, release the balloons." Tell the children to watch the balloons carefully. Ask: "What happened?" (The balloons flew all over.) "What caused the balloons to move?" (The air came out.) "If we can only cause something to move by pushing on it, what can we say the air did?" (The air pushed on the balloon, causing it to fly.) "How might this be like a rocket?" (Air, gases come out of a rocket and cause it to move.) Have the students draw a sketch of a rocket being propelled by escaping gas.

Lesson Plan ▪ I

Orientation:	Grades 3–6.
Content Objective:	The children will state that the thrust of a rocket engine is determined by the mass of the escaping gases and their velocities.
Skill Objective:	The children are required to *infer* a relationship between projectiles expelled from a vehicle and the motion of the vehicle.
Materials:	A skateboard or roller skates, a briefcase, books.
Evaluation:	Students' verbal interaction, reports.

Procedure

Have a boy stand on a skateboard or on roller skates, keeping them parallel. Ask him to hold an empty briefcase in front of him and toss it to you, using both hands. Now place six or eight books in the briefcase and ask the boy to repeat the procedure. Ask: "What was the difference in the reaction when an empty briefcase and one with books in it were thrown?" (John went backward faster, farther, when the books were in the briefcase.) "What was changed that made the difference in John's movement?" (The weight of the briefcase was increased.)[1] Now return the briefcase full of books to John and ask him to toss it to you

---

[1] It is appropriate to introduce children to the term *mass* at this point. The weight of an object is the force of attraction between the object and the earth or other planets. The weight of an object changes depending on where it is located in the universe. The mass of an object expresses the amount of stuff of which it is made. The mass of a body is best defined by the force required to speed it up, slow it down, or alter the direction of its motion. The mass of an object is the same everywhere in the universe.

continued on next page

as fast as he can. You may wish to place several children around him to prevent a fall. After John has tossed the briefcase, ask: "How was the result of this toss different from the last toss?" (John went backward faster.) "What two things appeared to make John go backward faster?" (Putting books in the briefcase [adding weight] and throwing the briefcase faster.) Now you may relate the children's observations to the thrust of a rocket engine. "How is this like a rocket engine?" The children may be led to conclude that thrust is determined by the weight of the escaping gases and the velocity with which they are ejected from the engine. Have the children write a statement that expresses what they learned about the thrust of a rocket.

Concept 5

The space program has achieved success in many areas of science and technology.

Discussion

Since the launch of the first Vanguard rockets at Cape Canaveral, Florida, in 1958, more than three hundred major flights have been launched into space from this and other facilities. Starting with the grapefruit-sized sphere that was the National Aeronautics and Space Administration's initial artificial satellite, there has been a progression of larger and more imaginative and daring ventures into space. Project Mercury was conceived in 1958, and several years later a series of flights sent astronauts orbiting the earth in a bell-shaped capsule that was less than two meters wide at the base and three meters in height. The orbiting mass of the entire loaded *Mercury* capsule was about 1,450 kilograms (3,200 lb), less than the weight of many mid-sized cars. The success of the Mercury program led to the development of larger rockets and capsules under the Gemini program, and earth-orbiting flights of capsules that contained two astronauts. When the series of nineteen flights of the Gemini program was completed, astronauts had logged nearly 1,000 hours in space. During this series of missions, astronauts conducted the first extravehicular activity (EVA) or space walk, made ten orbital rendezvous, and docked two spacecraft together nine times. The United States was ready to undertake the tremendous challenge of sending humans to the moon.

In May, 1961, President Kennedy announced the grand goal of sending humans to the moon and returning them to earth. Following his statement of national commitment to the space adventure were seven years of the most intense and dramatic research and development activity ever seen. In this brief time, the Saturn IB and Saturn V rockets were built to lift 126,418 kilograms (139 tons, or about the weight of three medium-sized houses) into orbit. Other prominent research efforts were in the areas of solar power, health and nutrition, computer technology, and materials development. Following a series of seven launches of manned and unmanned vehicles, on December 21, 1968, *Apollo 8* lifted off from the Space Center and took its three-man crew on a 147-hour, half-million-mile flight that included ten orbits around the moon. Men had gone to the moon and returned! Then, following several more earth- and moon-orbiting missions, the national goal set by President Kennedy was achieved by Astronaut Neil Armstrong in 1969 as he stepped from the lunar module of *Apollo 11* onto the moon's surface. Six more moon landings were accomplished without a loss of life. Men had walked, worked, and played on the moon. The Apollo program drew to a close in December, 1972.

After the Apollo moon landings were accomplished, there followed a slowdown in space exploration in the ensuing five or six years, with major launches limited to four Skylab missions, during which scientific experiments were conducted, and the Apollo-Soyuz mission that saw the rendezvous and hookup of Russian and American spacecraft. Current U.S. efforts in space are centered around the development of the Space Shuttle, a reusable vehicle that is half rocket and half aircraft, capable of reentering the earth's atmosphere at very high speeds and, after slowing down, gliding to a landing on the earth. The reusable nature of the Space Shuttle and the first-stage solid-rocket boosters is designed to greatly reduce the cost of sending people and materials into space. Eventually the Space Shuttle is intended to be economically self-sufficient, carrying communications satellites, experiments, and even production processes of private industry into space.

In addition to manned space flight, NASA has conducted a number of launches of unmanned vehicles for purposes of studying the sun, the earth, and other planets, and of positioning communications satellites. A summary of the types of launches conducted at the Spaceport at Cape Kennedy may be seen in Chart 21–2.

Chart 21–2 ▪ Major NASA Launches

Mission Name	Time Period(s)	Number of Flights
Space Applications and Technology: *Launch and Space Vehicle Development*		
SATURN	1961–64, 1966	6
CENTAUR	1962–66	8
FIRE (Flight Investigation of Reentry Environment)	1964–65	2
SERT (Space Electric Rocket Tests)	1970	1
TITAN III-CENTAUR	1974	1
Space Applications and Technology: *Applications Technology*		
ATS (Applications Technology Satellites)	1966–69, 1974	6
STRATEGIC DEFENSE INITIATIVE	1986, 1988	2
Manned Space Flights		
MERCURY (Suborbital)	1959–61	9
MERCURY (Orbital)	1961–63	8
GEMINI (Suborbital)	1965	1
GEMINI (Orbital)	1964–66	18
APOLLO (MSFN Test & Training Satellites)	1967–69, 1971	4
APOLLO (Suborbital)	1966	2
APOLLO (Earth Orbital)	1964–65, 1967–69	10
APOLLO (Lunar Orbital)	1968–69	2
APOLLO (Lunar Landing)	1969–72	7
SKYLAB	1973	4
APOLLO-SOYUZ TEST PROJECT	1975	1
SPACE SHUTTLE	1982–Present	30+
Earth Observations: *Meteorology*		
TIROS (Television Infrared Observations Satellites)	1960–65	9
TIROS OPERATIONAL	1965–69	10

continued on next page

IMPROVED TIROS OPERATIONAL	1970–76	8
NIMBUS	1964–78	8
GEOS (Geostationary Operational Environmental Satellites)	1974–87	10
INTERNATIONAL GEOSTATIONARY METEOROLOGICAL SATELLITES	1977	2

Earth Observations: *Geodesy*

GEOS (Geodetic Satellites)	1965, 1966, 1968, 1975	4
LAGEOS (Laser Geodynamic Satellites)	1976	1

Earth Observations: *Earth Resources Technology*

ERTS (Earth Resources Technology Satellites)	1972, 1975, 1978, 1982, 1984	5

Communications: *Technology Development*

ECHO	1960, 1962, 1964	5
TELSTAR	1962–63	2
RELAY	1962, 1964	2
SYNCOM	1963–64	3
SYMPHONIE (French-German Experimental Communications Satellites)	1974–75	2
COMMUNICATIONS TECHNOLOGY SATELLITES	1976–78	6

Communications: *Operational Systems*

INTERNATIONAL TELECOMMUNICATIONS SATELLITE ORGANIZATION	1965–78, 1980–85	37
WESTAR (U.S. Domestic Communications Satellites)	1974, 1979, 1982	5
RCA (U.S. Domestic Communications Satellites)	1975–76, 1979, 1981–83	8
MARISAT (U.S. Maritime Communications Satellites)	1976	3
FLTSATCOM (U.S. Fleet Satellite Communications Spacecraft)	1978–81, 1986–87, 1989	8
COMSTAR (U.S. Domestic Communications Satellites)	1976, 1978, 1981	4
SKYNET (British Communications Satellites)	1969–70, 1974	4
TELESAT (Canadian Domestic Communications Satellites)	1972–73, 1975, 1978, 1982	5
NATOSAT (North Atlantic Treaty Organization Communications Satellites)	1970–71, 1976–78, 1984	6
PALAPA (Indonesian Domestic Communication Satellites)	1976–77, 1987	3
SBS-A (Satellite Business Systems)	1980–81	2
INSAT	1982	1
TELSTAR	1983	1

Space Science: *Physics and Astronomy*

BEACON	1958–59	2
VANGUARD	1959	4
EXPLORER	1959, 1969, 1971–73, 1975, 1977–78, 1981, 1988	38

continued on next page

OSO (Orbiting Solar Observatories)	1962, 1965, 1967, 1969, 1971, 1975	8
OGO (Orbiting Geophysical Observatories)	1964–69	6
OAO (Orbiting Astronomical Observatories)	1966, 1968, 1970, 1972	4
HEAO (High Energy Astronomy Observatories)	1977–79	3
SCATHA (Spacecraft Charging at High Altitude)	1979	1
SMM (Solar Maximum Mission)	1980	1
Space Science: *International Space Science*		
AERIEL (British)	1962	1
ALOUETTE (Canadian)	1962, 1965	2
ISIS (Canadian)	1969, 1971	2
ESA (European Space Agency)	1968, 1972, 1975, 1977–78	6
INTASTAT (Spanish)	1974	1
HELIOS (German)	1974, 1976	2
IRAS (Infrared Astronomical Satellite)	1983	1
EXOSAT	1984	1
ACTIVE MAGNETOSPHERIC PARTICLE TRACER EXPLORERS	1984	1
Space Science: *Bioscience*		
BIOFLIGHTS (Suborbital Primate Flights)	1958–59	2
BIOS (Biological Satellites)	1966, 1967, 1969	3
Space Science: *Lunar and Planetary*		
PIONEER (Lunar)	1958–60	7
PIONEER (Interplanetary)	1960, 1965–69, 1972–73, 1978	10
RANGER	1961–62, 1964–65	9
SURVEYOR	1967–68	7
LUNAR ORBITER	1966–67	5
MARINER	1962, 1964, 1967, 1969, 1971, 1973	10
VIKING	1975	2
VOYAGER	1977	2

Some Setbacks in the Space Shuttle Program

Three different space shuttles had flown a total of twenty-four successful test flight and operational missions between March 1981 and January 1986, when on January 28 the *Challenger* exploded in the air just a minute and a half after lift-off killing all seven members of the crew. Flights were halted for two and a half years so that problems related to the accident could be investigated and general safety concerns ad-

dressed. In 1990 the *Hubble Telescope* was placed in orbit. The $1.5 billion, 43-foot-long, 25-pound telescope was designed to give astronomers their clearest view ever of distant stars and galaxies from its orbit 370 miles above the earth's surface. Unfortunately, scientists discovered that an error had been made in the manufacture of the large eight-foot mirror contained in the telescope, allowing it to focus on only the closest objects, such as the planets of the solar system. Plans have been made to send astronauts into space to replace the faulty mirror and

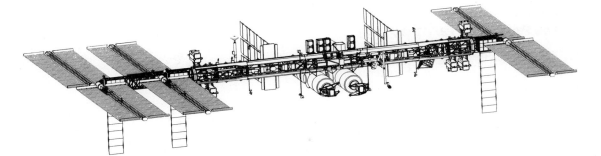

Figure 21–12 ■ The Space Station

perform any other necessary repairs to make the telescope operational.

These events have caused NASA officials to evaluate the role of the shuttle in the total space program. In the future the space shuttle will remain as a valuable part of the space effort, but will share the task with disposable launch vehicles such as updated versions of the Atlas.

The Space Station

NASA is now working to build a space station that will orbit the earth at an altitude of about 300 miles. This multipurpose facility will serve as a laboratory for conducting basic research, an observatory for exploring the earth and the vast reaches of space, a repair garage for satellites and other space vehicles, an industrial facility to manufacture exotic metal alloys, perfect crystals, and pure medicines, a station to assemble structures too large to haul in the space shuttle, and a storage facility for all manner of equipment and spare parts required for repair, replacement equipment, and to maintain support systems necessary for those who work and visit there.

The Structure of the Space Station

The dimensions and scope of the functions the space station will serve will change due to budgetary considerations, but the basic structure of the space station will be designed around the "power tower" model. This model features a 122-meter-long spine (about the length of a football field, including the end zones) to which is attached two 90-meter-tall "keels" that form the appearance of a huge rectangular wing. These structures, which are constructed of materials in the shape of beams and struts, give the space station the overall look of a huge airplane built from an erector set. (See Figure 21-12.) Two pressurized modules 13.6 meters long and 5 meters in diameter are placed near the intersection of the keels and the spine to serve as a laboratory and living quarters. The space station will support a crew of eight persons, who will be rotated every three months. An environmental control and life support system (ECLSS) will recycle and remove contaminates from the air as well as liquid wastes such as urine and atmospheric water vapor. Two large panels containing photovoltaic cells will supply electricity for the space station. A docking facility will enable the space shuttle to resupply the facility with personnel, food, and supplies.

The Unmanned Platform

Two or more unmanned platforms will be placed in polar orbits and will be serviced by the space station. The unmanned platforms will provide additional changeable accommodations for activities that require conditions free from disturbance and contamination. An Orbiting Maneuvering Vehicle (OMV) will be used to travel between the space station and its platforms.

Activities to Learn
Space Program Terminology

The following activities may be used to teach or reinforce student knowledge of the terminology associated with space.

A	S	Y	R	U	C	R	E	M	E	P	X	I	N	U
S	E	T	I	L	L	E	T	A	S	D	W	A	O	A
T	T	A	L	F	O	X	E	R	U	C	A	X	I	B
E	A	R	A	L	O	S	L	S	N	V	O	I	T	S
R	T	S	G	S	A	M	E	T	E	O	R	S	A	A
O	O	U	R	A	N	U	S	K	V	J	U	T	L	T
I	R	E	A	R	T	H	C	O	M	E	T	S	L	U
D	G	L	V	A	M	O	O	J	U	P	I	T	E	R
S	U	N	I	E	C	A	P	S	H	I	B	S	T	N
N	A	S	T	A	R	S	E	O	M	A	R	A	S	E
M	R	D	Y	N	S	I	R	S	N	O	O	M	N	N
T	I	N	S	T	E	N	A	L	P	L	U	T	O	E
R	I	Q	N	E	P	T	U	N	E	Z	A	N	C	P

SUN	METEORS	MARS	ROTATES	PLANETS
EARTH	GRAVITY	URANUS	TELESCOPE	SPACE
SATURN	SATELLITES	SOLAR	VENUS	COMETS
PLUTO	AXIS	STARS	JUPITER	ORBIT
MOONS	MERCURY	ASTEROIDS	NEPTUNE	CONSTELLATION

Word Search

Directions

Before you work this seek-a-word, write the words in alphabetical order on another sheet of paper.

X	Y	I	G	L	I	F	T	O	F	F	M	C
S	B	J	N	I	R	A	V	N	N	Q	O	P
H	P	U	O	L	L	O	P	A	C	Z	R	H
U	K	U	P	S	R	E	T	S	O	O	B	J
T	F	O	T	E	T	X	T	A	Y	Y	I	B
T	S	P	S	N	L	A	U	N	C	H	T	D
L	L	E	M	D	I	X	R	R	L	Z	E	Y
E	W	B	R	O	C	K	E	T	E	M	R	O
X	G	S	A	X	N	W	Q	W	R	T	B	U
T	L	P	W	R	I	G	H	T	N	E	P	N
X	E	A	H	O	R	B	T	E	R	P	K	G
O	N	C	V	R	A	S	E	W	G	A	Q	C
U	N	E	P	P	I	R	C	R	A	N	U	L

Word Search

Directions

Find the twenty aerospace names or terms in the grid. Words may be found horizontally, vertically, diagonally, or backwards.

Lost on the Moon[2]

Orientation:	Grades 3–6.
Concept:	Survival in space depends on equipment available.
Purpose:	To determine by group censensus the rank importance of survival items.
Background Information:	The students are members of a space crew originally scheduled to rendezvous with a mother ship on the lighted surface of the moon. However, because of mechanical difficulties, their ship has been forced to land at a spot some 200 miles from the rendezvous point. During the moon landing, much of the equipment on board was damaged, and since survival depends on reaching the mother ship, the fifteen most critical items available must be chosen for the 200-mile trip.
Materials:	Copy of "Lost on the Moon Survival Items" for each student (see below), pencils.
Procedure:	1. Divide class into workable groups (five to six students per group).
	2. Explain that this is an exercise in group decision making. Each group is to use the method of group consensus in reaching its decision. This means that the rating for each of the fifteen survival items must be agreed on by each group member before it becomes a part of the group decision. Consensus is difficult to reach, therefore not every ranking will meet with everyone's approval. Try, as a group, to make each ranking one with which all group members can at least partially agree. *Note:* This should be done as individual decisions first, *then* as a group activity.
	3. Allow fifteen minutes for group decisions.
	4. *Postlab.* Review each item, check group decisions, compile data, then compare to NASA ranking (see Key to "Lost on the Moon").
Evaluation:	Students' verbal interaction, students' group problem-solving skills.

"Lost on the Moon" Survival Items

Your spaceship has just crash-landed on the dark side of the moon. You were scheduled to rendezvous with your mother ship 200 miles away on the lighted surface of the moon, but the rough landing has ruined your ship and destroyed all the equipment on board, except for the fifteen items listed below.

Your crew's survival depends on reaching the mother ship, so you must choose the most critical items available for the 200-mile trip. Your task is to rank the fifteen items in terms of their importance for your survival.

Scoring

Error points = absolute difference between your ranks and NASA's (no + or −).

0–25	Excellent—The force is with you!
26–32	Good
33–45	Average
46–55	Fair
56–70	Poor
71–112	Very poor—Did you fake it or just use earth-bound logic?

---

[2]"Lost on the Moon" is a noncopyrighted activity of the National Aeronautics and Space Administration (NASA).

"Lost on the Moon" Survival Items

Items	Your Own Ranking	Error Points	Your Group Ranking	Error Points
Box of matches	_____	_____	_____	_____
Food concentrate	_____	_____	_____	_____
Fifty feet of nylon rope	_____	_____	_____	_____
Parachute silk	_____	_____	_____	_____
Solar-powered portable heating unit	_____	_____	_____	_____
Two 45-caliber pistols	_____	_____	_____	_____
One case of condensed milk	_____	_____	_____	_____
Stellar map (of the moon's constellation)	_____	_____	_____	_____
Two 100-pound tanks of oxygen	_____	_____	_____	_____
Self-inflating life raft	_____	_____	_____	_____
Magnetic compass	_____	_____	_____	_____
Five gallons of water	_____	_____	_____	_____
Signal flares	_____	_____	_____	_____
First-aid kit containing injection needles	_____	_____	_____	_____
Solar-powered FM receiver/transmitter	_____	_____	_____	_____
TOTALS	_____	_____	_____	_____

Key to "Lost on the Moon"

NASA'S Ranking	Items	NASA's Reasons
15	Box of matches	No oxygen to sustain the flame.
4	Food concentrate	Good food energy source, efficient.
6	Fifty feet of nylon rope	Useful in scaling cliffs, tying together the injured.
8	Parachute silk	Will provide protection from sun's rays.
13	Solar-powered portable heating unit	Useless on dark side, not needed on lighted side.
11	Two 45-caliber pistols	Possible means of propulsion.
12	One case of condensed milk	Bulky duplication of food concentrate.
3	Stellar map (of the moon's constellation)	Primary means of navigation.
1	Two 100-pound tanks of oxygen	Most pressing need.
9	Self-inflating life raft	CO_2 bottle in raft may be used for propulsion.
14	Magnetic compass	Magnetic field on moon is not polarized, worthless.
2	Five gallons of water	Replacement for high water loss on light side.
10	Signal flares	Distress signal when mother ship sighted.
7	First-aid kit containing injection needles	For injecting vitamins—special aperture in suit.
5	Solar-powered FM receiver/transmitter	Talk to mother ship; FM needs short range and line of sight.

Summary

Airplanes are able to fly through the earth's atmosphere because of differences in atmospheric pressure created by air moving over and on the plane's wing surfaces. Fast-moving air over the curved upper surfaces is at a slightly lesser atmospheric pressure than the air moving across the lower surfaces. Four forces act on an airplane in flight—thrust, drag, lift, and weight. The lift must exceed the weight of the loaded aircraft, and the thrust must exceed the force of the drag in order for the craft to remain in the air and fly in a forward direction. Movable surfaces on the wing and tail sections of the airplane permit the pilot to control the direction of flight. The rudder, located at the rear of the vertical stabilizer, controls flat right and left turns by pushing the tail in the desired direction. The elevators, located on the trailing edges of the horizontal stabilizers, control the up-and-down orientation of the aircraft by allowing the airstream moving over them to push the tail in the desired direction. Banked turns are accomplished with the simultaneous use of the rudder and the ailerons, located on the trailing edges of both wings. The moving airstream pushes on the ailerons, tilting the wings while it pushes the tail around in the desired direction. Airplanes are propelled by propellers that are turned by internal-combustion, piston-driven engines; by high-speed, high-energy emission of hot gases from a jet engine; or by a combination of jet and propeller effects created by a turboprop engine. The flight of airplanes is confined to the earth's atmosphere by the requirements of the engine for oxygen and by the fact that the force that provides an airplane's lift depends on atmospheric gases moving over its wing surfaces.

Rocket engines permit vehicles to leave the earth's atmosphere and fly into the vacuum of space for they carry their own fuel and oxygen. The propulsion of the rocket engine comes from the unequal distribution of forces within its combustion chamber as hot gases exit the chamber at the rear. Rockets may use solid or liquid fuels and a supply of oxygen in a pure-liquid or combined-chemical form.

The path of an object moving through space is dependent on its velocity and the attractive forces of bodies in its vicinity. The inertia of a body moving through space is dependent on its velocity. When the inertia of a body that comes into the earth's gravitational field is equal to the force of gravity, the body circles the earth and becomes a satellite, its distance from the earth being dependent solely on its velocity.

The space program of the National Aeronautics and Space Administration has many varied and often spectacular accomplishments. Programs include rocket and vehicular design, earth observation, communications, human space flight, and interplanetary flight and observation.

Extending Activities

Chapter 9 deals with many of the important issues facing our society as we move from an industrially oriented economy toward an electronic-information-oriented, high-technology-based economy. Children may be involved with the major issues in a variety of ways. Group research projects on specific issues provide information and experience with processes useful for dealing with societal problems. After the children have gathered information concerning an issue, the teacher may organize culminating activities, such as written and oral project reports, debates wherein children utilize gathered information, general discussions of issues, or action projects, such as writing or visiting responsible authorities.

Suggested Topics for Investigation

1. Noise and air pollution caused by airplanes.

2. Safety issues of jumbo jets carrying up to 1,000 passengers.

3. The role of women in the space program.

4. The cost of the space program versus such benefits as new technologies (communications satellites, computers, nutrition, solar energy cells, efficient storage batteries, and so on) and new knowledge (such as that supplied by the probes to Venus, Mars, Jupiter, and Saturn, and information gathered from space observatories).

Teaching Metric Measurement

Look What's in This Chapter

In this chapter we'll discuss some important topics related to the study of the metric system, including the history of the metric system, the system of metric linear measurement, the system of metric volume (capacity) measurement, the system of metric mass measurement, and the system of metric temperature (Celsius) measurement. We'll also present lesson plans that are designed to teach metric measurement to children.

Out with the Old

The English System of Measurement — How It Got That Way

5,280 English king's feet = 1,000 paces of a Roman soldier

36 barley corns = 1 English king's foot

16 freeholder's feet = 1 rod

36 thumbs' widths = 1 arm's length

Do these statements appear to be nonsensical? They represent the roots of actual relationships that were incorporated into the English system of measure. The English system of weights and measures resulted from the standardization of commonly used units. Many units of the English system of measurement have roots in ancient Middle Eastern civilizations dating back 6,000 to 8,000 years. Most units are related to the human body and the geography of the earth. Ancient Chaldeans, for instance, established the *cubit* (the distance from the tip of the middle finger to the elbow). The *meridian mile* was established as 4,000 cubits prior to the building of the Egyptian pyramids. Ancient Egyptians also employed the *span* (the distance between the thumb and little finger of the outstretched hand), the *palm* (combined width of four fingers), the *digit* (the width of the knuckle of the middle finger), and the *fathom* (distance between the fingertips of a person's outstretched arms). Many of the units of measurement of Egypt were adopted by the Romans and transmitted to the English during the Roman occupation of that land. Mileposts still exist along English country roads that were built by the Roman army. Each post is 1,000 paces (double steps) from the other. After England became a nation, King James decreed the length of his foot as the standard foot. King Edward II, in 1324, established the inch as three barleycorns taken from the middle of the ear and placed end to end. King Henry I declared the yard to be the distance from the tip of his nose to the tip of his outstretched thumb. Prior to this, the yard was

often measured using the length of the sash that fashionable men wore about their waists. By 1500, these various units of measurement were standardized to some degree in England and later transported to the colonies of America. The adoption of the English system of weights and measures is evidence of the strong influence England had upon the heritage of our country.

In with the New

The decimal metric system was established in France under Napoleon in 1790. The system was imposed upon the French by the Republican Convention. Strong measures were taken to rigidly enforce its use. People went to jail for using the old calendar or for selling eggs by the dozen. The population was so incensed with the strong measures taken to institute the metric system that they succeeded in having the metrication committee disbanded in 1793. The principal member of the committee was subsequently guillotined. The decimal metric system was reimposed in France in 1837. The new system retained the established units for measuring time based on seconds, hours, days.

The adoption of the metric system in Holland and Belgium dates back to 1795, in Italy to 1859, Portugal, 1868, and Germany, 1872. The use of the system has spread around the world so that today the United States is the last industrialized nation that has not adopted it. Adoption by the United States will be the last step in establishing a global system of weights and measures based upon the metric system. The new system is formally called the System International, or SI.

Metric Linear Measurement

Discussion

The standard unit of linear measurement in the metric system is the meter. The meter was originally established as a unit of length equal to one

Chart 22–1 ▪ Seven Linear Units of the Metric System

Symbol*	Unit Name	Relationship to the Meter
km	kilometer	1000 meters
hm	hectometer	100 meters
dam	dekameter	10 meters
m	meter	1 meter
dm	decimeter	1/10 meter
cm	centimeter	1/100 meter
mm	millimeter	1/1000 meter

*Our discussion will be limited to these seven units of the metric system. Other prefixes used for very large and very small units are: *mega,* one million units; *giga,* one billion units; *tera,* one trillion units: *micro,* one millionth of a unit; *nano,* one billionth of a unit; and *pico,* one trillionth of a unit.

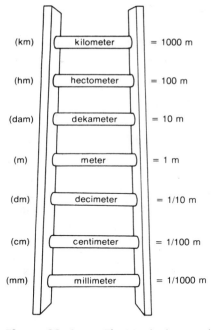

Figure 22–1 ▪ The Metric Linear Ladder

ten-millionth of the distance from the North Pole to the equator. In more accurate, but less understandable terms, the meter is now defined as 1,650,763.73 wavelengths in a vacuum of the orange-red line of the spectrum of krypton-36. The meter is a little over one yard in length.

Since the meter is not appropriate to measure very short or very long distances, other units were established. All units of length in the metric system are multiples of ten or submultiples of ten of the meter. Figure 22–1 contains a "ladder" of the metric units of length.

You will need to know the unit names' prefixes and the relationship of the units of the met-

ric ladder. Do you see that the unit on each rung of the metric ladder is ten times as large as the unit on the rung below it? Another way to state the same concept is: "Each rung unit of the metric ladder contains ten of the units of the rung below it." Thus, one kilometer contains ten hectometers; one hectometer contains ten dekameters; one dekameter contains ten meters, and so on. (See also Chart 22–1.)

Lesson Plan ▪ A

Orientation:	Grades K–6.
Content Objective:	The children will relate parts of their bodies to the meter.
Skill Objective:	The children will *measure* using a meter stick or meter-long string.
Materials:	Meter sticks or meter-long strings, worksheets.
Evaluation:	Students' verbal interaction, worksheets.

continued on next page

Procedure

Group children in pairs. Give each pair a one-meter-long piece of string or a meter stick. Ask them to fill in the blanks on the following worksheet.

Directions: Measure and find out. Write *longer* or *shorter* in the blank spaces.

1. My hop is _____ than a meter.

2. My step is _____ than a meter.

3. My reach is _____ than a meter.

4. My leg is _____ than a meter.

5. Two of my hops are _____ than a meter.

6. Three of my hops are _____ than a meter.

Lesson Plan ▪ B

Orientation:	Grades K–6.
Content Objective:	The children will relate dimensions of common classroom objects to the meter.
Skill Objective:	The children will *measure* using a meter stick or meter-long string.
Materials:	Meter sticks or meter-long strings, worksheets.
Evaluation:	Students' verbal interaction, worksheets.

Procedure

Provide each pair of children with a meter-long string or meter stick and the following worksheet.

Directions: Look around the classroom. Name some objects that are about one meter in length.

With a partner, estimate and then measure some things in your classroom using a meter stick. Fill in the chart. Your answers should be written to the nearest whole meter.

1. __A stool__ is about one meter __tall__ .

2. _____ is about one meter _____ .

3. _____ is about one meter _____ .

4. _____ is about one meter _____ .

	Door	Window	Chalkboard	Room
5. My estimate	____	____	____	____
6. Partner's estimate	____	____	____	____
7. Our measurement	____	____	____	____

Lesson Plan ■ C

Orientation:	Grades 3–6.
Content Objective:	The children will relate dimensions of common objects to the centimeter.
Skill Objective:	The children will *measure* using a meter stick or metric ruler.
Materials:	Meter sticks or metric rulers, worksheets.
Evaluation:	Students' verbal interaction, worksheets.

Procedure

Provide each pair of children with a meter stick or 30-centimeter ruler and the following worksheet.

Directions: Using a centimeter ruler, measure some objects and complete the chart.

Object   Length

1. My desk _____ _____ centimeters

2. My chair _____ _____ centimeters

3. _____ _____ centimeters

4. _____ _____ centimeters

5. _____ _____ centimeters

6. _____ _____ centimeters

7. _____ _____ centimeters

8. _____ _____ centimeters

Lesson Plan ■ D

Orientation:	Grades 3–6.
Content Objective:	The children will relate parts of their bodies to the meter and centimeter.
Skill Objective:	The children will *measure* using a meter tape or meter stick.
Materials:	Meter tape measures or meter sticks and string, worksheets.
Evaluation:	Students' verbal interaction, worksheets.

Procedure

Provide a ditto that contains a line drawing of a child. Provide blanks for measurement of the height, head, neck, chest, forearm, wrist, waist, hand span, thigh, length of little finger, circumference of calf, length of foot, length of big toe, others (see Figure 22-2).

Directions: On the drawing write your measurements in meters or centimeters. You may also state a measurement as a combination of meters and centimeters.

continued on next page

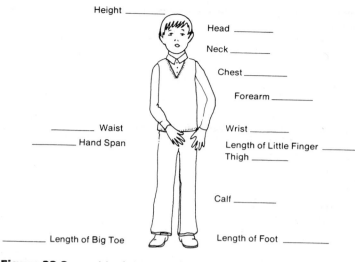

Height _____

Head _____

Neck _____

Chest _____

Forearm _____

_____ Waist

Wrist _____

_____ Hand Span

Length of Little Finger _____

Thigh _____

Calf _____

_____ Length of Big Toe

Length of Foot _____

Figure 22-2 ■ Metric Measurements of Body Parts

Lesson Plan ■ E

Orientation:	Grades 3–6.
Content Objective:	The children will relate dimensions of common objects to the meter and centimeter.
Skill Objective:	The children will *estimate* and *measure* using a meter stick.
Materials:	Meter sticks, worksheets.
Evaluation:	Students' verbal interaction, students' group problem-solving skills, worksheet.

Procedure

Have pairs of students estimate, measure using a meter stick, and fill in Chart 22-2.

Chart 22–2 ■ Using a Meter Stick

	Hall Length	Hall Width
Our estimate	_____	_____
Our discovery	_____	_____

continued on next page

Chart 22–2 ■ Using a Meter Stick (*continued*)

	Locker Length	Locker Width
Our estimate	_____	_____
Our discovery	_____	_____

	Bulletin Board Height	Bulletin Board Width
Our estimate	_____	_____
Our discovery	_____	_____

	Water Fountain Height	Window Width
Our estimate	_____	_____
Our discovery	_____	_____

Lesson Plan ■ F

Orientation:	Grades 5–6.
Content Objective:	The children will combine meter and centimeter measurements using the decimal.
Skill Objective:	None.
Type of Inquiry:	None.
Materials:	Worksheet from completed Lesson Plan E.
Evaluation:	Students' verbal interaction, students' group problem-solving skills, worksheet.

Procedure

Have children work in pairs to complete the following exercise.

Tell the class that meters and centimeters can be written without using both words. For instance, a measurement of 1 meter plus 68 centimeters may be written 1.68 meters. (Write the example on the board.) Tell the children they can write the number of meters followed by a point and the number of centimeters and label it meters. The point separates the meters and centimeters. Write other examples on the board:

3 meters and 21 centimeters = 3.21 meters

12 meters and 3 centimeters = 12.03 meters

0 meters and 37 centimeters = 0.37 meter

Directions: Change your hallway measures to this new way to write meters and centimeters. Meters are abbreviated m and centimeters are abbreviated cm.

continued on next page

1. Hall length = _____ m _____ cm = _____ meters
2. Hall width = _____ m _____ cm = _____ meters
3. Water fountain height = _____ m _____ cm = _____ meters
4. Locker length = _____ m _____ cm = _____ meters
5. Locker width = _____ m _____ cm = _____ meters
6. Bulletin board width = _____ m _____ cm = _____ meters
7. Bulletin board height = _____ m _____ cm = _____ meters

Lesson Plan ▪ G

Orientation: Grades 4–6.

Content Objective: The children will state the relationships between the millimeter and the meter.

Skill Objective: The children will recognize the millimeter on a metric ruler or meter stick.

Materials: Metric rulers or meter sticks, worksheets.

Evaluation: Students' verbal interaction, worksheets.

Procedure

Provide each child with the following activity sheet.

Directions: Examine the centimeter ruler. We know that the numbered divisions are *centimeters*. The smaller divisions between the centimeter markings are *millimeters*. Count and see how many millimeter spaces make up one centimeter. Then complete the following statements:

1. 1 centimeter = _____ millimeters.

   Jane's thumb is 5 cm long. So, Jane's thumb is 50 millimeters long.

2. __8 cm__ = _____ millimeters (mm)
3. __6 cm__ = _____ millimeters (mm)
4. __3 cm__ = _____ millimeters (mm)
5. _____ = __40__ millimeters (mm)
6. _____ = __70__ millimeters (mm)
7. _____ = __90__ millimeters (mm)
8. Since there are 10 millimeters in a centimeter and 100 centimeters in a meter, how many millimeters are there in 1 meter? _____
   Did you count the number of millimeters in a meter, or did you understand that 10 millimeters in each one of the 100 centimeters is the same as:
   100 × 10?
9. So, 100 × 10 = _____ millimeters in a meter.

Lesson Plan ▪ H

Orientation:	Grades 4–6.
Content Objective:	The children will recognize the relationship among metric units.
Skill Objective:	The children will demonstrate the ability to convert metric units using a number line.
Materials:	Worksheets containing sample conversion problems.
Evaluation:	Students' verbal interaction, worksheets.

Procedure

Write the metric units on the chalkboard as follows:

km	hm	dam	m	dm	cm	mm
—	—	—	—	—	—	—

Tell the class: "If I want to show I have 1 kilometer I can write the numeral 1 in the km space followed by a decimal point. The rest of the units could be 0 since they have no value."

km	hm	dam	m	dm	cm	mm
1.	0	0	0	0	0	0

Then ask, "This represents 1 kilometer. How many hectometers are equal to 1 kilometer? (Ten.) "So we can change 1 kilometer to its equivalent value in hectome-ters by moving the decimal point one place to the right." Demonstrate the other equivalents of 1 km.

"Now suppose we have 12 decimeters. We would write it like this:"

km	hm	dam	m	dm	cm	mm
0	0	0	1	2.	0	0

Ask: "How many centimeters is this?" (120.) "How many hectometers is this?" (.012.) "All you have to do is move the decimal point and fill in the blank spaces with zeros."

Add as many more examples as are necessary.

Lesson Plan ▪ I

Orientation:	Grades 5–6.
Content Objective:	The children will be able to combine meter, centimeter, and millimeter units.
Skill Objective:	None.
Materials:	Posterboard circle, paper clip, brass paper brad.
Evaluation:	Students' verbal interaction and ability to participate in the game.

Procedure

Make a spinner by attaching a paper clip to a cardboard circle with a brass paper brad as in Figure 22–3. Divide the circle into eight parts and mark the parts with the units millimeter, centimeter, and meter. Provide the children with directions and permit them to play the Metric Game.

continued on next page

Directions: Permit each child to spin the spinner in turn. The spinner must turn at least one complete revolution. Each player should keep track of where the spinner stops on each of his turns. After seven turns, each player should tally the total of the units acquired during his turns. The winner is the player whose units add up to the greatest total distance.

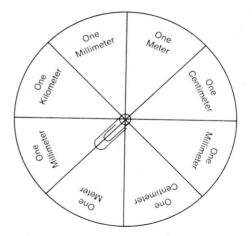

Figure 22–3 ■ A Metric Spinner

Lesson Plan ■ J

Orientation:	Grades 3–6.
Content Objective:	The children will write the names, symbols, and numerical relationships of metric linear units in order.
Skill Objective:	None.
Materials:	Posterboard strips, Magic Marker, magnets or tape.
Evaluation:	Seat work.

Procedure

Copy the metric ladder from Figure 22–1 on the chalkboard. Make posterboard rungs by writing a unit of the metric ladder on each of seven pieces of posterboard. Make the rungs stick by adding a magnet or masking tape loops on the back of each piece of posterboard. Permit the children several minutes to memorize the metric ladder, then erase the unit names. Now hand out the posterboard rungs one at a time in random order and ask a child to place each rung in the proper place on the ladder. Make a contest to see which group can make the ladder properly first.

Repeat the exercise using the proper symbols for the seven metric ladder units.

Repeat the exercise using the numerical relationships of the units and the meter (intermediate grades).

A metric ladder of liquid volume may also be constructed. Point out that the prefixes and tens relationships are the same for units of liquid volume as they are for length. (See Chart 22–3.) Only the basic unit changes. This consistency across the various areas of measurement is one of the primary advantages of the metric system.

Finally, construct a correct ladder of units, symbols, and numerical relationships and leave it on the chalkboard.

Chart 22–3 ▪ Measuring Volume: The Metric System

Symbol	Unit Name	Relationship to the Liter
kL	kiloliter	1000 liters
hL	hectoliter	100 liters
daL	dekaliter	10 liters
L	liter	1 liter
dL	deciliter	1/10 liter
cL	centiliter	1/100 liter
mL	milliliter	1/1000 liter

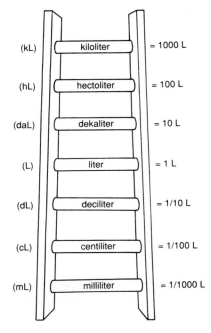

(kL)	kiloliter	= 1000 L
(hL)	hectoliter	= 100 L
(daL)	dekaliter	= 10 L
(L)	liter	= 1 L
(dL)	deciliter	= 1/10 L
(cL)	centiliter	= 1/100 L
(mL)	milliliter	= 1/1000 L

Figure 22–4 ▪ The Metric Liquid Volume Ladder

Metric Liquid Volume (Capacity) Measurement

Discussion

The basic unit of liquid volume, or capacity, of the metric system is the *liter*. The liter is equal to the volume of a cube that is ten centimeters (one decimeter) on each side. So a liter is said to equal one cubic decimeter or 1,000 cubic centimeters (cm³). Remember, to find the volume of the decimeter cube in centimeters, we must multiply ten centimeters by ten centimeters by ten centimeters to get the 1,000 cubic centimeters (cm³). The liter is slightly larger than a quart. The ladder of metric liquid volume is shown in Figure 22–4.

Lesson Plan ▪ K

Orientation:	Grades 2–6.
Content Objective:	The children will relate the capacity of common objects to the liter.
Skill Objective:	The children will *estimate* and *measure* using a liter container.
Materials:	Various sizes of containers from medicine cups to gallon jars, decimeter cubes, sand, rice, puffed wheat, marbles, or any other "fluid." If a watertight liter container is available, water may be used as the fluid. Worksheets.
Evaluation:	Students' verbal interaction, students' group problem-solving skills, worksheets.

Procedure

Divide the class into groups of three to five students. Provide each group with a decimeter cube (these cubes may be constructed by the children with poster-board and masking tape [see Figure 22–5]; also some

continued on next page

typewriter ribbons are packaged in boxes that are decimeter cubes) and about one-half gallon of water or substitute "fluid." Provide them with copies of Chart 22—4 and the following directions:

1. Fill the decimeter box level.

2. This volume of sand (or other material) is called a *liter*. It is the basic unit of measurement of liquid volume in the metric system. You are going to use your liter container to find out about the volume of other common containers.

3. First estimate the volume of each of the containers in liters. Then, using your liter container to pour "fluid" into them, measure in liters the volume of various containers. You may estimate fractions of liters.

List the containers that were larger than one liter: _____

_____

_____

List the containers that were about one liter in volume:

_____

_____

_____

Permit the children to measure as many containers as time permits.

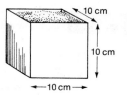

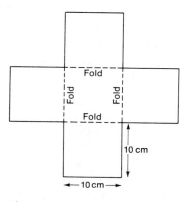

Figure 22—5 ▪ A Decimeter Box

Chart 22—4 ▪ Measuring the Volume of Various Containers

Container*	Estimate (Liters)	Measurement (Liters)	Smaller or Larger Than 1 Liter
A quart jar or bottle			
A pint jar or bottle			
A saucepan			
A coffee pot			
A paper cup			
A coffee cup			
A mayonnaise jar			
An olive bottle			

*You may add to or change this list of common containers.

Lesson Plan ▪ L

Orientation: Grades 3–6.

Content Objective: The children will relate the capacities of common objects to liter and milliliter units of measurement.

Skill Objective: The children will *measure* using a liter container and a graduated cylinder.

Materials: Liter container, graduated cylinder, miscellaneous containers, worksheets.

Evaluation: Students' verbal interaction, students' group problem-solving skills, worksheets.

Procedure

Divide the class into groups of six to eight children. Provide each group of children with a graduated cylinder (a 100-milliliter graduated cylinder is preferred), fluid, and the same containers used in Lesson Plan K. Instruct the children to use the liter container (decimeter box) and the graduated cylinder to determine the actual capacity of the common containers, entering their figures in Chart 22–5.

Chart 22–5 ▪ Capacity (Volume)

Containers	Liters	Milliliters
1. Plastic jar	_____	_____
2. Baby bottle	_____	_____
3. ⎫ Other containers	_____	_____
4. ⎭	_____	_____

Lesson Plan ▪ M

Orientation: Grades 3–6.

Content Objective: Children will relate the capacities of common objects to the liter and milliliter.

Skill Objective: The children will *estimate* and *measure* volumes of common objects.

Materials: Six containers, graduated cylinders, fluid, set of directions, worksheets.

Evaluation: Students' verbal interaction, students' group problem-solving skills, worksheets.

Procedure

Provide each group of children with the following directions.

Directions: Fill six containers *partially* with water. Let each player guess the volume of water in each container. Then measure the water to determine its actual volume.

Scoring

10 points—"best guesser" on each volume

5 points—second-place "guesser"

2 points—third-place "guesser"

After the volume of each of the six containers has been estimated, add up the scores. Declare the winner the "Liter Leader."

Lesson Plan ■ N

Orientation:	Grades 5–6.
Content Objective:	The children will combine liter and milliliter units using decimal notation.
Skill Objective:	None.
Materials:	Worksheet from Lesson Plan L.
Evaluation:	Students' verbal interaction, worksheet.

Procedure

Provide each child with the following worksheet for Chart 22–6.

Liters and milliliters can be written without using both words. Sometimes the measures are written 1.685 liters. This means 1 liter and 685 milliliters. The decimal point separates liters and milliliters.

Other examples are:

3 liters and 82 milliliters =   3.082 liters
12 liters and   7 milliliters = 12.007 liters

Directions: Change your answers to Lesson Plan L to this new way of writing liters and milliliters.

Chart 22–6 ■ Capacity (Volume)

Containers	Liters	Milliliters	Decimal Notations
1. Plastic jar	_____	_____	_____ . _____ liters
2. Baby bottle	_____	_____	_____ . _____ liters
3. _____	_____	_____	_____ . _____ liters
4. _____	_____	_____	_____ . _____ liters

Any large container may be substituted for the containers named in this exercise, such as a coffee pot, sprinkling can, pail, salad bowl, saucepan, frying pan, mixing bowl, or tea kettle.

Chart 22–7 ▪ Measuring Mass: The Metric System

Symbol	Unit Name	Relationship to the Gram
kg	kilogram	1000 grams
hg	hectogram	100 grams
dag	dekagram	10 grams
g	gram	1 gram
dg	decigram	1/10 gram
cg	centigram	1/100 gram
mg	milligram	1/1000 gram

Metric Mass Measurement

Discussion

The basic unit of mass in the metric system is the *gram*. The gram is the mass (weight) of one cubic centimeter (or one milliliter) of water. The gram is a mass approximately equal to the weight of a large paper clip or a half sheet of tablet paper. The ladder of metric mass units is shown in Figure 22–6. The same prefixes and

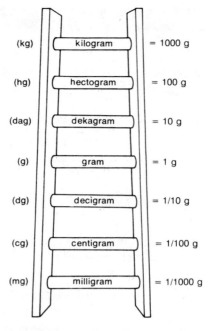

Figure 22–6 ▪ The Metric Mass Ladder

tens relationships are true for the metric mass units as they are for the linear and volume units (see Chart 22–7).

Lesson Plan ▪ O

Orientation:	Grades K–6.
Content Objective:	The children will relate the mass of common objects to the kilogram.
Skill Objective:	The children will compare the masses of common objects with the kilogram.
Materials:	Large plastic bowl, cut-off milk or bleach container, graduated cylinder.
Evaluation:	Students' verbal interaction, students' group problem-solving skills.

Procedure

Divide the class into groups of four to six children. Provide each group with a large (greater than one liter), light plastic bowl and a graduated cylinder. In-struct the children to use the graduated cylinder to put a total of 1,000 mL of water into the plastic bowl. Tell them that the mass of this much water is equal to one

continued on next page

kilogram. Permit each child to hold the bowl of water in turn. Ask each group to name three objects that have a mass of *about* one kilogram. The children should be allowed to manipulate many objects available in the classroom. (If a standard kilogram mass is available, permit the children to use it as a comparison. Standard kilogram, one-half kilogram, and other masses may be made by pouring sand into a large soda or Pringles can as it is balanced against 1,000 mL, 500 mL, and so on of water). You may make a master chart of those objects lighter than one kilogram, and objects having about the same mass as one kilogram.

Lesson Plan ▪ P

Orientation:	Grades 4–6.
Content Objective:	The children will relate the masses of common objects to the gram.
Skill Objective:	The children will *compare* masses of common objects with the gram.
Materials:	Medicine dropper, graduated cylinder, classroom objects.
Evaluation:	Students' verbal interaction, students' group problem-solving skills.

Procedure

Ask the class, "How could we obtain a single mL of water using a medicine dropper and a graduated cylinder?" Instruct each child to place one milliliter of water in his or her cupped hand. "How much does this water weigh?" (One gram.) (You may have to remind the class that if 1,000 milliliters of water has a mass of 1,000 grams, then one milliliter of water would have a mass of one gram.) "Is a gram a large or small unit of mass?" Tell the children to find three objects in the classroom that have a mass of about one gram (sheet of paper, small paper clip, thumbtack, stick of gum, and so on). To conclude the lesson, call on individual students to name the objects that they think weigh about one gram.

Lesson Plan ▪ Q

Orientation:	Grades 4–6.
Content Objective:	The children will relate the masses of common objects to the gram and kilogram.
Skill Objective:	The children will use a platform balance to determine the masses of common objects.
Materials:	Platform balances, graduated cylinders, foam cups, common objects, worksheets.
Evaluation:	Students' verbal interaction, students' group problem-solving skills, worksheet.

continued on next page

Procedure

Provide each group of children with a platform balance, a graduated cylinder, four foam or paper cups. Paper clips (small and jumbo), whole sticks of chalk, light books such as spelling books, and heavier books such as science books should be available to be tested.

Tell each group they are to find the mass of the following list of objects. To do this they are to place a foam cup on each side of the platform balance, put

Chart 22–8 ▪ Calculating Mass

Object	Mass
Paper clip (small)	_____
Paper clip (jumbo)	_____
Chalk	_____
Spelling book	_____
Others	_____

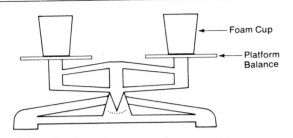

Figure 22–7 ▪ Finding the Mass of Small Objects

the object in (or, in the case of large objects, under) one cup. The approximate mass of the object may be determined by adding measured amounts of water poured from the graduated cylinder to the second cup until the scale is balanced. For heavier objects, add foam cups as needed to each side of the platform balance until the amount of water necessary balances the scale. Enter the mass in Chart 22–8.

Lesson Plan ▪ R

Orientation:	Grades 3–6.
Content Objective:	The children will relate masses of common objects to the gram and kilogram.
Skill Objective:	The children will *estimate* the masses of common objects and then *determine* their mass by *weighing* them.
Materials:	Objects of known mass from Lesson Plan P, platform balances, "mystery objects," copies of Chart 22–9.
Evaluation:	Students' verbal interaction, students' group problem-solving skills, worksheet.

Procedure

Provide the groups of children with the same materials used in Lesson Plan P, and give them the following directions: Select five objects from your desks (pens, pencils, book, and so on). These will be "mystery masses." Each student should handle each "mystery mass" and estimate its mass in grams. After all the

students have made their estimates, find the approximate mass of each "mystery mass" by balancing it on a platform balance with known masses from Lesson Plan P. (Some children prefer to use measured amounts of water as the standard weight.) Put the "mystery

continued on next page

mass" on one side of the balance scale and add known masses to the other side until the scale is balanced.

Then add up the known weights to determine the mass of the "mystery mass." Fill in your worksheet.

Chart 22–9 ▪ "Mystery Mass"

"Mystery Mass"	Estimated Mass	Measured Mass	Difference
_____	_____	_____	_____
_____	_____	_____	_____
_____	_____	_____	_____

If time permits, have a contest with others in your group to see who can come the closest in estimating the mass of small objects.

Lesson Plan ▪ S

Orientation: Grades 5–6.

Content Objective: The children will combine kilogram and gram masses using decimal notation.

Skill Objective: None.

Materials: Worksheets.

Evaluation: Students' verbal interaction, worksheet.

Procedure

Tell the class that they may combine kilograms and grams as decimal forms of the kilogram. First write the number of whole kilograms followed by a decimal, then the grams.

Some examples are:

$$3 \text{ kg and } 165 \text{ g} = 3.165 \text{ kg}$$
$$0 \text{ kg and } 220 \text{ g} = 0.220 \text{ kg}$$
$$1 \text{ kg and } 23 \text{ g} = 1.023 \text{ kg}$$
$$10 \text{ kg and } 9 \text{ g} = 10.009 \text{ kg}$$

Help your students to complete the following:

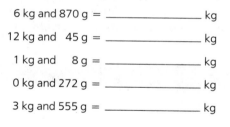

$$6 \text{ kg and } 870 \text{ g} = \underline{\hspace{2cm}} \text{ kg}$$
$$12 \text{ kg and } 45 \text{ g} = \underline{\hspace{2cm}} \text{ kg}$$
$$1 \text{ kg and } 8 \text{ g} = \underline{\hspace{2cm}} \text{ kg}$$
$$0 \text{ kg and } 272 \text{ g} = \underline{\hspace{2cm}} \text{ kg}$$
$$3 \text{ kg and } 555 \text{ g} = \underline{\hspace{2cm}} \text{ kg}$$

Orientation:	Grades 3–6.
Content Objective:	The children will write the names, symbols, and numerical relationships of metric mass units in order.
Skill Objective:	None.
Materials:	Posterboard strips, Magic Marker, magnets or tape.
Evaluation:	Students' verbal interaction, students' group problem-solving skills.

Procedure

Repeat the activities of Lesson Plan J, using mass units and symbols.

Metric Temperature Measurement

Discussion

The Celsius thermometer (formerly called the centigrade thermometer) is employed in the metric system of measurement. The Celsius thermometer has a scale of 100 degrees between the freezing and boiling points of water. On this scale, room temperature is usually in the range of 19°C to 23°C, warm water about 40°C, cold water 10°C, and hot water perhaps 80°C. The beginning letter of the word Celsius and the symbol C are both capital letters. This is unlike the names and symbols of the other units with which you are now familiar. The reason for capitalizing Celsius is that the scale was named for Anders Celsius, the Swedish astronomer who first suggested its use.

Orientation:	Grades K–4.
Content Objective:	The children will read temperatures from a model Celsius thermometer.
Skill Objective:	The children will be able to use the Celsius thermometer to *measure* temperatures.
Materials:	Model Celsius thermometer (posterboard, red and white elastic ribbons).
Evaluation:	Students' verbal interaction.

Procedure

On a piece of posterboard 30 cm × 100 cm construct a temperature scale as in Figure 22–8. Attach a 90-cm red elastic ribbon to a 90-cm white elastic ribbon by sewing the ends together. Thread the elastic ribbon through slots cut near the top and bottom of the posterboard. Then attach the loose ends of the elastic

continued on next page

ribbon behind the posterboard. The model thermometer may be stiffened by stapling it to a meter stick placed behind the board.

You may now simulate various temperatures by adjusting the height of the red elastic ribbon.

Show the class the model thermometer. Have individual children read the temperatures from the model thermometer as you adjust it between 0°C and 100°C. After a number of children have read temperatures from the model thermometer, you may show them various pairs of temperatures and ask them: "How many degrees did the temperature increase (rise)?" or "How many degrees did the temperature decrease (fall)?"

Discuss the significance of the 0° and 100° markings on the Celsius thermometer. (The freezing point of water is 0°, and 100° is the boiling point.)

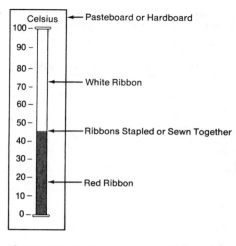

Figure 22–8 ■ Posterboard Thermometer

Lesson Plan ■ V

Orientation: Grades 2–6.

Content Objective: The children will state temperatures of various common environments.

Skill Objective: The children will *measure* temperatures using the Celsius thermometer.

Materials: Celsius thermometers, ice, warm water, cups or other containers, worksheets.

Evaluation: Students' verbal interaction, students' group problem-solving skills, worksheets.

Procedure

Divide the class into groups, and provide each group of children with the following directions to accompany Chart 22–10.

Directions

Hold your Celsius thermometer lightly near the top. Examine it carefully. Notice the lowest and highest temperature markings. How many degrees is it between the markings on the thermometer scale? ____. What is normal room temperature? _____. What is the room temperature now? _____. Place your finger on the bulb at the bottom of the glass stem.

What happens? _____. What is the highest reading you can obtain from holding the thermometer in your hand? _____.

Place the Celsius thermometer in the following environments. Take turns reading the temperature of each environment. Record your observations.

continued on next page

Chart 22–10 ■ Recording Celsius Temperatures

Environment	Celsius Temperature	Change from Room Temperature
Room temperature	_____	_____
Hand temperature	_____	_____
Tap water	_____	_____
Ice water	_____	_____
Warm water	_____	_____
Sunlight (near windowsill)	_____	_____
Desk top	_____	_____
Near heater or air conditioner	_____	_____
Sunlight (outdoors)	_____	_____
Others	_____	_____

The Earth,
the Solar System,
and the Universe

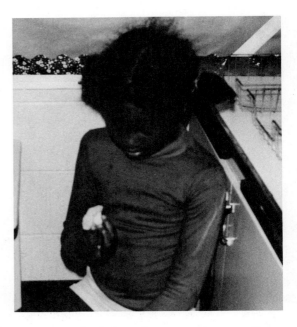

"Nature and wisdom always say the same."
—JUVENAL

The Solar System and the Universe Beyond

Look What's in This Chapter

In this chapter we'll discuss some important concepts and subconcepts related to the study of the solar system and the universe. We'll also present lesson plans that are designed to teach these concepts and subconcepts to children.

Concept 1   Our universe appears to be expanding.

Concept 2   The universe is composed chiefly of hydrogen; stars are formed from hydrogen gas.

Concept 3   The stars' source of energy is nuclear fusion.

Concept 4   Distances between parts of the universe are vast.

Concept 5   Stars appear to form pictures in the sky.

Concept 6   The earth is part of the solar system.

Subconcept 6–1   The planets are very small and very far away from the sun.

Subconcept 6–2   Planets differ from one another.

Subconcept 6–3   Planets orbit about the sun.

Subconcept 6–4   Time is measured by the motions of heavenly bodies.

Subconcept 6–5   The earth has seasons.

Subconcept 6–6   The moon interacts with the earth.

The heavens have long inspired us to wonder and to speculate. The apparent movement of the sun across the daytime sky, the sweep of the moon and stars across the sky at night are constant sources of delight to ordinary people and subjects of study for the scientist. Though the cosmos has been observed and studied from before the dawn of civilization, we have not yet learned all its secrets. We have yet to penetrate much of the vast unknown that lies beyond our planet.

Though we *know* very little of the universe beyond our own planet, we have *inferred* a great deal. Much of this chapter is speculative theory, usually based upon rather large assumptions. As one of the real frontiers of science, the study of the heavens moves scientists to hypothesize boldly about the origin of the cosmos and the nature of its parts. The mysteries of the universe tax the very limits of the human intellect.

As some of the inferences of modern astronomers are described, the nature of the evidence upon which they are based will also be presented. Teachers should attempt to understand as many as possible of the processes whereby inferences are made from observations for they will surely find it necessary to answer such questions as: "If we have never been there, how do we know what stars are made of?" "How do we know how far away the nearest star is?" "How do we know there is no life on Jupiter?"

Concept 1

Our universe appears to be expanding.

Discussion

Light is assumed to be a series of waves of energy that travel in space. When separated by prisms, as the colors of the rainbow are separated by raindrops, the light from distant stars and galaxies looks redder than the light from nearby stars. The colors are of slightly longer wavelengths. Or put another way, the distance between each wave appears to be greater. The universe may be assumed to be uniform throughout, for there is no good reason to suppose that distant stars are different from nearby stars. Therefore, astronomers reason that the apparently greater wavelength of the light from more distant stars may be because the stars emitting the light are moving away from the earth at a rapid rate. An analogy may help to clarify this concept.

A boy is sitting in a motorboat anchored in the middle of a large lake. He notices that twenty waves pass his boat each minute. The boy starts the motor and moves slowly in the same direction as the waves. He notices that now only eighteen waves pass his boat in one minute. The boy increases his speed until only fifteen waves pass his boat in one minute, then ten. The faster the boy moves in the same direction as the waves, and away from the source of the waves, the greater the distance seems between each pair of waves. From this analogy, illustrated in Figure 23–1, the question arises: "Since the color of light depends upon the frequency with which light waves strike our eyes, how would the color of light be changed by moving rapidly away from its source? Would not the color of light from a star shift in the direction of the lower red-wave frequencies as we moved away from the star?" The same phenomenon would occur if the boat were stationary and the source of the waves were moving away from the boat. The number of waves per minute would be reduced.

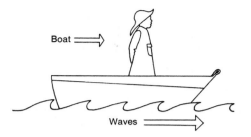

Boat ➡

Waves ➡

Fewer Waves per Minute Passing By

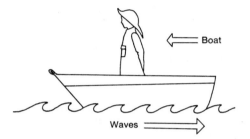

⬅ Boat

Waves ➡

More Waves per Minute Passing By

Figure 23–1 ■ An Analogy of the Red Shift

The shift in the apparent frequency of light energy due to the motion of the source is called the red shift or Doppler effect. Because the light that comes from the stars is red, astronomers believe that the stars are moving away from the earth. The universe is believed to be expanding.

The Big Bang Theory

The red shift in the light of distant stars has caused astronomers to speculate that the entire universe is expanding from some central point. And, as would be true of an explosion, the more distant stars are traveling faster than those closer to the point of the explosion. The most distant galaxies we can observe with powerful photographic telescopes appear to be traveling through space at about one-fifth the speed of light. Extending present observations back to a point of origin, some astronomers conclude that the universe began some 5 billion years ago when all matter, at that time condensed into

a tiny volume of space, exploded with a "big bang" that sent it off in all directions. An extension of the big bang theory is that at some point in the future, gravitational forces among the matter of the universe will slow down, and finally stop, the expansion. At this point, all the matter in the universe will collapse back to a tiny volume, and the process will begin again.

The Steady State Theory

A second theory of the nature of the universe holds that the universe is not expanding. According to the steady state theory, there is only a recession of individual stars and galaxies. The universe maintains a constant density as hydrogen atoms are created out of nothingness to fill the voids left by the moving stars and galaxies. The steady state theory recognizes evolutionary processes in stars and galaxies— that they change with age—but it does not recognize an evolution of the universe as a whole. According to this theory, the universe is constant in size and uniform throughout.

Concept 2

The universe is composed chiefly of hydrogen; stars are formed from hydrogen gas.

Discussion

Hydrogen is the simplest of the atoms. It is usually composed of one proton and one neutron. All of space contains traces of this gas though its density is usually less than the best vacuum created on the earth.

Huge clouds of dust and gas exist in some regions of space. It is in these clouds, called nebulae, that stars are believed to be born. As the gas-dust cloud begins to condense, a *red giant star* is formed. The red giants are huge masses of gas with densities only about one-millionth that of water. It is only because they are so huge that we can see them on earth at all. If the center of a red giant star such as Antares or Betelgeuse were in the position of the sun, its edge would extend beyond the orbit of the planet Jupiter (see

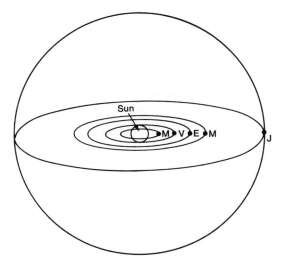

Figure 23–2 ■ The Size of a Red Giant Star

the future the sun will explode, blowing outward hot gases that will destroy the planets of the solar system. Then the sun will appear as a nova to other forms of life on other planets of other stars.

Quasars and Pulsars

In recent years, powerful radio receivers (radio telescopes) on earth have been receiving signals from a kind of heavenly body that was previously unknown. The radio waves come to earth in pulses from the farthest reaches of space. It is theorized that these newly discovered bodies must be composed of neutrons and are so dense and possess so much energy that they stagger the imaginations of even the astronomers who work constantly with outsized numbers and concepts. Intensive searches are being conducted to locate more of these very interesting bodies.

Figure 23–2). Red giants are much cooler than the other stars.

Stars comparable to the sun in general size and temperature are called *main sequence stars.* Some astronomers hypothesize that main sequence stars are formed by red giant stars that have been pulled in by gravitational attraction. After many billions of years, a main sequence star may explode and be seen on earth as a brilliant light illuminating the night sky. These brilliant stars are called *novas.* After throwing off a great deal of gaseous matter, the star will condense to a *white dwarf* about the size of a planet. It will then have a density about 100,000 times that of water. This density is so great that one cupful of a white dwarf star would weigh up to thirty tons on earth (Figure 23–3).

If this hypothesized evolutionary theory of stars is true, at some point millions of years into

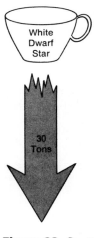

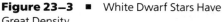

Figure 23–3 ■ White Dwarf Stars Have Great Density

Orientation: Grades 3–6.

Content Objective: The children will state that the temperature of stars may be inferred from their color.

continued on next page

Skill Objective:	The children are required to *observe* the changes in color of the heated metal and to *infer* the relationship of color and temperature.
Materials:	A nail or iron wire, tongs or a wooden clothespin, a propane torch.
Evaluation:	Students' verbal interaction, report.

Procedure

Using a pair of insulated pliers or a wooden clothespin, hold a thin nail (or iron wire) in the flame of a propane torch. Instruct the class to observe the process carefully and to write down their observations. The students will observe the nail turn dark red, then cherry red, and finally almost white in some parts. The teacher may ask: "What did you observe?" (The nail turned dull red, then bright red, then almost white.) "Remember, the nail is giving off the light that you see. How can we relate the temperature of the nail and the color of the light it gives off?" (As a nail gets hotter, the color of the light it gives off goes from dull red to white.) "Can we tell the range of temperature of the nail by the color of light?" (Yes.) "How is this like the stars?" (We can tell the temperature of the stars by their color.) "What color stars are coolest?" (Red.) "What color stars are hottest?" (White.) *Note:* Stars range from coolest to hottest in the following order: red, yellow, blue, and white. Ask the students to write a brief paragraph describing how the color of stars is related to their temperature.

Concept 3

The stars' source of energy is nuclear fusion.

Discussion

A star begins its life as a gas cloud composed chiefly of hydrogen atoms. As the gas cloud condenses into a smaller volume, an increase in pressure creates a heating effect, causing the hydrogen atoms to move about at high speed. When the nuclei of atoms smash into one another at high speed, they *fuse* and release a great deal of energy (Figure 23–4). Similar *fusions* of larger atoms are also believed to occur. These form atoms of heavy elements with an accompanying release of energy.

Energy coming from nuclear fusions occurring deep inside the stars is absorbed by an envelope of gaseous matter that surrounds them. The gaseous envelope emits the radiations that are broadcast as *radio, light, heat,* and *cosmic rays.*

Concept 4

Distances between parts of the universe are vast.

Discussion

The commonest unit for measuring astronomical distances is the *light-year.* Simply defined, the light-year is the distance light travels in one

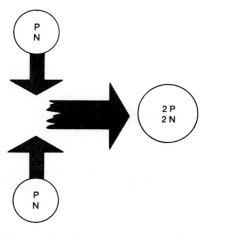

Figure 23–4 ■ The Fusion of Two Hydrogen Atoms

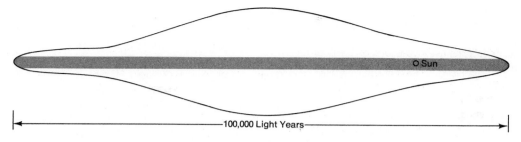

Figure 23–5 ▪ The Milky Way Galaxy

year at a velocity of 186,000 miles per second. The light-year is equal to approximately 6 trillion miles.

Distributed more or less uniformly in space are countless thousands of islands of matter called *galaxies*. Each galaxy is composed of millions of *stars,* plus clouds of dust and gas. The *sun* is a star of medium brightness residing in a galaxy called the *Milky Way* (Figure 23–5). When viewed from the edge, the Milky Way galaxy is shaped like a flying saucer. It is 100,000 light-years in diameter. Our sun is located about one-third of the length of the diameter from one edge. From above, the Milky Way would look like a huge spiral, just as its nearest neighbor galaxy, Andromeda, does. Andromeda is believed to be separated from the Milky Way by 1,700,000 light-years of space. This distance is equal to about seventeen Milky Way diameters.

As far as we have been able to see with our most powerful telescopes, there are galaxies like Andromeda and the Milky Way scattered throughout space. They occur at intervals of about 2 billion light-years. They appear to be randomly but uniformly distributed, and as far as we are able to see them, their numbers do not diminish.

Stars in the same part of the Milky Way as the sun are an average of about 5 light-years, or 30 trillion miles, apart. Our nearest stellar neighbor, Alpha Centauri, is about 4.5 light-years, or 26 trillion miles, from the sun, although there is a possibility that we may discover dim stars some day that are closer.

Children often wonder, "How can such large distances be measured?" Several methods are used to establish interstellar distances, but the method of parallax is probably the easiest to illustrate to elementary school children.

Lesson Plan ▪ B

Orientation:	Grades 4–6.
Content Objective:	The children will describe how to measure the distance between two stars by parallax.
Skill Objective:	The children are required to *measure* and to establish the *spatial relationship* that near stars appear to move against a background of distant stars.
Materials:	Chalkboard, chalk, pencils.
Evaluation:	Students' verbal interaction, sketch, report.

continued on next page

Procedure

Draw a vertical chalk line five inches long on the board. Ask each child to close one eye and hold a pencil in front of the open eye so that it is lined up with the chalkmark. With the pencil about six inches from the eye, instruct the children to close and open first one eye and then the other. Ask: "What do you see?" (The pencil moves away from the chalkmark.) Now instruct the children to hold the pencil at arm's length away from their eye and repeat the exercise. Ask: "What do you notice has changed?" (The distance the pencil moves away from the chalkmark is shorter.) Permit the children to repeat the exercise while varying the distance between the pencil and their eye. Ask: "What can we say about the relationship between the distance of the pencil from the eye and the distance the pencil seems to move away from the chalkmark?" (The farther the pencil is from the eye, the less it moves

away from the chalkmark.) "Now let us imagine that the distance between our eyes is the diameter of the earth's orbit about the sun. The pencil represents a near star, and the chalkmark a distant star. What can we say about the distance between the earth and the near star, and how much the near star seems to move away from the distant star?" (The farther the near star is from the earth, the less it would appear to move away from the distant star.) "The movement of the near star in relation to the far star is called parallax. The amount of parallax of a near star allows astronomers to estimate its distance from the earth." (See Figure 23–6.) Have the students draw a sketch and explain the relationship between a near star and a distant star, and how the distance that the near star appears to move away from the distant star depends on how far the near star is from the earth.

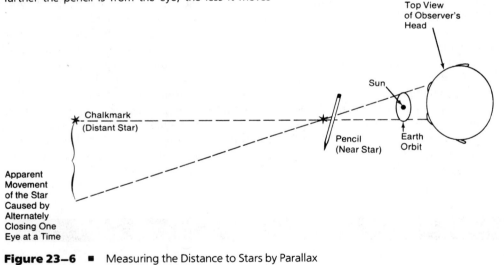

Figure 23–6 ■ Measuring the Distance to Stars by Parallax

Lesson Plan ■ C

Orientation:	Grades 5–6.
Content Objective:	The children will describe how distances may be measured indirectly using parallax.
Skill Objective:	The children are required to *measure*, to *communicate* by constructing a graph, and to *interpret data* from the graph.

continued on next page

Materials: Pencils, rulers, graph paper or prepared graph axes.

Evaluation: Students' group problem-solving skills, laboratory worksheets, log, and reports.

Procedure

A class of able students can extend the concept of parallax to determine the distance of an object using graphing procedures.

One child acts as the observer, a second child measures the distance between a pencil and the observer's eye, and a third measures the apparent displacement of the pencil from a mark on the chalkboard. The observer should shut one eye and hold the pencil 15 cm from the other, in line with the chalk-

mark. Then he closes the open eye and opens the shut one. He then tells the student at the chalkboard to place a pointer on the spot where the pencil now appears to be. The third student measures the distance from this spot to the chalkmark. Repeat the operation, having the observer hold the pencil 30, 45, and 60 cm from his eye. Have the children record the data on a chart and then construct a graph as in Figure 23–7.

continued on next page

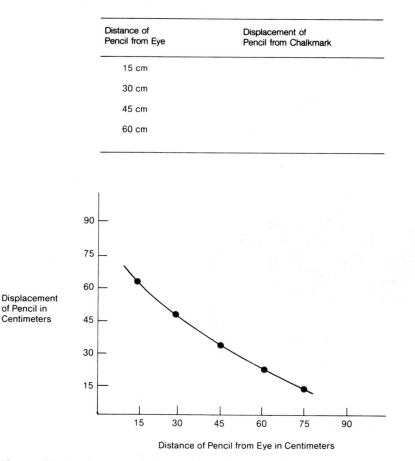

Distance of Pencil from Eye	Displacement of Pencil from Chalkmark
15 cm	
30 cm	
45 cm	
60 cm	

Figure 23–7 ■ Determining Parallax by Graphical Analysis

The graph should look approximately like the graph in Figure 23–7. The teacher may ask the children to interpolate and extrapolate answers to such questions as: "A displacement of 80 cm on the chalkboard would mean the pencil was how far from the eye?" "A displacement of x inches (some number larger than any experimental displacement) would mean the pencil was how far from the eye?"

Concept 5

Stars appear to form pictures in the sky.

Discussion

All of the heavenly bodies look to humans like points of light on a large sphere whose center is the earth. The stars' positions on such a celestial sphere (Figure 23–8) may be described by means of latitude and longitude or some similar scheme.

Ancient people saw patterns in the stars—kings and beasts and lovers—and told stories about them. These purely contrived patterns of stars are called constellations. In reality, the points of light we think of as single stars may be pairs of stars or triplets or even whole galaxies. Furthermore, the stars of a constellation may not be associated with one another in any stellar sense. Some may be nearby, in the Milky Way, and some may be far distant, outside it. The only relationship the individual stars of a constellation may have to each other is in the apparent

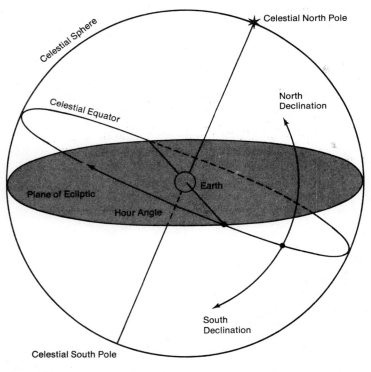

Figure 23–8 ■ Celestial Sphere

arrangement they seem to have to an observer on earth.

The stars on the side of the earth away from the sun (the night side) appear to rise in the eastern sky as the earth turns upon its axis and to move toward the west. As the earth migrates in orbit about the sun, different stars fill the night sky. Except for the position of the planets, the night sky on a given date in one year is identical to the night sky on the same date in any other year.

Lesson Plan ▪ D

Orientation:	Grades 3–6.
Content Objective:	The children will identify the common constellations of stars by naming them.
Skill Objective:	The children are required to *observe* star patterns and to develop *spatial relationships* that permit them to identify constellations.
Materials:	Shoe box, heavy construction paper, flashlight.
Evaluation:	Students' group problem-solving skills, seat work, and sketches.

Procedure

Cut off one end of a large shoe box. Cut a circular hole about three inches in diameter in the opposite end. With a pin, puncture holes in pieces of black construction paper in the patterns of some common constellations. Hold one of these over the cut-off end of the box. Darken the room and shine a flashlight through the hole as in Figure 23–9. Change the patterns until the children can recognize a few of the constellations. Have them draw sketches of at least five constellations.

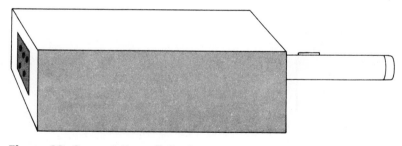

Figure 23–9 ▪ A Constellation Box

Orientation: Grades 3–6.

Content Objective: The children will point out the North Star and other familiar objects and constellations in the night sky.

Skill Objective: The children are required to *observe* a simulation of the night sky and to develop an awareness of the *spatial relationships* that exist among heavenly bodies.

Materials: Constellation box, star chart, flashlight.

Evaluation: Students' verbal interaction.

Procedure

The night skies vary according to the region and the time of year. However, when the atmosphere is clear, the North Star (Polaris) and some nearby constellations are visible in all northern latitudes in all seasons. Using pictures and a constellation box, help the children to recognize the circumpolar constellations. Then present the problem of locating the North Star in the evening sky. The North Star will be found as high off the northern horizon as the latitude of the observer. For instance, New York is at a latitude of 42° above the northern horizon. Therefore, the North Star will be located 42° above the northern horizon. Polaris is a star of only medium brightness, so an observer may need to use certain circumpolar constellations to locate it. (See Figure 23–10.)

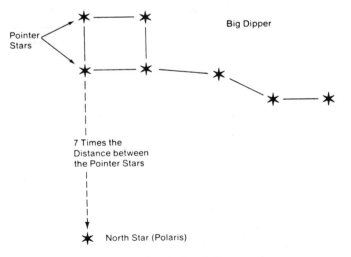

Figure 23–10 ■ Locating the North Star

Concept 6

The earth is part of the solar system.

Discussion

The earth is one of nine planets rotating at various distances around the sun. Astronomers speculate that the planets were torn from the sun by a passing star (tidal theory) or condensed to their present state from a cloud of dust, gas, and meteoroids at about the same time as the sun was formed (dust-cloud theory).

Some Facts about the Solar System

The Explorer and Voyager missions have added much to our knowledge of the solar system in recent years. Following is a brief summary of some important facts, including information gained through the space exploration programs of the National Aeronautics and Space Administration (NASA).

Sun

The sun is a medium-sized star in the Milky Way Galaxy; its gravity controls the orbits of nine planets that move about it in elliptical orbits. The sun is a huge rotating nuclear furnace and is composed mainly of hydrogen, helium (a product of the fusion of hydrogen atoms), and traces of heavier elements such as the metals iron and nickel. The sun's surface includes sunspots, flares, and solar prominences. Sunspots occur where magnetic fields emerge from the surface, resulting in locally cooler temperatures. They appear in eleven-year cycles and are believed to affect the earth's weather and the amount of cosmic particles that strike its atmosphere. Solar flares are regions of intense heat. Prominences are pinnacles of solar matter thrown high above the sun's surface, presumably by explosions. The *period of rotation* of the sun is 25 days at the equator. Its *diameter* is 1,400,000 km, about 875,000 miles. It has a *mass* 353,000 times as great as that of the earth.

And its *temperature* is 15,000,000° Celsius in the core and 5,500° Celsius on the surface. The source of the sun's energy is the fusion of atoms, principally hydrogen.

Mercury

Mercury is the planet whose orbit is closest to the sun. It is a small planet, less than one-half the diameter of the earth, nearly devoid of atmosphere (except for traces of sodium and helium), and very hot. It is a "dead" planet, having had no volcanic activity for several billion years and pocked by countless craters created by meteor strikes. Mercury, like the other three "inner" planets, Venus, Earth and Mars, has a metal core that is surrounded by a silicate shell.

Distance from the Sun: 57,900,000 km—about 37,000,000 miles.

Period of Revolution Around the Sun: 88 days.

Rotation: 59 days.

Diameter: 4,800 km—about 3,000 miles.

Mass: 1/20 that of the earth.

Surface Temperature: 450°C on day side, minus 180°C on the night side.

Moons: None.

Venus

Venus, the second planet from the sun, is most notable for its dense cloud cover, about 100 times as dense as the earth's, that renders its surface invisible except to radar and other scanning devices. The Venusian atmosphere is composed mostly of carbon dioxide. The clouds are droplets of sulfuric acid. The greenhouse effect of the dense cloud cover causes the surface of Venus to be very warm, and its reflection of sunlight makes it appear to be the brightest "star" in the morning and evening sky. Evidence of volcanism and meteor strikes has been observed, although it is believed Venus no longer has active volcanoes.

Distance from the Sun: 108,200,000 km—about 68,000,000 miles.

Period of Revolution Around the Sun:
225 days.

Rotation: 243 days.

Diameter: 12,100 km—about 7,560 miles.

Mass: 0.8 that of the earth.

Surface Temperature: 480°C.

Moons: None.

Earth

Our favorite planet; the only one known to support life. The earth's atmosphere is four-fifths nitrogen and one-fifth oxygen, with traces of other gases. Clouds of water vapor and oceans that cover nearly four-fifths of its surface make the earth the "water planet." The earth is still volcanically active, and huge continental plates drift slowly about on a molten mantle of rock.

Distance from the Sun: 149,000,000 km—about 90,000,000 miles.

Period of Revolution Around the Sun:
365.2 days.

Rotation: 23.9 hours.

Diameter: 12,750 km—about 7,980 miles.

Mass: 6 × 10 to the 21st power metric tons.

Surface Temperature: Averages 15°C.

Moons: 1.

Mars

Called the "Red Planet" because of windblown, iron-rich dust covering its surface, and possessing surface features visible with small telescopes, Mars has long excited the curiosity of earth dwellers. It has a thin atmosphere composed mainly of carbon dioxide and water vapor. Features observed on Mars include polar ice caps of frozen water and carbon dioxide, a 25 km-high extinct volcano, a 5,000 km-long canyon system, and a channel system and dunes probably formed by actions of water in the past. The composition of Mars is similar to that of the earth, having a metal core surrounded by a shell of silicate material.

Distance from the Sun: 227.9 million km—about 142.4 million miles.

Period of Revolution Around the Sun:
687 days.

Rotation: 24.6 hours.

Diameter: 6,787 km—about 4,242 miles.

Mass: 0.1 that of the earth.

Surface Temperature: Averages −50°C.

Moons: None.

Asteroids

Separating the inner planets, which are composed of metal cores surrounded by silicate shells, and the four giant outer planets, which are composed chiefly of hydrogen and helium, is a belt of asteroids. Countless in number, the asteroids, composed mainly of rock and iron, range in size from 1 km in diameter to more than 1,000 km. These small objects orbit about the sun in the same manner as the larger planets. They are believed to be debris left over from the formation of the solar system billions of years ago.

Comets

Comets were called "the wanderers" by ancient astronomers, because their orbits, greatly affected by the gravitational effects of the sun and planets, are elongated and they appear to wander among the stars in the night sky. Comets have a nucleus of ice and dust and a small body, or coma, of gases and dust. As these celestial objects approach close to the sun, much of the material that forms the coma vaporizes and forms a tail that always points away from the sun due to the pressure of light and solar wind upon it.

Jupiter

Jupiter is the closest to the sun of a group of four giant outer planets that include Jupiter, Saturn, Uranus, and Neptune. These four planets contain 99 percent of all the matter that makes up the solar system outside the sun. Jupiter, like each of these four planets, is a rotating gaseous sphere composed chiefly of hydrogen and helium with traces of ammonia, methane, and water, which are compressed into liquid and even metallic forms deep under its surface. Scientists suspect that Jupiter and the other giant planets possess a core of metals and silicates. Jupiter is the largest planet, one-tenth the size of the sun. The atmosphere of Jupiter is turbulent, with huge violent windstorms that last for centuries. One such storm, the Great Red Spot, which is three times as large as the earth's diameter, was first observed about 300 years ago.

Distance from the Sun: 778.3 million km—about 486.4 million miles.

Period of Revolution Around the Sun: 11.86 years.

Rotation: 9.9 hours.

Diameter: 142,000 km—about 88,750 miles.

Mass: 318 times that of the earth.

Temperature: −130°C at cloud tops.

Moons: 16. Four moons of Jupiter—Io, Europa, Ganymede, and Galileo—are very large, about the size of the planet Pluto. Io was observed by Voyager I to have volcanic activity with sulfur and sulfur compounds being ejected hundreds of kilometers above the surface. All four of Jupiter's large satellites are thought to have silicate cores, and all but Io are covered by layers of ice, which may overlie oceans of water.

Saturn

The second largest planet in the solar system, Saturn is well known for its majestic rings made up of a countless number of orbiting, icy particles. Like Jupiter, Saturn is composed mainly of hydrogen and helium gases with traces of ammonia, methane, and water that are compressed into liquid and metallic forms deep under the surface. Silicates and metals are likely to make up its core. Saturn's mostly hydrogen atmosphere is churned by large-scale, violent storms.

Distance from the Sun: 1,427 million km—about 892 million miles.

Period of Revolution Around the Sun: 29.46 years.

Rotation: 10.7 hours.

Diameter: 120,000 km—about 75,000 miles.

Mass: 95 times that of the earth.

Temperature: −185°C at cloud tops.

Moons: 17. Titan, the largest of all planetary satellites, has an atmosphere composed of nitrogen.

Uranus

Composed chiefly of hydrogen and helium and traces of ammonia, methane, water, and other volatiles, Uranus likely has a silicate and metallic core. Strangely, Uranus is tilted on its axis at an angle of 98°; that is, it rotates lying on its side. Uranus and Neptune both have a green-blue color due to the absorption of red light by methane gas contained in their atmospheres. Uranus has a system of rings, much less spectacular than Saturn's, that is believed held in place by tiny orbiting moons.

Distance from the Sun: 2,870 million km—about 1,794 million miles.

Period of Revolution Around the Sun: 84 years.

Rotation: 17.2 hours.

Diameter: 51,300 km—about 32,000 miles.

Mass: 14.4 times that of the earth.

Temperature: −200°C at cloud tops.

Moons: 15. Uranus' moon Miranda is a very odd appearing body. Its surface is broken and jumbled as though it has been shattered by one or more collisions with other bodies and reassembled under the force of gravity.

Neptune

Neptune has a composition like that of the other great planets. Composed of hydrogen, helium, ammonia, methane, and water, it is believed to have a silicate and metallic core. Like Uranus, Neptune has a blue-green appearance due to the presence of methane in its atmosphere. And like Jupiter and Saturn its surface is covered by large, violent atmospheric storms. Neptune also has rings much less pronounced than those of Saturn and three bright arc segments imbedded in its outermost ring.

Distance from the Sun: 4,497 million km—about 2,811 million miles.

Period of Revolution Around the Sun: 165 years.

Rotation: 16.1 hours.

Diameter: 49,100 km—about 30,687 miles.

Mass: 17.2 times that of the earth.

Temperature: −200°C at cloud tops.

Moons: 8. Triton, the largest of the moons, has a thin atmosphere composed chiefly of nitrogen. Geyserlike plumes spurt some ten kilometers above the sparkling nitrogen–frost-covered surface of Triton.

Pluto

The outermost planet in the solar system is also the smallest. It is a ball of frozen methane and water mixed with rock. Pluto has a single moon, Charon, which is more than half its size and similar in composition. Pluto has a thin atmosphere of methane gas. It is considered by some astronomers to be a double planet. It is a unique intermediate object lying between the planets and a "belt" of comets that exist in the darkness at the limits of the sun's gravitational field. During each revolution, Pluto passes inside Neptune's orbit for a twenty-year period; the most recent one began in 1979.

Distance from the Sun: 5,900 million km—about 3,688 million miles.

Period of Revolution Around the Sun: 248 years.

Rotation: 6.4 days.

Diameter: 2,300 km—about 1,438 miles.

Mass: .003 that of the earth.

Temperature: −230°C at surface.

Moons: One, Charon, which has a diameter of 1,200 km (about 750 miles) and is composed of icy water, methane, and rocks, similar in structure to Pluto.

Note: A more comprehensive account of the Voyager missions and a more comprehensive account of current knowledge of the solar system may be found in *National Geographic* 172, no. 2 (August 1990).

Subconcept 6–1

The planets are very small and very far away from the sun.

Discussion

Most adults have a poor concept of the relationship between the size of the planets and their distance from the sun. The sizes of the planets are shown in Chart 23–1, along with information related to size-distance concepts.

Using the diameters of the planets as an index, it may be seen that Mercury is over 9,000 of its diameters away from the sun. Venus is over 8,000 Venusian diameters from the sun; the earth is over 11,000 earth diameters away; and the outermost planet, Pluto, is 900,000 Plutonian diameters away from the sun. The size and distance relationships of the solar system are very difficult to visualize because the distances are vast in comparison to the size of the planets. No classroom model can demonstrate them properly. There is simply not enough room. To establish the spatial relationships among the bodies of the solar system, the teacher must move outside to the playground.

Chart 23–1 ▪ Temperature, Distance from the Sun, Diameter, and the Length of the Year of the Planets

	Temp. °F	Distance from Sun (Millions of Miles)	Diameter (Miles)	Length of Year
Sun			875,000	
Mercury	770	37	3,000	88 days
Venus	130	68	7,600	225 days
Earth	55	90	7,980	365.25 days
Mars	30	142	4,200	1.88 years
Asteroids		200–300	up to 600	1.75–13 years
Jupiter	−225	486	89,000	11.86 years
Saturn	−250	892	75,000	29.50 years
Uranus	−300	1,794	32,000	84 years
Neptune	−350	2,800	31,000	165 years
Pluto	−400	3,700	1,400	250 years

Lesson Plan ▪ F

Orientation: Grades 5–6.

Content Objective: The children will verbally describe the size-distance relationships among the bodies that comprise the solar system.

Skill Objective: The children are required to *observe* a model of the solar system and to *describe* the *spatial relationships* that exist among its parts.

Materials: One volleyball, two straight pins, two seamstress pins with plastic heads, one Ping-Pong ball.

Evaluation: Students' verbal interaction.

Procedure

Take the class to one side of the playground. Give one child a volleyball to hold. Tell the children: "This represents the sun." Pace off twelve large paces and place a child at that point, holding a straight pin. Tell them: "This pinhead represents Mercury." Pace off another ten large paces and place a child holding a seamstress pin. Ask: "What planet does the seamstress pinhead represent?" (Venus.) Pace off nine more paces and place a child holding a second seamstress pin. "This is?" (Earth.) Pace off fourteen more paces and place a child with a second straight pin. "This is?" (Mars.) An-

other 115 paces and a Ping-Pong ball would add Jupiter to the model, although most playgrounds will not accommodate this. (See Chart 23–2.) Let the children look at the abbreviated model of the solar system. You may point out that Jupiter would be a Ping-Pong ball one and one-half football fields away from the volleyball and that Pluto would be a pinhead at some appropriate spot three-quarters of a mile from the volleyball. Emphasize the emptiness of space and the great distances between the planets. Figure 23–11 illustrates the relative sizes of the sun and the planets.

continued on next page

Chart 23–2 ▪ Relative Positions of the Planets

Body	Distance from Sun in Large Paces	Diameter of Body (Inches)	Object to Represent
Sun		12	Volleyball
Mercury	12	$\frac{1}{32}$	Straight Pinhead
Venus	22	$\frac{1}{16}$	Seamstress Pinhead
Earth	31	$\frac{1}{16}$	Seamstress Pinhead
Mars	45	$\frac{1}{24}$	Straight Pinhead
Jupiter	160	$1\frac{1}{2}$	Ping-Pong Ball

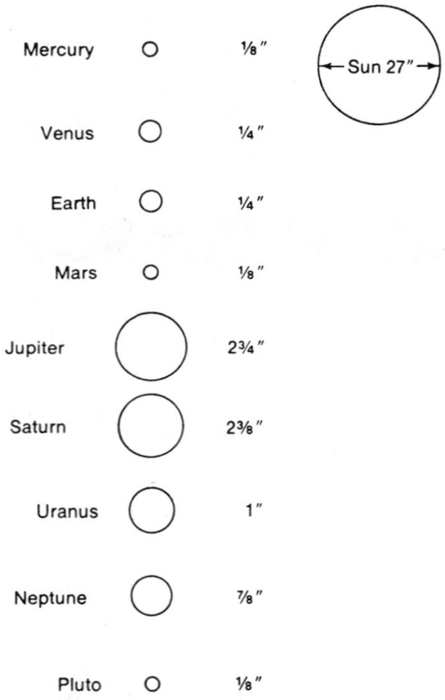

Mercury ○	$\frac{1}{8}$"	
		Sun 27"
Venus ○	$\frac{1}{4}$"	
Earth ○	$\frac{1}{4}$"	
Mars ○	$\frac{1}{8}$"	
Jupiter ◯	$2\frac{3}{4}$"	
Saturn ◯	$2\frac{3}{8}$"	
Uranus ◯	1"	
Neptune ◯	$\frac{7}{8}$"	
Pluto ○	$\frac{1}{8}$"	

Figure 23–11 ▪ The Relative Sizes of the Bodies of the Solar System

Subconcept 6–2

Planets differ from one another.

Discussion

The planets' atmospheres are made up of gases. These gases are held to a planet by gravitational attraction. The extent of the gravitational force exerted by a planet upon its atmosphere is determined by the planet's mass. Small planets such as Mercury have too little gravity to hold their atmospheres. They have lost any gases they might once have had. Furthermore, molecules of atmospheric gases at high temperatures have a great velocity. The high velocity of such molecules causes them to escape into space.

The pattern appears to be that small planets such as Mercury, Mars, and Pluto have almost no atmosphere. Middle-sized planets such as Earth and Venus have moderately dense atmospheres. And the larger outer planets—Jupiter, Saturn, Uranus, and Neptune—appear to have very dense atmospheres.

The temperature of a planet is primarily a function of its distance from the sun, although a planet with a dense atmosphere tends to retain more of the sun's energy that strikes its surface and is therefore somewhat warmer. Mercury, the planet closest to the sun, is extremely hot, while Pluto, the planet farthest from the sun, is extremely cold.

Lesson Plan ■ G

Orientation:	Grades 4–6.
Content Objective:	The children will state the relative temperature and atmospheric density of the planets.
Skill Objective:	The children are required to *infer* a pattern of relationships between planet size and atmospheric density and between distance from the sun and temperature.
Materials:	Worksheets containing Chart 23–3 as well as a reference source that gives each planet's size and its distance from the sun.
Evaluation:	Seat work, chart.

Procedure

Make a copy of Chart 23–3, leaving blanks where terms are now in parentheses. Ask your students to complete the chart. They should draw the best inferences they can from the information you give them. They may describe temperature as being "very hot," "hot," "warm," "cold," and "very cold." They may describe the atmosphere as being "none," "light," "medium," and "very dense." The children should have a reference available that gives each planet's size and its distance from the sun.

After the children have filled in the chart by inference, have them check their inferences by locating the correct answers in some source book. You may ask the children: "Why might the earth be the only planet of the solar system that is suited for life as we know it?" (It is the only planet that has an atmosphere and temperature suited to supporting life.)

Chart 23–3 ■ Atmosphere and Temperature of the Planets

Planet	Amount of Atmosphere	Temperature
Mercury	none	very hot
Venus*	(dense)†	(hot)†
Earth	medium	warm
Mars	(light)†	(warm-cold)†
Jupiter	(very dense)†	(cold–very cold)†
Saturn	(very dense)†	(very cold)†
Uranus	(dense)†	(very cold)†
Neptune	(dense)†	(very cold)†
Pluto	none	very cold

*Scientists think that the Venusian atmosphere may have been formed from internal gases in relatively recent times. This would account for its unusual density.

†Leave these blank for the children to fill in.

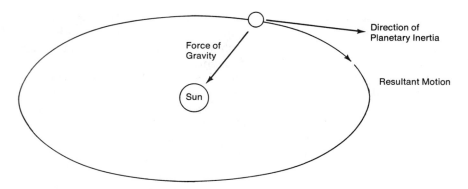

Figure 23–12 ■ Planetary Motion

Subconcept 6–3

Planets orbit about the sun.

Discussion

Planets follow a nearly circular path as they orbit about the sun. What forces hold them in that path? Why do all the planets, as well as artificial satellites, enter into the same kind of orbit? Let us see.

We know that if we whirl an object tied to a string around our head and let go of the string, the object will fly away from us. This is because the object has inertia. Inertia causes a moving object to continue to move in a straight line unless some force acts upon it. So moving planets would fly away from the sun in a straight line if it were not for a force acting upon them. That force is gravity. The gravitational attraction between the planet and the sun changes the direction of the planet's motion so that it follows a nearly circular path about the sun.

Two factors, then, keep a planet in motion about the sun. One is the inertia that would cause the planet to fly off into space. The second is gravity, which continually alters the direction of the planet's motion so that it follows a circular path about the sun. (See Figure 23–12.)

Lesson Plan ■ **H**	
Orientation:	Grades 3–6.
Content Objective:	The children will state that the two forces that keep a planet in orbit are inertia and gravity. They will state that the velocity of the planet determines its distance from the sun.
Skill Objective:	The children are required to *observe* a model of planetary motion, to *analyze* the motion, and to *infer* the relationship of the model to the solar system.
Materials:	Four chalkboard erasers, string, thread spool.
Evaluation:	Students' verbal interaction.

continued on next page

Procedure

Tie a string around the middle of a chalkboard eraser, leaving an end about two feet long. Insert this free end through the hole of a thread spool. Hold the end of the string where it emerges from the bottom of the spool and use the spool to whirl the eraser in circles. Ask the children: "What would happen if I released the string?" (The eraser would fly off.) "Let us see." Release the string and watch the eraser fly away in a straight line. Repeat. "What does an object that is orbiting about a central point have a tendency to do when it is released?" (Fly off in a straight line. Refer to Newton's laws of motion, Chapter 20.)

Now tie two chalkboard erasers to the end of the string where it emerges from the bottom of the spool as in Figure 23–13. Hold the two bottom erasers lightly in one hand and continue using the spool to whirl the single eraser around in circles as before. Release the bottom erasers and continue to whirl the top eraser around the spool. "We know the eraser would fly off if it could because of its inertia. What is holding it in its circular path?" (The string tied to it.) "If the orbiting eraser were a planet, what force would the string represent?" (The force of gravity between the sun and the planet.) "So what may we say are the two forces that determine the orbit of a planet?" (The inertia of the planet and the force of gravity between the planet and the sun.)

Resume whirling the eraser slowly around the spool. Ask the children: "I wonder what would happen if I increased the speed of the eraser?" (Accept the

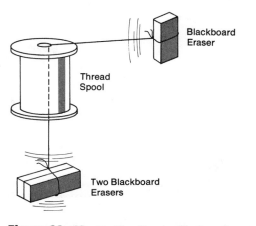

Figure 23–13 ■ The Circular Motion of an Orbiting Object

children's guesses and then increase the speed of the whirling eraser.) "What happens when the eraser moves faster?" (It moves farther away from the spool.) Slow down and speed up the motion of the eraser. Ask: "The distance at which an object orbits about a central point appears to depend chiefly upon what?" (Its speed.) "Then the distance that each planet maintains from the sun is due to what factor?" (The speed of a planet determines its distance from the sun.)

The teacher may wish to extend the discussion to artificial satellites that are governed by exactly the same physical laws. The radius of the orbit of an artificial satellite is determined by the velocity imparted to the satellite by rocket engines.

Subconcept 6–4

Time is measured by the motions of heavenly bodies.

Discussion

Ancient cavemen must have noticed that such natural events as the changing of the seasons and the phases of the moon recur regularly.

Egyptian astronomers charted the heavens and noticed that the same star would appear in the same position every 365 days.

Except for the polar regions, any position on earth is exposed to some hours of sunlight and some hours of darkness each day as it is turned alternately toward and away from the sun. The earth rotates a full circle, 360°, each day. It is therefore convenient to call the time it takes the earth to rotate 15° one hour.

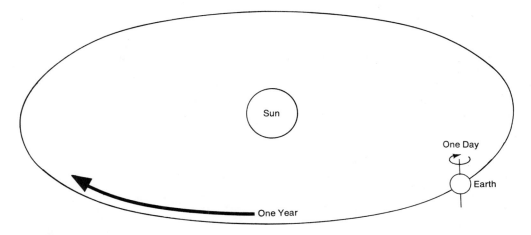

Figure 23–14 ■ Two Motions of the Earth

Thus, there are twenty-four hours in one day $\left(\dfrac{360°}{15° \text{ per hour}}\right)$, and each hour time zone is 15° wide.

The earth makes 365¼ rotations in one year—the time it takes to complete one orbit of the sun. The length of the month is the approxi- mate time required for the moon to complete one orbit of the earth. Thus, days, months, and years are all measured by the motions of heav- enly bodies.

Figure 23–14 illustrates the two motions of the earth.

Lesson Plan ■ I

Orientation:	Pre-K—2.
Content Objective:	The children will describe shadows as places where the sun is blocked out; they will describe how shadows are different at various times of the day; and they'll understand the relationship between the position of an object, its shadow, and the sun.
Skill Objective:	The children will *investigate*, *observe*, and make *inferences*.
Materials:	Meter or yard sticks or a blank stick of the approximate same length.
Evaluation:	Students' group problem-solving skills, verbal interaction.

Procedure

Activity 1—Morning shadows: Take the children out- side on a sunny day at about nine o'clock in the morn- ing. Have them stand so that there are several feet of space between them. Tell them, "Each of us has a 'friend' with us who likes to play with us. This friend does everything you do and goes with you wherever

continued on next page

you go. Do you know what friend I am talking about?" Give them clues until the children guess you are talking about their shadows. Have them attempt to move their arms, heads, legs, and their whole bodies without their shadows moving. Have them attempt to step on their shadows and run away from them.

After they have had time to explore their shadows in this way, pair each student with a partner and give each pair a meter stick or a plain stick that is about as long as a meter stick. Ask them which is longer, "you or your shadow." Have them use the meter sticks to make comparisons between their heights and the lengths of their shadows. Ask them to test other children and objects on the playground to see if their shadows are longer or shorter.

Gather the class together again and lead them to where they can view the shadow of a prominent object such as the flagpole or a tree. Ask them to describe the direction in which the shadow of the object is pointing (toward the school, road, playground, and so on.) Then ask them if their shadows are pointing in the same direction as the object. Also ask, "Do all the shadows point in the same direction?" "Where is the sun?" (Do *not* permit the children to stare at the sun.) Have them point in its general direction.) See if the children understand the relationship between the position of the sun, objects, and their shadows—that shadows are the places where the sun is blocked out.

Activity 2—Shadows at noontime: As close as possible to twelve o'clock noon, take the children outdoors. (If it has become very cloudy, put off this activity until a day when the sun is shining at noontime.) Ask the children to pair themselves with the same partners they had in the morning and have them repeat Activity 1, starting with where they compared their heights with the length of their shadows. Of course, at noon they will find their shadows to be much shorter than they were in the morning. Discuss this with them to see if they might know why this is true. Do not press them if this is not apparent to them. Next, take them to the same place they observed the flagpole or other object. Repeat this portion of Activity 1. Ask them which direction the shadow of the flagpole is pointing, and which is longer—the flagpole or its shadow. Discuss with them whether the shadows of all objects would be shorter at noon than in the morning.

Activity 3—Shadows in the afternoon: At about three o'clock (or as late as possible in the afternoon), repeat Activity 2. The children will find their shadows have grown longer again, and the direction in which the shadows are pointing has changed. Ask them if they think what they found about shadows is true for shadows every day or if shadows are different each day. Ask them questions such as, "If the sun is over there (pointing), which direction would your shadow point?" and "If your shadow is pointing that direction, where would the sun be?"

Lesson Plan ▪ J

Orientation:	Grades 2–6.
Content Objective:	The children will say what time of day it is when the sun is in various positions in relation to the earth.
Skill Objective:	The children are required to *observe* some *spatial relationships* presented by an earth-sun model and to *infer* their meaning in terms of time.
Materials:	Earth globe, flashlight, chalk or crayon.
Evaluation:	Students' verbal interaction.

continued on next page

Procedure

Darken the classroom and shine a flashlight on a globe. Tell the children: "We are going to investigate day and night. What does the globe represent?" (The earth.) "Can you find our position on the globe?" (Mark this position clearly with a crayon or chalk.) "What does the flashlight represent?" (The sun.) Direct one child to hold the flashlight so that it shines on the globe. Rotate "our location" so that it is on the lighted side of the globe and directly in line with the flashlight. Ask: "What time would it be when we are in this position?" (Noon.) Rotate the globe until "our position" is on the dark side of the globe, directly opposite the flashlight. "What time is it now?" (Midnight.) Rotate the globe slowly so that "our position" approaches the terminal line of the light. Remember to turn the globe so that "our position" moves toward the east. Ask: "What time of day is it when we are just entering into the sunlight?" (Dawn, morning.) Rotate the globe until "our position" is approaching the opposite terminal line and moving into the darkness. Ask: "What time of day is it now?" (Dusk, evening, twilight.) "Now using our earth-sun model, let's go through a whole day." Rotate the globe slowly and

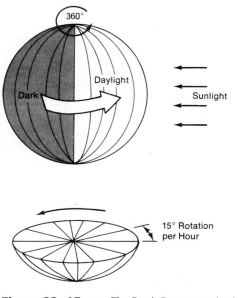

Figure 23–15 ■ The Earth Rotates on Its Axis

have the children name the time of day that various positions represent. (See Figure 23–15.)

Lesson Plan ■ K

Orientation:	Grades 2–6.
Content Objective:	When told the time of day at one spot on a globe, the children will state the time of day at other spots on the globe.
Skill Objective:	The children are required to *observe* some *spatial relationships* presented by an earth-sun model and to *infer* their meaning in terms of time.
Materials:	Earth globe, flashlight, chalk or crayon.
Evaluation:	Students' verbal interaction, seat work, and sketches.

Procedure

Set up the sun-earth model as in Lesson Plan J and Figure 23–16. Place "our location" directly under the flashlight beam at the noon position. Ask the children:

"What time is it now?" (Noon.) "At some place on earth it must be midnight. Can you guess where that might be?" (Japan, China, Asia.) "When it is midnight

continued on next page

here, what time would it be in Japan?" (Noon.) "Let us see." Then rotate the globe to place "our location" at the midnight position.

"Now let us look at the time at different places in the United States." Mark the locations of New York, Chicago, Denver, and San Francisco on the globe. Rotate the globe so that New York is in the dawn position, coming into the light. "What time is it in New York?" (Dawn.) "Is it dawn yet in San Francisco? Denver? Chicago?" (No.) "If it is still night in Chicago when it is dawn in New York, must it be earlier or later on the clock in Chicago than in New York?" (Earlier.) The

teacher may continue to establish time relationships in this way with various combinations of locations until she is satisfied that the children comprehend the time relationship concept.

You may also wish to provide the children with a worksheet on which they will write the words *dawn, noon, evening*, and *midnight* to describe the time of day at certain locations on the globe. (Allow them to use the globe themselves: Ask them to set the globe in one position, write the correct time of day for one location, and then write the correct time of day for a second location with the globe in the same position.)

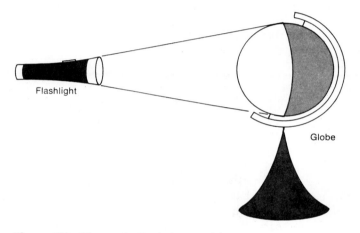

Flashlight

Globe

Figure 23–16 ■ An Earth-Sun Model

Lesson Plan ■ L

Orientation:	Grades K–2.
Content Objective:	The children will state that the length and the position of shadows change during the day—that shadows are longer in the morning and afternoon and shorter at noon.
Skill Objective:	The children are required to *observe* the length and position of shadows and to *infer* the relationship that exists between length and position of shadows and the time of day.
Materials:	Chalk.
Evaluation:	Students' verbal interaction, seat work, and sketches.

continued on next page

Procedure

On a sunny morning, take the class outdoors. Tell the children that you would like them to discover as many things about shadows as they can. Outside, instruct the children to face in such a direction that they can see their own shadows. Say: "Raise your arm. What does your shadow do? Lift your leg. What does your shadow do?" Have the children bend over, hop up and down, and perform other movements while watching their shadows. Ask: "What does your shadow do?"

Next, have all the children stand in the shadow of a large tree or the building. Then move them out of the shadow into the sunlight. "Do you notice anything different about being in the shadow and in the sunlight?" (It is warmer in the sunlight than in the shadow.)

Using chalk, draw a small circle on the sidewalk. Have one child stand in the circle. Ask a second child to draw a line where the shadow of the child in the circle ends. Write "MORNING" beside the line. About noon, and again in the afternoon, take the class back to the same spot. Ask the same child to stand in the circle, draw lines that mark the end of the shadow each time, and write beside the marks, "NOON" and "AFTERNOON." After completing the exercise in the afternoon, ask the children: "What did we find out about shadows?" (Shadows are long in the morning and afternoon, but short at noon. Shadows move and are different places during the day. My shadow does whatever I do. It is colder in a shadow than in the sunlight.) Try to get the children to guess what a shadow is. Write the three major concepts on the chalkboard and have the children copy them.

Subconcept 6–5

The earth has seasons.

Discussion

The earth moves about the sun in a roughly circular orbit. This orbit might be thought of as a huge, flat saucer with the sun at the center and the earth on the outer rim. A close examination would show that the earth's equator does not correspond to the plane formed by the saucer. Rather, it lies at an angle of 23.5 degrees to the saucer. The earth is, in fact, tilted upon its axis.

Because the earth's equator and the plane of its orbit are not aligned, different parts of the earth receive the direct rays of the sun at different times of year. The average temperature of the earth and the atmosphere is highest in the part that receives the direct rays of the sun. As the earth moves through its orbit, the part of the earth that receives the direct rays changes. This gives us our seasons. Summer occurs in the hemisphere that is tilted toward the sun. Winter occurs in the hemisphere that is tilted away from the sun.

Lesson Plan ▪ M

Orientation:	Grades 2–5.
Content Objective:	The children will state that the earth has seasons because different parts of the earth receive more sunlight at different times of the year. The children will describe the characteristics of their environment during the various seasons.
Skill Objective:	The children will *observe* a sun-earth model and *infer* that different places on earth receive varying amounts of sunlight during the year.

continued on next page

Materials:	Large globe, flashlight, chalk, three paper doll figures.
Evaluation:	Students' verbal interaction.

Procedure

Cut three doll figures from paper and tape them to a globe, one in the United States, one at the equator, and one in South America. You may name the figures Joe, Carlos, and Juan, respectively. Hold a flashlight about one foot away from the globe, changing its position so that it shines directly above each figure. Ask the class: "What does the flashlight represent?" (The sun.) "When the sun is directly over Joe's head, who would be warmest, Joe or Juan?" (Joe.) "If the sun remained over Joe's head for a long time, what season of the year would it be? What is the warm time of the year?" (Summer.) "When the earth tilts so that the sun is above Carlos's head, what season is it for Joe? What season follows summer?" In this way, move the position of the globe and the discussion through the four seasons. To conclude, ask the children: "Can we name the four seasons of the year in order? What might we say is the cause of the seasons on the earth?" (The sun is not over one person's head all the time.) As an extending activity, write the names of the four seasons on the chalkboard and have the children describe the characteristics of each season: summer—hot, no school, no rain, flowers grow, vegetables grow, and so on.

Figure 23–17 shows how the sun strikes the earth's surface at different times of the year.

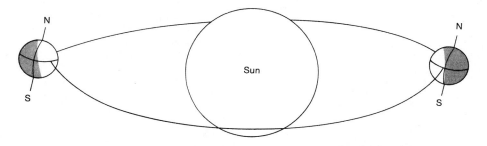

Figure 23–17 ■ The Sun Strikes the Earth at Varying Angles Throughout the Year

Lesson Plan ■ N

Orientation:	Grades 3–6.
Content Objective:	The children will state that light that strikes a paper at an angle is more spread out than light that strikes it directly.
Skill Objective:	The children are required to *investigate* by manipulating the angle at which a light strikes a surface, to *communicate* by constructing a data table, and to *interpret* the *data* they have acquired.
Materials:	Six to eight small flashlights, graph paper, eight dowel rods or pencils, tape, worksheets.
Evaluation:	Students' verbal interaction, laboratory worksheets, log, and reports.

continued on next page

Procedure

Arrange the children in groups of two or three. Provide each group with several sheets of graph paper with large ruled squares, a small (pencil) flashlight, and a copy of Chart 23–4. Have each group tape a dowel rod or pencil to the flashlight so that it extends about three inches beyond the light. Direct the children to hold the flashlight directly above the graph paper so that the projecting rod touches the paper. Each group is to trace around the lighted area with a pencil and count the number of squares within the outline. Portions of squares may be estimated and added together. Now have the children tilt the light at increasingly sharp angles. With the projecting rod still touching the graph paper, have them trace an outline of the lighted area each time and count the number of squares within the outline.

Each experimental group should discuss the following questions: "Why should the rod be taped on the flashlight?" (So the light will be at the same distance from the graph paper each time.) "What appears to be the relationship between the angle of the light and the number of squares within the lighted area?" (The more slanted the flashlight, the more squares within the lighted area.) (See Figure 23–18.) "Can you see a difference in the brightness of the light striking the graph paper at the different angles?" (The light reflected from the graph paper is brightest when it shines directly down upon the paper and becomes less bright as the angle of tilt increases.) "Could the temperature at certain places on the earth be affected if the sun strikes at different angles?" (Yes. Earth's seasons are caused by the differences in the angle at which the sun's rays strike.)

Chart 23–4 ▪ Relationship of Angle of Light to Area Illuminated

Position of Light	Area Within the Outlined Shape in Squares
Straight down	
Slightly tilted	
Tilted about 45°	

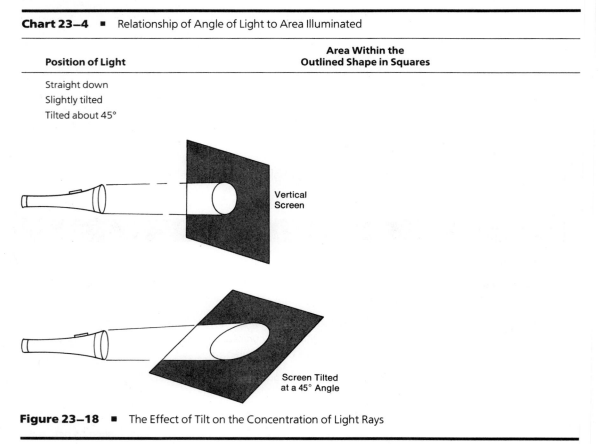

Figure 23–18 ▪ The Effect of Tilt on the Concentration of Light Rays

Subconcept 6–6

The moon interacts with the earth.

Discussion

The earth has one natural satellite. Although humans have now set foot upon this satellite, we know very little about it. What is it made of? What is its origin? What is the origin of its surface features? Is there any sign of life? Though we now have considerable data to aid our speculations, none of these questions has been answered with absolute certainty.

There are two current theories concerning the moon's origin. One is that the moon was torn from the Pacific Ocean basin while the earth was yet in a molten state. The second is that the moon condensed from gases and dust at about the same time as the earth. Most of the physical features of the moon appear to be caused by the impact of meteors, although some of the mountains and craters may be due to volcanic activity.

Rocks returned to the earth from the Apollo moon missions revealed no traces of microfossils. This leads authorities to speculate that no life in any form has ever existed on the moon.

Tides

The phases of the moon and the earth's tides are determined by the positions of three bodies: the earth, the moon, and the sun (see Figure 23–19). The ocean tides are caused by the gravitational pull of both the sun and the moon. However, because it is closer to the earth, the moon's gravitational influence is greater than the sun's.

As the earth rotates on its axis, the moon pulls on the ocean. The result is a bulge in the water level directly beneath the moon. There is also a bulge in the water level on the side of the earth opposite the moon. This second bulge is caused by the tendency of the water to remain in place (its inertia) and by a decrease with distance in the moon's gravitational attraction. As the earth rotates once upon its axis, the two bulges in the water level move, following the moon. This creates two high and two low tides.

The highest tides will occur then the moon, earth, and sun are aligned. This occurs when the moon is in positions A and C in Figure 23–19. These highest tides are called *spring tides*. When the sun and the moon are pulling at right angles to each other, as when the moon is in positions B and D, the high tides will be lower. These moderate tides are known as *neap tides*.

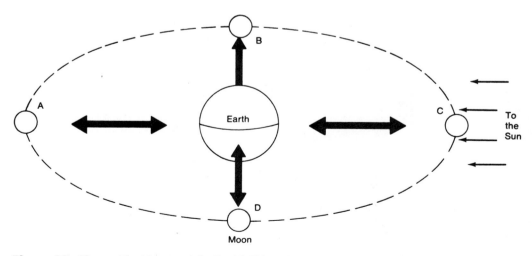

Figure 23–19 ■ The Moon and the Earth's Tides

Orientation:	Grades 3–6.
Content Objective:	The children will state that the phases of the moon are caused by the way the sunlight falls upon this body as it orbits the earth.
Skill Objective:	The children are required to *observe* the *spatial relationships* presented by a sun-earth-moon model and *infer* that the same relationships exist among the real bodies.
Materials:	Basketball or large globe, flashlight.
Evaluation:	Students' verbal interaction, seat work, and sketches.

Procedure

Have one child stand at the front of the room. Have a second child hold a basketball or large globe at about head height and three feet away from the first child as in position 1, Figure 23–20. Tell the children: "John is going to be the earth, and the basketball is the moon. I will hold a flashlight that will represent the sun. Let us see what happens." Darken the room and hold the flashlight beam on the basketball. Ask John: "What do you see?" (The ball is half dark and half light.) Move the basketball to positions 2, 3, and 4 and ask John each time to describe the ball. The flashlight beam should always come from the same direction. You may ask John to sketch the ball on the chalkboard in each

of its four positions. These will be the phases of the moon. Permit several more children to be "earths." Then say that the center of the room is the earth and position the basketball on each side of the room consecutively. The flashlight beam should come from the same general direction each time. The children may draw their own sketches of the basketball in each of the four positions.

To conclude the lesson, ask the children: "Why does the moon appear to have different shapes?" (Because of the position of the earth, sun, and moon.) On a worksheet showing sun, earth, and moon positions, have the children shade in the dark parts of the moon, leaving the lighted, visible parts white.

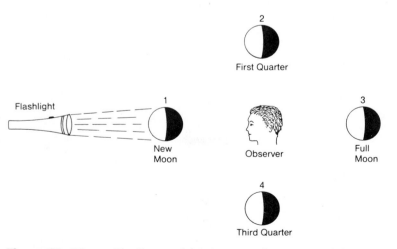

Figure 23–20 ■ The Phases of the Moon—A Classroom Model

Orientation:	Grades 2–6.
Content Objective:	The children will describe the positions of the sun, moon, and earth during solar and lunar eclipses.
Skill Objective:	The children are required to *observe* the *spatial relationships* of a moon-sun-earth model during eclipses of the sun and moon and to *infer* the transfer of these relationships to actual bodies.
Materials:	A globe, a flashlight, a small ball.
Evaluation:	Students' verbal interaction, seat work, and sketches.

Procedure

Arrange a globe, a flashlight, and a small ball as in Figure 23–21, with the moon at position 1. Ask the children: "Is it daylight or dark on the side of the earth where the sun is located?" (Daylight.) "What would the people see who were in the place on the earth where the moon's shadow is falling?" (They would be in darkness.) "This is called an eclipse of the sun because the sun's light is blocked in this small area by the moon." Then move the moon to position 2. Ask: "What time of day is it on the side of the earth where the moon is now?" (Nighttime.) "Could the people on this side of the earth see the moon?" (No, it is in the earth's shadow.) Move the ball in and out of the earth's shadow and allow the children to observe how the darkness moves across the face of the moon. Point out that this is a lunar eclipse. Have the children draw a picture of a lunar eclipse.

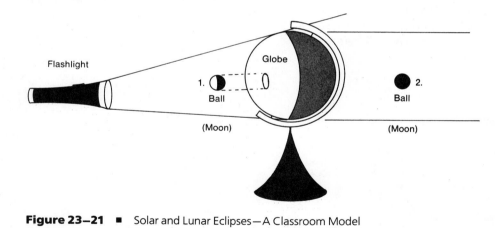

Figure 23–21 ▪ Solar and Lunar Eclipses—A Classroom Model

Lesson Plan ▪ Q

Orientation: Grades 3–6.

Content Objective: The children will state that each point on earth experiences two high and two low tides each day.

Skill Objective: The children are required to *observe* a model depicting earth tides and to *infer* the transfer of the relationships expressed to the actual earth.

Materials: A circle of brown paper one foot in diameter, an ellipse of green or blue paper cut so that the short axis is one foot long and the long axis is one foot and four inches, a tack.

Evaluation: Students' verbal interaction, seat work, and sketches.

Procedure

Cut a circle with a diameter of at least one foot from brown construction paper. Locate the North Pole in the center of the circle and points A, B, C, and D as shown in Figure 23–22. Now cut out an ellipse from blue or green construction paper with the short diameter equal to the diameter of the circle and the long diameter exceeding the diameter of the circle by two to four inches. Place the circle on top of the ellipse and attach them both to the bulletin board with a tack through their centers. Tell the children that the model will allow them to discuss the tides. Ask: "Where are the high tides now?" (At B and D.) "The low tides?" (At A and C.) "Where must the moon be located?" (Above points B and D.) Instruct the children to watch point A as the earth rotates one full turn. Ask: "How many high tides did A pass through?" (Two.) "How many low tides?" (Two.) "How many tides occur at any point on the earth during one day?" (There are two high tides and two low tides each day.) Have the children write (or copy from the board) statements that describe the causes of tides on earth, the names of the tides, and the number of tides per day.

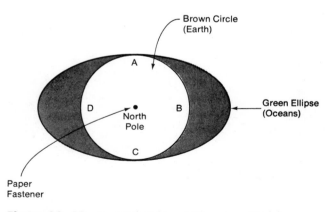

Figure 23–22 ▪ Earth Tides—A Classroom Model

Summary

What is the origin of the universe? We have formulated many highly speculative answers. The two most generally accepted ones are:

1. All the matter in the universe was once concentrated in a small region of space; it exploded outward and is continuing to expand in all directions.

2. Matter is constantly created out of nothingness to fill the void where local movement of galaxies occurs; the universe is constant in size and uniform throughout.

Stars appear to form out of clouds of hydrogen gas and dust. They evolve from red giants to main sequence and then to white dwarfs. As they become more compressed they also become hotter. Their source of energy is the fusion of the nuclei of atoms, with an accompanying loss of mass.

The sun is a star in the Milky Way galaxy. A galaxy is an island of stars, dust, and gases separated from other galaxies by vast regions of space. Man has probed 2 billion light-years into space with photographic and radio telescopes. There is no discernible reduction in the numbers of galaxies in those far regions. Within the Milky Way, there are many millions of stars extending in a saucer-shaped spiral over 100,000 light-years of space. The average distance between stars in the sun's part of the Milky Way is about 5 light-years.

When viewed from earth, the stars look like points of light on a celestial sphere, forming interesting patterns that suggest people, animals, and objects. These patterns are called constellations.

The solar system is composed of one medium star, the sun, and nine small planets. The planets orbit the sun. They are very far away from it if one measures the distance in relation to their diameters. Conditions of temperature and atmosphere appear to be functions primarily of a planet's mass and distance from the sun. Planetary motion is determined by the interaction of the planet's inertia and the sun's gravitational pull.

Common units of time measurement are derived from the periodic motions of heavenly bodies—the rotation of the earth on its axis, its orbiting motion around the sun, and the moon's orbiting motion around the earth.

Earth tides are bulges of water that remain in position beneath the moon as the earth rotates upon its axis. The tides thus appear to flow around the earth. A solar eclipse occurs when the moon is between the sun and the earth. A lunar eclipse occurs when the moon moves into the earth's shadow on the side of the earth away from the sun.

The Earth: Its Structure and History

Look What's in This Chapter

In this chapter we'll discuss some important concepts and subconcepts related to the study of the earth, and we'll present lesson plans that are designed to teach these concepts and subconcepts to children.

Concept 1 The earth began as a hot, liquid ball.

Concept 2 The earth's surface is constantly changing.

Concept 3 The record of the changing earth is preserved in rocks.

    Subconcept 3–1 All rocks may be classified into three groups.

Concept 4 Life has existed upon the earth for only a small fraction of the planet's history.

    Subconcept 4–1 Fossils are evidence of life in the earth's history.

The earth changes so little in any one person's lifetime that many people assume it has always been much as it is today—a constant environment of lands, seas, and air in which we have thrived. This is not true. Though the changes that occur in a lifetime are barely perceptible, change is taking place. The lifespan of a person compared to the lifespan of the earth is like a drop of water compared to an ocean. Over eons the earth's structure and surface have altered in ways that challenge the imagination. Step by step, the planet has evolved from a ball of hot gases to the warm, hospitable environment that spawned and permitted the development of the life forms that we know today.

Concept 1

The earth began as a hot, liquid ball.

Discussion

Whether the earth was pulled from the sun by a passing star (*tidal theory*) or was formed at the same time and from the same material as the sun (*dust-cloud* or *planetesimal theory*) is open to debate. It is generally agreed, however, that the earth began its existence as a ball of hot gases that gradually cooled to a liquid and then to a plasticlike state. Lighter materials floated to the surface of this *magma*, cooled, and solidified to form the *continental masses*. Heavier materials such as iron and nickel were pulled by *gravity* toward the center of the sphere to form a heavy, plastic core. Between the core and the continental crust a *mantle* of dense rock was formed (see Figure 24–1). In the early stages of formation all of the continents may have been part of one huge land mass that subsequently split into pieces that are even now drifting apart atop the hot mantle.

As the thin crust that covered the hot, molten rock mantle continued to cool and contract, great wrinkles and cracks were formed. Through them the molten rock flowed to the

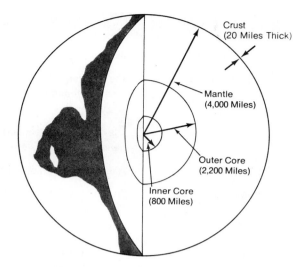

Figure 24–1 ■ The Earth's Structure

surface. This molten rock cooled and solidified to thicken the crust where the outpourings occurred.

Water vapor was released from the depths below the planet's crust to form tiny water droplets as it cooled in the empty space beyond the earth's surface. Water droplets and carbon dioxide formed dense clouds that blocked the sun's rays from the earth. After a long period of cooling, water fell as rain upon the surface of the earth and formed lakes and oceans. This precipitation helped to cool the still-hot sphere even further.

If an observer had been present at this stage of the earth's development, he would probably have seen great expanses of very warm ocean and a large, hot, steaming and lifeless land mass of *granite* and *basalt* rock. The entire surface would have been enveloped by clouds so thick as to virtually blot out the sun. Tremendous rainstorms would occur with regularity, accompanied by spectacular displays of lightning and thunder. It would be several billion more years before the first primitive life would appear on this ball of matter isolated in space and whirling at great speed about the sun.

Lesson Plan ▪ A

Orientation:	Grades 3–6.
Content Objective:	The children will state that we have been upon the earth for a very short time and that during most of its history the earth was a ball of lifeless rock and water.
Skill Objective:	The children are required to establish *time relationships* for the very long periods of earth history.
Materials:	A ten-foot length of roll paper, crayons or colored chalk, a ruler.
Evaluation:	Students' verbal interaction, student sketches.

Procedure

On a long sheet of roll paper draw a line ten feet long. This line will represent 5 billion years, the age of the earth. Starting at the left, measure off eight feet and draw a vertical line. At this point (1 billion years ago) primitive one-celled life appeared on earth. Measure to the right one foot and draw a second verticle line. This line represents when fishes first appeared in the oceans (500 million years ago). Now draw a line seven inches from the right end of the time line to represent the appearance of reptiles (300 million years ago). Draw the last line one and one-half inches from the right end of the time line to represent the appearance of mammals (60 million years ago). (See Figure 24–2.)

A line approximately 1/20,000 of an inch thick on the right end of the time line would represent the point in time when man appeared on the earth (2–5 million years ago).

If space permits, a twenty-foot time line may be constructed by doubling each dimension. Additional points may be added to the line as the teacher wishes. After completing the time line, the teacher may lead a discussion by asking such questions as: "What was the earth like for most of its existence?" "Compared to the whole earth history, how long have we been on earth?" Permit the children to draw sketches on the time line that are appropriate to each era.

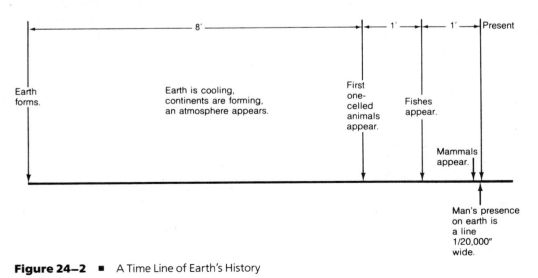

Figure 24–2 ▪ A Time Line of Earth's History

Lesson Plan ▪ B

Orientation:	Grades K–6.
Content Objective:	The children will construct a clay model of the earth's structure and label the core, mantle, and crust.
Skill Objective:	The children are required to establish the *spatial relationship* necessary for understanding a model of the earth's structure.
Materials:	Three colors of Plasticine or clay.
Evaluation:	Students' verbal interaction, student model.

Procedure

On the chalkboard draw three concentric circles with the following radii: two and one-half inches, six and one-half inches, and two feet. The inner circle represents the inner core of the earth, the middle circle is the outer core, and the third circle is the mantle. The crust is represented by the outer line that is ⅛" thick. Label each of the layers of the drawing as in Figure 24–3, and discuss the fact that the deepest oil well does not reach the bottom of the crust. We have created a model of the earth. Next, give each child or group three colors of clay and ask the children to construct a clay model of the earth using the chalkboard model as a guide. They should choose one color of clay and form a small ball for the inner core. This ball should be covered with a layer of a different color, and so on until a three-dimensional model of the earth is formed. You can then use a sharp knife to cut one of the models in half to discuss it with the students.

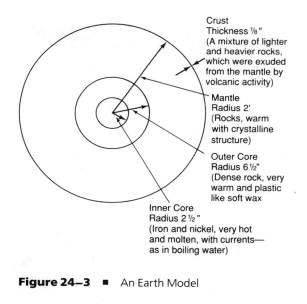

Crust
Thickness ⅛"
(A mixture of lighter and heavier rocks, which were exuded from the mantle by volcanic activity)

Mantle
Radius 2'
(Rocks, warm with crystalline structure)

Outer Core
Radius 6½"
(Dense rock, very warm and plastic like soft wax

Inner Core
Radius 2½"
(Iron and nickel, very hot and molten, with currents—as in boiling water)

Figure 24–3 ▪ An Earth Model

Lesson Plan ▪ C

Orientation:	Grades 2–5.
Content Objective:	The children will state that the continents were formed when lighter molten rock floated upon heavier rock and hardened.
Skill Objective:	The children are required to *observe* the change as a boiling mixture of paraffin and water cools and to *infer* the relationship between what they see and the formation of the continents.
Materials:	A pan, hot plate, water, wax candles.
Evaluation:	Students' verbal interaction, sketch. *continued on next page*

Procedure

Boil several birthday candles vigorously in a small glass baking dish filled one-half full of water. When the candles are nearly melted, tell the class that this is what the earth was like 5 billion years ago. It was composed of several liquid substances all mixed together and very hot. Ask: "What do you think will happen when we allow the water and wax mixture to cool?" Accept guesses from the class and then allow the mixture to cool. After the mixture has cooled nearly to room temperature, ask these questions: "What do we see?" (The wax is floating on the water and is growing hard.)

"If the water represents the hot, molten rocks of the earth's mantle, what does the wax represent?" (The crust.) "What could we say about how heavy (dense) the crust of the earth is compared to the mantle and the core?" (The crust is lighter [less dense] than the mantle.) "What would you guess about how heavy the core of the earth is compared to the mantle?" "Could we say that when the earth was formed the densest material went to the central core, the next densest formed the mantle, and the least dense material the crust?" Have the children draw a sketch of the earth as it was when it was a cooling molten ball.

Lesson Plan ■ D

Orientation:	Grades 3–6.
Content Objective:	The children will state that all of the earth's land masses were originally joined together as one "master continent" that split and drifted apart.
Skill Objective:	The children are required to establish *spatial relationships* by working with a paper model of the earth's continents.
Materials:	Paper cutouts of the outlines of the earth's continents.
Evaluation:	Students' verbal interaction, students' group problem-solving skills.

continued on next page

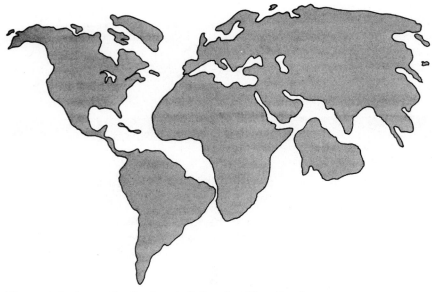

Figure 24–4 ■ The Continents Fit Together Like a Puzzle

Procedure

Provide the children with a paper containing outlines of the earth's continents. Ask them to cut out the shapes. Label the various continents. Then let the children, working in small groups, attempt to fit the continents together to form one large continent as in Figure 24–4. They should be permitted to look at a map or globe to ensure that the coastlines that are being matched are opposite one another, making the matches reasonable in terms of the continental drift theory. (All of the continents on earth were once joined together as one large land mass. Over thousands of years, this land broke apart; even today, the continents continue to drift apart.) See Chapter 25 for a more complete presentation of plate tectonics.

Concept 2

The earth's surface is constantly changing.

Discussion

As soon as they rose to the surface of the mantle and solidified, the earth's masses were subjected to erosive forces. The cold rains beat down upon the hot rock, chipping and cracking it and washing it away. Soluble materials dissolved in the running surface water and washed out to sea. The winds drove rain and rock particles against the land, further wearing away material that was subsequently deposited in low areas. At some later date, the low, sediment-bearing areas were uplifted to form mountains and high plateaus. The erosion continued until layers of sediments were formed, often several miles thick, covering nearly the whole land mass.

Today, the forces of erosion are still at work. If they were not offset by other forces that build up the land mass, all of the earth today might be covered by shallow seas.

Forces That Build Up the Land Masses

Crustal movements of the earth heave up large plateaus and mountain ranges. When the crust is bent and contorted, folding is said to have taken place. There are two reasons for such upheavals. The earth is slowly shrinking as it cools, and the solid crust must wrinkle and bend as the supporting mantle sinks beneath it. And the continents lose mass and weight as sediments and dissolved salts are washed out to sea.

This increases the weight on the thin crust of the ocean floor, creating a force upon the mantle that raises the continental mass.

Magma flows result when cracks develop in the earth's crust. This occurs when a reduction of the pressure on the mantle permits this hot rock to become molten. The magma follows the *fissures* in the overlying rock to the surface and spreads out over large areas.

Volcanoes spew forth *lava* in much the same way, but the area affected by a single volcano is comparatively small. However, whole island chains have been built from volcanic activity. *Earthquakes* result when forces along breaks in the crustal rock (*faults*) become large enough to cause a shift in the rock masses. Some amount of uplift often occurs along a fault line during an earthquake. (See Figure 24–5.)

Forces That Wear Down the Land Masses/Physical and Chemical Erosion

There are many examples of physical erosion. *Ocean tides* and wave action have a great eroding effect upon the coastlines of continents. These forces may have been an even greater eroding factor in the past when the moon is believed to have been closer to the earth, and huge, twenty-foot tides swept around the planet twice a day. The *wind* and the dust and sand particles that it bears also have an abrasive effect upon exposed rock formations. *Running water* is perhaps the most effective eroding agent. As rainwater runs over the ground surface, it dissolves minerals and pushes along small particles. The water and its sediments pour into

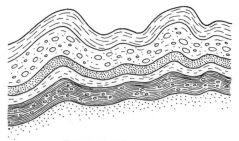

Folds in Rock Layers

A Fault in Rock Layers

Figure 24–5 ■ Folding and Faulting

creeks and streams, which empty into rivers. The rivers wear away their beds to form canyons and wide valleys. Limestone and other rocks dissolve and are carried away as groundwater seeps through their layers. In the colder regions of the earth, *freezing* and *thawing* chip and split rocks, and huge *glaciers* move down mountain valleys and across wide land areas, pushing and gouging the rock layers before them.

Chemical erosion or *weathering* occurs as surface water becomes acidic due to decaying vegetation and/or certain minerals that dissolve and then wear away rock formations. Most of the large caves and caverns on earth were formed in this way.

All these erosive forces move huge quantities of earthen materials. Where they are dropped by the carrier agent, these materials form stratified deposits many hundreds of feet thick.

Lesson Plan ■ E

Orientation:	Grades K–6.
Content Objective:	The children will describe at least five ways in which they see erosion occurring on the playground.
Skill Objective:	The children are required to *observe* evidence of erosion on the school grounds.
Materials:	Playground (field trip) pictures of erosion in nature.
Evaluation:	Students' verbal interaction.

Procedure

Take your class out on the playground. Ask them to look for any signs that soil has been disturbed or moved by rain or wind. Some things to look for are:

1. Sand and dirt deposited by the splash effect of falling rain at the base of the outside walls of the building.

2. Crevasses and depressions caused by the runoff of rainwater.

3. Puddles or depressions where water stands after a rain. Look for sediments that were deposited in the depression by running water.

4. Sidewalks that have been uplifted by the roots of trees and hedges.

Interested students may measure the width, depth, and length of a crevasse and *estimate* the volume of the eroded material by multiplying the three factors

continued on next page

together. You may also want to show students pictures of the Grand Canyon, rocky sea coasts, sand dunes, and other examples of erosion. Discuss how erosion affects the earth's surface. What happens to mountains? Where does the material from an eroding mountain go?

Lesson Plan ■ F

Orientation: Grades 1–6.

Content Objective: The children will state that erosion will occur when limestone is dissolved in running water.

Skill Objective: The children are required to *observe* the effect of running water on limestone and to *infer* the relationship of their observation to erosion.

Materials: One large metal can, cotton cloth, crushed limestone, rubber band, small containers such as jar lids.

Evaluation: Students' verbal interaction, students' group problem-solving skills, written report.

Procedure

Remove the top of a can, and punch holes in the bottom. Cover the bottom with cotton cloth, fastened securely with a heavy rubber band. Fill the can with crushed limestone. Slowly pour distilled water or rainwater over the limestone and collect it in a pan after it has passed over the limestone and through the cloth (see Figure 24–6). Give each child or group of children two jar lids, one containing a small quantity of rainwater, and one limewater. Direct the children to label the water samples and place them in the sunlight to allow the water to evaporate.

After evaporation is complete (you may hasten the process by using only small quantities of water), ask the children: "What is the difference between your two containers?" (The lid with the water that passed over the limestone has a white deposit on it; the other lid does not.) "What do you think that white deposit is?" (Limestone.) "Where must the limestone have come from?" (From the water. The limestone dissolved in the water.) "I wonder what might happen if we put the limestone under the faucet and let the water run for many days?" (The limestone would dissolve in the water and disappear.) "From what we have

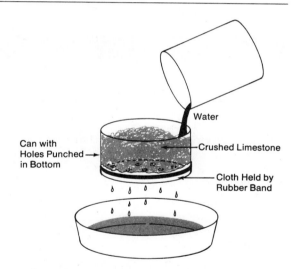

Water

Can with Holes Punched in Bottom

Crushed Limestone

Cloth Held by Rubber Band

Figure 24–6 ■ Water Dissolves Limestone

seen here, what might happen if water in the ground were to pass through a layer of limestone for many years?" (The limestone would dissolve. A cave would be formed.) Have the students write a brief report of what they did, what they observed, and what they think.

Lesson Plan ▪ G

Orientation:	Grades K–6.
Content Objective:	The children will state that rocks may be cracked and broken by freezing water.
Skill Objective:	The children are required to *observe* the effect of freezing water on a closed container and *infer* that this same effect may cause erosion in rocks.
Materials:	One quart jar with lid, one towel.
Evaluation:	Students' verbal interaction.

Procedure

Wrap a towel around a small jar that has been filled with water and covered with a lid. Place the jar in a freezer overnight. Unwrap the jar in front of the class while telling them what you have done. Ask: "What happened to the jar?" (It broke.) "I wonder what caused it to break?" (The ice. When water freezes, it expands and exerts a pressure.) "Could water break rocks?" (Yes. Water can get in the cracks of rocks and freeze.)

Lesson Plan ▪ H

Orientation:	Grades K–6.
Content Objective:	The children will state that heating and cooling will cause rocks to crack and break apart.
Skill Objective:	The children are required to *observe* the effect of heating and cooling upon a rock or marble and *infer* how this same effect will cause erosion.
Materials:	Tongs, marbles, propane torch, glass jar, water.
Evaluation:	Students' verbal interaction.

Procedure

Hold a glass marble in a flame with tongs or tweezers until it is very hot. Then plunge it into a glass of cold water. Ask the class: "What happened?" (The marble has cracks all through it.) "Can temperature changes cause some things to crack?" (Yes.) With a fourth-, fifth-, or sixth-grade class the teacher may ask: "Why did the marble crack?" (It expanded when it was heated and contracted rapidly when it was cooled.) "What does this have to do with erosion?" (Heating and cooling can cause rocks to crack and break up.)

This exercise may be done with rock samples if available. Shale is a rock that demonstrates the effect of heat and cold very dramatically.

Concept 3

The record of the changing earth is preserved in rocks.

Discussion

Most of the earth's crust is made up of hard material called rocks. Rocks are generally classified into three main groups—igneous, sedimentary, and metamorphic—according to the manner in which they were formed.

Subconcept 3–1

All rocks may be classified into three groups.

Discussion

Igneous rocks are formed from molten material from the earth's mantle that intrudes into fissures of the crust. This material, called *magma*, frequently pushes the crust upward and solidifies. Such intrusions of magma (Figure 24–7) are often small but are sometimes large enough to create mountains. When normal processes of erosion wear away the sedimentary rock layers that overlie the *intrusion*, igneous rock is exposed. *Granite* is the most common igneous rock. When the magma finds its way to the surface before it cools and solidifies, it is said to be an *extrusive* rock. These outpourings of magma from fissures and volcanoes produce such igneous rocks as *basalt*, *pumice*, and *obsidian*.

Sedimentary rocks are formed when sediments previously laid down are cemented together by chemicals and/or great pressure from overlying layers of material. The nature of the sedimentary rock depends upon the nature of the deposits and the conditions under which it was formed. *Sandstone*, a common sedimentary rock, is composed of grains of sand that have been cemented together. *Shale* is a sedimentary rock composed of compressed clay materials. *Limestone* is a sedimentary rock composed of

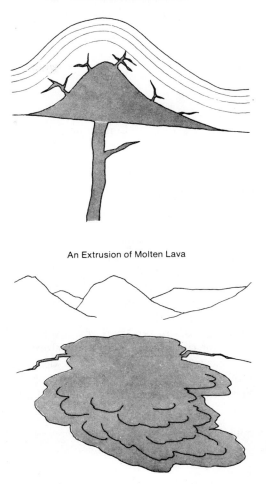

An Intrusion of Molten Lava

An Extrusion of Molten Lava

Figure 24—7 ■ Intrusions and Extrusions

the shells of tiny animals and plants that settled to the sea bottom after the plant or animal died. Other examples of sedimentary rock are *conglomerate*, made of cemented pebbles and gravel; *coquina*, made of the shells of larger sea animals; and *rock salts* that are precipitated from saturated sea water.

Metamorphic rocks are any igneous or sedimentary rocks that have been changed in structure or composition by heat combined with pressure from overlying rock strata. Here is a list of some common metamorphic rocks and the original rock from which each was formed:

Metamorphic Rock	Original Rock
Gneiss	Granite
Quartzite	Sandstone
Slate	Shale
Marble	Limestone
Hard Coal	Soft Coal
Graphite	Hard Coal

Evidence of Change

Geologists can tell much about the history of a region from the kinds of rocks that exist there and from their arrangement. For instance, the glacial periods on the American and European continents left fairly clear geological evidence. During this period, soil and sedimentary rock deposits were removed from large areas of Canada by the bulldozing action of huge ice sheets. Large beds of sand and gravel were deposited by the runoff water from the melting ice when a glacier began to recede. These deposits of sand and gravel mark the terminus of the glacier's southern-most advance.

Layers of coal in the Appalachian Mountains tell us much about the geologic history of this region. Once it was low-lying marshland. Gradually beds of dead vegetation were covered and compressed by the accumulation of overlying sediments. A tremendous folding of the sedimentary rock layers distorted and uplifted the rock strata as the mountain range was formed.

The presence of seashells in all but the highest of the mountain ranges appears to indicate that the North American and European continents have been periodically submerged beneath the sea. Large salt beds are believed to be deposits left by the evaporation of huge inland seas.

Through oil well drilling operations, mining, seismic research, and field study, we have accumulated more and more evidence concerning the rock strata that compose the upper crust of the earth. With such evidence we can piece together the series of geological events that took place in a region over billions of years. The nature of the materials that compose the rock, the ways in which the rocks have been changed, and the order in which the layers were laid down over one another all furnish valuable information for the trained geologist.

Lesson Plan ▪ I

Orientation:	Primary Grades K–6.
Content Objective:	The children will state that rock crystals will form when water that contains salts is permitted to evaporate.
Skill Objective:	The children are required to *observe* the growth of crystals and to *infer* that rocks may be formed by this process.
Materials:	Sugar, borax, alum, photographic fixer, salt, saltpeter, jars, six saucers, cotton twine, hand lenses or microscope.
Evaluation:	Students' verbal interaction, sketch.

Procedure

Prepare hot, saturated solutions of as many of the following substances as possible: sugar, borax, alum, photographic fixer (hypo), salt, and saltpeter. Saturated solutions are prepared by adding each agent to an individual jar of hot water and stirring until no more can be dissolved. Pour small amounts of each solution

continued on next page

into separate saucers. Place a piece of cotton twine in the solution with one end extending over the edge of the saucer (see Figure 24–8). Allow the solutions to sit for several days as the water evaporates and crystals form on the twine. Ask the children to observe the crystals of several substances with the aid of a hand lens and to attempt to sketch each type of crystal. Ask them: "What does this tell us about how some rocks are formed?" (Some rocks are made of crystals that come out of water solutions.) "What kind of rock would we say these crystals are—sedimentary, igneous, or metamorphic?" (Sedimentary.)

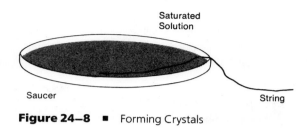

Figure 24–8 ■ Forming Crystals

Lesson Plan ■ J

Orientation:	Grades 4–6.
Content Objective:	The children will state that rocks may change their form with the addition of heat.
Skill Objective:	The children are required to *observe* the change that takes place in sulfur as the result of heating and cooling and to *infer* the relation between their observations and metamorphic rock.
Materials:	One large test tube, one propane burner, one pint jar, hand lenses.
Evaluation:	Students' verbal interaction, students' group problem-solving skills, sketches, reports.

Procedure

Heat a test tube nearly full of flowers of sulfur over a burner until the yellow powder liquefies and turns brown. *Caution:* THIS SHOULD BE DONE NEAR AN OPEN WINDOW WITH GOOD VENTILATION. Pour the liquid sulfur slowly into a jar of cold water (see Figure 24–9). Permit the children to pull off a piece of the rubbery substance and examine it. Ask the children: "What is the sulfur like now? How has it changed?" (It was yellow; now it is brown. It was a powder; now it is a rubbery solid.) Let the rubbery sulfur set for fifteen to twenty minutes and allow the children to examine it again. Ask the class: "Is the sulfur the same?" (No. Crystals are forming. It is losing its rubbery property.) "We have seen sulfur change its properties because of changes in temperature. How is this like the rocks of the earth?" (Metamorphic rocks are rocks that have been changed due to heat and pressure.) Permit the

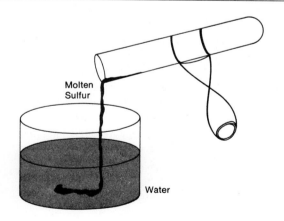

Figure 24–9 ■ Changing the Properties of Sulfur

continued on next page

children to examine the sulfur crystals with a hand lens throughout the day. They will see long needlelike crystals change to smaller diamond-shaped crystals. Have them sketch the various forms of sulfur they observed and write a brief paragraph describing how their observations relate to the metamorphoses of rocks in nature.

Lesson Plan ■ K

Orientation:	Grades 2–6.
Content Objective:	The children will state that sediments settle out of running water in order of size and weight—gravel first, then sand, then fine particles of soil.
Skill Objective:	The children are required to *hypothesize* about how sediments suspended in moving water settle out, to *observe* an experiment that tests their hypothesis, and to *infer* the relationship of their conclusions to sedimentation in nature.
Materials:	One-gallon, wide-mouthed jar with lid, coarse gravel, fine gravel, sand, soil, water.
Evaluation:	Students' verbal interaction, report.

Procedure

Put a handful of fine gravel, a handful of sand, and a handful of dirt into a large wide-mouthed jar (see Figure 24–10). Fill the jar about three-fourths full of water, screw on lid, and shake it vigorously. Ask the class: "What happens while the water is stirring about very vigorously in the jar?" (All of the sediments are suspended.) "What do you think will happen when we permit the water to become calm?" Accept the children's guesses. Then set the jar on a desk or window sill for three to five minutes. Ask the children: "Can you describe the appearance of the sediments?" (The sediments have settled out in layers with the coarse gravel on the bottom, the fine gravel next, the sand next, and the dirt on top. Some of the dirt is still in the water.) "Now let us picture a stream emerging from some high, hilly country. A swift current is carrying along sediment like this in the jar. As the stream reaches a level valley the current slows more and more until it empties into a large lake. Can you describe what might happen to the sediments in this stream? How is this like our model?" (Most of the coarse gravel would settle out where the current begins to slow.

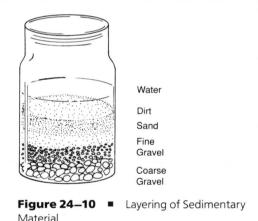

Figure 24–10 ■ Layering of Sedimentary Material

Next would be the fine gravel. The sand would settle out where the stream enters the lake. The dirt would settle on the bottom of the lake.) Discuss how seasonal changes in the amount of water runoff would vary the nature of the sediments deposited at any point in the stream or lake. Have the students write a brief explanation of how some sedimentary rocks are formed.

Concept 4

Lift has existed upon the earth for only a small fraction of the planet's history.

Discussion

Primitive, one-celled life has existed on earth for something over 1 billion years, or about one-fifth of the planet's lifetime. We have existed on earth for about 2 million years, or about 1/2500 of the planet's lifetime. Or, to think about geological time relationships in another way, if a line from the earth to the moon represents the time the earth has existed, a line one mile long would represent time since the birth of Christ. Over these millions of years the environment has undergone innumerable changes. Each new set of conditions favored the growth of some forms of plant and animal life over others, and life on earth has changed with each change in the environment.

Subconcept 4–1

Fossils are evidence of life in the earth's history.

Discussion

Fossils provide evidence that life existed in earlier ages. They also show what kind of life it was. A tree falls into a swamp and is covered by sediments before it can rot away. A fish dies, settles to the bottom of a muddy stream, and is quickly covered by silt and sand. A dinosaur walks across a mud flat along a river, leaving huge footprints in the mud that soon fill with sand. Worms bore tunnels through soft soil; the soil dries and is covered with sediments. The tree and the fish will later decompose, and the organic matter will be replaced with minerals through the action of seeping groundwater. The forms of such organisms are often preserved in great detail. The dinosaur footprints and the worm borings, though they are not replicas of

Chart 24–1 ■ Divisions of Geologic Time

Era	Age	Years Ago
Cenozoic	People	
		2,000,000
	Mammals	
		60,000,000
Mesozoic	Reptiles	
		300,000,000
Paleozoic	Fishes	
		450,000,000
		600,000,000
Proterozoic	Invertebrates	
		1,000,000,000
Archeozoic		

once-living things, provide evidence of the nature of earlier forms of life. All these traces of prehistoric life are called fossils.

Fossils are found in sedimentary, but not in igneous or metamorphic rocks. The great heat and pressure that form the latter destroy fossil evidence.

The Archeozoic and Proterozoic Eras

Granite and sedimentary rock layers of the Archeozoic and Proterozoic eras may be as much as twenty miles thick. The rocks have been faulted, folded, and metamorphosed and therefore show little fossil evidence. Investigators sometimes find organic molecules among the rocks of these eras, indicating that one-celled life probably existed then. The Archeozoic and Proterozoic eras comprise the first 4½ billion years of the earth's geologic history.

The Paleozoic Era

Sediments laid down in the Paleozoic era offer a fairly complete chronology of the geological and biological events that occurred one-quarter to one-half billion years ago. At the beginning of this era, the North American continent was uplifted beyond its present boundaries so that land extended several hundred miles into the Atlantic and Pacific Oceans. Later the continent subsided and was almost completely submerged beneath salty ocean water for millions of years. Some commercially valuable deposits of that submerged epoch are: Pennsylvania, New York, and Vermont slates; Vermont marble; Ohio, New York, and Michigan salt deposits; and some of the gas and oil deposits of the southwest United States. Toward the middle of the Paleozoic era, the sea withdrew from the New American continent, and great deposits of limestone were laid down in the present Mississippi Valley. Later the central portion of the continent became swampy bog land. It was then that the great coal deposits of the present Appalachian region were formed as were the extensive oil and gas deposits from Pennsylvania to the Rocky Mountains.

For millions of years the biotic organisms of the Paleozoic era consisted of *invertebrate sea animals* and *seaweeds*. Later, some animal forms developed shells of *calcium carbonate*. The shells of these animals left the first definite evidence of life forms in sedimentary rocks. The warm, shallow seas were dominated by the *trilobite*, the ancestor of the modern crab, shrimp, and lobster.

As land continued to emerge from the seas in the middle and late Paleozoic era, dense growths of *club mosses, ferns*, and *horsetails* began to cover the low, swampy ground. Some of these plants were 100 feet high and had trunks 4 feet in diameter. In the late Paleozoic, the first *vertebrate fishes* developed. Some species of vertebrates emerged from the water to wander about on land. These *amphibians* were the first land animals. Some amphibians flourished greatly, but they largely disappeared in the Mesozoic era. Only frogs, toads, and salamanders remain as their modern descendants.

The Mesozoic Era

The Mesozoic, or Middle Life, era is defined geologically in the United States by two great uplifts of the Appalachian Mountain chain. Between these two uplifts there was a prolonged period of submergence. During the Mesozoic era many new forms of vertebrate and invertebrate life appeared. *Reef-building corals* became abundant. Snail-like *ammonites*, now extinct, were the most abundant of the shellfish. On land, in the dense swamps, the small *amphibians* and *reptiles* of the late Paleozoic era developed into the great reptiles called *dinosaurs*. Some of these animals were 100 feet long and weighed 50 tons. For unexplained reasons these great reptiles became extinct at the end of the Mesozoic era. Their direct living descendants are *lizards, snakes, alligators*, and *crocodiles*. Modern birds appear to be descended from certain of the lizards that developed wings, feathers, and hollow bones. The Mesozoic era began about 300 million years ago and ended 60 million years ago.

The Cenozoic Era

We live in the Cenozoic era. This era began only about 60 million years ago yet it has seen many geologic changes. Most of the high mountain ranges that exist today were formed in either the late Mesozoic or the early Cenozoic eras. The great mountain ranges that extend along the west coasts of North, Central, and South America were formed by a tremendous *folding* and *faulting* process followed by a *general uplift*. This mountain building was accompanied by tremendous *volcanic activity*. Much of Washington, Oregon, and Idaho was covered with layers of *lava* thousands of feet thick during this period. The Gulf area of the United States remained submerged beneath the sea for millions of years during the Cenozoic period.

Sediments deposited in this area contain important quantities of *gas, oil,* and *sulfur.*

The four great ice advances of the late Cenozoic era left some interesting deposits and geomorphic forms. *Glacial sheets* thousands of feet thick covered all of Canada and the United States to a line that runs roughly from southern Pennsylvania to southern Oregon. The *scraping action* of the advancing ice removed all sedimentary rock layers from Canada and deposited them in the form of *sand, gravel,* and *silt* in the northern United States. Where rock formations were softest, depressions were created that filled with water when the ice receded. The *Great Lakes* were formed in this way. Many major rivers were created as glacial *melt water* poured from the receding ice sheet.

The Cenozoic era is generally referred to as the *age of mammals.* Mammals are animals that nourish their young with milk. The first mammals were tiny shrews no bigger than mice. Some species of mammals have modern descendants; others have become extinct. In terms of intelligence, we are the most highly developed of the mammals. According to most of the evidence, we have been on earth about 2 million years. However, some fossil remains uncovered in Africa indicate that there may have been primitive humanlike beings much longer than that—perhaps as long as 5 million years ago.

Lesson Plan ▪ L

Orientation:	Grades K–6.
Content Objective:	The children will state that scientists can infer many things from examining fossils.
Skill Objective:	The children are required to *experiment* by creating fossil casts, to *observe* a cast of a fossil, and to *infer* the nature of the "animal" associated with the fossil.
Materials:	Plaster of Paris, paper cups or milk cartons, objects such as seashells and leaves, a penknife, a hair clasp, Vaseline.
Evaluation:	Students' verbal interaction, students' group problem-solving skills, "fossil" molds.

Procedure

Mix water with plaster of Paris to form a paste. Pour the plaster into waxed containers to a depth of about one inch and distribute them to groups of children. The waxed containers may be drinking cups or milk cartons with the tops removed. Have the children cover the surface of a seashell or other object with Vaseline and push it gently into the plaster of Paris as in Figure 24—11. Have them allow the paste to dry and remove the object carefully. A mold of the object will be left in the plaster cast.

Make casts of several common objects out of the children's sight. Show the children one cast. "We are going to see how scientists make inferences about fossils. Can you tell me what made this imprint?" (A penknife, and so on.) "Do you *know* that the impression was made by a penknife?" (No. It looks like it was made by a penknife. We inferred it.) "What kind of animal did the object probably belong to?" (A human.) "How large is the animal that uses such an object likely to be? As big as a mouse, an elephant?" Discuss with

continued on next page

the class further inferences that might be drawn from examining the mold. Examples: the animal has fingernails to open the knife; the animal has fingers to hold the knife. Repeat the process with several other molds. Show how scientists can infer a great many things from a fossil and the material in which it is found.

An extending activity to demonstrate the skill of inferring and its importance is to provide each child with a penny. Give the children a few minutes to examine the penny and then say: "If a scientist were to find this penny 50,000 years from now, what could she tell (infer) from it?" (That there were people and their appearance. That they had buildings, a number system, an alphabet; they could refine metals, and so forth.)

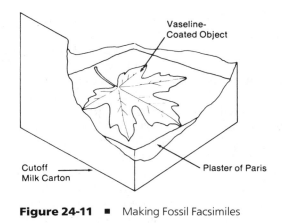

Figure 24-11 ▪ Making Fossil Facsimiles

Lesson Plan ▪ M

Orientation:	Grades 5–6.
Content Objective:	The children will state that many inferences concerning prehistoric life may be made from fossil evidence.
Skill Objective:	The children are required to *infer* as many things as they can about fossil specimens and to verify their inferences using established reference sources.
Materials:	A collection of fossil specimens.
Evaluation:	Students' verbal interaction, students' group problem-solving skills.

Procedure

Show the children some real fossils. Ask them to make all the inferences they can about the animals or plants that made the fossils. Permit them to find scientists' inferences about the same type of fossil in a sourcebook. Have them evaluate their own inferences. Discuss the kinds of evidence on which the scientists base other inferences about other fossils.

Summary

The earth was born as a hot, molten ball. We do not know how it originated. The two most prominent explanations are the tidal theory and the dust-cloud (planetesimal) theory. According to the tidal theory, the earth and the other planets were torn from the sun by the gravitational attraction of a passing star. According to the dust-cloud theory, the planets condensed from rings of dust, gas, and rock particles at about the same time as the sun was forming. Regardless of which theory one subscribes to, it is generally agreed that an extremely long cooling process took place. During this time, hot, molten material cooled to form a thin outer crust of lightweight material, a core of heavy iron-nickel, and a mantle of dense, rocklike substance. Continental land masses formed, floated upon the mantle rock, and apparently drifted over the earth's surface. After many tens of millions of years of cooling and contracting, water and gases were extruded from the material of the earth to form the oceans and the atmosphere.

The earth's surface has been subjected to many agents and forces that have changed, and continue to change, the appearance of its crustal layer. The cooling mantle has shrunk, causing uplifting, folding, and faulting of the outer rock layers. Hot, liquid magma has issued from large fissures in the crust and from volcanoes, adding solidified materials several thousand feet thick to the continental land mass. Forces that tend to erode away the land mass are ocean tides; running water in the form of rainfall, streams, and rivers; wind; chemical action; and freezing and thawing.

The earth's crust has also undergone a series of submergences when the seas inundated most of the continental land mass, and upheavals when the seas receded to the ocean basins and great mountain chains were formed. The story of the major geological and biological events is written in the rocks and fossils of the earth's crust.

The rocks of the earth's crust may be classified as igneous—those extruded from molten, subsurface material; sedimentary—those laid down by the forces of erosion; and metamorphic—those changed in structure and appearance by heat and pressure.

Traces of prehistoric animal and plant life found in sedimentary rock layers are called fossils. Fossil evidence indicates that the nature of living organisms on earth has changed as the surface environment of the earth has changed. Life began as one-celled sea forms. With the passing of time, shellfish, then vertebrate fish, dominated the vast oceans of the earth. Some animals and plants appear to have made the transition from sea to land in the Paleozoic era, more than 300 million years ago. The animals were the forerunners of modern amphibians. The plants of the Paleozoic era were primarily mosses and ferns. The Mesozoic era is called the age of reptiles. Giant dinosaurs dominated the landscape, and the prototypes of modern birds could be seen in the skies. Mammals appeared over 60 million years ago, late in the Mesozoic era, in the form of tiny, mouselike shrews. Primitive people appeared late in the Cenozoic era, only about 2 million years ago.

CHAPTER 25

The Earth's Oceans

Look What's in This Chapter

In this chapter we'll discuss some important concepts and subconcepts related to the study of the earth's oceans, and we'll present lesson plans that are designed to teach these concepts and subconcepts to children.

Concept 1 Ocean basin floors have a wide variety of geologic features.

Concept 2 Island chains or arcs are formed through volcanic activity.

Concept 3 Underwater mountain ridges are formed on the ocean floor by lava that extrudes from fractures in the ocean floor.

Concept 4 The ocean floor is spreading.

Concept 5 The earth's crust is made of large moving sections called plates.

Concept 6 Ocean water has movement and energy.

> Subconcept 6–1 Energy is transported by ocean waves.

Subconcept 6–2 Ocean waves transport energy, not water.

Concept 7 Oceans have streams or currents that flow for great distances.

Concept 8 Vertical currents exist in deep ocean water.

Concept 9 The margins of continents are constantly changing.

Concept 10 There is diversity among the plants and animals that live in the ocean.

Prior to 1940 scientists knew very little about the vast oceans that cover nearly three-fourths (71 percent) of the earth's surface. Now as the result of extensive activities such as dredging up samples of sediments from the ocean floor, extracting cores from drilling far into the earth's surface beneath the oceans, and examining their depths with sonar and television, we now know a great deal about what lives in the ocean and what lies on and beneath the ocean basins. The work of all the scientists who have spent their lives studying the mysteries of the vast regions beneath and along the shores of the earth's oceans has created a new branch of science called *oceanography*.

Concept 1

Ocean basin floors have a wide variety of geologic features.

Discussion

Many people picture the ocean floor as a vast flat, sandy plain devoid of life or geologic features. But oceanic studies reveal that in addition to such regions, there are some of the most spectacular geologic forms found on earth. Among them are volcanoes that rise more than 20,000 feet from the ocean floor and then extend another 12,000 feet above the ocean's surface into the atmosphere. Mauna Loa and Mauna Kea on the island of Hawaii are two of many examples. Under the ocean waters exist mountain chains that dwarf the European Alps and the American Rockies and extend for thousands of miles in length. In places the floor of the ocean gives way to great, deep trenches that sometimes extend miles beneath the earth's surface. The Challenger Deep in the western Pacific is the deepest trench yet discovered, with a depth of eleven kilometers or nearly seven miles. Sediments from the great rivers of the continental land masses form great underwater deltas (fan-sloped deposits hundreds of feet thick), and the moving water and sediments cut deep valleys into the accumulated deposits. Pressure on the rock layers of the ocean floor cause upheavals and fractures like those that occur on the continent and create another form of subsurface mountains. You can see that many regions of the ocean basins are spectacular geologic phenomena.

Lesson Plan ▪ A

Orientation:	Grades 3–6.
Content Objective:	The children will state that the landforms that occur on the continents also occur on the ocean floor.
Skill Objective:	The children will make *inferences* concerning the nature of the environment if the United States were submerged under the ocean.
Materials:	Pictures of oceanic submarine landforms, topographical map of the United States.
Evaluation:	Students' verbal interaction.

continued on next page

Show the children a topographical map of the United States. Say: "Use your imaginations. What would the United States be like if it were submerged under the ocean?" "Would there be erosion of the Rocky Mountains? Would rocks tumble to the bottom of cliffs as they do on land?" "What kinds of plants would grow?" "Would coral reefs form on the sides of mountains near the surface of the warm ocean in Mexico?" "Can volcanoes exist under water? Could they erupt?" "Are there mountains under the present ocean? Are there cliffs and valleys and other landforms, or is the ocean floor all flat?"

After the children have speculated, show pictures of ocean floor landforms. Ask: "What have we found out about the ocean floor?" (It contains many different geological forms.)

Concept 2

Island chains or arcs are formed through volcanic activity.

Discussion

In recent decades exploratory vessels equipped with sonar and other equipment have discovered deep trenches stretching for hundreds of miles across the ocean floors. These huge chasms often parallel the edge of continents, have widths of several miles, and extend downward into the basin crust for nearly seven miles. Along these deep trenches volcanic activity is common. Many islands of the world are products of this extensive outpouring of lava from the earth's mantle and the mountain building that results from it.

Figure 25–1, for example, shows the deep trench that lies just off the coast of South and

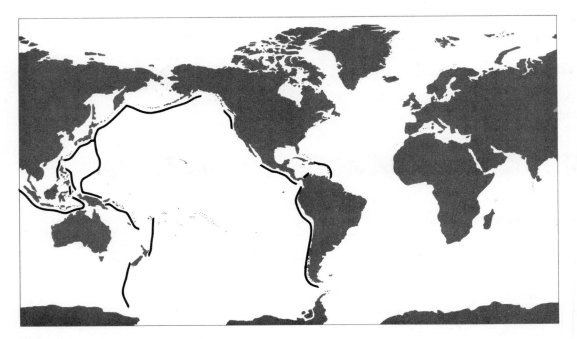

Figure 25–1 ■ Ocean Trenches and Island Chains

Central America. In this region volcanic activity occurs chiefly in the mountainous terrain that extends the length of this continental margin. Volcanic activity along the coasts of Chile, Ecuador, Colombia, Panama, and Mexico is very common, and dozens of peaks of volcanic origin rise to heights of more than 19,000 feet. (In 1943 a young Mexican boy reported to his family that a hole had formed on their small farm. Lava began to spew from the opening and today a mountain, Parícutin, which is more than 9,000 feet in elevation, stands as testimony to the landbuilding forces of volcanic activity.) In the ocean basins volcanic activity produces mountains that thrust upward nearly 40,000 feet from the ocean floor to altitudes 12,000 feet above the ocean waves. The height and mass of these volcanic cones dwarfs the tallest mountains found on the continents of the world.

Most of the deep oceanic trenches that exist are found along the edge of the Pacific Ocean basin. The Aleutian Islands lie along a deep ocean trench. So too do the islands of Japan. The Philippine Islands and the islands of Java and Sumatra lie along the Mindanao trench. The myriad small islands of Marianas and the Marshall archipelagoes are in the vicinity of the world's deepest trench, the 35,000-foot Marianas. The Kermadec-Tonga trench extends north along the ocean floor from New Zealand. Along its margins is an underwater mountain ridge extending to the Samoan Islands.

The Role of Coral in Island Building

Corals are tiny, one-celled marine animals that secrete calciferous substances to build colonial protective shells. Figure 25–2 shows different types of coral. Over time each new generation of coral builds upon the "dead" coral deposits of its predecessors, forming great deposits of limestone on the shallow ocean floors. Figure 25–3 illustrates the sequence of coral building on a mountain that has emerged above the waters of the ocean. Coral grows in the shallow and warm waters of the flanks of the mountain, forming a limestone ring or collar just below the ocean's surface. In some places coral

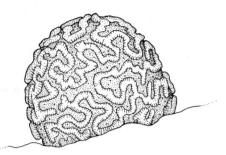
Brain Coral

Astrangia Polyp

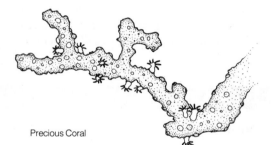
Precious Coral

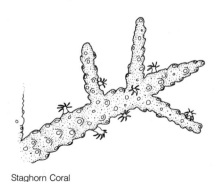
Staghorn Coral

Figure 25–2 ■ Types of Coral

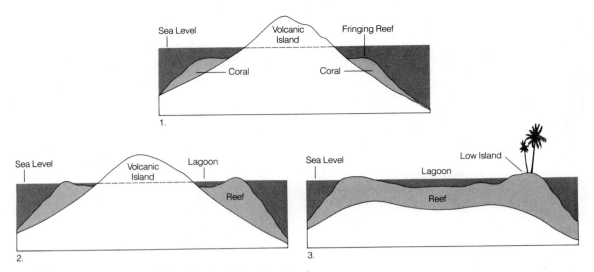

Figure 25–3 ■ Stages of Development of a Coral Reef

deposits appear above the water level at low tide. The aggregated coral limestone and the rich collection of other organisms form a new marine environment called a *reef.* As the volcanic materials inside the reef erode, shallow waters are formed and are protected by the reef from the ocean waves. These are called *lagoons.*

An area in which a number of coral islands exist is called an *atoll.*

Coral reefs are also formed along the continental shelves where the water is shallow and warm and has moving currents that nourish organisms.

Lesson Plan ■ B

Orientation: Grades 3–6.

Content Objective: The children will state that island chains or arcs are often located along deep ocean trenches.

Skill Objective: The children are required to *observe* a globe with the Pacific Ocean basin trenches drawn on it, and to *infer* a relationship between ocean trenches and island formation.

Materials: Several world globes, wax crayons, map of Pacific Ocean basin trenches.

Evaluation: Students' verbal interaction, students' group problem-solving skills, tracings on a globe.

Procedure

Divide the class into small groups, and provide each group with a world globe and a map showing the Pacific Ocean basin trenches. Direct the children to use a wax crayon to draw the location of the trenches on

continued on next page

the globes. Have different members of each group draw the various trenches. After all groups have marked the trenches on their globes, say: "Carefully examine your globe and tell me what you think about the locations of the deep ocean trenches." (The trenches form a circle around the Pacific Ocean.) If necessary, guide the children to focus on the relationship of island locations and the trenches: "Are islands commonly located far away from the trenches?" (Islands are located along the deep ocean trenches in the Pacific Ocean.)

You may also provide information related to the process of oceanic volcanic island building.

Lesson Plan ■ C

Orientation:	Grades 3–6.
Content Objective:	The children will describe the development of a tropical reef.
Skill Objective:	The children are required to *communicate* their understanding of coral reef building by drawing the development of a tropical reef.
Materials:	Drawing paper, crayons, pencils, and erasers.
Evaluation:	Students' verbal interaction, students' group problem-solving skills, sketches.

Procedure

On the chalkboard sketch a line drawing of a volcanic mountain with sloping sides jutting above the water line of the ocean (as in Figure 25–3). Direct the children to copy the line drawing. If samples of coral are available, show them to the children and tell them that the hard material is built from the shells of tiny animals that live in the sea. In the absence of coral samples, show the children pictures of coral. Tell them that the coral deposits grow as new animals build their shells on top of those of their ancestors. Tell them that coral grows (1) in warm ocean water, (2) in shallow water, and (3) where ocean currents can wash over them. Now say, "Can you draw some coral in your picture?" After they have added coral in their drawings, have some children show and describe their pictures to the class. Point out that the coral should be shown living under water or in the shallow water on the slopes of the mountain. Have students whose sketches did not conform to these conditions change them.

Now tell the children that new coral material is added as new corals build their shelters. Remind them that the volcanic lava that makes up the mountain can erode away and not be replaced. Ask: "What other changes might take place?" (Rocks from the land might fall or be washed up on the coral. Shells and plants from the ocean floor might be washed up on the coral. Ocean waves might erode the shoreline.) Tell the children to change their pictures to show how their scene might look after a long time. Again, have some children show their drawings to the class. Correct the pictures as necessary. Write the words *reef, lagoon*, and *atoll* on the board, and explain their meanings. Have the children label their drawings.

Concept 3

Underwater mountain ridges are formed on the ocean floor by lava that extrudes from fractures in the ocean floor.

Discussion

Scientists have known for several centuries that underwater mountain ridges existed in the oceans of the world. But it was not until the 1950s that the great range of the oceanic ridge system was discovered. Figure 25—4 depicts the oceanic ridges. Note that the mid-Atlantic ridge system begins at about 70 degrees north latitude far above the Arctic Circle and extends down the center of the Atlantic Ocean to about 55 degrees south latitude, where it circles the southern tip of Africa. From its extension into the Indian Ocean the ridge continues to enter the Red Sea, and it disappears at the narrow strip of land at the Red Sea's northern edge. You can trace a second major ridge system eastward between Australia and Antarctica, then northward where it becomes the eastern Pacific ridge.

The outpouring of basaltic materials from the earth's mantle along the oceanic ridges is tremendous in terms of volume, and it is very important in creating new crustal materials on the earth's surface. Although most of the extrusions of lava occur deep underwater, humans have witnessed the phenomenon on a number of occasions.

Volcanic activity in Iceland, which is situated on the mid-Atlantic ridge, has provided spectacular displays for observers for centuries. The atmospheric effects of Iceland's volcanic activities—ash, dust, and gases—have been recorded from as early as the twelfth century. People in Scandinavia, Europe, and even Africa have witnessed the darkened midday skies and striking red sunsets that resulted from volcanic activity in the Iceland area. In some Scandinavian and European literature, Iceland was de-

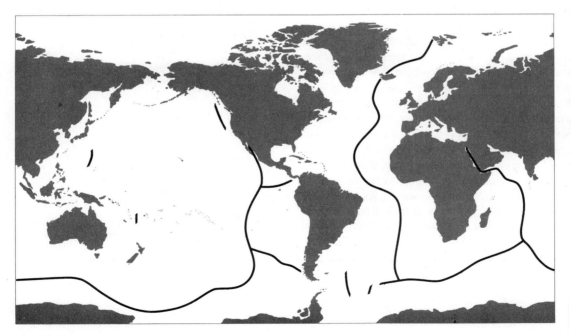

Figure 25—4 ▪ Oceanic Ridges of the Earth

picted as the entrance to Hell, or as Hell itself. Iceland's most recent extraordinary display occurred in 1963 when amid clouds of billowing steam and sulfurous gases lava appeared on the ocean's surface south of Iceland. The outpouring of basaltic material continued for two years. At that time the new island, named Surtsey, rose 568 feet above sea level and more than 1,000 feet above the ocean floor. The geologic events on Iceland and the formation of Surtsey are a vivid display of those that occur regularly along thousands of miles of underwater ocean ridges.

The Formation of the Hawaiian Islands

Partly because they make up the fiftieth state of the United States, but mostly due to their somewhat mysterious geological features, the islands of Hawaii hold particular interest. The Hawaiian Island arc is of volcanic origin. The youngest of the islands, the "Big Island" of Hawaii, is situated at the southwestern end of a ridge that includes its neighbors, Maui, Molokai, Lanai, Oahu, Kauai, and many smaller islands. Beyond the islands to the northwest extends a ridge of underwater volcanic mountains that can be followed in a gentle arc across the northeastern Pacific Ocean to where it disappears at the Aleutian trench south of the Aleutian Islands. Some scientists speculate that all of the islands of the Hawaiian ridge were formed in the approximate location of the island of Hawaii. Because of the slow rotation of the crustal plate on which they are located, they were rotated toward the northeast. One by one, mountains and islands were formed in the single location and transported away to be weathered by wind, waves, and ocean currents until they disappeared beneath the surface. On the island of Hawaii the volcano Mauna Loa continues to spew forth island-building lava, though the volcanic activity has moved down the 12,000-foot peak to form a number of active craters. If the volcanologists who work at Volcano National Park on the island of Hawaii are correct, perhaps 10,000 years into the future Mauna Loa will no longer be an active volcano and a new island will have appeared on the island's southwest flank.

Lesson Plan ■ D

Orientation:	Grades 4–6.
Content Objective:	The children will state that mountains extend for thousands of miles on the ocean floor and that the mountain ridges are locations of great volcanic activity.
Skill Objective:	The children are required to *observe* oceanic ridges drawn on a globe and to *infer* that the earth's crust has many fractures (faults).
Materials:	Several world globes, wax crayons, copies of Figure 25–4.
Evaluation:	Students' verbal interaction, students' group problem-solving skills, group globes.

Procedure

Divide the class into groups, and provide each group with a globe, crayons, and a copy of Figure 25–4. (*Note:* If globes are still available from Lesson Plan B, with the ocean trenches marked on them, you may wish to have the children use the same globes and use another color of crayon for this activity.) Direct the

continued on next page

groups to draw lines on the globe that represent the oceanic ridges as shown in the sketch. After all the groups have completed drawing the ridges, ask: "What can we observe about mountain ridges in the oceans of the earth?" "If these mountain ridges were formed (and are being formed) by volcanic activity, what can we say about the amount of volcanic activity on earth?" "If we learned that volcanic lava comes from deep within the earth and is forced by pressure through fractures in the earth's surface, what can we say about the crust of the earth along the oceanic ridges?" (The earth's crust has breaks or fractures for long distances where the oceanic ridges occur.)

Concept 4

The ocean floor is spreading.

Discussion

The oceanic ridges extend for thousands of miles along the ocean floor. Sonic exploration has revealed that these ridges are also not simple, single-stranded mountain chains. Instead they appear to be formed along deep rifts that appear in the earth's crust. On each side of the rifts are mountains made of more recent lava flows. Along the sides of these young mountains, away from the central valley or rift, are successive peaks each older than the ones closer to the rift. On the large *abyssal plain* (the extensive flat, sedimented expanse that comprises much of the oceanic basin floors) are lines of what appear to be heavily eroded mountain structures called *guyots*. Guyots have flat tops that are thought to be the result of the action of surface waves as the mountains were pushed farther and farther from the rift valleys where they were formed. Over tens of thousands of years these outer ridgelines not only were nudged away from the rift but also sank slowly beneath the surface as they moved down the slope to the abyssal plain. When their tops lay just beneath the ocean's surface, the wave action eroded away the volcanic rock and formed the flat-topped surfaces. Even farther onto the abyssal plain are rounded structures called *seamounts* that are much shorter in elevation than the guyots and may be the remains of even older volcanic ridges that were pushed ahead of the guyot ridges.

Evidence is mounting that the seafloor along the entire range of oceanic mountain ridges has been spreading; that is, new crustal material is being spewed from the earth's interior to form successions of great undersea mountains that shove the neighboring peaks away from the central valley. Currently the best estimate is that this ocean-floor-spreading activity has been going on for about 200 million years and has created new ocean floors for many hundreds of miles on each side of the mid-ocean ridges.

Evidence in Support of the Theory of Seafloor Spreading

Magnetic Orientation

Volcanic lava frequently contains iron deposits. As the molten material cools, the iron deposits align themselves with the earth's magnetic field. As layer after layer of lava spewed onto the ocean floor and cooled, the iron took on different north-south alignments because of fluctuations in the earth's magnetic field. From these layers of magnetic materials scientists can tell that the layers on the top are the newest and that each layer is older than the one above it. The magnetic materials also indicate that the rock that makes up the oceanic ridges is volcanic in nature.

Sedimentation

The abyssal plain on the ocean floor is heavily deposited with sediments that have drifted down from the water's surface. The high ridges along the central rifts show almost no evidence of sedimentary deposits, and the deposits appear to be heavier as one moves away from the high ridges down the slopes toward the abyssal plain. This indicates that the central high ridges have more recently been formed and that age increases as one moves away from the central rift valley.

Water Temperature

The temperature of the deep ocean water in the vicinity of the rift valleys is much higher than that of the water elsewhere on the outer ridge slopes or abyssal plain. This indicates that the rift valleys and the ridge areas immediately adjacent to them are areas of ongoing volcanic or extrusive activity.

Earthquake Activity

Records of seismologists show the rift valley regions to be the centers of a major part of the earthquake activity in the world. This finding supports the theory that these fissures are the center of volcanism.

Lesson Plan ■ E

Orientation:	Grades 3–6.
Content Objective:	The children will state that ocean ridges and other geological formations occur on both sides of rift valleys because of volcanic activity.
Skill Objective:	The children are required to *observe* a sketch of features of the ocean floor, *read* an information sheet, and make *inferences* about oceanic geological structures.
Materials:	Copies of Figure 25–5 and information sheets.
Evaluation:	Students' verbal interaction, students' group problem-solving skills, group globes.

Procedure

Divide the class into small groups. Provide each group with a copy of Figure 25–5 (or sketch it on the chalk-board) and an information sheet. The sheet should contain the following information:

continued on next page

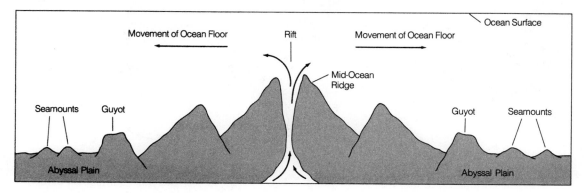

Figure 25–5 ■ Topographical Features of the Ocean Floor

1. The mountain ridges in the figure are made of material from beneath the earth's crust.

2. The temperature of the water in the rift valley and along the ridge is higher than that farther away from the rift.

3. The rock material at the top of the ridge is younger (newer) than the rock material deeper in the ridge.

4. The rocks in the ridges farther away from the rift are younger than those closer to the rift.

5. The sedimentary material that has settled on the bottom is thicker on the abyssal plain and less thick the closer one comes to the rift.

Tell the children to use the sketch and the information to make inferences about the origins of the structures that appear on the ocean floor. Have each group write a list or summary of its conclusions. Lead a class discussion about the lists. The children should conclude that oceanic ridges are formed on both sides of deep rifts as the result of volcanic extrusions; that newer ridge formations along the rifts push the older ones away from the rifts; that the ridge system may extend far from the rifts onto the floor of the abyssal plain; and that new ocean floor crust is formed in the process of ridge building.

Concept 5

The earth's crust is made of large moving sections called plates.

Discussion

All of the previous concepts are related and unified by the concept of global *plate tectonics*. It is now believed that the crust of the earth is broken

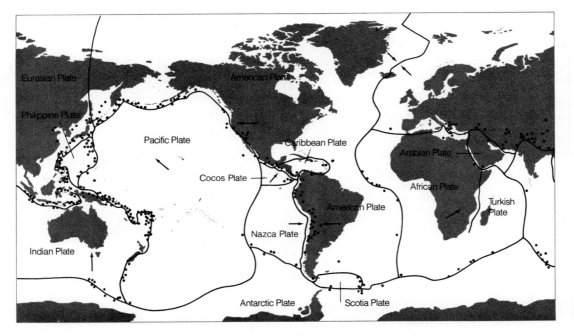

Figure 25–6 ■ Crustal Plates and Earthquake Activity (Represented by Dots)

into six massive pieces that are suspended independently on a mantle of hot, pliable rock. The plates are identified as the *American, Eurasian, Pacific, African, Indian,* and *Antarctic.* The plates are in motion, rotating, and separating in places. At their margins tremendous forces are exerted as the plates collide. At some places along the plate margins they rub, causing great faults and fractures; at other places, such as along the western margin of the American plate, a second plate, the Pacific, is being forced underneath the more massive continental plate, causing earthquakes, uplifting, and mountain building. Figure 25–6 shows the earth's crustal plate system and the locations of major earthquake activity.

As you review the chapter, note the relationships among the several observed phenomena: locations of deep oceanic trenches, volcanic activity, island building, and oceanic ridges. All are near the margins of the crustal plates and are the result of the tremendous energy released there in the form of volcanic activity—the extrusion of material from deep under the earth's crust that forms new crustal material.

Lesson Plan ▪ F

Orientation:	Grades 3–6.
Content Objective:	The children will state that the earth's crust is broken into six independent moving parts called plates.
Skill Objective:	The children are required to *observe* the positions of the crustal plates and evidence of earthquake and volcanic activity and to *infer* the *relationship* to the theory of plate tectonics.
Materials:	World globes, wax crayons, copies of Figure 25–6.
Evaluation:	Students' verbal interaction, students' group problem-solving skills, globes.

Procedure

Divide the class into groups. Give each group a globe, crayons, and a copy of Figure 25–6. (*Note:* if the globes from Lesson Plans C and E are still available, use them.) Tell the children to draw the outlines of the six crustal plates on their globes. Then have them place dots on the globe to indicate major earthquake activity. Ask: "How do the outlines of the plates correspond to the lines you made in Lesson Plans B and D that showed deep ocean trenches, island chains, and volcanic activity?" The children should conclude that the margins of the six plates are the sites of much of the earth's geological phenomena. Tell them that the theory of plate tectonics explains the relationships that exist among these phenomena.

Concept 6

Ocean water has movement and energy.

Discussion

Ocean water is constantly on the move, both on the surface and at great depths. Ocean waves can carry a surfer along for hundreds of meters on their crests. They can also tumble huge concrete blocks weighing hundreds of tons and lift the largest ships hundreds of feet on their upward swells. The oceans also transport floating icebergs from the arctic region far south. In fact, an object that floats low in the water where the wind will not affect it can be transported from the Florida Keys to New Jersey in two weeks' time. The energy of the oceans may be a friend to the surfer or a terrible threat to anything in its path when its kinetic force is at a high level.

Subconcept 6–1

Energy is transported by ocean waves.

Discussion

When asked, "What is an ocean wave?" most people describe the whitecaps that roll onto the beach or crash against a rocky coastline. That is, they see the effect of moving water meeting the resistance of rocks and beach sands and dissipating their energy. As the ocean waves strike the countless miles of shorelines, their energy "eats away" the sand dunes and wears away the rocks. Waves are a form of kinetic energy. It is not the water that acts upon the shoreline, but the *energy* of the water. Some properties of wave energy are:

1. Waves are *reflected* when they strike a solid surface. For instance, when an ocean wave strikes a concrete seawall on the shoreline, a wave is formed that moves back toward the ocean.
2. Waves pass through one another when they meet. When the reflected wave meets the

next incoming wave, they will appear to combine together momentarily before each wave will emerge to continue on its separate way.

3. When waves meet, their energies are momentarily combined. Thus, when two wave crests meet, the resulting momentary result is a wave that has the combined energy of both waves, and we observe a higher wave. But when a crest of one wave meets the trough of a second, their combined energies tend to momentarily cancel one another, and a flattened wave will be observed.

4. Ocean waves can be *diffracted*. That is, when an ocean wave meets an obstruction that has only a narrow opening through it, a wave will be formed on the other side of the obstruction with the narrow opening as its source. We can see this happen in bays and inlets and even in tidal pools on the beach.

5. Waves may be *refracted* or *bent* as they move from the deep ocean to strike a sloping beach at an angle. The portion of the wave that strikes the sloping bottom first is slowed while the portion of the wave still in deep water continues to move at the greater speed. This bends the wave.

Each of these wave properties can be demonstrated by generating waves in a shallow baking dish as suggested in Lesson Plan C of Chapter 16. (You can choose to use that lesson here to have the children discover these properties of waves.)

Subconcept 6–2

Ocean waves transport energy, not water.

Discussion

When a pebble is dropped into a quiet pond, it strikes the water's surface and displaces an amount of water equal to its own volume. The displaced water is forced to bulge above the pond's surface. Each molecule of elevated water now has kinetic energy because of the force of gravity and is pulled back to the surface of the pond, forming a circular motion. As each molecule of water falls back to the pond's surface, it acts just as the original pebble, causing the upward displacement of adjacent molecules. The effect is the transfer of energy from one molecule to another. The wave in the still pond will continue to expand from its center in a circular fashion until it strikes the pond's shore. Waves in the ocean are the same as those in a pond or in a baking dish: they transport energy in the same fashion, but the source of their energy is usually different.

Most waves in the ocean are formed by the wind blowing across its surface. As the wind blows steadily or with great velocity, the waves take on greater energy and become larger both in width and height (*amplitude*). The earth's prevailing winds cause the oceans to be in constant motion much of the time. And once a wave is formed it can travel great distances across the open water. Waves formed by the winds from a storm around the Antarctic may move north to strike the shores of California. The waves of the famous surfing beach on the north side of the island of Oahu, Hawaii, originate thousands of miles away in the northern Pacific Ocean. Wind-generated waves usually have a height of about three feet. However, a U.S. Navy ship once recorded storm-generated ocean waves that were more than a hundred feet in height. The energy of even a four-foot-high wave as it strikes the shore is impressive. Such a normal wave expends about 4,000 foot-pounds of work on each foot of beach length. Multiply that number of foot-pounds times the length in feet of a beach and you will be astonished at the tremendous amount of work the ocean waves expend on the coastlines of the world each day.

A second, but infrequent source of ocean waves is underwater geological events. For example, volcanoes erupt on ocean floors far below the surface; landslides occur on the steep cliffs of underwater ridges; and earthquakes take place under the ocean surfaces. Each of these may be the cause of waves, sometimes of great height, being generated on the surface. Waves generated by cataclysmic undersea geological events are called *tsunamis*. Tsunamis of more than fifty feet in height struck around Japan as the result of the underwater eruption that destroyed the volcano Krakatau off the coast of Java.

Lesson Plan ■ G

Orientation:	Grades 2–6.
Content Objective:	The students will state that waves transport energy, but not water.
Skill Objective:	The children are required to *observe* waves passing floating objects, *record* their observations, and *infer* that the water does not move (much).
Materials:	Deep glass baking dishes, corks, string, metal washers or fish sinkers, water.
Evaluation:	Students' verbal interaction, students' group problem-solving skills, sketch.

Procedure

Divide the class into groups. Provide each group with the materials listed above. Show them how to attach a weight (washers or sinkers) to the cork so it floats about level with the water's surface. Have the children observe the floating cork from the sides of the dish. Tell them to make waves of various sizes and record

continued on next page

their observations. Ask such questions as: "What happens to the cork when the waves pass over it?" "How would you describe the motion of the cork?" "Did the cork move along with the wave?" "What sort of geometric pattern did the cork make with its motion?" "How is the motion of the cork related to the motion of the water around the cork?" The children should state that the water makes a circular motion within a wave; that the water in a wave has motion but does not move along the surface with the wave. Have the children draw a sketch of the motion within a wave.

Concept 7

Oceans have streams or currents that flow for great distances.

Discussion

The movement of ocean water as "streams" or surface currents occurs wherever water is forced to "pile up" so its level is higher than the surrounding water. Ocean surface levels can be raised by strong, steady winds that push water before them until its movement is obstructed by a large landform. The trade winds that blow steadily from east to west in a band 30 degrees on each side of the equator create the movement that causes the major ocean currents of the world.

Another major cause of ocean currents is the expansion of surface water along the equator. Although water expands only slightly with an increase in temperature, this effect is enough to raise the level of the ocean surface in a zone along the equator several centimeters in height. This elevation, added to the effect of the trade winds as they pile up surface water on the western margins of oceans, causes the band of ele-

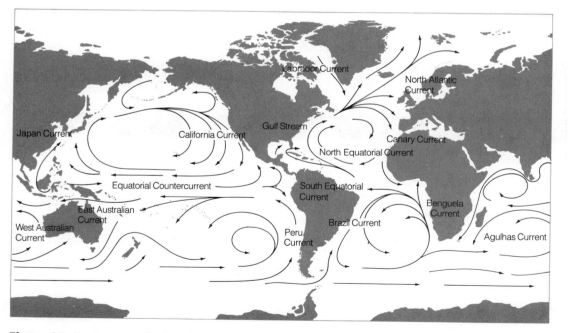

Figure 25–7 ■ Ocean Surface Currents

vated water to flow both to the north and to the south, creating currents in both hemispheres. (See Chapter 26 for a discussion of the earth's prevailing wind patterns.)

The Gulf Stream

One of the most important and best understood of the ocean currents is the *Gulf Stream*. The warm, slightly elevated tropical waters along the equator and the prevailing trade winds create an ocean current that flows westward along the equator. When this current reaches the edge of the ocean basin off northern South and Central America, the flow is channeled northward along the Central American coast. The current continues along the coasts of Mexico and the Gulf states to emerge through the Florida Straits into the Atlantic Ocean.

The waters of the Gulf Stream flow northward along the south Florida coast at a speed of seven miles per hour. The current is about five hundred miles wide and nearly a thousand feet deep. The volume of water of the Gulf Stream at this point is equal to about ten Mississippi Rivers.

As the Gulf Stream makes its long journey around the northern Atlantic Ocean basin, it loses a great deal of heat, slows, and spreads out over an expanse of ocean surface. The heat from the Gulf Stream has a moderation effect on the climates of the many nations that lie adjacent to its path. Among the greatest recipients of its heat energy are England and other countries of northern Europe. Even though these nations lie at about the same latitude as Newfoundland, their climate is considerably less cold.

Figure 25–7 shows the other ocean currents of the world that result from the piling up of water against the western shorelines of land masses because of the earth's rotation.

Lesson Plan ■ H

Orientation:	Grades 1–6.
Content Objective:	Students will state that ocean currents are created by the wind.
Skill Objective:	The children are required to *observe* the effect of their breath on a movable object and to make *inferences* about the wind's effect on ocean currents.
Materials:	Deep baking pans, corks or small floating objects, water.
Evaluation:	Students' verbal interaction, students' group problem-solving skills, written paragraph.

Procedure

Divide the class into groups. Give each group a deep baking pan and several corks with weights attached so that the corks float with their tops at the level of the water's surface. Tell the groups to place the corks in the water and observe what happens as they blow across the water's surface. Direct them not to blow directly on the floating corks. If they do so, have them place the corks near one end of the baking dish and blow across the water's surface from the other end.

Ask: "What happens to the corks?" "Do they move because of the air you blow or from the water's movement?" "If your breath were a strong wind across the ocean and the side of the baking dish were a shoreline, what would this represent?" (A steady, strong wind pushes water against shorelines and currents are created as the water flows away along the shoreline.) Have the students write a brief paragraph describing the ways in which ocean currents are formed.

Concept 8

Vertical currents exist in deep ocean water.

Lesson Plan ▪ I

Orientation:	Grades K–6.
Content Objective:	The students will state that vertical currents occur in ocean water.
Skill Objective:	The children are required to *observe* the effects of changing the temperature and density of water and to make *inferences* about ocean convection currents.
Materials:	Clear tumblers, warm water, ice cubes, salt, tissues.
Evaluation:	Students' verbal interaction, students' group problem-solving skills, report.

Procedure

Divide the class into groups. Give each group a clear tumbler two-thirds full of warm tap water. Have someone in each group place about half a teaspoon of table salt into a tissue. The corners of the tissue should be twisted to form a "ball" of salt as in Figure 25–8. The tissue should be held so the salt is just under the surface of the water in the tumbler. After they have watched for several minutes, ask: "What do you see?" "What makes the water under the tissue fall toward the bottom of the tumbler?" As the salty water falls,

continued on next page

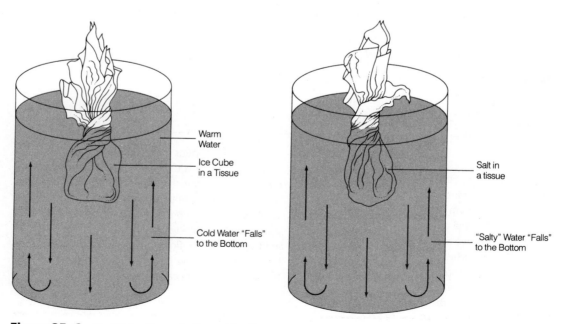

Labels (left): Warm Water; Ice Cube in a Tissue; Cold Water "Falls" to the Bottom

Labels (right): Salt in a tissue; "Salty" Water "Falls" to the Bottom

Figure 25–8 ▪ Water Currents Caused by Changes in Temperature and Salt Content

where does the warmer water that was on the bottom go?" "What would happen in the ocean when very salty water from the ocean is blown by the wind on top of fresh water running from rivers into the ocean?" (The salty ocean water would sink, forming a convection current.)

Now have the children empty their tumblers. Fill them again two-thirds full of warm water from the tap. Give each group a tissue and several ice cubes. Instruct them to suspend the ice cubes in the water as they did the salt. Let them watch what happens for several minutes. Ask: "What did you see?" "Why does the water around the ice cubes flow toward the bottom of the tumbler?" "What happens to the warmer water that was on the bottom of the tumbler?" "What would happen when cold water from the far north Atlantic Ocean is carried to the warmer Gulf Stream?" (A convection current will occur in the ocean water.) You may wish to have the children write a paragraph describing how vertical currents are formed in the ocean water.

Concept 9

The margins of continents are constantly changing.

Discussion

The land that meets the sea along the margins of continents may have many forms; for example, there are the granite cliffs of the northern Pacific coast of the United States, the wide sandy beaches and mangrove estuaries of the Gulf and south and middle Atlantic states, and the rocky coastline of New England. The common characteristic of all continental margins is the evidence of the erosive forces of the wind and sea. On many shorelines a wave strikes the rocky barrier or rolls up onto a sandy beach every fifteen to twenty seconds under average conditions. This represents about 4 waves each minute, 240 waves per hour, and more than 5,000 waves per day that may average five feet in height. The total forces that act upon the shorelines in a 24-hour period are incredible. And when gale or hurricane winds drive before them waves that are twenty or more feet tall and only several seconds apart, it is little wonder that the hardest granite is broken and washed away. A single storm can wash away millions of tons of sand along a few miles of coastline that can take dredges months to restore. In shallow inland seas such as the Gulf of Mexico, the forces of erosion of generally smaller waves are less strong, but still create many changes in the configuration of the sandy beaches and mangrove estuaries of that region.

The Sandy Beach

Figure 25–9 shows the profile of a typical sandy beach. The long and often gradual slope

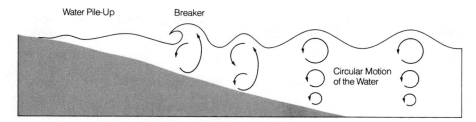

Figure 25–9 ■ Waves Striking a Sloped Beach. As a wave approaches a sloped beach, its circular motion is disrupted by the ocean floor. The pressure of the water piled up against the bottom breaks up the wave motion and provides lift.

of the offshore bottom makes contact with the waves coming from the open ocean and drains much of their energy. As waves striking the sand are slowed, faster waves catch up and combine periodically to form the large waves that are the delight of surfers. Sand picked up from the foreshore and beach face is carried toward the ocean and dumped as the outrushing water loses its energy. This sand forms offshore *sandbars* that may appear above the water level at low tides. Along the many miles of shoreline of the Gulf and Atlantic coastal states, these sandbars have become islands as mangroves and other plants take root and flourish. These *barrier islands* help protect the mainland from the forces of wind and waves.

Sometimes the sandbars help form channels called *inland waterways*. The Indian River along the east coast of Florida and the Albemarle and Pamlico Sounds on the coasts of Virginia and North Carolina are some examples of inland waterways protected by barrier islands.

Of course, what nature has built it can also tear down, and some of the most exposed sandbars and barrier islands have been washed away during violent storms.

Riptides

When ocean waves spill over a slightly submerged longshore sandbar, the surge of water is prevented from flowing back out to sea. Sometimes the trapped water will wash a narrow channel through the sandbar through which the backwash from the waves may flow. Water fun-

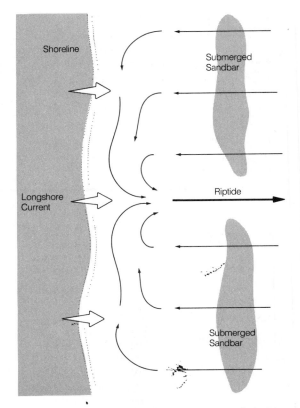

Figure 25–10 ■ Longshore Currents and Riptides

neled through this narrow opening forms a very strong current called a *riptide* (Figure 25–10). Riptides can carry swimmers or boats away from the beach and into the open ocean. Luckily, once through the narrow opening, the water quickly spreads out and loses its energy.

Lesson Plan ■ J

Orientation:	Grades 5–6.
Content Objective:	The children will demonstrate a knowledge of facts and terms that deal with continental margins.
Skill Objective:	None.
Materials:	Copies of Figure 25–11.
Evaluation:	Worksheet of Figure 25–11.

continued on next page

Procedure

Following a discussion of the nature of shorelines or continental margins, give each student a copy of Figure 25–11 with the answers deleted.

Across Clues

2. An inland waterway on the coast of North Carolina is the Albemarle _____ .

3. Winds pile up water against the shoreline causing longshore _____ .

7. An expanse of water protected by barrier islands is called an inland _____ .

10. Fast-moving water returning to the ocean through a narrow channel is a _____ .

11. The channel that occurs in the shoreward side of an offshore sandbar is called a _____ .

13. The main force that causes coastal erosion is the _____ .

15. Sandy hills that serve as buffers against ocean waves are called _____ .

Down Clues

1. Winds pile up water against the shoreline and cause longshore _____ .

4. Offshore sandbars that rise above sea level are called _____ islands.

5. What hard, rocky sea cliffs are made of: _____ .

6. The region of a sandy beach from the berm to the sea cliff is called the _____ .

8. A soft rock that is easily eroded by ocean waves is _____ .

Figure 25–11 ▪ Coastline Facts

9. Ocean waves are a form of _____ energy.

13. The second most effective coastal erosion agent is _____ .

14. The flat or sloping underwater plateau extending from the shore of a continent is called a _____ .

Concept 10

There is diversity among the plants and animals that live in the ocean.

Discussion

A number of different environments exist in the oceans. The *estuaries* provide a protected, shallow, warm, organically rich environment that is conducive to the prolific reproduction of marine plants and animals. *Tidal pools* are another rich habitat for marine animals and plants capable of living part of the time exposed and part submerged. Far out in the oceans are fishes and sea mammals. And colonial *coral* create *reefs* that support a complex and rich tropical ecosystem. As on land, we find all living things are interdependent, each being a part of complex food webs, and each uniquely adapted to its existence in the strange (at least to humans) environment of the ocean.

The Mangrove Estuary

The *mangrove*, a low-growing, shrublike tree, thrives in the brackish, shallow waters of coastal islands and bays. The roots of these plants provide shelter for the hatchlings of fishes and shrimp, and their leaves decay into the organic matter that is essential for numerous animals. Plant-eating organisms such as small fish (mullet, sheepshead, killifish, and so on), crustaceans (crabs, shrimp, crayfish, and so on), and shellfish (oysters, mussels, and so on) feed on the decayed leaves as well as on certain algae and other one-celled organisms called *phytoplankton*. Feeding on the small herbivorous animals are such fish as pinfish, adult sheepshead, flatfish, and blue crabs. And wading birds, such as storks, herons, and ibis; reptiles, such as alligators and snakes; and larger fish, such as the weakfish, redfish, mangrove snapper, and others eat the fish. When the many animal species that live in the mangrove estuarian environment mature, they migrate to deeper water. Thus, the mangrove estuary is an important breeding ground for countless numbers of animals that live in the ocean.

The Ocean Food Chain

The nutritional basis for much of the animal life in the ocean is the small organism called *plankton*. Some plankton possess animal characteristics (*zooplankton*) and some possess plant characteristics (*phytoplankton*). Most plankton are microscopic, though one, the *jellyfish*, may grow to be several feet across. These organisms grow in great abundance in the warm waters near the surface of the ocean. A few very large sea animals, such as the blue whale and certain sharks, feed directly on these tiny organisms. But the plankton most commonly are the foundation of a complex food web whereby small fishes feed upon the plankton and become the source of food for larger carnivorous fish and sea mammals.

Plankton even provide nutrition for the deep ocean dwellers, the seldom seen fish (often blind and sometimes emitting light and possessing other unusual characteristics) that have adapted to life thousands of feet under water. These bottom dwellers forage on the remains of countless plankton that die and drift downward to come to rest on the ocean floor. Should the plankton disappear from our oceans, so too would much of the other life that exists there.

Lesson Plan ■ K

Orientation:	Grades 3–6.
Content Objective:	The children will state that small organisms (plankton) are the first stage of the food web of the sea.
Skill Objective:	The children are required to make *inferences* about a marine food web.
Materials:	Figure 25–12.
Evaluation:	Students' verbal interaction, student food web.

Procedure

Copy Figure 25–12 on the chalkboard. Ask the children to describe each organism. Have the children suggest some relationships. Ask: "What organisms do not feed on any other organisms?" (Plankton. Algae.)

continued on next page

"What do they eat?" (They make their own food by photosynthesis.) "What would happen to the other animals if the plankton and algae would one day disappear from the ocean?" (The animals would die.)

"How important are plankton and algae to life in the ocean?" Have the students create a simple ocean food web of their own.

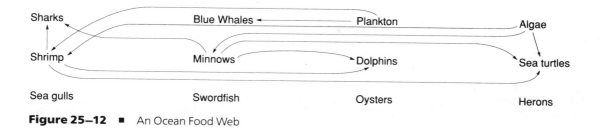

Figure 25–12 ■ An Ocean Food Web

Lesson Plan ■ L

Orientation:	Grades K–5.
Content Objective:	The children will state that there are many kinds of living things in the sea.
Skill Objective:	The children are required to *observe* pictures of marine life and to *infer* that there are many kinds of animals and plants in the ocean.
Materials:	Assorted pictures of marine plants and animals.
Evaluation:	Students' verbal interaction, sketch.

Procedure

Show the students pictures of marine plants and animals. Ask them if they think each plant or animal lives in the ocean or on land. Tell them the names of some of the organisms. After showing the pictures, ask the children what they have found out about plants and animals that live in the ocean. (There are many kinds of plants and animals that live in the ocean.)

Lesson Plan ■ M

Orientation:	Grades K–6.
Content Objective:	Students will state that ocean mammals have different characteristics than fish.
Skill Objective:	The children are required to *observe* pictures of ocean mammals and fishes and to make *inferences*.
Materials:	Pictures of a variety of fish and sea mammals.
Evaluation:	Students' verbal interaction, students' group problem-solving skills, sketches, worksheet.

continued on next page

Procedure

Show the children pictures of different fish. Ask: "What characteristics do they have in common?" After the children discuss the common characteristics of fish, show pictures of several sea mammals. Ask: "Are these fish? Why or why not?" List the different properties on the chalkboard. Ask such questions as: "Do fish breathe air?" "Do sea mammals have to come to the surface to breathe?" "Do fish have scales or fur?" You may wish to have the children write a paragraph in which they differentiate between fish and sea mammals. Primary (K–2) children can match pictures of mammals and fish to these terms on a worksheet you give them. (*Note:* Chapters 9, 10, and 11 contain examples that apply general scientific concepts and principles to life in the sea.)

Lesson Plan ■ N

Orientation:	Grades 4–6.
Content Objective:	Students will describe how an ocean food pyramid demonstrates the quantitative relationships of a food chain.
Skill Objective:	Students are required to *observe* quantitative relationships and make *inferences.*
Materials:	Figure 25–13.
Evaluation:	Students' verbal interaction, students' food pyramid.

continued on next page

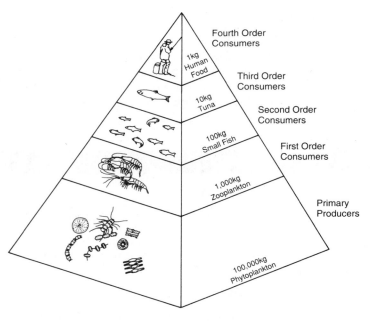

Figure 25–13 ■ An Ocean Food Pyramid

Procedure

Using a large chart or a line drawing that you've drawn on the chalkboard, show the class Figure 25–13. If necessary, show the children pictures and describe the terms *phytoplankton* and *zooplankton*. (Phytoplankton are one-celled organisms, the simplest form of life in the ocean [diatoms]. Zooplankton are tiny animals, such as the prolific, shrimplike krill, that feed on phytoplankton and are a source of food for many larger species of animals.) Ask questions such as: "Which organism is at the bottom of the food chain, and which is at the top?" "How many kilograms of diatoms must exist to feed one kilogram of krill in our food pyramid?" "How many kilograms of diatoms must exist to create one kilogram of food for humans according to our food pyramid?" "What does the food pyramid show?" "What would happen if a pollutant, such as an oil spill, killed off most of the diatoms in one region of the ocean?" Discuss the quantitative interrelationships of food chains in the ocean environment. Have the students draw a food pyramid using the following food chain: mangrove leaves, shrimp, small fish, otters, and hawks. They may omit the hypothetical quantities of each producer and consumer but should make some statement about the general relationship that exists among them.

Summary

The ocean floor is not simply a wide expanse of flat sand or sediment. It has instead a topography that is as varied and even more spectacular than that of the continents. Ocean trenches that reach depths of about seven miles are found on the ocean floors, especially in the Pacific Ocean basin. Along the edges of these trenches are often found islands of volcanic origin, and in the tropics coral atolls often form on the peaks of volcanoes. There are long mountain ridges that cross the ocean floors for thousands of miles. These ridges are the result of the extrusion of lava from deep rifts that lie along the center of the ridgeline. As new mountains are formed over thousands of years of time, the older mountains are pushed away from the center rift and form such features as ridgelines that parallel the newly formed ridge, flat-topped mountains called guyots, and short, rounded rises in the ocean floor called seamounts.

Measurements from satellites in space have verified that the land masses on earth are moving very slowly away from one another, that the ocean floor is spreading. The earth's crust is now thought to be made of six separate plates, each associated with a continental land mass, except for the Pacific plate, which corresponds in its dimensions to the Pacific Ocean basin. The model of moving crustal plates is called the tectonic plate theory.

Wind blowing on the surface of the ocean creates waves that contain amounts of energy. This energy is most often expended on the margins of continents and island land masses where it wears away the rocks and sand, altering coastlines. Currents caused by prevailing winds push water that piles up against the western margins of the ocean basins. These currents are channeled by the landforms, winds, and the rotation of the earth to follow a circular path. The oceans also have vertical currents that result from the differences in density between salty and less salty water and between cold and warmer water. The more dense cold, salty water sinks toward the bottom of the ocean, displacing the warmer, less salty water and producing convection currents.

Life in the sea is as diverse as life on land. Living things in the oceans have interdependent relationships as do living things on land.

The Earth's Atmosphere and Weather

Look What's in This Chapter

In this chapter we'll discuss some important concepts and subconcepts related to the study of the earth's atmosphere and weather, and we'll present lesson plans that are designed to teach these concepts and subconcepts to children.

Concept 1 The earth is surrounded by a sea of gases.

Concept 2 Atmospheric conditions determine the earth's weather.

Subconcept 2–1 Cold air is heavier than warm air; warm air rises and cold air falls.

Subconcept 2–2 Wind currents are caused by the unequal heating of the earth's surface.

Subconcept 2–3 Water vapor moves between the earth's surface and its atmosphere in a continuous cycle.

Subconcept 2–4 Cold air may contain less water vapor than warm air contains.

Subconcept 2–5 Weather may be predicted.

Concept 1

The earth is surrounded by a sea of gases.

Discussion

The earth is covered with a layer of gases and vapors called the *atmosphere*. The atmosphere is very thin compared to the size of the planet as illustrated in Figure 26–1. Ninety-nine percent of the gases that surround the earth lie below an altitude of twenty miles, while the earth's diameter is nearly eight thousand miles. The thickness of the atmosphere is only about one-four-hundredth of the earth's diameter.

The atmosphere is composed of a mixture of gases. *Nitrogen* makes up about 78 percent of the mixture, *oxygen* 20 percent, and *carbon dioxide* and *inert* gases 2 percent. These gases are heavy enough to exert a force on the surface of the earth at sea level of nearly *fifteen pounds per square inch*. Because it is not a solid or liquid

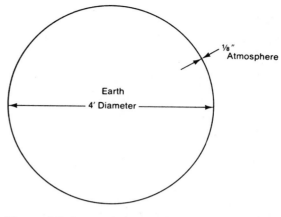

Figure 26–1 ■ The Atmosphere Is Thin

substance, many elementary school children think of air as being nothing. They should be made to realize that air is something. It has weight, exerts pressure, and occupies space.

Lesson Plan ■ A

Orientation:	Pre-K–2.
Content Objective:	The children will state that air is real, that it is around us, it fills bubbles, it can be felt, and it can push on things.
Skill Objective:	The children will *experiment, observe,* and make *inferences.*
Materials:	Two dozen clear plastic bags about 11 inches across, common materials such as newspaper and play dough to fill three plastic bags, six toy horns, two balloons per child, construction paper, a large box or plastic bag to hold inflated balloons, one styrofoam cup per child, bubble solution, several soda straws per child, six large plastic bowls, six clear plastic tumblers, several inflatable balls and toys.
Evaluation:	Students' verbal interaction, students' group problem-solving skills.

Procedure

Activity 1—Air is real; it can be trapped in a bag: Lay several large (about 11 inches wide) plastic bags on a table. Ask the children to describe them. They should note that the bags are empty. Next, wave a plastic bag

through the air to catch some air inside; "choke" the top to close the bag. Ask the children, "How is the bag different?" "What makes it bulge?" Permit several children to feel the inflated bag and describe it to their

continued on next page

classmates. Now give each child a plastic bag. Be sure to warn them to refrain from placing the plastic bag over their heads, and continue to monitor the children during this activity. Ask them to wave their bags in the air and trap some air, then close off the top of the bag. Have them feel their inflated bags and perhaps place a book on top of their bag as they lay on a table. Again discuss the contents of the bag. "What is in the bag?" "What is making it bulge?" "What holds up the book?"

Activity 2—Air is real; it can blow a horn and move things: Pass out a plastic bag to each group of three to four children. Have one child in each group inflate the plastic bag and trap the air. Let each child in the group feel the bag. Discuss the contents of the bag.

While the children are involved with their plastic bags, blow into a toy horn. Ask how they might blow the horn without placing it in their mouths. If they do not guess, place the horn in the opening of an inflated plastic bag and squeeze the bag. (Check the toy horns prior to this activity to be sure they are capable of making a noise in this fashion.) Now hang a wind chime or mobile from some piece of furniture or light fixture. Ask, "How can we make the mobile move or wind chimes chime without blowing with our mouths?" The children will guess that they might do this with their inflated plastic bags. Permit groups of children to blow the horns and the wind chimes/ mobile. Tell them the rules do not allow them to use their mouth to do this. After each group has had an opportunity to perform the assigned tasks, ask them, "What caused the horn to blow? the wind chimes/ mobile to move?" How do we know that air is a real substance?"

If there is a breeze take the children outside. Walk around the playground as the children search for evidence that the air is making things move (some examples are the leaves of trees, the school flag, dust, leaves, and scrap paper moving along the ground, children's hair and scarves). Back in the classroom, discuss the things that the wind moves and the fact that the wind is moving air.

Activity 3—Wind can blow streamers: Cut two-inch-wide strips of newspaper the long way across the double sheet to make them 3 feet to 4 feet long. Staple four to six strips together on one end. Make a multiple-strip streamer for each child. You may wish to allow the children to decorate their streamers with crayons or tempera paints. Then tape or staple each streamer to a pencil or short dowel rod. Show the children how to hold the streamers by the dowel rod so the streamers can hang free. Permit the children to wave their streamers about while they are in the classroom. Ask them to find ways to make the streamers fly out behind their moving hand. Take them outside on a day when there is a breeze. First have the children stand still and let the breeze blow their streamers. Then permit them to run about freely, waving their streamers in the air. Back in the room ask them, "What made your streamer go from a hanging position to a horizontal one?" showing them the meaning of *horizontal* with your hand or a streamer. (The wind blows the streamer and moving it about through the air also does this.)

Activity 4—Air is real; it can be used to inflate things: Before class, inflate a balloon for each child plus five or six extra ones. Tie a three-foot-long string on each. Deflate several inflatable balls and toys. In class, inflate a balloon while the children are watching. Ask, "What is making the balloon grow?" "What is inside?" Help them to see that you are blowing air into the balloon. Then hold up an inflatable ball that may be inflated by blowing into it. Ask the children how they might inflate a ball. Permit several children to inflate balls if they can. (If they are too young to do this, have the balls and toys inflated prior to class.) Tell the children that during their outdoor time they may play with balloons and with the inflated balls. As the children leave the classroom, give each one an inflated balloon. Outdoors, permit the children free play to throw or kick the inflated balls and play with the balloons. When they return to the classroom, ask them to tell what things they did with the balloons and balls. Ask them if these objects would have been as much fun to play with if they were not full of air. What changes did the air make in the balloons and balls?

Activity 5—Air can make bubbles: This activity can be conducted inside or outside. Obtain some bubble soap or make it using the following directions. For each group of children mix together two cups of water, two tablespoons of liquid soap, and one-fourth cup of glycerine, if available. Provide each small child with a small styrofoam cup and a pencil. Show the children how to pierce the side of their cups near the bottom (the hole should be just large enough so a soda straw can be inserted through it). Instruct them to insert the soda straw through the hole. For each small group of children, provide a shallow pan such as an aluminum pie pan, which contains the bubble solution. Show them how they might make a bubble by placing the cup, open end down, into the bubble solution, lifting it slowly from the liquid and then blowing gently into the soda straw. Permit the children to explore making bubbles this way. As they are making bubbles, walk among them and suggest that they see how big a bubble they can make.

If there is bubble solution remaining after this activity, you may wish to pour some into small plastic bowls (butter or margarine containers will do) and permit three or four children to gather around each bowl, insert their straws into the liquid, and blow bubbles until the solution is used up. Discuss the nature of bubbles with the children. Have them describe a bubble, how they made a large bubble, and other interesting things they learned about bubbles. Ask them how a bubble is like a balloon; what makes the covering of an inflated balloon; what makes the covering of a bubble.

Lesson Plan ▪ B

Orientation:	Grades K–4.
Content Objective:	The children will state such generalizations about air as: (1) Air occupies space. (2) Air exerts a force. (3) Air has weight.
Skill Objective:	The children are required to *experiment* by manipulating materials, to *observe* the effect of air upon the materials, and to *infer* some generalizations concerning air from their observations.
Materials:	Cleansing tissues, six soda straws, six plastic baggies, assorted balloons, string.
Evaluation:	Students' verbal interaction, students' group problem-solving skills.

Procedure

Provide each child or small group of children with the following materials: a cleansing tissue, a soda straw, a plastic baggie, several balloons, a string, and a ruler. Tell the children that they may investigate the materials to see what they can discover. After the children have had ample time to manipulate the materials, ask them to report on what they discovered. Have the children generalize from their observations. For example: "The balloon or baggie becomes larger when we blow into it." (Air occupies space. Air exerts a force.) "The tissue blows away when I blow on it with the straw." (Air exerts a force.) "When I blow up the balloon and let it go, I feel air on my face." (Air exerts a force.)

To conclude the lesson, the teacher may ask the class if air is real, even though we cannot see it. Ask them for other examples that show that air can exert a force.

Orientation:	Grades 2–6.
Content Objective:	The children will state that air exerts a force.
Skill Objective:	The children are required to *observe* as a flat-sided can is crumpled and *infer* that the crumpling was caused by air pressure.
Materials:	One flat-sided can, water, hot plate.
Evaluation:	Students' verbal interaction, report.

Procedure

Put about one-half cup of water into a clean, flat-sided can like the ones in which duplicating fluid is packaged. *With the lid off,* boil the water vigorously for about a minute. Remove the can from the heat and place the lid tightly over the opening. Ask the class: "What happened inside the can?" (Water turned to steam and filled the can.) "What do you think will happen when we permit the can to cool off?" Let the children speculate upon this as the can begins to cool. As the can cools and begins to crumple (the collapse of the can may be speeded up by pouring cold water over its sides), ask the children what is happening to the steam inside the can. (It is condensing, turning back to water.) "If much of the air has been removed and the steam is turning back to water, what can we say is inside the can?" (A vacuum.) "What is causing the can to collapse?" (The air [atmosphere] is pushing on it.) "What can we say about air from this observation?" (Air exerts a force, pressure.) Ask the children to list other examples showing how air exerts a force.

Orientation:	Grades 2–6.
Content Objective:	The children will state that air exerts a force.
Skill Objective:	The children are required to *observe* as the water in an inverted glass tumbler is held in place by an index card and to *infer* that air exerts a force.
Materials:	A glass tumbler, water, an index card.
Evaluation:	Students' verbal interaction.

Procedure

Fill a glass tumbler with water. Place a *stiff* index card over the mouth of the tumbler (see Figure 26–2). Announce to the class: "I am going to turn this glass upside down and take away my hand from under the card. What do you think will happen?" (The water will spill out.) After eliciting a number of guesses from the children, hold the index card in place with the palm of

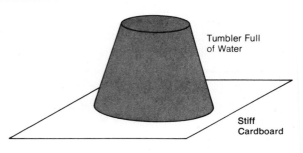

Tumbler Full of Water

Stiff Cardboard

continued on next page
Figure 26–2 ■ Air Exerts Force

one hand and the tumbler with the other hand. Invert the glass, and remove the hand that holds the index card in place. "What happened?" (The card stayed in place.) "I wonder why? What force is there that could hold the card in place? What is all around the card?" (Air must supply the force that holds the card in place. Air exerts a force.)

Lesson Plan ▪ E

Orientation:	Grades K–6.
Content Objective:	The children will state that air has weight.
Skill Objective:	The children are required to *observe* a loss of equilibrium as one of two balloons suspended from a yardstick is broken and to *infer* a generalization from the observation.
Materials:	Two large balloons, one lightweight yard- or meterstick, string, one sharp object.
Evaluation:	Students' verbal interaction.

Procedure

Suspend a large, partially inflated balloon from each end of a yard- or meterstick (see Figure 26–3). Suspend the whole system by a string tied to the center of the stick. Introduce or review the concept of balance (equilibrium of forces) by referring to a teeter-totter. With a sharp object break one of the balloons. The partially inflated balloon probably will not break into pieces when pierced with the pin. If possible no section of the balloon should be "lost" when pierced. Ask: "What happened?" (One side fell down. The system is no longer balanced.) "What is the thing we have lost that makes the system unbalanced?" (The air from the broken balloon.) "Does air have weight if it can do this?" (Yes. Air has weight.) Ask the children to think of other examples that show that air has weight.

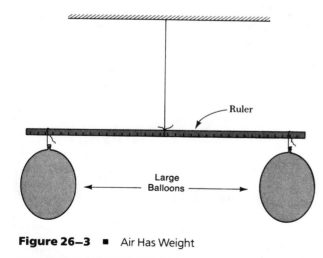

Ruler

Large Balloons

Figure 26–3 ▪ Air Has Weight

Orientation: Grades 2–6.

Content Objective: The children will state that air occupies space.

Skill Objective: The children are required to *observe* that the paper in an inverted tumbler immersed in a tank of water remains dry and to *infer* a generalization from their observations.

Materials: Large glass container or aquarium, glass tumbler, sheet of paper.

Evaluation: Students' verbal interaction.

Procedure

Crumple a piece of paper and push it into the bottom of a glass tumbler so that it stays there when the tumbler is inverted (see Figure 26–4). Push the inverted tumbler into a large glass container filled with water until it is completely submerged. Ask: "I wonder what is happening to the paper?" Accept student comments, then remove the tumbler from the water and permit several students to feel the paper. "Is the paper wet or dry?" (Dry.) "Why didn't the water come up in the tumbler?" (There was air in the tumbler. The air occupied the space.) Ask the children for other examples that show that air occupies space.

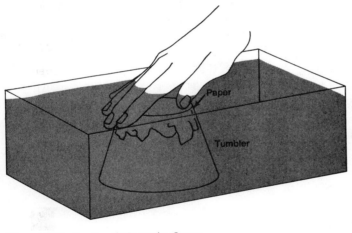

Figure 26–4 ▪ Air Occupies Space

Concept 2

Atmospheric conditions determine the earth's weather.

Subconcept 2–1

Cold air is heavier than warm air; warm air rises and cold air falls.

Discussion

Convection currents are created when air is heated unequally. This is because the molecules of warm air move faster than the molecules of cold air and have more space between them. This means that warm air is not as heavy (is less dense than) cold air. The warm air rises, forced up by the heavier cold air, and the cold air rushes into the space formerly occupied by the warm air. As it rushes in, the cool air is heated and also rises, and a continuous upward flow of air is created above a heat source. Such thermal currents account for nearly all winds.

Lesson Plan ▪ G

Orientation:	Grades K–5.
Content Objective:	The children will state that warm air rises.
Skill Objective:	The children will *observe* and make *inferences*.
Materials:	Glass chimney used with a kerosene lamp, tissue paper, heat source such as a 100-watt electric light bulb or alcohol burner.
Evaluation:	Students' verbal interaction, sketch.

Procedure

Plug in an extension cord that is attached to a socket and a 100- or 150-watt bulb. Have a number of children hold their hands close to but not touching the bulb and describe what they feel. (The bulb is giving off heat. The air close to the bulb is warm or hot.) Now lay the bulb on a small sheet of wood or a book and place the glass chimney over it. Attach a strip of tissue paper to a pencil with plastic tape and hold it over the top of the chimney. Ask the class, "What do you see?" (The tissue paper is being "blown up into the air.") "What is causing it to do this?" (The heat from the light bulb makes the air hot, and it blows up the chimney.) "What did we learn about hot air?" (Hot air rises.) Tell the children this is called a convection current, and ask them to think where convection currents might occur in nature. Then ask them to draw a sketch of a convection current. Some examples of convection currents are those that are formed over parking lots, beaches, or even over warm ocean or lake water.

Lesson Plan ▪ H

Orientation:	Grades K–5.
Content Objective:	The children will state that as air is warmed it expands and that warm air does not weigh as much as cold air.
Skill Objective:	The children are required to *observe* the expansion of a balloon filled with warm air and the contraction of a balloon filled with cold air and to *infer* from their observations.

continued on next page

Materials: Two soft drink bottles, two balloons, two pans, hot water, ice water.

Evaluation: Students' verbal interaction, laboratory worksheets, log, and reports.

Procedure

Fit the mouth of a balloon over the open top of a soft drink bottle. Place the bottle in a pan containing several inches of hot water. Fit a second balloon over the top of a second soft drink bottle and place this bottle in a pan containing several inches of ice water. Ask the children: "What happened?" (One balloon expanded, the other balloon went into the bottle.) "Why did this happen?" Have the children ask questions that you can answer "yes" or "no" until they arrive at the reason. Examples of such questions are: "Are both bottles empty?" (No.) "Do both bottles contain air?" (Yes.) "Is the water in both pans the same temperature?" (No.)

"Did the air in one bottle expand and fill the balloon?" (Yes.) "Did the air in the second bottle contract?" (Yes.)

The teacher may then review the generalization that warm air expands and cool air contracts. To pursue the generalization that cold air is heavier than warm air, the teacher may ask: "Did the air in both bottles weigh the same at the beginning of the experiment?" (Yes.) "Which bottle had more air after the heating and cooling?" (The cold air bottle.) "Which bottle of air weighed the most?" (The bottle of cold air.) "Which weighs the most, cold air or warm air?" (Cold air weighs more than warm air.) Ask the children in grades 3–6 to write statements describing what they learned about warm and cold air.

Subconcept 2–2

Wind currents are caused by the unequal heating of the earth's surface.

Discussion

The temperature of a land mass will increase much more than the temperature of a water mass when exposed to the same amount of heat. In the absence of heat, a land mass will cool more rapidly than a water mass. Dark substances absorb more radiant heat than do light substances. Furthermore, surfaces exposed to the direct rays of the sun absorb more heat than do surfaces exposed to slanted rays. For all of these reasons, the surface of the earth is heated unequally. This causes the formation of convection currents and winds.

Prevailing winds are illustrated in Figure 26–5. Warm air around the equator rises vertically (doldrums), cools, returns to the surface, and rushes back toward the equator. If it were not for the earth's rotation on its axis, all prevailing winds would blow in a north-south direction. Because of the rotation, however, the

trade winds between 10 and 25 degrees north latitude blow from the northeast, and trade winds between 10 and 25 degrees south latitude blow from the southeast. Cold, heavy air pushes along the earth's surface toward the temperate zones from both poles. This air heats up, rises, and returns to the surface at the poles.

Local winds may occur any time two adjacent masses of air possess different temperatures. Breezes occur at the shores of large bodies of water. A shore breeze blows from the cool air above the water to the warm air above the land in the daytime, and from the cool air above the land to the warm air above the water at night. The temperature of the land mass varies greatly between day and night while the temperature of the water mass changes only a little.

To discuss convection currents and their effects on the weather, conduct the activity of Lesson Plan K in this chapter. At the conclusion of this lesson, ask the children what would happen if the source of the heat were a hot, sandy beach or hot, sun-drenched rocks. Convection currents that cover a large area of the earth's surface are called *winds*.

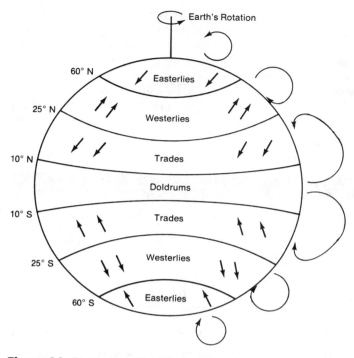

Figure 26–5 ■ Prevailing Winds of the Earth

Lesson Plan ■ I

Orientation:	Grades 4–6.
Content Objective:	The children will state that the rotation of the earth on its axis affects the direction of the prevailing winds.
Skill Objective:	The children are required to *observe* what happens when a globe is spun in the path of water droplets and to *infer* the relationship of the earth's rotation to the direction of the prevailing winds.
Materials:	A large globe that may be spun on its axis, a medicine dropper, food coloring.
Evaluation:	Students' verbal interaction, seat work.

Procedure

Put some food coloring in a half cup of water. Hold the globe motionless. Poise a medicine dropper full of colored water above the north pole and ask the children:

"What will happen to a drop of water that falls upon the globe?" Accept the children's suggestions. Then allow a few drops of colored water to fall upon the

continued on next page

globe. "The water appears to flow in the same general direction as what lines on the globe?" (The longitude lines.) "Let us see what will happen when the water drops are allowed to fall upon the globe while it is spinning." Spin the globe slowly from west to east and drop a few drops of water upon the surface. Stop the globe and ask: "What effect did spinning the globe have upon the path of the water drops?" (They now run diagonally across the longitude lines.) "If the water drops represent cold air falling upon the earth's surface, how would the air tend to move?" (Diagonally across the surface.) "In what way do you suppose the prevailing winds move across the earth?" (Diagonally.) Now show a globe or chart that demonstrates the prevailing winds of the earth; discuss them. On a line drawing of a world globe, have the children draw arrows to show the prevailing winds.

Lesson Plan ▪ J

Orientation:	Grades 3–6.
Content Objective:	The children will state that the temperature of sand or soil increases faster than the temperature of an equal volume of water.
Skill Objective:	The children are required to *hypothesize, name,* and *control variables, experiment, communicate* by putting data in graphical form, and *interpret* the data.
Materials:	Sand or soil, water, two pans, sunlight or sunlamp, two thermometers.
Evaluation:	Students' verbal interaction, student group problem-solving skills, laboratory worksheets, log, and reports.

Procedure

You may introduce the problem by announcing: "We would like to investigate the effect of sunlight upon water and various kinds of soil. Can anyone guess how these substances are affected by sunlight?" (The class may say that paving, beaches, and other surfaces become very warm in the sunlight. Water does not become so warm.) "Can we make some hypotheses about the heating effect of sunlight upon various surfaces?" The class may offer such *hypotheses* as: Sunlight causes white sand to become hotter than water; sunlight causes topsoil to become hotter than water. You might then ask: "How can we test our hypotheses?" The class may be directed to suggest putting thermometers in samples of the materials and placing the samples in the sunlight.

To *control variables* you may ask such questions as: "Which materials do we want to test?" (Water, sand, soil, and any other materials that are available.) "How much of each should we use?" (It is easy to use equal amounts of materials by volume.) "May we use different shapes for the containers?" (No. The containers should be the same. The areas exposed to sunlight should be equal.) "Where should we place the samples?" (In the direct sunlight.) "How long should we expose each material to sunlight?" (Half an hour to an hour is sufficient.) "How often should we read the thermometers?" (Every ten to fifteen minutes.) *After establishing and providing means for controlling variables,* allow the children, working in groups, to set up the experiment.

To *interpret* data you may suggest that the children construct line graphs showing the temperature of the various materials at different time intervals (see Figure 26–6). This activity may be extended to include data covering the speed with which the materials cool off when they are removed from the sunlight.

During the concluding discussion, you may ask the children to relate what they have learned to the

continued on next page

study of weather. They should conclude that land masses become hotter on sunny days than bodies of water. "If land masses become hotter, what about the air above the land masses?" (It will become hotter, too.) "What do we know happens to warm or hot air?" (It expands and rises.) The discussion may go on to include thunderstorms and land and sea breezes.

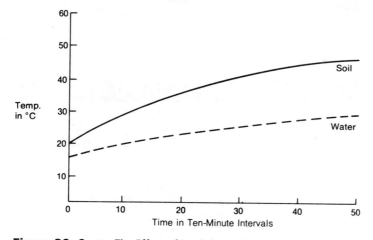

Figure 26–6 ■ The Effect of Sunlight on Various Substances

Lesson Plan ■ K

Orientation:	Grades 3–6.
Content Objective:	The children will state that black (dark) surfaces absorb more heat energy than white (light) surfaces.
Skill Objective:	The children are required to *hypothesize* concerning the heating effect of the sun on light and dark objects, to *control variables* as they *experiment*, and to *infer* a generalization from their data.
Materials:	Six cans painted white, six cans of equal size painted black, six Celsius thermometers, a clock.
Evaluation:	Students' verbal interaction, students' group problem-solving skills, laboratory worksheets, log, and reports.

Procedure

Select twelve cans of equal size. Paint six of them black on the outside and six of them white. Without showing the cans to the children, ask: "Does the color of an object affect the rate at which it will absorb heat energy?" Accept all student comments (*hypotheses*) and then ask: "How could we use these painted cans to find out?" Direct the students' suggestions to some promising procedure.

One such procedure would be to place equal amounts of water and a thermometer in each can and expose the cans to sunlight for some period of time (controlling variables). Divide the class into groups.

continued on next page

Provide each group with a black can, a white can, and a thermometer. Let the groups record the temperatures of the cans of water at ten-minute intervals for about an hour while they are doing another assignment. Discuss the data gathered. The groups should discover that the temperature of the water in the black can increased the most. Black objects absorb more radiant energy than white objects. Ask the children: "How may what we learned here be related to winds?" The children should be led to conclude that the unequal heating of the earth's surface due to differences in color causes convection currents. As cold air moves in to replace warm air that is rising, winds are created.

Lesson Plan ▪ L

Orientation:	Grades 2–6.
Content Objective:	The children will state that direct rays of the sun produce a greater heating effect than slanted rays.
Skill Objective:	The children are required to *hypothesize* concerning the heating effect of direct and slanted sun rays, to *control variables* as they *experiment*, and to *interpret* their *data* to form a generalization.
Materials:	Twelve baking pans, soil, six thermometers, clock.
Evaluation:	Students' verbal interaction, students' problem-solving skills, laboratory worksheet, log, and reports.

Procedure

You might start this activity by saying: "I have some soil, two bread pans (or other containers with a large surface area), and two thermometers. I would like to find out if sunlight falling directly on a surface will cause a different heating effect than sunlight that strikes the surface at an angle. Would anyone care to offer a hypothesis?" (Example: Surfaces that have direct sunlight on them will have a higher temperature than those that have slanted sunlight.) After accepting the children's hypotheses, ask: "How might I proceed to test these hypotheses?" Shape the children's suggestions to form some likely procedure such as the following:

Divide the class into groups. Give each group two bread pans, soil, and one thermometer. Direct the children to stir the soil thoroughly and fill each container. Stirring ensures equal starting temperatures. Have them place one container flat on a window sill or table in the sunlight. The soil in this container will receive slanted sunlight. Have them prop up one end of the second container so that it receives the sunlight at nearly a right angle as in Figure 26–7. Have them record the temperature of each soil sample at fifteen-minute intervals for one hour. Tell them to record the temperature near the surface of the soil in each instance.

After the children have reported the results of their experiment, hold a class discussion to *interpret the data.* (Direct sunlight has a greater heating effect than slanted sunlight.) Ask: "If some parts of the earth receive direct sunlight and other parts receive slanted sunlight, what could we say about the heating effect of the sun upon the earth?" (Some parts of the earth are heated more than other parts.) "What effect might this cause in the atmosphere?" (It might cause winds.) "What if a large part of the earth receives direct sunlight for several months, while another part receives slanted sunlight?" (One part of the earth would become warmer than the other.) See Chapter 23, Subconcept 6–5 (the earth has seasons), for additional related activities.

continued on next page

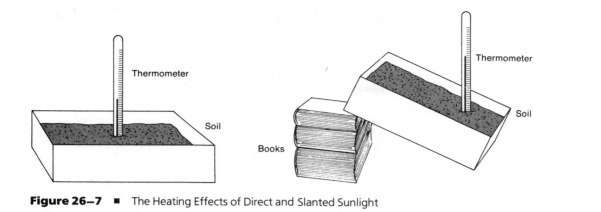

Figure 26–7 ■ The Heating Effects of Direct and Slanted Sunlight

Subconcept 2–3

Water vapor moves between the earth's surface and its atmosphere in a continuous cycle.

Discussion

An important aspect of weather is *precipitation*. Water vapor precipitates as rain, snow, hail, sleet, dew, and frost. Two questions come to mind. How does water vapor get into the atmosphere in the first place? Why does it precipitate out of the atmosphere?

Water vapor gets into the earth's atmosphere by the process of *evaporation*. During evaporation, individual water molecules gain enough kinetic energy to be ejected from the liquid. They then travel freely among the gas molecules of the atmosphere. Nearly 80 percent of the earth's surface is covered by oceans, lakes, and streams. Thus, there is ample opportunity for evaporation to take place on a large scale. Evaporation also occurs over land masses where moist soil and living plants yield large amounts of water vapor to the atmosphere.

The opposite of evaporation is *condensation*. Condensation takes place when the water molecules lose kinetic energy (movement) and begin to join together into droplets. When the droplets are large enough, precipitation will occur. The rate of condensation appears to depend on both the number of water molecules and the temperature of the air in a given place. The more molecules of water vapor in the air, the greater the chance that they will collide and stick together. Thus, the more water vapor there is, the greater the probable rate of condensation.

The temperature of the air is an important factor in determining the rate of condensation. Warm water molecules move faster through the air than cold water molecules. There is therefore less chance that warm water molecules will join together to form droplets, and so warm air may contain more water molecules than cold air without condensation occurring. The ratio of the amount of moisture the atmosphere contains to the amount it would contain at the saturation (condensation) level is called *relative humidity*. This term is defined by the relationship:

$$\text{Relative humidity (in percent)} = \frac{\text{Amount of H}_2\text{O in the air}}{\text{Amount of H}_2\text{O the air can contain at that temperature}} \times 100$$

Lesson Plan ■ M

Orientation: Grades K–6.

Content Objective: The children will state that the rate of evaporation is increased by air movement, heat, and increased surface area.

Skill Objective: The children are required to *observe* the changes that occur in the evaporation rate under various conditions, to *hypothesize* concerning the effect of certain variables on evaporation, and to *infer* a generalization from the observations.

Materials: Wet rag or sponge, chalkboard, floodlamp or heat lamp, tablet, glass tumbler, shallow baking dish.

Evaluation: Students' verbal interaction, students' group problem-solving skills, reports.

Procedure

Wipe a damp rag or sponge across the chalkboard, telling the children to observe any change that occurs. Ask: "What happened?" (The wet place disappeared.) "Where did the water go?" (Into the air.) You may introduce the term *evaporation* at this point. Continue with the lesson by asking: "Can anyone think of any way we could speed up the rate at which the water evaporates?" Accept the children's ideas. Be sure to include the suggestions that the evaporation rate may be increased by heat and by air movement.

"Let us see how heat affects the rate of evaporation." Wipe two water marks upon the blackboard and hold a floodlamp or heat lamp on one of the marks. Ask: "Why did I make two water marks and hold the lamp on only one of them?" (So we can see the effect of heat on evaporation. The unheated mark is a control.) "What effect did heating have upon the rate of evaporation?" (The heated mark evaporated faster.) "Now let us see what effect moving air (wind) has on evaporation." Again make two wet marks on the chalkboard and have a child fan one of the marks vigorously with a tablet. Ask: "What effect does moving air have upon the rate of evaporation?" (Moving air increases the rate of evaporation.)

continued on next page

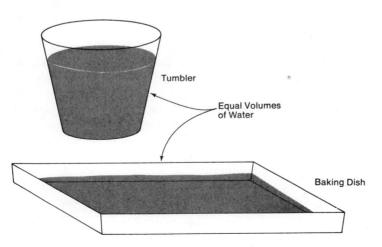

Figure 26–8 ■ Area and the Rate of Evaporation

Now let the class watch as you carefully measure out two equal volumes of water, about 100 mL. Pour one into a drinking glass and the other into a shallow baking dish (see Figure 26–8). Place both containers in the sunlight and tell the children: "We are going to have an evaporation race. I wonder which container will win, the glass or the pan?" Allow the children to vote for their choice of containers. Check on the containers periodically to see which is winning the race. Remember: the less water used, the shorter the evap-

oration time required for the exercise. After the water has been completely evaporated from the baking dish, ask the children which container won the race and why. (The water in the baking dish evaporated first because there was more surface from which the water molecules could escape. Ask the children to copy statements about the things that affect the evaporation of water. Intermediate-grade children may write out the statements on their own.

Lesson Plan ▪ N

Orientation:	Grades K–4.
Content Objective:	The children will state that condensation occurs when water vapor from the air collects upon cold surfaces.
Skill Objective:	The children are required to *observe* that water vapor collects upon a cold surface and to *infer* that the water came from the air.
Materials:	One cold soft drink bottle, one soft drink bottle at room temperature.
Evaluation:	Students' verbal interaction, report.

Procedure

Place two soft drink bottles in front of the class, one containing cold water and the other water at room temperature. Wipe the outside of both bottles with a cloth or paper towel. Ask the children to observe the bottles and report anything that is happening. They will report that one of the bottles is getting wet or has water on it while the other bottle does not. Ask: "I wonder why this is happening. Can you guess?" Accept the children's suggestions. If they do not guess that one of the bottles is cold, permit them to feel both bottles.

Take away the warmer bottle and discuss the fact that moisture is collecting on the colder bottle. Ask the

children: "Where does the moisture come from?" If they guess that it comes from inside the bottle and is seeping through the glass, put sugar or salt in the water and let several of the children taste the moisture by touching the surface of the bottle with their fingers. (The water comes from the air.) "What kinds of objects does water collect upon?" (Cold objects.) Remind the class that the grass is often wet in the morning when there has been no rain, and ask them to explain. Introduce the term *condensation* and discuss how it is the opposite of evaporation. Have the students copy or write the words *evaporation* and *condensation* and their meanings.

Subconcept 2–4

Cold air may contain less water vapor than warm air.

Discussion

The kinetic energy that air and water vapor molecules possess depends on the temperature. The gas and water molecules of warm air move about more rapidly and are farther apart than those of cold air. This makes it less likely that the water molecules contained in warm air will collide and join to form droplets. Conversely, because the gas and water molecules of cold air are closer together and move more slowly, any water molecules that are present are more likely to collide and join together to form droplets. Because its molecules have more kinetic energy and more space, warm air is able to hold more water vapor than cold air. When warm air is cooled, the water and gas molecules slow down. When this occurs, the water molecules tend to stick together when they collide. In this way, water vapor in a warm air mass may condense to form clouds when the air is cooled. This cooling effect and the resultant cloud formation generally occur in two situations: where there are rising convection currents and where cold and warm air meet.

Thunderstorms, Hurricanes, and Tornadoes

Thermal or convection currents spawn thunderstorms, tornadoes, and hurricanes. When the surface of the earth is heated by the sun, the warm air near the surface rises. When it reaches higher altitudes, it cools. With this cooling comes condensation and cloud formation. When temperature differences and vapor content are moderate, the clouds formed by thermal currents are white and fluffy cumulus clouds. When temperature differences are extreme and water content is high, dark and turbulent cumulonimbus thunderheads are formed. The winds that normally accompany a thunderstorm occur when the cooler, heavier air surrounding the hot air mass rushes in to occupy the space vacated by the warm, rising air as illustrated in Figure 26–9.

When thermal updrafts occur over a large area of the tropical ocean, *hurricanes* are sometimes formed. (Such tropical storms are called *typhoons* in the Pacific Ocean.) Water vapor condensing at high altitudes gives hurricanes their tremendous energy. As water evaporates at sea level, it absorbs heat energy that is stored in the kinetic energy of its molecules. When these

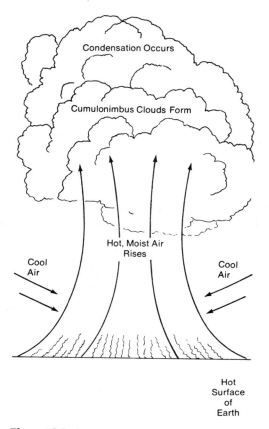

Figure 26–9 ■ How a Thunderstorm Forms

water molecules join to form droplets at higher altitudes, they give up their energy to the surrounding air. This makes the air heat up. As it grows hotter, this air rises still higher, creating thermal updrafts of great velocity. As cool air rushes in to fill the void left by the rising warm air, a huge, whirlpool air mass is formed. When surface winds reach seventy-two miles per hour, the storm is said to be of hurricane force.

Tornadoes occur under special or unusual conditions where a cold air mass is forced up and over a warm air mass. When the warm air pushes its way up through the cold air, violent air currents are formed. These air currents rotate at speeds thought to exceed 400 miles per hour.

Frontal Systems

A frontal system is said to occur where two air masses meet. Where a cold air mass is pushing along a warm air mass, a narrow front occurs. In such a situation—called a *cold front* (Figure 26–10)—an observer might find himself surrounded by hot, humid air with the skies clear or hazy. Puffy white cumulus clouds appear. As time passes, the clouds become progressively darker and finally spawn a thunderstorm. After the thunderstorm is over, the observer finds himself surrounded by comparatively cool, dry air with clear skies. All of this might occur within several hours as such frontal systems are typically less than 100 miles wide.

A *warm front* (Figure 26–11) takes much longer to pass through a region. When a warm air mass is pushing along a cold air mass, the warm air has a tendency to rise over the cooler air, and the air masses join over a long, ascending front. As a warm front approaches, an observer who is in a mass of cool, dry air will see high, wispy, white cirrus clouds (mare's tails) that are composed of ice crystals. As time passes, a large, sheetlike cloud, dark and of medium altitude, moves across to cover the sky from horizon to horizon. A steady rain may fall,

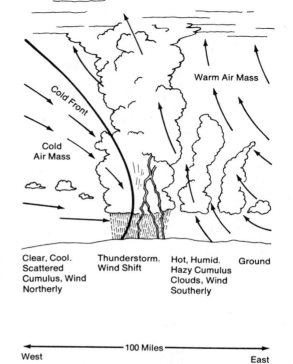

Figure 26–10 ■ A Cold Front

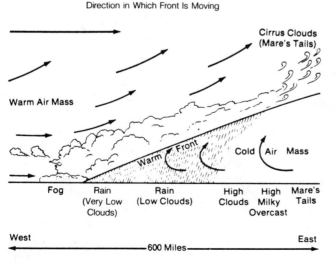

Figure 26–11 ■ A Warm Front

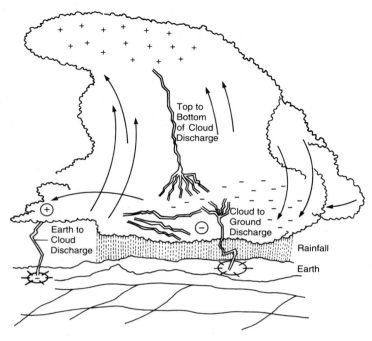

Figure 26–12 ■ Anatomy of a Thunderhead

sometimes for a whole day. After the front passes, the observer finds himself in a sea of warm, moist air. Such warm fronts are typically 600 miles across.

The Products of Severe, Large-scale Convection Currents (Thermal Updrafts)— Lightning and Hail

Cumulonimbus clouds, or thunderheads, are the products of extremes in temperature and water content of thermal updrafts. Giant columns of air rushing up from the earth's surface sometimes reach speeds of more than 200 miles per hour and heights of 40,000 feet. These extreme conditions often result in lightning storms and hail.

Lightning is the visible light generated by a great discharge of electrical energy through the atmosphere. These electrical discharges may take place within a cloud, between two clouds, from a cloud to the earth, or from the earth to a cloud (see Figure 26–12). The discharges may have an electric potential of more than 15 million volts. (House current, by contrast, has an

electric potential of 110 or 220 volts.) The discharge of the tremendous electrical energies is much like the smaller scale discharge of static electricity resulting from a plastic comb that has been rubbed on a wool sweater, or the discharge of an automobile sparkplug. These very large electrical charges are built up by water and ice particles as they are blown upward and downward within a thunderhead.

Scientists do not entirely understand how electrical charges are created in a thunderhead. There are several conflicting theories. One commonly accepted theory is that when large raindrops fall through a thermal updraft, they break up into smaller drops of unequal size. The larger ones possess a positive charge, the smaller ones a negative charge. The updraft separates these charged drops into different regions of the cloud, where they accumulate. When the charges become great enough to overcome the insulating properties of the air, a great bolt of electrical charges takes place. Such bolts may be up to eight miles long when they occur between a cloud and the earth and over twenty miles long between two clouds. Lightning flashes occur, in order of frequency, (1) from the front of a storm to the back, (2) from upper to lower clouds, (3) into the surrounding air ("glow" discharge), (4) between a low cloud and the earth, (5) between a squall or satellite cloud and the earth, and (6) between an upper cloud and the earth. Lightning bolts have been photographed going from the earth to the clouds as well as from the clouds downward. It is most common for several flashes to occur very close together rather than for a single discharge to occur, as it appears to an observer. "Sheet" lightning and "heat" lightning are forms of glow discharges of electrical charges into the surrounding air.

Hailstones that fall to earth appear to be small spheroid masses of ice. Close examination reveals, however, that the structure of a hailstone is more complex than one might first suspect. A hailstone is built up layer upon layer as it falls through the updraft of a thunderhead accumulating moisture and is then hoisted upward again by the convection currents. At higher altitudes the aggregated water freezes to its surface, forming an additional layer. This cycle is repeated until at last the hailstone falls to earth. Hail is found commonly as "stones" as large as a golf ball. In rare instances hailstones as large as tennis balls are reported, and in rarer instances yet huge ice balls several feet in diameter have been reported falling from the sky.

Lesson Plan ■ O

Orientation:	Grades K–5.
Content Objective:	The children will state that clouds form when warm air is cooled because cold air cannot hold as much water vapor as warm air.
Skill Objective:	The children are required to *observe* a "cloud" being formed in a jar and *infer* the reason for its formation.
Materials:	Glass bottle, hot water, match, ice cubes, flashlight.
Evaluation:	Students' verbal interaction, report.

Procedure

Pour hot water into a glass bottle until it is about three-quarters full. Pour off all but about two inches of the hot water. Strike a match and throw it into the bottle. This will provide colloidal particles for the water droplets to collect on. Place several ice cubes at the mouth of the bottle (see Figure 26–13). Hold the bottle in strong sunlight or a flashlight. A cloud will be seen to have formed inside. Ask the children to explain why the cloud formed. (The cool air created by the ice cubes cannot contain as much water vapor as the warm air in the bottle. When the air in the bottle is cooled, the cloud forms.) Have the children copy a simple statement that explains the formation of clouds.

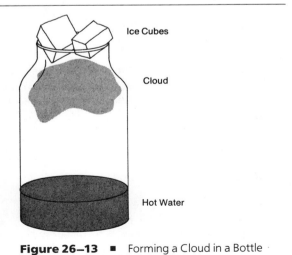

Figure 26–13 ■ Forming a Cloud in a Bottle

Subconcept 2–5

Weather may be predicted.

Discussion

The science of meteorology is not as exact as some of the other sciences because the meteorologist cannot control variables as a laboratory scientist can. He is also hampered by the fact that he must often work with very incomplete data. However, weather can often be predicted from temperature, humidity, and related conditions. One can chart the speed and direction of the movement of air masses to predict the arrival of frontal systems. Severe winds and tornadoes may be predicted for regions where cold air is forced to override a warm air mass. Thunderstorms are known to occur when a high ground temperature is accompanied by high humidity. Such examples indicate that certain temperature-humidity conditions create specific and predictable weather. In general, a meteorologist's job is to furnish weather data to observers in other parts of the country, to compile data from charts and maps of weather conditions over a large area, and to employ the accumulated information to predict the weather in the area where he or she is located.

The meteorologist will acquire data on wind and temperature conditions at various altitudes. He or she will also acquire information on cloud cover, relative humidity, barometric pressure, and precipitation. To obtain information on weather conditions at high altitudes, the meteorologist releases instrumented balloons equipped with radio transmitters (radiosondes). For ground level observations, instruments such as the *thermometer* (temperature), *anemometer* (wind velocity), *wind vane* (wind direction), *wet-bulb thermometer* (relative humidity), and *barometer* (air pressure) are employed.

Lesson Plan ▪ P

Orientation:	Grades 3–6.
Content Objective:	The children will name four instruments used to predict weather, describe their construction, and tell how they are used.
Skill Objective:	The children are required to construct instruments and use them to *observe* weather conditions, to *communicate* by compiling data, and to *predict* the approaching weather.
Materials:	Pint jar, rubber sheet from a balloon, soda straw, glue, matchstick, glass tubing, four paper cups, large straight pins or small nails, posterboard, staple gun, wire clothes hanger, two thermometers, cotton cloth, glass tumbler.
Evaluation:	Students' verbal interaction, constructed instruments, report.

Procedure

Provide children with the following directions:

Making an aneroid barometer. Fasten a rubber sheet from a balloon with a rubber band to the mouth of a pint jar. Flatten both ends of a soda straw and glue one end to the center of the rubber sheet. The straw should rest on a matchstick that is glued in place at the rim of the jar. Place the barometer out of the sunlight in a spot where the temperature is fairly constant.

continued on next page

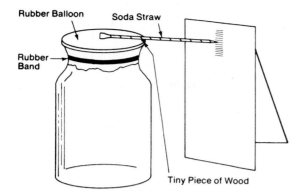

Figure 26–14 ■ A Homemade Aneroid Barometer

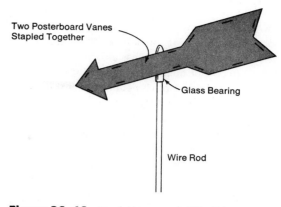

Figure 26–16 ■ A Homemade Wind Vane

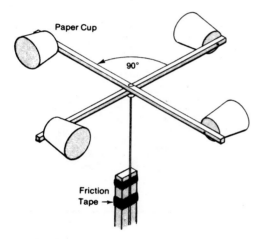

Figure 26–15 ■ A Homemade Anemometer

Set up a card beside it as in Figure 26–14. On the first rainy day, have the children make a mark on the card where the end of the soda straw points. Label this point Low (Rain). Do the same on a bright, sunny day. Mark this point High (Clear). Have the children observe and record the position of their barometer several times each day for several days. Can they predict the weather with the data gained from their barometer?

Making an anemometer. See Figure 26–15. The wood may be balsa, pine, or any other light wood. The bearing upon which the crossarms rest may be made by heating the end of a two-inch piece of glass tubing in an open flame until the opening fuses closed. Be sure to position the paper cups as shown in the illustration. The instrument may be roughly calibrated by counting the number of turns it makes per minute in a wind of known velocity as reported by a nearby weather bureau. The number of turns per minute the anemometer will make for each mile per hour of wind velocity may be found by dividing the number of revolutions per minute by the number of miles per hour. The wind velocity may be reported each day for several days as part of a class weather report.

Making a wind vane. See Figure 26–16. The glass bearing may be made by fusing closed one end of a two-inch piece of glass tubing as described above. Make sure the tail of the wind vane is larger than the head. This ensures that the vane will point in the direction *from* which the wind is coming. Orient the wind vane with a compass. The direction of the wind may be reported each day as part of a class weather report.

Making wet- and dry-bulb thermometers. Suspend two identical thermometers side by side. Wrap the bulb of one thermometer with one end of a piece of soft cotton cloth. Suspend the other end of the cloth in a glass of water (see Figure 26–17). Record the reading of each thermometer after allowing ample time for the temperatures to stabilize. Use the dry-bulb reading and the *difference* between the wet- and dry-bulb readings to determine the relative humidity (see Chart 26–1).

continued on next page

The wet-bulb thermometer will always show a lower temperature than the dry-bulb thermometer as long as water is evaporating from the cotton cloth. The process of evaporation has a cooling effect upon the thermometer bulb. The rate at which water will evaporate from the cloth is determined to a great extent by the relative humidity of the air—the greater the humidity, the slower the evaporation rate, and vice versa. So the temperature recorded by the wet-bulb thermometer indicates the relative humidity of the air.

The teacher may assign committees to construct and obtain data from the four instruments described above. A fifth committee might catch precipitation in wide-mouthed containers and measure its depth. Yet another committee would be responsible for putting all data on a master chart and comparing the class findings to the weather reports of the U.S. Weather Bureau.

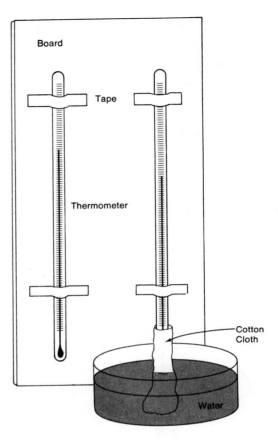

Figure 26–17 ▪ Wet- and Dry-Bulb Thermometers

Chart 26–1 ▪ Relative Humidity Index in Percent

Dry-Bulb Readings	Difference Between Wet- and Dry-Bulb Readings																								
°F	1	2	3	4	5	6	7	8	9	10	11	12	13	14	15	16	17	18	19	20	21	22	23	24	25
65	95	90	85	80	75	70	66	62	57	53	48	44	40	36	32	28	25	21	17	13	10	7	3		
68	95	90	85	81	76	72	67	63	59	55	51	47	43	39	35	31	28	24	21	17	14	11	8	4	1
71	95	90	86	82	77	73	69	64	60	56	53	49	45	41	38	34	31	27	24	21	18	15	11	8	5
74	95	91	86	82	78	74	70	66	62	58	54	51	47	44	40	37	34	30	27	24	21	18	15	12	9
77	96	91	87	83	79	75	71	67	63	60	56	52	49	46	42	39	36	33	30	27	24	21	18	15	13
80	96	91	87	83	79	76	72	68	64	61	57	54	51	47	44	42	38	35	32	29	27	24	21	18	16
84	96	92	88	84	80	77	73	70	66	63	59	56	53	50	47	44	41	38	35	32	30	27	25	22	20
88	96	92	88	85	81	78	74	71	67	64	61	58	55	52	49	46	43	41	38	35	33	30	28	25	23
92	96	92	89	85	82	78	75	72	69	65	62	59	57	54	51	48	45	43	40	38	35	33	30	28	26
96	96	93	89	86	82	79	76	73	70	67	64	61	58	55	53	50	47	45	42	40	37	35	33	31	29
100	96	93	90	86	83	80	77	74	71	68	65	62	59	57	54	52	49	47	44	42	40	37	35	33	31

Lesson Plan ▪ Q

Orientation: Grades K–3.

Content Objective: The children will describe three weather conditions that may be used to help predict weather. They will describe cumulus, stratus, and nimbus clouds.

Skill Objective: The children are required to *observe* weather conditions, to *classify* information according to *operational* definitions, to *communicate* by maintaining a weather chart, and to *predict* weather from a set of conditions.

Materials: Weather chart, two thermometers, copies of Chart 26–2.

Evaluation: Students' verbal interaction, students' group problem-solving skills, laboratory worksheets, log, and reports.

Procedure

To begin this activity, discuss the weather with the children. Let them offer answers to such questions as: "What causes rain?" "What are clouds?" "Where does the wind come from?" Tell them they are going to learn to be good weather observers and to help you keep a record of the weather for one (or two) weeks. Give each child a copy of Chart 26–2. Describe the three different types of cloud. Draw pictures of each type and post them on the bulletin board. (Cumulus clouds are low, white, and puffy in appearance; they darken as the water content increases. Stratus clouds are gray and sheetlike. They occur at medium height and may extend from horizon to horizon. Cirrus clouds occur at high altitudes. They are white; initially they appear as wispy fragments, gradually becoming more widespread and sheetlike.)

You may also wish to create *operationalized definitions* of wind conditions with such statements as:

continued on next page

Chart 26–2 ▪ A Weather Chart

Day		Clouds Cumulus/Cirrus/Stratus/Clear	Rain Yes/No	Wind Strong/Breezy/No	Temp.	Other Conditions Fog/Frost/Hail/Etc.
Monday	Morning					
	Afternoon					
Tues.	Morning					
	Afternoon					
Wed.	Morning					
	Afternoon					
Thurs.	Morning					
	Afternoon					
Friday	Morning					
	Afternoon					

"We will call a strong wind one that will make the flag stand straight out from the flagpole." The class will have to make many decisions during the observation period while attempting to *classify* their observations. New categories may be originated where established classifications are not descriptive enough. Temperature measurements may be made if the children can use a thermometer or if there is time for them to learn.

After completing the *observation period,* use the data from the chart for discussion purposes. The children should *infer* some relationships among the various weather conditions. (Rain comes from dark clouds. Cumulus clouds form or become thicker in the afternoon. Cirrus clouds come before stratus clouds.) Caution the class that their data are limited, that what they observed may not always happen just that way. Their generalizations may have only limited application.

Summary

The earth is surrounded by a thin layer of gases and water vapor. The density of the gases is greatest at the surface and diminishes rapidly with altitude. Nearly all of the gases lie within twenty miles of mean sea level.

Weather is caused by fluctuations in atmospheric conditions. Unequal heating of the earth's surface over either large or small areas creates convections or thermal air currents. Prevailing winds are caused by differences in regional heating effects; local winds by differences in local heating effects. Convection currents carry moisture-laden air to higher altitudes where the vapor condenses to form clouds. When a region of the atmosphere contains all the water vapor it can hold at a particular temperature, the addition of more water vapor or a reduction in temperature will cause condensation and precipitation in the form of rain, snow, sleet, and so on. After falling to earth, the precipitation evaporates and the cycle begins again.

Violent convection currents cause high winds and heavy rainfall: thunderstorms, tornadoes, and hurricanes. Noticeable changes in weather occur where air masses with different pressures, temperatures, and/or humidities meet. A cold front occurs when a cold air mass pushes along a warm air mass, generally with accompanying thundershowers. A warm front occurs when a warm air mass pushes along a cold air mass, usually with accompanying stratus clouds and prolonged rain.

Weather conditions may be predicted in advance. The job of the U.S. Weather Bureau is to collect and disseminate data concerning weather conditions throughout the world. Local weather stations also maintain weather charts and predict local weather conditions.

Appendixes

APPENDIX A
Selected Commercial Suppliers of Science Materials

Carolina Biological Supply Co.
2700 York Rd.
Burlington, NC 27215

Center for Multisensory Learning
Lawrence Hall of Science
University of California
Berkeley, CA 94720

Central Scientific Co.
11222 Melrose Ave.
Franklin Park, IL 60131

Connecticut Valley Biological Supply Co., Inc.
P.O. Box 326
Southampton, MA 01073

Delta Biologicals
P.O. Box 26666
Tucson, AZ 85726-6666

Delta Education, Inc.
P. O. Box 915
Hudson, NH 03051-0915

Estes Industries
1295 H Street
Penrose, CO 81240

Fisher Scientific Co.
4901 LeMoyne St.
Chicago, IL 60651

Hubbard Scientific
P.O. Box 104
Northbrook, IL 60062

Ideal School Supply Co.
11000 S. Lavergne Ave.
Oak Lawn, IL 60453

Lab-Aids, Inc.
249 Trade Zone Dr.
Ronkonkoma, NY 11779

Lab Safety Supply Co.
P.O. Box 1368
Janesville, WI 53547-1368

Nasco
901 Janesville Ave.
Fort Atkinson, WI 53538

Nasco West, Inc.
P.O. Box 3837
Modesto, CA 95352

Nystrom
3333 Elston Ave.
Chicago, IL 60618

Ohaus Scale Corp.
29 Hanover Rd.
Florham Park, NJ 07932

Owls, Etc.
P.O. Box 665
Great River, NY 11739

Sargent-Welch Scientific Co.
7300 N. Linder Ave.
Skokie, IL 60077

Science Kit and Boreal Labs
777 E. Park Dr.
Tonawanda, NY 14150

Silver Burdett/Ginn
250 James St. CN 1918
Morristown, NJ 07960-1918

Ward's Natural Science Establishment, Inc.
P.O. Box 92912
Rochester, NY 14692-9012

APPENDIX B
Selected Suppliers of Audiovisual Materials

American Cancer Society, Inc.
219 E. 42nd Street
New York, NY 10017

American Dental Association
Bureau of AV Services
222 E. Superior St.
Chicago, IL 60614

American Gas Assn. Ed. Prog.
1515 Wilson Blvd.
Arlington, VA 22209

American Heart Association Film Library
267 W. 25th Street
New York, NY 10001

American Museum of Natural History
Central Park W. at 79th St.
New York, NY 10024

Bullfrog Films
Oley, PA 19547

Carolina Biological Supply Co.
Burlington, NC 27215

Cenco Educational Films
11222 Melrose Avenue
Franklin Park, IL 60131

Coronet/MTI Film & Video
108 Wilmot Rd.
Deerfield, IL 60016

D. C. Heath
125 Spring St.
Lexington, MA 02173

Delta Education, Inc.
P.O. Box 915
Hudson, NH 03051-0915

Denoyer-Geppert Science Co.
5215-35 N. Ravenswood Ave.
Chicago, IL 60640-2028

Encyclopedia Britannica Education Corp.
301 S. Michigan Ave.
Chicago, IL 60604

ESS Elementary Science Study
55 Chapel St.
Newton, MA 02160

Ford Motor Co. Film Library
3000 Schaefer Rd.
Dearborn, MI 48122

Frey Scientific Co.
905 Hickory Ln.
Mansfield, OH 44905

Gamco Industries
Box 1911
Big Spring, TX 79720

Hubbard Scientific Co.
P.O. Box 104
Northbrook, IL 60062

Instructional Video
P.O. Box 21
Maumee, OH 43537

MMI Corp.
2950 Wyman Pkwy.
P.O. Box 19907
Baltimore, MD 21211

Modern Talking Picture Service
5000 Park St. N.
St. Petersburg, FL 33709

Nasco
901 Janesville Ave.
Fort Atkinson, WI 53538

National Aeronautics & Space Administration
Washington, DC 20546
(Apply to national office for address of
regional centers)

National Dairy Council
6300 N. River Road
Chicago, IL 60606
(Apply to state dairy council for information)

National Wildlife Federation
1400 Sixteenth St. NW
Washington, DC 20036

Nystrom
3333 Elston Ave.
Chicago, IL 60618

Owl/TV
c/o Bullfrog Films
Oley, PA 19547

Science Kit and Boreal Laboratories
777 E. Park Drive
Tonawanda, NY 14150

Sierra Club
730 Polk Street
San Francisco, CA 94109

Silver Burdett & Ginn
250 James St. CN 1918
Morristown, NJ 07960-1918

Society for Visual Education, Inc.
1345 Diversey Pkwy.
Chicago, IL 60614-1299

Troll Associates
100 Corporate Dr.
Mahwah, NJ 07430

United Learning, Inc.
6633 W. Howard St.
Niles, IL 60648

U.S. Department of Agriculture
Motion Picture Services
Washington, DC 20250

Videodiscovery, Inc.
1515 Dexter Ave. N. Suite 400
Seattle, WA 98109

Walt Disney, 16mm Films
800 Sonora Ave.
Glendale, CA 91201

Ward's Natural Science
5100 West Henrietta Rd.
P.O. Box 92912
Rochester, NY 14692-9012

APPENDIX C
Elementary Science Textbook Directory

Publisher's Name and Address	Textbook Series	Grade Level	Regional Office in
Addison-Wesley Publishing Co. 2725 Sand Hill Rd. Menlo Park, CA 94025	Addison-Wesley Science	K–6	Atlanta, GA; Barrington, IL; Dallas, TX; Don Mills, Ontario, Canada; Menlo Park, CA; Reading, MA
Delta Education, Inc. P.O. Box 915 Hudson, NH 03051-0915	SAPA II (Science: A Process Approach); SCIS (Science Curriculum Improvement Study)	K–6	Nashua, NH
Harcourt Brace Jovanovich, Inc. School Dept. Orlando, FL 32887	HBJ	K–6	Atlanta, GA; Chicago, IL; Dallas, TX; New York, NY; Petaluma, CA
D. C. Heath and Co. 125 Spring St. Lexington, MA 02173	Heath Science	K–6	Atlanta, GA; Dallas, TX; Lexington, MA; New York, NY; Novato, CA; Skokie, IL
Macmillan/McGraw-Hill	Science in Your World Journeys in Science	K–6	Columbus, Ohio

continued on next page

Publisher's Name and Address	Textbook Series	Grade Level	Regional Office in
Scott, Foresman and Co. 1900 E. Lake Ave. Glenview, IL 60025	Scott Foresman Science Discover Science	K–6	Dallas, TX; Glenview, IL; Oakland, NJ; Sunnyvale, CA; Tucker, GA
Silver Burdett & Ginn Lexington, MA 02173 Morristown, NJ 07960	Silver Burdett & Ginn Science Science Horizons	K–6	Atlanta, GA; Dallas, TX; Glenview, IL; Palo Alto, CA

APPENDIX D
Selected Sources of Free and Inexpensive Science Teaching Materials

Alabama, State of
Dept. of Conservation & Natural Resources
Information Education Section
64 N. Union St.
Montgomery, AL 36130

Allied Signal, Inc.
Engineered Materials Section
P.O. Box 1087R
Morristown, NJ 07960

Aluminum Assoc. Inc.
Mgr. Educational Services
818 Connecticut Ave. N.W.
Washington, DC 20006

Alyeska Pipeline Service Co.
Corporate Affairs Dept.
MS #542
1835 S. Bragaw St.
Anchorage, AK 99512

American Coal Foundation
1130 17th St. N.W. Suite 220
Washington, DC 20036

American Gas Assoc.
Education Programs
1515 Wilson Blvd.
Arlington, VA 22209

American Petroleum Institute
Public Relations Dept.
12220 L Street, NW
Washington, DC 20005

American Water Works Association
Mgr. of Youth Education
6666 West Quincy Ave.
Denver, Colorado 80235

Animal Welfare Institute
P.O. Box 3650
Washington, DC 20007

Brown Swiss Cattle Breeders' Assoc.
P.O. Box 1038
Beloit, WI 53511-1038

Detroit Consumer Affairs Dept.
1600 Cadillac Tower
Detroit, MI 48226

Georgia Penaut Commission
P.O. Box 967
Tifton, GA 31793

GTE Products Corp.
Marketing Services Center
70 Empire Dr.
West Seneca, NY 14224

Izaak Walton League of America, Inc.
Save Our Streams Program
1401 Wilson Blvd. Level B
Arlington, VA 22209

Kalmbach Publishing Co.
Patty Montbriand
P.O. Box 1612
Waukesha, WI 53187

National Aeronautics & Space Admin.
Education Services Branch LFC-9
Washington, DC 20546

National Cotton Council of America
Communications Services
P.O. Box 12285
Memphis, TN 38182-0285

National Institute of Dental Research
Health Promotion and Science Transfer Section,
Room 536
Westwood Blvd.
Bethesda, MD 20892

Ohaus Corporation
Customer Service
29 Hanover Road
Florham Park, NJ 07932-0900

Oklahoma Penaut Commission
P.O. Box D
Madill, OK 73446

Research Products Corp.
1015 E. Washington Ave.
P.O. Box 1467
Madison, WI 53701-1467

Reynolds Metals Co.
Public Relations Mgr.
Recycling
P.O. Box 27003
Richmond, VA 23261-7003

U.S. Dept. of Commerce
National Ocean Service/Distribution Branch
Physical Science Services Section
Riverdale, MD 20737-1199

APPENDIX E
Sources of Materials for Environmental and Energy Education

Periodicals

Audubon, National Audubon Society
1130 Fifth Ave.
New York, NY 10028

Conservation Report, Conservation News, National Wildlife, and *Ranger Rick's Nature Magazine,*
National Wildlife Federation
1412 Sixteenth St. N.W.
Washington, DC 20036

Earthlight, A Weekly Environmental Newspaper for Children
13 Columbus
San Francisco, CA 94111

Environment, Committee for Environmental Information
438 N. Skinker Blvd.
St. Louis, MO 63130

Environmental Education News
Michigan Dept. of Natural Resources
Lansing, MI 48926

Natural History, The American Museum of Natural History
Central Park W. at 79th St.
New York, NY 10024

Nature Conservancy News, Nature Conservancy
2039 K St. N.W.
Washington, DC 20006

Outdoor News Bulletin, Wildlife Management Institute
709 Wire Bldg.
Washington, DC 20005

Regional Conservation Education Newsletter,
Forest Service, U.S. Dept. of Agriculture
633 W. Wisconsin Ave.
Milwaukee, WI 53203

Environmental and Energy Resource Organizations

American Assoc. for the Advancement of Science
1515 Massachusetts Ave. N.W.
Washington, DC 20005

American Assoc. of University Women
2410 Virginia Ave. N.W.
Washington, DC 20006

American Chemical Society
1155 Sixteenth St. N.W.
Washington, DC 20036

American Forestry Assoc.
919 17th St. N.W.
Washington, DC 20006

American Geological Institute
2201 M St. N.W.
Washington, DC 20037

American Industrial Arts Assoc.
1201 Sixteenth St.
Washington, DC 20036

American Institute of Architects
1735 Massachusetts Ave. N.W.
Washington, DC 20036

American Institute of Biological Sciences
3900 Wisconsin Ave. N.W.
Washington, DC 20016

American Iron and Steel Institute
Education Dept.
150 East 42nd St.
New York, NY 10017

American Museum of Natural History
Education Dept.
Central Park W. at 79th St.
New York, NY 10024

American Petroleum Institute
2101 L St. N.W.
Washington, DC 20037

American Society for Engineering Education
1 Dupont Circle N.W.
Washington, DC 20036

Assoc. of Classroom Teachers, NEA
1201 Sixteenth St. N.W.
Washington, DC 20036

Biological Sciences Curriculum Study
University of Colorado
P.O. Box 930
Boulder, CO 80302

Committee on Environmental Information
138 N. Skinker Blvd.
St. Louis, MO 63130

The Conservation Foundation
1717 Massachusetts Ave. N.W.
Washington, DC 20036

Council on Education in the Geological Sciences
2201 M Street N.W.
Washington, DC 20036

Council of State Governments
1735 DeSales St. N.W.
Washington, DC 20036

Earth Science Education Program
P.O. Box 1559
Boulder, CO 80302

ERIC Information Analysis Center for Science and Mathematics Education
1460 West Lane Ave.
Columbus, OH 43221

Humble Oil and Refining Co.
P.O. Box 2180
Houston, TX 77001

The Izaak Walton League of America
1326 Waukegan Rd.
Glenview, IL 60025

Keep America Beautiful, Inc.
99 Park Ave.
New York, NY 10016

Manufacturing Chemists Assoc.
1825 Connecticut Ave. N.W.
Washington, DC 20009

National Assoc. of Biology Teachers
1420 N St. N.W.
Washington, DC 20005

National Coal Assoc., Coal Bldg.
1130 17th St. N.W.
Washington, DC 20036

National Council for the Social Studies
1201 Sixteenth St. N.W.
Washington, DC 20036

National Education Assoc.
1201 Sixteenth St. N.W.
Washington, DC 20036

National Park Service
C between 18th and 19th Sts. N.W.
Washington, DC 20006

National Science Foundation
1800 G St. N.W.
Washington, DC 20006

National Science Teachers Assoc.
1201 Sixteenth St. N.W.
Washington, DC 20036

National Wildlife Federation
1412 Sixteenth St. N.W.
Washington, DC 20036

New York Alliance to Save Energy, Inc.
36 West 44th St.
New York, NY 10036

Resources for the Future, Inc.
1775 Massachusetts Ave. N.W.
Washington, DC 20036

St. Regis Paper Company
150 East 42nd St.
New York, NY 10017

Sierra Club
730 Polk St.
San Francisco, CA 94109

Standard Oil Company
30 Rockefeller Plaza
New York, NY 10020

Thomas Alva Edison Foundation
Cambridge Office Plaza, Suite 143
182 West Ten Mile Rd.
Southfield, MI 48075

Total Education in the Total Environment
15 West Washington St., Box 423
Norwalk, CT 06856

U.S. Dept. of Energy
P.O. Box 62
Oak Ridge, TN 37830

U.S. Dept. of the Interior, Information Office
Interior Bldg.
Washington, DC 20242

U.S. Office of Education
GSA Building, 7th and D Sts. S.W.
Washington, DC 20202

U.S. Office of Education, HEW,
Environmental Task Force
Room 3600, ROB—37th and D St. S.W.
Washington, DC 20202

Walt Disney Educational Media Company
500 South Buena Vista St.
Burbank, CA 91521

APPENDIX F
Professional Publications for Teachers

Books

Cain, Sandra E. & Jack M. Evans. *Sciencing, An Involvement Approach to Elementary Science Methods*. Columbus, OH: Charles E. Merrill Publishing Company, 1984.

Henson, Kenneth T. & Delmar Janke. *Elementary Science Methods*. New York: McGraw-Hill Book Co., 1984.

Wolfinger, Donna M. *Teaching Science in the Elementary School*. Boston: Little, Brown and Company, 1984.

Periodicals

Current Science, Science and Math Weekly, and *My Weekly Reader*. Columbus, Ohio, American Education Press. Published weekly during school year.

Geographic School Bulletins. Washington, DC, National Geographic Society. Published weekly by School Service Division.

Journal of Research in Science Teaching. Easton, PA, National Association for Research in Science Teaching. Published quarterly.

National Geographic School Bulletin. Washington, DC, National Geographic Society. Published each week (October to May).

School Science and Mathematics. Menasha, WI. Published monthly, except July, August, and September.

Science and Children. Washington, DC, National Science Teachers Association. Published eight times a year.

Science Digest. Chicago. Published monthly.

Bibliographies

American Association for the Advancement of Science, "The Science Book List for Children." 1515 Massachusetts Ave., Washington, DC 20005.

Board of Education of the City of New York, Bureau of Curriculum Research, "A Selected Bibliography in Elementary Science." Curriculum Center, 130 W. 55th St., New York, NY.

Science and Children. 1742 Connecticut Avenue N.W., Washington, DC 20009. Bibliography of outstanding science tradebooks for children, published annually in the March issue.

APPENDIX G
Selected Suppliers of Microcomputer Software for Elementary Science

Apple Computer, Inc.
20525 Mariani Ave.
Cupertino, CA 95014

Astronomical Society of the Pacific
1290 24th Ave.
San Francisco, CA 94122

Cambridge Development Lab.
214 Third Ave.
Waltham, MA 02154

Cross Educational Software
P.O. Box 1536
Ruston, LA 71270

Educational Activities, Inc.
P.O. Box 392
Freeport, NY 11520

Fisher Scientific
4901 W. LeMoyne St.
Chicago, IL 60651

Focus Media, Inc.
P.O. Box 865
Garden City, NY 11530

Frey Scientific Co.
905 Hickory Ln.
Mansfield, OH 44905

Harcourt Brace Jovanovich, School Dept.
Orlando, FL 32887

D.C. Heath & Co.
125 Spring St.
Lexington, MA 02173

Holt, Rinehart and Winston
383 Madison Ave.
New York, NY 10017

MECC
3490 Lexington Ave.
St. Paul, MN 55126

Micro Power and Light Co.
8814 Sunshine Ave.
Dallas, TX 75231

Milliken Publishing Co.
P.O. Box 21579
St. Louis, MO 63132-0579

Nasco
901 Janesville Ave.
Fort Atkinson, WI 53538

Nasco West, Inc.
P.O. Box 3837
Modesto, CA 95352

Sargent-Welch Scientific Co.
7300 N. Linder Ave.
Skokie, IL 60077

Scholastic Software
730 Broadway
New York, NY 10003

Scott Foresman and Co.
1900 E. Lake Ave.
Glenview, IL 60025

Silver Burdett/Ginn
250 James St. CN 1918
Morristown, NJ 07960-1918

Sunburst Communications
39 Washington Ave.
Pleasantville, NY 10570-9971

Tandy/Radio Shack
1600 One Tandy Center
Fort Worth, TX 76102

Videodiscovery, Inc.
1515 Dexter Ave. N.
Suite 400
Seattle, WA 98109

Video Vision Assoc., Ltd.
7 Waverly Pl.
Madison, NJ 07940

APPENDIX H
Selected Trade Book Publishers

Addison-Wesley Publishing Co.
2725 Sand Hill Rd.
Menlo Park, CA 94025

Atheneum Publishers/Macmillan Children's
Book Group
866 Third Ave.
New York, NY 10022

Carnegie Museum of Natural History
Division of Education
4400 Forbes Ave.
Pittsburgh, PA 15213

Carolrhoda Books, Inc.
241 First Ave. N.
Minneapolis, MN 55401

Crowell Junior Books
Education Dept.
10 E. 53rd St.
New York, NY 10022

Enslow Publishers, Inc.
P.O. Box 777
Hillside, NJ 07205

Harper Collins Publishers
10 E. 53rd St.
New York, NY 10022

Houghton Mifflin Co.
One Beacon Street
Boston, MA 02108

Learning Spectrum
1390 Westridge
Portola Valley, CA 94025

Lippincott Junior Books
Dept. 128
10 E. 53rd St.
New York, NY 10022

Macmillan's Children's Book Group
866 Third Ave.
New York, NY 10022

Julian Messner
c/o Silver Burdett Press
Prentice-Hall Bldg.
Englewood Cliffs, NJ 07632

National Geographic Society
Box 89
Washington, DC 20036

Raintree Publishers, Inc.
310 W. Wisconsin Ave.
Milwaukee, WI 53203

Charles Scribner's Sons
866 Third Ave.
New York, NY 10022

Silver Burdett Press
Prentice-Hall Bldg.
Englewood Cliffs, NJ 07632

Troll Assoc.
100 Corporate Dr.
Mahwah, NJ 07430

Walker and Company
720 Fifth Ave.
New York, NY 10019

Ward's Natural Science Establishment, Inc.
P.O. Box 92912
Rochester, NY 14692-9012

APPENDIX I
Keeping Animals in the Classroom

Reasons for Keeping Animals in a Classroom

Some children do not have pets at home.

Children enhance their tactile development through handling and petting.

Children learn how to take care of a pet.

Children learn how animals grow, eat, drink, sleep, play, hide, and (sometimes) reproduce.

Children can become acquainted with animals of many kinds.

Children can conduct scientific observations and maintain records of animal behavior.

Caring for the Animals

Animals must be properly fed and watered. (See the information that follows.)

Animals must not be overly handled by children.

Animals must have a clean, healthy environment. In the case of wild animals, their surroundings should be as much like their natural habitat as possible.

Animals should have a place they can hide.

Responsibilities Involved in Caring for Classroom Animals

The teacher, of course, is ultimately responsible for the care of animals in her or his classroom. Caring for animals is a daily responsibility for as long as they are maintained in the classroom.

Remember that keeping animals in a classroom is unlawful in some states.

Children may be assigned responsibility for feeding, watering, and cleaning the cages of classroom animals.

Wild animals must never be kept longer than a few days before they are released into a suitable habitat.

Provisions must be made for the classroom animals over holidays and vacations. Parents of children may be solicited to care for classroom pets during holidays and vacations.

Providing for the animals' welfare after they are no longer wanted is an additional responsibility.

Proper Food for Some Common Classroom Animal Pets

Ants—miscellaneous food scraps, sugar or honey water, dead insects, bread crumbs. Place the food in a shallow dish or in a jar lid.

Birds—clean water, commercial bird seed (for wild birds, use wild bird seed), lettuce, carrot, apple, bone of cuttlefish, bread crumbs, find sand (grit).

Caterpillars and moth larvae—leaves of the plant from which they were taken; for commercial specimens, consult the supplier.

Butterflies—sugar or honey water, flower nectar.

Chickens—clean water, commercial chicken feed, vegetables, fine sand.

Chameleons and lizards—Spray water into the terraria with a spray bottle (chameleons drink the water droplets from the leaves of plants), live insects, especially crickets and roaches, small bits of hamburger dangled on a string.

Frogs and toads—earthworms, grubs, caterpillars, mealworms, and other live larvae.

Gerbils—a small amount of clean water, commercial gerbil food, seeds, carrots, lettuce.

Guppies and goldfish—Although goldfish will eat finely ground dog biscuits and grain cereals, we recommend that you feed them only commercial fish food. Be careful not to overfeed the fish! Follow the directions on the package.

Guinea pigs or cavies—clean water, commercially prepared food, green, leafy vegetables, fresh grasses, and clover.

Hamsters—clean water, hamster pellets, dog biscuits, dried corn or wheat. (Gnawing maintains hamsters' dental health.) Carrots, cabbage, and lettuce may be used to supplement the diet.

Rabbits—clean water, commercial rabbit pellets, green, leafy vegetables, clover. Wild rabbits do not require as much water as domestic rabbits.

Rats and mice—clean water, grains or breakfast cereal, bacon or other fatty meat, carrots and other vegetables.

Snakes—insects, lizards, chameleons, boiled egg, earthworms. Larger snakes eat mice and other rodents. Snakes do not eat every day; some may not eat for weeks. Consult a local herpetologist to determine whether to release a snake that is reluctant to eat.

Turtles—*Caution:* There are sporadic reports of pet turtles being contaminated with a salmonella bacterium, which could be passed on to children; check with health officials in your area. Turtles eat all types of insects, commercial turtle food, boiled egg, worms, grubs, berries, and lettuce. Let them float on the surface of the water in their habitat.

APPENDIX J
Selected Children's Magazines

3–2–1 Contact (school monthly)—elementary
Children's Television Workshop
P.O. Box 2933
Boulder, CO 80322

Cricket (monthly)—ages 6–12
Open Court Publishing Co.
Box 100
La Salle, IL 61301

The Curious Naturalist (nine issues per year)—elementary
Massachusetts Audubon Society
South Lincoln, MA 01773

Ladybug (monthly)—ages 3–7
Carus Publishing Company
315 Fifth Street
Peru, IL 61354

Odyssey (monthly)—elementary
AstroMedia
625 E. St. Paul Ave.
Milwaukee, WI 53202

Ranger Rick's Nature Magazine (eight issues per year)—elementary
1412 16th Street NW
Washington, DC 20036

National Geographic World (monthly)—elementary
17 and M Streets, NW
Washington, DC 20036

Science Scope (eight issues per year)—elementary
National Science Teachers Association
1201 Sixteenth St. NW
Washington, DC 20036

APPENDIX K
Selected Science Teachers Organizations

National Science Teachers Association
1742 Connecticut Avenue N.W.
Washington, DC 20009-1171

NSTA Affiliates (correspond with the parent organization for more information):

Association for the Education of Teachers in Science (AETS)

Council for Elementary Science International (CESI)

Council of State Science Supervisors (CSSS)

National Association for Research in Science Teaching (NARST)

National Science Supervisors Association (NSSA)

Society for College Science Teachers (SCST)

I N D E X

Ohm's law, 382–383
Optical illusions, 275
Orbits, of planets, 502–503
Organizing science supplies
  central storage, 121
  shoebox kits, 121
Osteichthyes, 222
Oswego plan, 9
Output, of simple machines, 416–417

P

Paper airplane, 438
Parallax, to determine distance to
  stars, 490–491
Parallel circuit, 385–386
Parasite, 248
  fungus, 205
Pharynx, 258
Photosynthesis, 216, 254
Phototropism, 216
Piagetian theory of cognitive
  development
  brain research and, 39
  child study exercises, 34–36
  concrete operations stage, 35–36
  formal operations stage, 36
  implications for instruction, 38–39
  preoperational stage, 34
  sensory-motor stage, 33
Pinwheel, construction of, 414–415
Pitch
  as related to length of vibrating air
    column, 405, 408
  as related to length of vibrating
    string, 407
Planets, characteristics of, 492, 499,
  501
  orbits, 502–503
Plates, earth's crust, 544–546
Platyhelminthes, 223
Pond water organisms, 227
Populations, sampling, 247
Porifera, 222
Potential energy, 415–416
Predators, 248
Primary-grade science, teaching,
  73–80
Primary process skills, 73–76
Problem solving, general
  activities, planning and conducting,
    182, 184
  collecting data, procedures for, 185
  determining sources of information,
    185
  developing a formal project, 186
  formulating the problem question,
    184
  interpreting data, 185
  making decisions and formulating
    solutions, 183
    costs/benefits/risks method, 183
    force field method, 183

skills, chart, 178
  values, 181
Problem-solving skills, relationship
  between, and the science
  processes, 177
Processes, life
  of animals, 231–233
  of plants, 209–212
  in the human digestive system, 258
Project 2061, 20
Proteins, broken down by acids, 260
Protons, in atoms, 296–302
Protozoa, 222
Psychomotor domain, 32
Psychomotor objectives, 96
Ptolemy, 8
Pulleys, 425–427

Q

Questioning, oral, in classroom
  closure-seeking questions, 68
  eliciting questions, 66–67
  probing questions, 67–68

R

Rational inquiry teaching, 53–55
  type one, 53
  type two, 55
Reading skills (chart), 136
Red giant star, 486–489
Reef, coral, 537–538
Reflection
  of light, 345–348
  of light energy, 345–346
Refraction, of light, 348–349
Relative humidity, 571–572
  chart, 580
Reproduction
  of animals, 228
  of humans, 278–279
  of plants, 209
    asexual, 209
    sexual, 209–210
Reptilia, 222
Resistance, of simple machines, 417
Respiration
  animal, 231
  plant, 216
  human, 270–271
    lung capacity, 271
    lung structure, operation, 270
Rift, oceanic, 543
Rocket power
  staging, 449
  as weapons of war, 448
Rocks
  classification of, 525–526
  crystals in, 526
  layering of, 528
  as record of earth history, 525–526

S

Safety
  in elementary classroom, 98
  precautions and guidelines, 105
Science, nature of, 8
Science—A Process Approach (SAPA),
  12
Science and Technology for Children
  (STC), 17
Science-based whole-language
  approach, 140
Science Curriculum Improvement
  Study (SCIS), 13
Science education, 21st century, 16, 17
Science fair, 159–164
  nature of projects, 159–160
Science, technology, and the human
  experience, 176
Seamount, 543
Seasons, 508–510
Secretion, animal, 232
Senses, human, 271–273
Sensitivity
  of animals, 232
  of humans, to touch, 276
Series circuit, 384–385
Set, 97
Simple machines,
  efficiency of, 417
  effort of, 417
Skeleton, human, 267–270
Solar cooker, 412–413
Solar system, 495–502
  model of, 500
Sound
  through air, 397–399
  through water, 397–399
Sound, produced by vibrating object,
  395–396
Sound, properties of
  intensity, 394–395
  pitch, 394–395
  quality, 394–395
Sound wave properties, 399–404
  bending around corners, 403–404
  echos, 402
  joining together, 404
  traveling in all directions, 401
Sources of materials
  general science kits, 119
  inquiry-based science, 118
  publisher's kits, 119
  science supply houses, 119
Space
  major NASA launches chart,
    452–454
  space station, 455
Spaceflight, 445–455
  activities, 456–459
  National Aeronautics and Space
    Administration, 449–455